# MONGODB FUNDAMENTALS

A hands-on guide to using MongoDB and Atlas in the real world

Amit Phaltankar, Juned Ahsan, Michael Harrison, and Liviu Nedov

# MONGODB FUNDAMENTALS

**Authors:** Amit Phaltankar, Juned Ahsan, Michael Harrison, and Liviu Nedov

**Reviewer:** Rolson Quadras

**Managing Editors:** Megan Carlisle and Saumya Jha

**Acquisitions Editors:** Karan Wadekar and Alicia Wooding

**Production Editor:** Shantanu Zagade

**Editorial Board:** Megan Carlisle, Samuel Christa, Mahesh Dhyani, Heather Gopsill, Manasa Kumar, Alex Mazonowicz, Monesh Mirpuri, Bridget Neale, Dominic Pereira, Shiny Poojary, Abhishek Rane, Brendan Rodrigues, Erol Staveley, Ankita Thakur, Nitesh Thakur, and Jonathan Wray

First published: December 2020

Production reference: 1211220

ISBN: 978-1-83921-064-8

Published by Packt Publishing Ltd.

Livery Place, 35 Livery Street

Birmingham B3 2PB, UK

# Table of Contents

# Chapter 2: Documents and Data Types 47

## Chapter 3: Servers and Clients                    93

# Chapter 5: Inserting, Updating, and Deleting Documents 213

# Chapter 7: Data Aggregation           311

# Chapter 9: Performance     419

# Chapter 12: Data Visualization 561

## Chapter 13: MongoDB Case Study     621

# PREFACE

## ABOUT THE BOOK

MongoDB is one of the most popular database technologies for handling large collections of data. This book will help MongoDB beginners develop the knowledge and skills to create databases and process data efficiently.

Unlike other MongoDB books, *MongoDB Fundamentals* dives into cloud computing from the very start – showing you how to get started with Atlas in the first chapter. You will discover how to modify existing data, add new data into a database, and handle complex queries by creating aggregation pipelines. As you progress, you'll learn about the MongoDB replication architecture and configure a simple cluster. You will also get to grips with user authentication, as well as techniques for backing up and restoring data. Finally, you'll perform data visualization using MongoDB Charts.

You will work on realistic projects that are presented as bitesize exercises and activities, allowing you to challenge yourself in an enjoyable and attainable way. Many of these mini-projects are based around a movie database case study, while the last chapter acts as a final project where you will use MongoDB to solve a real-world problem based on a bike-sharing app.

By the end of this book, you'll have the skills and confidence to process large volumes of data and tackle your own projects using MongoDB.

## ABOUT THE AUTHORS

*Amit Phaltankar* is a software developer and a blogger with more than 13 years of experience in building lightweight and efficient software components. He specializes in wiring web-based applications as well as handling large-scale data sets using traditional SQL, NoSQL, and big data technologies. He has work experience in a wide range of technology stack and loves learning and adapting to newer technology trends. Amit has a huge passion for improving his skill set and also loves guiding and grooming his peers and contributing to blogs. During the last 6 years, he has effectively used MongoDB in various ways to build faster systems.

*Juned Ahsan* is a software professional with more than 14 years of experience. He has built software products and services for companies and clients such as Cisco, Nuamedia, IBM, Nokia, Telstra, Optus, Pizza Hut, AT&T, Hughes, Altran, and others. Juned has vast experience in building software products and architecting platforms of different sizes from scratch. He loves to help and mentor others and is a top 1% contributor on Stack Overflow. Juned is passionate about cognitive CX, cloud computing, artificial intelligence, and NoSQL databases.

*Michael Harrison* started his career at the Australian telecommunications leader Telstra. He worked across their networks, big data, and automation teams. He is now a lead software developer and the founding member of Southbank Software, a Melbourne based startup that builds tools for the next generation of database technologies. As a full-stack engineer, Michael led the development of an open-sourced, platform-agnostic IDE for MongoDB (dbKoda ), as well as a Blockchain-enabled database built on top of MongoDB, called ProvenDB. Both these products were exhibited at the MongoDB World conference in New York. Given that Michael owns a pair of MongoDB socks, it's safe to say he's an enthusiast.

*Liviu Nedov* is a senior consultant with more than 20 years of experience in database technologies. He has provided professional and consulting services to customers in Australia and Europe. Throughout his career, he has designed and implemented large enterprise projects for customers like Wotif Group, Xstrata Copper/Glencore, and the University of Newcastle and Energy, Queensland. He is currently working at Data Intensity, which is the largest multi-cloud service provider for applications, databases, and business intelligence. In recent years, he is actively involved in MongoDB, NoSQL database projects, database migrations, and cloud DBaaS (Database as a Service) projects.

## WHO THIS BOOK IS FOR

*MongoDB Fundamentals* is targeted at readers with a basic technical background who are approaching MongoDB for the first time. Any database, JavaScript, or JSON experience will be useful, but not required. *MongoDB Fundamentals* may briefly dip into these technologies as well as more advanced topics, but no background knowledge is needed to gain value from this book.

## ABOUT THE CHAPTERS

*Chapter 1, Introduction to MongoDB*, contains the history and context of MongoDB, essential concepts, and a guide to setting up your first MongoDB instance.

*Chapter 2, Documents and Data Types*, will teach you about the critical components in MongoDB data and commands.

*Chapter 3, Servers and Clients*, provides you with the information needed to manage MongoDB access and connections, including the creation of databases and collections.

*Chapter 4, Querying Documents*, is where we get to the core of MongoDB: querying the database. This chapter provides hands-on exercises to get you working with the query syntax, operators, and modifiers.

*Chapter 5, Inserting, Updating, and Deleting Documents*, expands on querying, allowing you to change a query into an update, modifying existing data.

*Chapter 6, Updating with Aggregation Pipelines and Arrays*, covers more complex update operations, using pipelines and bulk updates.

*Chapter 7, Data Aggregation*, demonstrates one of MongoDB's most powerful advanced features, allowing you to create reusable, complex query pipelines that can't be solved with more straightforward queries.

*Chapter 8, Coding JavaScript in MongoDB*, takes you from direct database interactions to a method more commonly found in the real world: queries from an application. In this chapter, you will create a simple Node.js application that can programmatically interact with MongoDB.

*Chapter 9, Performance*, provides you with the information and tools to ensure your queries are running effectively, primarily by using indexes and execution plans.

*Chapter 10, Replication*, takes a closer look at the standard MongoDB configurations you may encounter in production environments, namely clusters and replica sets.

*Chapter 11, Backup and Restore*, covers the information needed as part of managing database redundancy and migration. This is integral for database administration but is also useful for loading sample data and development life cycles.

*Chapter 12, Data Visualization*, explains how you can turn raw data into meaningful visualizations that aid in discovering and communicating insights within the data.

*Chapter 13, MongoDB Case Study*, is an end-of-course case study that will tie together all the skills covered in the previous chapters in a real-world example.

## CONVENTIONS

Code words in text form, database and collection names, file and folder names, shell commands, and user input use the following formatting: "The **db.myCollection. findOne()** command will return the first document from **myCollection**."

Smaller blocks of sample code and their output will be formatted in blocks like this:

```
use sample_mflix
var pipeline = []
var options  = {}
var cursor   = db.movies.aggregate(pipeline, options);
```

In most cases, where the output is a separate block, it will be formatted as a figure like this:

```
> db.users.replaceOne(
...    {"name" : "Margaery Baratheon"},
...    {"name": "Margaery Tyrell", "email": "Margaery.Tyrell@got.es"},
...    { upsert: true }
... )
{ "acknowledged" : true, "matchedCount" : 1, "modifiedCount" : 1 }
>
> db.users.replaceOne(
...    {"name" : "Tommen Baratheon"},
...    {"name": "Tommen Baratheon", "email": "Tommen.Baratheon@got.es"},
...    { upsert: true }
... )
{
        "acknowledged" : true,
        "matchedCount" : 0,
        "modifiedCount" : 0,
        "upsertedId" : ObjectId("5f21f41b19421fdf08471445")
}
>
```

Figure 0.1: Output as a figure

Often, at the beginning of chapters, key new terms will be introduced. In these cases, the following formatting will be used: "The **aggregate** command operates on a collection like the other **Create, Read, Update, Delete** (**CRUD**) commands like so."

## BEFORE YOU BEGIN

As mentioned earlier, MongoDB is more than just a database. It's a vast and sprawling set of tools and libraries. So, before we dive headfirst into MongoDB, we'd better make sure we're fully equipped for the adventure.

## INSTALLING MONGODB

1. Download the MongoDB Community tarball (**tgz**) from https://www.mongodb.com/try/download/community. In the **Available Downloads** section, select the current (4.4.1) version, your platform, and click **download**.

2. Place the downloaded **tgz** file in any folder of your choice and extract it. On a Linux-based operating system, including macOS, the **tgz** file can be extracted to a folder using Command Prompt. Open the terminal, navigate to the directory where you copied the **tgz** file, and issue the following command:

```
tar -zxvf mongodb-macos-x86_64-4.4.1.tgz
```

Note that the name of the **tgz** can vary based on your operating system and the version you have downloaded. If you peep into the extracted folder, you will find all the MongoDB binaries, including **mongod** and **mongo**, are placed in the **bin** directory.

3.  The executables, such as **mongod** and **mongo**, are the launchers for the MongoDB database and Mongo Shell respectively. To be able to launch them from anywhere, you will need to add these commands to the **PATH** variable or copy the binaries into the **/usr/local/bin** directory. Alternatively, you can keep the binaries where they are and create symbolic links of these binaries into the **/usr/local/bin** directory. To create symbolic links, you need to open Terminal, navigate into the MongoDB installation directory, and execute this command:

```
sudo ln -s /full_path/bin/* /usr/local/bin/
```

4.  To run MongoDB locally, you must create a data directory. Execute the next command and create the data directory in any folder you want:

```
mkdir -p ~/mytools/mongodb
```

5.  To verify whether the installation was successful, run MongoDB locally. For that, you need to use the **mongo** command and provide the path of the data directory:

```
mongod --dbpath ~/mytools/mongodb
```

Once you execute this command, MongoDB starts on the default of port of **27017**, and you should see MongoDB boot logs; the last line contains **msg":"Waiting for connections**, which indicates that the database is up and waiting for clients, such as a Mongo shell, to make connections.

6.  Finally, you need to verify the Mongo shell by connecting it to the database. The next command is used to start the Mongo shell with default configurations:

```
mongo
```

Executing this command, you should see the shell prompt is started. By default, the shell connects to the database running on the **localhost 27017** port. In the coming chapters, you will learn how to connect the shell to a MongoDB Atlas cluster.

7.  Detailed instructions on installing MongoDB on Windows or any specific operating system can be found in MongoDB's official installation manual, located at https://docs.mongodb.com/manual/installation/.

## EDITORS AND IDES

The MongoDB shell allows you to directly interact with databases by merely typing commands into the console. However, this method will only get you so far and will end up being more of a burden as you perform more advanced operations. For this reason, we recommend having a text editor ready to write your commands down, and these can then be copied into the shell. Although any text editor will work, if you don't already have a preference, we recommend Visual Studio Code as it has some helpful plugins for MongoDB. That being said, whatever tools you are comfortable with will be more than enough for this book.

There is also a wide array of tools for MongoDB that will help you along your way. We don't prescribe a particular tool as the best way to learn, but we recommend doing some searches online to find tools and plugins that provide you with extra value during the learning process.

## DOWNLOADING AND INSTALLING VISUAL STUDIO CODE

Let's go ahead and get set up with a proper JavaScript IDE. You can choose whichever one you like, of course, but we are going to stick with Visual Studio Code for the initial chapters. It's an approachable editor dedicated to web technologies and is available on every major operating system:

1.  First, you need to acquire the installation package. This can be done in different ways depending upon your operating system, but the most direct way is to visit the Visual Studio Code website using https://code.visualstudio.com/.

2.  The website should detect your operating system and present you with a button that allows the direct download of a stable build. Of course, you can choose a different version by clicking the down arrow for additional options:

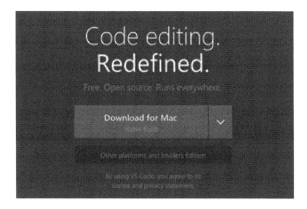

Figure 0.2: Download prompt for Visual Studio Code

3. Once downloaded, the installation will depend upon your operating system. Again, depending on your chosen operating system, the installation will differ slightly:

   **macOS**: The downloaded file is a `.ZIP` archive. You will need to unzip the package to expose the `.APP` application file.

   **Windows**: An executable `.EXE` file is downloaded to your local machine.

   **Linux**: Depending upon your download choice, you will have either a `.DEB` or `.RPM` package downloaded to your local environment.

4. With the installer package downloaded, you now have to run an installation routine dependent upon our chosen operating system:

   **macOS**: Drag the Visual Studio Code `.APP` to the `Applications` folder. This will make it available through macOS interface utilities such as **Spotlight Search**.

   **Windows**: Simply run the executable installer and follow the instructions to set everything up.

   **Linux**: There are many possibilities here; refer to your operating system instructions for the proper installation of the `.DEB` or `.RPM` package.

5. With Visual Studio Code installed, you now only need to pin it to the **Taskbar**, the **Dock**, or any other operating system mechanism that allows quick and easy access to the program.

That's it. Visual Studio Code is now available to use.

So far, we have had a look at a variety of integrated development environments available for use today when working with JavaScript. We also downloaded and installed Visual Studio Code, a modern JavaScript IDE from Microsoft. We'll now see why it is important to use proper filesystem preparation when beginning a new JavaScript project.

## DOWNLOADING NODE.JS

Node.js is open source and you can download it from its official website for all platforms. It supports all three major platforms: Windows, Linux, and macOS.

## WINDOWS

Visit their official website and download the latest stable **.msi** installer. The process is very simple. Just execute the **.msi** file and follow the instructions to install it on the system. There will be some prompts about accepting license agreements. You have to accept those and then click on **Finish**. That's it.

## MAC

The installation processes for Windows and Mac are very similar. You have to download the **.pkg** file from the official website and execute it. Then, follow the instructions. You may have to accept the license agreement. After that, follow the prompts to finish the installation process.

## LINUX

To install Node.js on Linux, execute the following commands in the same order they are mentioned:

- `$ cd /tmp`
- `$ wget http://nodejs.org/dist/v8.11.2/node-v8.11.2-linux-x64.tar.gz`
- `$ tar xvfz node-v8.11.2-linux-x64.tar.gz`
- `$ sudo mkdir -p /usr/local/nodejs`
- `$ sudo mv node-v8.11.2-linux-x64/* /usr/local/nodejs`

Note that you will need to use **sudo** in the last two commands only if you are *not* logged in as the admin. Here, you first change the current active directory to the temporary directory (**tmp**) of the system. Second, you download the **tar** package of **node** from their official distribution directory. Third, you extract the **tar** package to the **tmp** directory. This directory contains all the compiled and executable files. Fourth, you create a directory in the system for **Node.js**. In the last command, you are moving all the complied and executable files of the package to that directory.

## VERIFYING THE INSTALLATION

After the installation process, you can verify whether it is installed properly on the system by executing the following command:

```
$ node -v && npm -v
```

It will output the currently installed version of Node.js and npm:

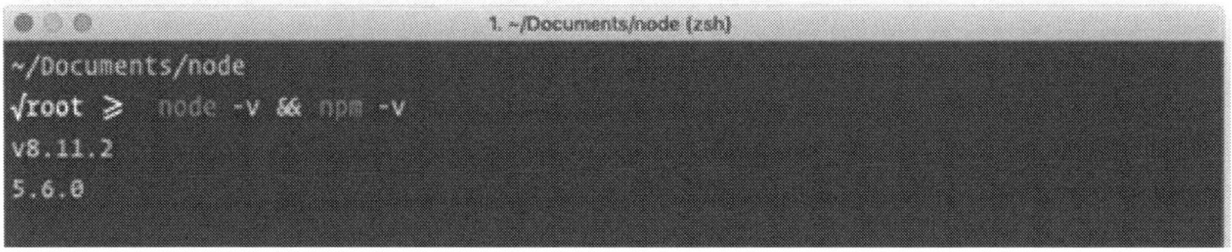

Figure 0.3: Installed versions of Node.js and npm

Here, it shows that the 8.11.2 version of Node.js is installed on the system, as is the 5.6.0 version of npm.

## INSTALLING THE CODE BUNDLE

Download the code files from GitHub at https://github.com/PacktPublishing/MongoDB-Fundamentals. The files here contain the exercises, activities, and some intermediate code for each chapter. This can be a useful reference when you become stuck.

You can use the **Download ZIP** option to download the complete code as a ZIP file. Alternatively, you can use the **git** command to check out the repository, as shown in the next snippet:

```
git clone https://github.com/PacktPublishing/MongoDB-Fundamentals.git
```

## GET IN TOUCH

Feedback from our readers is always welcome.

**General feedback**: If you have any questions about this book, please mention the book title in the subject of your message and email us at **customercare@ packtpub.com**.

**Errata**: Although we have taken every care to ensure the accuracy of our content, mistakes do happen. If you have found a mistake in this book, we would be grateful if you could report this to us. Please visit www.packtpub.com/support/errata and complete the form.

**Piracy**: If you come across any illegal copies of our works in any form on the Internet, we would be grateful if you could provide us with the location address or website name. Please contact us at `copyright@packt.com` with a link to the material.

**If you are interested in becoming an author**: If there is a topic that you have expertise in and you are interested in either writing or contributing to a book, please visit authors.packtpub.com.

## PLEASE LEAVE A REVIEW

Let us know what you think by leaving a detailed, impartial review on Amazon. We appreciate all feedback – it helps us continue to make great products and help aspiring developers build their skills. Please spare a few minutes to give your thoughts – it makes a big difference to us.

# 1

# INTRODUCTION TO MONGODB

## OVERVIEW

This chapter will introduce you to MongoDB fundamentals, first defining data and its types, then exploring how a database solves data storage challenges. You will learn about the different types of databases and how to select the right one for your task. Once you have a clear idea about these concepts, we will discuss MongoDB, its features, architecture, licensing, and deployment models. By the end of the chapter, you will have gained hands-on experience using MongoDB through Atlas—the cloud-based service used to manage MongoDB—and worked with its basic elements, such as databases, collections, and documents.

# INTRODUCTION

A database is a platform to store data in a way that is secure, reliable, and easily available. There are two types of databases used in general: relational databases and non-relational databases. Non-relational databases are often called as NoSQL databases. A NoSQL database is used to store large quantities of complex and diverse data, such as product catalogs, logs, user interactions, analytics, and more. MongoDB is one of the most established NoSQL databases, with features such as data aggregation, **ACID (Atomicity, Consistency, Isolation, Durability)** transactions, horizontal scaling, and Charts, all of which we will explore in detail in the upcoming sections.

Data is crucial for businesses—specifically, storing, analyzing, and visualizing the data while making data-driven decisions. It is for this reason that MongoDB is trusted and used by companies such as Google, Facebook, Adobe, Cisco, eBay, SAP, EA, and many more.

MongoDB comes in different variants and can be utilized for both experimental and real-world applications. It is easier to set up and simpler to manage than most other databases due to its intuitive syntax for queries and commands. MongoDB is available for anyone to install on their own machine(s) or to be used on the cloud as a managed service. MongoDB's cloud-managed service (called Atlas) is available to everyone for free, whether you are an established enterprise or a student. Before we start our discussion of MongoDB, let us first learn about database management systems.

## DATABASE MANAGEMENT SYSTEMS

A **Database Management System** (**DBMS**) provides the ability to store and retrieve data. It uses query languages to create, update, delete, and retrieve data. Let us look at the different types of DBMS.

### RELATIONAL DATABASE MANAGEMENT SYSTEMS

**Relational Database Management Systems** (**RDBMS**) are used to store structured data. The data is stored in the form of tables that consist of rows and columns. The tables can have relationships with other tables to depict the actual data relationships. For example, in a university relational database, the *Student* table can be related to the *Course* and *Marks Obtained* tables through a common columns such as *courseId*.

# NOSQL DATABASE MANAGEMENT SYSTEMS

NoSQL databases were invented to solve the problem of storing unstructured and semi-structured data. Relational databases enforce the structure of data to be defined before the data can be stored. This database structure definition is often referred to as schema, which pertains to the data entities, that is, its attributes and types. RDBMS client applications are tightly coupled with the schema. It is hard to modify the schema without affecting the clients. Contrastingly, NoSQL databases allow you to store the data without a schema and also support dynamic schema, which decouples the clients from a rigid schema, and is often necessary for modern and experimental applications.

The data stored in the NoSQL database varies depending on the provider, but generally, data is stored as documents instead of tables. An example of this would be databases for inventory management, where different products can have different attributes and, therefore, require a flexible structure. Similarly, an analytics database that stores data from different sources in different structures would also need a flexible structure.

## COMPARISON

Let us compare NoSQL databases and RDBMS based on the following factors. You will get an in-depth understanding of these as you read through this book. For now, a basic overview is provided in the following table:

| Feature | Relational Database | NoSQL Database |
|---|---|---|
| Schema | A relational database follows a rigid schema. The database tables should have a definition of all the desired columns and their types. Any data manipulation that deviates from the schema generates an error. | A NoSQL database does not impose a rigid schema and allows you to store the unstructured data with dynamic structures. This allows an evolving database structure. |
| Data model/ Storage Structure | The data is stored in tables. Each record is stored as a row that contains information about all the columns. Changing a table can affect the other tables and applications. | The data is stored in different formats, depending on the provider. The standard storage structures are documents, graphs, key-values, and wide columns. There is no alteration required as the database adapts to the dynamic nature of data and the application works seamlessly. |
| Normalization | Normalization is the process used to remove duplicate data and avoid data anomalies. A relational database prevents data anomalies, using normalization. It requires the data to be stored in different tables and to create relationships among them. | NoSQL databases focus more on fast data retrieval, and the data can be denormalized. |
| Scaling | Scaling is the ability of a database to grow or reduce in size, depending on the need. Relational databases are hard to scale and are generally scaled vertically, which means increasing the machine compute and storage. | NoSQL databases provide both vertical and horizontal scaling. In horizontal scaling, the data can be distributed across different machines/ clusters. |

Figure 1.1: Differences between relational databases and NoSQL

That concludes our discussion on databases and the differences between the various database types. In the next section, we will begin our exploration of MongoDB.

# INTRODUCTION TO MONGODB

MongoDB is a popular NoSQL database that can store both structured and unstructured data. Founded in 2007 by Kevin P. Ryan, Dwight Merriman, and Eliot Horowitz in New York, the organization was initially called 10gen and was later renamed MongoDB—a word inspired by the term **humongous**.

It provides both essential and extravagant features that are needed to store real-world big data. Its document-based design makes it easy to understand and use. It is built to be utilized for both experimental and real-world applications and is easier to set up and simpler to manage than most of the other NoSQL databases. Its intuitive syntax for queries and commands makes it easy to learn.

The following list explores these features in detail:

- **Flexible and Dynamic Schema**: MongoDB allows a flexible schema for your database. A flexible schema allows variance in fields in different documents. In simple terms, each record in the database may or may not have the same number of attributes. It addresses the need for storing evolving data without making any changes to the schema itself.

- **Rich Query Language**: MongoDB supports intuitive and rich query language, which means simple yet powerful queries. It comes with a rich aggregation framework that allows you to group and filter data as required. It also has built-in support for general-purpose text search and specific purposes like geospatial searches.

- **Multi-Document ACID Transactions**: **Atomicity, Consistency, Integrity, and Durability** (**ACID**) are features that allow your data to be stored and updated to maintain its accuracy. Transactions are used to combine operations that are required to be executed together. MongoDB supports ACID in a single document and multi-document transactions.

- **Atomicity** means all or nothing, which means either all operations are a part of a transaction as it happens or none of them are. This means that if one of the operations fails, then all the executed operations are rolled back to leave the data affected by transaction operation in the state it was in before the transaction started.

- **Consistency** in a transaction means keeping the data consistent as per the rules defined for the database. If a transaction breaks any database consistency rules, then it must be rolled back.

- **Isolation** enforces running transactions in isolation, which means that the transactions do not partially commit the data and any values outside the transactions change only after all the operations are executed and are fully committed.

- **Durability** ensures that the changes are committed by the transaction. So, if a transaction has executed then the database will ensure the changes are committed even if there is a system crash.

- **High Performance**: MongoDB provides high performance using embedded data models to reduce disk I/O usage. Also, extensive support for indexing on different kinds of data makes queries faster. Indexing is a mechanism to maintain relevant data pointers in an index just like an index in a book.

- **High Availability**: MongoDB supports distributed clusters with a minimum of three nodes. A cluster refers to a database deployment that uses multiple nodes/machines for data storage and retrieval. Failovers are automatic, and data is replicated on secondary nodes asynchronously.

- **Scalability**: MongoDB provides a way to scale your databases horizontally across hundreds of nodes. So, for all your big data needs, MongoDB is the perfect solution. With this, we have looked at some of the essential features of MongoDB.

> **NOTE**
>
> MongoDB 1.0 was first officially launched in February 2009 as an open source database. Since then, there have been several stable releases of the software. More information about different versions and the evolution of MongoDB can be found at the official MongoDB website (https://www.mongodb.com/evolved).

# MONGODB EDITIONS

MongoDB is available in two different editions to address the needs of developers and enterprises, as follows:

**Community Edition**: The Community Edition is released for the developer community, for those who want to learn and get hands-on experience with MongoDB. The Community Edition is free and is available for installation on Windows, Mac, and different Linux flavors, such as Red Hat, Ubuntu, and so on. You can run your production workload on community servers; however, for advanced enterprise features and support, you must consider the paid Enterprise Edition.

**Enterprise Edition**: The Enterprise Edition uses the same underlying software as the Community Edition but comes with some additional features, which include the following:

- *Security*: **Lightweight Directory Access Protocol** (**LDAP**) and Kerberos authentication. LDAP is a protocol that allows authentication from external user directories. This means that you do not need to create users in the database to authenticate them but can use external directories such as a corporate user directory. This saves a lot of time by not replicating users in different systems such as a database.

- *In-memory storage engine*: This provides high throughput and low latency.

- *Encrypted storage engine*: This lets you encrypt data at rest.

- *SNMP monitoring*: Centralized data collection and aggregation.

- *System event auditing*: This lets you record events in JSON format.

## MIGRATING COMMUNITY EDITION TO ENTERPRISE EDITION

MongoDB allows you to upgrade your Community Edition to the Enterprise Edition. This can be useful for scenarios in which you started with the Community Edition and eventually built a database that is now good for commercial use. For such cases, instead of installing the Enterprise Edition and building the database again, you can simply upgrade the Community Edition to the Enterprise Edition, saving time and effort. For more information about upgrading, you can visit this link: https://docs. mongodb.com/manual/administration/upgrade-community-to-enterprise/.

# THE MONGODB DEPLOYMENT MODEL

MongoDB can run on a variety of platforms, including Windows, macOS, and different flavors of Linux. You can install MongoDB on a single machine or a cluster of machines. Multiple machine installation provides high availability and scalability. The following list details each of these installation types:

**Standalone**

Standalone installation is a single-machine installation and is meant mainly for development or experimental purposes. You can refer to the *Preface* for the steps to install MongoDB on your system.

**Replica Set**

A replica set in MongoDB is a group of processes or servers that work together to provide data redundancy and high availability. Running MongoDB as a standalone process is not highly reliable because you may lose access to your data due to connectivity issues and disk failures. Using a replica set solves these problems as the data copies are stored on multiple servers. It requires at least three servers in a cluster. These servers are configured as the primary, secondaries, or arbiters. You will learn more about the replica set and its benefits in *Chapter 9, Replication*.

**Sharded**

Sharded deployments allow you to store the data in a distributed way. They are required for applications that manage massive data and expect high throughput. A shard contains a subset of the data, and each shard must use a replica set to provide redundancy of the data that it holds. Multiple shards working together provide a distributed and replicated dataset.

# MANAGING MONGODB

MongoDB provides the user with two options. Based on your requirements, you can either install it on your system and manage the database yourself or utilize the **Database as a Service** (**DBaaS**) option offered by MongoDB (Atlas). Let us learn more about these two options.

## SELF-MANAGED

MongoDB is available to be downloaded and installed on your machines. The machine can be a workstation, a server, a virtual machine in a data center, or on the cloud. You can install MongoDB as standalone, a replica set, or sharded clusters. All these deployments are possible with both the Community and Enterprise Editions. Each deployment has its advantages and associated complexity. A self-managed database can be useful for scenarios where you either want more granular control of your database or you just want to learn database management and operations.

## MANAGED SERVICE: DATABASE AS A SERVICE

A managed service is the concept of outsourcing some processes, functions, or deployments to a vendor. DBaaS is a term generally used for databases outsourced to an external vendor. A managed service enforces a shared responsibility model. The provider of the service manages the infrastructure, that is, the installation, deployment, failover, scalability, disk space, monitoring, and so on. You can manage the data and the settings for security, performance, and tuning. It allows you to save time managing databases and focus on other things, such as application development.

In this section, we learned about the history of MongoDB and its evolution. We also learned about different editions of MongoDB and the differences between them. We concluded the section by learning how MongoDB can be deployed and managed.

# MONGODB ATLAS

MongoDB Atlas is the DBaaS offering from MongoDB Inc. It allows you to provision a database on the cloud as a service, which can be used for your applications from anywhere. Atlas uses cloud infrastructures from different cloud vendors. You can choose the cloud vendor on which you want to deploy your database. Like any other managed service, you get the benefits of highly available secured environments with low or no maintenance needed.

## MONGODB ATLAS BENEFITS

Let us look at some of the benefits of MongoDB Atlas.

- **Simple Setup**: The database setup on Atlas is easy and can be done in just a few steps. Atlas runs a variety of automated tasks behind the scenes to set up your multi-node cluster.

- **Guaranteed Availability**: Atlas deploys at least three data nodes or servers per replica set. Each node is deployed in a separate availability zone (**Amazon Web Services** (**AWS**)), fault domains (Microsoft Azure), or zones (**Google Cloud Platform** (**GCP**)). This allows a highly available setup and continuous uptime in case of outages or routine updates.

- **Global Presence**: MongoDB Atlas is available across different regions in the AWS, GCP, and Microsoft Azure clouds. The support for different regions allows you to pick a region closer to you for low latency read and write.

- **Optimal Performance**: The founders of MongoDB manage Atlas, and they utilize their expertise and experience to keep the databases in Atlas running optimally. Also, single-click upgrades are available for upgrading to the latest versions of MongoDB.

- **Highly Secured**: Security best practices are implemented by default, such as a separate VPC (virtual private cloud), network encryption, access controls, and firewalls to restrict access.

- **Automated Backups**: You can configure automated backups with customizable schedules and data retention policies. Secure backups and restores are available for switching between different versions of your database.

## CLOUD PROVIDERS

MongoDB Atlas currently supports three cloud providers, namely **AWS**, **GCP**, and **Microsoft Azure**.

## AVAILABILITY ZONES

**Availability Zones** (**AZs**) are a group of physical data centers within close proximity, equipped with computational, storage, or networking resources.

## REGIONS

A region is a geographical area, for example, Sydney, Mumbai, London, and so on. A region generally consists of two or more AZs. The AZs are generally in different cities/towns away from each other, to provide fault tolerance in case of any natural disasters. Fault tolerance is the ability of a system to keep running when something goes wrong in one portion of the system. In terms of AZs, if one AZ goes down due to some reason, another AZ should still be able to serve the operations.

## MONGODB SUPPORTED REGIONS AND AVAILABILITY ZONES

MongoDB Atlas allows you to deploy your database in a multi-cloud global infrastructure from AWS, GCP, and Azure. It allows MongoDB to support a vast number of regions and AZs. Also, the number of supported regions and AZs keeps growing as cloud providers keep adding to them. Follow these links from the official MongoDB website about cloud providers' region support:

- AWS: https://docs.atlas.mongodb.com/reference/amazon-aws/#amazon-aws.

- GCP: https://docs.atlas.mongodb.com/reference/google-gcp/#google-gcp.

- Azure: https://docs.atlas.mongodb.com/reference/microsoft-azure/#microsoft-azure.

## ATLAS TIERS

To build a database cluster in MongoDB Atlas, you need to select a **tier**. A tier is a level of database power that you get from your cluster. When you provision your database in Atlas, you are given two parameters: RAM and storage. Depending on your selection of these parameters, an appropriate amount of database power is provisioned. The cost of your cluster is linked to the selection of RAM and storage; a higher selection means a higher cost and a lower selection means a lower cost.

M0 is the free tier available in MongoDB Atlas, which gives you shared RAM with storage of 512 MB. It is the tier that we will be using for our learning purposes. The free tier is not available in all regions, so if you do not find it in your region, select the closest free tier region. The proximity of your database determines the latency for your operations.

Selecting a tier requires an understanding of your database usage and how much you would like to spend. Under provisioned databases can exhaust your application's capacity at peak usage and can lead to application errors. Overprovisioned databases can help your application perform well but are more expensive. One of the advantages of using a cloud database is that you can always modify your cluster size as per your needs. But you still need to find what is the optimal capacity for your day-to-day database use. Determining the maximum number of concurrent connections is a critical decision factor that can help you choose the appropriate MongoDB Atlas tier for your use case. Let us look at the different tiers available:

| Maximum Number of Concurrent Incoming Connections | Tier Name | RAM | Storage size |
|---|---|---|---|
| 100 | M0 | Shared | 512 MB |
| 100 | M2 | Shared | 2 GB |
| 100 | M5 | Shared | 5 GB |
| 350 | M10 | 2 GB | 10 GB-100 GB |
| 700 | M20 | 4 GB | 20 GB – 200 GB |
| 2000 | M30 | 8 GB | 40 GB – 400 GB |
| 4000 | M40 / M40 Low CPU * | 16 GB / 15.24 GB | 80 GB – 800 GB |
| 16000 | M50 / M50 Low CPU * | 32 GB / 30.5 GB | 160 GB – 3000 GB |
| 32000 | M60 / M60 Low CPU* | 64 GB / 61 GB | 320 GB – 4000 GB |
| 64000 | M80 Low CPU* | 122 GB | 750 GB |
| 96000 | M100 | 160 GB | 1000 GB – 4000 GB |
| 128000 | M200 / M200 Low CPU* | 256 GB / 244 GB | 1500 GB – 4000 GB |
| 128000 | M400 Low CPU* | 488 GB | 3000 GB |

\* Low CPU tiers are available only with AWS clusters.

Figure 1.2: MongoDB Atlas tier configuration

## MONGODB ATLAS PRICING

Capacity planning is essential but estimating the cost of your database cluster is important too. We learned that an M0 cluster is free, with minimal resources, making it ideal for prototyping and learning purposes. For the paid cluster tiers, Atlas charges you on an hourly basis. The total cost is comprised of multiple factors, such as the type and number of servers. Let us look at an example to understand the cost estimation of an M30 type replica set (three servers) on Atlas.

## CLUSTER COST ESTIMATION

Let us try to understand how to estimate the cost of your MongoDB Atlas cluster. Identify the cluster requirements as follows:

- Machine type: M30

- Number of servers: 3 (replica set)

- Running time: 24 hours a day

- Estimation time period: 1 month

Once we have identified our requirements, the estimated cost can be calculated as follows:

- Cost of running a single M30 server per hour: $0.54

- Number of hours a server will run: 24 (hours) x 30 (days) = 720

- Cost of a single server for a month: 720 x 0.54 = $388.8

- Cost of running the three-server cluster: 388.8 x 3 = $1166.4

So, the total cost should come down to $1166.4.

> **NOTE**
>
> Apart from the running cost of your cluster, you should consider the cost of additional services such as backups, data transfer, and support contracts.

Let us implement our learning in an example scenario through the following exercise.

## EXERCISE 1.01: SETTING UP A MONGODB ATLAS ACCOUNT

MongoDB Atlas offers you free registration to set up a free cluster. In this exercise, you will create an account by executing the following steps:

1. Go to https://www.mongodb.com and click **Start free**. The following window appears:

Figure 1.3: MongoDB Atlas home page

2. You can sign up using your Google account or by providing your details manually as can be seen from the following screen. Provide your usage, **Your Work Email**, **First Name**, **Last Name**, and **Password** details in the respective fields, select the checkbox to agree to the terms of service and click **Get started free**.

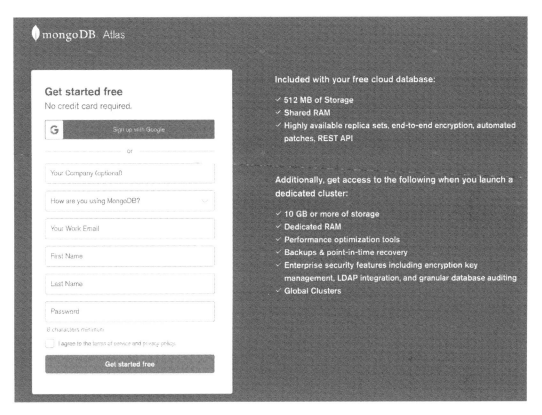

Figure 1.4: The Get started page

The following window appears in which you can enter your organization and project details:

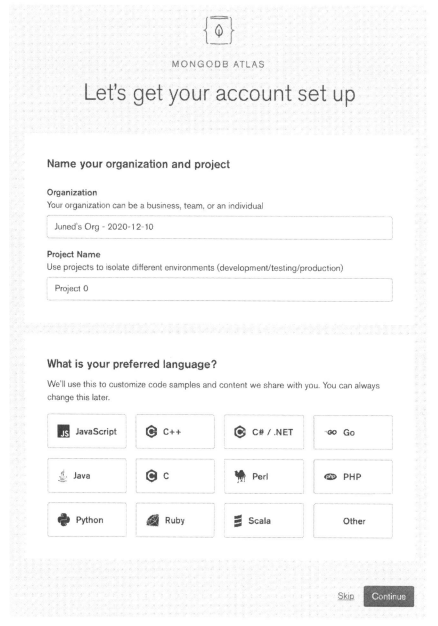

**Figure 1.5: Page to enter the organization and project details**

Next, you should see the following page, which means your account has been successfully created:

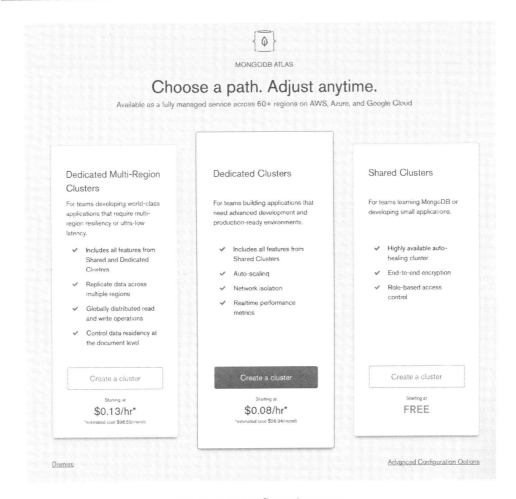

Figure 1.6: Confirmation page

In this exercise, you successfully created your MongoDB account.

# MONGODB ATLAS ORGANIZATIONS, PROJECTS, USERS, AND CLUSTERS

MongoDB Atlas enforces a basic structure for your environment. This includes the concepts of organizations, projects, users, and clusters. MongoDB provides a default organization and a project to help you get started easily. This section will teach you what these entities mean and how to set them up.

## ORGANIZATIONS

A MongoDB Atlas organization is the top-level entity in your account, containing other elements such as projects, clusters, and users. You need to set up an organization first before any other resources.

## EXERCISE 1.02: SETTING UP A MONGODB ATLAS ORGANIZATION

You have successfully created an account on MongoDB Atlas, and in this exercise, you will set up an organization based on your preferences:

1. Log on to your MongoDB account created in *Exercise 1.01*, *Setting Up a MongoDB Atlas Account*. To create an organization, select the **Organizations** option from your account menu as shown in the following figure:

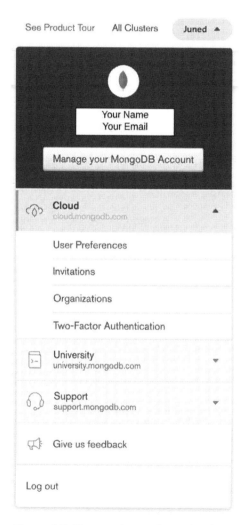

Figure 1.7: User options – Organizations

2. You will see the default organization in the list of organizations. To create a new organization, click the **Create New Organization** button in the top-right corner:

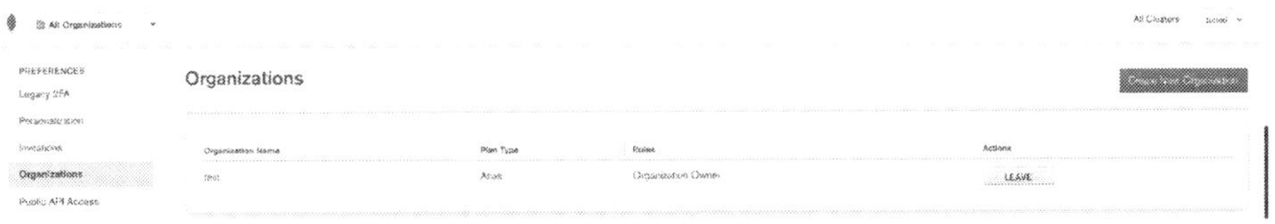

Figure 1.8: Organizations list

3. Type the organization name in the **Name Your Organization** field. Leave the default selection for **Cloud Service** as **MongoDB Atlas**. Click **Next** to proceed to the next step:

Figure 1.9: Organization Name

You will be presented with the following screen:

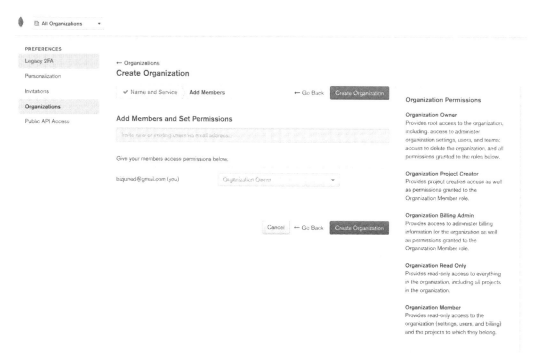

Figure 1.10: Create Organization page

4.  You will see your login as the **Organization Owner**. Leave everything as their defaults and click **Create Organization**.

    Once you have successfully created the organization, the following **Projects** screen will appear:

Figure 1.11: Projects page

So, in this exercise, you have successfully created the organization for your MongoDB application.

## PROJECTS

A project provides a grouping of clusters and users for a specific purpose; for example, you would like to segregate your lab, demo, and production environments. Similarly, you may like a different network, region, and user setup for different environments. Projects allow you to do this grouping as per your own organizational needs. In the next exercise, you will create a project.

### EXERCISE 1.03: CREATING A MONGODB ATLAS PROJECT

In this exercise, you will set up a project on MongoDB Atlas using the following steps:

1.  Once you have created an organization in *Exercise 1.02*, *Setting Up MongoDB Atlas Organization*, the **Projects** screen will appear on your next login. Click **New Project**:

Figure 1.12: Projects page

2.  Provide a name for your project on the **Name Your Project** tab. Name the project **myMongoProject**. Click **Next**:

Figure 1.13: Create a Project page

3.  Click **Create Project**. The **Add Members and Set Permissions** page is not mandatory, so leave it as the default. Your name should appear as the **Project Owner**:

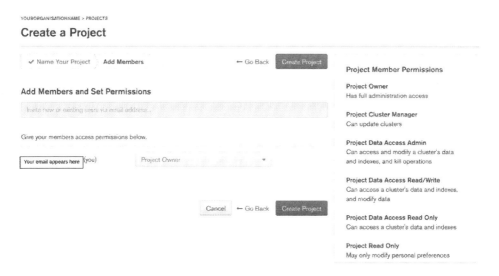

Figure 1.14: Add Members and Set Permissions for the project

Your project is now set up. A cluster setup splash screen appears as shown in the following figure:

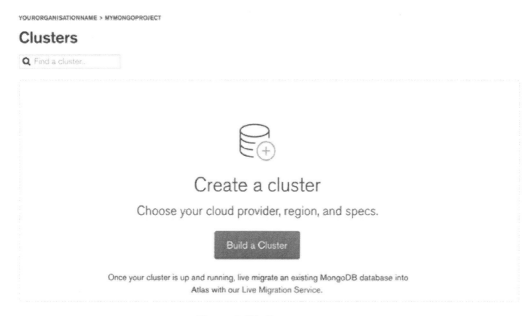

Figure 1.15: Clusters page

Now that you have created a project, you can create your first MongoDB cloud deployment.

## MONGODB CLUSTERS

A MongoDB cluster is the term used for a database replica set or shared deployments in MongoDB Atlas. A cluster is a distributed set of servers used for data storage and retrieval. A MongoDB cluster, at the minimum level, is a three-node replica set. In a sharded environment, a single cluster may contain hundreds of nodes/servers containing different replica sets with each replica set comprised of at least three nodes/servers.

## EXERCISE 1.04: SETTING UP YOUR FIRST FREE MONGODB CLUSTER ON ATLAS

In this section, you will set up your first MongoDB replica set on Atlas free tier (M0). Here are the steps to do this:

1. Go to https://www.mongodb.com/cloud/atlas and log on to your account using the credentials that you used in *Exercise 1.01, Setting Up a MongoDB Atlas Account*. The following screen appears:

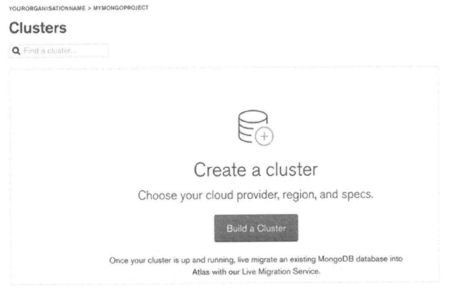

Figure 1.16: Clusters page

2. Click **Build a Cluster** to configure your cluster:

## Create a cluster

Choose your cloud provider, region, and specs.

Build a Cluster

Once your cluster is up and running, live migrate an existing MongoDB database into Atlas with our Live Migration Service.

Figure 1.17: Build a Cluster page

The following cluster options will appear:

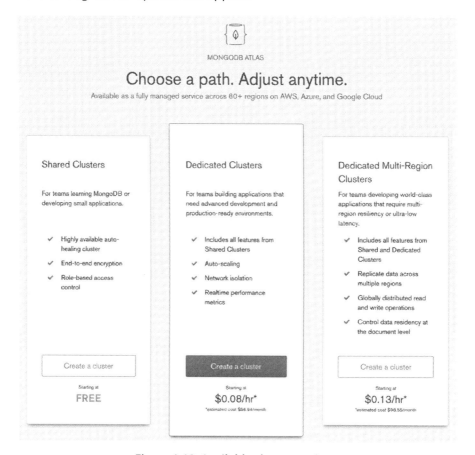

Figure 1.18: Available cluster options

3. Select the **Shared Clusters** option marked as **FREE** as shown in the previous figure.

4. A cluster configuration screen will be presented to select different options for your cluster. Select the cloud provider of your choice. For this exercise, you will be using AWS, as shown here:

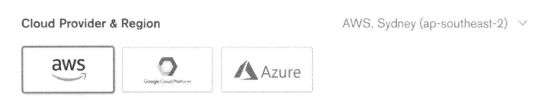

Figure 1.19: Selecting the cloud provider and region

5. Select the **Recommended region** that is closest to your location and is free. In this case, you are selecting **Sydney**, as can be seen from the following figure:

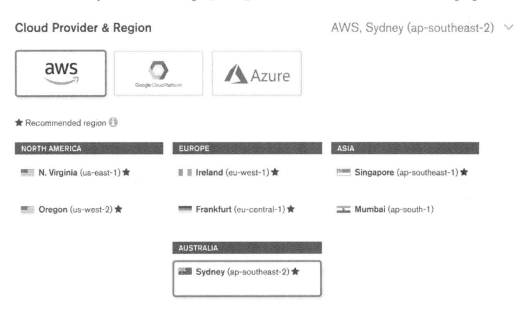

Figure 1.20: Selecting the recommended region

On the region selection page, you will see your cluster setting as per your selection. The **Cluster Tier** will be **M0 Sandbox (Shared RAM, 512 MB storage)**, **Additional Settings** will be **MongoDB 4.2 No Backup**, and **Cluster Name** will be **Cluster0**:

Figure 1.21: Additional Settings for the cluster

6. Ensure that the selections are made correctly in the preceding step so that the cost appears as **FREE**. Any selections different from what is recommended in the previous steps may add costs for your cluster. Click on **Create Cluster**:

Figure 1.22: FREE tier notification

A success message of **Your cluster is being created**... appears on the screen. It generally takes a few minutes to set up the cluster:

Figure 1.23: MongoDB Cluster getting created

After a few minutes, you should see your new cluster, as shown here:

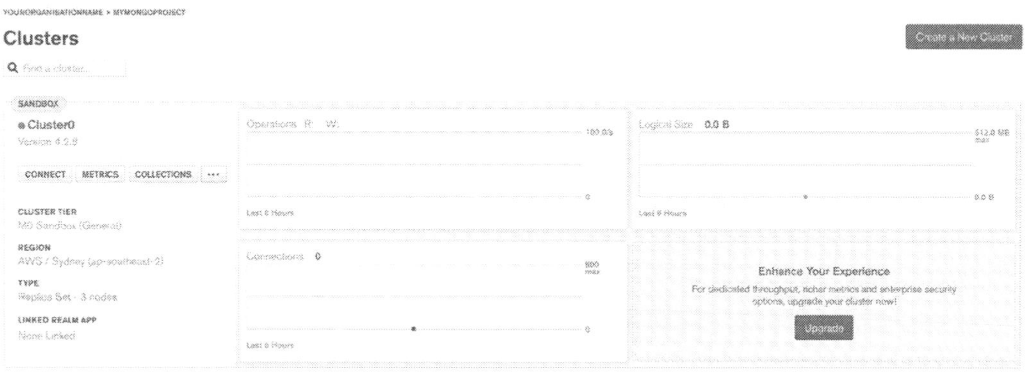

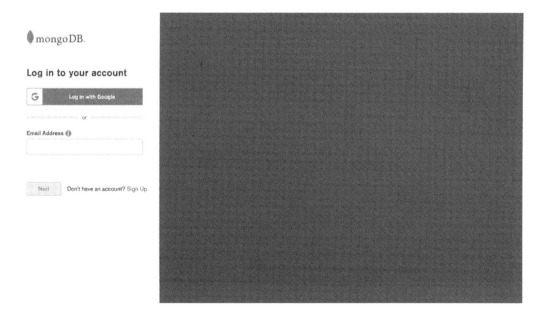

Figure 1.24: MongoDB cluster created

You have successfully created a new cluster.

## CONNECTING TO YOUR MONGODB ATLAS CLUSTER

Here are the steps to connect to your MongoDB Atlas cluster running on the cloud:

1. Go to https://account.mongodb.com/account/login. The following window appears:

Figure 1.25: MongoDB Atlas login page

2. Provide your email address and click **Next**:

Figure 1.26: MongoDB Atlas Login page (password)

3. Now type your **Password** and click **Login**. The **Clusters** window appears as shown here:

Figure 1.27: MongoDB Atlas Clusters screen

4. Click the **CONNECT** button under `Cluster0`. It will open a modal screen as follows:

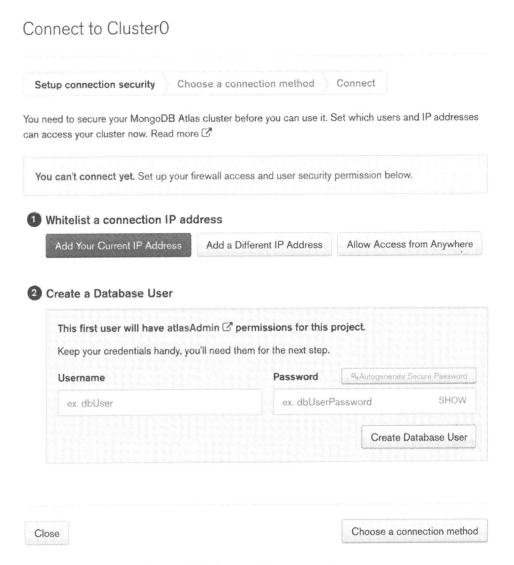

Figure 1.28: MongoDB Atlas modal screen

The first step before you connect to the cluster is to whitelist your IP address. MongoDB Atlas has a built-in security feature that is enabled by default, which blocks connectivity to the database from everywhere. So, the whitelisting of the client IP is necessary to connect to the database.

5.  Click **Add Your Current IP Address** to whitelist your IP as shown here:

Figure 1.29: Adding your current IP address

6.  The screen will show your current IP address; just click on the **Add IP Address** button. If you wish to add more IPs to the whitelist, you can add them manually by clicking the **Add a Different IP Address** option (see preceding figure):

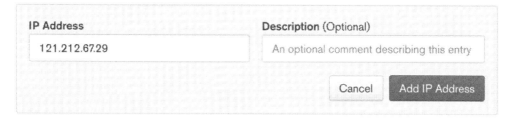

Figure 1.30: Adding your current IP address

The following message appears once the IP is whitelisted:

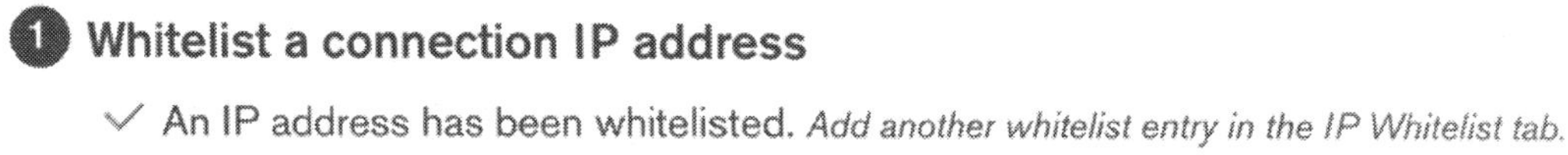

**Whitelist a connection IP address**

✓ An IP address has been whitelisted. *Add another whitelist entry in the IP Whitelist tab.*

Figure 1.31: IP whitelisted message

7.  To create a new MongoDB user, provide a **Username** and **Password** for a new user and click on the **Create Database User** button to create a user as shown here:

### 2 Create a Database User

**This first user will have atlasAdmin** ✷ **permissions for this project.**

Keep your credentials handy, you'll need them for the next step.

**Username**

> ex. dbUser

**Password**           ✷ Autogenerate Secure Password

> ex. dbUserPassword       SHOW

Create Database User

Figure 1.32: Creating a MongoDB user

Once the details are successfully updated, the following screen appears:

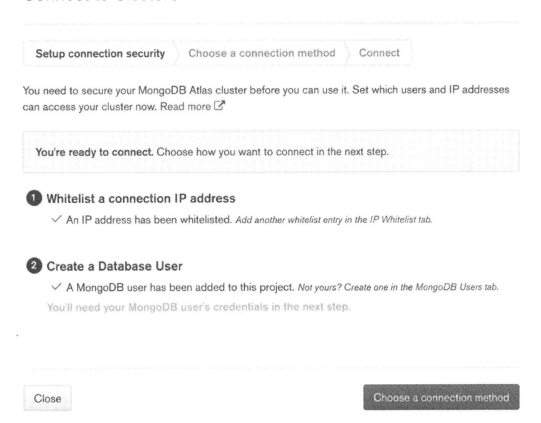

# Connect to Cluster0

**Setup connection security** > Choose a connection method > Connect

You need to secure your MongoDB Atlas cluster before you can use it. Set which users and IP addresses can access your cluster now. Read more ✷

**You're ready to connect.** Choose how you want to connect in the next step.

### 1 Whitelist a connection IP address

✓ An IP address has been whitelisted. *Add another whitelist entry in the IP Whitelist tab.*

### 2 Create a Database User

✓ A MongoDB user has been added to this project. *Not yours? Create one in the MongoDB Users tab.*

You'll need your MongoDB user's credentials in the next step.

Close

Choose a connection method

Figure 1.33: MongoDB user created screen

8. To choose a connection method, click on the **Choose a connection method** button. Select the Connect with the mongo shell option as shown here:

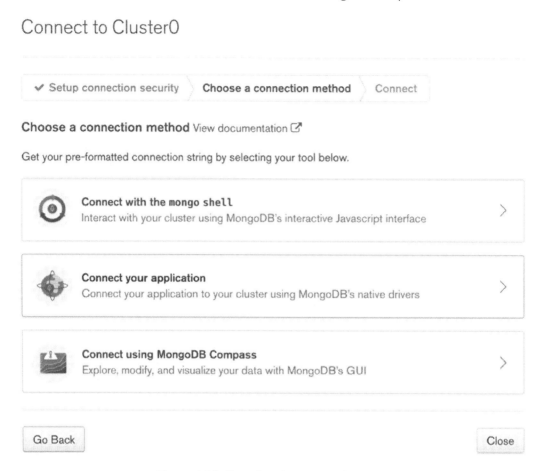

Figure 1.34: Choosing the connection type

9. Download and install the mongo shell by selecting the options for your workstation/client machine as shown in the following screenshot:

Figure 1.35: Installing the mongo shell

The mongo shell is a command-line client to connect to your Mongo server(s). You will be using this client throughout the book, so it is imperative that you install it.

10. Once you have the mongo shell installed, run the connection string you grabbed in the preceding step to connect to your database. When prompted, enter the password that you used for your MongoDB user in the previous step:

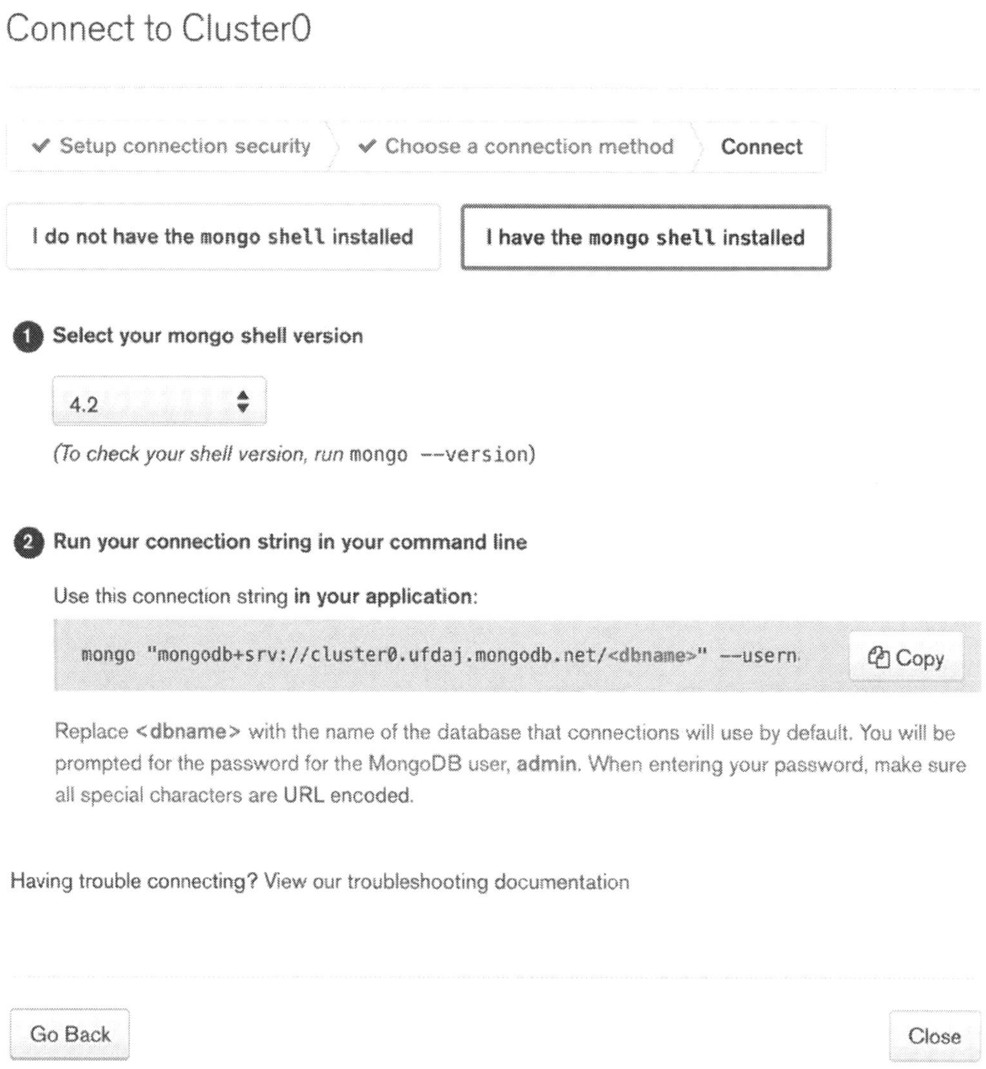

## Connect to Cluster0

✔ Setup connection security  ›  ✔ Choose a connection method  ›  **Connect**

| I do not have the mongo shell installed | **I have the mongo shell installed** |

**1** Select your mongo shell version

    4.2    ⬍

*(To check your shell version, run* mongo --version*)*

**2** Run your connection string in your command line

Use this connection string **in your application**:

```
mongo "mongodb+srv://cluster0.ufdaj.mongodb.net/<dbname>" --usern    ⧉ Copy
```

Replace **<dbname>** with the name of the database that connections will use by default. You will be prompted for the password for the MongoDB user, **admin**. When entering your password, make sure all special characters are URL encoded.

Having trouble connecting? View our troubleshooting documentation

    Go Back                                                                    Close

Figure 1.36: Installing the mongo shell

If everything goes well, you should see the mongo shell connected to your Atlas cluster. Here is a sample output of a connecting string execution:

```
MongoDB shell version v4.2.0
Enter password:
connecting to: mongodb://cluster0-shard-00-00.ufdaj.mongodb.net:27017,cluster0-shard-00-01.ufdaj.mongodb.net:27017,cluster0-shard-00-02.ufdaj.mongodb.net:27017/%3
Cdbname%3E?authSource=admin&compressors=disabled&gssapiServiceName=mongodb&replicaSet=atlas-ae64cx-shard-0&ssl=true
2020-08-12T21:09:44.569+1000 I  NETWORK  [js] Starting new replica set monitor for atlas-ae64cx-shard-0/cluster0-shard-00-00.ufdaj.mongodb.net:27017,cluster0-shar
d-00-01.ufdaj.mongodb.net:27017,cluster0-shard-00-02.ufdaj.mongodb.net:27017
2020-08-12T21:09:44.569+1000 I  CONNPOOL [ReplicaSetMonitor-TaskExecutor] Connecting to cluster0-shard-00-01.ufdaj.mongodb.net:27017
2020-08-12T21:09:44.569+1000 I  CONNPOOL [ReplicaSetMonitor-TaskExecutor] Connecting to cluster0-shard-00-02.ufdaj.mongodb.net:27017
2020-08-12T21:09:44.570+1000 I  CONNPOOL [ReplicaSetMonitor-TaskExecutor] Connecting to cluster0-shard-00-00.ufdaj.mongodb.net:27017
2020-08-12T21:09:44.649+1000 I  NETWORK  [ReplicaSetMonitor-TaskExecutor] Confirmed replica set for atlas-ae64cx-shard-0 is atlas-ae64cx-shard-0/cluster0-shard-00
-00.ufdaj.mongodb.net:27017,cluster0-shard-00-01.ufdaj.mongodb.net:27017,cluster0-shard-00-02.ufdaj.mongodb.net:27017
Implicit session: session { "id" : UUID("73ea8a62-0065-4d88-a273-b47da2786189") }
MongoDB server version: 4.2.8
Error while trying to show server startup warnings: user is not allowed to do action [getLog] on [admin.]
MongoDB Enterprise atlas-ae64cx-shard-0:PRIMARY> 
```

**Figure 1.37: Output of connecting string execution**

Ignore the warnings seen in *Figure 1.37*. At the end, you should see your cluster name and a command prompt. You can run the **show databases** command to list the existing database. You should see the two databases that are used by MongoDB for administrative purposes. Here is some sample output of the **show databases** command:

```
MongoDB Enterprise Cluster0-shard-0:PRIMARY> show databases
admin   0.000GB
local   4.215GB
```

You have successfully connected to your MongoDB Atlas instance.

## MONGODB ELEMENTS

Let us dive into some very basic elements of MongoDB, such as databases, collections, and documents. Databases are basically aggregations of collections, which in turn, are made up of documents. A document is the basic building block in MongoDB and contains information about the various fields in a key-value format.

## DOCUMENTS

MongoDB stores data records in documents. A document is a collection of field names and values, structured in a **JavaScript Object Notation (JSON)**-like format. JSON is an easy-to-understand key-value pair format to describe data. The documents in MongoDB are stored as an extension of the JSON type, which is called BSON (Binary JSON). It is a binary-encoded serialization of JSON-like documents. BSON is designed to be more efficient in space than standard JSON. BSON also contains extensions that allow the representation of data types that cannot be represented in JSON. We will look at these in detail in *Chapter 2, Documents and Data Types*.

## DOCUMENT STRUCTURES

MongoDB documents contain field and value pairs and follow a basic structure, as follows:

```
{

    "firstFieldName": firstFieldValue,

    "secondFieldName": secondFieldValue,

    ...

    "nthFieldName": nthFieldValue

}
```

The following is an example of a document that contains details about a person:

```
{

    "_id":ObjectId("5da26111139a21bbe11f9e89"),

    "name":"Anita P",

    "placeOfBirth":"Koszalin",

    "profession":"Nursing"


}
```

The following is another example with some fields and date types from BSON:

```
{

    "_id" : ObjectId("5da26553fb4ef99de45a6139"),

    "name" : "Roxana",

    "dateOfBirth" : new Date("Dec 25, 2007"),

    "placeOfBirth" : "Brisbane",

    "profession" : "Student"

}
```

The following example of a document contains an array and a sub-document. An array is a set of values and can be used when you need to store multiple values for a key such as hobbies. Sub-documents allow you to wrap related attributes in a document against a key, such as an address:

```
{
    "_id" : ObjectId("5da2685bfb4ef99de45a613a"),
    "name" : "Helen",
    "dateOfBirth" : new Date("Dec 25, 2007"),
    "placeOfBirth" : "Brisbane",
    "profession" : "Student",
    "hobbies" : [
     "painting",
     "football",
     "singing",
     "story-writing"],
    "address" : {
     "city" : "Sydney",
    "country" : "Australia",
    "postcode" : 2161
   }
}
```

The **_id** field shown in the preceding snippet is auto generated by MongoDB and is used as a unique identifier for the document. We will learn more about this in the upcoming chapters.

## COLLECTIONS

In MongoDB, documents are stored in collections. Collections are analogous to tables in relational databases. You need to use the collection name in your queries for operations such as insert, retrieve, delete, and so on.

## UNDERSTANDING MONGODB DATABASES

A database is a container for collections grouped together. Each database has several files on the filesystem that contain database metadata and the actual data stored in collections. MongoDB allows you to have multiple databases, and each of these databases can have various collections. In turn, each of these collections can have numerous documents. This is illustrated in the following figure, which shows an events database that contains collections for different event-related fields, such as *Person*, *Location*, and *Events*; these, in turn, contain various documents with all the granular data:

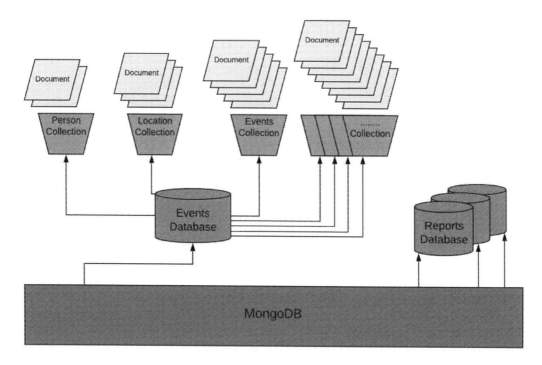

Figure 1.38: Pictorial representation of a MongoDB database

## CREATING A DATABASE

Creating a database in MongoDB is very simple. Execute the **use** command in the mongo shell as follows, by replacing **yourDatabaseName** with your own choice of database name:

```
use yourDatabaseName
```

If the database does not exist, Mongo will create the database and will switch the current database to the new database. If the database exists, Mongo will refer to the existing database. Here is the output of the last command:

```
switched to db yourDatabaseName
```

> **NOTE**
>
> Naming conventions and using logical names always help even if you are working on a learning project. The project name is meant to be replaced by something more meaningful for you and understandable for later use. This rule applies to the name of any asset that we create, so try to use logical names.

## CREATING A COLLECTION

You can use the **createCollection** command to create a collection. This command allows you to utilize different options for your collection, such as a capped collection, validation, collation, and so on. Another way to create a collection is by just inserting a document in a non-existent collection. In such a case, MongoDB checks whether the collection exists, and if not, it will create the collection before inserting the documents passed. We will try to utilize both methods to create a collection.

To create the collection explicitly, use the **createCollection** operation in the syntax as follows:

```
db.createCollection( '<collectionName>',
{
    capped: <boolean>,
    autoIndexId: <boolean>,
    size: <number>,
    max: <number>,
    storageEngine: <document>,
    validator: <document>,
    validationLevel: <string>,
    validationAction: <string>,
    indexOptionDefaults: <document>,
    viewOn: <string>,
```

```
    pipeline: <pipeline>,
    collation: <document>,
    writeConcern: <document>
})
```

In the following snippet, we are creating a capped collection with a maximum of 5 documents, with each document having a size limit of 256 bytes. The capped collection works like a circular queue, which means older documents will go out to make space for the latest inserts when the maximum size is reached:

```
db.createCollection('myCappedCollection',
{
    capped: true,
    size: 256,
    max: 5
})
```

Here is the output of the **createCollection** command:

```
{
    «ok» : 1,
    «$clusterTime» : {
            «clusterTime» : Timestamp(1592064731, 1),
            «signature» : {
                    «hash» : BinData(0,»XJ2DOzjAagUkftFkLQIT
                      9W2rKjc="),
                    «keyId» : NumberLong(«6834058563036381187»)
            }
    },
    «operationTime» : Timestamp(1592064731, 1)
}
```

Do not worry about the preceding options much as none of them are mandatory. If you do not need to set any of these, then your **createCollection** command can be simplified as follows:

```
db.createCollection('myFirstCollection')
```

The output of this command should look as follows:

```
{
    «ok» : 1,
    «$clusterTime» : {
            «clusterTime» : Timestamp(1597230876, 1),
            «signature» : {
```

```
                «hash» : BinData(0,»YO8Flg5AglrxCV3XqEuZG
                   aaLzZc="),
                «keyId» : NumberLong(«6853300587753111555»)
            }
        },
        «operationTime» : Timestamp(1597230876, 1)
}
```

## CREATING A COLLECTION USING DOCUMENT INSERTION

You do not need to create a collection before inserting documents. MongoDB creates a collection if it does not exist on the first document insertion. You would use this method as follows:

```
use yourDatabaseName;
db.myCollectionName.insert(
{
    "name" : "Yahya A",  "company" :  "Sony"}
);
```

The output of your command should look like this:

```
WriteResult({ "nInserted" : 1 })
```

The preceding output returns the number of documents inserted into the collection. As you have inserted a document in a non-existent collection, MongoDB must have created the collection for us before inserting this document. To confirm that, display your collections list using the following command:

```
show collections;
```

The output of your command should display the list of collections in your database, something like this:

```
myCollectionName
```

## CREATING DOCUMENTS

As you must have noticed in the previous section, we used the **insert** command to put a document in a collection. Let us look at a couple of variants of **insert** commands.

## INSERTING A SINGLE DOCUMENT

The **insertOne** command is used to insert one document at a time, as in the following syntax:

```
db.blogs.insertOne(
    { username: "Zakariya", noOfBlogs: 100, tags: ["science",
      "fiction"]
})
```

The **insertOne** operation returns the **_id** value of the newly inserted document. Here is the output of the **insertOne** command:

```
{
    "acknowledged" : true,
    "insertedId" : ObjectId("5ea3a1561df5c3fd4f752636")
}
```

> **NOTE**
>
> **insertedId** is the unique ID for the document that is inserted, and it will not be the same for you as mentioned in the output.

## INSERTING MULTIPLE DOCUMENTS

The **insertMany** command inserts multiple documents at once. You can pass an array of documents to the command as mentioned in the following snippet:

```
db.blogs.insertMany(
[
        { username: "Thaha", noOfBlogs: 200, tags: ["science",
          "robotics"]},
        { username: "Thayebbah", noOfBlogs: 500, tags: ["cooking",
    "general knowledge"]},
        { username: "Thaherah", noOfBlogs: 50, tags: ["beauty",
          "arts"]}
]
)
```

The output returns the **_id** values of all the newly inserted documents:

```
{
    «acknowledged» : true,
    «insertedIds» : [
```

```
    ObjectId(«5f33cf74592962df72246ae8»),
    ObjectId(«5f33cf74592962df72246ae9»),
    ObjectId(«5f33cf74592962df72246aea»)
  ]
}
```

## FETCHING DOCUMENTS FROM MONGODB

MongoDB provides the **find** command to fetch documents from a collection. This command is useful to check whether your inserts are actually saved in the collections. Here is the syntax for the **find** command:

```
db.collection.find(query, projection)
```

The command takes two optional parameters: **query** and **projection**. The **query** parameter allows you to pass a document to apply filters during the **find** operation. The **projection** parameter allows you to pick desired attributes from the returned documents instead of all the attributes. When no parameter is passed in the **find** command, then all the documents are returned.

## FORMATTING THE FIND OUTPUT USING THE PRETTY() METHOD

When the **find** command returns multiple records, it is sometimes hard to read them as they are not formatted properly. MongoDB provides the **pretty ()** method at the end of the **find** command to get the returned records in a formatted manner. To see it in action, insert a couple of records in a collection called **records**:

```
db.records.insertMany(
[
  { Name: "Aaliya A", City: "Sydney"},
  { Name: "Naseem A", City: "New Delhi"}
]
)
```

It should generate an output as follows:

```
{
  "acknowledged" : true,
  "insertedIds" : [
    ObjectId("5f33cfac592962df72246aeb"),
    ObjectId("5f33cfac592962df72246aec")
  ]
}
```

First, fetch these records using the **find** command without the **pretty** method:

```
db.records.find()
```

It should return an output as shown here:

```
{ "_id" : ObjectId("5f33cfac592962df72246aeb"), "Name" : "Aaliya A",
  "City" : "Sydney" }
{ "_id" : ObjectId("5f33cfac592962df72246aec"), "Name" : "Naseem A",
  "City" : "New Delhi" }
```

Now, run the same **find** command using the **pretty** method:

```
db.records.find().pretty()
```

It should return the same records, but in a beautifully formatted way as shown here:

```
{
    "_id" : ObjectId("5f33cfac592962df72246aeb"),
    "Name" : "Aaliya A",
    "City" : "Sydney"
}
{
    "_id" : ObjectId("5f33cfac592962df72246aec"),
    "Name" : "Naseem A",
    "City" : "New Delhi"
}
```

Clearly, the **pretty()** method can be quite useful when you are looking at multiple or nested documents, as the output is more easily readable.

## ACTIVITY 1.01: SETTING UP A MOVIES DATABASE

You are one of the founders of a company that builds software about movies from all over the world. Your team does not have much database administration skills and there is no budget to hire a database administrator. Your task is to provide a deployment strategy and basic database schema/structure and set up the movies database.

The following steps will help you complete the activity:

1. Connect to your database.

2. Create a movies database named **moviesDB**.

3. Create a movies collection and insert the following sample data: https://packt.live/3lJXKuE.

```
[
    {
        "title": "Rocky",
        "releaseDate": new Date("Dec 3, 1976"),
        "genre": "Action",
        "about": "A small-time boxer gets a supremely rare chance
            to fight a heavy-  weight champion in a bout in
            which he strives to go the distance for his self-respect.",
        "countries": ["USA"],
        "cast" : ["Sylvester Stallone","Talia Shire",
            "Burt Young"],
        "writers" : ["Sylvester Stallone"],
        "directors" : ["John G. Avildsen"]
    },
    {
        "title": "Rambo 4",
        "releaseDate ": new Date("Jan 25, 2008"),
        "genre": "Action",
        "about": "In Thailand, John Rambo joins a group of
            mercenaries to venture into war-torn Burma, and rescue
            a group of Christian aid workers who were kidnapped
            by the ruthless local infantry unit.",
        "countries": ["USA"],
        "cast" : [" Sylvester Stallone", "Julie Benz",
            "Matthew Marsden"],
        "writers" : ["Art Monterastelli",
            "Sylvester Stallone"],
        "directors" : ["Sylvester Stallone"]
    }
]
```

4. Check whether the documents are inserted by fetching the documents.

5. Create an **awards** collection with a few records using the following data:

```
{
    "title": "Oscars",
    "year": "1976",
    "category": "Best Film",
    "nominees": ["Rocky","All The President's Men","Bound For
        Glory","Network","Taxi Driver"],
    "winners" :
```

```
[
    {
        "movie" : "Rocky"
    }
]
}
{
    "title": "Oscars",
    "year": "1976",
    "category": "Actor In A Leading Role",
    "nominees": ["PETER FINCH","ROBERT DE NIRO",
      "GIANCARLO GIANNINI","WILLIAM  HOLDEN","SYLVESTER STALLONE"],
    "winners" :
    [
        {
            "actor" : "PETER FINCH",
            "movie" : "Network"
        }
    ]
}
```

6.  Check whether your inserts have saved the documents in the collection as desired by fetching the documents.

> **NOTE**
>
> The solution to this Activity can be found on Page 642

## SUMMARY

We began this chapter by covering the fundamentals of data, databases, RDBMS, and NoSQL databases. You learned the differences between RDBMS and NoSQL databases, and how to decide which database is a good fit for a given scenario. You learned that MongoDB can be used as self-managed or as DbaaS, set up your account in MongoDB Atlas, and reviewed MongoDB deployment on different cloud platforms and how to estimate its cost. We concluded the chapter with the MongoDB structure and its basic components, such as databases, collections, and documents. In the next chapter, you will utilize these concepts to explore MongoDB components and its data model.

# 2

# DOCUMENTS AND DATA TYPES

## OVERVIEW

This chapter introduces you to MongoDB documents, their structure, and data types. For those who are new to the JSON model, this chapter will also serve as a short introduction to JSON. You will identify the basic concepts and data types of JSON documents and compare the document-based storage of MongoDB with the tabular storage of relational databases. You will learn how to represent complex data structures in MongoDB using embedded objects and arrays. By the end of this chapter, you will understand the need for precautionary limits and restrictions on MongoDB documents.

# INTRODUCTION

In the previous chapter, we learned how MongoDB, as a NoSQL database, differs from traditional relational databases. We covered the basic features of MongoDB, including its architecture, its different versions, and MongoDB Atlas.

MongoDB is designed for modern-world applications. We live in a world where requirements change rapidly. We want to build lightweight and flexible applications that can quickly adapt to these new requirements and ship them to production as quickly as possible. We want our databases to become agile so that they can adapt to the ever-changing needs of our applications, reduce downtime, scale out easily, and perform efficiently. MongoDB is a perfect fit for all such needs.

One of the major factors that make MongoDB an agile database is its document-based data model. Documents are widely accepted as a flexible way of transporting information. You might have come across many applications that exchange data in the form of **JavaScript Object Notation (JSON)** documents. MongoDB stores data in Binary JSON (BSON) format and represents it in human readable JSON. This means that when we use MongoDB, we see the data in JSON format. This chapter begins with an overview of the JSON and BSON formats, followed by details of MongoDB documents and data types.

# INTRODUCTION TO JSON

JSON is a full-text, lightweight format for data representation and transportation. JavaScript's simple representation of objects gave birth to JSON. Douglas Crockford, who was one of the developers of the JavaScript language, came up with the proposal for the JSON specification that defines the grammar and data types for the JSON syntax.

The JSON specification became a standard in 2013. If you have been developing applications for a while, you might have seen the transition of applications from XML to JSON. JSON offers a human-readable, plain-text way of representing data. In comparison to XML, where information is wrapped inside tags, and lots of tags make it look bulky, JSON offers a compact and natural format where you can easily focus on the information.

To read or write information in JSON or XML format, the programming languages use their respective parsers. As XML documents are bound by schema definitions and tag library definitions, parsers need to do a lot of work to read and validate **XML Schema Definition (XSD)** and **Tag Library Descriptors (TLDs)**.

On the other hand, JSON does not have any schema definition, and JSON parsers only need to deal with opening and closing brackets and colons. Different programming languages have different ways of representing language constructs, such as objects, lists, arrays, variables, and more. When two systems, written in two different programming languages, want to exchange data, they need to have a mutually agreed standard for representing information. JSON provides that standard with its lightweight format. The objects, collections, and variables of any programming language can naturally fit into the JSON structure. Most programming languages have parsers that can translate their own objects to and from JSON documents.

> **NOTE**
>
> JSON does not impose JavaScript language internals on other languages. JSON is the syntax for language-independent data representation. The grammar that defines the JSON format was derived from JavaScript's syntax. However, to use JSON, programmers do not need to know JavaScript internals

## JSON SYNTAX

JSON documents or objects are a plain-text set of zero or more key-value pairs. The key-value pairs form an object, and if the value is a collection of zero or more values, they form an array. JSON has a very simple structure where, by only using a set of curly braces ( **{ }** ), square brackets ( **[ ]** ), colons ( **:** ), and commas( **,** ), you can represent any complex piece of information in a compact form.

In a JSON object, key-value pairs are enclosed within curly braces: **{ }**. Within an object, the key is always a string. However, the value can be any of JSON's specified types. The JSON grammar specification does not define any order for JSON fields and can be represented as follows:

```
{
  key : value
}
```

The preceding document represents a valid JSON object that has a single key-value pair. Moving on to JSON arrays, an array is a set of zero or more values that are enclosed within square brackets, `[]`, and separated by commas. While most programming languages have support for ordered arrays, JSON's specification does not specify the order for array elements. Let's take a look at an example array that has three fields separated by commas:

```
[
   value1,
   value2,
   value3
]
```

Now that we have looked at JSON syntax, let's consider a sample JSON document that contains the basic information of a company. The example demonstrates how naturally a piece of information can be presented in document format, making it easily readable:

```
{
   "company_name" : "Sparter",
   "founded_year" : 2007,
   "twitter_username" : null,
   "address" : "15 East Street",
   "no_of_employees" : 7890,
   "revenue" : 879423000
}
```

From the preceding document, we can see the following:

- Company name and address, both being string fields
- Foundation year, number of employees, and revenue as numeric fields
- The company's Twitter username as null or no information

## JSON DATA TYPES

Unlike many programming languages, JSON supports a limited and basic set of data types, as follows:

- **String**: Refers to plain text
- **Number**: Consists of all numeric fields
- **Boolean**: Consists of `True` or `False`

- **Object**: Other embedded JSON objects

- **Array**: Collection of fields

- **Null**: Special value to denote fields without any value

One of the major reasons for the wide acceptance of JSON is its language-independent format. Different languages have different data types. Some languages support **statically typed variables**, while some support **dynamically typed variables**. If JSON had many data types, it would be more in line with a number of languages—though, not all.

JSON is a data exchange format. When an application transmits a piece of information over the wire, the information gets serialized into plain strings. The receiving application then deserializes the information into its objects so that it becomes available to use. The presence of basic data types provided by JSON reduces complexity during this process.

Thus, JSON keeps it simple and minimal in terms of data types. JSON parsers specific to programming languages can easily relate basic data types to the most specific types the language provides.

## JSON AND NUMBERS

As per the JSON specification, a number is just a sequence of digits. It does not differentiate between numbers such as **integer**, **float**, or **long**. Additionally, it restricts the range limits of numbers. This leads to greater flexibility when data is transferred or represented.

However, there are some challenges involved. Most programming languages represent numbers in the form of **integer**, **float**, or **long**. When a piece of information is presented in JSON, the parsers cannot anticipate the exact format or range of a numeric field in the entire document. To avoid number format corruption or the loss of precision of numeric fields, the two parties exchanging data should agree and follow a certain contract in advance.

For instance, say you are reading a movie record set in the form of JSON documents. When you look at the first record, you find the **audience_rating** field is an **integer**. However, when you reach the next record, you realize it is a **float**:

```
{audience_rating: 6}
{audience_rating: 7.6}
```

We will look at how this issue can be overcome in an upcoming section, *BSON*.

## JSON AND DATES

As you may have noticed, JSON documents do not support the **Date** data type, and all dates are represented as plain strings. Let's look at an example of a few JSON documents, each of which has a valid date representation:

```
{"title": "A Swedish Love Story", released: "1970-04-24"}
{"title": "A Swedish Love Story", released: "24-04-1970"}
{"title": "A Swedish Love Story", released: "24th April 1970"}
{"title": "A Swedish Love Story", released: "Fri, 24 Apr 1970"}
```

Although all the documents represent the same date, they are written in a different format. Different systems, based on their local standards, use different formats to write the same date and time instances.

Like the examples of JSON numbers, the parties exchanging the information need to standardize the **Date** format during the transfers.

> **NOTE**
>
> Remember that the JSON specification defines syntax and grammar for data representation. However, how you read the data depends on the interpreters of the languages and their data exchange contracts.

## EXERCISE 2.01: CREATING YOUR OWN JSON DOCUMENT

Now that you have learned the basics of JSON syntax, it is time to put this knowledge into practice. Suppose your organization wants to build a dataset of movies and series, and they want to use MongoDB to store the records. As a proof of concept, they ask you to choose a random movie and represent it in JSON format.

In this exercise, you will write your first basic JSON document from scratch and verify whether it is a grammatically valid document. For this exercise, you will consider a sample movie, **Beauty and the Beast**, and refer to the **Movie ID**, **Movie Title**, **Release Year**, **Language**, **IMDb Rating Genre**, **Director**, and **Runtime** fields, which contain the following information:

```
Movie Id = 14253
Movie Title = Beauty and the Beast
Release Year = 2016
Language = English
IMDb Rating = 6.4
Genre = Romance
Director = Christophe Gans
Runtime = 112
```

To successfully create a JSON document for the preceding listed fields, first differentiate each field into key-value pairs. Execute the following steps to achieve the desired result:

1. Open a JSON validator—for example, https://jsonlint.com/.

2. Type the preceding information in JSON format, which looks as follows:

```
{
    "id" : 14253,
    "title" : "Beauty and the Beast",
    "year" : 2016,
    "language" : "English",
    "imdb_rating" : 6.4,
    "genre" : "Romance",
    "director" : "Christophe Gans",
    "runtime" : 112
}
```

Remember, a JSON document always starts with **{** and ends with **}**. Each element is separated by a colon (**:**) and the key-value pairs are separated by a comma (**,**).

3. Click on **Validate JSON** to validate the code. The following screenshot displays the expected output and validity of the JSON document:

```
1 ▾ {
2       "id": 14253,
3       "title": "Beauty and the Beast",
4       "year": 2016,
5       "language": "English",
6       "imdb_rating": 6.4,
7       "genre": "Romance",
8       "director": "Christophe Gans",
9       "runtime": 112
10  }
```

| Validate JSON | Clear | Support JSONLint for $2/Month |

Figure 2.1: The JSON document and its validity check

In this exercise, you modeled a movie record into a document format and created a grammatically valid JSON object. To practice it more, you can consider any general item, such as a product you recently bought or a book you read, and model it as a valid JSON document. In the next section, we will look at a brief overview of MongoDB's BSON.

# BSON

When you work with MongoDB using database clients such as mongo shell, MongoDB Compass, or the Collections Browser in Mongo Atlas, you always see the documents in human readable JSON format. However, internally, MongoDB documents are stored in a binary format called BSON. BSON documents are not human-readable, and you will never have to deal with them directly. Before we explore MongoDB documents in detail, let's have a quick overview of the BSON features that benefit the MongoDB document structure.

Like JSON, BSON was introduced in 2009 by MongoDB. Although it was invented by MongoDB, many other systems also use it as a format for data storage or transportation. BSON specifications are primarily based on JSON as they inherit all the good features of JSON, such as the syntax and flexibility. It also provides a few additional features, which are specifically designed for improving storage efficiency, ease of traversal, and a few data type enhancements to avoid the type conflicts that we saw in the *Introduction to JSON* section.

As we have already covered the JSON features in detail, let's focus on the enhancements that BSON provides:

- BSON documents are designed to be more efficient than JSON as they occupy less space and provide faster traversal.

- With each document, BSON stores some **meta-information**, such as the length of the fields or the length of the sub-documents. The meta-information makes the document parsing, as well as traversing, faster.

- BSON documents have **ordered arrays**. Each element in an array is prefixed by its index position and can be accessed using its index number.

- BSON provides many **additional data types**, such as dates, integers, doubles, byte arrays, and more. We will cover BSON data types later, in the next section.

> **NOTE**
> Because of the binary format, BSON documents are compact in nature. However, some smaller documents end up occupying more space compared to JSON documents with the same information. This is because of the meta-information added to each document. However, for large documents, BSON is more space efficient.

Now that we have completed a detailed introduction to JSON and BSON enhancements, let's now learn about MongoDB documents.

# MONGODB DOCUMENTS

A MongoDB database is composed of collections and documents. A database can have one or more collections, and each collection can store one or more related BSON documents. In comparison to RDBMS, collections are analogous to tables and documents are analogous to rows within a table. However, documents are much more flexible compared with the rows in a table.

RDBMSes consist of a tabular data model that comprises rows and columns. However, your applications may need to support more complex data structures, such as a nested object or a collection of objects. Tabular databases restrict the storage of such complex data structures. In such cases, you will have to split your data into multiple tables and change the application's object structures accordingly. On the other hand, the document-based data model of MongoDB allows your application to store and retrieve more complex object structures due to the flexible JSON-like format of the documents.

The following list details some of the major features of MongoDB's document-based data model:

1. The documents provide a flexible and natural way of representing data. The data can be stored as is, without having to transform it into a database structure.

2. The objects, nested objects, and arrays that are within a document are easily relatable to your programming language's object structure.

3. With the ability of a flexible schema, the documents are agile in practice. They continuously integrate with application changes and new features without any major schema changes or downtimes.

4. Documents are self-contained pieces of data. They avoid the need to read multiple relational tables and table-joins to understand a complete unit of information.

5. The documents are extensible. You can use documents to store the entire object structure, use it as a map or a dictionary, as a key-value pair for quick lookup, or have a flat structure that resembles a relational table.

## DOCUMENTS AND FLEXIBILITY

As stated earlier, MongoDB documents are a flexible way of storing data. Consider the following example. Imagine you are developing a movie service where you need to create a movie database. A movie record in a simple MongoDB document will look like this:

```
{"title" : "A Swedish Love Story"}
```

However, storing only the title is not enough. You need more fields. Now, let's consider a few more basic fields. With a list of movies in the MongoDB database, the documents will look like this:

```
{
  "id" : 1122,
  "title" : "A Swedish Love Story",
  "release_date" : ISODate("1970-04-24T00:00:00Z"),
  "user_rating" : 6.7
}
{
  "id" : 1123,
  "title" : "The Stunt Man",
  "release_date" : ISODate("1980-06-26T00:00:00Z"),
  "user_rating" : 7.8
}
```

Say you are using an RDBMS table instead. On an RDBMS platform, you need to define your schema at the beginning, and to do that, first, you must think about the columns and data types. You might then come up with a **CREATE TABLE** query as follows:

```
CREATE TABLE movies(
  id INT,
  title VARCHAR(250),
  release_date DATE,
  user_ratings FLOAT
);
```

This query is a clear indication that relational tables are bound by a definition called the **schema definition**. However, considering the restrictions, you cannot assign a float value in the **id** field and **user_ratings** can never be a string.

With a few records inserted, the table will appear as in *Figure 2.2*. This table is as good as a MongoDB document:

| id | title | release_date | user_ratings |
|----|-------|--------------|--------------|
| 1122 | A Swedish Love Story | 1970-04-24 | 6.7 |
| 1123 | The Stunt Man | 1980-06-26 | 7.8 |

Figure 2.2: The movies table

Now, say you want to include the IMDb ratings for each of the movies listed in the table, and going forward, all the movies will have **imdb_ratings** included in the table. For an existing list of movies, **imdb_ratings** can be set to **null**:

To meet this requirement, you will include an **ALTER TABLE** query in your syntax:

```
ALTER TABLE movies
ADD COLUMN imdb_ratings FLOAT default null;
```

The query is correct, but there can be instances where table alterations may block the table for some time, especially for large datasets. When a table is blocked, other read and write operations will have to wait until the table is altered, which may lead to downtime. Now, let's see how we can tackle the same situation in MongoDB.

MongoDB supports a flexible schema, and there is no specific schema definition. Without altering anything on the database or the collection, you can simply insert a new movie with the additional field. The collection will behave exactly like the modified table of the movies, where the latest insertions will have **imdb_ratings** and the previous ones will return a **null** value. In MongoDB documents, a non-existent field is always considered **null**.

Now, the whole collection will look similar to the following screenshot. You will notice that the last movie has a new field, **imdb_ratings**:

```
●  ●  ●                                    MongoDB
{
        "_id" : ObjectId("5dd2cb8567ea69a888f03f64"),
        "id" : 1122,
        "title" : "A Swedish Love Story",
        "release_date" : ISODate("1970-04-24T00:00:00Z"),
        "user_rating" : 6.7
}
{
        "_id" : ObjectId("5dd2cb8f67ea69a888f03f65"),
        "id" : 1123,
        "title" : "The Stunt Man",
        "release_date" : ISODate("1980-06-26T00:00:00Z"),
        "user_rating" : 7.8
}
{
        "_id" : ObjectId("5dd2cbb767ea69a888f03f66"),
        "id" : 1124,
        "title" : "Return of the Jedi",
        "release_date" : ISODate("1983-05-25T00:00:00Z"),
        "user_rating" : 6,
        "imdb_ratings" : 8.3
}
|>                                                                  ]
 > ▊
```

Figure 2.3: Result for imdb_ratings for the movies collection

The preceding examples clearly indicate that documents are extremely flexible in comparison to tabular databases. Documents can incorporate changes on the go without any downtime.

# MONGODB DATA TYPES

You have learned how MongoDB stores JSON-like documents. You have also seen various documents and read the information stored within them and seen how flexible these documents are to store different types of data structures, irrespective of the complexity of your data.

In this section, you will learn about the various data types supported by MongoDB's BSON documents. Using the right data types in your documents is very important as correct data types help you use the database features more effectively, avoid data corruption, and improve data usability. MongoDB supports all the data types from JSON and BSON. Let's look at each in detail, with examples.

## STRINGS

A string is a basic data type used to represent text-based fields in a document. It is a plain sequence of characters. In MongoDB, the string fields are UTF-8 encoded, and thus they support most international characters. The MongoDB drivers for various programming languages convert the string fields to UTF-8 while reading or writing data from a collection.

A string with plain-text characters appears as follows:

```
{
    "name" : "Tom Walter"
}
```

A string with random characters and whitespaces will appear as follows:

```
{
    "random_txt" : "a ! *& ) ( f s f @#$ s"
}
```

In JSON, a value that is wrapped in double quotes is considered a string. Consider the following example in which a valid number and date are wrapped in double quotes, both forming a string:

```
{
    "number_txt" : "112.1"
}
{
    "date_txt" : "1929-12-31"
}
```

An interesting fact about MongoDB string fields is that they support search capabilities with regular expressions. This means you can search for documents by providing the full value of a text field or by providing only part of the string value using regular expressions.

## NUMBERS

A number is JSON's basic data type. A JSON document does not specify whether a number is an integer, a float, or *long*:

```
{
    "number_of_employees": 50342
}
{
```

```
    "pi": 3.14159265359
}
```

However, MongoDB supports the following types of numbers:

- **double**: 64-bit floating point

- **int**: 32-bit signed integer

- **long**: 64-bit unsigned integer

- **decimal**: 128-bit floating point – which is IEE 754-compliant

When you are working with a programming language, you don't have to worry about these data types. You can simply program using the language's native data types. The MongoDB drivers for respective languages take care of encoding the language-specific numbers to one of the previously listed data types.

If you are working on the mongo shell, you get three wrappers to handle: **integer**, **long**, and **decimal**. The Mongo shell is based on JavaScript, and thus all the documents are represented in JSON format. By default, it treats any number as a 64-bit floating point. However, if you want to explicitly use the other types, you can use the following wrappers.

**NumberInt**: The **NumberInt** constructor can be used if you want the number to be saved as a 32-bit integer and not as a 64-bit float:

```
> var plainNum = 1299
> var explicitInt = NumberInt("1299")
> var explicitInt_double = NumberInt(1299)
```

- In the preceding snippet, the first number, **plainNum**, is initialized with a sequence of digits without mentioning any explicit data type. Therefore, by default, it will be treated as a *64-bit floating-point number* (also known as a **double**).

- **explicitInt**, however, is initialized with an integer-type constructor and a string representation of a number, and so MongoDB reads the number in an argument as a *32-bit integer*.

- However, in the **explicitInt_double** initialization, the number provided in the constructor argument doesn't have double quotes. Therefore, it will be treated as a *64-bit float*—that is, a **double**—and used to form a *32-bit integer*. But as the provided number fits in the integer range, no change is seen.

- When you print the preceding numbers, they look as follows:

```
                                                    MongoDB
> plainNum
1299
>
> explicitInt
NumberInt(1299)
>
> explicitInt_double
NumberInt(1299)
>
```

Figure 2.4: Output for the plainNum, explicitInt, and explicitInt_double

**NumberLong**: **NumberLong** wrappers are similar to **NumberInt**. The only difference is that they are stored as 64-bit integers. Let's try it on the shell:

```
> var explicitLong = NumberLong("777888222116643")
> var explicitLong_double = NumberLong(444333222111242)
```

Let's print the documents in the shell:

```
                                                    MongoDB
[> explicitLong                                           ]
 NumberLong("777888222116643")
[>                                                        ]
[> explicitLong_double                                    ]
 NumberLong("444333222111242")
 >
```

Figure 2.5: MongoDB shell output

**NumberDecimal**: This wrapper stores the given number as a 128-bit IEEE 754 decimal format. The **NumberDecimal** constructor accepts both a string and a double representation of the number:

```
> var explicitDecimal = NumberDecimal("142.42")
> var explicitDecimal_double = NumberDecimal(142.42)
```

We are passing a string representation of a decimal number to **explicitDecimal**. However, **explicitDecimal_double** is created using a **double**. When we print the results, they appear slightly differently:

```
●  ●  ●                                    MongoDB
> explicitDecimal
NumberDecimal("142.42")
>
> explicitDecimal_double
NumberDecimal("142.420000000000")
>
```

Figure 2.6: Output for explicitDecimal and explicitDecimal_double

The second number has been appended with trailing zeros. This is because of the internal parsing of the numbers. When we pass a double value to **NumberDecimal**, the argument is parsed to BSON's double, which is then converted to a 128-bit decimal with a precision of 15 digits.

During this conversion, the decimal numbers are rounded off and may lose precision. Let's look at the following example:

```
> var dec = NumberDecimal("5999999999.99999999")
> var decDbl = NumberDecimal(5999999999.99999999)
```

Let's print the numbers and inspect the output:

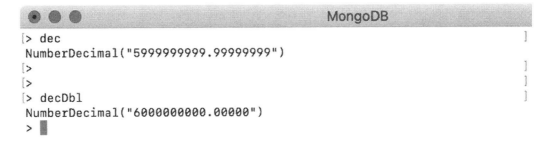

```
●  ●  ●                                    MongoDB
> dec
NumberDecimal("5999999999.99999999")
>
>
> decDbl
NumberDecimal("6000000000.00000")
>
```

Figure 2.7: Output for dec and decDbl

It is evident that when a double is passed to **NumberDecimal**, there is a chance of a loss of precision. Therefore, it is important to always use string-based constructors when using **NumberDecimal**.

## BOOLEANS

The Boolean data type is used to represent whether something is true or false. Therefore, the value of a valid Boolean field is either **true** or **false**:

```
{
    "isMongoDBHard": false
}
{
    "amIEnjoying": true
}
```

The values do not have double quotes. If you wrap them in double quotes, they will be treated as strings.

## OBJECTS

The object fields are used to represent nested or embedded documents—that is, a field whose value is another valid JSON document.

Let's take a look at the following example from the airbnb dataset:

```
{
    "listing_url": "https://www.airbnb.com/rooms/1001265",
    "name": "Ocean View Waikiki Marina w/prkg",
    "summary": "A great location that work perfectly for business,
        education, or simple visit.",
    "host":{
        "host_id": "5448114",
        "host_name": "David",
        "host_location": "Honolulu, Hawaii, United States"
    }
}
```

The value of the host field is another valid JSON. MongoDB uses a dot notation (.) to access the embedded objects. To access an embedded document, we will create a variable of the listing on the mongo shell:

```
> var listing = {
    "listing_url": "https://www.airbnb.com/rooms/1001265",
    "name": "Ocean View Waikiki Marina w/prkg",
    "summary": "A great location that work perfectly for business,
        education, or simple visit.",
    "host": {
        "host_id": "5448114",
```

```
        "host_name": "David",
        "host_location": "Honolulu, Hawaii, United States"
    }
}
```

To print only the host details, use the dot notation (.) to get the embedded object, as follows:

```
● ● ●                          MongoDB
> var listing = {
...      "listing_url": "https://www.airbnb.com/rooms/1001265",
...      "name": "Ocean View Waikiki Marina w/prkg",
...      "summary": "A great location that work perfectly for business, education, or simple
visit.",
...      "host": {
...           "host_id": "5448114",
...           "host_name": "David",
...           "host_location": "Honolulu, Hawaii, United States"
...      }
[... }
[>
[>
[> listing.host
{
        "host_id" : "5448114",
        "host_name" : "David",
        "host_location" : "Honolulu, Hawaii, United States"
}
> █
```

Figure 2.8: Output for the embedded object

Using a similar notation, you can also access a specific field of the embedded document as follows:

```
> listing.host.host_name
David
```

Embedded documents can have further documents within them. Having embedded documents makes a MongoDB document a piece of self-contained information. To record the same information in an RDBMS database, you will have to create the listing and the host as two separate tables with a foreign key reference in between, and join the data from both tables to get a piece of information.

Along with embedded documents, MongoDB also supports links between the documents of two different collections, which resembles having foreign key references.

## EXERCISE 2.02: CREATING NESTED OBJECTS

Your organization is happy with the movie representation so far. Now they have come up with a requirement to include the IMDb ratings and the number of votes that derived the rating. They also want to incorporate Tomatometer ratings, which include the user ratings and critics ratings along with fresh and rotten scores. Your task is to modify the document to update the **imdb** field to include the number of votes and add a new field called **tomatoes**, which contains the Rotten Tomato ratings.

Recall the JSON document of a sample movie record that you created in *Exercise 2.01, Creating Your Own JSON Document*:

```
{
  "id": 14253,
  "title": "Beauty and the Beast",
  "year": 2016,
  "language": "English",
  "imdb_rating": 6.4,
  "genre": "Romance",
  "director": "Christophe Gans",
  "runtime": 112
}
```

The following steps will help modify the IMDb ratings:

1.  The existing **imdb_rating** field indicates the IMDb rating score, so add an additional field to represent the vote count. However, both fields are closely related to each other and will always be used together. Therefore, group them together in a single document:

```
{
  "rating": 6.4,
  "votes": "17762"
}
```

2.  The preceding document with two fields represents the complete IMDb rating. Replace the current **imdb_rating** field with the one you just created:

```
{
  "id" : 14253,
  "Title" : "Beauty and the Beast",
  "year" : 2016,
  "language" : "English",
  "genre" : "Romance",
```

```
   "director" : "Christophe Gans",
   "runtime" : 112,
   "imdb" :
   {
     "rating": 6.4,
     "votes": "17762"
   }
 }
```

This **imdb** field with its value of an embedded object represents the IMDb ratings. Now, add the Tomatometer ratings.

3.  As stated previously, the Tomatometer rating includes viewer ratings and critics ratings, along with the fresh score and the rotten score. Like the IMDb ratings, both **Viewer Ratings** and **Critics Ratings** will have a **rating** field and a **votes** field. Write these two documents separately:

```
// Viewer Ratings
{
  "rating" : 3.9,
  "votes" : 238
}
// Critic Ratings
{
  "rating" : 4.2,
  "votes" : 8
}
```

4.  As both ratings are related, group them together in a single document:

```
{
  "viewer" : {
    "rating" : 3.9,
    "votes" : 238
  },
  "critic" : {
    "rating" : 4.2,
    "votes" : 8
  }
}
```

5. Add the **fresh** and **rotten** scores as per the description:

```
{
    "viewer" : {
      "rating" : 3.9,
      "votes" : 238
    },
    "critic" : {
      "rating" : 4.2,
      "votes" : 8
    },
    "fresh" : 96,
    "rotten" : 7
}
```

The following output represents the Tomatometer ratings with the new **tomatoes** field in our movie record:

```
{
    "id" : 14253,
    "Title" : "Beauty and the Beast",
    "year" : 2016,
    "language" : "English",
    "genre" : "Romance",
    "director" : "Christophe Gans",
    "runtime" : 112,
    "imdb" : {
        "rating": 6.4,
        "votes": "17762"
    },
    "tomatoes" : {
        "viewer" : {
            "rating" : 3.9,
            "votes" : 238
        },
        "critic" : {
            "rating" : 4.2,
            "votes" : 8
        },
```

```
        "fresh" : 96,
        "rotten" : 7
    }
}
```

6.  Finally, validate your document with any online JSON validator (in our case, https://jsonlint.com/). Click on **Validate JSON** to validate the code:

```
1 ▼ {
2       "id": 14253,
3       "title": "Beauty and the Beast",
4       "year": 2016,
5       "language": "English",
6       "genre": "Romance",
7       "director": "Christophe Gans",
8       "runtime": 112,
9 ▼     "imdb": {
10          "rating": 6.4,
11          "votes": 17762
12      },
13 ▼    "tomatoes": {
14 ▼        "viewer": {
15              "rating": 3.9,
16              "votes": 238
17          },
18 ▼        "critic": {
19              "rating": 4.2,
20              "votes": 8
21          },
22          "fresh": 96,
23          "rotten": 7
24      }
25  }
```

Validate JSON    Clear                                                    Support JSONLint for $2/Month

**Results**

Valid JSON

Figure 2.9: Validation of the JSON document

Your movie record is now updated with detailed IMBb ratings and the new **tomatoes** rating. In this exercise, you practiced creating two nested documents to represent IMDb ratings and Tomatometer ratings. Now that we have covered nested or embedded objects, let's learn about arrays.

## ARRAYS

A field with an **array** type has a collection of zero or more values. In MongoDB, there is no limit to how many elements an array can contain or how many arrays a document can have. However, the overall document size should not exceed 16 MB. Consider the following example array containing four numbers:

```
> var doc = {
    first_array: [
      4,
      3,
      2,
      1
    ]
}
```

Each element in an array can be accessed using its index position. While accessing an element on a specific index position, the index number is enclosed in square brackets. Let's print the third element in the array:

```
> doc.first_array[3]
1
```

> **NOTE**
>
> Indexes are always zero-based. The index position **3** denotes the fourth element in the array.

Using the index position, you can also add new elements to an existing array, as in the following example:

```
> doc.first_array[4] = 99
```

Upon printing the array, you will see that the fifth element has been added correctly, which contains the index position, **4**:

```
> doc.first_array
[ 4, 3, 2, 1, 99 ]
```

Just like objects having embedded objects, arrays can also have embedded arrays. The following syntax adds an embedded array into the sixth element:

```
> doc.first_array[5] = [11, 12]
[ 11, 12 ]
```

If you print the array, you will see the embedded array as follows:

```
> doc.first_array
[ 4, 3, 2, 1, 99, [11, 12]]
>
```

Now, you can use the square notation, [], to access the elements of a specific index in the embedded array, as follows:

```
> doc.first_array[5][1]
12
```

The array can contain any MongoDB valid data type fields. This can be seen in the following snippet:

```
// array of strings
[ "this", "is", "a", "text" ]

// array of doubles
[ 1.1, 3.2, 553.54 ]

// array of Json objects
[ { "a" : 1 }, { "a" : 2, "b" : 3 }, { "c" : 1 } ]

// array of mixed elements
[ 12, "text", 4.35, [ 3, 2 ], { "type" : "object" } ]
```

## EXERCISE 2.03: USING ARRAY FIELDS

In order to add comment details for each movie, your organization wants you to include full text of the comment along with user details such as name, email, and date. Your task is to prepare two dummy comments and add them to the existing movie record. In *Exercise 2.02, Creating Nested Objects*, you developed a movie record in a document format, which looks as follows:

```
{
    "id" : 14253,
    "Title" : "Beauty and the Beast",
```

```
    "year" : 2016,
    "language" : "English",
    "genre" : "Romance",
    "director" : "Christophe Gans",
    "runtime" : 112,
    "imdb" : {
      "rating": 6.4,
      "votes": "17762"
    },
    "tomatoes" : {
      "viewer" : {
        "rating" : 3.9,
        "votes" : 238
      },
      "critic" : {
        "rating" : 4.2,
        "votes" : 8
      },
      "fresh" : 96,
      "rotten" : 7
    }
}
```

Build upon this document to add additional information by executing the following steps:

1. Create two comments and list the details:

```
// Comment #1
Name = Talisa Maegyr
Email = oona_chaplin@gameofthron.es
Text = Rem itaque ad sit rem voluptatibus. Ad fugiat...
Date = 1998-08-22T11:45:03.000+00:00
// Comment #2
Name = Melisandre
Email = carice_van_houten@gameofthron.es
Text = Perspiciatis non debitis magnam. Voluptate...
Date = 1974-06-22T07:31:47.000+00:00
```

2. Split the two comments into separate documents as follows:

> **NOTE**
>
> The comment text has been truncated to fit it on a single line.

```
// Comment #1
{
    "name" : "Talisa Maegyr",
    "email" : "oona_chaplin@gameofthron.es",
    "text" : "Rem itaque ad sit rem voluptatibus. Ad fugiat...",
    "date" : "1998-08-22T11:45:03.000+00:00"
}
// Comment #2
{
    "name" : "Melisandre",
    "email" : "carice_van_houten@gameofthron.es",
    "text" : "Perspiciatis non debitis magnam. Voluptate...",
    "date" : "1974-06-22T07:31:47.000+00:00"
}
```

There are two comments in two separate documents, and you can easily fit them in the movie record as **comment_1** and **comment_2**. However, as the number of comments will increase, it will be difficult to count their number. To overcome this, we will use an array, which implicitly assigns an index position to each element.

3. Add both comments to an array as follows:

```
[
    {
        "name": "Talisa Maegyr",
        "email": "oona_chaplin@gameofthron.es",
        "text": "Rem itaque ad sit rem voluptatibus. Ad fugiat...",
        "date": "1998-08-22T11:45:03.000+00:00"
    },
    {
        "name": "Melisandre",
        "email": "carice_van_houten@gameofthron.es",
        "text": "Perspiciatis non debitis magnam. Voluptate...",
        "date": "1974-06-22T07:31:47.000+00:00"
```

```
    }
  ]
```

An array gives you the opportunity to add as many comments as you want. Also, because of the implicit indexes, you are free to access any comment via its dedicated index position. Once you add this array in the movie record, the output will appear as follows:

```
{
  "id": 14253,
  "Title": "Beauty and the Beast",
  "year": 2016,
  "language": "English",
  "genre": "Romance",
  "director": "Christophe Gans",
  "runtime": 112,
  "imdb": {
    "rating": 6.4,
    "votes": "17762"
  },
  "tomatoes": {
    "viewer": {
      "rating": 3.9,
      "votes": 238
    },
    "critic": {
      "rating": 4.2,
      "votes": 8
    },
    "fresh": 96,
    "rotten": 7
  },
  "comments": [{
    "name": "Talisa Maegyr",
    "email": "oona_chaplin@gameofthron.es",
    "text": "Rem itaque ad sit rem voluptatibus. Ad fugiat...",
    "date": "1998-08-22T11:45:03.000+00:00"
  }, {
    "name": "Melisandre",
    "email": "carice_van_houten@gameofthron.es",
    "text": "Perspiciatis non debitis magnam. Voluptate...",
```

```
        "date": "1974-06-22T07:31:47.000+00:00"
    }]


}
```

4. Now, validate the JSON document with an online validator (for example, https://jsonlint.com/). Click **Validate JSON** to validate the code:

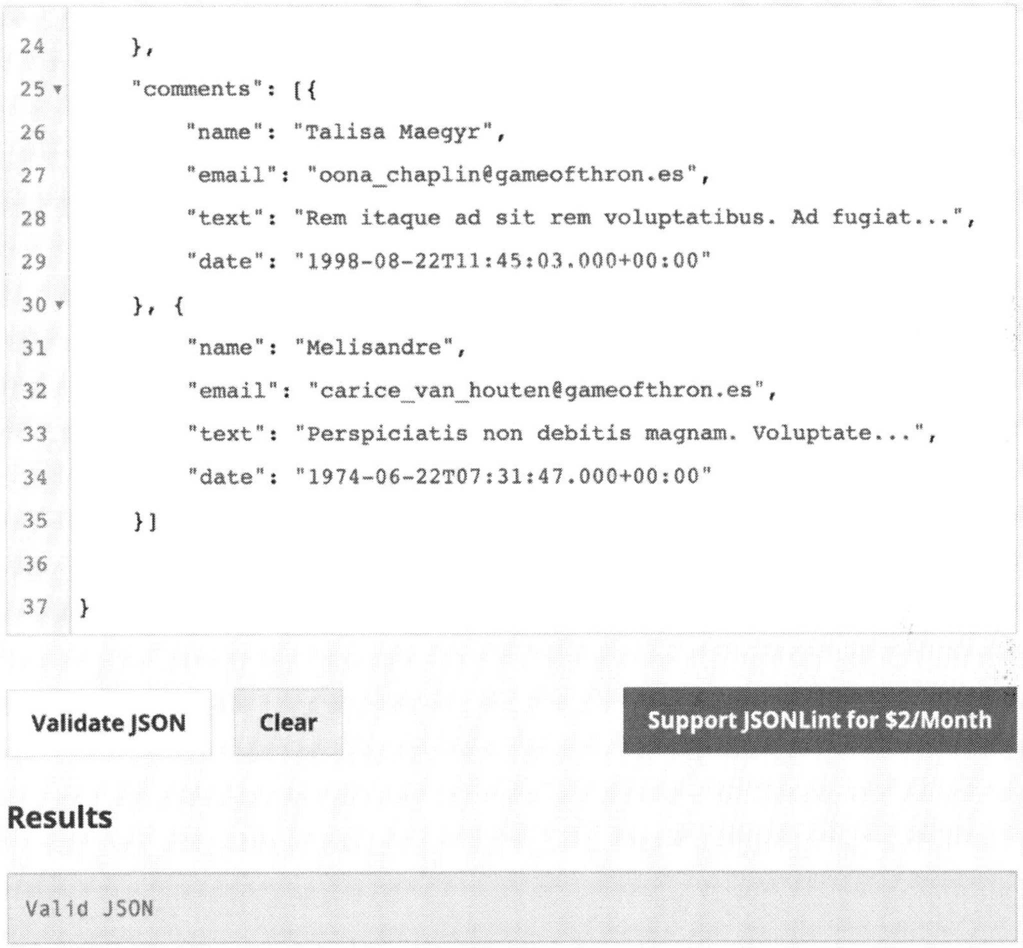

```
24        },
25 ▾      "comments": [{
26            "name": "Talisa Maegyr",
27            "email": "oona_chaplin@gameofthron.es",
28            "text": "Rem itaque ad sit rem voluptatibus. Ad fugiat...",
29            "date": "1998-08-22T11:45:03.000+00:00"
30 ▾      }, {
31            "name": "Melisandre",
32            "email": "carice_van_houten@gameofthron.es",
33            "text": "Perspiciatis non debitis magnam. Voluptate...",
34            "date": "1974-06-22T07:31:47.000+00:00"
35        }]
36
37 }
```

**Validate JSON**    **Clear**    **Support JSONLint for $2/Month**

**Results**

Valid JSON

Figure 2.10: Validation of the JSON document

We can see that our movie record now has user comments. In this exercise, we have modified our movie record to practice creating array fields. Now it is time to move on to the next data type, **null**.

## NULL

Null is a special data type in a document and denotes a field that does not contain a value. The **null** field can have only **null** as the value. You will print the object in the following example, which will result in the **null** value:

```
> var obj = null
>
> obj
Null
```

Build upon the array we created in the *Arrays* section:

```
> doc.first_array
[ 4, 3, 2, 1, 99, [11, 12]]
```

Now, create a new variable and initialize it to **null** by inserting the variable in the next index position:

```
> var nullField = null
> doc.first_array[6] = nullField
```

Now, print this array to see the **null** field:

```
> doc.first_array
[ 4, 3, 2, 1, 99, [11, 12], null]
```

## OBJECTID

Every document in a collection must have an **_id** that contains a unique value. This field acts as a *primary key* to these documents. The primary keys are used to uniquely identify the documents, and they are always indexed. The value of the **_id** field must be unique in a collection. When you work with any dataset, each dataset represents a different context, and based on the context, you can identify whether your data has a primary key. For example, if you are dealing with the users' data, the users' email addresses will always be unique and can be considered the most appropriate **_id** field. However, for some datasets that do not have a unique key, you can simply omit the **_id** field.

If you insert a document without an **_id** field, the MongoDB driver will autogenerate a unique ID and add it to the document. So, when you retrieve the inserted document, you will find **_id** is generated with a unique value of random text. When the **_id** field is automatically added by the driver, the value is generated using **ObjectId**.

The **ObjectId** value is designed to generate lightweight code that is unique across different machines. It generates a unique value of 12 bytes, where the first 4 bytes represent the timestamp, bytes 5 to 9 represent a random value, and the last 3 bytes are an incremental counter. Create and print an **ObjectId** value as follows:

```
> var uniqueID = new ObjectId()
```

Print **uniqueID** on the next line:

```
> uniqueID
ObjectId("5dv.8ff48dd98e621357bd50")
```

MongoDB supports a technique called sharding, where a dataset is distributed and stored on different machines. When a collection is sharded, its documents are physically located on different machines. Even so, **ObjectId** can ensure that the values will be unique in the collection across different machines. If the collection is sorted using the **ObjectId** field, the order will be based on the document creation time. However, the timestamp in **ObjectId** is based on the number of seconds to epoch time. Hence, documents inserted within the same second may appear in a random order. The **getTimestamp()** method on **ObjectId** tells us the document insertion time.

## DATES

The JSON specifications do not support date types. All the dates in JSON documents are represented as plain strings. The string representations of dates are difficult to parse, compare, and manipulate. MongoDB's BSON format, however, supports **Date** types explicitly.

The MongoDB dates are stored in the form of milliseconds since the Unix epoch, which is January 1, 1970. To store the millisecond's representation of a date, MongoDB uses a 64-bit integer (**long**). Because of this, the date fields have a range of around +/-290 million years since the Unix epoch. One thing to note is that all dates are stored in *UTC*, and there is no *time zone* associated with them.

While working on the mongo shell, you can create **Date** instances using **Date()**, **new Date()**, or **new ISODate()**:

```
var date = Date()// Sample output
Sat Sept 03 1989 07:28:46 GMT-0500 (CDT)
```

When a **Date()** type is used to construct a date, it uses JavaScript's date representation, which is in the form of plain strings. These dates represent the date and time based on your current time zone. However, being in string formats, they are not useful for comparison or manipulation.

If you add the **new** keyword to the **Date** constructor, you get the BSON date that is wrapped in **ISODate()** as follows:

```
> var date = new Date()
// Sample output
ISODate("1989-09-03T10:11:23.357Z")
```

You can also use the **ISODate()** constructor directly to create **date** objects as follows:

```
> var isoDate = new ISODate()
// Sample output
ISODate("1989-09-03T11:13:26.442Z")
```

These dates can be manipulated, compared, and searched.

## TIMESTAMPS

The timestamp is a 64-bit representation of date and time. Out of the 64 bits, the first 32 bits store the number of seconds since the Unix epoch time, which is January 1, 1970. The other 32 bits indicate an incrementing counter. The timestamp type is exclusively used by MongoDB for internal operations.

## BINARY DATA

Binary data, also called **BinData**, is a BSON data type for storing data that exists in a binary format. This data type gives you the ability to store almost anything in the database, including files such as text, videos, music, and more. **BinData** can be mapped with a binary array in your programming language as follows:

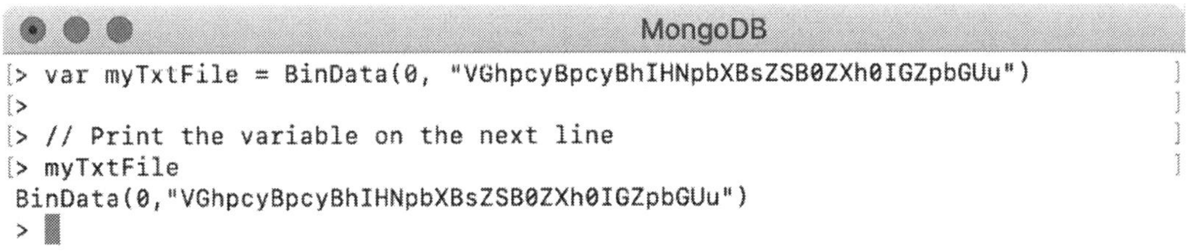

```
MongoDB
[> var myTxtFile = BinData(0, "VGhpcyBpcyBhIHNpbXBsZSB0ZXh0IGZpbGUu")
[>
[> // Print the variable on the next line
[> myTxtFile
 BinData(0,"VGhpcyBpcyBhIHNpbXBsZSB0ZXh0IGZpbGUu")
 >
```

Figure 2.11: Binary array

The first argument to **BinData** is a binary subtype to indicate the type of information stored. The zero value stands for plain binary data and can be used with text or media files. The second argument to **BinData** is a *base64*-encoded text file. You can use the binary data field in a document as follows:

```
{
    "name" : "my_txt",
    "extension" : "txt",
    "content" : BinData(0,/
      "VGhpcyBpcyBhIHNpbXBsZSB0ZXh0IGZpbGUu")
}
```

We will cover MongoDB's document size limit in the upcoming section.

# LIMITS AND RESTRICTIONS ON DOCUMENTS

So far, we have discussed the importance and benefits of using documents. Documents play a major role in building efficient applications, and they improve overall data usability. We know how documents offer a flexible way to represent data in its most natural form. They are often self-contained and can hold a complete unit of information. The self-containment comes from nested objects and arrays.

To use any database effectively, it is important to have the correct data structure. The incorrect data structures you build today may result in lots of pain in the future. In the long term, as your application's usage grows, the amount of data also grows, and the problems that seemed very small initially become more evident. Then comes the obvious question: how do you know whether your data structure is correct?

Your application will tell you the answer. If, to access a certain piece of information, your application must execute multiple queries to the database and combine all the results to get the final information, then it will slow down the overall throughput. Contrastingly, if a single query on the database returns too much information in a single result, your application will have to scan through the entire result set and grab the intended piece of information. This will cause higher memory consumption, stale objects, and finally, slower performance.

Thus, MongoDB has put some limits and restrictions on documents. One thing to note is that the restrictions are not because of database limitations or shortcomings. The restrictions are added so that the overall database platform can perform efficiently. We have already covered the flexibility that MongoDB documents offer; now it is important to know the restrictions.

## DOCUMENT SIZE LIMIT

A document with too much information is bad in many ways. For this reason, MongoDB puts a limit of 16 MB on the size of every document in the collection. The limit of 16 MB is enough to store the right information. A collection can have as many documents as you want. There is no limitation on the size of a collection. Even if a collection exceeds the space of the underlying system, you can use vertical or horizontal scaling to increase the capacity of the collection.

The flexibility and self-containment of documents may tempt developers to put in too much information and create bulky documents. Oversized documents are usually an indication of bad design. Most of the time, your applications do not need all the information. A good database design considers the needs of the application.

Imagine your application is an interface providing sales information from various stores, where users can search and find sold items by the item type or by the store location. Most of the time, it is your application that will be hitting the database and that too with a similar set of queries. Therefore, your application's needs play a major role in database design, especially when the user base grows, and your application starts getting thousands and millions of requests in a short period of time. All you want is faster queries, less processing, and less resource consumption.

Oversized documents are also expensive in terms of resource usage. When the documents are read from the system, they are held in memory and then transferred over the wire. Wire transfers are always slower. Then, your driver will map the received information to your programming language's objects. Larger documents will result in too many bulky objects. Consider a sample document from a dummy sales record, as follows:

```
{
    «_id" : ObjectId("5bd761dcae323e45a93ccff4"),
    «saleDate" : ISODate("2014-08-18T10:42:13.935Z"),
    «items" : [
        {
            «name" : "backpack",
            «tags" : [
                «school»,
                «travel»,
                «kids»
            ],
            «price" : NumberDecimal("187.16"),
            «quantity" : 2
        },
        {
            «name" : "printer paper",
            «tags" : [
                «office»,
                «stationary»
            ],
            «price" : NumberDecimal("20.61"),
            «quantity" : 10
        },
        {
            «name" : "notepad",
            «tags" : [
```

```
                    «office»,
                    «writing»,
                    «school»
            ],
            «price" : NumberDecimal("23.75"),
            «quantity" : 5
        },
        {
            «name" : "envelopes",
            «tags" : [
                    «stationary»,
                    «office»,
                    «general»
            ],
            «price" : NumberDecimal("9.44"),
            «quantity" : 5
        }
    ],
    «storeLocation" : "San Diego",
    «customer" : {
        «gender" : "F",
        «age" : 59,
        «email" : "la@cevam.tj",
        «satisfaction" : 4
    },
    «couponUsed" : false,
    «purchaseMethod" : "In store"
}
```

Although this document is just fine, there are some constraints. The **items** field is an array of the **items** object. If an order has too many **items**, the size of the array will increase, which will result in an increase in the size of the overall document. If your application allows multiple items per order and you have thousands of unique items in store, this document will easily become oversized. The best way to deal with such complex documents is to split the collection into two and have document links embedded within.

## NESTING DEPTH LIMIT

A MongoDB BSON document supports nesting up to 100 levels, which is more than enough. Nested documents are a great way to provide readable data. They provide complete information in one go and avoid multiple queries to gather a piece of information.

However, as the nesting level increases, performance and memory consumption issues arise. For example, consider a driver that is parsing the document to an object structure. During the scan, whenever a new sub-document is found, the scanner recursively enters the nested objects while maintaining a stack of already read information. This causes high memory utilization and slow performance.

By setting the nesting limit of 100 levels, MongoDB avoids such issues. However, if you can't avoid such deep nesting, you can consider splitting the collections into two, or more, and have document references.

# FIELD NAME RULES

MongoDB has a few rules about document field names, which are listed as follows:

1. The field name cannot contain a **null** character.

2. Only the fields in an array or an embedded document can have a name starting with the dollar sign (**$**). For the top-level fields, the name cannot start with a dollar (**$**) sign.

3. Documents with duplicate field names are not supported. According to the MongoDB documentation, when a document with duplicate field names is inserted, no error will be thrown, but the document won't be inserted. Even the drivers will drop the documents silently. On the mongo shell, however, if such a document is inserted, it gets inserted correctly. However, the resulting document will have only the second field. That means the second occurrence of the field overwrites the value of the first.

> **NOTE**
>
> MongoDB (as of version 4.2.8) does not recommend field names starting with a dollar (**$**) sign or a dot ( **.** ). The MongoDB query language may not work correctly with such fields. Additionally, the drivers do not support them.

## EXERCISE 2.04: LOADING DATA INTO AN ATLAS CLUSTER

Now that you have learned about documents and their structures, you can implement your learning on a business use case and observe MongoDB documents. In *Chapter 1*, *Introduction to MongoDB*, you created a MongoDB Atlas account and initiated a cluster on the cloud. You will load sample datasets into this cluster. MongoDB Atlas provides sample datasets that can be loaded into the cluster by executing a few simple steps. These sample databases are large, real-life datasets that are made available for practice. The sample dataset in MongoDB Atlas has the following databases, where each database has multiple collections:

- `sample_mflix`
- `sample_airbnb`
- `sample_geospatial`
- `sample_supplies`
- `sample_training`
- `sample_weatherdata`

Of all these datasets, it will be the **`sample_mflix`** dataset that you deal with throughout this book. This is a huge database with over 23,000 movies and series records along with their ratings, comments, and other details. Before you learn about the database, import the database into our cluster and familiarize ourselves with its structure and components.

The following are the steps to be executed in order to achieve the desired result:

1. Visit https://cloud.mongodb.com/ and click to log in to your account:

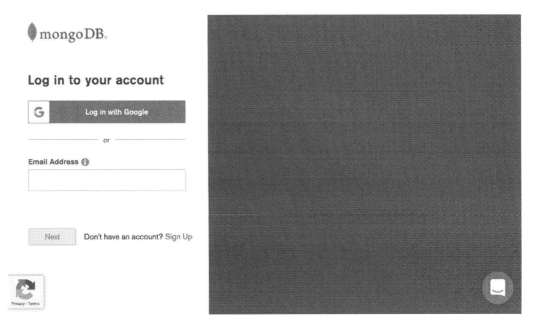

Figure 2.12: Atlas login page

Since you already have a cluster created on the cloud, upon login, the following screen displaying the cluster details will appear:

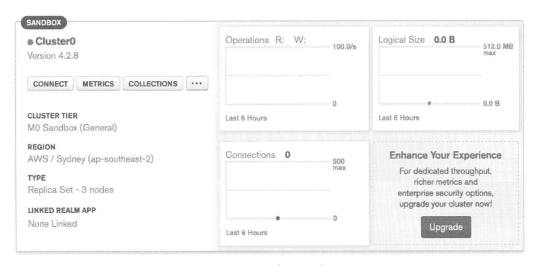

Figure 2.13: Cluster view

2. Click on the (...) option available next to **COLLECTIONS**. A drop-down list displaying the following options will appear. Click `Load Sample Dataset`:

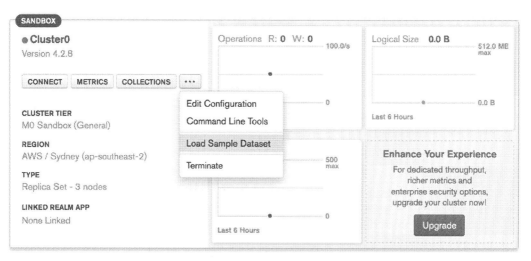

Figure 2.14: The Load Sample Dataset option

This opens a confirmation dialog that shows the total size of a sample dataset that will be loaded into your cluster:

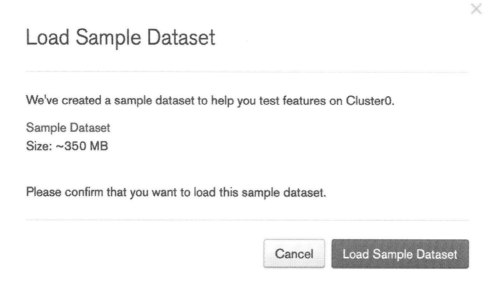

Figure 2.15: Load Sample Dataset confirmation

3. Click `Load Sample Dataset`. You will see a message saying `Loading your sample dataset...` on the screen:

Figure 2.16: Loading your sample dataset... window

It may take a few minutes to load the data and redeploy the cluster instances.

4.  Once the dataset has successfully loaded, you will see a success message saying **`Sample dataset successfully loaded`**:

Figure 2.17: Sample dataset successfully loaded

As the dataset is loaded, you can also see charts showing information about the number of read and write operations performed on the dataset, the total connections, and the total size of the dataset.

5.  Now, click **COLLECTIONS**. On the next screen, you will see the following list of available databases:

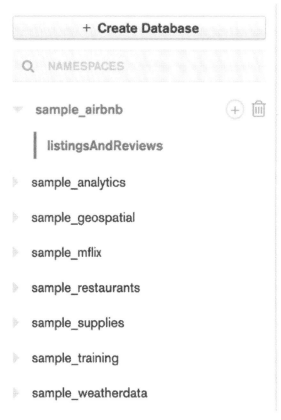

Figure 2.18: List of sample databases

6. Click the down arrow next to **sample_mflix**.

7. Select the **movies** collection.

   Your result for the first 20 documents will be displayed as follows:

Figure 2.19: Movies collection on the cluster

In this exercise, we were able to load the **sample_mflix** database into our cluster. Let's now perform a simple activity that will help us put our understanding of everything we've learned in this chapter to practice.

## ACTIVITY 2.01: MODELING A TWEET INTO A JSON DOCUMENT

Now that you understand JSON documents, the data types supported by MongoDB, and the document-based storage model, it's time to practice modeling a real-life entity into a valid JSON document format.

Your task is to prepare a valid JSON document to represent the data of a tweet. For this, use the dummy tweet shown in *Figure 2.20* From this tweet, identify all the various pieces of information that you can find, decide the field names and data types they can be represented with, prepare a JSON document with all the fields, and validate your document:

**Office of Ned Stark** ⬤
@Lord_Of_Winterfell

Tweeps in the #north. The long nights are upon us. Do stock enough warm clothes, meat and mead. Don't forget to take your flue shots, available for free at @MaesterLuwin's office. #WinterIsComing
Thanks Mylord @TheNedStark and Mylady @CatelynTheCat

#WinterfellCares #flueshots

4:29 PM - 17 Apr 2011

**12165** Retweets **14925** Likes

♡    ♺ 12K    ♡ 14K    ✉

Figure 2.20: Sample tweet

The following steps will help you achieve the desired result:

1. List all the objects that you see in the tweet, such as user ID, name, profile picture, tweet text, tags, and mentions.

2. Identify the set of closely related fields that can be grouped together. These groups of fields can be placed as embedded objects or arrays.

3. Once you have created the JSON document, validate it using any JSON validator available online (for example, https://jsonlint.com/).

The following code represents the final JSON document with only a few fields revealed:

```
{
  "id": 1,
  "created_at": "Sun Apr 17 16:29:24 +0000 2011",
  "text": "Tweeps in the #north. The long nights are upon us..",
  ...,
  ...,
  ...
}
```

> **NOTE**
>
> The solution to this activity can be found on page 650.

## SUMMARY

In this chapter, we have covered a detailed structure of MongoDB documents and document-based models, which is important before we dive into more advanced concepts in the upcoming chapters. We began our discussion with the transportation and storage of information in the form of JSON-like documents that provide a flexible and language-independent format. We studied an overview of JSON documents, the document structure, and basic data types, followed by BSON document specifications and differentiating between BSON and JSON on various parameters.

We then covered MongoDB documents, considering their flexibility, self-containment, relatability, and agility, as well as various data types provided by BSON. Finally, we made a note of MongoDB's limitations and restrictions for documents and learned why the limitations are imposed and why they are important.

In the next chapter, we will use the mongo shell and Mongo Compass to connect to an actual MongoDB server and manage user authentication and authorization.

# 3

# SERVERS AND CLIENTS

## OVERVIEW

This chapter introduces network and database access security for the MongoDB Atlas Cloud service. You will learn about MongoDB clients and how you can connect clients to cloud databases to run MongoDB commands. You will create and manage user authentication and authorization using Atlas Cloud security configuration and create a user account for MongoDB database. After you connect to MongoDB database, you will explore the Compass GUI client for MongoDB Server commands.

# INTRODUCTION

We have explored the basics of the MongoDB database in the cloud, and have seen how MongoDB is different from other databases. *Chapter 2, Documents and Data Types* explained the data structures used in MongoDB. By now, you know how to connect to your MongoDB Atlas Console and how to browse the database using Data Explorer. In this chapter, you will continue your journey into the world of MongoDB, and connect and access the new MongoDB database and discover its internal architecture and commands.

In today's world, internet and cloud computing are the main driving forces that dictate the rules for existing and future applications. So far, we have learned that MongoDB Atlas is a powerful cloud version of MongoDB, offering performance, security, and flexibility for clients. While cloud infrastructure provides many benefits for users, it also increases the security risk associated with data stored in the cloud. Cybersecurity incidents are frequently seen on the news. One such incident occurred with the Target Corporation in 2013, when they became the victim of a large cyber attack and the personal data of over 100 million customers was stolen.

One of the advantages of the MongoDB Atlas service is that many security features are enabled by default, thus protecting against attacks over the internet. Therefore, it is very important to understand the basics of configuring Atlas security.

Consider a scenario in which you are working on a project based on MongoDB. Your colleagues from the IT department have deployed a new MongoDB database in the Atlas Cloud and have sent you the connection details. However, after taking a look, you discover that you are not able to connect to the new database because of security rules for network and user access. The first thing to configure will be to provide yourself with access to the new database. You also need to make sure that access will continue to be disabled for unauthorized access over the internet.

To configure access to your project's database, there are two key aspects that you will have to keep in mind:

- **Network access**: Configures IP network access

- **Database access**: Configures users and database roles

# NETWORK ACCESS

The first step, after we have a database installed and running, is to be able to successfully connect to our database. Network access is a low-level security configuration that's available for databases deployed in the Atlas Cloud.

For a database installed locally on a laptop, we usually don't need to configure any network security. The connection is directed to the database installed locally. However, for a database that is deployed on cloud infrastructure, security is enabled by default and needs to be configured. It is very important to protect access to the database so that the data is protected from unauthorized access over the internet. Before we learn how to configure network access in MongoDB, let's go through some of its core underlying concepts.

## NETWORK PROTOCOLS

The **Internet Protocol** (**IP**) is a decades-old standard, and the **Transmission Control Protocol/Internet Protocol** (**TCP/IP**) is the transport protocol used by all applications to reliably communicate data packets over the internet. Each computer or device on the internet has its unique IP address or hostname. Communication between devices is possible by including the source IP address and the destination IP address in the network packet header.

> **NOTE**
>
> A network packet header is an additional piece of data found at the start of a data packet containing information about the data the packet carries. This information includes the source IP, destination IP, the protocol, and other information.

MongoDB makes no exception in using TCP/IP as its network protocol to transport data. Furthermore, there are currently two versions of the IP: IPv4 and IPv6. Both versions are supported by the Atlas Cloud platform. IPv4 defines a standard 4-byte (32-bit) address, whereas IPv6 defines a standard 16-byte (128-bit) address.

Both IPv4 and IPv6 are used to specify the complete address of a device on the internet. The latest standard, IPv6, is designed to overcome the limitations of the IPv4 protocol. An IP address has two parts: the IP network and the IP host address. A netmask is a sequence of bits (mask) that is used to indicate the network and host part of the IP address. The network address is the IP address' prefix, while the address of the host is the remainder (the suffix of the IP address):

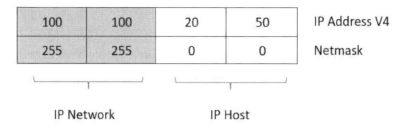

Figure 3.1: Diagrammatic representation of an IP address

In *Figure 3.1*, the netmask 255.255.0.0 (or (1111 1111).(1111 1111).(0000 0000)(0000 0000) in binary format) acts as a mask, indicating the IP network and IP host part of the address. The IP network part of the address (prefix) is composed of the first 16 bits of the general IPv4 address, 100.100, while the host address is the rest of the address – 20.50.

MongoDB Atlas uses **Classless Inter-Domain Routing** (**CIDR**) notation instead of an IP netmask to specify IP addresses. The CIDR format is a shorter format that is used to describe an IP network and host format. Moreover, CIDR is more flexible than the older IP netmask notation.

Here is an example of a netmask and its equivalent CIDR notation:

| **Netmask** | IP: 54.175.147.155 |
| | Netmask: 255.255.255.0 |
| **CIDR** | CIDR: 54.175.147.155 / 24 |

Figure 3.2: Netmask and its CIDR notation

They both describe the same IP network – 54.175.147.0 (24 bits from the left, or 3 bytes), and host number –155. There could be 254 hosts (from 1 to 254) in this network.

> **NOTE**
>
> It is beyond the goal of this course to present a comprehensive guide to internet network standards. For more details, refer to *Understanding TCP/IP* (https://www.packtpub.com/networking-and-servers/understanding-tcpip), which is a clear and comprehensive guide to TCP/IP protocols.

## PUBLIC VERSUS PRIVATE IP ADDRESSES

As explained previously, any device connected on the internet needs a unique IP address in order to communicate with other servers. Those types of IP addresses are called **public** IP addresses. Apart from public IPs, the internet standard also defines a few IP addresses that are reserved for private use, called **private** IP addresses. These are more commonly used in corporate environments that need to limit their employees' access to a private network (intranet) instead of giving them access to the public internet.

The following table describes the private IP addresses available for IP version 4.

| IP | Netmask | CIDR |
|---|---|---|
| 10.0.0.0 | 255.0.0.0 | /8 |
| 172.16.0.0 | 255.255.0.0 | /16 |
| 192.168.0.0 | 255.255.255.0 | /24 |

Figure 3.3: Private IP addresses for IP4

On the other hand, a public IP address is unique on the internet and can have any value that is different from the ones in *Figure 3.3*.

## DOMAIN NAME SERVER

Let's consider an example where the IP address **52.206.222.245** is the public IP address of the MongoDB website:

```
C:\>ping mongodb.com


Pinging mongodb.com [52.206.222.245] with 32 bytes of data:
Reply from 52.206.222.245: bytes=32 time=241ms TTL=48
```

```
Reply from 52.206.222.245: bytes=32 time=242ms TTL=48
Reply from 52.206.222.245: bytes=32 time=243ms TTL=48

Ping statistics for 52.206.222.245:
    Packets: Sent = 3, Received = 3, Lost = 0 (0% loss),
Approximate round trip times in milli-seconds:
    Minimum = 241ms, Maximum = 250ms, Average = 244ms
```

As you can see, we used the name **mongodb.com** to run the ping command, and not the IP address of the MongoDB website directly. The **Domain Name Server** (**DNS**) is the solution for resolving hostnames on the internet. The client queries the DNS servers for a specific hostname or domain (in this case, **mongodb.com**), and the DNS server responds with the public IP addresses registered for that host and domain: IP **54.175.147.155**.

## TRANSMISSION CONTROL PROTOCOL

The **Transmission Control Protocol** (**TCP**), part of the IP address, defines sockets, or ports, that can be used for different types of network connections. Every process that needs to communicate over the internet uses a TCP port to establish a connection.

The default TCP port for MongoDB Server is 27017. In the MongoDB Atlas free tier, the default TCP port cannot be changed. This is one of the limitations of the Atlas free-tier M0 server. However, on a local installation, the TCP listener port can be configured when the server is started.

MongoDB Atlas Cloud always encrypts network communication between the server and applications. Data is protected using a specialized network encryption protocol called TLS (Transport Layer Security).

There are a few important aspects of TCP/IP communication to remember:

- The server always listens for new connections from clients, usually on TCP port 27017.

- The client always initiates the connection to the server by sending a special TCP packet.

- If network access is configured, the client can establish a TCP connection with the database server.

- The server only accepts the connection if the client passes the security checks.

- The network communication is always encrypted for databases in the Atlas Cloud.

- Once the connection is established, the client communicates with the server by sending database commands and receiving data.

## THE WIRE PROTOCOL

Internally, MongoDB stores documents in a special binary format called **Binary JSON** (**BSON**). We learned about the structure of a JSON document in *Chapter 2, Documents and Data Types*. BSON is a more efficient way to store data than JSON. Therefore, BSON is used by MongoDB to store data in files and to transport data over the network.

The Wire Protocol is MongoDB's solution to encapsulate BSON data into network packets that can be sent over the internet. The Wire Protocol defines standard datagrams, or data packets, in a format that can be understood by both MongoDB servers and clients. The structure of a datagram is composed of a header and a body, with a simple but rigorous format defined by MongoDB. The Wire Protocol datagrams are also encapsulated in TCP/IP packets, as shown in the following diagram:

Figure 3.4: Encapsulated Wire Protocol datagrams

## NETWORK ACCESS CONFIGURATION

The Atlas project owner or cluster manager can modify network access from the Atlas web management console. After logging on to the Atlas console, you can access the **Network Access** tab from the Atlas web console, from the **SECURITY** menu:

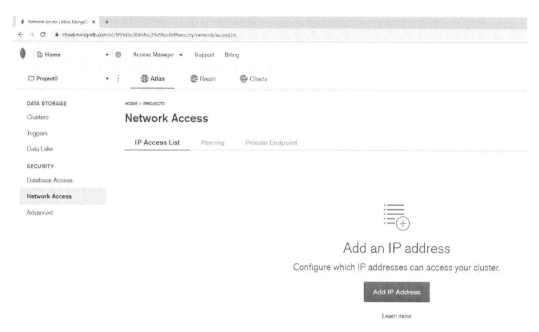

Figure 3.5: MongoDB Atlas console

The **Network Access** configuration page appears on the right side of the page. MongoDB Atlas consists of three methods to manage network access, which can be accessed using the following tabs:

- **IP Access List**
- **Peering**
- **Private Endpoint**

## THE IP ACCESS LIST

**IP Access List** helps the Atlas administrator to specify a list of valid IP addresses that are allowed to connect to the MongoDB database. To add your first IP addresses, you can click the green button **ADD IP ADDRESS**, which is in the middle of the page:

**NOTE**

If you already added one IP address (or a few of them), then **+ ADD IP ADDRESS** button is displayed on the right side of the network access IP list, as shown in *Figure 3.6*.

Figure 3.6: Adding an IP address list

When you click on the **ADD IP ADDRESS** button (or **+ ADD IP ADDRESS**), a pop-up window appears:

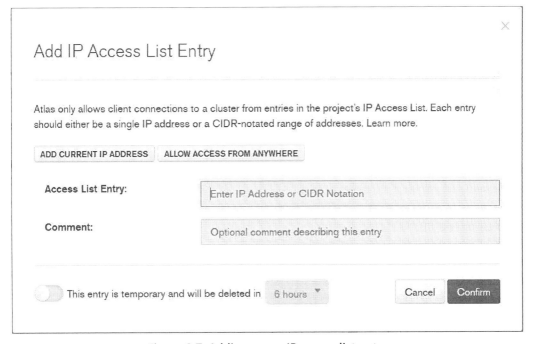

Figure 3.7: Adding a new IP access list entry

The following options are available in the Add IP Access List form:

- **ADD CURRENT IP ADDRESS**: This is the most common method that can be used for simple deployments. It allows you to add your own IP address to the IP access list, as shown in *Figure 3.7*. Atlas automatically detects the IP source address from the web management console's current session, so you don't have to remember the IP address. Most likely, your computer has an internal IP address from a private IP class, such as 192.168.0.xx, which is quite different from the address that Atlas has detected. This is because Atlas always detects the external IP address of your network gateway, instead of internal network private IP addresses. Private IP addresses are not visible from the internet. You can always verify your external IP address by searching **what is my IP?** in Google. The result in the Google search should match the address in Atlas.

- **ALLOW ACCESS FROM ANYWHERE**: As the name suggests, this option enables network access from any location by disabling the network protection for your database, as shown in *Figure 3.7*. The special IP class 0.0.0.0/0 is added to the IP access list.

> **NOTE**
>
> The option to allow access from anywhere is not recommended because it will disable network security protection and will expose our cloud database to possible attacks.

While adding a custom IP address to the **IP List Entry** field, the IP address needs to be in CIDR notation, as described in the introduction to this chapter. A short description can also be typed in the **Comment** field, as shown in *Figure 3.8*:

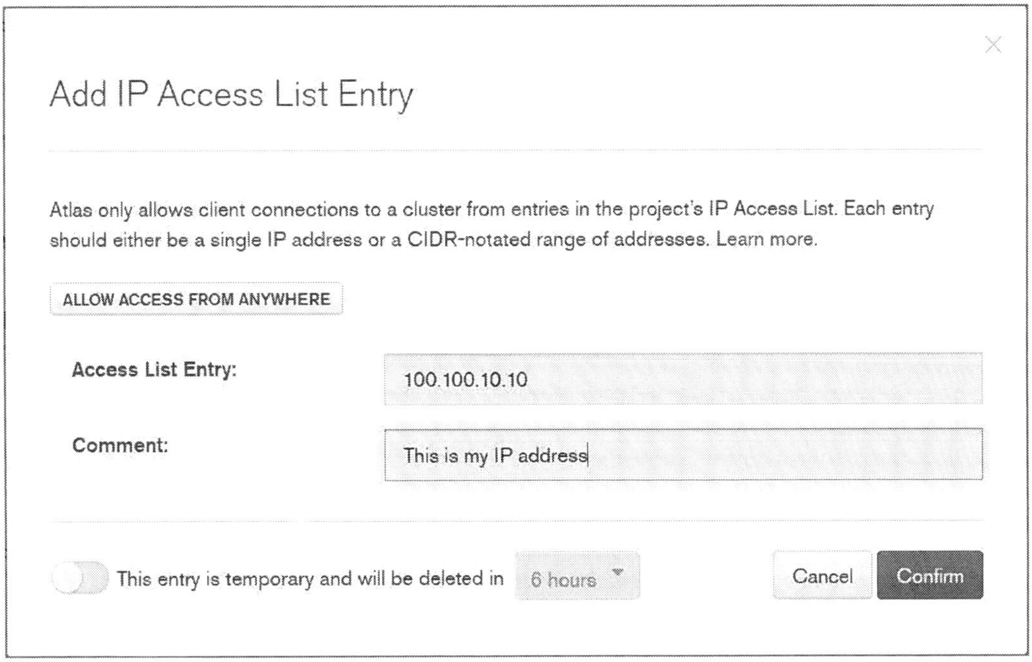

Figure 3.8: Filling in the Comment field in the IP Access list entry

**NOTE**

In the current version of the Atlas console, it is not possible to add a hostname or a **Fully Qualified Domain Name** (**FQDN**) to the IP access list. Only IP addresses are accepted as valid entries. Both IPv4 and IPv6 are supported for MongoDB Atlas. For example, it is not possible to add a hostname such as *server01prd* or *server01prd.mongodb.com* (including the domain), but rather the host public IP address. The IP address can be obtained from a DNS lookup or just a ping hostname.

## TEMPORARY ACCESS

Entries in the access list can be permanent or they can have an expiration time. Temporary entries are automatically removed from the list when they expire. If you wish to add a temporary IP address, check the switch **This entry is temporary and will be deleted in** option in the **Add IP Access List Entry** form, as shown in *Figure 3.9*. You can specify the expiration time using the dropdown:

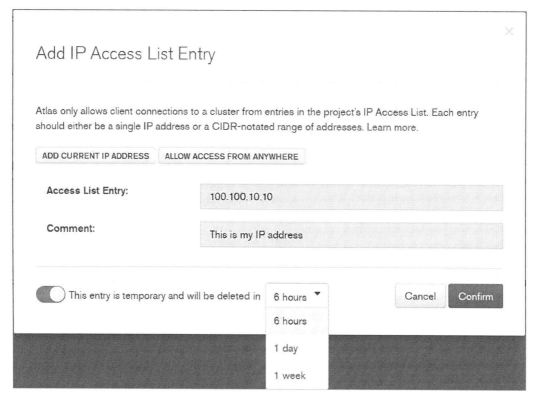

**Figure 3.9: Adding a temporary IP Access list entry**

When you click **Confirm**, the IP/host address is saved in the access list and the network configuration is activated. The process usually completes in less than a minute and during this time, the entry status will be **Pending** for a few seconds, as shown in *Figure 3.10*:

| IP Address | Comment | Status |
|------------|---------|--------|
| 100.100.10.10/32 | This is my IP address | ⟳ Pending |

Figure 3.10: Network access window displaying the Pending status

Once the network configuration is activated, **Status** will be **Active**, as shown in *Figure 3.11*:

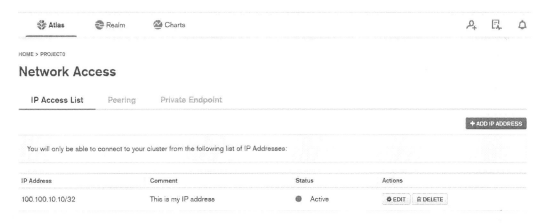

Figure 3.11: Network Access window

> **NOTE**
>
> A message saying **You will only be able to connect to your cluster from the following list of IP Addresses:** appears on the screen to notify the user of the list of available IP addresses, as shown in *Figure 3.11*.

After the IP was saved in the IP access list, the administrator can modify the entry. The permission of the following operations can be accessed from the **Actions** tab, as shown in *Figure 3.11*:

- Delete an existing entry from the IP access list by clicking **DELETE**.

- Edit an existing entry from the IP access list by clicking **EDIT**.

> **NOTE**
>
> You can add multiple IP addresses to the access list. For example, if you need to access your cloud database from your office and from your home, you can add both IP addresses to the access list table. Nevertheless, please note that there is a limit of 200 addresses that can be added to the list.

## NETWORK PEERING

Network peering is another method of controlling network access on the Atlas Cloud infrastructure, which is different from an IP access list. It enables companies to set up a **Virtual Private Cloud** (**VPC**) connection between the local company network and the Atlas network infrastructure, as follows:

- Private IP networks are used to configure VPC between the client's private network and MongoDB Atlas servers. Any type of private IP is supported for VPC network peering.

- All cloud providers are supported for network peering, such as AWS's, Microsoft's, or Google's cloud infrastructure.

- Network peering is appropriate only for large implementations (M10+), and therefore is not available for Atlas free-tier users.

> **NOTE**
>
> The details of network peering and private endpoint are beyond the scope of this introductory course.

# EXERCISE 3.01: ENABLING NETWORK ACCESS

In this exercise, you will use the Atlas web management console to enable network access for your new database in the cloud. This is necessary to permit network connections over the internet.

The exercise will guide you through the steps to add your own IP address to the access list. As a result, network access will be permitted from your location, and you'll be able to connect to the MongoDB database using a client running on your local computer. Follow these steps to complete this exercise:

1. Go to http://cloud.mongodb.com to connect to the Atlas console.

2. Log on to your new MongoDB Atlas web interface using your username and password, which was created when you registered for the Atlas Cloud:

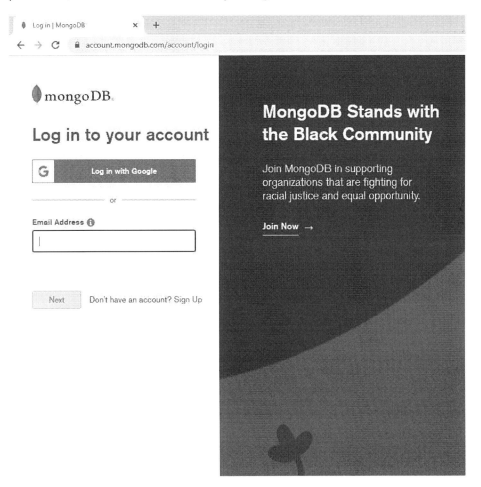

Figure 3.12: MongoDB Atlas login page

3.  From the **SECURITY** menu, click the **Network Access** tab:

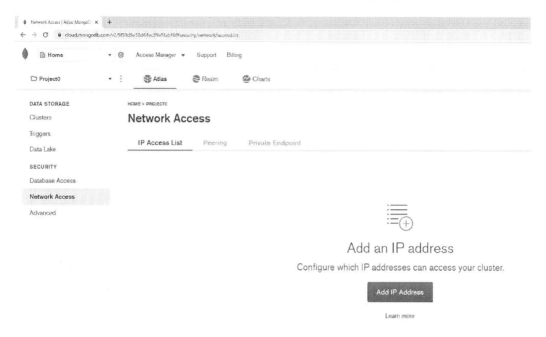

Figure 3.13: Network Access window

4.  Click **ADD IP ADDRESS** in the **IP Access List** tab.

5. From the **Add IP Access List Entry** window that appears, click the **ADD CURRENT IP ADDRESS** button:

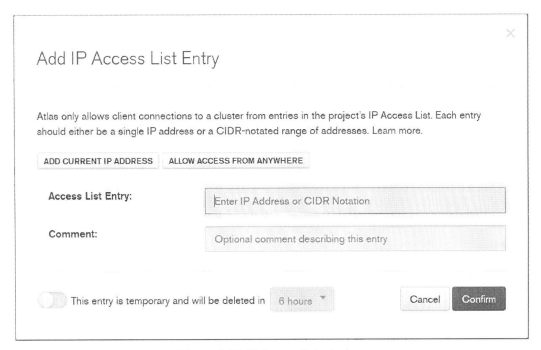

Figure 3.14: IP Access list window

The MongoDB web interface will automatically detect your external IP address and will reflect it in the **IP Access List Entry** field.

6. Type **This is my IP Address** in the **Comment** field (this is optional):

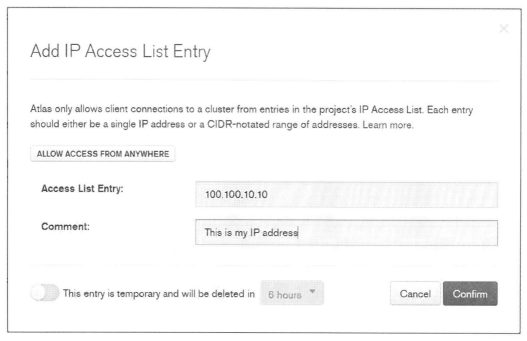

Figure 3.15: Typing in a comment in the Add IP Access List Entry window

7. Click the **Confirm** button to save the new entry. Atlas is deploying the new IP access list rules to the cloud system

8. The IP address will appear in the access list table (as active):

Figure 3.16: Network Access window

> **NOTE**
>
> The IP `100.100.10.10/32` is a dummy IP address as an example. In your practical case, the IP address will be your own public IP address, which is different. Moreover, your ISP (Internet Service Provider) may assign you a dynamic IP address, which is not permanent, and it may be changed after a period of time.

We have successfully "whitelisted" our current public IP address into the Atlas Cloud console so that TCP/IP connections will be allowed from our public IP address. If you have multiple locations, such as home and a work office, add multiple IP addresses to the access list in the Atlas console.

# DATABASE ACCESS

MongoDB databases deployed on the Atlas Cloud have several security features enabled by default, such as user access control. Database access control verifies user authentication credentials, such as the username and password. Therefore, even if network access is available from anywhere, you will still need to authenticate before successfully connecting to the MongoDB database in the cloud. This is necessary to protect databases deployed in the cloud from unauthorized access over the internet. More importantly, when compared with other security features, access control cannot be disabled for cloud databases and will always remain enabled.

Database access covers the following aspects of database security:

- Database users
- Database roles

When compared with other MongoDB installations, the management of user accounts in the Atlas Cloud is configured at the project level. Users created in one Atlas project are shared among all MongoDB database clusters created in that project. The basic methods to configure Atlas database security (users and roles) are both covered in this chapter.

> **NOTE**
>
> Database access refers only to the access to database services deployed in Atlas, and not to the Atlas Console itself. As an Atlas project owner, you will always be able to connect to the Atlas web console to manage your cloud database access. If you need to add more project team members to the Atlas project, then this is possible from the **PROJECT** tab on the Atlas web application. In the scope of this course, the examples are relevant when connected as an Atlas project owner.

## USER AUTHENTICATION

The validation of user identity is an essential aspect of database security and is necessary in order to protect data integrity and confidentiality. This is exactly the reason why all MongoDB databases deployed in the Atlas Cloud require users to be authenticated before they can create new database sessions. Therefore, only trusted database users are granted access to the cloud database.

The database authentication process consists of a procedure to validate the user identity prior to connection.

The user identity must qualify the following two parameters:

- A valid username must be provided at connection time.
- The user's identity must be confirmed via validation.

Declaring a valid username is straightforward. The only prerequisite is that the username must exist, which means the username must have been created previously and its account must be activated.

## USERNAME STORAGE

Users need to be declared in Atlas before they can be used. The username and password can either be stored internally (within the database) or externally (outside the database) as follows:

- **Internally**: The username is stored within the MongoDB database, in a special collection of the admin database. There are a few restrictions. The admin database is accessible only to system administrators. When a user tries to connect, the username must exist in the list of existing usernames in the admin database.

- **Externally**: The username is stored in an external system, such as **Lightweight Directory Access Protocol (LDAP)**. For example, the Microsoft Active Directory is an LDAP directory implementation that can be configured for MongoDB username authentication.

> **NOTE**
>
> LDAP authentication is only available for bigger Atlas clusters (M10+) and permits enterprise-specific configuration of many database users' accounts. This configuration is not covered in this introductory course.

## USERNAME AUTHENTICATION

Authentication is the process of validating user identity. If user authentication is successful, the user is confirmed and trusted to access the database. Otherwise, the user is rejected and will not be allowed to establish a database connection. The following are some authentication mechanisms, each one with a different technology and level of security.

**Password Authentication**

- Simple password authentication. The user needs to provide the correct password. The database system validates the password against the declared username. The process of securely validating user passwords over the internet is called a **handshake** or **challenge response**.

- Passwords are validated by the MongoDB database. In the case of LDAP authentication, passwords are validated externally. Since version 4.0, MongoDB has a new challenge-response method to validate passwords known as the **Salted Challenge Response Authentication Mechanism** (**SCRAM**). SCRAM guarantees that the user password can be validated securely over the internet without transferring or storing passwords in cleartext. This is because transferring cleartext passwords over the internet's public infrastructure is considered extremely insecure.

- In older versions of MongoDB, a different challenge-response method was used. If you upgrade your applications from MongoDB 2.0 or 3.0 to the latest version, verify the MongoDB client's compatibility with MongoDB version 4.0 or higher. At the time of writing, the current version on premises of MongoDB server is version 4.4.

### X.509 Certificate Authentication

- This refers to the use of cryptographic certificates for user authentication instead of simple passwords. Certificates are longer and far more secure than passwords.

- An X.509 certificate is a digitally encrypted key, created using a cryptographical standard **Public Key Infrastructure** (**PKI**). Certificates are created in a pair of keys (public-private).

- This method also permits password-less authentication for users, which allows users and applications to connect using a private key X.509 certificate.

## CONFIGURING AUTHENTICATION IN ATLAS

It is recommended to use only the Atlas web application to create and configure database users.

Atlas project owners can add users to an Atlas project and configure users' authentication from the Atlas web interface. Atlas users can be added to all database clusters within the respective Atlas project. Authentication settings can be made available by clicking **Database Access** from the Atlas application.

Here is a screenshot from the Atlas web application ([http://cloud.mongodb.com](http://cloud.mongodb.com)):

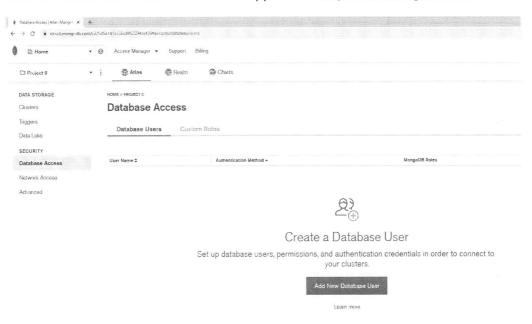

Figure 3.17: Database Access window

In *Figure 3.17*, you will notice two tabs, **Database Users** and **Custom Roles**. Let's first focus on the options available for **Database Users**. Once you click the **ADD NEW DATABASE USER** option to create a new user, the following window will appear:

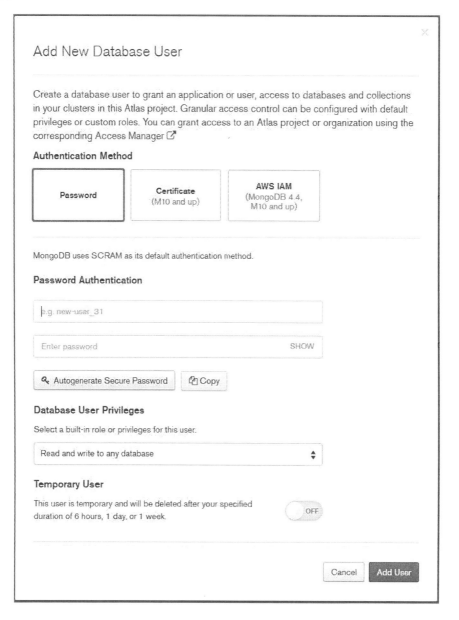

Figure 3.18: Add New Database User window

**NOTE**

Password SCRAM authentication is the only option available for Atlas M0 free-tier cluster, which is used for examples in this course. The other authentication method options, a certificate and AWS IAM, are available for larger Atlas M10+ clusters.

There are two fields in the window, as shown in *Figure 3.19*:

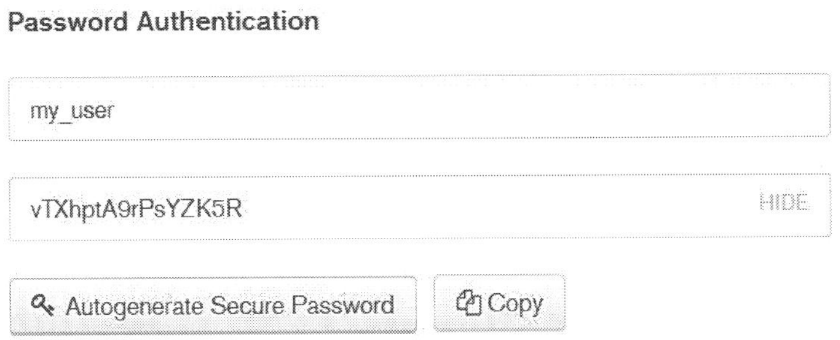

Password Authentication

> my_user

> vTXhptA9rPsYZK5R                                                                HIDE

> 🔑 Autogenerate Secure Password        📋 Copy

Figure 3.19: Username and password fields in the Add New Database User window

In the first field, you can type the new database username. The username should not contain spaces or special characters. Only ASCII letters, numbers, hyphens, and underscores are allowed.

The second field is for the user password. A password can be entered manually by the administrator or it can be generated by the Atlas application. The **Autogenerate Secure Password** button automatically generates a secure, complex password. The **SHOW** and **HIDE** options will either display or hide the password input on the screen. There is also an option to copy the password to the clipboard by clicking the **COPY** button, as shown in *Figure 3.19*.

## TEMPORARY USERS

The Atlas administrator can decide to add temporary user accounts. A temporary user account is an account that is valid only for a limited period. The account will be automatically deleted by Atlas after its expiration time:

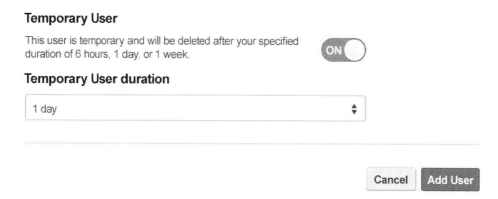

Figure 3.20: Temporary User option in the Add New User window

In the preceding example, the user account, **my_user**, is set to expire automatically in 1 day (24 hours). The checkbox for **Save as temporary user for** is selected, and the stipulated time is set.

> **NOTE**
>
> From the **built-in role or privilege** drop-down menu, the administrator can assign a database privilege when the new user is created. By default, the assigned privilege is **Read and write to any database**. Database privilege options are explained in detail in the next section.

The **Add User** button completes the add new user process. Once the user account is created, it will appear in the MongoDB user list, as shown in *Figure 3.21*. The user account can be changed or deleted if required. The user account details can be changed or removed using the **EDIT** or **DELETE** options in the **Actions** tab:

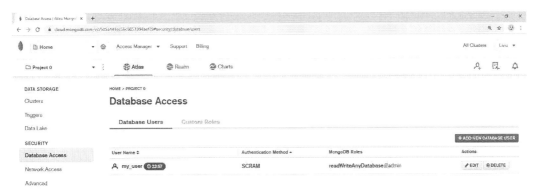

Figure 3.21: The Database Access window

> **NOTE**
>
> As you may observe, in my example in *Figure 3.21*, the **my_user** account is set to automatically expire after 24 hours (23:57). The user account will be automatically deleted after the expiration time.

## DATABASE PRIVILEGES AND ROLES

Database authorization is the part of database security that covers privileges and roles for MongoDB databases. Once you authenticate a user successfully and create a new database session, the database privileges and roles are assigned to the user. The accessibility of a database's collections and objects is verified against the database privileges that are assigned to the user.

A privilege (or action) is the right to perform a particular action or operation within the MongoDB database on a specific database resource. For example, the read privilege grants the right to query a specific database collection or view.

Multiple database privileges can be grouped within a role. There is a long list of database privileges, each one for a different function in MongoDB. Instead of directly assigning privileges to users, the privileges are assigned to roles, and these roles are then assigned to users. As a result, the management of privileges and roles in the database is easier to understand:

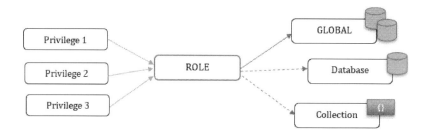

Figure 3.22: Pictorial representation of database privileges

Roles can have a global or local scope:

- **GLOBAL:** This role applies to all MongoDB databases and collections.

- **Database:** This role applies only to a specific database name.

- **Collection:** This role applies only to a specific collection name within a database. It has the most restrictive scope.

## PREDEFINED ROLES

There are a few predefined database roles, and for each role, there is a list of specific privileges assigned. For example, the administrator role contains all the privileges necessary to administer a MongoDB database. Assigning a predefined role is the most common way to manage your MongoDB database.

If none of the predefined roles fit the security requirements for your application, custom roles can be defined in MongoDB. The following roles are predefined in the Atlas application, and can be assigned when new database users are created:

- **Atlas admin**: This has all the permissions and roles necessary for MongoDB database administration in the cloud. The role is global, applicable to all database clusters created in one project Atlas account. It includes many database roles, such as **dbAdminAnyDatabase**, **readWriteAnyDatabase**, and **clusterMonitor**.

> **NOTE**
>
> The `Atlas admin` role is different from the MongoDB database `dbAdmin` role. The `Atlas admin` role includes the **dbAdmin** plus other roles, and is available only on the Atlas Cloud platform.

- **Read and write to any database**: This Atlas role has the read and write to any database role and is applicable to all database clusters created within one Atlas project account.

- **Only read any database**: This is a read-only Atlas role that is applicable to all database clusters created within one Atlas project account.

## CONFIGURING BUILT-IN ROLES IN ATLAS

The simplest way to assign a built-in role is at the time when a new user is created. Atlas offers a very simple and intuitive interface to add new database users. The default `built-in role or privilege` is assigned when a new user is created. Nevertheless, the administrator can assign a different role for a new user or can edit the privileges for existing users.

> **NOTE**
>
> It is highly recommended to use only the Atlas web interface to manage database roles and privileges. Atlas will automatically disable and roll back any changes to database roles that are not made through the Atlas web interface.

The user roles in Atlas can be managed in the **+ADD NEW USER** window or the **EDIT** user window, as presented in the previous section:

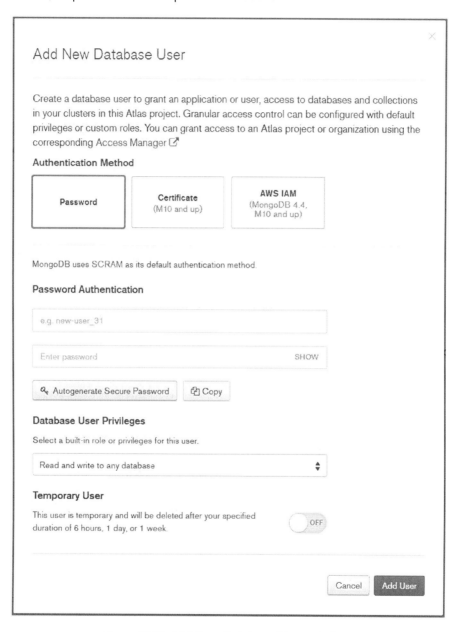

Figure 3.23: Add New Database User window

By default, the built-in **Read and write any database** role is automatically selected in the window, as you can see in *Figure 3.23*. Nevertheless, the administrator can assign a different role (for example, **Atlas admin**) by clicking in the drop-down menu, as shown in *Figure 3.24*:

Figure 3.24: Selecting a role in the Add New User window

## ADVANCED PRIVILEGES

Sometimes, none of the built-in Atlas database roles are suitable for the access we need for the database. There are cases when the intended database design requires a special user access, or applications require a specific security policy that needs to be implemented.

> **NOTE**
>
> Custom roles, which are presented later in this chapter, offer better functionality than advanced privileges. It is always recommended to create a custom role and assign individual permissions to a role rather than assigning specific privileges directly to users.

If you select **Grant specific privileges** from the drop-down list, the interface changes:

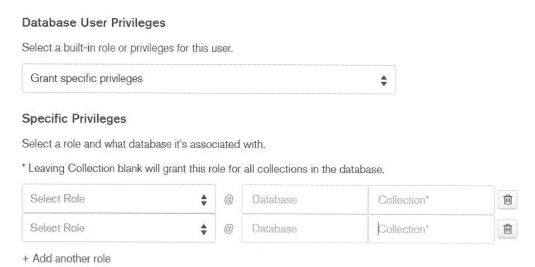

Figure 3.25: Granting specific privileges in the Add New User window

As you can see in *Figure 3.25*, administrators can quickly assign specific MongoDB privileges to a user. This advanced functionality is covered in the custom roles later in this chapter. For the moment, let's configure database access in the following exercise.

## EXERCISE 3.02: CONFIGURING DATABASE ACCESS

The goal of this exercise is to enable database access for your new MongoDB database. Your database now allows connections, and it is asking for username and password validation. In order to enable access, you need to create a new user and grant appropriate database permissions for access.

Create an admin user with the username **admindb**.

Follow these steps to complete this exercise:

1. Repeat *steps 1, 2*, and *3* from *Exercise 3.01, Enabling Network Access*, to log on to your new MongoDB Atlas web interface and select **project 0**.

2. From the **SECURITY** menu, select the **Database Access** option:

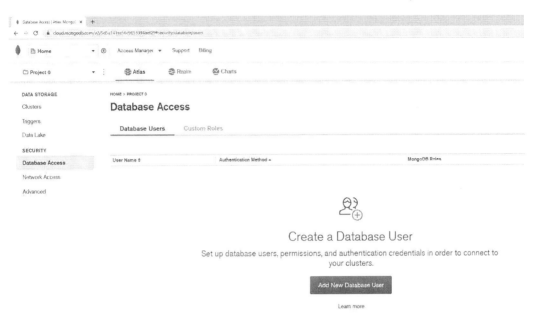

Figure 3.26: Selecting the Database Access option

3. Click **ADD NEW DATABASE USER** in the **Database Users** tab to add a new database user. The **Add New User** window opens.

4. Keep the default authentication method, **Password**.

5. Provide a username or type **admindb** as the username.

6.  Provide the password or click **Autogenerate Secure Password** to
    generate the password. Click **SHOW** to see the autogenerated password:

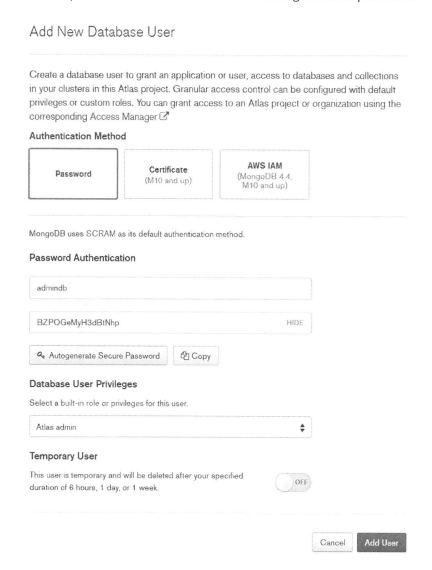

Figure 3.27: Add New Database User window

7.  Click on the drop-down menu under **Database User Privileges** and
    select the **Atlas admin** role.

8.  Click **Add User**. The system will apply the changes to the databases:

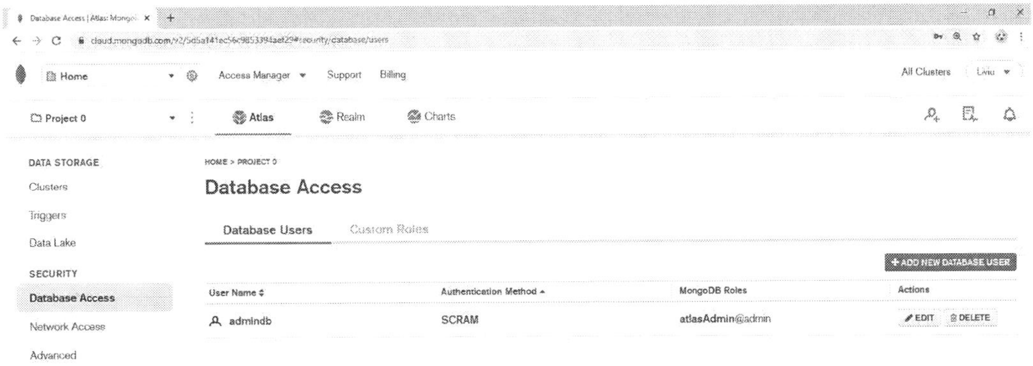

Figure 3.28: New admin user details

In *Figure 3.28*, you can see that a new user, **admindb**, has been created with **Authentication Method** of **SCRAM** and **MongoDB Role** (global) set to **atlasAdmin@admin** for all databases in the project.

The new database user is now configured and deployed in Atlas.

## CONFIGURING CUSTOM ROLES

As the name suggests, a custom role is a collection of selected database permissions that are not included in any of the built-in Atlas database roles. For example, if the read and update permissions are required, but without the right to delete and insert new documents, then a custom role needs to be created as this combination of permissions is not part of any built-in role.

From the **Database Access** window, click on the second tab in the application, **Custom Roles**. This option is used to create and modify custom Atlas roles.

> **NOTE**
>
> Custom roles need to be defined in Atlas before they can be assigned to users.

A new custom role can be created by clicking the **ADD NEW CUSTOM ROLE** button. The new custom role window appears:

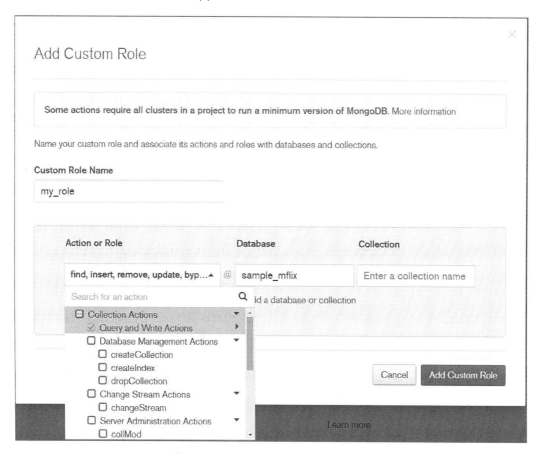

Figure 3.29: MongoDB custom roles

Actions can be selected based on the following categories:

- **Collection Actions**: Actions that are applicable to a collection database object

- **Database Actions**: Actions that are applicable to a database

- **Global Actions**: Actions that are applicable globally to all Atlas projects

For example, the database administrator permits users to only update a database collection. The user cannot delete or insert new documents in a collection. This specific combination of actions is not contained in any Atlas predefined role.

There could be many combinations of Collection/Database/Global actions defined under one complex role. When the definition is complete, click the **Add Custom Role** button to create the new role in Atlas. The new role becomes visible in the list, as shown in *Figure 3.30*:

Figure 3.30: Custom role list

> **NOTE**
>
> Once custom roles are created, they become visible in Atlas and can be assigned to database users. The new custom role can be assigned from the **ADD/EDIT** user window, in the **Database Privileges** drop-down list, under **Select pre-defined custom roles**.

# THE DATABASE CLIENT

Before we cover the specifics of the different types of clients of a MongoDB database, let's look at a short introduction to clarify the basics of a database client. A database client is a software application that is designed to do the following:

- Connect to a MongoDB database server
- Request information from the database server
- Modify data by sending MongoDB CRUD requests
- Send other database commands to the database server

Interaction and compatibility with the MongoDB database server are essential. A difference in compatibility between the client and the server—for example, different versions—could produce unexpected results or generate database or application errors. This is the reason why clients are usually tested and certified for compatibility with a specific version of the MongoDB database.

Let's categorize the MongoDB clients depending on the purpose for which they were created:

- **Basic**: This is a minimalist version of the client. Usually delivered with the database software, basic clients provide an interactive application to work with the database server.

- **Data-oriented**: This type of client is designed to work with data. It usually provides a **Graphical User Interface** (**GUI**), and the tools that assist you to efficiently query, aggregate, and modify data.

- **Drivers**: These are designed to provide the interface between the MongoDB database and another software system, such as a general-use programming language. The main use of drivers is in software development and application deployments.

You now have all the configuration changes in place for the new MongoDB database deployed in the Atlas Cloud. The installation of MongoDB client on a local computer has already been covered in previous chapters. If necessary, review *Chapter 1, Introduction to MongoDB*, for basic MongoDB installation. The next step is to use your local MongoDB client to connect to your new database in the cloud. Secondly, a custom collection of Python scripts will be used for data migration, so you need to know how you can connect from Python to a MongoDB database in Atlas. The next section discusses all aspects regarding client connection in MongoDB.

## CONNECTION STRINGS

What exactly is a connection string and why is it important? A connection string is nothing more than a method to identify the database service address and its parameters so that clients can connect to the server over the network. It is important because without a connection string, the client would have no clue how to connect to the database service.

Database clients, such as users and applications, need to form a valid connection string in order to be able to connect to the database service. Moreover, the MongoDB connection string follows the **Uniform Resource Identifier** (**URI**) format to pass all connection details to the database client.

Here is the general format of a MongoDB connection string: **`mongodb+srv://`**
**`user:pass@hostname:port/database_name?options`**

The elements of the connection string are described in the following table:

| Elements of the connection string | Description |
| --- | --- |
| `mongodb+srv`<br><br>or<br><br>`mongodb` | New DNS prefix: `mongodb+srv`<br><br>This indicates that a special **DNS Service** (**DNS SRV**) record is used for connection, which is the default connection string for databases deployed in the Atlas Cloud.<br><br>Standard prefix: `mongodb`<br><br>This is the older version of a connection string, for when DNS SRV is not used. DNS can still be used for hostname and domain resolution. |
| `user:pass` | Database authentication, username, and password details are required for a new database connection.<br><br>The username and password are required if:<br><br>The database is in the Atlas Cloud<br><br>The database is in authorization mode (that is, it started with an `--auth` parameter)<br><br>There are no default values. |
| `hostname` | This is the hostname or IP address of the database server. It can include the full DNS domain name.<br><br>Default value: `localhost (127.0.0.1)` |
| `port` | This is the TCP port on which the database service listens for new connection requests.<br><br>Default value: `TCP 27017` |
| `database_name` | This is the name of the database on the database server.<br><br>Default value: `admin` |
| `?options` | These are the connection string parameters that clients can send to the server at connection time. |

Figure 3.31: Elements of the connection string

> **NOTE**
>
> More details about the new prefix **`mongodb+srv`** and how DNS SRV records are used for identifying the MongoDB service will be covered in *Chapter 10, Replication*.

Let's now look at some of the examples of connection strings, as follows:

```
mongodb+srv://guest:passwd123@atlas1-u7xxx.mongodb.
net:27017/data1
```

This connection string is suitable to attempt a database connection with the following parameters:

- The server is running on the Atlas Cloud (the hostname is **mongodb.net**).

- The database cluster name is **atlas1**.

- The connection is attempted with the username **guest** and the password **passwd123**.

- The database service is presented on the standard TCP port **27017**.

- The default database name on the server is **data1**.

While the preceding connection string is valid for Atlas database connections, it is generally not a good idea to display the password in the connection string. Here is an example where the password is requested at connection time:

`mongodb+srv://guest@atlas1-u7xxx.mongodb.net:27017/data1`

Another example is as follows:

`mongodb+srv://atlas1-u7xxx.mongodb.net:27017/data1`
`--username guest`

In this case, the connection is attempted with the **guest username**. However, the password is not part of the connection string, and it will be requested by the server at connection time.

If the database name is omitted (or is invalid), connection to the default database is attempted, which is the admin database. Also, if the TCP port is omitted, it will attempt to connect to the default TCP port 27017, as in the following example:

`mongodb+srv://guest@atlas1-u7xxx.mongodb.net`

For non-cloud database connections or for legacy MongoDB connections, the simple **mongodb** prefix should be used instead. Here are a few examples of non-cloud connection strings:

`mongodb://localhost/data1`

In this example, the hostname is **localhost**, which means that the database server is running on the same computer as the application, and connecting to the database **data1** is attempted. Here is another example of a remote network connection on the non-default TCP port **5500**:

`mongodb://devsrv01.dev-domain-example.com:5500/data1`

As no username is specified in the connection string, connection is attempted without a username. This type of connection works for databases that have no authorization mode (no user security configured). Authorization mode is always configured for cloud databases.

> **NOTE**
>
> A MongoDB connection string can be different if the database service is configured in a replication or sharded cluster. Examples of connection strings for MongoDB clusters will be provided later, in *Chapter 10, Replication*.

## THE MONGO SHELL

Probably the simplest way to connect to a MongoDB database is to use the mongo shell. The mongo shell offers a simple terminal mode client for a MongoDB database:

- The mongo shell is included in all MongoDB installations.

- It can be used to run server interactive commands in terminal mode.

- It can be used to run JavaScript.

- The mongo shell has its own commands.

To start the mongo shell, run the **mongo** command in Command Prompt, as follows:

```
C:\>mongo --help
MongoDB shell version v4.4.0
usage: mongo [options] [db address] [file names (ending in .js)]
db address can be:
  foo                     foo database on local machine
  192.168.0.5/foo         foo database on 192.168.0.5 machine
  192.168.0.5:9999/foo    foo database on 192.168.0.5 machine on port 9999
  mongodb://192.168.0.5:9999/foo    connection string URI can also be used
Options:
  --ipv6                                enable IPv6 support (disabled by
....
```

## EXERCISE 3.03: CONNECTING TO THE CLOUD DATABASE USING THE MONGO SHELL

This simple exercise will show you the steps to connect to Atlas using the mongo shell. For this exercise, use the **mongodb+srv** prefix in the connection string. The first step is to obtain the cluster name (the DNS SRV record) for your Atlas Cloud database:

1. Log on to your new MongoDB Atlas web interface using your username and password, which was created when you registered for the Atlas Cloud:

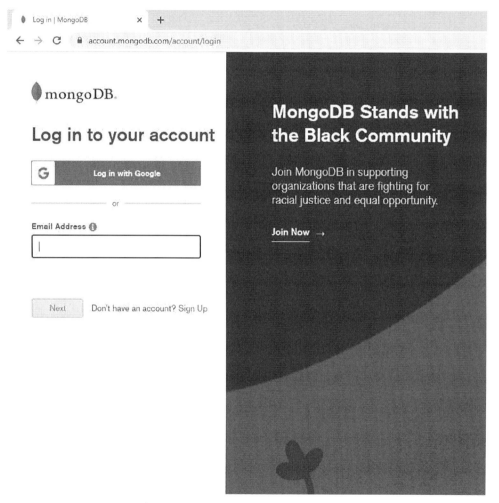

Figure 3.32: MongoDB Atlas login page

2. Click on the **Clusters** tab in the **Atlas** project menu, as shown in *Figure 3.33*.

3. Click on the **CONNECT** button in the **Clusters** menu. In the case of M0 free-tier, there is a single cluster called **Cluster0**:

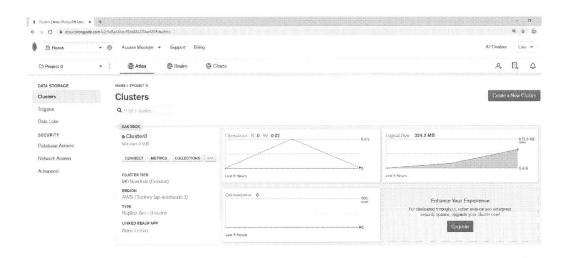

Figure 3.33: Clusters window

4. The **Connect to Cluster0** window appears:

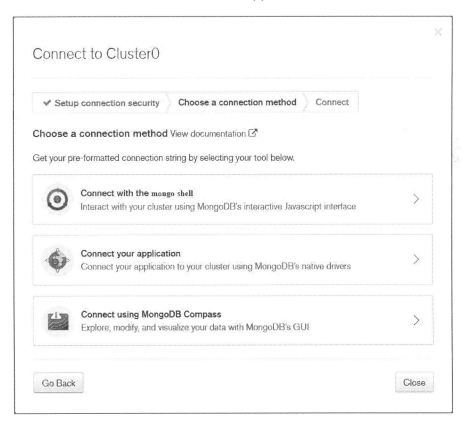

Figure 3.34: Connect to Cluster0 window

5. Click **Connect with the mongo shell**. The following window appears:

**Figure 3.35: Connect to Cluster0 page**

6. Select the **I have the mongo shell installed** option and select the correct mongo shell version (the latest mongo shell version is 4.4 at the time of writing). Alternatively, you can select **I do not have the mongo shell installed** and install the mongo shell, if you have not installed it yet.

7. Click **Copy** to copy the connection string to the clipboard.

8. Start a command prompt window or terminal in your operating system.

9. Start the mongo shell with the new connection string command line:

```
C:\>mongo "mongodb+srv://cluster0.u7n6b.mongodb.net/test" --username
admindb
```

The following details will appear:

```
MongoDB shell version v4.4.0
Enter password:
connecting to: mongodb://cluster0-shard-00-00.u7n6b.mongodb.
net:27017,cluster0-
Implicit session: session { "id" : UUID("7407ce65-d9b6-4d92-87b2-
754a844ae0e7") }
MongoDB server version: 4.2.8
WARNING: shell and server versions do not match
MongoDB Enterprise atlas-rzhbg7-shard-0:PRIMARY>
```

To connect to the Atlas database as the **admindb** database user created in *Exercise 3.02*, *Configuring Database Access*, when prompted, provide the password for the **admindb** user and complete the connection.

After the connection is established successfully, the shell prompt will display the following details:

```
MongoDB Enterprise atlas-rzhbg7-shard-0:PRIMARY>
```

The details for this are as follows:

- **Enterprise**: This refers to the MongoDB Enterprise edition.

- **atlas1-#####-shard-0**: This refers to the MongoDB replica set name. We will learn about this in more detail later.

- **PRIMARY>**: This refers to the state of the MongoDB instance, which is **PRIMARY**.

> **NOTE**
>
> You may see a message saying **WARNING: shell and server versions do not match**. This is because the latest version of mongo shell is 4.4, while the M0 Atlas cloud database is version 4.2.8. This warning can be ignored.

10. Type **exit** to exit the mongo shell.

In this exercise, you connected to a cloud database using the mongo shell client. For convenience, you used the Atlas interface to copy the connection string for our Atlas cluster. In practice, developers already have the database connection string prepared in advance, so they don't need to copy it from the Atlas application every time they connect to the database.

## MONGODB COMPASS

MongoDB Compass is a graphical tool for data visualization in MongoDB. It is installed together with MongoDB Server installation, as MongoDB Compass is part of the standard distribution. Alternatively, MongoDB Compass can be downloaded and installed separately, without the MongoDB Server software.

The simple and powerful GUI interface of MongoDB Compass helps you to easily query and analyze data in the database. MongoDB Compass has a query builder graphical interface that greatly simplifies the work of creating complex JSON database queries.

The MongoDB Compass version 1.23 is shown in the following screenshot:

Figure 3.36: MongoDB Compass connected to Atlas cloud

The following are the most important MongoDB Compass features in the standard version:

- Easy management of database connections
- Interaction with data, queries, and CRUD
- Efficient graphical query builder
- Management of query execution plans
- Aggregation builder
- Management of collection indexes
- Schema Analysis
- Real Time Server Stats

Apart from standard MongoDB Compass standard version, at the time when this chapter was written there are other two versions of MongoDB Compass available for download:

- Compass Isolated: For highly secure environments. The isolated version of Compass initiates network requests only to MongoDB server on which is connected.
- Compass Read Only: As the name suggests, the read only version of Compass does not change any data in the database and it is used only for queries.

> **NOTE:**
>
> MongoDB Compass Community version is now deprecated. Instead you can use full version of MongoDB Compass, which is free to use and includes enterprise edition features like MongoDB schema analysis.

## MONGODB DRIVERS

There is a misconception that MongoDB is only a database for the JavaScript stack. It is inappropriate to minimize the power of MongoDB and to use it only for JavaScript applications.

MongoDB is a multi-platform database with a flexible data model that can be used for any type of application. Also, there is great support for MongoDB in almost every programming language.

Probably the most useful and popular versions of MongoDB clients are represented by drivers. MongoDB drivers are the glue between the database and the world of software development. Currently, there are many drivers for the most popular programming languages, such as C/C++, C#, Java, Node, and Python.

The Driver API, which is the software library interface, makes it possible to use MongoDB database functions directly in programming language structures. For example, specific BSON data types from MongoDB are translated into a data format that can be used in a programming language such as Python.

## EXERCISE 3.04: CONNECTING TO A MONGODB CLOUD DATABASE USING THE PYTHON DRIVER

Business decisions are often made on the basis of data analysis. Sometimes, in order to obtain useful results, developers use a programming language such as Python to analyze data. Python is a powerful programming language, yet it is easy to learn and practice. In this exercise, you will connect to a MongoDB database from Python 3. Before you connect to MongoDB using Python, note the following points:

- You need not install MongoDB locally on your computer in order to connect using Python.

- The Python library uses the **pymongo** module to connect to MongoDB.

- The **pymongo** module is available for both Python 2 and Python 3. However, as Python 2 is now end-of-life, it is highly recommended to use Python 3 for new software development.

- MongoDB client is part of the **pymongo** Python library.

- You also need to install the DNSPython module because the Atlas connection string is a DNS SRV record. Therefore, the DNSPython module is needed to perform a DNS lookup.

Follow these steps to complete the exercise:

1. Verify that the Python version is 3.6 or higher, as follows:

```
# Check Python version - 3.6+
# On Windows
C:\>python --version
Python 3.7.3

# On MacOS or Linux OS
$ python3 --version
```

> **NOTE**
>
> For macOS or Linux, the Python shell can start with **python3** instead of **python**.

2. Before installing **pymongo**, make sure the Python package manager, **pip**, is installed:

```
# Check PIP version
# On Windows
C:\>pip --version
pip 19.2.3 from C:\Python\Python37\site-packages\pip (python 3.7)


# On MacOS and Linux
$ pip3 --version
```

3. Install **pymongo client**, as follows:

```
# Install PyMongo client on Windows
C:\>pip install pymongo


# Install PyMongo client on MacOS and Linux
$ pip3 install pymongo


# Example output (Windows OS)
C:\>pip install pymongo


Collecting pymongo
  Downloading https://files.pythonhosted.org/packages/
c9/36/715c4ccace03a20cf7e8f15a670f651615744987af62fad8b48bea8f65f9/
pymongo-3.9.0-cp37-cp37m-win_amd64.whl (351kB)
     358kB 133kB/s
Installing collected packages: pymongo
Successfully installed pymongo-3.9.0
```

4.  Install the **dnspython** module, as follows:

```
# Install dnspython on Windows OS
C:\> pip install dnspython

# Install dnspython on MacOS and Linux
$ pip3 install dnspython

# Example output (Windows OS)
C:\> pip install dnspython

Collecting dnspython
  Using cached https://files.pythonhosted.org/packages/ec/
d3/3aa0e7213ef72b8585747aa0e271a9523e713813b9a20177ebe1e939deb0/
dnspython-1.16.0-py2.py3-none-any.whl
Installing collected packages: dnspython
Successfully installed dnspython-1.16.0
```

Now that you have prepared the Python environment, the next step is to get the correct connection string for your cloud database. Test the MongoDB connection to confirm this.

5.  Edit the connection string and add your database name and password. The connection is attempted with the **admindb** username created in *Exercise 3.02, Configuring Database Access*:

```
mongodb+srv://admindb:<password>@<server_link>/<database_name>
```

6.  Replace **<server_link>** with your server link.

> **NOTE**
>
> For example, consider this case in which the connection string is as follows:
>
> **"mongodb+srv://admindb:xxxxxx@cluster0-u7xxx. mongodb.net/test?retryWrites=true&w=majority"**
>
> Here, the server link can be quickly identified as : **cluster0-u7xxx. mongodb.net**

7.  Replace **<database_name>** with your database name, in this case, **sample_mflix**.

8. Replace **\<password\>** with the **admindb** user password.

9. Edit a test script in Python to test your connection and execute the Python script. In Windows, open the Notepad text editor and type in the following Python code:

```python
# Python 3 script to test MongoDB connection
# MongoDB Atlas connection string needs to be edited with your
connection

from pymongo import MongoClient
uri="mongodb+srv://admindb:xxxxxx@cluster0-u7xxx.mongodb.net/
test?retryWrites=true&w=majority"
client = MongoClient(uri)

# switch to mflix database
mflix = client['sample_mflix']

# list collection names
print('Mflix Collections: ')
for name in mflix.list_collection_names():
    print(name)
```

10. Save the text script with the name **mongo4_atlas.py**—for example, in **C:\Temp\mongo4_atlas.py**.

11. Run the test script.

    In Windows' Command Prompt, type:

```
"python C:\Temp\mongo4_atlas.py"
```

In a macOS/Linux shell prompt, type:

```
"$ python3 ./mongo4_atlas.py "
```

The output of the script will show the collections in the database, as follows:

```
C:\>python C:\Temp\mongo4_atlas.py
Mflix Collections:
comments
users
theaters
sessions
movies
>>>
```

In this exercise, you practiced working with MongoDB in the cloud in practical terms using a programming language such as Python. The possibilities are unlimited in terms of using the extended Python library; you can create web applications, perform data analytics, and much more.

## SERVER COMMANDS

MongoDB is a database server that has clients that connect to the server over the network. The database server manages the database, while clients are used by applications or users to query data from the database. If you're wondering whether there are only databases (without a server), then yes, there are. For example, Microsoft Access is an example of a relational database without a database server. The main advantage of the client-server architecture is that the server consolidates control data management, user security, and concurrency for parallel access.

There is also a separation of physical and logical structures. The database server manages the database's physical structures, such as storage and memory. On the other hand, database clients usually have access only to logical database structures, such as collections, indexes, and views.

This section will briefly explain the physical and logical structures in MongoDB 4.4.

## PHYSICAL STRUCTURE

The physical structure of the database consists of computing resources allocated for MongoDB Server, such as processor threads, memory allocation, and database file storage. Computing requirements and tuning are important parts of database management, especially for on-premises database servers. Nevertheless, in the case of databases deployed on the MongoDB Atlas Cloud, the physical structure of the database is not visible to users. The database is managed internally by MongoDB. Therefore, cloud users can focus exclusively on database utilization and application development rather than spending time on the database management of physical resources such as storage and memory.

As described in the introduction, MongoDB Atlas allocates physical resources based on cluster tier size. Resource management is done entirely through the cloud Atlas application. If more resources are needed, the cluster can be extended to a larger size.

The free-tier M0 cluster has no dedicated resources (only shared CPU and memory). However, the free-tier M0 cluster is a great database cluster because it's always available for learning about and testing MongoDB.

## DATABASE FILES

MongoDB automatically creates many types of files, such as data files and log files, on disk. In the case of Atlas Cloud databases, all database files are managed internally by MongoDB:

- **Datafiles:** These are files used for database collections and other database objects. MongoDB has a configurable storage engine for data files, and WiredTiger is a high-performance storage engine, that has been introduced in MongoDB since version 3.0.

- **Oplog:** These are files used for transaction replication between cluster members. We will learn about these in detail in *Chapter 10, Replication.*

- **Other files:** These are files such as config files, database logs, and audit files.

## DATABASE METRICS

While data files and memory management are not topics for databases deployed in the cloud, it is necessary to monitor the utilization of allocated cloud resources. Atlas resource monitoring provides a graphical interface where performance metrics are displayed. There are many metrics available in Atlas, such as logical database metrics, physical database metrics, and network bandwidth.

The content coverage of this topic is beyond the scope of this book. For more details, you can refer to the MongoDB Atlas documentation, *Monitoring and Alerts* (https://docs. atlas.mongodb.com/monitoring-alerts/).

## LOGICAL STRUCTURE

The logical structure of the database consists of databases, collections, and other database objects. The following diagram represents the main logical structure of MongoDB:

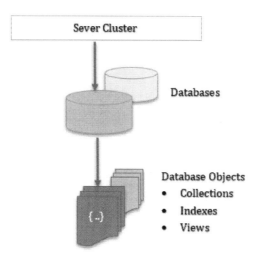

Figure 3.37: Logical structure of MongoDB

**MongoDB Server:** Physical or virtual computer where the MongoDB server instance is running. For a MongoDB cluster, there is a set of few MongoDB instances when a client connects to MongoDB

**Database:** A MongoDB cluster contains many databases. Each database is a logical storage container in MongoDB for database objects. There are a few system databases, created when a database is deployed. System databases are used internally by MongoDB Server for database configuration and security, and they cannot be used for user data.

**Objects:** A database contains the following objects:

- Collections of JSON documents

- Indexes

- Views

The basic logical entity in MongoDB is the JSON document. Multiple documents are grouped in a collection, and multiple collections are grouped in a database. In MongoDB version 4, more objects were introduced, such as database views, which add more functionality to the database. We will learn about database view objects with a suitable example in *Exercise 3.05*, *Creating a Database View Object*.

## SERVER COMMANDS

In a client-server database server architecture, such as MongoDB Server, clients send requests to the database server and MongoDB Server executes the requests on the server side. Therefore, there is no client processing involved when a server executes a client request. Once the request is complete, the server sends the execution results or messages back to the client.

While MongoDB Server has many functions, there are a few different categories:

- **CRUD operations**: Database **Create, Read, Update, Delete** (**CRUD**) operations are commands that modify data documents.

- **Database Commands**: These are all the commands that differ from data queries and CRUD operations. Database commands have other functions, such as database management, security, and replication.

Most database commands are executed in the background by Atlas every time a user changes a database configuration. For example, when the Atlas project owner adds a new user, the Atlas application runs database commands in the background to create the user in the database. Nevertheless, it is possible to execute server commands from MongoDB Shell or from MongoDB Driver.

In general, the syntax to run a database command is as follows:

```
>>> db.runCommand( { <db_command> } )
```

**db_command** is the database command.

For example, if we want to retrieve the current operations being executed in MongoDB, we can run a command with the following syntax:

```
>>> db.runCommand( {currentOp: 1} )
```

The server will return a JSON formatted document with the operations in progress.

Some database commands have their own shorter syntax and can run without the general **db.runCommand** syntax. This is used for convenience to remember the syntax for commands that are used more often. For example, the syntax for the command to list all collections in the current database is:

```
>>> db.getCollectionNames()
```

For databases deployed in the Atlas Cloud, there are some database admin commands that cannot be executed directly from the mongo shell. The complete list of commands is available in the MongoDB Atlas documentation, *Unsupported Commands in M0/M2/M5 Clusters* (https://docs.atlas.mongodb.com/reference/unsupported-commands/).

## EXERCISE 3.05: CREATING A DATABASE VIEW OBJECT

In this exercise, you will practice database commands. The goal of the exercise is to create a new database object from the mongo shell terminal. You will create a database view object to display only three columns: movie name, release year, and collection information. You will use the MongoDB console to execute all the database commands.

The following are the steps to execute this exercise:

1.  Connect to the Atlas database using the connection string for the MongoDB console. Repeat *steps 1 to 9* from *Exercise 3.03, Connecting to the Cloud Database using the Mongo Shell*, to connect using the mongo shell client. If you have the connection string already prepared for your Atlas database, start the mongo shell and connect as described in *step 8* of *Exercise 3.03, Connecting to the Cloud Database using the Mongo Shell*.

2. Select the **mflix** movie database using the **use** database command:

```
>>> use sample_mflix
```

3. List the existing collections using the **getCollectionNames** database command to return a list of all the collections in the current database:

```
>>> db.getCollectionNames()
```

4. Create a **short_movie_info** view from the movies collection:

```
db.createView(
    "short_movie_info",
    "movies",
    [ { $project: { "year": 1, "title":1, "plot":1}}]
)
```

> **NOTE**
>
> The **$project** operator is used to select only three fields (**year**, **title**, and **plot**) from the movie collection.

5. Execute the **createView** code:

```
MongoDB Enterprise Cluster0-shard-0:PRIMARY> db.createView(
...      "short_movie_info",
...      "movies",
...      [ { $project: { "year": 1, "title":1, "plot":1}}]
... )
```

A response of **"ok"** : **1** indicates that the command to create and view the database was executed successfully with no errors, as in the following code output:

```
# Command Output
{
        "ok" : 1,
        "operationTime" : Timestamp(1569982200, 1),
        "$clusterTime" : {
                "clusterTime" : Timestamp(1569982200, 1),
                "signature" : {
```

```
                                "hash" :
    BinData(0,"brozBUoH099xryq5l439woGcL3o="),
                            "keyId" : NumberLong("6728292437866840066")

                    }
            }
    }
```

**NOTE**

The output details may vary based on the server runtime values.

6. Verify that the view was created. The view just shows as a collection:

```
>>> db.getCollectionNames()
```

This command returns an array with the view name in the collection list.

7. Query the view, as follows:

```
>>> db.short_movie_info.findOne()
```

The view database object behaves exactly like a normal collection. You can query a view in the same way you query a database collection. You will run a short query to return just one document.

The output for this query will show only the document **id**, **plot**, **year**, and **title**. The complete session output is as follows:

```
Command Prompt - mongo  "mongodb+srv://cluster0.u7n6b.mongodb.net/test" --username admindb

C:\>mongo "mongodb+srv://cluster0.u7n6b.mongodb.net/test" --username admindb
MongoDB shell version v4.4.0
Enter password:
connecting to: mongodb://cluster0-shard-00-00.u7n6b.mongodb.net:27017,cluster0-shard-00-01.u7n6b.mongodb.net:27017,cluster0-sh
rviceName=mongodb&replicaSet=atlas-rzhbg7-shard-0&ssl=true
Implicit session: session { "id" : UUID("1cd0a64c-d2c6-434d-8238-ba9546716386") }
MongoDB server version: 4.2.8
WARNING: shell and server versions do not match
MongoDB Enterprise atlas-rzhbg7-shard-0:PRIMARY> use sample_mflix
switched to db sample_mflix
MongoDB Enterprise atlas-rzhbg7-shard-0:PRIMARY> db.getCollectionNames()
[
        "comments",
        "movies",
        "sessions",
        "short_movie_info",
        "theaters",
        "users"
]
MongoDB Enterprise atlas-rzhbg7-shard-0:PRIMARY>
MongoDB Enterprise atlas-rzhbg7-shard-0:PRIMARY> db.createView(
...     "short_movie_info",
...     "movies",
...     [ { $project: { "year": 1, "title":1, "plot":1}}]
... )
{
        "operationTime" : Timestamp(1598155777, 1),
        "ok" : 0,
        "errmsg" : "a view 'sample_mflix.short_movie_info' already exists",
        "code" : 48,
        "codeName" : "NamespaceExists",
        "$clusterTime" : {
                "clusterTime" : Timestamp(1598155777, 1),
                "signature" : {
                        "hash" : BinData(0,"QlpPmNAGMvynpJH/7HZspGKTQBE="),
                        "keyId" : NumberLong("6817874997416034306")
                }
        }
}
MongoDB Enterprise atlas-rzhbg7-shard-0:PRIMARY> db.short_movie_info.findOne()
{
        "_id" : ObjectId("573a1390f29313caabcd4135"),
        "plot" : "Three men hammer on an anvil and pass a bottle of beer around.",
        "title" : "Blacksmith Scene",
        "year" : 1893
}
MongoDB Enterprise atlas-rzhbg7-shard-0:PRIMARY>
```

Figure 3.38: Session output

This was an example of how to create a new database object, such as a simple view. Views can be very useful for users and developers to join multiple collections and to limit visibility to just some fields in JSON documents. Once we have learned more about MongoDB queries and aggregation, we can apply all those techniques to create more complex views in the database, from multiple collections to using the aggregation pipeline.

## ACTIVITY 3.01: MANAGING YOUR DATABASE USERS

Imagine you are in charge of managing your company's MongoDB database, which is in the MongoDB Atlas Cloud infrastructure in **Amazon Web Services** (**AWS**). Recently, you've been informed that a new developer, Mark, has joined the team. As a new team member, Mark needs access to the MongoDB movie database for a new project.

Execute the following high-level steps to complete the activity:

1.  Create a new database called **dev_mflix**, which will be used for development.

2.  Create a new custom role for developers, called **developers**.

3.  Grant read-write permissions on the **dev_mflix** database to the **developers** role.

4.  Grant read-only permissions on the **sample_mflix** movie database to the **developers** role.

5.  Create a new database account for Mark.

6.  Grant the **developers** custom role to Mark.

7.  Verify the account by connecting to the database with Mark as the user and verify the access permissions.

Mark should not be able to modify the production movie database, nor should he see any other databases on the server except **sample_mflix** and **dev_mflix**.

Once Mark is successfully added to the Atlas project, you should be able to test the connection with that account. Connect with the mongo shell using the following command:

```
C:\> mongo "mongodb+srv://cluster0.u7n##.mongodb.net/admin" --username
Mark
```

> **NOTE**
>
> Your actual connection string is different and needs to be copied from the Atlas connect window, as explained in this chapter.

This is an example of the output terminal (from the mongo shell):

```
Command Prompt - mongo "mongodb+srv://cluster0.u7n6b.mongodb.net/admin" --username Mark
C:\>mongo "mongodb+srv://cluster0.u7n6b.mongodb.net/admin" --username Mark
MongoDB shell version v4.4.0
Enter password:
connecting to: mongodb://cluster0-shard-00-00.u7n6b.mongodb.net:27017,cluster0-shard-00-01.u7n6b.mongodb.
erviceName=mongodb&replicaSet=atlas-rzhbg7-shard-0&ssl=true
Implicit session: session { "id" : UUID("238da0ec-fbc0-4e4f-88d2-68589a70d861") }
MongoDB server version: 4.2.8
WARNING: shell and server versions do not match
Error while trying to show server startup warnings: user is not allowed to do action [getLog] on [admin.]
MongoDB Enterprise atlas-rzhbg7-shard-0:PRIMARY> db.getUser("Mark")
{
        "_id" : "admin.Mark",
        "user" : "Mark",
        "db" : "admin",
        "roles" : [
                {
                        "role" : "Developers",
                        "db" : "admin"
                }
        ]
}
MongoDB Enterprise atlas-rzhbg7-shard-0:PRIMARY>
MongoDB Enterprise atlas-rzhbg7-shard-0:PRIMARY>
```

Figure 3.39: Connecting the MongoDB Shell

> **NOTE**
>
> The solution to this activity can be found on page 653.

## SUMMARY

In this chapter, you learned the basics of Atlas service management. As security is a very important aspect of cloud computing, controlling network access and database access is essential for the Atlas platform, and you should now be able to set up new users and grant permissions to database resources. Database connections and MongoDB database commands were also explored in detail. The next chapter will introduce you to the world of MongoDB query syntax. The MongoDB NoSQL language is a rich and powerful database language that integrates very well with all programming languages.

# 4

# QUERYING DOCUMENTS

## OVERVIEW

This chapter discusses how to prepare and execute queries in MongoDB. You will learn how to find documents from a collection and limit the fields shown in the output. You will use various conditional and logical operators, as well as combinations of them, in a query and use regular expressions to find documents in a collection. By the end of this chapter, you will be able to run queries on arrays and nested objects, as well as limit, skip, and sort the records in the result set.

# INTRODUCTION

In the previous chapters, we covered the basics of MongoDB, its document-based data model, data types, clients, and the MongoDB server. We created an Atlas cluster on the cloud, loaded sample datasets, and connected using different clients. Now that we have the data, we can start writing queries to retrieve documents from the collections. Queries are used to retrieve meaningful data from the database. We will begin by learning about query syntax, how to use operators, and the techniques we can use to format the result sets. Practicing and mastering the query language will help you find any required document quickly and efficiently.

For any database management system, having a powerful query language is as important as its storage model, or its scalability. Consider that you are working on a database platform that offers an excellent storage model or an extremely high-performance database engine. However, it has very poor query language support, because of which you cannot easily retrieve the required pieces of information. Clearly, such a database is not going to be very useful. One of the primary purposes of storing information in a database is to be able to retrieve it as and when required. MongoDB provides a lightweight query language, which is totally different from the SQL queries that are used in relational databases. Let's start by taking a look at its query structure.

# MONGODB QUERY STRUCTURE

MongoDB queries are based on JSON documents in which you write your criteria in the form of valid documents. With the data stored in the form of JSON-like documents, the queries seem more natural and readable. The following diagram is an example of a simple MongoDB query that finds all the documents where the **name** field contains the value **David**:

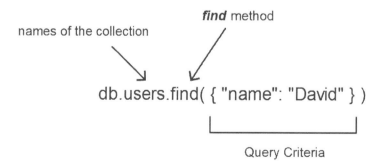

Figure 4.1: MongoDB Query Syntax

To draw a comparison with SQL, let's rewrite the same query in SQL format. This query finds all the rows from the **USERS** table that contain the **name** column where the value of **name** is **David**, as follows:

```
SELECT * FROM USERS WHERE name = 'David';
```

The most notable difference between the preceding queries is that the MongoDB queries do not have keywords such as **SELECT**, **FROM**, and **WHERE**. Thus, you need not remember a lot of keywords and their uses.

The absence of keywords makes the queries less wordy and hence more focused, and less error-prone. When you are reading or writing MongoDB queries, you can easily focus on the most important parts of the query; that is, the conditions and the logic. Also, because of fewer keywords, the chances of introducing syntactical errors are smaller.

As the queries are represented in a document format, they can be easily mapped with the object structure of the respective programming language. When you write the query in your application, the MongoDB driver maps the objects provided by the application's programming language into the MongoDB query. Hence, to build a MongoDB query, all you need to do is prepare an object that represents the query conditions.

In contrast, SQL queries are written in the form of plain strings. To build a SQL query, you will have to join the keywords, field and table names. and variables together into a string. Such string concatenations are prone to errors. Even a missing space between two joining keywords can introduce syntactical errors. Now that we have explored the basic advantages of MongoDB's query structure, let's start writing and executing basic queries against a collection.

# BASIC MONGODB QUERIES

All the queries in this section are top-level queries; that is, they are based on the top-level (also known as root-level) fields in the documents. We will learn about the basic query operators by writing queries against the root fields.

## FINDING DOCUMENTS

The most basic query in MongoDB is performed with the **find()** function on the collection. When this function is executed without any argument, it returns all the documents in a collection. For example, consider the following query:

```
db.comments.find()
```

This query calls the **find()** function on the collection named **comments**. When executed on a mongo shell, it will return all the documents from the collection. To return only specific documents, a condition can be provided to the **find()** function. When this is done, the **find()** function evaluates it against each and every document in the collection and returns the documents that match the condition.

For example, consider that instead of retrieving all the comments, we only want to find comments that have been added by a specific user, **Lauren Carr**. In short, we want to find all the documents in which the **name** field has the value **Lauren Carr**. We will connect to the MongoDB Atlas cluster and use the **sample_mflix** database. The query should be written as follows:

```
db.comments.find({"name" : "Lauren Carr"})
```

This will result in the following output:

```
● ● ●                              MongoDB
> db.comments.find({"name" : "Lauren Carr"})                                    }
{ "_id" : ObjectId("5a9427648b0beebeb6962d2e"), "name" : "Lauren Carr", "email" : "lauren_carr@fakegmail.com"
, "movie_id" : ObjectId("573a139af29313caabcf0d74"), "text" : "Temporibus iste error id molestias. Et quia qu
as voluptate asperiores. Consectetur quisquam rerum est suscipit ullam.", "date" : ISODate("1986-10-26T11:31:
17Z") }
{ "_id" : ObjectId("5a9427648b0beebeb6962d2f"), "name" : "Lauren Carr", "email" : "lauren_carr@fakegmail.com"
, "movie_id" : ObjectId("573a139af29313caabcf0d74"), "text" : "Quo odio ipsum officiis cumque commodi ipsum.
Repudiandae ratione magni ab minima suscipit excepturi quos. Facilis cupiditate modi optio soluta sunt molest
iae.", "date" : ISODate("1972-03-23T02:37:03Z") }
{ "_id" : ObjectId("5a9427648b0beebeb6962d2d"), "name" : "Lauren Carr", "email" : "lauren_carr@fakegmail.com"
, "movie_id" : ObjectId("573a139af29313caabcf0d74"), "text" : "Sit ullam tenetur atque delectus. Pariatur eos
 sequi enim. Quasi eligendi labore saepe rerum modi incidunt accusamus ex. Expedita temporibus consequatur do
lore modi.", "date" : ISODate("1978-03-25T06:29:47Z") }
> ▮
```

Figure 4.2: Resulting comments after using the find() function

The query returned three comments that were added by **Lauren Carr**. However, the output is unformatted, which makes it difficult to read and interpret. To overcome this, the **pretty()** function can be used to print a well-formatted result, as follows:

```
db.comments.find({"name" : "Lauren Carr"}).pretty()
```

When this query is executed on a mongo shell, the output will look like this:

```
● ● ●                              MongoDB
> db.comments.find({"name" : "Lauren Carr"}).pretty()
{
        "_id" : ObjectId("5a9427648b0beebeb6962d2e"),
        "name" : "Lauren Carr",
        "email" : "lauren_carr@fakegmail.com",
        "movie_id" : ObjectId("573a139af29313caabcf0d74"),
        "text" : "Temporibus iste error id molestias. Et quia quas voluptate asperiores. Consectetur quisquam
 rerum est suscipit ullam.",
        "date" : ISODate("1986-10-26T11:31:17Z")
}
{
        "_id" : ObjectId("5a9427648b0beebeb6962d2f"),
        "name" : "Lauren Carr",
        "email" : "lauren_carr@fakegmail.com",
        "movie_id" : ObjectId("573a139af29313caabcf0d74"),
        "text" : "Quo odio ipsum officiis cumque commodi ipsum. Repudiandae ratione magni ab minima suscipit
excepturi quos. Facilis cupiditate modi optio soluta sunt molestiae.",
        "date" : ISODate("1972-03-23T02:37:03Z")
}
{
        "_id" : ObjectId("5a9427648b0beebeb6962d2d"),
        "name" : "Lauren Carr",
        "email" : "lauren_carr@fakegmail.com",
        "movie_id" : ObjectId("573a139af29313caabcf0d74"),
        "text" : "Sit ullam tenetur atque delectus. Pariatur eos sequi enim. Quasi eligendi labore saepe reru
m modi incidunt accusamus ex. Expedita temporibus consequatur dolore modi.",
        "date" : ISODate("1978-03-25T06:29:47Z")
}
> █
```

Figure 4.3: Structured result after using find() with pretty()

As you can see, the output is the same as in the previous example, but the documents are well formatted and easily readable.

## USING FINDONE()

MongoDB provides another function, called **findOne()**, that returns only one matching record. This function is very useful when you are looking to isolate a specific record. The syntax of this function is similar to the syntax of the **find()** function, as follows:

```
db.comments.findOne()
```

This query is executed without any condition and matches all the documents in the **comments** collection, returning only the first:

```
●  ●  ●                                    MongoDB
|> db.comments.findOne()                                                          ]
 {
         "_id" : ObjectId("5a9427648b0beebeb69579d0"),
         "name" : "Talisa Maegyr",
         "email" : "oona_chaplin@gameofthron.es",
         "movie_id" : ObjectId("573a1390f29313caabcd41b1"),
         "text" : "Rem itaque ad sit rem voluptatibus. Ad fugiat maxime illum optio iure alias minus. Optio ra
 tione suscipit corporis qui dicta.",
         "date" : ISODate("1998-08-22T11:45:03Z")
 }
 > █
```

Figure 4.4: Finding a single document with the findOne() function

As you can see, the output of **findOne()** is always well formatted because it returns a document. Compare this with the **find()** function, which is designed to return multiple documents. The results of **find()** are enclosed in a collection, and a cursor to that collection is returned from the function. A cursor is an iterator for a collection that is used to iterate or traverse through the collection's elements.

> **NOTE**
>
> When you execute the **find()** query on the mongo shell, the shell automatically iterates through the cursor and shows the first 20 records. When you are using **find()** from a programming language, you will always have to iterate through the result set on your own.

On a mongo shell, you can capture the cursor returned by the **find()** function in a variable. By using the variable, we can iterate through the elements. In the following snippet, we are executing a **find()** query and capturing the resulting cursor in a variable named **comments**:

```
var comments = db.comments.find({"name" : "Lauren Carr"})
```

You can use the **next()** function on the cursor, which moves the cursor to the next index position and returns the document from there. By default, the cursor is set at the beginning of the collection. When called for the first time, the **next()** function moves the cursor to the first document in the collection, and that document is returned. When called again, the cursor will be moved to the second position and the second document will be returned. The following is the syntax for calling the **next()** function on our comments cursor:

```
comments.next()
```

When the cursor reaches the last document in the collection, calling **next()** will result in an error. To avoid this, the **hasNext()** function can be used before calling **next()**. The **hasNext()** function returns **true** if the collection has a document at the next index position, and false if not. The following snippet shows the syntax for calling the **hasNext()** function on the cursor:

```
comments.hasNext()
```

The following screenshot shows the result of using this function on a mongo shell:

```
●●●                          MongoDB
> var comments = db.comments.find({"name" : "Lauren Carr"})
>
> comments.hasNext()
true
>
> comments.next()
{
        "_id" : ObjectId("5a9427648b0beebeb6962d2e"),
        "name" : "Lauren Carr",
        "email" : "lauren_carr@fakegmail.com",
        "movie_id" : ObjectId("573a139af29313caabcf0d74"),
        "text" : "Temporibus iste error id molestias. Et quia quas voluptate asperiores. Consectetur quisquam
  rerum est suscipit ullam.",
        "date" : ISODate("1986-10-26T11:31:17Z")
}
> ▮
```

Figure 4.5: Iterating through a cursor

As we can see, first, we captured the cursor in a variable. Then, we verified whether the cursor had a document at the next position, which resulted in **true**. Finally, we printed the first document using the **next()** function.

## EXERCISE 4.01: USING FIND() AND FINDONE() WITHOUT A CONDITION

In this exercise, you will use **find()** and **findOne()** without any conditions on a mongo shell by connecting to the **sample_mflix** database on MongoDB Atlas. Follow these steps:

1. First, use **find()** without a condition. So, here, do not pass any document or pass an empty document to the **find()** function. We will also execute the **find()** function to query for a non-existent field in our documents. All the queries shown here have the same behavior:

```
// All of the queries have the same behavior
db.comments.find()
db.comments.find({})
db.comments.find({"a_non_existent_field" : null})
```

When executing any of these queries, all the documents are matched and returned in a cursor. The following screenshot shows the first 20 documents from the mongo shell, printed along with a **Type "it" for more** message at the end. Typing **it** every time will return the next set of 20 documents until the collection contains more elements:

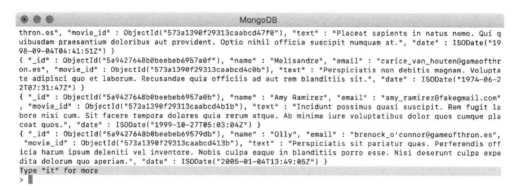

Figure 4.6: First 20 documents in the mongo shell

> **NOTE**
>
> Did you wonder why **{"a_non_existent_field" : null}** matches all documents?
>
> This is because, in MongoDB, a non-existent field is always considered to have a null value. The **"a_non_existent_field"** field does not exist in any document in our collection. Hence, the null check of the field stands true for all the documents and they are returned.

2. Next, use the **findOne()** function without any document, with an empty document, and with a document querying on a non-existing field:

```
// All of the queries have same behaviour
db.comments.findOne()
db.comments.findOne({})
db.comments.findOne({"a_non_existent_field" : null})
```

Similar to the previous step, all the preceding queries will have the same effect, except **findOne()** will output only the first document from the collection.

In the next section, we will explore how we can project only some fields in the output.

## CHOOSING THE FIELDS FOR THE OUTPUT

So far, we have observed many queries and their outputs. You might have noticed that every time a document is returned, it contained all the fields by default. However, in most real-life applications, you may only want a few fields in the resulting documents. In MongoDB queries, you can either include or exclude specific fields from the result. This technique is called **projection**. Projection is expressed as a second argument to the **find()** or **findOne()** functions. In the projection expression, you can explicitly exclude a field by setting it to **0** or include one by setting it to **1**.

For example, the user **Lauren Carr** may only want to know the dates on which she posted comments and may not be interested in the comment text. The following query finds all the comments posted by the user and returns only the **name** and **date** fields:

```
db.comments.find(
    {"name" : "Lauren Carr"},
    {"name" : 1, "date": 1}
)
```

Upon executing the query, the following result can be seen:

```
                                    MongoDB
> db.comments.find(
...     {"name" : "Lauren Carr"},
...     {"name" : 1, "date": 1}
[... )
{ "_id" : ObjectId("5a9427648b0beebeb6962d2e"), "name" : "Lauren Carr", "date" : ISODate("1986-10-26T11:31:1
7Z") }
{ "_id" : ObjectId("5a9427648b0beebeb6962d2f"), "name" : "Lauren Carr", "date" : ISODate("1972-03-23T02:37:0
3Z") }
{ "_id" : ObjectId("5a9427648b0beebeb6962d2d"), "name" : "Lauren Carr", "date" : ISODate("1978-03-25T06:29:4
7Z") }
>
```

Figure 4.7: Output showing only the name and date fields

Here, we have only specific fields in the result. However, the **_id** field is still visible, even though it was not specified. That is because the **_id** field is included by default in the resulting documents. If you do not want it to be present in the result, you must exclude it explicitly:

```
db.comments.find(
    {"name" : "Lauren Carr"},
    {"name" : 1, "date": 1, "_id" : 0}
)
```

The preceding query specifies that the **_id** field should be excluded from the result. When executed on a mongo shell, we get the following output, which shows that the **_id** field is absent from all documents:

```
                                    MongoDB
> db.comments.find(
...     {"name" : "Lauren Carr"},
...     {"name" : 1, "date": 1, "_id" : 0}
[... )
{ "name" : "Lauren Carr", "date" : ISODate("1986-10-26T11:31:17Z") }
{ "name" : "Lauren Carr", "date" : ISODate("1972-03-23T02:37:03Z") }
{ "name" : "Lauren Carr", "date" : ISODate("1978-03-25T06:29:47Z") }
> █
```

Figure 4.8: _id field excluded from the output

It is important to note the three behaviors of field projections, listed as follows:

- The **_id** field will always be included, unless excluded explicitly

- When one or more fields are explicitly included, the other fields (except **_id)** get excluded automatically

- Explicitly excluding one or more fields will automatically include the rest of the fields, along with **_id**

> **NOTE**
>
> Projection helps to compact the result set and focus on specific fields. The documents from the **sample_mflix** collections that we will query are quite big. Therefore, for most of our sample outputs, we will use projection to include only the specific fields of documents, which are required to demonstrate the query's behavior.

## FINDING THE DISTINCT FIELDS

The **distinct()** function is used to get the distinct or unique values of a field with or without query criteria. For the purpose of this example, we will use the **movies** collection. Each movie is assigned an audience suitability rating that is based on the content and viewers' age. Let's find the unique ratings that exist in our collection with the help of the following query:

```
db.movies.distinct("rated")
```

Executing the preceding query gives us all the unique ratings from the **movies** collection:

```
●  ●  ●                              MongoDB
[> db.movies.distinct("rated")
[
        "TV-G",
        "UNRATED",
        "TV-PG",
        "G",
        "PASSED",
        "NOT RATED",
        "APPROVED",
        "PG-13",
        "TV-14",
        "PG",
        "Approved",
        "M",
        "R",
        "TV-MA",
        "GP",
        "X",
        "NC-17",
        "AO",
        "TV-Y7",
        "OPEN",
        "Not Rated"
]
```

Figure 4.9: List of all movie ratings

The **distinct()** function can also be used along with a query condition. The following example finds all the unique ratings the films that were released in 1994 have received:

```
db.movies.distinct("rated", {"year" : 1994})
```

The first argument to the function is the name of the required field, while the second is the query expressed in the document format. Upon executing the query, we get the following output:

```
db.movies.distinct("rated", {"year" : 1994})
> [ "R", "G", "PG", "UNRATED", "PG-13", "TV-14", "TV-PG", "NOT RATED" ]
```

It is important to note that the result of **distinct** is always returned as an array.

## COUNTING THE DOCUMENTS

In some cases, we may not be interested in the actual documents but just the number of documents in a collection, or documents that match some query criteria. MongoDB collections have three functions that return the count of documents in the collection. Let's take a look at them one by one.

## COUNT()

This function is used to return the count of the documents within a collection or a count of the documents that match the given query. When executed without any query argument, it returns the total count of documents in the collection, as follows:

```
// Count of all movies
db.movies.count()
> 23539
```

Without a query, this function will not physically count the documents. Instead, it will read through the collection's metadata and return the count. The MongoDB specification does not guarantee that the metadata count will always be accurate. Cases such as the abrupt shutdown of a database or an incomplete chunk migration in sharded collections can lead to such inaccuracy. A sharded collection in MongoDB is partitioned and distributed across the different nodes of a database. We will not be going into details here as this is outside the scope of this book.

When the function is provided with a query, the count of documents that match the given query is returned. For example, the following query will return the count of movies that have exactly six comments:

```
// Counting movies that have 6 comments
> db.movies.count({"num_mflix_comments" : 6})
17
```

Upon executing this query, the actual count of documents is internally calculated by executing an aggregation pipeline with the same query. You will learn more about aggregation pipelines in *Chapter 7, Aggregations*.

In MongoDB v4.0, these two behaviors are separated into different functions: **countDocuments()** and **estimatedDocumentCount()**.

## COUNTDOCUMENTS()

This function returns the count of documents that are matched by the given condition. The following is an example query that returns the count of movies released in 1999:

```
> db.movies.countDocuments({"year": 1999})
542
```

Unlike the **count()** function, a query argument is mandatory for **countDocuments()**. Hence, the following query is invalid, and it will fail:

```
db.movies.countDocuments()
```

To count all the documents in the collections, we can pass an empty query to the function, as follows:

```
> db.movies.countDocuments({})
23539
```

An important thing to note about **countDocuments()** is that it never uses collection metadata to find the count. It executes the given query on the collection and calculates the count of matched documents. This provides accurate results but may take longer than the metadata-based counts. Even when an empty query is provided, it is matched against all documents.

## ESTIMATEDDOCUMENTCOUNT()

This function returns the approximate or estimated count of documents in a collection. It does not accept any query and always returns the count of all documents in the collection. The count is always based on the collection's metadata. The syntax for this is as follows:

```
> db.movies.estimatedDocumentCount()
23539
```

As the count is based on metadata, the results are less accurate, but the performance is better. The function should be used when performance is more important than accuracy.

# CONDITIONAL OPERATORS

Now that you have learned how to query MongoDB collections, as well as how to use projection to return only specific fields in the output, it is time to learn more advanced ways of querying. So far, you've tried to query the **comments** collection using the value of a field. However, there are more ways to query documents. MongoDB provides conditional operators that can be used to represent various conditions, such as equality, and whether a value is less than or greater than some specified value. In this section, we will explore these operators and learn how to use them in queries.

## EQUALS ($EQ)

In the preceding section, you saw examples of equality checking where the queries used a key-value pair. However, queries can also use a dedicated operator (**$eq**) to find documents with fields that match a given value. For example, the following queries find and return movies that have exactly **5** comments. Both queries have the same effect:

```
db.movies.find({"num_mflix_comments" : 5})
db.movies.find({ "num_mflix_comments" : {$eq : 5 }})
```

## NOT EQUAL TO ($NE)

This operator stands for **Not Equal To** and has the reverse effect of using an equality check. It selects all the documents where the value of the field doesn't match with the given value. For example, the following query can be used to return movies whose count for comments is not equal to 5:

```
db.movies.find(
    { "num_mflix_comments" :
        {$ne : 5 }
    }
)
```

## GREATER THAN ($GT) AND GREATER THAN OR EQUAL TO ($GTE)

The **$gt** keyword can be used to find documents where the value of the field is greater than the value in the query. Similarly, the **$gte** keyword is used to find documents where the value of the field is the same as or greater than the given value. Let's find the number of movies released after **2015**:

```
> db.movies.find(
    {year : {$gt : 2015}}
).count()
1
```

To find the movies that had been released in or after **2015**, the following line of code can be used:

```
> db.movies.find(
    {year : {$gte : 2015}}
).count()
485
```

With these operators, we can also count movies that were released in the 21st century. For this query, we also want to include the movies that have been released since January 1, 2000, so we will use **$gte**, as follows:

```
// On or After 2000-01-01
> db.movies.find(
    {"released" :
        {$gte: new Date('2000-01-01')}
    }
).count()
13767
```

## LESS THAN ($LT) AND LESS THAN OR EQUAL TO ($LTE)

The **$lt** operator matches the documents with the value of the field that's less than the given value. Similarly, the **$lte** operator selects the documents where the value of the field is the same as or less than the given value.

To find how many movies have less than two comments, enter the following query:

```
> db.movies.find(
    {"num_mflix_comments" :
        {$lt : 2}
    }
).count()
8514
```

Similarly, to find the number of movies that have a maximum of two comments, enter the following query:

```
> db.movies.find(
    {"num_mflix_comments" :
        {$lte : 2}
    }
).count()
13185
```

Again, to count the movies that were released in the previous century, simply use **$lt**:

```
// Before 2000-01-01
> db.movies.find(
    {"released" :
        {$lt : new Date('2000-01-01')}
    }
).count()
9268
```

# IN ($IN) AND NOT IN ($NIN)

What if a user wants a list of all movies that have been rated G, PG, or PG-13? In this case, we can use the **$in** operator, along with multiple values given in the form of an array. Such queries find all the documents where the value of the field matches at least one of the given values. Prepare a query that returns movies rated as either of G, PG, or PG-13 by entering the following:

```
db.movies.find(
    {"rated" :
        {$in : ["G", "PG", "PG-13"]}
    }
)
```

The **$nin** operator stands for **Not In** and matches all the documents where the value of the field does not match with any of the array elements:

```
db.movies.find(
    {"rated" :
        {$nin : ["G", "PG", "PG-13"]}
    }
)
```

The preceding query returns movies that are not rated as **G**, **PG**, or **PG-13**, including the ones that do not have the **rated** field.

To see what happens when you use **$nin** with a non-existent field, first, find the total documents you have, as follows:

```
> db.movies.countDocuments({})
23539
```

Now, use **$nin** with some values, except null, on a non-existent object. This means that all the documents are matched, as shown in the following snippet:

```
> db.movies.countDocuments(
    {"nef" :
        {$nin : ["a value", "another value"]}
    }
)
23539
```

In the following example, add a **null** value to the **$nin** array:

```
> db.movies.countDocuments(
    {"nef" :
        {$nin : ["a value", "another value", null ]}
    }
)
0
```

This time, it did not match any document. This is because, in MongoDB, a non-existent field always has a value of null, hence why the **$nin** condition did not stand true for any of the documents.

## EXERCISE 4.02: QUERYING FOR MOVIES OF AN ACTOR

Imagine that you're working for a popular entertainment magazine and their upcoming issue is dedicated to Leonardo DiCaprio. The issue will contain a special article, and you quickly need some data, such as the number of movies he has acted in, the genre of each, and more. In this exercise, you will write queries to count documents by given conditions, find distinct documents, and project different fields in the documents. Query on the **sample_mflix** movies collection for the following:

- The number of movies the actor has acted in

- the genre of these movies

- Movie titles and their respective years of release

- The number of movies he has directed

1. Find the movies in which Leonardo DiCaprio appears by using the **cast** field. Enter the following query to do so:

```
db.movies.countDocuments({"cast" : "Leonardo DiCaprio"})
```

The following output states that Leonardo has acted in 25 movies:

```
> db.movies.countDocuments({"cast" : "Leonardo DiCaprio"})
25
```

2. The genres of the movies in the collection are represented by the **genres** field. Use the **distinct()** function to find the unique genres:

```
db.movies.distinct("genres", {"cast" : "Leonardo DiCaprio"})
```

Upon executing the preceding code, you will receive the following output. As we can see, he has acted in movies of 14 different genres:

```
> db.movies.distinct("genres", {"cast" : "Leonardo DiCaprio"})
[
        "Biography",
        "Drama",
        "Action",
        "Thriller",
        "Western",
        "Romance",
        "Adventure",
        "Crime",
        "History",
        "Documentary",
        "Comedy",
        "Mystery",
        "Sci-Fi",
        "Short"
]
>
```

Figure 4.10: Genres of movies Leonardo DiCaprio has starred in

3. Using movie titles, you can now find the year of release for each of the actor's movies. As you are only interested in the titles and release years of his movies, add a projection clause to the query:

```
db.movies.find(
    {"cast" : "Leonardo DiCaprio"},
    {"title":1, "year":1, "_id":0}
)
```

The output will be generated as follows:

```
●  ●  ●                          MongoDB
> db.movies.find({"cast" : "Leonardo DiCaprio"}, {"title":1, "year":1, "_id":0})
{ "year" : 1993, "title" : "This Boy's Life" }
{ "title" : "What's Eating Gilbert Grape", "year" : 1993 }
{ "title" : "The Quick and the Dead", "year" : 1995 }
{ "title" : "Total Eclipse", "year" : 1995 }
{ "title" : "Marvin's Room", "year" : 1996 }
{ "year" : 1996, "title" : "Romeo + Juliet" }
{ "year" : 1997, "title" : "Titanic" }
{ "year" : 1998, "title" : "The Man in the Iron Mask" }
{ "year" : 2000, "title" : "The Beach" }
{ "title" : "Gangs of New York", "year" : 2002 }
{ "year" : 2002, "title" : "Catch Me If You Can" }
{ "title" : "The Aviator", "year" : 2004 }
{ "year" : 2006, "title" : "The Departed" }
{ "title" : "Blood Diamond", "year" : 2006 }
{ "year" : 2007, "title" : "The 11th Hour" }
{ "year" : 2008, "title" : "Body of Lies" }
{ "year" : 2008, "title" : "Revolutionary Road" }
{ "year" : 2013, "title" : "The Wolf of Wall Street" }
{ "year" : 2008, "title" : "Body of Lies" }
{ "year" : 2010, "title" : "Shutter Island" }
Type "it" for more
>
```

Figure 4.11: Titles and release years of Leonardo DiCaprio's movies

4. Next, you need to find the number of movies Leonardo has directed. To gather this information, count the number of movies he directed once again, this time using the director's field instead of the actor's field. The query document for this question should be as follows:

```
{"directors": "Leonardo DiCaprio"}
```

5. Write a query that counts the movies that match the preceding query:

```
db.movies.countDocuments({"directors" : "Leonardo DiCaprio"})
```

Execute the query. This shows that Leonardo DiCaprio has directed **0** movies:

```
> db.movies.countDocuments({"directors" : "Leonardo DiCaprio"})
0
```

In this exercise, you found and counted documents based on some conditions, found distinct values of a field, and projected specific fields in the output. In the next section, we will learn about logical operators.

# LOGICAL OPERATORS

So far, we have learned about various operators used for writing comparison-based queries. The queries we have written so far had only one criterion at a time. But in practical scenarios, you may need to write more complex queries. MongoDB provides four logical operators to help you build logical combinations of multiple criteria in the same query. Let's have a look at them.

## $AND OPERATOR

Using the **$and** operator, you can have any number of conditions wrapped in an array and the operator will return only the documents that satisfy all the conditions. When a document fails a condition check, the next conditions are skipped. That is why the operator is called a short-circuit operator. For example, say you want to determine the count of unrated movies that were released in 2008. This query must have two conditions:

* The field rated should have a value of **UNRATED**

* The field year must be equal to **2008**

In the document format, both queries can be written as **{ "rated" : "UNRATED" }** and **{ "year" : 2008 }**. Put them in an array using the **$and** operator:

```
> db.movies.countDocuments (
    {$and :
        [{"rated" : "UNRATED"}, {"year" : 2008}]
    }
)
37
```

The preceding output shows that in 2008, there were 37 unrated movies. In MongoDB queries, the **$and** operator is implicit and included by default if a query document has more than one condition. For example, the following query can be rewritten without using the **$and** operator and gives the same result:

```
> db.movies.countDocuments (
    {"rated": "UNRATED", "year" : 2008}
)
37
```

The output is exactly the same, so you do not have to use the **$and** operator explicitly, unless you want to make your code more readable.

## $OR OPERATOR

With the **$or** operator, you can pass multiple conditions wrapped in an array and the documents satisfying either of the conditions will be returned. This operator is used when we have multiple conditions and we want to find documents that match at least one condition.

In the example we used in the *In ($in) and Not In ($nin)* section, you wrote a query to count movies that are rated either G, PG, or PG-13. With the **$or** operator, rewrite the same query, as follows:

```
db.movies.find(
    { $or : [
        {"rated" : "G"},
        {"rated" : "PG"},
        {"rated" : "PG-13"}
    ]}
)
```

Both operators are different and are used in different scenarios. The **$in** operator is used to determine whether a given field has at least one of the values provided in an array, whereas the **$or** operator is not bound to any specific fields and accepts multiple expressions. To understand this better, write a query that will find movies that are either rated **G**, were released in **2005**, or have at least **5** comments. There are three conditions in this query, as follows:

- **{"rated" : "G"}**
- **{"year" : 2005}**
- **{"num_mflix_comments" : {$gte : 5}}**

To use these expressions in an **$or** query, combine these expressions in an array:

```
db.movies.find(
    {$or:[
        {"rated" : "G"},
        {"year" : 2005},
        {"num_mflix_comments" : {$gte : 5}}
    ]}
)
```

## $NOR OPERATOR

The **$nor** operator is syntactically like **$or** but behaves in the opposite way. The **$nor** operator accepts multiple conditional expressions in the form of an array and returns the documents that do not satisfy any of the given conditions.

The following is the same query you wrote in the previous section, except that the **$or** operator is replaced with **$nor**:

```
db.movies.find(
    {$nor:[
        {"rated" : "G"},
        {"year" : 2005},
        {"num_mflix_comments" : {$gte : 5}}
    ]}
)
```

This query will match and return all the movies that are not rated **G**, were not released in **2005**, and do not have more than **5** comments.

## $NOT OPERATOR

The **$not** operator represents the logical NOT operation that negates the given condition. Simply put, the **$not** operator accepts a conditional expression and matches all the documents that do not satisfy it.

The following query finds movies with **5** or more comments:

```
db.movies.find(
    {"num_mflix_comments" :
        {$gte : 5}
    }
)
```

Use the **$not** operator in the same query and negate the given condition:

```
db.movies.find(
    {"num_mflix_comments" :
        {$not : {$gte : 5} }
    }
)
```

This query will return all the movies that do not have 5 or more comments and the movies that do not contain the **num_mflix_comments** field. You will now use the operators you have learned about so far in a simple exercise.

## EXERCISE 4.03: COMBINING MULTIPLE QUERIES

The upcoming edition of the magazine has a special focus on Leonardo's collaborations with director Martin Scorsese. Your task for this exercise is to find the titles and release years of drama or crime movies in the production of which Leonardo DiCaprio and Martin Scorsese have collaborated. To complete this exercise, you will need to use a combination of multiple queries, as detailed in the following steps:

1.  The first condition is that Leonardo DiCaprio must be one of the actors and that Martin Scorsese must be the director. So, you have two conditions that need to have an *AND* relationship. As you have seen earlier, the *AND* relationship is the default relationship when two queries are combined. Enter the following query:

```
db.movies.find(
    {
        "cast": "Leonardo DiCaprio",
        "directors" : "Martin Scorsese"
    }
)
```

2.  Now, there is one more *AND* condition to be added, which is that the movies should be of the drama or crime genres. You can easily prepare two filters for the genre field: **{"genres" : "Drama"}** and **{"genres" : "Crime"}**. Bring them together in an *OR* relationship, as follows:

```
"$or" : [{"genres" : "Drama"}, {"genres": "Crime"}]
```

3.  Add the genre filter to the main query:

```
db.movies.find(
    {
        "cast": "Leonardo DiCaprio",
        "directors" : "Martin Scorsese",
        "$or" : [{"genres" : "Drama"}, {"genres": "Crime"}]
    }
)
```

4.  The preceding query contains all the expected conditions, but you are only interested in the title and release year. For this, add the projection part:

```
db.movies.find(
    {
        "cast": "Leonardo DiCaprio",
```

```
        "directors" : "Martin Scorsese",
        "$or" : [{"genres" : "Drama"}, {"genres": "Crime"}]
    },
    {
      "title" : 1, "year" : 1, "_id" : 0
    }
)
```

5.  Execute the query on a mongo shell. The output should look as follows:

```
●  ●  ●                        MongoDB
> db.movies.find(
...     {
...         "cast": "Leonardo DiCaprio",
...         "directors" : "Martin Scorsese",
...         "$or" : [{"genres" : "Drama"}, {"genres": "Crime"}]
...     },
...     {
...         "title" : 1, "year" : 1, "_id" : 0
...     }
... )
{ "title" : "Gangs of New York", "year" : 2002 }
{ "title" : "The Aviator", "year" : 2004 }
{ "year" : 2006, "title" : "The Departed" }
{ "year" : 2013, "title" : "The Wolf of Wall Street" }
> ▊
```

**Figure 4.12: Movies in which Leonardo DiCaprio and Martin Scorsese collaborated**

This output provides the required information; there are four movies that match our criteria. The actor and the director last worked together in 2013 on the movie *The Wolf of Wall Street*. With that, you have practiced using multiple query conditions together with different logical relationships. In the next section, you will learn how to query text fields using regular expressions.

# REGULAR EXPRESSIONS

In a real-world movie service, you will want to provide auto-completion search boxes where, as soon as the user types in a few characters of the movie title, the search box suggests all the movies whose titles match the character sequence typed in. This is implemented using regular expressions. A regular expression is a special string that defines a character pattern. When such a regular expression is used to find string fields, all the strings that have the matching pattern are found and returned.

In MongoDB queries, regular expressions can be used with the **$regex** operator. Imagine you have typed the word **Opera** into the search box and want to find all the movies whose titles contain this character pattern. The regular expression query for this will be as follows:

```
db.movies.find(
    {"title" : {$regex :"Opera"}}
)
```

Upon executing this query and using projection to print only the titles, the result will appear as follows:

```
>  db.movies.find(
...       {"title" : {$regex :"Opera"}},
...       {"title" : 1}
... )
{ "_id" : ObjectId("573a1391f29313caabcd806b"), "title" : "The Phantom of the Opera" }
{ "_id" : ObjectId("573a1391f29313caabcd9651"), "title" : "The 3 Penny Opera" }
{ "_id" : ObjectId("573a1392f29313caabcda998"), "title" : "A Night at the Opera" }
{ "_id" : ObjectId("573a1393f29313caabcdce88"), "title" : "Phantom of the Opera" }
{ "_id" : ObjectId("573a1394f29313caabcde81f"), "title" : "Operation Disaster" }
{ "_id" : ObjectId("573a1394f29313caabce0736"), "title" : "Operation Mad Ball" }
{ "_id" : ObjectId("573a1394f29313caabce08ab"), "title" : "What's Opera, Doc?" }
{ "_id" : ObjectId("573a1395f29313caabce1063"), "title" : "Operation Petticoat" }
{ "_id" : ObjectId("573a1395f29313caabce28b8"), "title" : "Operation Crossbow" }
{ "_id" : ObjectId("573a1395f29313caabce28ba"), "title" : "Operation 'Y' & Other Shurik's Adventures" }
{ "_id" : ObjectId("573a1398f29313caabce9ed1"), "title" : "Peking Opera Blues" }
{ "_id" : ObjectId("573a1398f29313caabcea906"), "title" : "Opera" }
{ "_id" : ObjectId("573a1398f29313caabceb98a"), "title" : "The Phantom of the Opera" }
{ "_id" : ObjectId("573a1398f29313caabcebf0b"), "title" : "Armour of God 2: Operation Condor" }
{ "_id" : ObjectId("573a1399f29313caabcec223"), "title" : "The Phantom of the Opera" }
{ "_id" : ObjectId("573a13a6f29313caabd17c1d"), "title" : "Pistol Opera" }
{ "_id" : ObjectId("573a13a6f29313caabd198c3"), "title" : "The Phantom of the Opera" }
{ "_id" : ObjectId("573a13acf29313caabd279bf"), "title" : "Fighter Pilot: Operation Red Flag" }
{ "_id" : ObjectId("573a13b4f29313caabd3fdf1"), "title" : "Alex Rider: Operation Stormbreaker" }
{ "_id" : ObjectId("573a13bbf29313caabd5325a"), "title" : "Standard Operating Procedure" }
Type "it" for more
>
```

Figure 4.13: Movies with titles containing the word "Opera"

The output from a mongo shell indicates that the regular expression correctly returned movies whose title contains the word **Opera**.

## USING THE CARET (^) OPERATOR

In the previous example of regular expressions, the titles in the output contained the given word **Opera** at any position. To find only the strings that start with the given regular expression, the caret operator (^) can be used. In the following example, you are using it to find only those movies whose titles start with the word **Opera**:

```
db.movies.find(
    {"title" : {$regex :"^Opera"}}
)
```

When you execute the preceding query and project the **title** field, you will get the following output:

```
> db.movies.find(
...     {"title" : {$regex :"^Opera"}},
...     {"title" : 1}
... )
{ "_id" : ObjectId("573a1394f29313caabcde81f"), "title" : "Operation Disaster" }
{ "_id" : ObjectId("573a1394f29313caabce0736"), "title" : "Operation Mad Ball" }
{ "_id" : ObjectId("573a1395f29313caabce1063"), "title" : "Operation Petticoat" }
{ "_id" : ObjectId("573a1395f29313caabce28b8"), "title" : "Operation Crossbow" }
{ "_id" : ObjectId("573a1395f29313caabce28ba"), "title" : "Operation 'Y' & Other Shurik's Adventures" }
{ "_id" : ObjectId("573a1398f29313caabcea906"), "title" : "Opera" }
{ "_id" : ObjectId("573a13bcf29313caabd56f73"), "title" : "Operation Homecoming: Writing the Wartime Experie
nce" }
>
```

Figure 4.14: Projecting only the title field for the preceding query

The preceding output from a Mongo shell shows that only the movie titles that start with the word "Opera" are returned.

## USING THE DOLLAR ($) OPERATOR

Similar to the caret operator, you can also match the strings that end with the given regular expression. To do this, use a dollar operator (**$**). In the following example, you are trying to find movie titles that end with the word "Opera":

```
db.movies.find(
    {"title" : {$regex :"Opera$"}}
)
```

The preceding query uses the dollar (**$**) operator after the regular expression text. When you execute and project the title fields, you will receive the following output:

```
> db.movies.find(
...     {"title" : {$regex :"Opera$"}},
...     {"title" : 1}
... )
{ "_id" : ObjectId("573a1391f29313caabcd806b"), "title" : "The Phantom of the Opera" }
{ "_id" : ObjectId("573a1391f29313caabcd9651"), "title" : "The 3 Penny Opera" }
{ "_id" : ObjectId("573a1392f29313caabcda998"), "title" : "A Night at the Opera" }
{ "_id" : ObjectId("573a1393f29313caabcdce88"), "title" : "Phantom of the Opera" }
{ "_id" : ObjectId("573a1398f29313caabcea906"), "title" : "Opera" }
{ "_id" : ObjectId("573a1398f29313caabceb98a"), "title" : "The Phantom of the Opera" }
{ "_id" : ObjectId("573a1399f29313caabcec223"), "title" : "The Phantom of the Opera" }
{ "_id" : ObjectId("573a13a6f29313caabd17c1d"), "title" : "Pistol Opera" }
{ "_id" : ObjectId("573a13a6f29313caabd198c3"), "title" : "The Phantom of the Opera" }
{ "_id" : ObjectId("573a13bcf29313caabd56956"), "title" : "Repo! The Genetic Opera" }
>
```

Figure 4.15: Movies whose titles end with "Opera"

Thus, by using the dollar (**$**) operator, we have found all the movie titles that end with the word **Opera**.

## CASE-INSENSITIVE SEARCH

Searching with regular expressions is case-sensitive by default. The casing of the characters in the provided search pattern is matched exactly. However, quite often, you will want to provide a word or pattern to the regular expression and find documents irrespective of their casing. MongoDB provides the **$options** operator for this, which can be used for case-insensitive regular expression searches. For example, say you want to find all the movies whose titles contain the word "the", first in a case-sensitive way and then in a case-insensitive way.

The following query retrieves the titles containing the word **the** in lowercase:

```
db.movies.find(
    {"title" : {"$regex" : "the"}}
)
```

The following output in mongo shell shows that this query returns the titles containing the word **the** in lowercase:

```
                              MongoDB
> db.movies.find(
...     {"title" : {"$regex" : "the"}},
...     {"title" : 1}
... )
{ "_id" : ObjectId("573a1390f29313caabcd4323"), "title" : "The Land Beyond the Sunset" }
{ "_id" : ObjectId("573a1390f29313caabcd4803"), "title" : "Winsor McCay, the Famous Cartoonist of the N.Y. H
erald and His Moving Comics" }
{ "_id" : ObjectId("573a1390f29313caabcd50e5"), "title" : "Gertie the Dinosaur" }
{ "_id" : ObjectId("573a1390f29313caabcd5c0f"), "title" : "Intolerance: Love's Struggle Throughout the Ages"
 }
{ "_id" : ObjectId("573a1390f29313caabcd516c"), "title" : "In the Land of the Head Hunters" }
{ "_id" : ObjectId("573a1390f29313caabcd680a"), "title" : "Broken Blossoms or The Yellow Man and the Girl" }
{ "_id" : ObjectId("573a1391f29313caabcd6d90"), "title" : "The Last of the Mohicans" }
{ "_id" : ObjectId("573a1391f29313caabcd70b4"), "title" : "The Four Horsemen of the Apocalypse" }
{ "_id" : ObjectId("573a1391f29313caabcd7586"), "title" : "Nanook of the North" }
{ "_id" : ObjectId("573a1391f29313caabcd7e6e"), "title" : "Clash of the Wolves" }
{ "_id" : ObjectId("573a1391f29313caabcd806b"), "title" : "The Phantom of the Opera" }
{ "_id" : ObjectId("573a1391f29313caabcd821b"), "title" : "Ben-Hur: A Tale of the Christ" }
{ "_id" : ObjectId("573a1391f29313caabcd830e"), "title" : "Flesh and the Devil" }
{ "_id" : ObjectId("573a1391f29313caabcd8521"), "title" : "The Son of the Sheik" }
{ "_id" : ObjectId("573a1391f29313caabcd8792"), "title" : "The Kid Brother" }
{ "_id" : ObjectId("573a1391f29313caabcd8acf"), "title" : "The Fall of the House of Usher" }
{ "_id" : ObjectId("573a1391f29313caabcd91b4"), "title" : "All Quiet on the Western Front" }
{ "_id" : ObjectId("573a1391f29313caabcd94b1"), "title" : "Under the Roofs of Paris" }
{ "_id" : ObjectId("573a1392f29313caabcd98c3"), "title" : "Tabu: A Story of the South Seas" }
{ "_id" : ObjectId("573a1392f29313caabcd9bcf"), "title" : "Murders in the Rue Morgue" }
Type "it" for more
> 
```

Figure 4.16: Titles containing the word "the" in lowercase

Now, try the same query with case-insensitive search. To do so, provide the **$options** argument with a value of **i**, where **i** stands for case-insensitive:

```
db.movies.find(
    {"title" :
        {"$regex" : "the", $options: "i"}
    }
)
```

The preceding query uses the same regular expression pattern (**the**) but with an additional argument; that is, **$options**. Execute the query along with projection on the **title** field:

```
                                   MongoDB
> db.movies.find(
...      {"title" :
...          {"$regex" : "the", $options: "i"}
...      },
...      {"title" : 1}
[... )
{ "_id" : ObjectId("573a1390f29313caabcd4323"), "title" : "The Land Beyond the Sunset" }
{ "_id" : ObjectId("573a1390f29313caabcd4803"), "title" : "Winsor McCay, the Famous Cartoonist of the N.Y. H
erald and His Moving Comics" }
{ "_id" : ObjectId("573a1390f29313caabcd50e5"), "title" : "Gertie the Dinosaur" }
{ "_id" : ObjectId("573a1390f29313caabcd5293"), "title" : "The Perils of Pauline" }
{ "_id" : ObjectId("573a1390f29313caabcd42e8"), "title" : "The Great Train Robbery" }
{ "_id" : ObjectId("573a1390f29313caabcd548c"), "title" : "The Birth of a Nation" }
{ "_id" : ObjectId("573a1390f29313caabcd56df"), "title" : "The Italian" }
{ "_id" : ObjectId("573a1390f29313caabcd5501"), "title" : "The Cheat" }
{ "_id" : ObjectId("573a1390f29313caabcd5c0f"), "title" : "Intolerance: Love's Struggle Throughout the Ages"
 }
{ "_id" : ObjectId("573a1390f29313caabcd516c"), "title" : "In the Land of the Head Hunters" }
{ "_id" : ObjectId("573a1390f29313caabcd6223"), "title" : "The Poor Little Rich Girl" }
{ "_id" : ObjectId("573a1390f29313caabcd60e4"), "title" : "The Immigrant" }
{ "_id" : ObjectId("573a1390f29313caabcd63d6"), "title" : "The Blue Bird" }
{ "_id" : ObjectId("573a1390f29313caabcd680a"), "title" : "Broken Blossoms or The Yellow Man and the Girl" }
{ "_id" : ObjectId("573a1391f29313caabcd6d90"), "title" : "The Last of the Mohicans" }
{ "_id" : ObjectId("573a1391f29313caabcd6f98"), "title" : "The Ace of Hearts" }
{ "_id" : ObjectId("573a1391f29313caabcd6ea2"), "title" : "The Saphead" }
{ "_id" : ObjectId("573a1391f29313caabcd70b4"), "title" : "The Four Horsemen of the Apocalypse" }
{ "_id" : ObjectId("573a1391f29313caabcd715c"), "title" : "The Kid" }
{ "_id" : ObjectId("573a1391f29313caabcd7586"), "title" : "Nanook of the North" }
Type "it" for more
> 
```

Figure 4.17: Querying for case-insensitive results

Executing the query and printing the titles shows that the regular expression is matched, irrespective of casing. So far, we have learned about querying on basic objects. In the next section, we will learn how to query arrays and embedded documents.

# QUERY ARRAYS AND NESTED DOCUMENTS

In *Chapter 2, Documents and Data Types*, we learned that MongoDB documents support complex object structures such as arrays, nested objects, arrays of objects, and more. The arrays and nested documents help store self-contained information. It is extremely important to have a mechanism to easily search for and retrieve the information stored in such complex structures. The MongoDB query language allows us to query such complex structures in the most intuitive manner. First, we will learn how to run queries on the array elements, and then we will learn how to run them on nested object fields.

## FINDING AN ARRAY BY AN ELEMENT

Querying over an array is similar to querying any other field. In the **movies** collection, there are several arrays, and the **cast** field is one of them. Consider that, in your movies service, the user wants to find movies starring the actor **Charles Chaplin**. To create the query for this search, use an equality check on the field, as follows:

```
db.movies.find({"cast" : "Charles Chaplin"})
```

When you execute this query and project only the **cast** field, you'll get the following output:

```
                            MongoDB
[> db.movies.find({"cast" : "Charles Chaplin"}, {"cast" : 1, "_id": 0})                        ]
{ "cast" : [ "Charles Chaplin", "Edna Purviance", "Eric Campbell", "Albert Austin" ] }
{ "cast" : [ "Carl Miller", "Edna Purviance", "Jackie Coogan", "Charles Chaplin" ] }
{ "cast" : [ "Charles Chaplin", "Mack Swain", "Tom Murray", "Henry Bergman" ] }
{ "cast" : [ "Charles Chaplin", "Paulette Goddard", "Henry Bergman", "Tiny Sandford" ] }
{ "cast" : [ "Charles Chaplin", "Jack Oakie", "Reginald Gardiner", "Henry Daniell" ] }
{ "cast" : [ "Charles Chaplin", "Mady Correll", "Allison Roddan", "Robert Lewis" ] }
{ "cast" : [ "Charles Chaplin", "Claire Bloom", "Nigel Bruce", "Buster Keaton" ] }
{ "cast" : [ "Charles Chaplin", "Maxine Audley", "Jerry Desmonde", "Oliver Johnston" ] }
> ▓
```

Figure 4.18: Finding movies starring Charles Chaplin

Now, imagine the user wants to search for movies with the actors **Charles Chaplin** and **Edna Purviance** together. For this query, you will use the **$and** operator:

```
db.movies.find(
    {$and :[
        {"cast" : "Charles Chaplin"},
        {"cast": "Edna Purviance"}
    ]}
)
```

Executing and projecting only the array fields produces the following output:

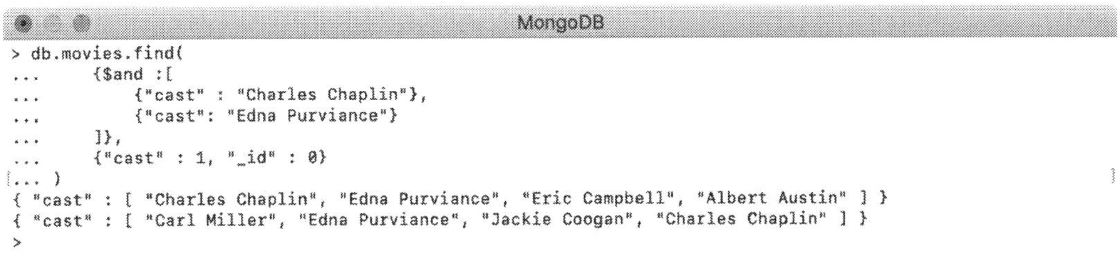

```
● ● ●                              MongoDB
> db.movies.find(
...     {$and :[
...         {"cast" : "Charles Chaplin"},
...         {"cast": "Edna Purviance"}
...     ]},
...     {"cast" : 1, "_id" : 0}
... )
{ "cast" : [ "Charles Chaplin", "Edna Purviance", "Eric Campbell", "Albert Austin" ] }
{ "cast" : [ "Carl Miller", "Edna Purviance", "Jackie Coogan", "Charles Chaplin" ] }
>
```

Figure 4.19: Finding movies starring Charles Chaplin and Edna Purviance

We can conclude that when an array field is queried using a value, all those documents are returned where the array field contains at least one element that satisfies the query.

## FINDING AN ARRAY BY AN ARRAY

In the previous examples, we were searching for arrays using the value of an element. Similarly, array fields can also be searched using array values. However, when you search an array field using an array value, the elements and their order must match. Let's try a few examples to demonstrate this.

The documents in the **movies** collection have an array to indicate how many languages the movie is available in. Let's assume that your user wants to find movies that are available in both **English** and **German**. Prepare an array of both values and query the **languages** field:

```
db.movies.find(
    {"languages" : ["English", "German"]}
)
```

Print the results while projecting the **languages** and **_id** fields:

```
MongoDB
> db.movies.find(
...      {"languages" : ["English", "German"]},
...      {"languages" : 1}
[... )
{ "_id" : ObjectId("573a1392f29313caabcd9fc4"), "languages" : [ "English", "German" ] }
{ "_id" : ObjectId("573a1392f29313caabcda64c"), "languages" : [ "English", "German" ] }
{ "_id" : ObjectId("573a1392f29313caabcdbabd"), "languages" : [ "English", "German" ] }
{ "_id" : ObjectId("573a1393f29313caabcdc13b"), "languages" : [ "English", "German" ] }
{ "_id" : ObjectId("573a1393f29313caabcdc5dc"), "languages" : [ "English", "German" ] }
{ "_id" : ObjectId("573a1393f29313caabcdca03"), "languages" : [ "English", "German" ] }
{ "_id" : ObjectId("573a1393f29313caabcdcb64"), "languages" : [ "English", "German" ] }
{ "_id" : ObjectId("573a1393f29313caabcdccb6"), "languages" : [ "English", "German" ] }
{ "_id" : ObjectId("573a1393f29313caabcdcd4e"), "languages" : [ "English", "German" ] }
{ "_id" : ObjectId("573a1393f29313caabcdcd6b"), "languages" : [ "English", "German" ] }
{ "_id" : ObjectId("573a1393f29313caabcdcf84"), "languages" : [ "English", "German" ] }
{ "_id" : ObjectId("573a1393f29313caabcdd009"), "languages" : [ "English", "German" ] }
{ "_id" : ObjectId("573a1393f29313caabcdd329"), "languages" : [ "English", "German" ] }
{ "_id" : ObjectId("573a1393f29313caabcdd482"), "languages" : [ "English", "German" ] }
{ "_id" : ObjectId("573a1393f29313caabcdd6e5"), "languages" : [ "English", "German" ] }
{ "_id" : ObjectId("573a1393f29313caabcdde5a"), "languages" : [ "English", "German" ] }
{ "_id" : ObjectId("573a1393f29313caabcdde97"), "languages" : [ "English", "German" ] }
{ "_id" : ObjectId("573a1393f29313caabcde04e"), "languages" : [ "English", "German" ] }
{ "_id" : ObjectId("573a1393f29313caabcde169"), "languages" : [ "English", "German" ] }
{ "_id" : ObjectId("573a1394f29313caabcde5c7"), "languages" : [ "English", "German" ] }
Type "it" for more
>
```

Figure 4.20: Movies available in English and German

The preceding output shows that when we search by using an array, the value is matched exactly.

Now, let's change the order of the array elements and search again:

```
db.movies.find(
    {"languages" : ["German", "English"]}
)
```

Note that this query is the same as the previous one except for the order of array elements, which is reversed. You should see the following output:

```
  ● ● ●                                   MongoDB
> db.movies.find(
...       {"languages" : ["German", "English"]},
...       {"languages" : 1}
... )
{ "_id" : ObjectId("573a1394f29313caabce0e55"), "languages" : [ "German", "English" ] }
{ "_id" : ObjectId("573a1395f29313caabce1082"), "languages" : [ "German", "English" ] }
{ "_id" : ObjectId("573a1395f29313caabce1bb0"), "languages" : [ "German", "English" ] }
{ "_id" : ObjectId("573a1395f29313caabce206e"), "languages" : [ "German", "English" ] }
{ "_id" : ObjectId("573a1396f29313caabce3bca"), "languages" : [ "German", "English" ] }
{ "_id" : ObjectId("573a1396f29313caabce531a"), "languages" : [ "German", "English" ] }
{ "_id" : ObjectId("573a1396f29313caabce5b83"), "languages" : [ "German", "English" ] }
{ "_id" : ObjectId("573a1397f29313caabce71c8"), "languages" : [ "German", "English" ] }
{ "_id" : ObjectId("573a1397f29313caabce7f70"), "languages" : [ "German", "English" ] }
{ "_id" : ObjectId("573a1397f29313caabce8700"), "languages" : [ "German", "English" ] }
{ "_id" : ObjectId("573a1398f29313caabce9201"), "languages" : [ "German", "English" ] }
{ "_id" : ObjectId("573a1398f29313caabcea78e"), "languages" : [ "German", "English" ] }
{ "_id" : ObjectId("573a1399f29313caabcec880"), "languages" : [ "German", "English" ] }
{ "_id" : ObjectId("573a1399f29313caabcec9e9"), "languages" : [ "German", "English" ] }
{ "_id" : ObjectId("573a139af29313caabceffdf"), "languages" : [ "German", "English" ] }
{ "_id" : ObjectId("573a139af29313caabcf0770"), "languages" : [ "German", "English" ] }
{ "_id" : ObjectId("573a139af29313caabcf0a53"), "languages" : [ "German", "English" ] }
{ "_id" : ObjectId("573a139bf29313caabcf2a4a"), "languages" : [ "German", "English" ] }
{ "_id" : ObjectId("573a139ef29313caabcfcca8"), "languages" : [ "German", "English" ] }
{ "_id" : ObjectId("573a139ef29313caabcfe05e"), "languages" : [ "German", "English" ] }
Type "it" for more
> ▊
```

Figure 4.21: Query to demonstrate the impact of the order of array elements

The preceding output shows that by changing the order of the elements in the array, different records have been matched.

This has happened because, when array fields are searched using an array value, the value is matched using an equality check. Any two arrays only pass the equality check if they have the same elements in the same order. Hence, the following two queries are not the same and will return different results:

```
// Find movies languages by [ "English", "French", "Cantonese", "German"]
db.movies.find(
    {"languages": [ "English", "French", "Cantonese", "German"]}
)


// Find movies languages by ["English", "French", "Cantonese"]
db.movies.find(
    {"languages": ["English", "French", "Cantonese"]}
)
```

The only difference between these two queries is that the second query doesn't contain the last element; that is, **German**. Now, execute both queries in a mongo shell and view the output:

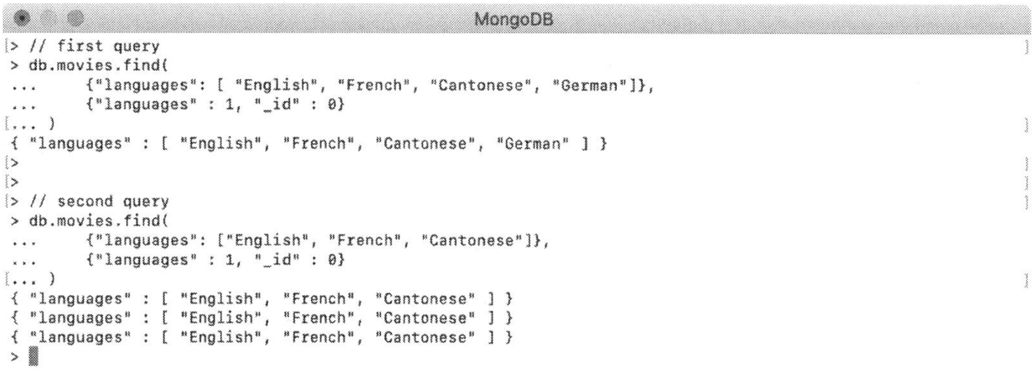

```
● ● ●                                    MongoDB
> // first query
> db.movies.find(
...     {"languages": [ "English", "French", "Cantonese", "German"]},
...     {"languages" : 1, "_id" : 0}
... )
{ "languages" : [ "English", "French", "Cantonese", "German" ] }
>
>
> // second query
> db.movies.find(
...     {"languages": ["English", "French", "Cantonese"]},
...     {"languages" : 1, "_id" : 0}
... )
{ "languages" : [ "English", "French", "Cantonese" ] }
{ "languages" : [ "English", "French", "Cantonese" ] }
{ "languages" : [ "English", "French", "Cantonese" ] }
> █
```

Figure 4.22: Different queries to demonstrate that array values are matched exactly

The preceding output shows both queries executed one after the other and proves that the array values are matched exactly.

## SEARCHING AN ARRAY WITH THE $ALL OPERATOR

The **$all** operator finds all those documents where the value of the field contains all the elements, irrespective of their order or size:

```
db.movies.find(
    {"languages":{
        "$all" :[ "English", "French", "Cantonese"]
    }}
)
```

The preceding query uses **$all** to find all the movies available in **English**, **French**, and **Cantonese**. You will execute this query, along with projection, to display only the **languages** field:

```
                                    MongoDB
> db.movies.find(
...     {"languages":{
...         "$all" :[ "English", "French", "Cantonese"]
...     }},
...     {"languages" : 1, "_id" : 0}
[... )
{ "languages" : [ "English", "French", "Cantonese", "German" ] }
{ "languages" : [ "Cantonese", "English", "Vietnamese", "French" ] }
{ "languages" : [ "French", "Cantonese", "English", "Hakka" ] }
{ "languages" : [ "Cantonese", "English", "French" ] }
{ "languages" : [ "French", "English", "Cantonese", "Italian" ] }
{ "languages" : [ "English", "Cantonese", "Italian", "Japanese", "Mandarin", "French" ] }
{ "languages" : [ "English", "German", "Arabic", "French", "Cantonese" ] }
{ "languages" : [ "Cantonese", "Mandarin", "English", "Korean", "French", "Turkish" ] }
{ "languages" : [ "English", "Cantonese", "French", "German", "Hindi", "Turkish" ] }
{ "languages" : [ "French", "English", "Cantonese" ] }
{ "languages" : [ "French", "English", "Cantonese" ] }
{ "languages" : [ "English", "French", "Cantonese" ] }
{ "languages" : [ "English", "French", "Cantonese", "Gujarati", "Yiddish" ] }
{ "languages" : [ "English", "French", "Cantonese" ] }
{ "languages" : [ "French", "English", "Cantonese" ] }
{ "languages" : [ "Cantonese", "English", "French" ] }
{ "languages" : [ "English", "French", "Cantonese" ] }
{ "languages" : [ "Cantonese", "Mandarin", "English", "Shanghainese", "French" ] }
{ "languages" : [ "Cantonese", "Mandarin", "English", "Shanghainese", "French" ] }
> █
```

Figure 4.23: Query using the $all operator on the languages field

The preceding output indicates that the **$all** operator has matched arrays, irrespective of the order and size of the elements.

## PROJECTING ARRAY ELEMENTS

So far, we have seen that whenever we search an array field, the output always contains the complete array. There are a few ways to limit how many elements of an array are returned in the query output. We have already practiced projecting fields in the resulting documents. Similar to this, elements in an array can also be projected. In this section, we will learn how to limit the result set when we search with an array field. After this, we will learn how to return specific elements from an array based on their index position.

## PROJECTING MATCHING ELEMENTS USING ($)

You can search an array by an element value and use projection to exclude all but the first matching element of the array using the **$** operator. To do this, execute a query without the **$** operator first, and then execute it with this operator. Prepare a simple element search query, as follows:

```
db.movies.find(
     {"languages" : "Syriac"},
     {"languages" :1}
)
```

This query uses element search on the **languages** array and projects the field to produce the following output:

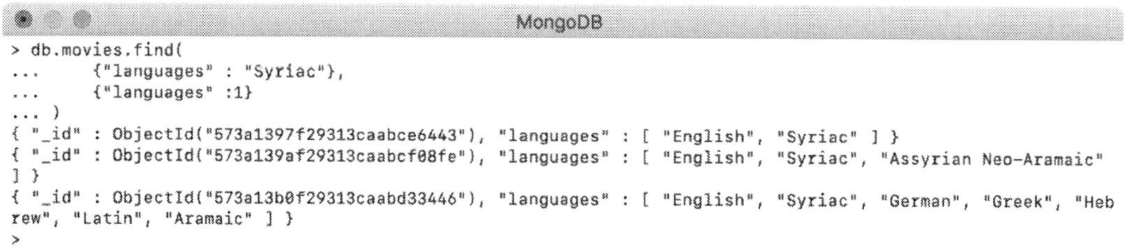

```
MongoDB
> db.movies.find(
...      {"languages" : "Syriac"},
...      {"languages" :1}
... )
{ "_id" : ObjectId("573a1397f29313caabce6443"), "languages" : [ "English", "Syriac" ] }
{ "_id" : ObjectId("573a139af29313caabcf08fe"), "languages" : [ "English", "Syriac", "Assyrian Neo-Aramaic"
] }
{ "_id" : ObjectId("573a13b0f29313caabd33446"), "languages" : [ "English", "Syriac", "German", "Greek", "Heb
rew", "Latin", "Aramaic" ] }
>
```

Figure 4.24: Movies available in the Syriac language

Although the query is intended to find Syriac-language movies, the output array contains other languages as well. Now, see what happens when you use the **$** operator:

```
db.movies.find(
     {"languages" : "Syriac"},
     {"languages.$" :1}
)
```

You have modified the query to add the **$** operator in the projection part. Now, execute the query, as follows:

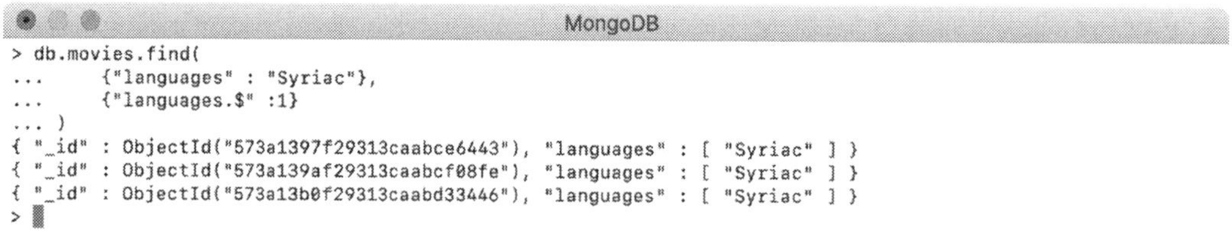

```
MongoDB
> db.movies.find(
...      {"languages" : "Syriac"},
...      {"languages.$" :1}
... )
{ "_id" : ObjectId("573a1397f29313caabce6443"), "languages" : [ "Syriac" ] }
{ "_id" : ObjectId("573a139af29313caabcf08fe"), "languages" : [ "Syriac" ] }
{ "_id" : ObjectId("573a13b0f29313caabd33446"), "languages" : [ "Syriac" ] }
>
```

Figure 4.25: Movies available only in the Syriac language

The array field in the output only contains the matching element; the rest of the elements are skipped. Thus, the **languages** array in the output only contains the **Syriac** element. The most important thing to remember is that if more than one element is matched, the **$** operator projects only the first matching element.

## PROJECTING MATCHING ELEMENTS BY THEIR INDEX POSITION ($SLICE)

The **$slice** operator is used to limit the array elements based on their index position. This operator can be used with any array field, irrespective of the field being queried or not. This means that you may query a different field and still use this operator to limit the elements of the array fields.

To see this, we will use the movie **Youth Without Youth** as an example, which has 11 elements in the **languages** array. The following output from the mongo shell shows what the array field looks like in the movie record:

```
a lightning storm. Not only does Dominic find love again, but her new abilities hold the key to his research.
Is the sweetness of life finally at hand?",
        "languages" : [
                "English",
                "Sanskrit",
                "German",
                "French",
                "Italian",
                "Russian",
                "Romanian",
                "Mandarin",
                "Latin",
                "Armenian",
                "Egyptian (Ancient)"
        ],
        "released" : ISODate("2007-10-26T00:00:00Z"),
        "directors" : [
                "Francis Ford Coppola"
        ],
```

Figure 4.26: List of languages for the movie Youth Without Youth

In the following query, use **$slice** to print only the first three elements of the array:

```
db.movies.find(
    {"title" : "Youth Without Youth"},
    {"languages" : {$slice : 3}}
).pretty()
```

The output for the preceding query shows that the **languages** field only contains the first three elements, as follows:

```
"languages" : [
        "English",
        "Sanskrit",
        "German"
    ]
"released" : ISODate("2007-10-26T00:00:00Z"),
"directors" : [
```

The **$slice** operator can be used in a few more ways. The following projection expression will return the last two elements of the array:

```
{"languages" : {$slice : -2}}
```

The following output shows that the array has been sliced down to the last two elements only:

```
"languages" : [
        "Armenian",
        "Egyptian (Ancient)",
    ]
"released" : ISODate("2007-10-26T00:00:00Z"),
```

The **$slice** operator can also be passed with two arguments, where the first argument indicates the number of elements to be skipped and the second one indicates the number of elements to be returned. For example, the following projection expression will skip the first two elements of the array and return the next four elements after it:

```
{"languages" : {$slice : [2, 4]}}
```

When we execute this query, we get the following output:

```
"languages" : [
        "German",
        "French",
        "Italian"
        "Russian"
    ]
"released" : ISODate("2007-10-26T00:00:00Z"),
"directors" : [
```

The two-argument slice can also be used with a negative value for skip. For example, in the following projection expression, the first number is negative. If the value of skip is negative, the counting starts from the end. So, in the following expression, five elements counting from the last index will be skipped and four elements starting from that index will be returned:

```
{"languages" : {$slice : [-5, 4]}}
```

Note that because of the negative skip value, the skip index will be calculated from the last index. Skipping five elements from the last index gives us **Romanian** and from this index position, the next four elements will be returned, as shown here:

```
    "languages" : [
            "Romanian",
            "Mandarin",
            "Latin"
            "Armenian"
    ]
    "released" : ISODate("2007-10-26T00:00:00Z"),
```

In this section, we have covered how to query array fields and how to project the results in various ways. In the next section, we will learn how to query nested objects.

## QUERYING NESTED OBJECTS

Similar to arrays, nested or embedded objects can also be represented as values of a field. Hence, fields that have other objects as their values can be searched using the complete object as a value. In the **movies** collection, there is a field named **awards** whose value is a nested object. The following snippet shows the **awards** object for a random movie in the collection:

```
    "rated" : "TV-G",
    "awards"  :  {
            "wins" : 1,
            "nominations" : 0,
            "text" : "1 win."
    }
```

The following query finds the **awards** object by providing the complete object as its value:

```
db.movies.find(
    {"awards":
        {"wins": 1, "nominations": 0, "text": "1 win."}
    }
)
```

The following output shows that there are several movies whose **awards** field has an exact value of **{"wins": 1, "nominations": 0, "text": "1 win."}**:

```
> db.movies.find(
...     {"awards":
...         {"wins": 1, "nominations": 0, "text": "1 win."}
...     },
...     {"awards" : 1}
... )
{ "_id" : ObjectId("573a1390f29313caabcd4323"), "awards" : { "wins" : 1, "nominations" : 0, "text" : "1 win." } }
{ "_id" : ObjectId("573a1390f29313caabcd446f"), "awards" : { "wins" : 1, "nominations" : 0, "text" : "1 win." } }
{ "_id" : ObjectId("573a1390f29313caabcd4eaf"), "awards" : { "wins" : 1, "nominations" : 0, "text" : "1 win." } }
{ "_id" : ObjectId("573a1390f29313caabcd4803"), "awards" : { "wins" : 1, "nominations" : 0, "text" : "1 win." } }
{ "_id" : ObjectId("573a1390f29313caabcd4135"), "awards" : { "wins" : 1, "nominations" : 0, "text" : "1 win." } }
{ "_id" : ObjectId("573a1390f29313caabcd50e5"), "awards" : { "wins" : 1, "nominations" : 0, "text" : "1 win." } }
{ "_id" : ObjectId("573a1390f29313caabcd5293"), "awards" : { "wins" : 1, "nominations" : 0, "text" : "1 win." } }
{ "_id" : ObjectId("573a1390f29313caabcd42e8"), "awards" : { "wins" : 1, "nominations" : 0, "text" : "1 win." } }
{ "_id" : ObjectId("573a1390f29313caabcd56df"), "awards" : { "wins" : 1, "nominations" : 0, "text" : "1 win." } }
{ "_id" : ObjectId("573a1390f29313caabcd5501"), "awards" : { "wins" : 1, "nominations" : 0, "text" : "1 win." } }
{ "_id" : ObjectId("573a1390f29313caabcd5a93"), "awards" : { "wins" : 1, "nominations" : 0, "text" : "1 win." } }
{ "_id" : ObjectId("573a1390f29313caabcd587d"), "awards" : { "wins" : 1, "nominations" : 0, "text" : "1 win." } }
{ "_id" : ObjectId("573a1390f29313caabcd5b9a"), "awards" : { "wins" : 1, "nominations" : 0, "text" : "1 win." } }
{ "_id" : ObjectId("573a1390f29313caabcd5c0f"), "awards" : { "wins" : 1, "nominations" : 0, "text" : "1 win." } }
{ "_id" : ObjectId("573a1390f29313caabcd516c"), "awards" : { "wins" : 1, "nominations" : 0, "text" : "1 win." } }
{ "_id" : ObjectId("573a1390f29313caabcd5ea4"), "awards" : { "wins" : 1, "nominations" : 0, "text" : "1 win." } }
{ "_id" : ObjectId("573a1390f29313caabcd6377"), "awards" : { "wins" : 1, "nominations" : 0, "text" : "1 win." } }
{ "_id" : ObjectId("573a1390f29313caabcd6223"), "awards" : { "wins" : 1, "nominations" : 0, "text" : "1 win." } }
{ "_id" : ObjectId("573a1390f29313caabcd60e4"), "awards" : { "wins" : 1, "nominations" : 0, "text" : "1 win." } }
{ "_id" : ObjectId("573a1390f29313caabcd63d6"), "awards" : { "wins" : 1, "nominations" : 0, "text" : "1 win." } }
[Type "it" for more
>
```

Figure 4.27: List of movies without a nomination and one award

When nested object fields are searched with object values, there must be an exact match. This means that all the field-value pairs, along with the order of the fields, must match exactly. For example, consider the following query:

```
db.movies.find(
    {"awards":
        {"nominations": 0, "wins": 1, "text": "1 win."}
    }
)
```

This query has a change in order regarding the query object; hence, it will return an empty result.

## QUERYING NESTED OBJECT FIELDS

In *Chapter 2, Documents and Data Types*, we saw that fields of nested objects can be accessed using dot (.) notation. Similarly, dot notation can be used to search nested objects by providing the values of its fields. For example, to find movies that have won four awards, you can use dot notation like so:

```
db.movies.find(
    {"awards.wins" : 4}
)
```

The preceding query uses dot (.) notation on the **awards** field and refers to the nested field named **wins**. When you execute the query and project only the **awards** field, you get the following output:

```
                                      MongoDB
> db.movies.find(
...      {"awards.wins" : 4},
...      {"awards" : 1, "_id" : 0}
[... )
{ "awards" : { "wins" : 4, "nominations" : 0, "text" : "Nominated for 1 Oscar. Another 3 wins." } }
{ "awards" : { "wins" : 4, "nominations" : 1, "text" : "Won 3 Oscars. Another 1 win & 1 nomination." } }
{ "awards" : { "wins" : 4, "nominations" : 3, "text" : "Won 1 Oscar. Another 3 wins & 3 nominations." } }
{ "awards" : { "wins" : 4, "nominations" : 0, "text" : "Nominated for 2 Oscars. Another 2 wins." } }
{ "awards" : { "wins" : 4, "nominations" : 0, "text" : "Nominated for 3 Oscars. Another 1 win." } }
{ "awards" : { "wins" : 4, "nominations" : 4, "text" : "Won 1 Oscar. Another 3 wins & 4 nominations." } }
{ "awards" : { "wins" : 4, "nominations" : 0, "text" : "Nominated for 2 Oscars. Another 2 wins." } }
{ "awards" : { "wins" : 4, "nominations" : 1, "text" : "Nominated for 3 Oscars. Another 1 win & 1 nomination." } }
{ "awards" : { "wins" : 4, "nominations" : 0, "text" : "Nominated for 1 Oscar. Another 3 wins." } }
{ "awards" : { "wins" : 4, "nominations" : 5, "text" : "Won 3 Oscars. Another 1 win & 5 nominations." } }
{ "awards" : { "wins" : 4, "nominations" : 0, "text" : "Nominated for 2 Oscars. Another 2 wins." } }
{ "awards" : { "wins" : 4, "nominations" : 0, "text" : "Nominated for 3 Oscars. Another 1 win." } }
{ "awards" : { "wins" : 4, "nominations" : 1, "text" : "4 wins & 1 nomination." } }
{ "awards" : { "wins" : 4, "nominations" : 0, "text" : "Nominated for 2 Oscars. Another 2 wins." } }
{ "awards" : { "wins" : 4, "nominations" : 0, "text" : "Nominated for 3 Oscars. Another 1 win." } }
{ "awards" : { "wins" : 4, "nominations" : 7, "text" : "Won 1 Oscar. Another 3 wins & 7 nominations." } }
{ "awards" : { "wins" : 4, "nominations" : 0, "text" : "Nominated for 1 Oscar. Another 3 wins." } }
{ "awards" : { "wins" : 4, "nominations" : 0, "text" : "Nominated for 3 Oscars. Another 1 win." } }
{ "awards" : { "wins" : 4, "nominations" : 0, "text" : "Won 2 Oscars. Another 2 wins." } }
{ "awards" : { "wins" : 4, "nominations" : 5, "text" : "Won 2 Oscars. Another 2 wins & 5 nominations." } }
Type "it" for more
> 
```

Figure 4.28: Projecting only the awards field for preceding snippet

The preceding output indicates that the filter has been correctly applied to **wins** and that all the movies that have exactly four awards are returned.

The nested field search is performed independently on the given fields, irrespective of the order of the elements. You can search by multiple fields and use any of the conditional or logical query operators. For example, refer to the following query:

```
db.movies.find(
    {
        "awards.wins" : {$gte : 5},
        "awards.nominations" : 6
    }
)
```

This query uses a combination of two conditions on two different nested fields. Upon executing the query while excluding the rest of the fields, you should see the following output:

```
> db.movies.find(
...     {
...         "awards.wins" : {$gte : 5},
...         "awards.nominations" : 6
...     },
...     {"awards" : 1, "_id" : 0}
... )
{ "awards" : { "wins" : 6, "nominations" : 6, "text" : "Won 1 Oscar. Another 5 wins & 6 nominations." } }
{ "awards" : { "wins" : 19, "nominations" : 6, "text" : "Won 8 Oscars. Another 11 wins & 6 nominations." } }
{ "awards" : { "wins" : 9, "nominations" : 6, "text" : "Won 3 Oscars. Another 6 wins & 6 nominations." } }
{ "awards" : { "wins" : 9, "nominations" : 6, "text" : "Won 6 Oscars. Another 3 wins & 6 nominations." } }
{ "awards" : { "wins" : 9, "nominations" : 6, "text" : "Won 1 Golden Globe. Another 8 wins & 6 nominations." } }
{ "awards" : { "wins" : 13, "nominations" : 6, "text" : "Won 3 Oscars. Another 10 wins & 6 nominations." } }
{ "awards" : { "wins" : 6, "nominations" : 6, "text" : "Won 1 Oscar. Another 5 wins & 6 nominations." } }
{ "awards" : { "wins" : 11, "nominations" : 6, "text" : "Nominated for 5 Oscars. Another 6 wins & 6 nominations." }
}
{ "awards" : { "wins" : 8, "nominations" : 6, "text" : "Won 1 Oscar. Another 7 wins & 6 nominations." } }
{ "awards" : { "wins" : 21, "nominations" : 6, "text" : "Nominated for 3 Oscars. Another 18 wins & 6 nominations." }
}
{ "awards" : { "wins" : 16, "nominations" : 6, "text" : "Won 1 Oscar. Another 15 wins & 6 nominations." } }
{ "awards" : { "wins" : 12, "nominations" : 6, "text" : "Nominated for 9 Oscars. Another 3 wins & 6 nominations." }
}
{ "awards" : { "wins" : 7, "nominations" : 6, "text" : "Nominated for 2 Oscars. Another 5 wins & 6 nominations." } }
{ "awards" : { "wins" : 8, "nominations" : 6, "text" : "Nominated for 2 BAFTA Film Awards. Another 6 wins & 6 nomina
tions." } }
{ "awards" : { "wins" : 5, "nominations" : 6, "text" : "Won 1 Oscar. Another 4 wins & 6 nominations." } }
{ "awards" : { "wins" : 7, "nominations" : 6, "text" : "Nominated for 5 Oscars. Another 2 wins & 6 nominations." } }
{ "awards" : { "wins" : 7, "nominations" : 6, "text" : "Nominated for 3 Oscars. Another 4 wins & 6 nominations." } }
{ "awards" : { "wins" : 8, "nominations" : 6, "text" : "Won 2 Oscars. Another 6 wins & 6 nominations." } }
{ "awards" : { "wins" : 10, "nominations" : 6, "text" : "Nominated for 7 Oscars. Another 3 wins & 6 nominations." }
}
{ "awards" : { "wins" : 10, "nominations" : 6, "text" : "Nominated for 2 Oscars. Another 8 wins & 6 nominations." }
}
Type "it" for more
> 
```

Figure 4.29: Movies with six nominations and a minimum of five awards

This query performs a search on two fields using conditional operators and returns movies that have six nominations and have won at least five awards. Like array elements or any field in a document, nested object fields can also be projected as we want. We will explore this in detail in the next exercise.

## EXERCISE 4.04: PROJECTING NESTED OBJECT FIELDS

In this exercise, you will learn how to project only certain fields from nested objects. The following steps will help you implement this exercise:

1. Open a mongo shell and connect to the **sample_mflix** database on Mongo Atlas. Enter the following query to return all the records and project only the **awards** field, which is an embedded object:

```
db.movies.find(
    {},
    {
        "awards" :1,
        "_id":0
    }
)
```

The following output shows that only the **awards** field has been included in the result, while the rest of the fields (including **_id**) have been excluded:

```
                                    MongoDB
> db.movies.find(
...     {},
...     {
...         "awards" :1,
...         "_id":0
...     }
... )
{ "awards" : { "wins" : 1, "nominations" : 0, "text" : "1 win." } }
{ "awards" : { "wins" : 1, "nominations" : 0, "text" : "1 win." } }
{ "awards" : { "wins" : 1, "nominations" : 0, "text" : "1 win." } }
{ "awards" : { "wins" : 1, "nominations" : 0, "text" : "1 win." } }
{ "awards" : { "wins" : 1, "nominations" : 0, "text" : "1 win." } }
{ "awards" : { "wins" : 1, "nominations" : 0, "text" : "1 win." } }
{ "awards" : { "wins" : 1, "nominations" : 0, "text" : "1 win." } }
{ "awards" : { "wins" : 1, "nominations" : 0, "text" : "1 win." } }
{ "awards" : { "wins" : 2, "nominations" : 0, "text" : "2 wins." } }
{ "awards" : { "wins" : 1, "nominations" : 0, "text" : "1 win." } }
{ "awards" : { "wins" : 0, "nominations" : 1, "text" : "1 nomination." } }
{ "awards" : { "wins" : 1, "nominations" : 0, "text" : "1 win." } }
{ "awards" : { "wins" : 1, "nominations" : 0, "text" : "1 win." } }
{ "awards" : { "wins" : 1, "nominations" : 0, "text" : "1 win." } }
{ "awards" : { "wins" : 1, "nominations" : 0, "text" : "1 win." } }
{ "awards" : { "wins" : 1, "nominations" : 0, "text" : "1 win." } }
{ "awards" : { "wins" : 1, "nominations" : 0, "text" : "1 win." } }
{ "awards" : { "wins" : 1, "nominations" : 0, "text" : "1 win." } }
{ "awards" : { "wins" : 1, "nominations" : 0, "text" : "1 win." } }
Type "it" for more
> 
```

Figure 4.30: Projecting only the awards field for a query

2. To project only specific fields from embedded objects, you can refer to a field of an embedded object using dot notation. Type in the following query:

```
db.movies.find(
    {},
    {
        "awards.wins" :1,
        "awards.nominations" : 1,
        "_id":0
    }
)
```

When you execute this query on a mongo shell, the output will look like this:

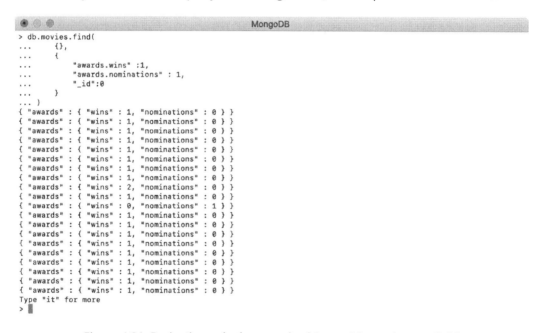

Figure 4.31: Projecting only the awards object, without the text field

The preceding output shows that only two of the nested fields are included in the response. The **awards** object in the output is still a nested object, but the **text** field has been excluded.

So far, we have seen how nested objects and their fields can be limited in the output. This concludes our discussion on querying arrays and nested objects in MongoDB. In the next section, we will learn how to skip, limit, and sort documents.

# LIMITING, SKIPPING, AND SORTING DOCUMENTS

So far, we have learned how to write basic and complex queries and to project fields in the resulting documents. In this section, you will learn how to control the number and order of documents returned by a query.

Let's talk about why the amount of data a query returns needs to be controlled. In most real-world cases, you won't be using all the documents your query matches to. Imagine that a user of our movie service is planning to watch a drama movie tonight. They will visit the movie store and search for drama movies and find that there are more than 13,000 of these in the collection. With such a large search result, they might spend the entire night just looking through the various movies and deciding which one to watch.

For a better user experience, you may want to show the 10 most popular movies in the drama category at a time, followed by the next 10 in the sequence, and so on. This technique of serving data is known as pagination. This is where a large result is divided into small chunks (also known as pages) and only one page is served at a time. Pagination not only improves the user experience, but also the overall performance of the system, and reduces the overhead on a database, network, or a user's browser or mobile application. To implement pagination, you must be able to limit the size of result, skip the already served records, and have them served in a definite order. In this section, we will practice all three of these techniques.

## LIMITING THE RESULT

To limit the number of records a query returns, the resulting cursor provides a function called `limit()`. This function accepts an integer and returns the same number of records, if available. MongoDB recommends the use of this function as it reduces the number of records that result from the cursor and improves the speed.

To print the titles of movies starring **Charles Chaplin**, enter the following query, which finds the actor's name in the **cast** field:

```
db.movies.find(
    {"cast" : "Charles Chaplin"},
    {"title": 1, "_id" :0}
)
```

The query is also adding a projection to the **title** field. When you execute the query, you will see the following output:

```
●●●                                MongoDB
> db.movies.find(
...     {"cast" : "Charles Chaplin"},
...     {"title": 1, "_id" :0}
[... )
{ "title" : "The Immigrant" }
{ "title" : "The Kid" }
{ "title" : "The Gold Rush" }
{ "title" : "Modern Times" }
{ "title" : "The Great Dictator" }
{ "title" : "Monsieur Verdoux" }
{ "title" : "Limelight" }
{ "title" : "A King in New York" }
>
```

Figure 4.32: Output showing movies starring Charles Chaplin

As can be seen, there are a total of eight movies that **Charles Chaplin** has acted in. Next, you will use the limit function to restrict the result size to **3**, as follows:

```
db.movies.find(
    {"cast" : "Charles Chaplin"},
    {"title": 1, "_id" :0}
).limit(3)
```

When this query is executed, only three records are returned:

```
●●●                                MongoDB
> db.movies.find(
...     {"cast" : "Charles Chaplin"},
...     {"title": 1, "_id" :0}
... ).limit(3)
{ "title" : "The Immigrant" }
{ "title" : "The Kid" }
{ "title" : "The Gold Rush" }
> ▊
```

Figure 4.33: Using limit() to show only three movies starring Charles Chaplin

Let's look at the behavior of the **limit()** function when it's used with different values.

When the limit size is larger than the actual records within the cursor, all the records will be returned, irrespective of the set limit. For example, the following query will return **8** records, even when the limit is set to **14**, as there are only **8** records present in the cursor:

```
db.movies.find(
    {"cast" : "Charles Chaplin"},
    {"title": 1, "_id" :0}
).limit(14)
```

The preceding query results in the following output, which shows that the query has returned all eight records:

```
                                        MongoDB
> db.movies.find(
...     {"cast" : "Charles Chaplin"},
...     {"title": 1, "_id" :0}
... ).limit(14)
{ "title" : "The Immigrant" }
{ "title" : "The Kid" }
{ "title" : "The Gold Rush" }
{ "title" : "Modern Times" }
{ "title" : "The Great Dictator" }
{ "title" : "Monsieur Verdoux" }
{ "title" : "Limelight" }
{ "title" : "A King in New York" }
>
```

Figure 4.34: Output when limit is set to 14

Note that setting the limit to zero is equivalent to not setting any limit at all. The following query will therefore return all eight records that match the criteria:

```
db.movies.find(
    {"cast" : "Charles Chaplin"},
    {"title": 1, "_id" :0}
).limit(0)
```

The output of the preceding query is as follows:

```
                                        MongoDB
> db.movies.find(
...     {"cast" : "Charles Chaplin"},
...     {"title": 1, "_id" :0}
... ).limit(0)
{ "title" : "The Immigrant" }
{ "title" : "The Kid" }
{ "title" : "The Gold Rush" }
{ "title" : "Modern Times" }
{ "title" : "The Great Dictator" }
{ "title" : "Monsieur Verdoux" }
{ "title" : "Limelight" }
{ "title" : "A King in New York" }
>
```

Figure 4.35: Output when limit is set to 0

Now, are you wondering what will happen if the limit size is set to a negative number? For queries returning smaller records, as in our case, a negative size limit is considered equivalent to the limit of a positive number. The following query demonstrates this:

```
db.movies.find(
    {"cast" : "Charles Chaplin"},
    {"title": 1, "_id" :0}
).limit(-2)
```

When you execute this query (which has a negative limit of **-2** on a mongo shell), you should get the following output:

```
> db.movies.find(
...     {"cast" : "Charles Chaplin"},
...     {"title": 1, "_id" :0}
... ).limit(-2)
{ "title" : "The Immigrant" }
{ "title" : "The Kid" }
>
```

Figure 4.36: Output when limit is -2

The output shows that the query returned two documents and the behavior is equivalent to using **limit** of size **2**. However, the result set's batch size can affect this behavior. The next section will explore this in detail.

## LIMIT AND BATCH SIZE

When a query is executed in MongoDB, the results are processed and returned in the form of one or more batches. The batches are allotted internally, and the results will be displayed all at once. One of the main purposes of batching is to avoid high resource utilization, which may happen while processing a large number of record sets.

Also, it keeps the connection between the client and server active, because of which timeout errors are avoided. For large queries, when the database takes longer to find and return the result, the client just keeps on waiting. After a certain threshold value for waiting is reached, the connection between the client and server is broken and the query is failed with a timeout exception. Using batching avoids such timeouts as the server keeps retuning the individual batches continuously.

Different MongoDB drivers can have different batch sizes. However, for a single query, the batch size can be set, as shown in the following snippet:

```
db.movies.find(
    {"cast" : "Charles Chaplin"},
    {"title": 1, "_id" :0}
).batchSize(5)
```

This query uses the **batchSize()** function on the cursor to provide a batch size of **5**. The output of executing this query is as follows:

```
> db.movies.find(
...     {"cast" : "Charles Chaplin"},
...     {"title": 1, "_id" :0}
... ).batchSize(5)
{ "title" : "The Immigrant" }
{ "title" : "The Kid" }
{ "title" : "The Gold Rush" }
{ "title" : "Modern Times" }
{ "title" : "The Great Dictator" }
{ "title" : "Monsieur Verdoux" }
{ "title" : "Limelight" }
{ "title" : "A King in New York" }
>
```

Figure 4.37: Output when batch size is 5

The query in the preceding output adds a batch size of **5**, but it has no effect on the output. However, there was a difference in how the results were prepared internally.

## POSITIVE LIMIT WITH BATCH SIZE

When the preceding query is executed, which specifies a batch size of **5**, the database starts finding the documents that match the given condition. As soon as the first five documents are found, they are returned to the client as the first batch. Next, the remaining three records are found and returned as the next batch. However, for the users, the results are printed at once and the change is unnoticeable.

The same thing happens when a query is executed with a positive limit that is larger than the batch size and the records are internally fetched in multiple batches:

```
db.movies.find(
    {"cast" : "Charles Chaplin"},
    {"title": 1, "_id" :0}
).limit(7).batchSize(5)
```

This query uses a limit of **7**, which is larger than the provided batch size of **5**. When the query is executed, we get the expected **7** records, without any noticeable changes. The following screenshot shows the output:

```
●  ●  ●                                          MongoDB
> db.movies.find(
...        {"cast" : "Charles Chaplin"},
...        {"title": 1, "_id" :0}
... ).limit(7).batchSize(5)
{ "title" : "The Immigrant" }
{ "title" : "The Kid" }
{ "title" : "The Gold Rush" }
{ "title" : "Modern Times" }
{ "title" : "The Great Dictator" }
{ "title" : "Monsieur Verdoux" }
{ "title" : "Limelight" }
> █
```

Figure 4.38: Output when limit is 7 and batch size is 5

So far, we have learned how to perform batching without specifying a limit, and then specifying a positive limit value. Now, we will see what happens when we use a negative limit value, whose positive equivalent is larger than the given batch size.

## NEGATIVE LIMITS AND BATCH SIZE

As we learned in the previous examples, MongoDB uses batches if the total number of records in the result exceeds the batch size. However, when we use a negative number to specify the limit size, only the first batch is returned and the next batch, even if it is required, will not be processed.

We will demonstrate this by using the following query:

```
db.movies.find(
    {"cast" : "Charles Chaplin"},
    {"title": 1, "_id" :0}
).limit(-7).batchSize(5)
```

This query uses a limit of negative **7** and batch of **5**, which means it should take two batches to return the results. To observe this behavior, execute this query on a mongo shell:

```
●  ●  ●                                          MongoDB
> db.movies.find(
...        {"cast" : "Charles Chaplin"},
...        {"title": 1, "_id" :0}
... ).limit(-7).batchSize(5)
{ "title" : "The Immigrant" }
{ "title" : "The Kid" }
{ "title" : "The Gold Rush" }
{ "title" : "Modern Times" }
{ "title" : "The Great Dictator" }
> █
```

Figure 4.39: Output when limit is -7 and batch size is 5

The output indicates that the query returned only the first five records instead of the expected seven records. This is because the database returned only the first batch and the next batch was not processed.

This proves that the negative limit is not exactly equivalent to providing the number in positive form. The results will be the same if the number of records returned by the query is smaller than the specified batch size. In general, you should avoid using a negative limit, but if you do, make sure to use an appropriate batch size so that such scenarios can be avoided.

## SKIPPING DOCUMENTS

Skipping is used to exclude some documents in the result set and return the rest. The MongoDB cursor provides the **skip()** function, which accepts an integer and skips the specified number of documents from the cursor, returning the rest. In the previous examples, you prepared queries to find the titles of movies starring Charles Chaplin. The following example uses the same query with the **skip()** function:

```
db.movies.find(
      {"cast" : "Charles Chaplin"},
      {"title": 1, "_id" :0}
).skip(2)
```

Since the **skip()** function has been provided with the value **2**, the first two documents will be excluded from the output, as shown in the following screenshot:

```
> db.movies.find(
...       {"cast" : "Charles Chaplin"},
...       {"title": 1, "_id" :0}
... ).skip(2)
{ "title" : "The Gold Rush" }
{ "title" : "Modern Times" }
{ "title" : "The Great Dictator" }
{ "title" : "Monsieur Verdoux" }
{ "title" : "Limelight" }
{ "title" : "A King in New York" }
>
```

Figure 4.40: Output with a skip value of 2

Similar to **limit()**, passing zero to **skip()** is equivalent to not calling the function at all, and the entire result set is returned. However, **skip()** has a different behavior for negative numbers; it does not allow the use of negative numbers. Thus, the following query is invalid:

```
db.movies.find(
    {"cast" : "Charles Chaplin"},
    {"title": 1, "_id" :0}
).skip(-3)
```

When you execute this query, you'll get an error, as shown in the following screenshot:

```
> db.movies.find(
...     {"cast" : "Charles Chaplin"},
...     {"title": 1, "_id" :0}
... ).skip(-3)
Error: error: {
        "ok" : 0,
        "errmsg" : "Skip value must be non-negative, but received: -3",
        "code" : 2,
        "codeName" : "BadValue"
}
>
```

Figure 4.41: Output with a skip value of -3

The **skip()** operation does not make use of any indexes, so it performs nicely on a smaller collection but may lag noticeably on larger collections. We will cover the topic of indexing in detail in *Chapter 9, Performance*.

## SORTING DOCUMENTS

Sorting is used to return documents in a specified order. Without using explicit sorting, MongoDB does not guarantee the order in which the documents will be returned, which may vary, even if the same query is executed twice. Having a specific sort order is important, especially during pagination. During pagination, we execute the query with a specified limit and serve. For the next query, the previous records are skipped, and the next limit is returned. During this process, if the order of the records changes, some movies may appear on multiple pages and some movies may not appear at all.

The MongoDB cursor provides a **sort()** function that accepts an argument of the document type, where the document defines a sort order for specific fields. See the following query, which prints Charles Chaplin's movie titles with a sort option:

```
db.movies.find(
    {"cast" : "Charles Chaplin"},
    {"title" : 1, "_id" :0}
).sort({"title" : 1})
```

In the preceding query, you are calling the **sort()** function on the resulting cursor. The argument to the function is a document where the **title** field has a value of **1**. This specifies that the given field should be sorted in ascending order. When the query is executed after it's been sorted, the results are evident, as follows:

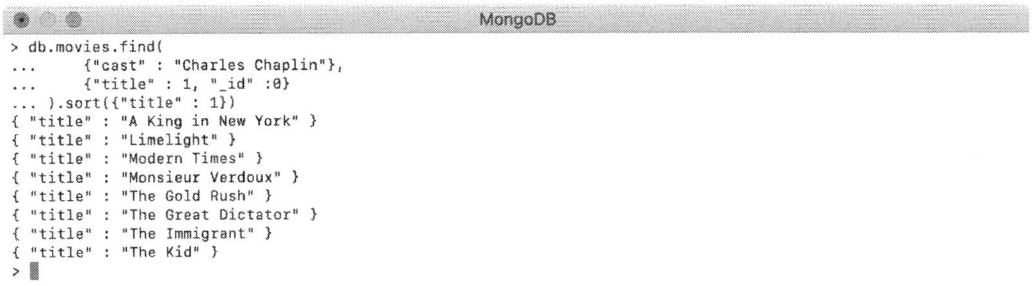

```
> db.movies.find(
...     {"cast" : "Charles Chaplin"},
...     {"title" : 1, "_id" :0}
... ).sort({"title" : 1})
{ "title" : "A King in New York" }
{ "title" : "Limelight" }
{ "title" : "Modern Times" }
{ "title" : "Monsieur Verdoux" }
{ "title" : "The Gold Rush" }
{ "title" : "The Great Dictator" }
{ "title" : "The Immigrant" }
{ "title" : "The Kid" }
>
```

Figure 4.42: Sorting in ascending order

Now, pass **-1** to the **sort** argument, which represents sorting in descending order:

```
db.movies.find(
    {"cast" : "Charles Chaplin"},
    {"title" : 1, "_id" :0}
).sort({"title" : -1})
```

The output for this is as follows:

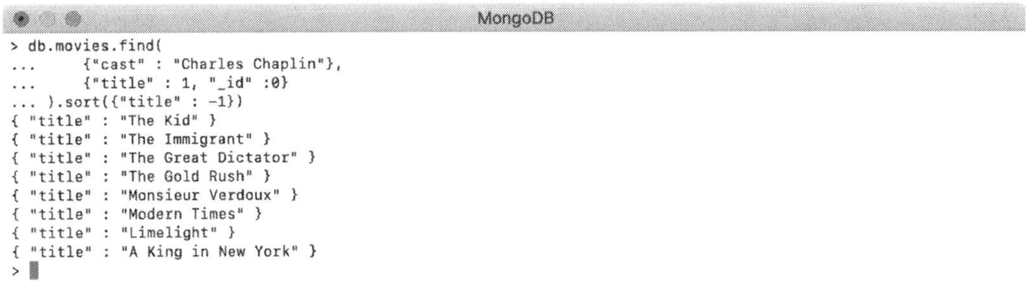

```
> db.movies.find(
...     {"cast" : "Charles Chaplin"},
...     {"title" : 1, "_id" :0}
... ).sort({"title" : -1})
{ "title" : "The Kid" }
{ "title" : "The Immigrant" }
{ "title" : "The Great Dictator" }
{ "title" : "The Gold Rush" }
{ "title" : "Monsieur Verdoux" }
{ "title" : "Modern Times" }
{ "title" : "Limelight" }
{ "title" : "A King in New York" }
>
```

Figure 4.43: Sorting in descending order

Sorting can be performed on multiple fields, and each field can have a different sorting order. Let's look at an example that sorts the IMDb ratings of movies in descending order, and the year by ascending order. The query should return 50 movies where the movie with the highest IMDb rating appearing at the top. If two movies have the same ratings, then the older movie should take precedence. The following query can be used to implement this:

```
db.movies.find()
    .limit(50)
    .sort({"imdb.rating": -1, "year" : 1})
```

Before we conclude this section, it is worth noting that any number other than a positive or negative integer, including zero, is considered invalid for sorting in MongoDB. If such a value is used, the query fails and we see the message **"bad sort specification error"**, shown as follows:

```
Error: error: {
        "ok" : 0,
        "errmsg" : "bad sort specification",
        "code" : 2,
        "codeName" : "BadValue"
}
```

In the next activity, we will use everything we've learned in this chapter to implement pagination for a genre-based movie search.

## ACTIVITY 4.01: FINDING MOVIES BY GENRE AND PAGINATING RESULTS

Your organization is planning to provide a new feature to its users where they will be able to find movies in their favorite genre. Since the movies database is huge, there's a lot of movies from each genre, and returning all the matching movie titles is not very useful. The requirement is to serve the results in small chunks.

Your task for this activity is to create a JavaScript function on the mongo shell. The function should accept a genre of the user's choice and print all the matching titles, where the titles with the highest IMDb ratings should appear at the top. Along with the genre, the function will accept two more parameters for the page size and page number. The page size defines how many records need to be displayed on one page, while the page number indicates which page the user is currently on. The following steps will help you complete this activity:

1. Write a **findMoviesByGenre** function that accepts three arguments: **genre**, **pageNumber**, and **pageSize**:

```
var findMoviesByGenre = function(genre, pageNumber, pageSize){

    ...

}
```

2. Write a query to filter the result based on **genre** and return the titles.

3. Sort the results to show the highest rated movies at the top.

4. Use the logic of skipping and limiting the results using the **pageNumber** and **pageSize** parameters.

5. Convert the result cursor into an array using the **toArray()** method.

6. Iterate through the resulting array and print all the titles.

7. Create the function in the mongo shell by copying and pasting it into the shell and executing it.

Consider that the genre provided by the user is **Action**. Here, as shown in the following output, the function is executed and shows the first page of results, showing the top five action movies:

```
●  ●  ●                          MongoDB
|> findMoviesByGenre("Action", 1, 5)
************* Page : 1
Another World
SuperBob
The Masked Saint
Band of Brothers
The Real Miyagi
> ▊
```

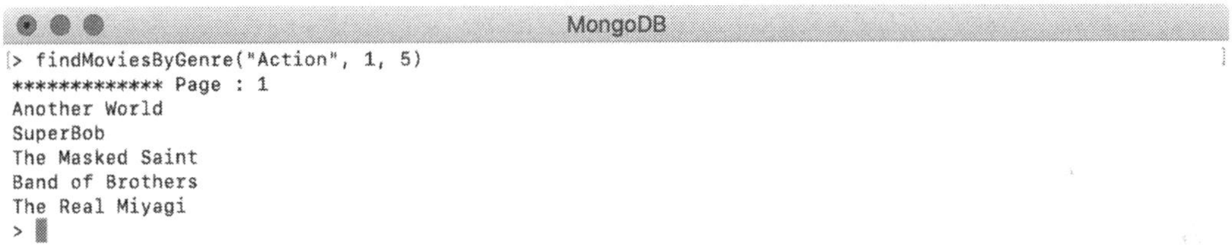

Figure 4.44: First page showing the top five action movies

Similarly, the following output shows the function returning the second page of five action movies:

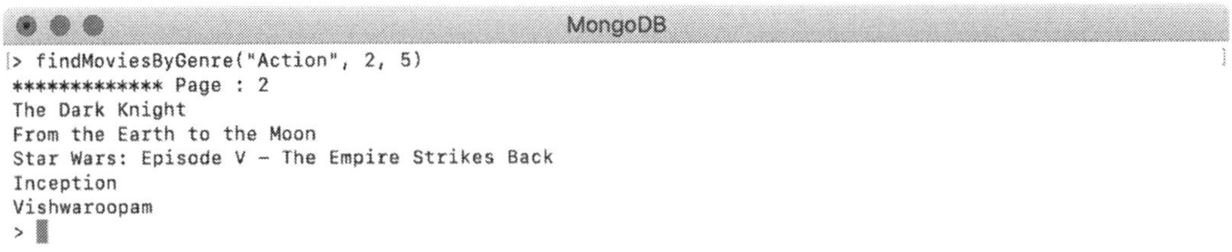

```
●  ●  ●                          MongoDB
|> findMoviesByGenre("Action", 2, 5)
************* Page : 2
The Dark Knight
From the Earth to the Moon
Star Wars: Episode V — The Empire Strikes Back
Inception
Vishwaroopam
> ▊
```

Figure 4.45: Second page of action movies

> **NOTE**
>
> The solution to this activity can be found on page 660.

# SUMMARY

We started this chapter with a detailed study of the structure of MongoDB queries and how different they are from SQL queries. Then, we implemented these queries to find and count the documents and limit the number of fields returned in the result using various examples. We also learned about the various conditional and logical operators and practiced using them in combination to notice the difference in results.

We then learned how to provide a text pattern using regular expressions to filter our search results, and covered how to query arrays and nested objects and include their specific fields in the results. Finally, we learned how to paginate large result sets by using limiting, sorting, and skipping on the documents in the result.

In the next chapter, we will learn how to insert, update, and delete documents from MongoDB collections.

# 5

# INSERTING, UPDATING, AND DELETING DOCUMENTS

## OVERVIEW

This chapter introduces you to the core operations in MongoDB, namely inserting, updating, and deleting documents in a collection. You will learn how to insert a single document or a batch of multiple documents into a MongoDB collection. You will add or autogenerate an `_id` field, replace existing documents, and update specific fields in the documents of an existing collection. Finally, you will learn how you can delete all or delete specific documents in a collection.

# INTRODUCTION

In previous chapters, we covered various database commands and queries. We learned to prepare query conditions and use them to find or count the matching documents. We also learned to use various conditional operators, logical operators, and regular expressions on fields, nested fields, and arrays. In addition to these, we learned how to format, skip, limit, and sort the documents in the result set.

Now that you know how to correctly find and represent the required documents from a collection, the next step is to learn how to modify the documents in the collection. When working on any database management system, you will be required to modify the underlying data. Consider this: you are managing our movies dataset and are often required to add new movies to the collection as they release. You will also be required to permanently remove some movies or remove incorrectly inserted movies from the database. Over a period of time, some movies may receive new awards, reviews, and ratings. In such cases, you will need to modify the details of existing movies.

In this chapter, you will learn how to create, delete, and update documents in a collection. We will start by creating new collections, adding one or more documents to a collection, and consider the importance of the unique primary key. We will then cover deleting all or deleting specific documents from a collection, as well as various delete functions provided by MongoDB and their characteristics. Next, you will learn how to replace existing documents from a collection and understand how MongoDB keeps the primary key unchanged. You will also see how to use the replace operation to perform an update or insert, which is also called upsert. Finally, you will learn to modify documents. MongoDB provides various update functions and a wide range of update operators that can be used in specific requirements. We will cover all of these functions in depth and practice with the operators.

## INSERTING DOCUMENTS

In this section, you will learn to insert new documents into a MongoDB collection. MongoDB collections provide a function named **insert()**, which is used to create a new document in a collection. The function is executed on the collection and takes the document to be inserted as an argument. The syntax of this function is shown in the next command:

```
db.collection.insert( <Document To Be Inserted>)
```

To see this in an example, open the mongo Shell, connect to the database cluster, and create a new database by using the **use CH05** command. You can give a different name to the database as per your preference. The database mentioned in this command will be created if it is not present earlier. In the following operation, we are inserting a movie with a **title** field and an **_id**, and the output is printed on the next line:

```
> db.new_movies.insert({"_id" : 1, "title" : "Dunkirk"})
WriteResult({ "nInserted" : 1 })
```

> **NOTE**
>
> In this chapter, we will be inserting, updating, and deleting a lot of documents in collections, and we do not want to corrupt the existing **sample_mflix** dataset. For this reason, we are creating a different database and using it throughout the chapter. Exercises and activities are focused on real-world scenarios and will therefore use the **sample_ mflix** dataset.

This mongo shell snippet shows the execution of the **insert** command and the result on the next line. The result (**WriteResult**) shows that one record was successfully inserted. First perform a **find()** query and confirm whether the record was created as we wanted:

```
> db.new_movies.find({"_id" : 1})
{ "_id" : 1, "title" : "Dunkirk" }
```

The preceding query and its output verify the correct insertion of our document. However, notice that the collection of **new_movies** was never present, nor did we create it. Where did the document go?

To find that, you execute the **show collections** command on the shell. This command prints the names of all collections in the current database:

```
> show collections
new_movies
```

The preceding snippet shows a new collection of **new_movies** is added to the database. This proves that, when a document **insert** command is executed, MongoDB will also create the given collection, if it does not exist already.

> **NOTE**
>
> When a new document is inserted, MongoDB does not validate the name of the collection. A typo in the collection name will result in the document being added to a completely new collection. Also, by default, MongoDB does not have any schema associated with a collection. Because of this, by giving an incorrect collection name, you may accidentally end up adding your document to any other existing collection, and MongoDB will not complain. This is why you should always be careful about the collection names in your **insert** commands.

## INSERTING MULTIPLE DOCUMENTS

When multiple documents need to be inserted into a collection, you can call the **insert()** function that you saw in the previous section multiple times, as shown here:

```
db.new_movies.insert({"_id": 2, "title": "Baby Driver"})
db.new_movies.insert({"_id": 3, "title": "title" : "Logan"})
db.new_movies.insert({"_id": 4, "title": "John Wick: Chapter 2"})
db.new_movies.insert({"_id": 5, "title": "A Ghost Story"})
```

MongoDB collections also provide the **insertMany()** function, which is a function specifically meant for inserting multiple documents into a collection. As shown in the syntax that follows, this function takes one argument of an array containing one or more documents to be inserted:

```
db.movies.insertMany(< Array of One or More Documents>)
```

To use this function, create an array of all the documents to be inserted and then pass this array to the function. The array of the same four movies will look like this:

```
[
    {"_id" : 2, "title": "Baby Driver"},
    {"_id" : 3, "title": "Logan"},
    {"_id" : 4, "title": "John Wick: Chapter 2"},
    {"_id" : 5, "title": "A Ghost Story"}
]
```

Now, you insert these four new movies into the collection:

```
db.new_movies.insertMany([
    {"_id" : 2, "title": "Baby Driver"},
    {"_id" : 3, "title": "Logan"},
    {"_id" : 4, "title": "John Wick: Chapter 2"},
    {"_id" : 5, "title": "A Ghost Story"}
])
```

The preceding command uses **insertMany()** and passes an array of four movies to it. You can see the result in the following figure:

```
●●●                              MongoDB
> db.new_movies.insertMany(
...   [
...     {"_id": 2, "title": "Baby Driver"},
...     {"_id": 3, "title": "Logan"},
...     {"_id": 4, "title": "John Wick: Chapter 2"},
...     {"_id": 5, "title": "A Ghost Story"}
...   ]
... )
{ "acknowledged" : true, "insertedIds" : [ 2, 3, 4, 5 ] }
>
```

Figure 5.1: Using insertMany() to pass an array of four movies

The result in the preceding operation contains two things. The first field is **acknowledged** with the value of **true**. This confirms the write operation was successfully performed. The second field of the result lists down all the **IDs** of the inserted documents. To insert multiple documents, it is preferable to use the **insertMany()** function, because insertion happens as a single operation. On the other hand, the insertion of each document separately will be executed as a number of different database commands and will make the process slower.

> **NOTE**
>
> You can insert as many documents as you want using the function
> **insertMany()**. However, the batch size should not exceed 100,000. On
> a mongo shell, if you try to insert more than 100,000 documents in a single
> batch, the query will fail. If you do the same thing using a programming
> language, the MongoDB driver will internally split a single operation into
> multiple batches of permissible sizes and perform the batch insert.

## INSERTING DUPLICATE KEYS

In any database system, a primary key is always unique in the table. Similarly, in
MongoDB collections, the value expressed by the **_id** field is a primary key, and so it
must be unique. If you try to insert a document whose key is already present in the
collection, you will get a *Duplicate Key Error*.

In the previous examples, we have already inserted a movie whose **_id** is **2**. Now we
will try to duplicate the primary key in another **insert** operation:

```
db.new_movies.insert({"_id" : 2, "title" : "Some other movie"})
```

This **insert** operation inserts a dummy movie into the collection and explicitly
mentions the **_id** field as **2**. When the command is executed, we get a duplicate key
error with a detailed message, as can be seen in the following figure:

```
● ● ●                                    MongoDB
> db.new_movies.insert({"_id": 2, "title": "Some other movie"})
WriteResult({
        "nInserted" : 0,
        "writeError" : {
                "code" : 11000,
                "errmsg" : "E11000 duplicate key error collection: test.new_movies index: _id_ dup key: { _id
 : 2.0 }"
        }
})
> ▮
```

Figure 5.2: Error message for the duplicate _id field

Similarly, the operation of a bulk insert fails when one or more of the documents in the given array has a duplicate **_id**. For example, consider the following snippet:

```
db.new_movies.insertMany([
    {"_id" : 6, "title" : "some movie 1"},
    {"_id" : 7, "title" : "some movie 2"},
    {"_id" : 2, "title" : "Movie with duplicate _id"},
    {"_id" : 8, "title" : "some movie 3"},
])
```

Here, using the **insertMany()** operation, you will insert four different movies into your collection. However, the third movie has an **_id** of **2**, and we know that another movie with the same **_id** already exists. This leads to an error, as can be seen in the following figure:

```
●  ●  ●                        MongoDB
> db.new_movies.insertMany([
...     {"_id" : 6, "title" : "some movie 1"},
...     {"_id" : 7, "title" : "some movie 2"},
...     {"_id" : 2, "title" : "Movie with duplicate _id"},
...     {"_id" : 8, "title" : "some movie 3"},
[... ])                                                                    ]
2020-01-27T06:21:48.105+1100 E  QUERY    [js] uncaught exception: BulkWriteError
({
        "writeErrors" : [
                {
                        "index" : 2,
                        "code" : 11000,
                        "errmsg" : "E11000 duplicate key error collection: array
.new_movies index: _id_ dup key: { _id: 2.0 }",
                        "op" : {
                                "_id" : 2,
                                "title" : "Movie with duplicate _id"
                        }
                }
        ],
        "writeConcernErrors" : [ ],
        "nInserted" : 2,
        "nUpserted" : 0,
        "nMatched" : 0,
        "nModified" : 0,
        "nRemoved" : 0,
        "upserted" : [ ]
}) :
BulkWriteError({
        "writeErrors" : [
                {
                        "index" : 2,
                        "code" : 11000,
                        "errmsg" : "E11000 duplicate key error collection: array
.new_movies index: _id_ dup key: { _id: 2.0 }",
                        "op" : {
                                "_id" : 2,
                                "title" : "Movie with duplicate _id"
```

Figure 5.3: Error message for the duplicate _id field

When you execute the command, it fails with a detailed error message. The error message clearly indicates that the value of **2** is duplicated in the **_id** field. However, the value of **nInserted** indicates that two documents have been inserted successfully. To confirm this, you will query the database and observe the output:

```
> db.new_movies.find({"_id" : {$in : [6, 7, 2, 8]}})
{ "_id" : 2, "title" : "Baby Driver" }
{ "_id" : 6, "title" : "some movie 1" }
{ "_id" : 7, "title" : "some movie 2" }
```

From the **find()** command and its output, shown in the previous snippet, we can conclude that the command failed while inserting the third document. However, the documents inserted before the third one will remain in the database.

## INSERTING WITHOUT _ID

So far, we have learned the basics of creating new documents in a collection. In all the examples we showed up till now, we explicitly added a primary key (**_id** field). However, in Chapter 2, Documents and Data Types, we learned that while creating a new document, MongoDB verifies the presence and uniqueness of a given primary key and, if the primary key is not already present, the database autogenerates it and adds it into the document.

The following is a snippet from the mongo shell where an **insert** command is executed. The **insert** command is trying to push a new movie into the collection, but the document does not have an **_id** field. The result on the very next line shows that the document is successfully created inside the collection:

```
> db.new_movies.insert({"title": "Thelma"})
WriteResult({ "nInserted" : 1 })
```

Now, you query the newly inserted document and see if it has the **_id** field. To do so, query the collection using the value of the **title** field:

```
> db.new_movies.find({"title" : "Thelma"})
{ "_id" : ObjectId("5df6a0e1b32aea114de21834"), "title" : "Thelma" }
```

In the previous snippet, the result shows that the document exists in the collection and an autogenerated **_id** field is added to the document. As we learned in Chapter 2, Documents and Data Types, the autogenerated primary is derived from the **ObjectId** constructor and it is globally unique. The same is true for bulk inserts. For instance, consider the following snippet:

```
db.new_movies.insertMany([
    {"_id" : 9, "title" : "movie_1"},
    {"_id" : 10, "title" : "movie_2"},
    {"title" : "movie_3"},
    {"_id" : 8, "title" : "movie_4"},
])
```

Here, the **insertMany()** command is pushing four movies into the collection. Out of the four new documents, the third document does not have a primary key; however, the rest of the documents have respective primary keys. The result of this can be seen as follows:

```
MongoDB
> db.new_movies.insertMany([
...      {"_id" : 9, "title" : "movie_1"},
...      {"_id" : 10, "title" : "movie_2"},
...      {"title" : "movie_3"},
...      {"_id" : 8, "title" : "movie_4"},
[... ])                                                              ]
{
        "acknowledged" : true,
        "insertedIds" : [
                9,
                10,
                ObjectId("5e2decafc0e6d22f1778865f"),
                8
        ]
}
>
```

Figure 5.4: Inserting a movie without _id

The output of the query indicates the query was successful, and the **insertedIds** field shows that all documents except the third were inserted with the given keys and the third document has got an autogenerated primary key.

While working on datasets, our documents will have unique fields that can be used as primary keys. Primary keys are the ones that can uniquely identify a record. MongoDB's autogenerated keys are useful in terms of uniqueness, but they are meaningless in terms of the data the respective document represents. Also, these autogenerated keys are lengthy and thus tedious to type in or remember. Therefore, we should always try to use the primary keys that already exist in the datasets. For example, in a user's dataset, the **email_address** field is the best example of a primary key. However, in the case of movies, there is no field that can be unique. So, for the purpose of movies, we can use autogenerated primary keys.

In this section, we covered how to create a single as well as multiple documents in a collection. During this, we learned that in MongoDB an **insert** command also creates the underlying collection if it does not exist. We also learned that the primary keys need to be unique in a collection, and if a new document does not have a primary key, MongoDB autogenerates and adds it.

# DELETING DOCUMENTS

In this section, we will see how to remove the documents from a collection. To delete one or more documents from a collection, we have to use one of the various delete functions provided by MongoDB. Each of these functions has different behaviors and purposes. To delete documents from a collection, we have to use one of the delete functions and provide a query condition to specify which documents should be deleted. Let's take a look at this in detail.

## DELETING USING DELETEONE()

As the name suggests, the function **deleteOne()** is used to delete a single document from a collection. It accepts a document representing a query condition. Upon successful execution, it returns a document containing the total number of documents deleted (represented by the field **deletedCount**) and whether the operation was confirmed (given by the field **acknowledged**). However, as the method deletes only one document, the value of **deletedCount** is always one. If the given query condition matches more than one document in the collection, only the first document will be deleted.

To see this, write a delete command using **deleteOne()** and see the results:

```
> db.new_movies.deleteOne({"_id": 2})
{ "acknowledged" : true, "deletedCount" : 1 }
```

In the preceding code snippet, you executed the **deleteOne()** command and passed a query condition of **{_id : 2}**. This means that you want to delete a document for which the value of **_id** is **2**. The output on the next line indicates that the deletion was successful.

## EXERCISE 5.01: DELETING ONE OF MANY MATCHED DOCUMENTS

In this exercise, you will use a query that matches more than one document and verify that only the first document is deleted when you do this. Perform the following steps to complete this exercise:

1. Use a regular expression in a query to match all movies where the **title** field starts with the word **movie**, as follows:

```
({"title" : {"$regex": "^movie"}}
```

The following snippet from the mongo shell shows that when you use the preceding query condition in a **find()** query, you get four movies:

```
> db.new_movies.find({"title" : {"$regex": "^movie"}})
{ "_id" : 9, "title" : "movie_1" }
{ "_id" : 10, "title" : "movie_2" }
{ "_id" : ObjectId("5ef2666a6c3f28e14fddc816"), "title" : "movie_3" }
{ "_id" : 8, "title" : "movie_4" }
```

2. Use the same query condition with **deleteOne()** to match all movies with titles starting with the word **movie**:

```
> db.new_movies.deleteOne({"title" : {"$regex": "^movie"}})
{ "acknowledged" : true, "deletedCount" : 1 }
```

The output in the second line here confirms that only one document is deleted successfully.

3. To find out which document is deleted, execute the same **find()** query on your collection:

```
> db.new_movies.find({"title" : {"$regex": "^movie"}})
{ "_id" : 10, "title" : "movie_2" }
{ "_id" : ObjectId("5ef2666a6c3f28e14fddc816"), "title" : "movie_3" }
{ "_id" : 8, "title" : "movie_4" }
```

The preceding snippet confirms that, although all four documents matched the query condition, only the first document is deleted.

## DELETING MULTIPLE DOCUMENTS USING DELETEMANY()

To delete multiple documents that match the given criteria, you can execute the **deleteOne()** function multiple times. However, in that case, each document will be deleted in a separate database command, which can slow down the performance. MongoDB collections provide the function **deleteMany()** to delete multiple documents in a single command.

The **deleteMany()** function must be provided with a query condition, and all the documents that match the given query will be removed:

```
> db.new_movies.deleteMany({"title" : {"$regex": "^movie"}})
{ "acknowledged" : true, "deletedCount" : 3 }
```

The **deleteMany()** command in the previous snippet uses the same regular expression used in the previous examples. The output in the next line indicates that all three movies whose titles start with the word "movie" are deleted.

The behavior of both of the delete functions, in terms of matching the documents to given query expressions, is similar to finding documents, as we saw in the previous chapter. Passing an empty query document is equivalent to not passing any filter, and thus, all the documents are matched.

In the following example, both of the commands have been given an empty query document:

```
db.new_movies.deleteOne({})
db.new_movies.deleteMany({})
```

The **deleteOne()** function will delete the document that is found first. However, the **deleteMany()** function will delete all the documents in the collection. In the same manner, the following queries perform a **null** check on a non-existent field. In MongoDB, a non-existent field is considered to be **null** and so the given condition will match all of the documents in the collection:

```
db.new_movies.deleteOne({"non_existent_field" : null})
db.new_movies.deleteMany({"non_existent_field" : null})
```

> **NOTE**
>
> Unlike finding documents, delete operations are **write** operations, and they permanently change the state of the collection. Therefore, while writing query conditions, which include null checks, you should always ensure that there is no typo in the field name. An incorrect field name may lead to the removal of all documents from the collection.

## DELETING USING FINDONEANDDELETE()

Apart from the two delete methods we saw previously, there is another function named **findOneAndDelete()**, which, as the name indicates, finds and deletes one document from the collection. Although it behaves similarly to the **deleteOne()** function, it provides a few more options:

* It finds one document and deletes it.

* If more than one document is found, only the first one will be deleted.

* Once deleted, it returns the deleted document as a response.

* In the case of multiple document matches, the **sort** option can be used to influence which document gets deleted.

* Projection can be used to include or exclude fields from the document in response.

Here, use **findOneAndDelete()** to delete a record and get the deleted document as a response:

```
> db.new_movies.findOneAndDelete({"_id": 3})
{ "_id" : 3, "title" : "Logan" }
```

In the preceding snippet, the delete command finds a document by its **_id**. The response in the next line shows that the deleted document is returned in the response. This is a very useful feature. Firstly, because it clearly indicates which record was matched and deleted. Secondly, it allows you to further process the deleted record. In some cases, you may want to store the record in an archive collection, or you may want to inform some other system about this deletion. If the query matches multiple documents, only the first document gets deleted. However, you can use an option to sort the matched documents and control which document gets deleted, as can be seen in the following snippet:

```
db.new_movies.insertMany([
    { "_id" : 11, "title" : "movie_11" },
    { "_id" : 12, "title" : "movie_12" },
    { "_id" : 13, "title" : "movie_13" },
    { "_id" : 14, "title" : "movie_14" },
    { "_id" : 15, "title" : "series_15" }
])
```

Using the preceding **insert** command, you have inserted five new documents into your collection. In the following snippet, you use the **findOneAndDelete()** command, which uses a regular expression to find those titles in the collection that start with the word **movie**. The query will match four documents; however, you will sort the **_id** field in descending order so that the document with the **_id** of 14 gets deleted:

```
> db.new_movies.findOneAndDelete(
        {"title" : {"$regex" : "^movie"}},
        {sort : {"_id" : -1}}
    )
{ "_id" : 14, "title" : "movie_14" }
```

This operation demonstrates how a sort option can influence which documents get deleted. Without providing the sort option, the document with an **_id** of 11 will be deleted.

As we have seen, this delete function always returns the deleted document in the response. We can also use the projection option to control the fields that are included or excluded in the document in response:

```
> db.new_movies.findOneAndDelete(
        {"title" : {"$regex" : "^movie"}},
```

```
      {sort : {"_id" : -1}, projection : {"_id" : 0, "title" : 1}}
  )
{ "title" : "movie_13" }
```

In this delete command, we are using the option of projection to include only the **title** field in the response. The output on the next line confirms the successful deletion and the document in response shows only the **title** field.

## EXERCISE 5.02: DELETING A LOW-RATED MOVIE

The movie archives team in your organization is the team that ensures that most highly rated movies are present in the database. In order to improve the user experience, they want to frequently perform quality checks on the database and remove the movies with the lowest ratings. To measure quality, they want to consider IMDb ratings and the total number of votes because a higher number of votes means a more reliable rating.

Based on this, they asked you to remove a movie with a high number of IMDb votes, a low average rating, and the least awards won from the list of low-rated movies. Your task for this exercise is to connect to the **sample_mflix** cluster and execute a delete command so that a movie with least awards won, an IMDb rating of less than 2, and more than 50,000 votes gets deleted. Then, record the **title** and **_id** of the deleted movie. The following steps will help you complete this exercise:

1. As you have to delete one movie, you can use either the **deleteOne()** or **findOneAndDelete()** function and prepare a query filter using the IMDb rating and votes. However, to ensure that the movie with the least awards gets deleted, you need to sort the films in ascending order of awards won and let the first movie in the resulting list be deleted. This means you will need to use **findOneAndDelete()**. First, open any text editor and start writing the query. Begin by writing the query filter. The first condition is to find movies with less than a two-point rating in IMDb:

```
("imdb.rating" : {$lt : 2}}
```

   The IMDb rating is a nested field; therefore, you will use the dot notation to access the field and then write the condition using the **$lt** operator.

2. Next, the second condition says the total number of IMDb votes should be more than 50,000. Add this condition to your query:

```
("imdb.rating" : {$lt : 2}, "imdb.votes" : {$gt : 50000}}
```

   The second condition is expressed using the **$gt** operator.

3. Now, write a **findOneAndDelete()** function and add the preceding query into it:

```
db.movies.findOneAndDelete(
   {"imdb.rating" : {$lt : 2}, "imdb.votes" : {$gt : 50000}}
)
```

The preceding command will find movies with less than 2-star ratings and more than 50,000 votes and delete the first one. However, you also want to ensure that the movie with the least awards gets deleted.

4. To delete the movie with the least awards won, add a **sort** option:

```
db.movies.findOneAndDelete(
   {"imdb.rating" : {$lt : 2}, "imdb.votes" : {$gt : 50000}},
   {"sort" : {"awards.won" : 1}}
)
```

This command sorts the filtered movies in ascending order of awards won.

5. Now, add a projection option to return only the **_id** and **title** field of the deleted movie:

```
db.movies.findOneAndDelete(
   {"imdb.rating" : {$lt : 2},"imdb.votes" : {$gt : 50000}},
   {
      "sort" : {"awards.won":1},
      "projection" : {"title" : 1}
   }
)
```

The preceding command has a projection option wherein the **title** field is explicitly included. This means that all the other fields will be excluded, while **_id** is included by default.

6.  Finally, open the mongo shell and connect to the Atlas cluster. Use the **sample_mflix** database and execute the preceding command. You should see the following output:

```
MongoDB
> db.movies.findOneAndDelete(
...      {"imdb.rating" : {$lt : 2},"imdb.votes" : {$gt : 50000}},
...      {
...          "sort" : {"awards.won":1},
...          "projection" : {"title" : 1}
...      }
[... )
{ "_id" : ObjectId("573a13c1f29313caabd64b87"), "title" : "Disaster Movie" }
>
```

Figure 5.5: Deleting the low-rated movie

As seen in the preceding output, the command was executed successfully. The document returned in the response correctly includes the **_id** and **title** of the deleted movie.

In this exercise, you used one of the delete functions to correctly delete a specific record from the real-world collection of movies.

# REPLACING DOCUMENTS

In this section, you will learn how you can completely replace the documents in a collection.

Sometimes you may want to replace an incorrectly inserted document in a collection. Or consider that, often, the data stored in documents is changed over time. Or, perhaps, to support your product's new requirements, you may want to alter the way your documents are structured or change the fields in your documents. In all such cases, you will need to replace the documents.

In the previous section, we used a new database of **CH05** which we will continue using in this section. In the same database, create a collection named **users** and insert a few users into it, as follows:

```
> db.users.insertMany([
  {"_id": 2, "name": "Jon Snow", "email": "Jon.Snow@got.es"},
  {"_id": 3, "name": "Joffrey Baratheon", "email":
    "Joffrey.Baratheon@got.es"},
  {"_id": 5, "name": "Margaery Tyrell", "email":
    "Margaery.Tyrell@got.es"},
```

```
    {"_id": 6, "name": "Khal Drogo", "email": "Khal.Drogo@got.es"}
])


{ "acknowledged" : true, "insertedIds" : [ 2, 3, 5, 6 ] }
```

You can see that the command is successful, and four users are added. Before going any further, quickly use the **find()** command to ensure no other documents are present in the collection except for the newly inserted ones:

```
> db.users.find()
{ "_id" : 2, "name" : "Jon Snow", "email" : "Jon.Snow@got.es" }
{ "_id" : 3, "name" : "Joffrey Baratheon", "email" :
  "Joffrey.Baratheon@got.es" }
{ "_id" : 5, "name" : "Margaery Tyrell", "email" :
  "Margaery.Tyrell@got.es" }
{ "_id" : 6, "name" : "Khal Drogo", "email" : "Khal.Drogo@got.es" }
```

In the documents in the preceding snippet, each user has a unique ID, name, and email address. Now, suppose the user **Margaery Tyrell** gets married to **Joffrey Baratheon**, and she wishes to change her surname to her husband's. To accomplish this, you will have to change her name as well as her email.

As per the requirement, the new record for **Margaery Tyrell** should look like this:

```
{"_id": 5, "name": "Margaery Baratheon", "email": "Margaery.Baratheon@
got.es"}
```

To replace a single document in a collection, MongoDB provides the method **replaceOne()**, which accepts a query filter and a replacement document. The function finds the document that matches the criteria and replaces it with the provided document. The following example demonstrates this:

```
> db.users.replaceOne(
  {"_id" : 5},
  {"name": "Margaery Baratheon", "email": "Margaery.Baratheon@got.es"}
)


{ "acknowledged" : true, "matchedCount" : 1, "modifiedCount" : 1 }
```

Here, the first argument is the query filter to identify the document to be replaced, and the second argument is the new document. The output clearly indicates that the given query matched one document and one document was updated. The query filter need not always be the **_id** field. It can be any query that filters using any field or combination of multiple fields and operators. For example, the following replace command will have the same effect as the previous one, as long as there is only one user with the name of **Margaery Tyrell**. If there is more than one document that matches the query, then only the first one will be replaced:

```
db.users.replaceOne(
   {"name": "Margaery Tyrell },
   {"name": "Margaery Baratheon", "email": "Margaery.Baratheon@got.es"}
)
```

## _ID FIELDS ARE IMMUTABLE

In the previous example, you will have noticed that there was no **_id** field in the replacement document. In that case, do you think MongoDB must have added and autogenerated a primary key field? Query the document and find out:

```
> db.users.find({"name" : "Margaery Baratheon"})
{"_id": 5, "name": "Margaery Baratheon", "email":
  "Margaery.Baratheon@got.es" }
```

The preceding output indicates that the **_id** of the original document is retained in the new document.

This is because **_id** fields are immutable in MongoDB. Immutable fields are like normal fields; however, once assigned with a value, their value cannot be changed again. The **_id** field serves as a unique identifier of a document and so should not be changed as long as the document exists.

It is similar to the user accounts you create on the various online portals, where your username is your unique identifier. You can change your password, or any other information in your profile, however, most portals won't allow you to change your username. Even if they allow you to modify your username, the old username cannot be assigned to anyone because there might be someone who still knows you by your old username.

This was the theory of why the **_id** fields in MongoDB are immutable. However, try modifying the field and observe what happens:

```
db.users.replaceOne(
   {"name" : "Margaery Baratheon"},
   {"_id": 9, "name": "Margaery Baratheon", "email":
   "Margaery.Baratheon@got.es"}
)
```

Here, the replace command finds a document named **Margaery Baratheon**. In the replacement document, it also provides a new value for the **_id** field:

```
> db.users.replaceOne(
...    {"name": "Margaery Baratheon"},
...    {"_id": 9, "name": "Margaery Baratheon", "email": "Margaery.Baratheon@got.es"}
[... )
2019-12-17T07:05:02.252+1100 E  QUERY    [js] WriteError({
        "index" : 0,
        "code" : 66,
        "errmsg" : "After applying the update, the (immutable) field '_id' was found to have been altered to
_id: 9.0",
        "op" : {
                "q" : {
                        "name" : "Margaery Baratheon"
                },
                "u" : {
                        "_id" : 9,
                        "name" : "Margaery Baratheon",
```

Figure 5.6: Error when _id is being modified

In this example, you executed a replace command, as shown in the preceding snippet, where the replacement document now has an explicit **_id** field. The command failed with a very detailed error message. The preceding snapshot highlights the most important part of the error message, which indicates that the field is immutable. Hence, the update was rolled back, and no change happened to the record.

## UPSERT USING REPLACE

In the previous sections, we learned that we can find an existing document in a collection and replace it with a new document. However, there will be times you want to replace an existing document with a new one and, if the document does not already exist, insert the new document. This operation is called an update (if found) or insert (if not found), which is further shortened to upsert. Upsert is a feature provided by many databases and MongoDB supports it as well.

# WHY USE UPSERT?

For the simple scenarios that we have seen above, upsert sounds a bit unnecessary—especially when the same operation can be performed easily using two different commands. For example, we can first execute a replace command and check the results. The value of the matched count will tell whether the document is found in the collection. If the document is not found, we can then execute an **insert** command.

However, in real-world scenarios, you will mostly be doing these operations in large numbers. Consider that your system receives daily updates from a user server, where the server sends you all the documents that were modified during the day. These daily updates might include records of the new users signed up with the server as well as changes to the existing users' profiles. On a large-scale system, performing a two-step update or insert operation for each of the records will be very time-consuming and error prone. However, having a dedicated command, you can simply prepare and execute an upsert command for each of the records you receive and let MongoDB do the update or insert.

Consider the following records in the **users** collection:

```
> db.users.find()
{"_id": 2, "name": "Jon Snow", "email": "Jon.Snow@got.es"}
{"_id": 3, "name": "Joffrey Baratheon", "email":
 "Joffrey.Baratheon@got.es"}
{"_id": 5, "name": "Margaery Baratheon", "email":
 "Margaery.Baratheon@got.es"}
{"_id": 6, "name": "Khal Drogo", "email": "Khal.Drogo@got.es"}
```

At the end of an episode, King Joffrey has been killed. As a result, **Margaery** wants to switch back to her old surname, and **Tommen Baratheon** becomes the new king. The update you receive from the user server contains the updated record for **Margaery** and the new record for **Tommen**, as follows:

```
{"name": "Margaery Tyrell", "email": "Margaery.Tyrell@got.es"}
{"name": "Tommen Baratheon", "email": "Tommen.Baratheon@got.es"}
```

In the following commands, you pass an additional argument of **{upsert: true}**, which makes these commands upsert commands:

```
db.users.replaceOne(
    {"name" : "Margaery Baratheon"},
    {"name": "Margaery Tyrell", "email": "Margaery.Tyrell@got.es"},
    { upsert: true }
)

db.users.replaceOne(
    {"name" : "Tommen Baratheon"},
    {"name": "Tommen Baratheon", "email": "Tommen.Baratheon@got.es"},
    { upsert: true }
)
```

When you execute the commands one after the other on a mongo shell, you see the following output:

```
> db.users.replaceOne(
...    {"name" : "Margaery Baratheon"},
...    {"name": "Margaery Tyrell", "email": "Margaery.Tyrell@got.es"},
...    { upsert: true }
... )
{ "acknowledged" : true, "matchedCount" : 1, "modifiedCount" : 1 }
>
> db.users.replaceOne(
...    {"name" : "Tommen Baratheon"},
...    {"name": "Tommen Baratheon", "email": "Tommen.Baratheon@got.es"},
...    { upsert: true }
... )
{
        "acknowledged" : true,
        "matchedCount" : 0,
        "modifiedCount" : 0,
        "upsertedId" : ObjectId("5f21f41b19421fdf08471445")
}
>
```

Figure 5.7: Output for the upsert operation

The result of the first upsert indicates that there was a match found, and the document has been updated. However, the second one denotes the match was not found, and a new document was upserted with an autogenerated primary key.

# REPLACING USING FINDONEANDREPLACE()

We have seen the **replaceOne()** function, which, after successful execution, returns the counts of matched and updated documents. MongoDB provides another operation, **findOneAndReplace()**, to perform the same operations. However, it provides more options. Its main features are as follows:

- As the name indicates, it finds one document and replaces it.

- If more than one document is found matching the query, the first one will be replaced.

- A sort option can be used to influence which document gets replaced if more than one document is matched.

- By default, it returns the original document.

- If the option of **{returnNewDocument: true}** is set, the newly added document will be returned.

- Field projection can be used to include only specific fields in the document returned in response.

To see the **findOneAndReplace()** function in action, add five documents to a movie collection:

```
db.movies.insertMany([
    { "_id": 1011, "title" : "Macbeth" },
    { "_id": 1513, "title" : "Macbeth" },
    { "_id": 1651, "title" : "Macbeth" },
    { "_id": 1819, "title" : "Macbeth" },
    { "_id": 2117, "title" : "Macbeth" }
])
```

Now, say that these five movies, all having the same **title**, were released and inserted in different calendar years. When these records were originally inserted, the field for the year of release wasn't added. As a result, to find the latest movie with this **title**, you need to use the incremental **_id** field, where the movie with the largest **_id** value is the latest one. To make future find queries simpler, you have been instructed to find the document of the latest movie with this **title** and add a flag of **latest: true** to that document. So, when someone tries to find that movie, they can pass this additional filter to get the latest one in the response, as follows:

```
db.movies.findOneAndReplace(
    {"title" : "Macbeth"},
```

```
    {"title" : "Macbeth", "latest" : true},
    {
        sort : {"_id" : -1},
        projection : {"_id" : 0}
    }
)
```

In the previous snippet, you found the document for a movie by its **title** and replaced it with another document that contains an additional field—that is, **latest : true**. Apart from that, the command used the option of **sort** so that the record with the largest value **_id** appears on top. The command also uses a projection option to include only the **title** field in the response. The output is as follows:

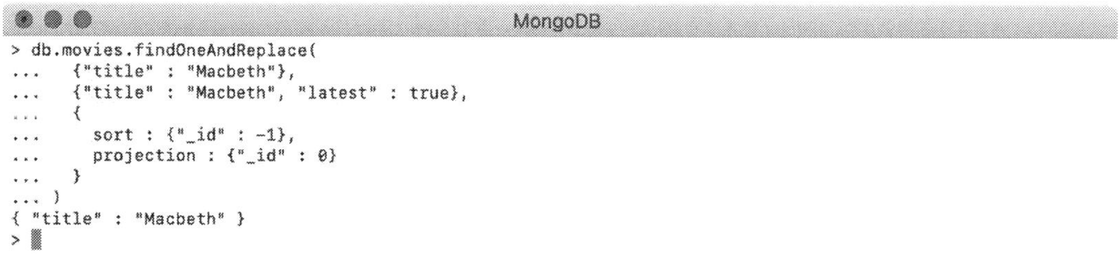

```
● ● ●                           MongoDB
> db.movies.findOneAndReplace(
...    {"title" : "Macbeth"},
...    {"title" : "Macbeth", "latest" : true},
...    {
...        sort : {"_id" : -1},
...        projection : {"_id" : 0}
...    }
... )
{ "title" : "Macbeth" }
>
```

Figure 5.8: Output for the findOneAndReplace command

The preceding snapshot confirms that the operation is successful, and the **title** of the old document is included in the response. Alternatively, if you are required to get the updated document in the response, you can make use of the **returnNewDocument** flag in the command. Setting this flag to true will return the replaced document from the collection, as follows:

```
db.movies.findOneAndReplace(
    {"title" : "Macbeth"},
    {"title" : "Macbeth", "latest" : true},
    {
        sort : {"_id" : -1},
        projection : {"_id" : 0},
        returnNewDocument : true
    }
)
```

This replace command works similarly to the previous one, but the only difference is that it is using an additional option of **returnNewDocument**, which is set to **true**:

```
> db.movies.findOneAndReplace(
...    {"title" : "Macbeth"},
...    {"title" : "Macbeth", "latest" : true},
...    {
...      sort : {"_id" : -1},
...      projection : {"_id" : 0},
...      returnNewDocument : true
...    }
... )
{ "title" : "Macbeth", "latest" : true }
>
```

Figure 5.9: Output after setting returnNewDocument to true

This output shows that having the **returnNewDocument** flag set to **true** returns the new document. Now, quickly query the database and see whether the replace command did actually work:

```
> db.movies.find({"title" : "Macbeth"})


{ "_id" : 1011, "title" : "Macbeth" }
{ "_id" : 1513, "title" : "Macbeth" }
{ "_id" : 1651, "title" : "Macbeth" }
{ "_id" : 1819, "title" : "Macbeth" }
{ "_id" : 2117, "title" : "Macbeth", "latest" : true }
```

The preceding output shows the latest record now has the desired flag.

## REPLACE VERSUS DELETE AND RE-INSERT

As we have seen in the previous sections, there are dedicated functions to find and replace documents in a collection. It is possible to replace a document using a combination of delete and insert, where you delete an existing document and insert a new one. This two-step operation of the delete and **insert** combination gives you the same results; let's see how.

To perform the two-step, replace operation using delete and **insert**, use the same example that you saw in the **findOneAndReplace()** section.

First, delete all the previously inserted or modified documents from the collection:

```
> db.movies.deleteMany({})
{ "acknowledged" : true, "deletedCount" : 5 }
```

Now, insert the five documents again:

```
db.movies.insertMany([
    { "_id": 1011, "title" : "Macbeth" },
    { "_id": 1513, "title" : "Macbeth" },
    { "_id": 1651, "title" : "Macbeth" },
    { "_id": 1819, "title" : "Macbeth" },
    { "_id": 2117, "title" : "Macbeth" }
])
```

Now, find the document of the latest movie titled **Macbeth** and add the flag **"latest" : true** to it:

```
var deletedDocument = db.movies.findOneAndDelete(
                            {"title" : "Macbeth"},
                            {sort : {"_id" : -1}}
    )



db.movies.insert(
   {"_id" : deletedDocument._id, "title" : "Macbeth", "latest" : true}
)
```

This snippet shows two different commands. The first is a **findOneAndDelete()** command that finds a movie by its **title** and also uses the sort option so that only the movie with largest **_id** gets deleted. The result of the deletion operation, which is the deleted document, is stored in a variable of **deletedDocument**.

The next command in the preceding snippet is an insert operation that re-inserts the same movie along with the flag **latest : true**. While doing so, it uses the **_id** value from the deleted document, so that the new record is inserted with the same primary key:

```
●●●                              MongoDB
> var deletedDocument = db.movies.findOneAndDelete(
...                          {"title" : "Macbeth"},
...                          {sort : {"_id" : -1}}
...    )
> db.movies.insert(
...    {"_id" : deletedDocument._id, "title" : "Macbeth", "latest" : true}
... )
WriteResult({ "nInserted" : 1 })
>
```

Figure 5.10: Output for delete first and then insert

The preceding output indicates that you have executed both commands sequentially, and the response shows that one document was inserted successfully, which can be verified using the **find** operation:

```
> db.movies.find()
{ "_id" : 1011, "title" : "Macbeth" }
{ "_id" : 1513, "title" : "Macbeth" }
{ "_id" : 1651, "title" : "Macbeth" }
{ "_id" : 1819, "title" : "Macbeth" }
{ "_id" : 2117, "title" : "Macbeth", "latest" : true }
```

The result of a **find** operation on the collection confirms that the two-step replacement operation worked perfectly.

Although the results are exactly the same, the two-step operation is more error prone. The two-step operation executes two totally different commands, one after the other. In the first command, your MongoDB client or your programming language's driver sends the **delete** command to the server. The server then validates and processes the command to remove the document. Then the deleted document is sent back to the client over the network. The client or driver then parses the returned result into the language-specific object. In our case, we are executing commands from a mongo shell, and so the results are parsed into the JSON format and stored in the variable **deleteDocument**.

Next, your MongoDB client or the driver sends another command to insert the new document. The new document, which is in JSON format in our case, gets transformed into BSON and sent over the wire to the server. For the MongoDB server, this **insert** command is like any other fresh **insert** commands. The server performs the initial validation of the document, checks whether the **_id** field is present, and also validates the uniqueness of the value in the collection. If the document is found to be valid, the insert will happen.

Now that you are familiar with the details of the two-step replace operation, consider the following potential shortfalls of using it over dedicated replace functions:

1.  First of all, in the delete and insert method, the data is transferred over the wire multiple times. This involves the drivers or clients to parse the data in multiple stages. This will slow down the overall performance.

2.  When multiple clients are constantly reading and writing to your collections, concurrency issues may arise. As an example, say you have successfully deleted a record and before you insert the new record, some other client accidentally inserts a different record with the same **_id**.

3. Your database client or driver may lose its connection to the database in the middle of two operations. For example, the delete operation was successful but insertion could not happen. To avoid such issues, you will have to run your commands in a transaction so that the failure of one operation can revert the previously successful operations in the same transaction.

The dedicated replace functions, on the other hand, are effectively atomic and are therefore safe to use in concurrent environments. An atomic operation is the smallest unit of operation that cannot be divided further. For this reason, when an atomic operation is performed, it is executed in one go as a single unit. Thus, dedicated replace functions are safer as compared to the delete and insert combination.

The dedicated functions first find a document to be replaced and lock it. The lock is then released only after the operation is finished. Because of this, no other client or process is able to modify that particular document while it is locked. Also, the replace operation replaces only the rest of the fields in the documents, keeping **_id** untouched. There is no chance that other processes will be able to push a different document with the same **_id** value.

Thus, it is always preferable to use the specialty functions provided by MongoDB.

# MODIFY FIELDS

In the previous sections, we learned that we could replace any document in a MongoDB collection once it has been inserted. During the replace operation, a document in the database will be replaced with a completely new document while keeping the same primary key. The replacement operations are quite useful when it comes to rectifying errors and to incorporating data changes or updates. However, in most cases, updates will affect only one or a few fields of a document. Think about any movie record from the **sample_mflix** dataset, where most of its fields (such as the title, cast, directors, duration, and so on) may never change. However, over a period of time, the movie may receive new comments, new reviews, and ratings.

The find and replace operation is very useful when all or most fields of a document are modified. But, using it to update only particular fields in the documents will not be easy. To do so, the replacement document you provide will need to have all the unchanged fields with their existing values and the changed fields with their new values. For a smaller document, this doesn't sound like a problem, but for large documents, like our movie records, the command will be bulky and error prone. We will see this with an example of a command that we will not execute on the database.

Say a record of a movie was added to the database, but the value of the field **year** is incorrect. The following is an example of how the command will look if the replace operation is used to correct the value. In the first statement, we find the movie document and assign it to a variable. Next is the actual replace command where the replacement document with all of its fields needs to be provided. We use the variable **movie** that we assigned in the first line and refer to all of its unchanged fields. The last field in the replacement document is the field of **year** with the new value:

```
// Find the movie and assign it to a variable
var movie = db.movies.findOne({"title" : "The Italian"})

// A replace function that keeps all the fields same except "year"
db.movies.replaceOne(
  {"title" : "The Italian"},
  {
    "plot" : movie.plot,
    "genres" : movie.genres,
    "runtime" : movie.runtime,
    "rated" : movie.rated,
    "cast" : movie.cast,
    "title" : movie.title,
    "fullplot" : movie.fullplot,
    "language" : movie.language,
    "released" : movie.released,
    "directors" : movie.directors,
    "writers" : movie.writers,
    "awards" : movie.awards,
    "imdb" : movie.imdb,
    "countries" : movie.countries,
    "type" : movie.type,
    "tomatoes" : movie.tomatoes,
    "year" : 1915
  }
)
```

The problem with the command is that it is too bulky, especially since we only want to update a single field. It re-enters all the fields, even if they are not changed, and there is a good possibility of a typo being introduced when we are re-assigning the unchanged field values. Moreover, this is a two-step operation and introduces concurrency problems that are hard to debug.

To understand the concurrency problem, imagine that the find operation in the first statement is successful, and the next statement is a replace command that refers to all the unchanged fields from the existing documents; but before the second statement is executed, the actual document in the database was modified by some other client or thread. Once your statement is executed, the updates added by the other client will be lost forever.

This is why the replace operation should only be used when all or most of the fields are being modified. To modify one or only a few fields of a document, MongoDB provides the **update** command. Let's explore this in the next section.

## UPDATING A DOCUMENT WITH UPDATEONE()

To update the fields of a single document in a collection, we can use the function **updateOne()**. This function, which is provided by MongoDB collections, accepts a query condition to find the record to be updated, and a document that specifies the field-level update expressions. The third argument to the function is to provide miscellaneous options and is optional. The syntax of this function looks like this:

```
db.collection.updateOne(<query condition>,
  <update expression>, <options>)
```

Like the replace commands, **updateOne()** cannot be used to update the **_id** field of a document because it is immutable. Once the update is performed, it returns a detailed result in the form of a document, which indicates how many records were matched and how many records were updated.

Before using this function, first delete all the previously inserted and modified records from the collection:

```
> db.movies.deleteMany({})
{ "acknowledged" : true, "deletedCount" : 5 }
```

Now, use the following **insert** command to add four new records to the collection:

```
> db.movies.insertMany([
  {"_id": 1, "title": "Macbeth", "year": 2014, "type": "series"},
```

```
    {"_id": 2, "title": "Inside Out", "year": 2015,
      "type": "movie", "num_mflix_comments": 1},
    {"_id": 3, "title": "The Martian", "year": 2015,
      "type": "movie", "num_mflix_comments": 1},
    {"_id": 4, "title": "Everest", "year": 2015,
      "type": "movie", "num_mflix_comments": 1}
])


{ "acknowledged" : true, "insertedIds" : [ 1, 2, 3, 4 ] }
```

Write and execute your first update command to change the field **year** for the movie **Macbeth**:

```
db.movies.updateOne(
    {"title" : "Macbeth"},
    {$set : {"year" : 2015}}
)
```

In the preceding command, the first argument to the **updateOne()** function is the query condition, wherein you specify that the name of the movie should be **Macbeth**. The second argument is a document that specifies a new field of **year** and its value. Here, we are using a new operator, **$set**, to assign values to the fields provided in a document. In the upcoming sections, we will learn more about the **$set** operator and also a few other operators that are supported by all the update functions.

When the command is executed on a mongo shell, the output looks like this:

```
> db.movies.updateOne(
    {"title" : "Macbeth"},
    {$set : {"year" : 2015}}
)
{ "acknowledged" : true, "matchedCount" : 1, "modifiedCount" : 1 }
```

The output is a document that denotes the following:

- **"acknowledged"** : **true** indicates that the update was performed and confirmed.

- **"matchedCount"** : **1** shows the number of documents found and chosen for the update (1 in this case.)

- **"modifiedCount"** : **1** refers to the number of documents modified (1 in this case.)

The following query and the output that follows confirm that the update command was executed correctly:

```
> db.movies.find({"title" : "Macbeth"})
{ "_id" : 1, "title" : "Macbeth", "year" : 2015, "type" : "series" }
```

In the preceding record, the field **year** is correctly set to **2015**, which was previously **2014**. If we execute the same command again, no update will be performed as the value is already **2015**:

```
> db.movies.updateOne(
    {"title" : "Macbeth"},
    {$set : {"year" : 2015}}
)
{ "acknowledged" : true, "matchedCount" : 1, "modifiedCount" : 0 }
```

*Figure 5.12* shows the output of executing the same update command again. The resulting document indicates that there was one document that was matched as eligible for the update; however, no document was updated.

## MODIFYING MORE THAN ONE FIELD

The **$set** operator that we used to update a field of a document can also be used to modify multiple fields of a document. As seen in the previous examples, **$set** is provided with a document that contains the update expression. Similarly, to modify more than one field, the update expression can contain more than one field and value pair. For example, consider this snippet:

```
db.movies.updateOne(
    {"title" : "Macbeth"},
    {$set : {"type" : "movie", "num_mflix_comments" : 1}}
)
```

In the preceding operation, the update expression **{"type": "movie", "num_mflix_comments": 1}}** specifies two fields and their values. Out of these, the **num_mflix_comment** field does not exist in the respective movie. Execute the command on our movie collection and see the output:

```
> db.movies.updateOne(
   {"title" : "Macbeth"},
   {$set : {"type" : "movie", "num_mflix_comments" : 1}}
)
{ "acknowledged" : true, "matchedCount" : 1, "modifiedCount" : 1 }
```

The preceding figure shows that the operation was successful, and one record is modified as expected. Now, query the document and see if the fields are modified correctly:

```
> db.movies.find({"title" : "Macbeth"}).pretty()
{
   "_id" : 1,
   "title" : "Macbeth",
   "year" : 2015,
   "type" : "movie",
   "num_mflix_comments" : 1
}
```

The document from the collection indicates that the movie type has been modified correctly, and a new field named **num_mflix_comments** has been added with the given value. Thus, you have seen that **$set** can be used to update multiple fields in the same command, and if a field is new, it will be added to the document with the specified value.

Before we move on to the next section, it is important to know that, in an update operation, updating the same field multiple times is valid, irrespective of the field's value. As seen in the previous output, the **year** field of the movie **Macbeth** is set to 2015. Modify the same field multiple times in the same command:

```
db.movies.updateOne(
   {"title" : "Macbeth"},
   {$set : {"year" : 2015, "year" : 2015, "year" : 2016, "year" : 2017}}
)
```

The preceding update command, which uses the **$set** operator, sets the year multiple times. The first two expressions set the field to its current value; however, the last two expressions have different values. Execute the command and observe the behavior:

```
db.movies.updateOne(
   {"title" : "Macbeth"},
   {$set : {"year" : 2015, "year" : 2015, "year" : 2016, "year" : 2017}}
)
{ "acknowledged" : true, "matchedCount" : 1, "modifiedCount" : 1 }
```

As expected, the operation is valid, and one document is modified. Query the document from the collection and see the value of the **year** field:

```
> db.movies.find({"title" : "Macbeth"}).pretty()
{
   "_id" : 1,
   "title" : "Macbeth",
   "year" : 2017,
   "type" : "movie",
   "num_mflix_comments" : 1
}
```

In the preceding output, we prove that, when the same field is provided multiple times, the update happens from left to right. First, the **year** field (which was already 2015) is set to 2015 twice; then with the third expression, the year is set to 2016; and lastly, with the rightmost expression, it is set to 2017.

In any valid scenario, you will hardly ever update a field twice in an update operation. However, even if you do so, perhaps accidentally, you now know the behavior, and this will help you in debugging.

## MULTIPLE DOCUMENTS MATCHING A CONDITION

As the name of the **updateOne()** function indicates, it always updates only one document in the collection. If the given query condition matches more than one document, only the first document will be modified:

```
db.movies.updateOne(
    {"type" : "movie"},
    {$set : {"flag" : "modified"}}
)
```

The preceding operation finds documents where **type** is **movie** and sets the value of **flag** as **modified**. Remember, we have a total of three documents of type **movie** in our movie collection. When the command is executed on our collection, the result will look like this:

```
db.movies.updateOne(
    {"type" : "movie"},
    {$set : {"flag" : "modified"}}
)
{ "acknowledged" : true, "matchedCount" : 1, "modifiedCount" : 1 }
```

The result of the execution indicates that one document was matched and chosen for the update, and one document was actually modified. Thus, it proves that even if there is more than one document that matches the given query condition, only one document is chosen and updated.

## UPSERT WITH UPDATEONE()

In the previous section, we learned in detail about the upsert operation. When upsert-based updates are executed, the document will be updated if it is found; however, if the document is not found, a new document is created inside the collection. Similar to the replace operations, **updateOne()** also supports upserts with an additional flag in the command. Consider the following snippet:

```
db.movies.updateOne(
    {"title" : "Sicario"},
    {$set : {"year" : 2015}}
)
```

The preceding operation executes an update command on the movie **Sicario**, which does not exist in our collection. When the command is executed without any **upsert** flag, no update is performed:

```
> db.movies.updateOne(
    {"title" : "Sicario"},
    {$set : {"year" : 2015}}
)
{ "acknowledged" : true, "matchedCount" : 0, "modifiedCount" : 0 }
```

The output indicates that no document was matched, and no document was updated. Now, we will execute the same command with an **upsert** flag:

```
db.movies.updateOne(
    {"title" : "Sicario"},
    {$set : {"year" : 2015}},
    {"upsert" : true}
)
```

The preceding operation uses a third argument, which contains a document with the **upsert** flag set to **true**, which is false by default. The output can be seen here:

```
                                    MongoDB
> db.movies.updateOne(
...     {"title" : "Sicario"},
...     {$set : {"year" : 2015}},
...     {"upsert" : true}
[... )
{
        "acknowledged" : true,
        "matchedCount" : 0,
        "modifiedCount" : 0,
        "upsertedId" : ObjectId("5ef5484b76db1f20a60917d2")
}
>
```

Figure 5.11: Update a non-existing movie with the upsert flag

So, the output of executing the command is slightly different this time. It indicates that no document was matched, and no document was updated. However, **"upsertedId" : ObjectId("5e…")** indicates that one document was inserted with an autogenerated primary key.

The following query finds the document using the autogenerated primary key. When you execute this query on your shell, you will have to use the **ObjectId** that was generated in the previous command:

```
> db.movies.find({"_id" : ObjectId("5ef5484b76db1f20a60917d2")}).pretty()
{
   "_id" : ObjectId("5ef5484b76db1f20a60917d2"),
   "title" : "Sicario",
   "year" : 2015
}
```

When we query the collection with the newly created primary key value, we get the newly inserted record.

One thing to notice here is that the new document has two fields, out of which the field **year** was part of the update expression; however, **title** was part of the query condition. When MongoDB creates a new document as part of an **upsert** operation, it combines fields from the update expressions as well as query conditions.

## UPDATING A DOCUMENT WITH FINDONEANDUPDATE()

We have seen the function **updateOne()**, which modifies one document from a collection. MongoDB also provides the **findOneAndUpdate()** function, which is capable of doing everything that **updateOne()** does with a few additional features, which we'll explore now. The syntax of this function is the same as **updateOne()**:

```
db.collection.findOneAndUpdate (
   <query condition>,
   <update expression>,
   <options>
)
```

**findOneAndUpdate()** needs at least two arguments where the first one is a query condition to find the document to be modified and the second one is the update expression. By default, it returns the old document in the response. In some scenarios, getting back the old document is really useful, especially when it needs to be archived somewhere. However, by passing a flag as an argument, the behavior of the function can be changed to return the new document in the response. Consider the following example.

The record for the movie **Macbeth** in our collection has only one comment, given by the field **num_mflix_comments**. Modify the count of these comments using the update command as follows:

```
db.movies.findOneAndUpdate(
    {"title" : "Macbeth"},
    {$set : {"num_mflix_comments" : 10}}
)
```

The preceding command finds a movie by its **title** and sets **num_mflix_comments** to the value of 10. We can see that it looks pretty similar to the **updateOne()** commands, and the effects on the collection will be exactly the same. However, the only difference we will see here is the response, as can be seen in the following figure:

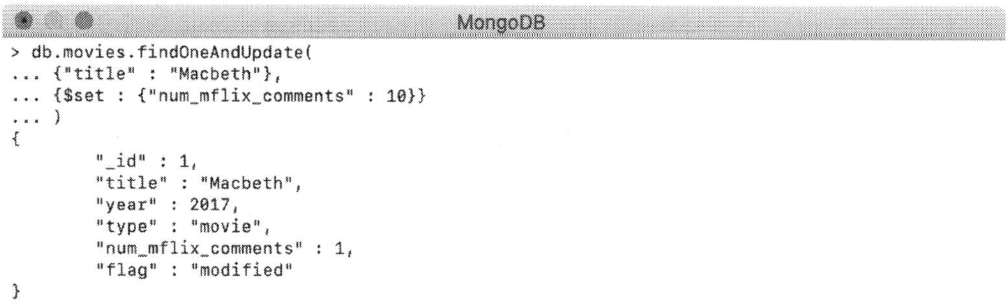

```
●●●                                   MongoDB
> db.movies.findOneAndUpdate(
... {"title" : "Macbeth"},
... {$set : {"num_mflix_comments" : 10}}
... )
{
        "_id" : 1,
        "title" : "Macbeth",
        "year" : 2017,
        "type" : "movie",
        "num_mflix_comments" : 1,
        "flag" : "modified"
}
```

Figure 5.12: Update using fineOneAndUpdate()

The output shows that the **findOneAndUpdate()** function did not return the query stats, such as how many records were matched and how many records were modified. Instead, it returns the document in its old state. Now query and verify whether the update was successful:

```
> db.movies.find({"title" : "Macbeth"}).pretty()
{
    "_id" : 1,
    "title" : "Macbeth",
    "year" : 2017,
    "type" : "movie",
    "num_mflix_comments" : 10,
    "flag" : "modified"
}
```

The query and its output here confirm that the number of comments is modified to its new value.

## RETURNING A NEW DOCUMENT IN RESPONSE

So far, we have used the function with two arguments where the first is the query condition and the second is the update expression. However, the function also supports an optional third argument, which is used to provide miscellaneous options to the commands. Out of these options, the **Boolean** flag `returnNewDocument` can be used to control which document should be returned in the response. By default, the value of this flag is set to false, which is why we get the old document without passing the options. However, setting this flag to true, we get back the modified or new document in the response. For example, consider the following snippet:

```
db.movies.findOneAndUpdate(
    {"title" : "Macbeth"},
    {$set : {"num_mflix_comments" : 15}},
    {"returnNewDocument" : true}
)
```

The preceding operation sets the comments count to 15 and also passes the flag of **returnNewDocument** set to true. The output can be seen as follows:

```
> db.movies.findOneAndUpdate(
...       {"title" : "Macbeth"},
...       {$set : {"num_mflix_comments" : 15}},
...       {"returnNewDocument" : true}
... )
{
        "_id" : 1,
        "title" : "Macbeth",
        "year" : 2017,
        "type" : "movie",
        "num_mflix_comments" : 15,
        "flag" : "modified"
}
>
```

Figure 5.13: findOneAndUpdate() with the returnNewDocument flag

The output shows that by setting the flag **returnNewDocument** to **true**, the response shows the modified document, which also confirms that the count of comments has been modified correctly.

With the optional third argument to the function, we can also provide an expression to limit the number of fields returned in the documents (also called a projection expression). The projection expression can be used for both cases—that is, returning an old or new document as a response:

```
db.movies.findOneAndUpdate(
    {"title" : "Macbeth"},
```

```
{$set : {"num_mflix_comments" : 20}},
{
    "projection" : {"_id" : 0, "num_mflix_comments" : 1},
    "returnNewDocument" : true
}
)
```

The preceding update command finds the movie by **title** and sets the count of comments to 20. As the third argument, it passes two options to the command. The first option is the projection expression, which includes only **num_mflix_comments** in the response and excludes the **_id** explicitly. By using the second operation, the function will return the modified document. The output can be seen here:

```
●  ●  ●                              MongoDB
> db.movies.findOneAndUpdate(
... {"title" : "Macbeth"},
... {$set : {"num_mflix_comments" : 20}},
...     {
...           "projection" : {"_id" : 0, "num_mflix_comments" : 1},
...           "returnNewDocument" : true
...     }
[... )
{ "num_mflix_comments" : 20 }
> ▐
```

Figure 5.14: findOneAndUpdate() with projection

We can see that the projection expression has excluded the **_id** and included only the **num_mflix_comments** field, as expected.

## SORTING TO FIND A DOCUMENT

So far, we have covered two update functions, and both are capable of updating a single document at a time. If more than one document is matched by the given query condition, the first document will be chosen for modification. This behavior is common between both functions. However, the **findOneAndUpdate()** function provides an additional option to sort the matching documents in a specific order. Using the sort option, you can influence which document is selected for the modification.

The sort option is specified as a field under the optional third argument of the **findOneAndUpdate()** function. The value of the sort field must be a document containing valid sort expressions. We will now see an example of using the sort option in an update command.

*Figure 5.15* shows that our collection has four records, which are of the movie type. Each one has a sequential **_id** field where the record inserted latest has the largest value in the sequence:

```
●  ●  ●                          MongoDB
> db.movies.find({"type" : "movie"})
{ "_id" : 1, "title" : "Macbeth", "year" : 2017, "type" : "movie", "num_mflix_comments" : 20, "fl
ag" : "modified" }
{ "_id" : 2, "title" : "Inside Out", "year" : 2015, "type" : "movie", "num_mflix_comments" : 1 }
{ "_id" : 3, "title" : "The Martian", "year" : 2015, "type" : "movie", "num_mflix_comments" : 1 }
{ "_id" : 4, "title" : "Everest", "year" : 2015, "type" : "movie", "num_mflix_comments" : 1 }
>
```

Figure 5.15: A collection having four records

Write a command that will use the same filter of **{"type" : "movie"}** and put the flag **"latest" : true** to the last inserted record:

```
db.movies.findOneAndUpdate(
   {"type" : "movie"},
   {$set : {"latest" : true}},
   {
      "returnNewDocument" : true,
      "sort" : {"_id" : -1}
   }
)
```

The update command in the preceding snippet sets the **latest** flag to true. The query condition finds a document with a **type** of **movie**. The options argument sets a flag to return the modified document in the response and also specifies a sort expression to sort documents by descending order of the primary key:

```
●  ●  ●                          MongoDB
> db.movies.findOneAndUpdate(
...      {"type" : "movie"},
...      {$set : {"latest" : true}},
...      {
...          "returnNewDocument" : true,
...          "sort" : {"_id" : -1}
...      }
... )
{
        "_id" : 4,
        "title" : "Everest",
        "year" : 2015,
        "type" : "movie",
        "num_mflix_comments" : 1,
        "latest" : true
}
>
```

Figure 5.16: Update one record by sorting matched documents

The response to the update command, as shown in *Figure 5.16*, indicates that the record with **_id : 4** has the latest flag. This is due to the specified sort option, which ordered the matching records so that the largest IDs will appear first. The function picked up the first record and modified it.

## EXERCISE 5.03: UPDATING THE IMDB AND TOMATOMETER RATING

Your movie database has records of a large number of worldwide movies along with their details. Your product owners want you to keep the database updated with the most recent changes. People still love to watch some of the timeless classic movies and rate them or post their reviews, so the ratings of some of the popular movies, which were released a few decades ago, keep changing on a daily basis. Your organization has decided to incorporate rating updates for all movies irrespective of their release date. As a proof of concept, they have chosen *The Godfather*, one of the all-time great movies, and asked you to update it with the latest IMDb and Tomatometer ratings. If your product team is happy with the update, they will sign off on receiving regular updates from these platforms. Your task is to write and execute an update operation to update these ratings.

These are the latest IMDb and Tomatometer viewer ratings of the movie:

**IMDb rating**

Rating: 9.2 and Votes: 1,565,120

**Tomatometer viewer rating**

Rating: 4.76, number of reviews: 733, 777, meter 98

Take a look at the database to find the current values of these ratings:

```
db.movies.find(
   {"title" : "The Godfather"},
   {"imdb" : 1, "tomatoes.viewer" : 1, "_id" : 0}
).pretty()
```

This query finds and prints the IMDb and Tomatometer viewer rating of the movie **The Godfather**:

```
●  ●  ●                          MongoDB
> db.movies.find(
...     {"title" : "The Godfather"},
...     {"imdb" : 1, "tomatoes.viewer" : 1, "_id" : 0}
... ).pretty()
{
        "imdb" : {
                "rating" : 9.2,
                "votes" : 1038358,
                "id" : 68646
        },
        "tomatoes" : {
                "viewer" : {
                        "rating" : 4.4,
                        "numReviews" : 725773,
                        "meter" : 98
                }
        }
}
>
```

Figure 5.17: Ratings of the movie The Godfather

The output shows the current ratings from the **sample_mflix** database.

1. Open any text editor and write a **findOneAndUpdate()** command along with a query parameter:

```
db.movies.findOneAndUpdate(
   {"title" : "The Godfather"}
)
```

2. Now, use the **$set** operator to set the IMDb fields. As the IMDb rating is still the same, you will only update the field **votes** field. To refer to the nested field of **votes**, use the dot notation:

```
db.movies.findOneAndUpdate(
   {"title" : "The Godfather"},
   {
     $set: {"imdb.votes" : 1565120}
   }
)
```

3. Next, add another update expression for Tomatometer ratings. For the Tomatometer viewer rating, you only need to update the fields of **rating** and **numReviews**. As these are two separate fields, add two separate update expressions to the **$set** operator. As these fields are nested within a nested object, use dot notation two times:

```
db.movies.findOneAndUpdate(
  {"title" : "The Godfather"},
  {
    $set: {
      "imdb.votes" : 1565120,
      "tomatoes.viewer.rating": 4.76,
      "tomatoes.viewer.numReviews": 733777
    }
  }
)
```

4. Now that your update query is complete, add the flag to return the modified document in response along with projection on specific fields:

```
db.movies.findOneAndUpdate(
  {"title" : "The Godfather"},
  {
    $set: {
      "imdb.votes" : 1565120,
      "tomatoes.viewer.rating": 4.76,
      "tomatoes.viewer.numReviews": 733777
    }
  },
  {
    "projection" : {"imdb" : 1, "tomatoes.viewer" : 1, "_id" : 0},
    "returnNewDocument" : true
  }
)
```

5. Open the mongo shell and connect to the Atlas **sample_mflix** database. Copy the previous command and execute it:

```
> db.movies.findOneAndUpdate(
...     {"title" : "The Godfather"},
...     {
...         $set: {
...             "imdb.votes" : 1565120,
...             "tomatoes.viewer.rating": 4.76,
...             "tomatoes.viewer.numReviews": 733777
...         }
...     },
...     {
...         "projection" : {"imdb" : 1, "tomatoes.viewer" : 1, "_id" : 0},
...         "returnNewDocument" : true
...     }
... )
{
        "imdb" : {
                "rating" : 9.2,
                "votes" : 1565120,
                "id" : 68646
        },
        "tomatoes" : {
                "viewer" : {
                        "rating" : 4.76,
                        "numReviews" : 733777,
                        "meter" : 98
                }
        }
}
>
```

Figure 5.18: Updated ratings

The previous output shows that the respective fields have been updated correctly.

In this exercise, you have practiced using **findOneAndUpdate()** and **$set** to update the values of nested fields. Next, we will learn to update multiple documents using **updateMany()**.

## UPDATING MULTIPLE DOCUMENTS WITH UPDATEMANY()

In the previous sections, we learned to find one document and modify or update its fields. Many times though, you will want to perform the same update operation on multiple documents in a collection. MongoDB provides the **updateMany()** function, which updates multiple documents at a time. Similar to **updateOne()**, the **updateMany()** function takes two mandatory arguments. The first argument is the query condition, and the second is the update expression. The third argument, which is optional, is used to provide miscellaneous options. Upon execution, this function updates all the documents that match the given query condition. The syntax of the function looks like this:

```
db.collection.updateMany(<query condition>,
  <update expression>, <options>)
```

We will write and execute an update operation on our movie collection. Consider that our movie collection has four movies that were released in 2015. Add a field named **languages** to these movies, as follows:

```
db.movies.updateMany(
    {"year" : 2015},
    {$set : {"languages" : ["English"]}}
)
```

This update operation uses two arguments. The first is to find all the movies that were released in 2015. The second argument is an update expression, which uses the **$set** operator, to add a new field named **languages**. The value of the **languages** field is an array containing English as the only language. The output can be seen here:

```
db.movies.updateMany(
    {"year" : 2015},
    {$set : {"languages" : ["English"]}}
)
{ "acknowledged" : true, "matchedCount" : 4, "modifiedCount" : 4 }
```

The output indicates that the operation was successful, and, like the **updateOne()** function, a similar document is returned in the response. The response indicates that the query condition matched a total of four documents, and all were modified.

In this section, we learned about modifying fields of one or more documents in MongoDB collections. We have covered three update functions, out of which **updateOne()** and **findOneAndUpdate()** are used to update one document in a collection while **updateMany()** is used to update multiple documents in a collection. The following are a few important points about the update operations and are applicable to all three functions:

- None of the update functions allows you to change the **_id** field.

- The order of the fields in a document is always maintained, except when the update includes renaming a field. However, the **_id** field will always appear first. (We will cover renaming fields in the next section).

- Update operations are atomic on a single document. A document cannot be modified until another process has finished updating it.

- All of the update functions support upsert. To execute an upsert command, **upsert : true** needs to be passed as an option.

In the next section, we will cover various update operators and their usages.

# UPDATE OPERATORS

In order to facilitate different types of update commands, MongoDB provides various update operators or update modifiers such as set, multiply, increment, and more. In the previous sections, we used the operator **$set**, which is one of the update operators provided by MongoDB. In this section, we will learn some of the most commonly used operators and examples. Before we go through the operators, we will discuss their syntax. The following code snippet shows the basic syntax of an update expression that uses an update operator:

```
{
    <update operator>: {<field1> : <value1>, ... }
}
```

As per the preceding syntax, an operator can be assigned a document containing one or more pairs of field and value. The operator is then applied to each field using the respective value. An update expression like the previous one is useful when all the given fields need to be updated with the same operator. You may also want to update different fields of a document using different operators. For such cases, an update expression can contain multiple update operators, each separated by a comma.

```
{
    <update operator 1>: {<field11> : <value11>, ... },
    <update operator 2>: {<field21> : <value21>, ... },
    ...,
}
```

The preceding snippet shows the syntax for using multiple operators in the same update expression. In an update operation, each of these operators will be executed in sequence.

Let's go through each of the update operators in detail now.

## SET ($SET)

As we have already seen, the **$set** operator is used to set the values of fields in a document. It is the most commonly used operator, as it can be easily used to set values of any type of field or add new fields in a document. The operator takes a document that contains pairs of field names and their new values. If the given field is not already present, it will be created.

## INCREMENT ($INC)

The increment operator **($inc)** is used to increment the value of a numeric field by a specific number. The operator accepts a document containing pairs of a field name and a number. Given a positive number, the value of the field will be incremented and if a negative number is provided, the value will be decremented. It is obvious but worth mentioning that the **$inc** operator can only be used with numeric fields; if attempted for non-numeric fields, the operation fails with an error.

Currently, in our collection, the document for a **Macbeth** movie looks as shown here:

```
> db.movies.find({"title" : "Macbeth"}).pretty()
{
  "_id" : 1,
  "title" : "Macbeth",
  "year" : 2017,
  "type" : "movie",
  "num_mflix_comments" : 20,
  "flag" : "modified"
}
```

Now, write an update using the **$inc** operator on two fields, out of which one exists in the document and the other does not:

```
db.movies.findOneAndUpdate(
  {"title" : "Macbeth"},
  {$inc : {"num_mflix_comments" : 3, "rating" : 1.5}},
  {returnNewDocument : true}
)
```

The preceding update operation finds a movie by its **title**, increments the **num_mflix_comments** field by 3 and a non-existent field called **rating** by **1.5**. It also sets **returnNewDocument** to **true**, so that the updated record will be returned in the response. You can see the output in the following screenshot:

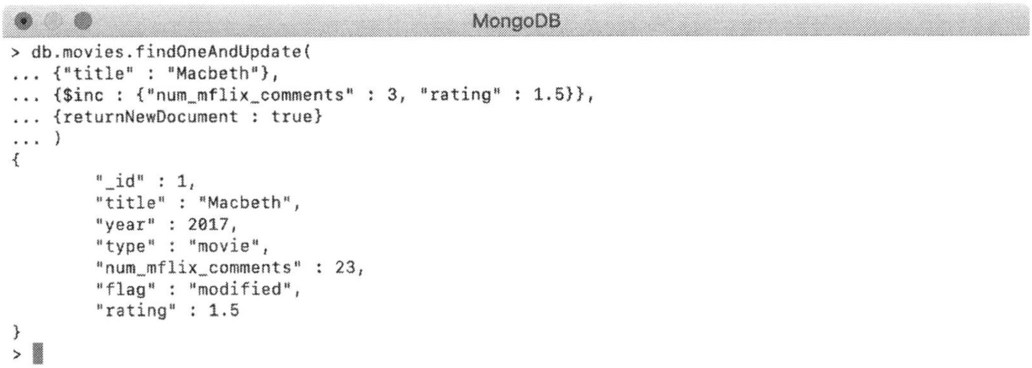

```
●  ●  ●                          MongoDB
> db.movies.findOneAndUpdate(
... {"title" : "Macbeth"},
... {$inc : {"num_mflix_comments" : 3, "rating" : 1.5}},
... {returnNewDocument : true}
... )
{
        "_id" : 1,
        "title" : "Macbeth",
        "year" : 2017,
        "type" : "movie",
        "num_mflix_comments" : 23,
        "flag" : "modified",
        "rating" : 1.5
}
> █
```

Figure 5.19: Incrementing the number of comments and the rating score

So, the update command was successful. The field of **num_mflix_comments** is correctly incremented by 3 and **rating** (which was a nonexistent field) is now added to the document with a specified value. We will see an example of decrementing the field values:

```
db.movies.findOneAndUpdate(
    {"title" : "Macbeth"},
    {$inc : {"num_mflix_comments" : -2, "rating" : -0.2}},
    {returnNewDocument : true}
)
```

The preceding command uses the **$inc** operator on two fields and provides negative numbers:

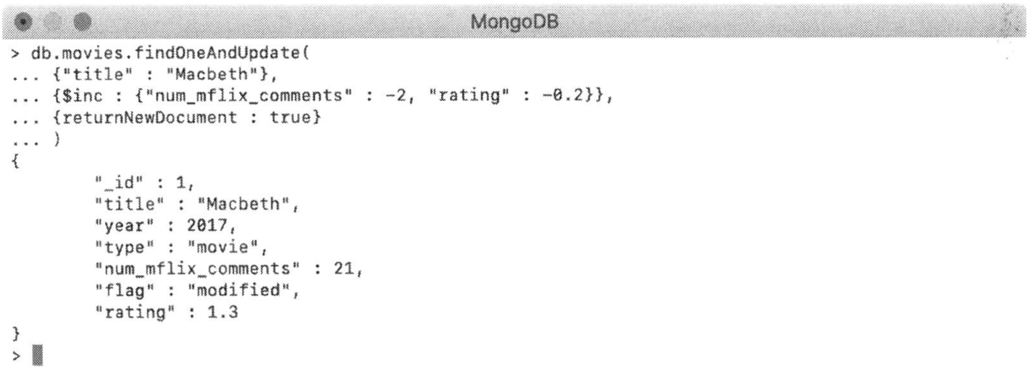

```
●  ●  ●                          MongoDB
> db.movies.findOneAndUpdate(
... {"title" : "Macbeth"},
... {$inc : {"num_mflix_comments" : -2, "rating" : -0.2}},
... {returnNewDocument : true}
... )
{
        "_id" : 1,
        "title" : "Macbeth",
        "year" : 2017,
        "type" : "movie",
        "num_mflix_comments" : 21,
        "flag" : "modified",
        "rating" : 1.3
}
> █
```

Figure 5.20: Decrementing the number of comments and rating score

As seen in *Figure 5.20*, the negative increments lead to the response. The **rating**, which was 1.5, is now reduced by 0.2 and **num_mflix_comments** is reduced to 21.

## MULTIPLY ($MUL)

The multiplication **($mul)** operator is used to multiply the value of a numeric field by the given number. The operator accepts a document containing pairs of field names and numbers and can only be used on numeric fields. For example, consider the following snippet:

```
db.movies.findOneAndUpdate(
   {"title" : "Macbeth"},
   {$mul : {"rating" : 2}},
   {returnNewDocument : true}
)
```

The preceding update operation finds a movie by its **title**, uses **$mul** to multiply the value of the field of **rating** by 2, and adds an option to return the modified document in the response. You can see this as follows:

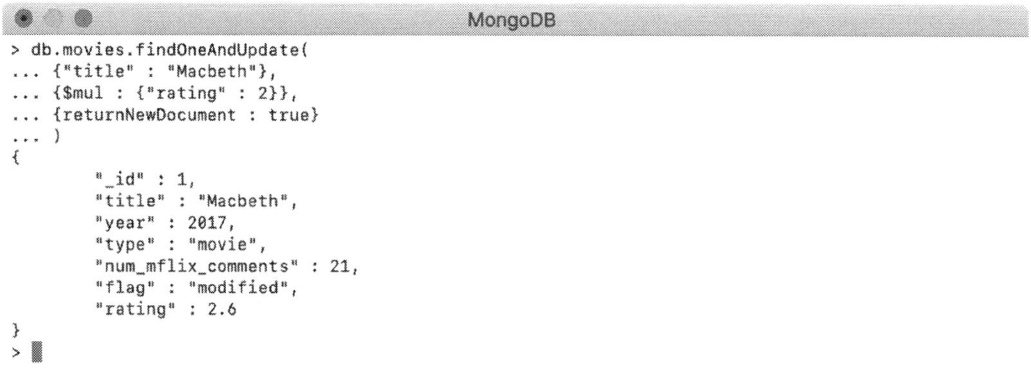

```
●  ●  ●                              MongoDB
> db.movies.findOneAndUpdate(
... {"title" : "Macbeth"},
... {$mul : {"rating" : 2}},
... {returnNewDocument : true}
... )
{
        "_id" : 1,
        "title" : "Macbeth",
        "year" : 2017,
        "type" : "movie",
        "num_mflix_comments" : 21,
        "flag" : "modified",
        "rating" : 2.6
}
>
```

Figure 5.21: Doubling the rating score

The output shows the value of the field **rating** is multiplied by 2. When using a non-existent field with **$mul**, we should always remember that no matter what multiplier we provide, the field will be created and always set to zero. This is because, with a multiplication operation, the value of a nonexistent numeric field is assumed to be zero. Thus, using any multiplier on zero results in zero:

```
db.movies.findOneAndUpdate(
   {"title" : "Macbeth"},
   {$mul : {"box_office_collection" : 16.3}},
   {returnNewDocument : true}
)
```

This update operation multiplies a nonexistent field **box_office_collection** by a given value:

```
                                        MongoDB
> db.movies.findOneAndUpdate(
... {"title" : "Macbeth"},
... {$mul : {"box_office_collection" : 16.3}},
... {returnNewDocument : true}
... )
{
        "_id" : 1,
        "title" : "Macbeth",
        "year" : 2017,
        "type" : "movie",
        "num_mflix_comments" : 21,
        "flag" : "modified",
        "rating" : 2.6,
        "box_office_collection" : 0
}
>
```

Figure 5.22: Multiplying the value of a non-existing field

The output in *Figure 5.22* proves that irrespective of the provided value, the nonexistent field of **box_office_collection** has been added with a value of zero.

## RENAME ($RENAME)

As suggested by the name, the **$rename** operator is used to rename fields. The operator accepts a document containing pairs of field names and their new names. If the field is not already present in the document, the operator ignores it and does nothing. The provided field and its new name must be different. If they're the same, the operation fails with an error. If a document already contains a field with the provided new name, the existing field will be removed.

To try various scenarios of the **$rename** operator, first, insert a field named **imdb_rating** for **Macbeth**. The following update operation sets the new field and the output shows that the field is correctly added:

```
> db.movies.findOneAndUpdate(
  {"title" : "Macbeth"},
  {$set : {"imdb_rating" : 6.6}},
  {returnNewDocument : true}
)
{
  "_id" : 1,
  "title" : "Macbeth",
  "year" : 2017,
```

```
    "type" : "movie",
    "num_mflix_comments" : 21,
    "flag" : "modified",
    "rating" : 2.6,
    "box_office_collection" : 0,
    "imdb_rating" : 6.6
}
```

Now, rename the field **num_mflix_comments** to **comments** and rename the field **imdb_rating** to **rating**, as follows:

```
db.movies.findOneAndUpdate(
    {"title" : "Macbeth"},
    {$rename : {"num_mflix_comments" : "comments",
      "imdb_rating" : "rating"}},
    {returnNewDocument : true}
)
```

The update operation uses the **$rename** operator and passes a document containing two pairs of field names and new names. Note that the second field name and new name combination is trying to rename the field of **imdb_rating** to **rating**; however, the record already has a field with the name of **rating**. The output can be seen as follows:

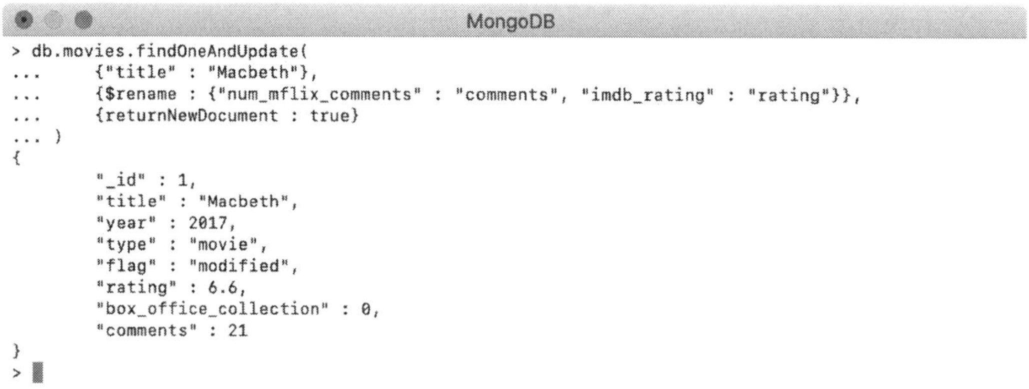

```
> db.movies.findOneAndUpdate(
...     {"title" : "Macbeth"},
...     {$rename : {"num_mflix_comments" : "comments", "imdb_rating" : "rating"}},
...     {returnNewDocument : true}
... )
{
        "_id" : 1,
        "title" : "Macbeth",
        "year" : 2017,
        "type" : "movie",
        "flag" : "modified",
        "rating" : 6.6,
        "box_office_collection" : 0,
        "comments" : 21
}
>
```

Figure 5.23: Renaming fields

The output shows that the rename operation was successful. As stated above, the original field of **rating** is removed and the **imdb_rating** field is now renamed to **rating**. Using this operator, a field can also be moved to and from nested documents. To do so, you have to use a dot notation, like this:

```
db.movies.findOneAndUpdate(
    {"title" : "Macbeth"},
```

```
    {$rename : {"rating" : "imdb.rating"}},
    {returnNewDocument : true}
)
```

Here, the update operation is renaming the **rating** field. However, the new name contains a dot notation:

```
                            MongoDB
> db.movies.findOneAndUpdate(
...     {"title" : "Macbeth"},
...     {$rename : {"rating" : "imdb.rating"}},
...     {returnNewDocument : true}
... )
{
        "_id" : 1,
        "title" : "Macbeth",
        "year" : 2017,
        "type" : "movie",
        "flag" : "modified",
        "box_office_collection" : 0,
        "comments" : 21,
        "imdb" : {
                "rating" : 6.6
        }
}
>
```

Figure 5.24: Renaming nested fields

Because of the dot notation, the field **rating** has been moved under the nested document **imdb**. Similarly, a field can be moved from a nested document to the root or to any other nested document.

## CURRENT DATE ($CURRENTDATE)

The operator **$currentDate** is used to set the value of a given field as the current date or timestamp. If the field is not present already, it will be created with the current date or timestamp value. Providing a field name with a value of **true** will insert the current date as a **Date**. Alternatively, a **$type** operator can be used to explicitly specify the value as a **date** or **timestamp**:

```
db.movies.findOneAndUpdate(
    {"title" : "Macbeth"},
    {$currentDate : {
      "created_date" : true,
        "last_updated.date" : {$type : "date"},
        "last_updated.timestamp" : {$type : "timestamp"},
    }},
    {returnNewDocument : true}
)
```

The preceding **findOneAndUpdate** operation sets three fields using the **$currentDate** operator. The field **created_date** has a value of true, which defaults to a **Date** type. The other two fields use a dot notation and explicit **$type** declaration. The output can be seen in the following figure:

```
●  ●  ●                              MongoDB
> db.movies.findOneAndUpdate(
...     {"title" : "Macbeth"},
...     {$currentDate : {
...         "created_date" : true,
...         "last_updated.date" : {$type : "date"},
...         "last_updated.timestamp" : {$type : "timestamp"},
...     }},
...     {returnNewDocument : true}
[... )
{
        "_id" : 1,
        "title" : "Macbeth",
        "year" : 2017,
        "type" : "movie",
        "flag" : "modified",
        "box_office_collection" : 0,
        "comments" : 21,
        "imdb" : {
                "rating" : 6.6
        },
        "created_date" : ISODate("2020-06-26T01:22:35.457Z"),
        "last_updated" : {
                "date" : ISODate("2020-06-26T01:22:35.457Z"),
                "timestamp" : Timestamp(1593134555, 1)
        }
}
> █
```

Figure 5.25: Setting the current date and timestamp

We can see that the field **created_date** has a value of the **Date** type. A new field, **last_updated**, has been added and has a nested document. Under the nested document, another field has been initialized as a **Date** type and the other as **Timestamp**.

## REMOVING FIELDS ($UNSET)

The **$unset** operator removes given fields from a document. The operator accepts a document containing pairs of field names and values and removes all the given fields from the matched document. As the provided fields are being removed, their specified values have no impact. For instance, consider the following snippet:

```
> db.movies.find({"title" : "Macbeth"}).pretty()
{
  "_id" : 1,
  "title" : "Macbeth",
  "year" : 2017,
  "type" : "movie",
  "flag" : "modified",
  "box_office_collection" : 0,
  "comments" : 21,
  "imdb" : {
    "rating" : 6.6
  },
  "created_date" : ISODate("2020-06-26T01:22:35.457Z"),
  "last_updated" : {
    "date" : ISODate("2020-06-26T01:22:35.457Z"),
  "timestamp" : Timestamp(1593134555, 1)
  }
}
```

Execute an update operation using the **$unset** operator to remove unwanted fields:

```
db.movies.findOneAndUpdate(
  {"title" : "Macbeth"},
  {$unset : {
    "created_date" : "",
    "last_updated" : "dummy_value",
    "box_office_collection": 142.2,
    "imdb" : null,
    "flag" : ""
  }},
  {returnNewDocument : true}
)
```

The preceding update operation removes four fields from the document. As stated previously, it doesn't matter whether and what value is provided to the field while it is being removed. Here, you are trying to remove multiple fields and providing them with different values, and you will observe that their values have no impact. The first field, **created_date**, is provided with a value of an empty string. The next two fields have some dummy values, and the field **imdb** has a null value. The last field, **flag**, is also provided with an empty string. Out of these five fields, **imdb** and **last_updated** are nested fields. You will now execute the operation and observe the output, as follows:

```
MongoDB
> db.movies.findOneAndUpdate(
...     {"title" : "Macbeth"},
...     {$unset : {
...         "created_date" : "",
...         "last_updated" : "dummy_value",
...         "box_office_collection": 142.2,
...         "imdb" : null,
...         "flag" : ""
...     }},
...     {returnNewDocument : true}
[... )
{
        "_id" : 1,
        "title" : "Macbeth",
        "year" : 2017,
        "type" : "movie",
        "comments" : 21
}
>
```

Figure 5.26: Removing multiple fields

The output indicates that all five fields are correctly removed from the document. The operation and the response prove that the values specified for the fields have no impact on field removal. Also, specifying a field with a value of a nested object removes the respective object and contained fields.

## SETTING WHEN INSERTED ($SETONINSERT)

The operator **$setOnInsert** is similar to **$set**; however, it only sets the given fields when an insert happens during an **upsert** operation. It has no impact when the **upsert** operation results in the update of existing documents. To understand this better, consider the following snippet:

```
db.movies.findOneAndUpdate(
  {"title":"Macbeth"},
  {
    $rename:{"comments":"num_mflix_comments"},
```

```
    $setOnInsert:{"created_time":new Date()}
  },
  {

    upsert : true,
    returnNewDocument:true

  }
)
```

Here, the upsert operation finds and updates the *Macbeth* movie record. It renames a field with a new name and also uses **$setOnInsert** on the field **created_time**, which is initialized to the current **Date**. As the movie is already present in the collection, this operation will result in an update:

```
> db.movies.findOneAndUpdate(
...     {"title":"Macbeth"},
...     {
...         $rename:{"comments":"num_mflix_comments"},
...         $setOnInsert:{"created_time":new Date()}
...     },
...     {
...         upsert : true,
...         returnNewDocument:true
...     }
[... )
{
        "_id" : 1,
        "title" : "Macbeth",
        "year" : 2017,
        "type" : "movie",
        "num_mflix_comments" : 21
}
>
```

Figure 5.27: Using $setOnInsert with upsert on an existing document

The output shows that **$setOnInsert** did not change the document, however, the field **comment** is now renamed to **num_mflix_comments**. Also, the field **created_time** is not added because the upsert operation was used to update an existing document. Now try an example of an insert using the upsert operation:

```
db.movies.findOneAndUpdate(
  {"title":"Spy"},
  {

    $rename:{"comments":"num_mflix_comments"},
    $setOnInsert:{"created_time":new Date()}
  },
  {
```

```
    upsert : true,
    returnNewDocument:true

  }
)
```

The only difference between this snippet and the previous one is that this operation finds a movie named **Spy**, which is not present in our collection. Because of the upsert, the operation will result in adding a document to the collection. The output can be seen in the following figure:

```
●  ●  ●                               MongoDB
> db.movies.findOneAndUpdate(
...     {"title":"Spy"},
...     {
...         $rename:{"comments":"num_mflix_comments"},
...         $setOnInsert:{"created_time":new Date()}
...     },
...     {
...         upsert : true,
...         returnNewDocument:true
...     }
... )
{
        "_id" : ObjectId("5e21e3928cb975719326c5cb"),
        "title" : "Spy",
        "created_time" : ISODate("2020-01-17T16:40:50.144Z")
}
> █
```

Figure 5.28: Using $setOnInsert with upsert on a new document

As we can see, a new movie record has been created along with the field **created_time**. With the preceding example and the output, we have seen that the **$setOnInsert** operator sets a field only when a record is inserted as part of an upsert operation.

## ACTIVITY 5.01: UPDATING COMMENTS FOR MOVIES

Some of the users of your database have complained that their comments on a movie are not found on the website. Your customer support team did some investigating and found that there is a total of three comments incorrectly posted on a movie that actually belong to some other movie. The IDs of the incorrect comments are as follows:

```
ObjectId("5a9427658b0beebeb6975eaa")
ObjectId("5a9427658b0beebeb6975eb3")
ObjectId("5a9427658b0beebeb6975eb4")
```

The following **find** query returns those three comments:

```
db.comments.find(
    {"_id" :
     {$in : [
        ObjectId("5a9427658b0beebeb6975eaa"),
        ObjectId("5a9427658b0beebeb6975eb3"),
        ObjectId("5a9427658b0beebeb6975eb4")
        ]
      }
    }
).pretty()
```

Execute the preceding query on the MongoDB Atlas **sample_mflix** database and the output should look as follows:

```
●  ●  ●                              MongoDB
> db.comments.find(
...      {"_id" :
...          {$in : [
...                ObjectId("5a9427658b0beebeb6975eaa"),
...                ObjectId("5a9427658b0beebeb6975eb3"),
...                ObjectId("5a9427658b0beebeb6975eb4")
...                ]
...          }
...      }
[... ).pretty()                                                                    ]
{
        "_id" : ObjectId("5a9427658b0beebeb6975eaa"),
        "name" : "Amy Phillips",
        "email" : "amy_phillips@fakegmail.com",
        "movie_id" : ObjectId("573a13abf29313caabd25582"),
        "text" : "Porro aspernatur nobis velit iste. Rerum ipsum non quam nam architecto nisi. Qu
idem quia nemo ipsa quibusdam nesciunt.",
        "date" : ISODate("2005-07-09T13:03:10Z")
}
{
        "_id" : ObjectId("5a9427658b0beebeb6975eb3"),
        "name" : "Barristan Selmy",
        "email" : "ian_mcelhinney@gameofthron.es",
        "movie_id" : ObjectId("573a13abf29313caabd25582"),
        "text" : "Delectus doloribus inventore tempore cumque. Repellendus dolor sapiente volupta
s explicabo et delectus rem qui. Odio atque quam tempore repellat delectus.",
        "date" : ISODate("1986-05-28T11:17:06Z")
}
{
        "_id" : ObjectId("5a9427658b0beebeb6975eb4"),
        "name" : "Barristan Selmy",
        "email" : "ian_mcelhinney@gameofthron.es",
        "movie_id" : ObjectId("573a13abf29313caabd25582"),
        "text" : "Voluptate iure illo nihil. Aliquid aspernatur quae id cumque fugit officia pari
atur. Nam sequi soluta occaecati nam facilis sunt quasi.",
        "date" : ISODate("1999-11-03T00:36:40Z")
}
> ▊
```

Figure 5.29: Incorrect comments

All three comments above are posted against a 2009 movie, **Sherlock Holmes** (**ObjectId("573a13bcf29313caabd57db6")**), however, they belong to a 2014 movie, **50 First Dates** (**ObjectId("573a13abf29313caabd25582")**).

Your task for this activity is to correct **movie_id** in all three comments as well as to update the **num_mflix_comments** fields of these movies, respectively. The following steps will help you complete this activity:

1. Update the **movie_id** field in all three documents.

2. Find the movie **Sherlock Holmes** by its ID and reduce the number of comments by 3.

3. Execute the command you used in *step 2* on the mongo shell and confirm the results.

4. Find the movie **50 First Dates** and increase the number of comments by 3.

5. Execute the command you used in *step 3* on the mongo shell and confirm the results.

> **NOTE**
>
> The solution to this activity can be found on Page 665.

## SUMMARY

We started this chapter with the creation of documents in a collection. We saw that, during an insert operation, MongoDB creates the underlying collection if it does not exist, and autogenerates an **_id** field if the document does not have one already. We then covered various functions provided by MongoDB to delete and replace one or more documents in a collection, as well as the concept of upsert, its benefits, its support in MongoDB, and how an upsert operation differs from delete and insert. Then we learned how to add, update, rename, or remove fields in MongoDB documents using various functions and operators.

In the next chapter, we will execute some complex update commands using the aggregation pipeline support that was added in MongoDB 4.2, and learn how to modify the elements in an array field.

# 6

# UPDATING WITH AGGREGATION PIPELINES AND ARRAYS

## OVERVIEW

This chapter introduces you to two additional features of update operations in MongoDB. You will first learn how to perform some complex update operations using pipeline support. Using pipeline support, you will be able to write a multi-step update expression and also refer to the values of other fields. Next, the chapter covers the updating of array fields in documents, which involves adding elements to an array, updating or deleting all or specific elements, creating arrays as a set, and sorting array elements. You will practice pushing unique elements to an array and sorting its elements as part of the final activity. By the end of this chapter, you will be able to derive update expressions based on the values of other fields and manipulate array fields in the documents of a collection.

# INTRODUCTION

So far, we have covered querying using various operators to prepare query expressions. We have also learned how to create, delete, and modify documents in the collection, used various delete and update functions, and considered their differences and usability. We have also covered how to replace documents and how to perform upsert operations using a number of update operators. Now it is time to practice more complex update operations using the aggregation pipeline support, and learn how to modify arrays in a document.

We will begin this chapter with MongoDB pipeline support, where we will briefly introduce the aggregation pipeline and how it helps you to perform more complex update operations. We will then cover how to update array fields, how to add and sort elements of an existing array, and use an array as a set of unique elements. Next, you will learn how to remove the first, last, or another specific element from an array. Finally, you will learn how to prepare an array filter with a query criterion and use it to modify only specific elements in an array.

## UPDATING WITH AN AGGREGATION PIPELINE (MONGODB 4.2)

In the previous chapter, we covered update functions that are used to modify fields from one or more documents. We also wrote a lot of update operations using various operators. As you have seen in the examples, where we assigned a field with a new value, we either used hardcoded values (for example, while updating `num_mflix_comments`) or dynamically derived values using operators such as `$inc`. However, in more complex update operations, you may need to use dynamically derived fields that are based on the values of other fields. Or, the update operation may involve multiple steps of update expressions.

In the previous versions of MongoDB, referring to other fields' values or writing multi-step update operations was not possible, but, with the release of MongoDB 4.2, all of its update functions have started supporting aggregation pipelines. The aggregation pipelines and various aggregation operators will be covered in `detail` in *Chapter 7, Aggregation Pipelines*. For now, we will limit the discussion to writing update expressions using pipeline support.

A pipeline is composed of multiple update expressions called stages. When an update operation containing multiple stages of update expressions is executed, each of the matched documents is processed and transformed through each stage sequentially. The output of the first stage is input for the next stage, until the last stage in the pipeline produces the final output. Apart from writing multi-stage update expressions, pipeline support also allows the use of field references in the update expressions.

In previous update expressions, we have either set hardcoded values on the fields, or for numeric fields, we have used various operators to manipulate their existing values. However, using pipeline support, we can read and use the values of other fields in an update expression.

The following code snippet shows the syntax for using aggregation pipelines in **updateMany()**. It is the same for all other update functions:

```
db.collection.updateMany(
    <query condition>,
    [<update expression 1>, <update expression 2>, ...],
    <options>
)
```

You may have noticed that the second argument to the function, which specifies an update expression, is now an array of multiple update expressions or stages. As stated, the syntax is only valid if your MongoDB version is 4.2 or later. Instead of passing an array, if a document with a single update expression is provided, it will be executed as a normal update command.

Let's consider how the aggregation pipeline allows us to write complex update queries and enables us to use field expressions and aggregation operations with an example. We have been using the *CH05* database in the previous chapter's examples and will continue using it here. If you already have the **users** collection, delete all of its elements before we insert two records into it.

Let's add the following records to the collection:

```
db.users.insertMany([
    {_id: 1, full_name : "Arya Stark"},
    {_id: 2, full_name : "Khal Drogo"}
])
```

Both documents have an **_id** and **full_name** field, composed of first and last names separated by a white space. We will write an update command to split the full name into the respective fields of first name and last name, and update the **full_name** field so that only the first name appears in uppercase:

```
db.users.updateMany(
    {},
    [
        {
            $set : {"name_array" : {$split : ["$full_name", " "]}},
        },
        {
            $set: {
                "first_name" : {"$arrayElemAt" : ["$name_array", 0]},
                "last_name" : {"$arrayElemAt" : ["$name_array", 1]}
            }
        },
        {
            $project : {
                "first_name" : 1,
                "last_name" : 1,
                "full_name" : {
                    $concat : [{$toUpper : "$first_name"}, " ", "$last_
name"]
                }
            }
        }
    ]
)
```

Here, the **updateMany()** operation is updating all the documents in the **users** collection. The second argument to the function is an array containing three stages (**$set**, **$set**, and **$project**). Now, we will go through each of these stages and explore the pipeline.

> **NOTE**
>
> Operators such as **$project**, **$arrayElemAt**, and **$concat** are aggregation operators. These operators cannot be used on versions older than MongoDB 4.2 or in an update expression that is not part of the aggregation pipeline.

## STAGE 1 ($SET)

In this stage, we are using the **$split** operator to split the full name with a white space. This gives us a two-element array containing the first name and the last name. We are also creating a new field of **name_array** using the **$set** operator and assigning the newly created array to it. **name_array** is a temporary field for us.

## STAGE 2 ($SET)

In this stage, we refer to the array stored in **name_array** and create new fields for the first name and last name. To do so, we use **$arrayElemAt** on the name array to fetch its element from a specific index position. A new field called **first_name** is created using the zeroth position element, and the **last_name** field is created using the first index position element. At the end of this stage, each user's documents will have **first_name**, **last_name**, **name_array**, and the original **full_name** field.

## STAGE 3 ($PROJECT)

In the last stage, we project fields. We explicitly include the **first_name** and **last_name** fields and rewrite **full_name** by concatenating **first_name** in uppercase and **last_name**; note that we will not change the case for **last_name**.

The **$toUpper** operator refers to the value of **first_name** and returns the same string in uppercase. The **$concat** operator accepts an array of strings and returns a single string by concatenating all the elements in the same order. Here, we were concatenating **first_name** in uppercase, a white space, and **last_name**.

The **$project** operator is used to project fields and to assign them. In this stage, we project **first_name**, **last_name**, and **full_name**, meaning that **name_array** will be omitted automatically:

```
●  ●  ●                        MongoDB
> db.users.updateMany(
...      {},
...      [
...          {
...              $set : {"name_array" : {$split : ["$full_name", " "]}},
...          },
...          {
...              $set: {
...                  "first_name" : {"$arrayElemAt" : ["$name_array", 0]},
...                  "last_name" : {"$arrayElemAt" : ["$name_array", 1]}
...              }
...          },
...          {
...              $project : {
...                  "first_name" : 1,
...                  "last_name" : 1,
...                  "full_name" : {$concat : ["$first_name", " ", "$last_name"]}

...              }
...          }
...      ]
[... )
{ "acknowledged" : true, "matchedCount" : 2, "modifiedCount" : 2 }
> ▊
```

Figure 6.1: Updating using pipeline support

The preceding output shows that the operation was successful. It matched two documents and both of them were modified. We will now query the documents and see whether they have updated correctly:

```
> db.users.find({}, {_id : 0})
{ "first_name" : "Arya", "last_name" : "Stark", "full_name" : "ARYA Stark"
}
{ "first_name" : "Khal", "last_name" : "Drogo", "full_name" : "KHAL Drogo"
}
```

Here, the **find** query and the output shows that the documents are modified correctly. The original full name is correctly split into a first and a last name. Also, the first name in the **full_name** field is in uppercase.

In this section, we studied how to write complex update commands using pipeline stages and aggregation operator support provided by MongoDB 4.2. We also learned that the stages are executed in sequence and the output of a stage becomes the input of the next stage.

# UPDATING ARRAY FIELDS

In the previous sections, we learned about updating fields in one or more MongoDB documents. We also learned how to write update expressions using various operators and how to use MongoDB pipeline support. In this section, we will learn about updating array fields from a document.

To try some basic update operations on array fields, we will insert the following document into the **movies** collection:

```
db.movies.insert({"_id" : 111, "title" : "Macbeth"})
```

The document only has a **title** field and does not contain an array, so let's try creating one:

```
db.movies.findOneAndUpdate(
    {_id : 111},
    {$set : {"genre" : ["Unknown"]}},
    {"returnNewDocument" : true}
)
```

The preceding operation uses **$set** in the **genre** field. The value of **genre** is a single-element array—**["unknown"]**. The output can be seen here:

```
●●●                          MongoDB
> db.movies.findOneAndUpdate(
...     {_id : 111},
...     {$set : {"genre" : ["Unknown"]}},
...     {"returnNewDocument" : true}
[... )
{ "_id" : 111, "title" : "Macbeth", "genre" : [ "Unknown" ] }
>
```

Figure 6.2: Updating value of an array field

The output shows that the **genre** field is created and assigned the value of the given array. Next, we will remove the fields from the document, as follows:

```
db.movies.findOneAndUpdate(
    {_id : 111},
    {$unset : {"genre" : ""}},
    {"returnNewDocument" : true}
)
```

The preceding update command uses **$unset** to remove the **genre** field. You can see the output here:

```
> db.movies.findOneAndUpdate(
...      {_id : 111},
...      {$unset : {"genre" : ""}},
...      {"returnNewDocument" : true}
[... )
{ "_id" : 111, "title" : "Macbeth" }
>
```
MongoDB

Figure 6.3: Removing an array field

The output indicates that the field is correctly removed from the document. From these two examples, it is clear that when an array field is being updated using the array as a value, it is treated like any other field. Next, we will see how we can manipulate array elements.

We have seen how we can update fields with array values. It is useful when we want to fully replace an array value. However, to add more elements to an array, an operator called **$push** can be used. The operator pushes a given element to the end of an array, and if the given field is not present, it is created. Let's use this in the next exercise.

## EXERCISE 6.01: ADDING ELEMENTS TO ARRAYS

In this exercise, you will add elements to arrays using the following steps:

1. To insert a single document, add the following command:

```
db.movies.findOneAndUpdate(
     {_id : 111},
     {$push : {"genre" : "unknown"}},
     {"returnNewDocument" : true}
)
```

The update operation in the preceding snippet finds a document by its **_id** value and pushes an element to the **genre** array. This field is currently absent in the document. You should see the following output:

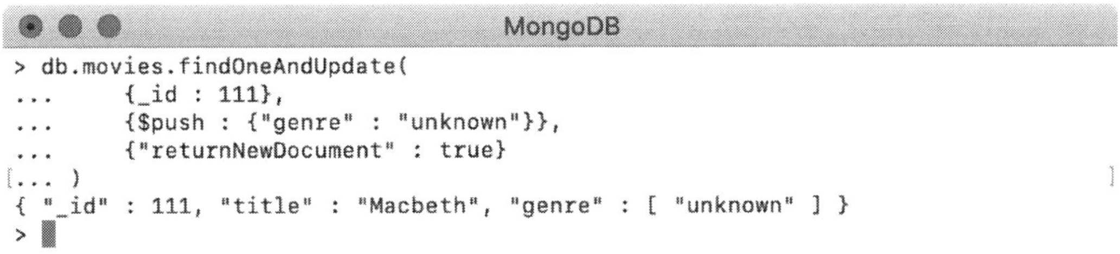

```
● ● ●                          MongoDB
> db.movies.findOneAndUpdate(
...       {_id : 111},
...       {$push : {"genre" : "unknown"}},
...       {"returnNewDocument" : true}
[... )                                                          ]
{ "_id" : 111, "title" : "Macbeth", "genre" : [ "unknown" ] }
> █
```

Figure 6.4: Adding one element into an array

2. As shown here, the **genre** array field is created successfully, and the given element is added to the array. Now add one more genre, as follows:

```
db.movies.findOneAndUpdate(
    {_id : 111},
    {$push : {"genre" : "Drama"}},
    {"returnNewDocument" : true}
)
```

The preceding command inserts another genre, **Drama**. You can see the output here, which shows that the **Drama** element has been added to the end of the existing array:

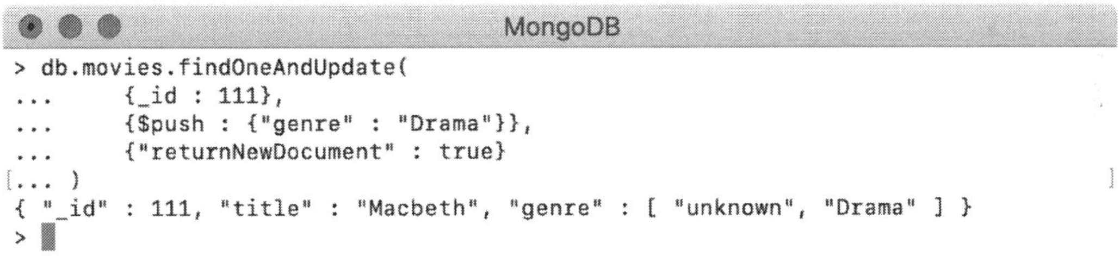

```
● ● ●                          MongoDB
> db.movies.findOneAndUpdate(
...       {_id : 111},
...       {$push : {"genre" : "Drama"}},
...       {"returnNewDocument" : true}
[... )                                                          ]
{ "_id" : 111, "title" : "Macbeth", "genre" : [ "unknown", "Drama" ] }
> █
```

Figure 6.5: Adding another element into the array

We dealt with adding single elements in this exercise. In the next section, we will add multiple elements at once.

## ADDING MULTIPLE ELEMENTS

As we have seen, **$push** can add one element at a time. To add multiple elements to an array in a single update command, we have to use **$push** along with **$each**. The following is the syntax for this:

```
$push : {<field_name> : {$each : [<element 1>, <element2>, ..]}}
```

The elements that need to be appended to the array are provided to the **$each** operator in the form of an array. When such an update expression is executed, **$each** iterates through each element, and the element is pushed to the array:

```
db.movies.findOneAndUpdate(
    {_id : 111},
    {$push : {
        "genre" : {
            $each : ["History", "Action"]
        }}
    },
    {"returnNewDocument" : true}
)
```

The preceding update operation finds and updates a document by its **_id** field and uses **$push** to add elements to the **genre** field. We add two elements to the array by providing those two elements to **$each**:

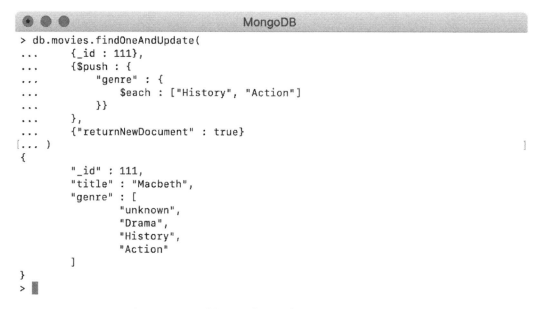

```
> db.movies.findOneAndUpdate(
...     {_id : 111},
...     {$push : {
...         "genre" : {
...             $each : ["History", "Action"]
...         }}
...     },
...     {"returnNewDocument" : true}
[... )
{
        "_id" : 111,
        "title" : "Macbeth",
        "genre" : [
                "unknown",
                "Drama",
                "History",
                "Action"
        ]
}
> 
```

Figure 6.6: Pushing multiple elements into an array

The document in the response (see the preceding screenshot) indicates that both the elements are correctly appended to the end of the array and are added in the same order.

## SORT ARRAY

Arrays in MongoDB, and in general, are an ordered but unsorted collection of elements. In other words, the elements of the array will always remain in the order in which they were inserted. However, while executing an update command with **$push**, we can also sort an array. To do that, we must use the **$sort** operator with **$each**. In the previous examples, we added four elements to the **genre** array. Now, we will try to sort the array alphabetically:

```
db.movies.findOneAndUpdate(
    {_id : 111},
    {$push : {
        "genre" : {
            $each : [],
            $sort : 1
        }}
    },
    {"returnNewDocument" : true}
)
```

In the preceding command, we use **$push** in the **genre** field. One thing to note is that this query is not pushing any element to the array because there are no elements provided to the **$each** operator. The new **$sort** operator is assigned the value **1**, which denotes ascending order:

```
                              MongoDB
> db.movies.findOneAndUpdate(
...      {_id : 111},
...      {$push : {
...          "genre" : {
...              $each : [],
...              $sort : 1
...          }}
...      },
...      {"returnNewDocument" : true}
[... )
{
        "_id" : 111,
        "title" : "Macbeth",
        "genre" : [
                "Action",
                "Drama",
                "History",
                "unknown"
        ]
}
>
```

Figure 6.7: Sorting an array

As shown, the **genre** array is now alphabetically sorted in ascending order of the elements. In the previous example, we sorted an array without adding an element to it, but we can also perform the sort while inserting one or more elements into an array. In that case, the new elements will be added to the array, and the array will be sorted based on the given sort order. Consider the following snippet:

```
db.movies.findOneAndUpdate(
    {_id : 111},
    {$push : {
        "genre" : {
            $each : ["Crime"],
            $sort : -1
        }}
    },
    {"returnNewDocument" : true}
)
```

In this update command, we pass a new element, **Crime**, to the genre. Note that the **$sort** operator has a value of **−1**. When we execute this command, the new element will be added to the array, and the array will be sorted in descending alphabetical order. This results in the following output:

```
                              MongoDB
> db.movies.findOneAndUpdate(
...      {_id : 111},
...      {$push : {
...          "genre" : {
...              $each : ["Crime"],
...              $sort : -1
...          }}
...      },
...      {"returnNewDocument" : true}
[... )                                                                    ]
{
         "_id" : 111,
         "title" : "Macbeth",
         "genre" : [
                 "unknown",
                 "History",
                 "Drama",
                 "Crime",
                 "Action"
         ]
}
> █
```

Figure 6.8: Sorting an array and pushing elements into it

As we can see from the response, the array is sorted in descending order and the new element, **Crime**, is part of the **genre** array. Without providing the **$sort** operator, the new element would be appended to the end of the array. In both the previous examples, the **genre** array contains plain string elements. However, if we have an array of objects that contains multiple fields, sorting can be performed based on the fields of nested objects. Consider the following record in an **items** collection:

```
> db.items.insert({_id : 11, items: [
    {"name" : "backpack", "price" : 127.59, "quantity" : 3},
    {"name" : "notepad", "price" : 17.6, "quantity" : 4},
    {"name" : "binder", "price" : 18.17, "quantity" : 2},
    {"name" : "pens", "price" : 60.56, "quantity" : 3},

]})
WriteResult({ "nInserted" : 1 })
```

The **items** field is an array of four objects, each containing three fields. We will sort the array by price now:

```
db.items.findOneAndUpdate(
    {_id : 11},
    {$push : {
        "items" : {
            $each : [],
            $sort : {"price" : -1}
        }}
    },
    {"returnNewDocument" : true}
)
```

The update command finds one document and sorts the array field. Unlike the previous examples, this time we want to sort the elements based on their nested field:

```
> db.items.findOneAndUpdate(
...        {_id : 11},
...        {$push : {
...            "items" : {
...                $each : [],
...                $sort : {"price" : -1}
...            }}
...        },
...        {"returnNewDocument" : true}
[... )
{
        "_id" : 11,
        "items" : [
                {
                        "name" : "backpack",
                        "price" : 127.59,
                        "quantity" : 3
                },
                {
                        "name" : "pens",
                        "price" : 60.56,
                        "quantity" : 3
                },
                {
                        "name" : "binder",
                        "price" : 18.17,
                        "quantity" : 2
                },
                {
                        "name" : "notepad",
                        "price" : 17.6,
                        "quantity" : 4
                }
        ]
}
>
```

Figure 6.9: Sorting an array based on a value of a nested field

Note the array field in the modified document. All the elements are now sorted in descending order by price. In the next section, we will learn about using arrays in MongoDB as sets.

## AN ARRAY AS A SET

An array is an ordered collection of elements that can be iterated over or accessed using its specific index position. A set is a collection of unique elements whose order is not guaranteed. MongoDB supports only plain arrays and no other types of collections. However, you may want your array to contain unique elements only. MongoDB provides a way to do that by using the **$addToSet** operator.

The **$addToSet** operator is like **$push**, with the only difference being that an element will be pushed only if it is not present already. This operator does not change the underlying array, but it ensures that only unique elements are pushed into it. Currently, the document for the movie **Macbeth** in our **movies** collection looks like this:

```
> db.movies.find({"_id" : 111}).pretty()
{
    "_id" : 111,
    "title" : "Macbeth",
    "genre" : [
        "unknown",
        "History",
        "Drama",
        "Crime",
        "Action"
    ]
}
```

The **genre** array is a really good example, wherein you want your array to have unique elements because duplicate genres for a movie do not make sense. Consider the following snippet:

```
db.movies.findOneAndUpdate(
    {_id : 111},
    {$addToSet : {"genre" : "Action"}},
    {"returnNewDocument" : true    }
)
```

Here, the update operation uses **$addToSet** to push an element of **Action** in the **genres** array. Note that the element is already part of the array:

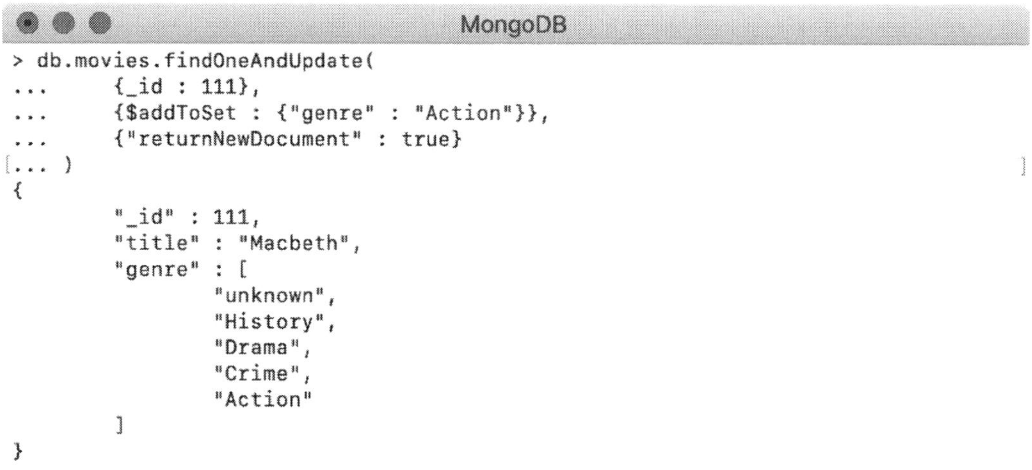

```
> db.movies.findOneAndUpdate(
...      {_id : 111},
...      {$addToSet : {"genre" : "Action"}},
...      {"returnNewDocument" : true}
[... )                                                                              ]
{
         "_id" : 111,
         "title" : "Macbeth",
         "genre" : [
                 "unknown",
                 "History",
                 "Drama",
                 "Crime",
                 "Action"
         ]
}
```

Figure 6.10: Adding element into an array as a set

As can be seen in the preceding screenshot, the **Action** element was not pushed to the array because the array already contains it. The same behavior is evident even when we use **$each** to push multiple elements into an array. For example, consider this snippet:

```
db.movies.findOneAndUpdate(
     {_id : 111},
     {$addToSet : {
         "genre" : {
             $each : ["History", "Thriller", "Drama"]
         }}
     },
     {"returnNewDocument" : true}
)
```

Here, we use **$each** to add three genres to the array, of which only the middle one is new:

```
●  ●  ●                            MongoDB
> db.movies.findOneAndUpdate(
...      {_id : 111},
...      {$addToSet : {
...          "genre" : {
...              $each : ["History", "Thriller", "Drama"]
...          }}
...      },
...      {"returnNewDocument" : true}
... )
{
         "_id" : 111,
         "title" : "Macbeth",
         "genre" : [
                 "Unknown",
                 "History",
                 "Drama",
                 "Crime",
                 "Action",
                 "Thriller"
         ]
}
>  █
```

Figure 6.11: Adding multiple elements into an array as a set

The modified document confirms that only the new genre, **Thriller**, has been added to the array.

## EXERCISE 6.02: NEW CATEGORY OF CLASSIC MOVIES

Recently, due to the re-release of **Casablanca**, there has been quite an upsurge in demand for classic movies. The analytics department at your company found that, not surprisingly, classics are the only movies that both critics and viewers have rated above 95. So, your company wants to assign all those movies in the database to a new genre, called "Classic." In your movie documents, a sample tomato rating looks like this:

```
"tomatoes" : {
"viewer" : {
        "rating" : 3.7,
        "numReviews" : 2559,
        "meter" : 75
    },
"fresh" : 6,
```

```
    "critic" : {
        "rating" : 7.6,
        "numReviews" : 6,
        "meter" : 100
    },
    "rotten" : 0,
    "lastUpdated" : ISODate("2015-08-08T19:16:10Z")
}
```

Your task is to put a filter on the meter field in both the **viewer** and **critic** sub-objects to find classic movies and assign them the new genre. The following steps will help you to complete this exercise:

1.  Open a text editor and start writing a query. You will have to prepare an update command to update multiple documents, so use **updateMany()**:

```
db.movies.updateMany()
```

2.  The first criterion in finding movies is that the tomato meter rating from viewers needs to be more than **95**. Type in the following command:

```
db.movies.updateMany(
    {"tomatoes.viewer.meter" : {$gt : 95}}
)
```

Here, you have added a filter to the viewer meter. As the field is nested within a nested field, you used the dot notations accordingly.

3.  According to the second criterion, you need to put the same filter on the **critic** ratings. Add the second criterion to the query, as follows:

```
db.movies.updateMany(
    {
        "tomatoes.viewer.meter" : {$gt : 95},
        "tomatoes.critic.meter" : {$gt : 95}
    }
)
```

In the preceding command, you have added the same filter to the critic meter. The command now has all the required filters.

4. Now, create an update expression to add a new genre called **Classic** to all the matching movies:

```
db.movies.updateMany(
    {
        "tomatoes.viewer.meter" : {$gt : 95},
        "tomatoes.critic.meter" : {$gt : 95}
    },
    {
        $addToSet : {"genres" : "Classic"}
    }
)
```

You have now added the update expression. Note that the genres in the array should always be unique and so you would use **$addToSet** instead of **$push** to add the **Classic** element to the **genres** array.

5. Now, open a MongoDB shell and connect to the Mongo Atlas cluster, and then go to the **sample_mflix** database. Execute the preceding command on the database. The output should be as follows:

```
●  ●  ●                              MongoDB
> db.movies.updateMany(
...      {
...              "tomatoes.viewer.meter" : {$gt : 95},
...              "tomatoes.critic.meter" : {$gt : 95}
...      },
...      {
...              $addToSet : {"genre" : "Classic"}
...      }
[... )
{ "acknowledged" : true, "matchedCount" : 30, "modifiedCount" : 30 }
>
```

Figure 6.12: Adding the new genre

You can see that all 30 records have been updated successfully.

6. To verify this, write a **find** query using the same condition and project the essential fields with the following command:

```
db.movies.find(
    {
        "tomatoes.viewer.meter" : {$gt : 95},
        "tomatoes.critic.meter" : {$gt : 95}
    },
    {
```

```
            "_id" : 0,
            "title" : 1,
            "genres" : 1
        }
    )
```

The **find** query here uses the same filter and displays only the **title** and **genres** fields. You can see the output as follows:

```
● ● ●                           MongoDB
> db.movies.find(
...     {
...          "tomatoes.viewer.meter" : {$gt : 95},
...          "tomatoes.critic.meter" : {$gt : 95}
...     },
...     {
...          "_id" : 0,
...          "title" : 1,
...          "genres" : 1
...     }
... )
[... )
{ "genres" : [ "Comedy", "Drama", "Family", "Classic" ], "title" : "The Kid" }
{ "genres" : [ "Comedy", "Drama", "Romance", "Classic" ], "title" : "City Lights" }
{ "genres" : [ "Drama", "Classic" ], "title" : "Ikiru" }
{ "genres" : [ "Drama", "Classic" ], "title" : "Seven Samurai" }
{ "genres" : [ "Crime", "Drama", "Classic" ], "title" : "12 Angry Men" }
{ "genres" : [ "Crime", "Drama", "Thriller", "Classic" ], "title" : "The Hole" }
{ "genres" : [ "Drama", "Classic" ], "title" : "Yojimbo" }
{ "genres" : [ "Action", "Drama", "History", "Classic" ], "title" : "Harakiri" }
{ "genres" : [ "Western", "Classic" ], "title" : "The Good, the Bad and the Ugly" }
{ "genres" : [ "Drama", "Classic" ], "title" : "Days and Nights in the Forest" }
{ "genres" : [ "Crime", "Drama", "Classic" ], "title" : "Investigation of a Citizen A
bove Suspicion" }
{ "genres" : [ "Documentary", "History", "War", "Classic" ], "title" : "The Sorrow an
d the Pity" }
{ "genres" : [ "Crime", "Drama", "Classic" ], "title" : "The Godfather" }
{ "genres" : [ "Crime", "Drama", "Classic" ], "title" : "The Godfather: Part II" }
{ "genres" : [ "Adventure", "Drama", "War", "Classic" ], "title" : "Das Boot" }
{ "genres" : [ "Documentary", "Biography", "Classic" ], "title" : "Marlene" }
{ "genres" : [ "Comedy", "Crime", "Drama", "Classic" ], "title" : "Time of the Gypsie
s" }
{ "genres" : [ "Biography", "Crime", "Drama", "Classic" ], "title" : "Goodfellas" }
{ "genres" : [ "Drama", "Classic" ], "title" : "The Stranger" }
{ "genres" : [ "Biography", "Drama", "History", "Classic" ], "title" : "Schindler's L
ist" }
Type "it" for more
> ▌
```

Figure 6.13: Output showing the movies belonging to the Classic genre

The output indicates that all of the movies now have the new genre, **Classic**. In this exercise, you used the concept of sets for a business use case. In the next section, let's look at the deletion of array elements.

## REMOVING ARRAY ELEMENTS

So far, we have studied the various means of adding elements to an array and sorting an array using various operators. MongoDB also provides the means of removing elements from arrays. In this section, we will go through different operators that allow you to remove all or specific elements from an array.

### REMOVING THE FIRST OR LAST ELEMENT ($POP)

The **$pop** operator, when used in an update command, allows you to remove the first or last element in an array. It removes one element at a time and can only be used with the values **1** (for the last element) or **−1** (for the first element):

```
> db.movies.find({"_id" : 111}).pretty()
{
    "_id" : 111,
    "title" : "Macbeth",
    "genre" : [
        "unknown",
        "History",
        "Drama",
        "Crime",
        "Action",
        "Thriller"
    ]
}
```

The output in the preceding snippet shows the movie record as having six elements in the **genre** array:

```
db.movies.findOneAndUpdate(
    {_id : 111},
    {$pop : {"genre" : 1}},
    {"returnNewDocument" : true   }
)
```

The preceding **findOneAndUpdate** operation makes use of **$pop** on the **genre** field with the value **1**, which will remove the last element from the array. All other aspects of the command are the same as we have seen in the previous examples:

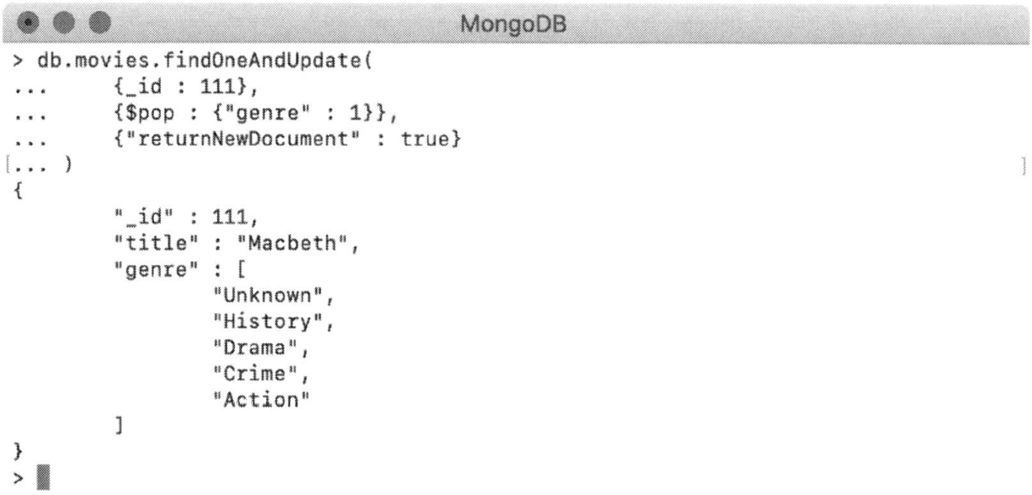

```
MongoDB
> db.movies.findOneAndUpdate(
...        {_id : 111},
...        {$pop : {"genre" : 1}},
...        {"returnNewDocument" : true}
[... )
{
          "_id" : 111,
          "title" : "Macbeth",
          "genre" : [
                  "Unknown",
                  "History",
                  "Drama",
                  "Crime",
                  "Action"
          ]
}
>
```

Figure 6.14: Removing the last element from an array

The modified document indicates that the last element (**Thriller**) has been successfully removed from the array. Now, use the following command with the value of **$pop** as **-1**:

```
db.movies.findOneAndUpdate(
     {_id : 111},
     {$pop : {"genre" : -1}},
     {"returnNewDocument" : true      }
)
```

Let's see what happens when we execute this command:

```
●●●                              MongoDB
> db.movies.findOneAndUpdate(
...     {_id : 111},
...     {$pop : {"genre" : -1}},
...     {"returnNewDocument" : true}
[... )                                                            ]
{
        "_id" : 111,
        "title" : "Macbeth",
        "genre" : [
                "History",
                "Drama",
                "Crime",
                "Action"
        ]
}
> █
```

Figure 6.15: Removing the first element from an array

The output shows that the first element of the array (**'Unknown'**) has now been removed. Remember that **$pop** only allows **1** or **-1** as a value and that providing any other number, including a zero, results in an error.

## REMOVING ALL ELEMENTS

When you only need to remove certain elements from an array, you can use the **$pullAll** operator. To do so, you provide one or more elements to the operator, which then removes all occurrences of those elements from the array. For instance, consider the following command:

```
db.movies.findOneAndUpdate(
    {_id : 111},
    {$pullAll : {"genre" : ["Action", "Crime"]}},
    {"returnNewDocument" : true     }
)
```

In this update operation, we use **$pullAll** in the **genre** field. We provide two elements, **Action** and **Crime**, in the form of an array. The output for this is as follows:

```
                                        MongoDB
> db.movies.findOneAndUpdate(
...      {_id : 111},
...      {$pullAll : {"genre" : ["Action", "Crime"]}},
...      {"returnNewDocument" : true}
... )
{ "_id" : 111, "title" : "Macbeth", "genre" : [ "History", "Drama" ] }
>
```

Figure 6.16: Removing all elements of an array

We can see that the specified genres, **Action** and **Crime**, are now removed from the underlying array.

## REMOVING MATCHED ELEMENTS

In the previous example, we saw how we can use **$pullAll** to remove specific elements from an array. In this example, we will use another operator, called **$pull**, to write a query condition, using various logical and conditional operators, and the array elements that match the query will then be removed. As an example, consider the following snippet, in which an array named **items** contains four objects:

```
> db.items.find({"_id" : 11}).pretty()
{
    "_id" : 11,
    "items" : [
        {
            "name" : "backpack",
            "price" : 127.59,
            "quantity" : 3
        },
        {
```

```
            "name" : "pens",
            "price" : 60.56,
            "quantity" : 3
        },
        {
            "name" : "binder",
            "price" : 18.17,
            "quantity" : 2
        },
        {
            "name" : "notepad",
            "price" : 17.6,
            "quantity" : 4
        }
    ]
}
```

Now, we will write a query to update the array with **$pull**. Remember that it allows us to use combinations of logical and conditional operators to prepare a query condition, just like any **find** query:

```
db.items.findOneAndUpdate(
    {_id : 11},
    {$pull : {
        "items" : {
            "quantity" : 3,
            "name" : {$regex: "ck$"}
        }
    }},
    {"returnNewDocument" : true     }
)
```

In this update command, the **$pull** operator is provided with a query condition in the array field **items**. The conditions filter the array elements, where the **quantity** is **3** and the **name** ends with 'ck'. The output should be as follows:

```
> db.items.findOneAndUpdate(
...        {_id : 11},
...        {$pull : {
...            "items" : {
...                "quantity" : 3,
...                "name" : {$regex: "ck$"}
...            }
...        }},
...        {"returnNewDocument" : true}
[... )
{
        "_id" : 11,
        "items" : [
                {
                        "name" : "pens",
                        "price" : 60.56,
                        "quantity" : 3
                },
                {
                        "name" : "binder",
                        "price" : 18.17,
                        "quantity" : 2
                },
                {
                        "name" : "notepad",
                        "price" : 17.6,
                        "quantity" : 4
                },
                {
                        "name" : "it"
                }
        ]
}
>
```

Figure 6.17: Removing elements that matched the given regular expression

The document in response shows that an element where the quantity was **3** and name ends with 'ck' is removed, as expected. Let's now look at updating array elements.

## UPDATING ARRAY ELEMENTS

In an array, each element is bound to a specific index position. These index positions start at zero, and we can use a pair of square brackets ( **[**, **]** ) with the respective index position to refer to an element from the array. Using such a pair of square brackets with **$** allows you to update elements of an array. Consider the following snippet, which shows how the **genres** array looks currently:

```
> db.movies.find({"_id" : 111})
{ "_id" : 111, "title" : "Macbeth", "genre" : [ "History", "Drama" ] }
```

The **genres** array has two elements, and we will update both of them using the following command:

```
db.movies.findOneAndUpdate(
    {_id : 111},
    {$set : {"genre.$[]" : "Action"}},
    {"returnNewDocument" : true}
)
```

In this operation, we use **$set** in the **genres** field. The field is referred to by using the expression **"genre.$[]"** expression and provided with the value **Action** value. The **$[]** operator refers to all the elements contained by the given array and the update expression will be applied to all of them:

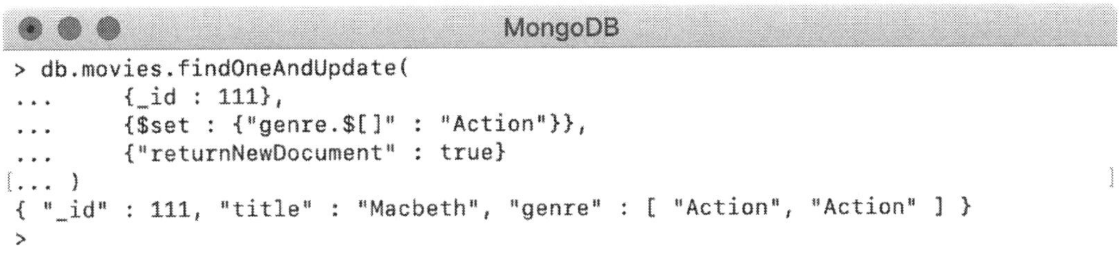

```
> db.movies.findOneAndUpdate(
...     {_id : 111},
...     {$set : {"genre.$[]" : "Action"}},
...     {"returnNewDocument" : true}
[... )
{ "_id" : 111, "title" : "Macbeth", "genre" : [ "Action", "Action" ] }
>
```

Figure 6.18: Replacing all elements from an array

The document, in response, indicates that **genre** is still a two-element array. However, both elements are now changed to **Action**. Therefore, we can use **$[]** to update all elements of an array with the same value.

Similarly, we can also update specific elements from an array. To do so, we first need to find such elements and identify them. To derive an element identifier, we can use the update option of **arrayFilters** to provide a query condition and assign it a variable (known as an identifier) to the matching elements. We then use the identifier along with **$[]** to update the values of those specific elements. To see an example of this, we will use the document from our **items** collection and add one more element to its array, as follows:

```
> db.items.findOneAndUpdate(
    {"_id" : 11},
    {$push : {"items" : {"name" : "it"}}},
    {"returnNewDocument": true}
)
{
    "_id" : 11,
    "items" : [
        {
            "name" : "pens",
            "price" : 60.56,
            "quantity" : 3
        },
        {
            "name" : "binder",
            "price" : 18.17,
            "quantity" : 2
        },
        {
```

```
            "name" : "notepad",
            "price" : 17.6,
            "quantity" : 4
        },
        {
            "name" : "it"
        }
    ]
}
```

Using the preceding **update** command, we have added a new element to the array. Notice that the newly added element does not have the **price** and **quantity** fields. In the following update command, we will find and update elements from this array:

```
db.items.findOneAndUpdate(
    {_id : 11},
    {$set : {
        "items.$[myElements]" : {
            "quantity" : 7,
            "price" : 4.5,
            "name" : "marker"
        }
    }},
    {
        "returnNewDocument" : true,
        "arrayFilters" : [{"myElements.quantity" : null}]
    }
)
```

In the preceding update operation, we use **$set** to update the elements of the
**items** array. The array element to be updated is referred to by an expression of
**$[myElements]** and assigned a new value, which is a nested object. The identifier
of **myElements** is defined using **arrayFilters** based on a query condition. All of
the elements that match the given condition are identified by **myElements**, which
are then updated using **$set**:

```
> db.items.findOneAndUpdate(
...       {_id : 11},
...       {$set : {
...          "items.$[myElements]" : {
...              "quantity" : 7,
...              "price" : 4.5,
...              "name" : "marker"
...          }
...       }},
...       {
...          "returnNewDocument" : true,
...          "arrayFilters" : [{"myElements.quantity" : null}]
...       }
... )
{
        "_id" : 11,
        "items" : [
              {
                      "name" : "pens",
                      "price" : 60.56,
                      "quantity" : 3
              },
              {
                      "name" : "binder",
                      "price" : 18.17,
                      "quantity" : 2
              },
              {
                      "name" : "notepad",
                      "price" : 17.6,
                      "quantity" : 4
              },
              {
                      "quantity" : 7,
                      "price" : 4.5,
                      "name" : "marker"
              }
        ]
}
>
```

Figure 6.19: Replacing elements that match given filters

The query condition of **{quantity: null}** is matched by the last element of the
array and has been updated with the new document.

## EXERCISE 6.03: UPDATING THE DIRECTOR'S NAME

On your movie website, people can find movies by their title or by names of actors or directors. Your task for this exercise is to connect to update the name of one of these directors from **H. C. Potter** to **H. C. Potter (Henry Codman Potter)**, so that users don't confuse him with another director who has a similar name. Remember, a movie or a series can be directed by multiple people. The **directors** field in your database is an array, and a person from the directors' team can appear at any index position:

```
db.movies.find(
    {"directors" : "H.C. Potter"},
    {_id : 0, title: 1, directors :1}
).pretty()
```

This **find** command finds all the movies by the director's abbreviated name and prints the movie title, followed by the director's name:

1.  Open the mongo shell and connect to the **sample_mflix** database on your Mongo Atlas cluster.

2.  As all six movies need to be updated, use the **updateMany()** update function. Open any text editor and write the following command:

```
db.movies.updateMany()
```

3.  Next, use the director's abbreviated name in the query condition, as follows:

```
db.movies.updateMany(
    {"directors" : "H.C. Potter"}
)
```

This command is still incomplete and syntactically invalid. So far, you have only added the query condition to the command.

4.  Next, add the update expression. As you are changing a field here, use the **$set** operator in the array field. Also, to change only a specific element in an array, use an element identifier:

```
db.movies.updateMany(
    {"directors" : "H.C. Potter"},
    {$set : {
        "directors.$[hcPotter]" : "H.C. Potter (Henry Codman Potter)"
    }}
)
```

In the preceding (and still incomplete) command, you have added an update expression that uses the **$set** operator on the array. Notice that the array element to which the **hcPotter** identifier refers is being assigned with the new value—that is, **Henry Codman Potter**.

5.  Now that you have used an element identifier in the update expression, define the identifier using **arrayFilters** as follows:

```
db.movies.updateMany(
    {"directors" : "H.C. Potter"},
    {$set : {
        "directors.$[hcPotter]" : "H.C. Potter (Henry Codman Potter)"
    }},
    {
        "arrayFilters" : [{hcPotter : "H.C. Potter"}]
    }
)
```

As can be seen from the preceding snippet, you have added an option of **arrayFilters**. The identifier of **hcPotter** is given a value of **H.C. Potter**—the value that currently exists in the arrays.

6.  Now, open the mongo shell and connect to the MongoDB Atlas cluster. Use the database of **sample_mflix** and execute the preceding command.

```
MongoDB
> db.movies.updateMany(
...     {"directors" : "H.C. Potter"},
...     {$set : {
...         "directors.$[hcPotter]" : "H.C. Potter (Henry Codman Potter)"
...     }},
...     {
...         "arrayFilters" : [{hcPotter : "H.C. Potter"}]
...     }
... )
{ "acknowledged" : true, "matchedCount" : 6, "modifiedCount" : 6 }
>
```

Figure 6.20: Updating the name of the director

The output indicates that all six records were found and updated correctly.

7.  Now, find the director's movies with his full name using a regular expression in the **directors** field:

```
db.movies.find(
    {"directors" : {$regex : "Henry Codman Potter"}},
```

```
        {_id : 0, title: 1, directors :1}
    ).pretty()
```

The query uses a regular expression to find the movies of the director according to his full name:

```
                                    MongoDB
> db.movies.find(
...      {"directors" : {$regex : "Henry Codman Potter"}},
...      {_id : 0, title: 1, directors :1}
[... ).pretty()                                                              ]
{
        "title" : "The Adventures of Tom Sawyer",
        "directors" : [
                "Norman Taurog",
                "George Cukor",
                "H.C. Potter (Henry Codman Potter)",
                "William A. Wellman"
        ]
}
{
        "title" : "The Cowboy and the Lady",
        "directors" : [
                "H.C. Potter (Henry Codman Potter)",
                "Stuart Heisler",
                "William Wyler"
        ]
}
{
        "title" : "The Story of Vernon and Irene Castle",
        "directors" : [
                "H.C. Potter (Henry Codman Potter)"
        ]
}
{
        "title" : "Victory Through Air Power",
        "directors" : [
                "James Algar",
                "Clyde Geronimi",
                "Jack Kinney",
                "H.C. Potter (Henry Codman Potter)"
        ]
}
{
        "title" : "The Farmer's Daughter",
        "directors" : [
                "H.C. Potter (Henry Codman Potter)"
        ]
}
{
        "title" : "Mr. Blandings Builds His Dream House",
        "directors" : [
                "H.C. Potter (Henry Codman Potter)"
        ]
}
>
```

Figure 6.21: Output showing the director's correct name

The output indicates that you have correctly updated the director's name in all the records. In this exercise, you practiced using array filters to modify only the matching elements in an array.

In this section, we studied how to update array fields in a document. We learned to add new elements, remove elements from an array, and update specific elements in an array. We also learned how to treat an array as a set and sort existing or new elements in an array.

## ACTIVITY 6.01: ADDING AN ACTOR'S NAME TO THE CAST

Recently, an error in the database came to your attention. The actor Nick Robinson played the character of **Zach** in the 2015 movie, **Jurassic World**. However, the **cast** field in the movie record does not attribute this actor to this movie:

```
MongoDB
> db.movies.find(
...     {"title" : "Jurassic World"},
...     {"_id" : 0, "title" : 1, "cast" : 1}
... ).pretty()
{
        "cast" : [
                "Chris Pratt",
                "Bryce Dallas Howard",
                "Irrfan Khan",
                "Vincent D'Onofrio"
        ],
        "title" : "Jurassic World"
}
>
```

Figure 6.22: Showing only casts of the movie

The output, as shown in the preceding screenshot, confirms that the actor's name is missing. Your task for this activity is to add **Nick Robinson** to the cast of this movie and sort this array by actor names. As a best practice, you should also ensure that the **cast** array has unique values. The following steps will help you to complete this activity:

1. Prepare a query expression based on the movie title and add an update expression to it. As you have to avoid duplicate insertions, you should treat the array as a set by using the **$addToSet** operator.

2. Next, you need to sort the array. Since sets are considered to be collections of unique and unordered elements, you cannot sort the elements while using **$addToSet**. So, first push the element in the array of unique elements.

3. Lastly, create another update command and sort all the arrays.

In this activity, you added unique elements to an array and sorted them. You also verified that it isn't possible to add elements to an array as a set and sort it at the same time.

> **NOTE**
>
> The solution to this activity can be found on page 669.

# SUMMARY

We started this chapter by learning how to update documents using aggregation pipeline support. Pipeline support, which was introduced in MongoDB version 4.2, helps us to perform some complex updates. Using pipeline support, we can write multi-stage update expressions, where the output of a stage is provided as input to the next stage. It also allows us to use field references and aggregation operators. We also learned how to manipulate elements in array fields, how to add, remove, and update elements in an array, how to sort an array, and how to add only unique elements to an array.

In the next chapter, we will learn about MongoDB aggregation framework and pipeline in detail.

# 7

# DATA AGGREGATION

## OVERVIEW

This chapter introduces you to the concept of aggregation and its implementation in MongoDB. You will learn how to identify the parameters and structure of the aggregate command, combine and manipulate data using the primary aggregation stages, work with large datasets using advanced aggregation stages, and optimize and configure your aggregation to get the best performance out of your queries.

# INTRODUCTION

In the previous chapters, we learned the fundamentals of interacting with MongoDB. With these basic operations (**insert**, **update**, and **delete**), we can now begin exploring and manipulating our data as we would with any other database. We also observed how, by fully leveraging the **find** command options, we can use operators to answer more specific questions about our data. We can also sort, limit, skip, and project on our query to create useful result sets.

In more straightforward situations, these result sets may be enough to answer your desired business question or satisfy a use case. However, more complex problems require more complex queries to answer. Solving such problems with just the **find** command would be highly challenging and would likely require multiple queries or some processing on the client side to organize or link the data.

The basic limitation is where you have data contained in two separate collections. To find the correct data, you would have to run two queries instead of one, joining the data on the client or application level. This may not seem like a big problem, but as your application or dataset increases in scale, performance and complexity also grow. Wherever possible, it is ideal for the server to do all the heavy lifting, returning only the data we are looking for in a single query. This is where the **aggregation pipeline** comes in.

The **aggregation pipeline** does precisely what the name implies. It allows you to define a series of stages that filter, merge, and organize data with much more control than the standard **find** command. Beyond that, the pipeline structure of aggregation allows developers and database analysts to easily, iteratively, and quickly build queries on ever-changing and growing datasets. If you want to accomplish anything significant at scale in MongoDB, you'll need to write complex, multi-stage aggregation pipelines. In this chapter, we will learn exactly how to do that.

> **NOTE**
>
> For the duration of this chapter, the exercises and activities included are iterations on a single scenario. The data and examples are based on the MongoDB Atlas sample database called **sample_mflix**.

Consider a scenario in which a cinema company is running its annual classic movie marathon and is trying to decide what their lineup should be. They need a variety of popular movies meeting specific criteria to satisfy their customer base. The company has asked you to research and determine the films they should show. In this chapter, we will use aggregations to retrieve data given a complex set of constraints, and then transform and manipulate data to create new results and answer business questions across our entire dataset with a single query. This will help the cinema company decide what movies they should be showing to satisfy their customers.

It's worth noting that the aggregation pipeline is robust enough that there are many ways to accomplish the same task. The exercises and activities covered in this chapter are just one solution to the scenarios posed and can be solved using different patterns. The best way to master the aggregation pipeline is to consider multiple methods to solve the same problem.

# AGGREGATE IS THE NEW FIND

The **aggregate** command in MongoDB is similar to the **find** command. You can provide the criteria for your query in the form of JSON documents, and it outputs a **cursor** containing the search result. Sounds simple, right? That's because it is. Although aggregations can become very large and complex, at their core, they are relatively simple.

The key element in aggregation is called the pipeline. We will cover it in detail shortly, but at a high level, a pipeline is a series of instructions, where the input to each instruction is the output of the previous one. Simply put, aggregation is a method for taking a collection and, in a procedural way, filtering, transforming, and joining data from other collections to create new, meaningful datasets.

## AGGREGATE SYNTAX

The **aggregate** command operates on a collection like the other **Create, Read, Update, Delete (CRUD)** commands, like so:

```
use sample_mflix;
var pipeline = [] // The pipeline is an array of stages.
var options  = {} // We will explore the options later in the
   chapter.
var cursor   = db.movies.aggregate(pipeline, options);
```

There are two parameters used for aggregation. The **pipeline** parameter contains all the logic to find, sort, project, limit, transform, and aggregate our data. The **pipeline** parameter itself is passed in as an array of JSON documents. You can think of this as a series of instructions to be sent to the database, and then the resulting data after the final stage is stored in a **cursor** to be returned to you. Each stage in the pipeline is completed independently, one after another, until none are remaining. The input to the first stage is the collection (**movies** in the preceding example), and the input into each subsequent stage is the output from the previous stage.

The second parameter is the **options** parameter. This is optional and allows you to specify the details of the configuration, such as how the aggregation should execute or some flags that are required during debugging and building your pipelines.

The parameters in an **aggregate** command are fewer than those in the **find** command. We will cover **options** as the final topic of this chapter, so for now, we can simplify our command by excluding **options** completely, as follows:

```
var cursor = db.movies.aggregate(pipeline);
```

In the preceding example, rather than writing the pipeline directly into the command, we are saving the pipeline as a variable first. Aggregation pipelines can become very large and difficult to parse during development. It can sometimes be helpful to separate the pipeline (or even large sections of the pipeline) into separate variables for code clarity. Although recommended, this pattern is completely optional, and is similar to the following:

```
var cursor = db.movies.aggregate([])
```

It is recommended that you follow along with these examples in a code or text editor, saving your scripts and then copying and pasting them into the MongoDB shell. For example, say we create a file called **aggregation.js** with the following content:

```
var MyAggregation_A = function() {
    print("Running Aggregation Script Ch7.1");
    var pipeline = [];
      // This next line stores our result in a cursor.
    var cursor = db.movies.aggregate(pipeline);
      // This line will print the next iteration of our cursor.
    printjson(cursor.next())
};
MyAggregation_A();
```

Then, copying this code directly into the MongoDB shell returns the following output:

```
MongoDB Enterprise atlas-nb3biv-shard-0:PRIMARY> MyAggregation_A();
Running Aggregation Script Ch7.1
{
        "_id" : ObjectId("573a1390f29313caabcd4135"),
        "plot" : "Three men hammer on an anvil and pass a bottle of beer around.",
        "genres" : [
                "Short"
        ],
        "runtime" : 1,
        "cast" : [
                "Charles Kayser",
                "John Ott"
        ],
        "num_mflix_comments" : 1,
        "title" : "Blacksmith Scene",
        "fullplot" : "A stationary camera looks at a large anvil with a blacksmith behind
it and one on either side. The smith in the middle draws a heated metal rod from the fire,
 places it on the anvil, and all three begin a rhythmic hammering. After several blows, th
e metal goes back in the fire. One smith pulls out a bottle of beer, and they each take a
swig. Then, out comes the glowing metal and the hammering resumes.",
        "countries" : [
                "USA"
```

Figure 7.1: Results of the aggreagation (output truncated for brevity)

We can see in this output that once the **MyAggregation_A.js** function is defined, we only need to call that function again to see the results of our aggregation (in this case, a list of movies). You can call this function again and again without having to write the entire pipeline every time.

By structuring your aggregations this way, you will not lose any of them. It also has the added benefit of letting you load all your aggregations into the shell interactively as functions. However, you can also copy and paste the entire function into the MongoDB shell if you prefer or simply enter it interactively. In this chapter, we will use a mix of both methods.

## THE AGGREGATION PIPELINE

As mentioned earlier, the key element in aggregation is the pipeline, which is a series of instructions to perform on the initial collection. You can think of the data as water flowing through this pipeline, being transformed and filtered at each stage until it is finally poured out the end of the pipeline as a result.

In the following diagram, the orange blocks represent the aggregation pipeline. Each of these blocks in the pipeline is referred to as an aggregation stage:

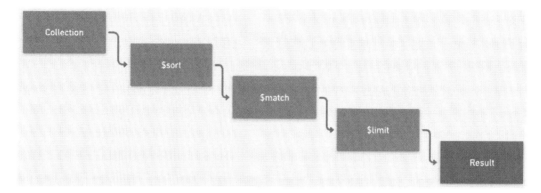

Figure 7.2: Aggregation pipeline

Something to note about aggregations is that, although the pipeline always begins with one collection, using certain stages, we can add collections further in the pipeline. We will cover joining collections later in this chapter.

Large multi-stage pipelines may look intimidating, but if you understand the structure of the command and the individual operations that can be performed at a given stage, then you can easily break the pipeline down into smaller parts. In this first topic, we will explore the construction of an aggregation pipeline, compare a query implemented using **find** with one created using **aggregate**, and identify some basic operators.

## PIPELINE SYNTAX

The syntax of an aggregation pipeline is very simple, much like the **aggregate** command itself. The pipeline is an array, with each item in the array being an object:

```
var pipeline = [
        { . . . },
        { . . . },
        { . . . },
];
```

Each of the objects in the array represents a single stage in the overall pipeline, with the stages being executed in their array order (top to bottom). Each stage object takes the form of the following:

```
{$stage : parameters}
```

The stage represents the action we want to perform on the data (such as **limit** or **sort**) and the parameters can be either a single value or another object, depending on the stage.

The pipeline can be passed in two ways, either as a saved variable or directly as a command. The following example demonstrates how the pipeline can be passed as a variable:

```
var pipeline = [
        { $match:    { "location.address.state": "MN"} },
        { $project: { "location.address.city": 1    } },
        { $sort:     { "location.address.city": 1    } },
        { $limit: 3 }
    ];
```

Then, typing in the **db.theaters.aggregate(pipeline)** command in the MongoDB shell will provide the following output:

```
MongoDB Enterprise atlas-nb3biv-shard-0:PRIMARY> var pipeline = [
...            { $match:    { "location.address.state": "MN"} },
...            { $project: { "location.address.city": 1    } },
...            { $sort:     { "location.address.city": 1    } },
...            { $limit: 3 }
...        ];
MongoDB Enterprise atlas-nb3biv-shard-0:PRIMARY>
MongoDB Enterprise atlas-nb3biv-shard-0:PRIMARY> db.theaters.
aggregate(pipeline)
{ "_id" : ObjectId("59a47287cfa9a3a73e51e94f"), "location" :
  { "address" : { "city" : "Apple Valley" } } }
{ "_id" : ObjectId("59a47287cfa9a3a73e51eb8f"), "location" :
  { "address" : { "city" : "Baxter" } } }
{ "_id" : ObjectId("59a47286cfa9a3a73e51e833"), "location" :
  { "address" : { "city" : "Blaine" } } }
MongoDB Enterprise atlas-nb3biv-shard-0:PRIMARY>
```

Passing it directly into the command, the output will look as follows:

```
MongoDB Enterprise atlas-nb3biv-shard-0:PRIMARY> db
  .theaters.aggregate([
... ...            { $match:    { "location.address.state": "MN"} },
... ...            { $project: { "location.address.city": 1    } },
... ...            { $sort:     { "location.address.city": 1    } },
... ...            { $limit: 3 }
... ...        ]
... );
```

```
{ "_id" : ObjectId("59a47287cfa9a3a73e51e94f"), "location" :
  { "address" : { "city" : "Apple Valley" } } }
{ "_id" : ObjectId("59a47287cfa9a3a73e51eb8f"), "location" :
  { "address" : { "city" : "Baxter" } } }
{ "_id" : ObjectId("59a47286cfa9a3a73e51e833"), "location" :
  { "address" : { "city" : "Blaine" } } }
MongoDB Enterprise atlas-nb3biv-shard-0:PRIMARY>
```

As you can see, you get the same output using either method.

## CREATING AGGREGATIONS

Let's begin to explore the pipeline itself. The following code, when pasted in the MongoDB shell, will help us get a list of all the theaters in the state of Minnesota (MN):

```
var simpleFind = function() {
    // Find command using filter, project, sort and limit.
    print("Find Result:")
    db.theaters.find(
        {"location.address.state" : "MN"},
        {"location.address.city" : 1})
    .sort({"location.address.city": 1})
    .limit(3)
    .forEach(printjson);
}
simpleFind();
```

This will give us the following output:

```
MongoDB Enterprise atlas-nb3biv-shard-0:PRIMARY> simpleFind();
Find Result:
{
        "_id" : ObjectId("59a47287cfa9a3a73e51e94f"),
        "location" : {
                "address" : {
                        "city" : "Apple Valley"
                }
        }
}
{
        "_id" : ObjectId("59a47287cfa9a3a73e51eb8f"),
        "location" : {
                "address" : {
                        "city" : "Baxter"
```

```
                    }
                }
        }
        {
                "_id" : ObjectId("59a47286cfa9a3a73e51e7e2"),
                "location" : {
                        "address" : {
                                "city" : "Blaine"
                        }
                }
        }
```

This syntax should look very familiar by now. This is quite a simple command, so let's look at the steps involved:

1. Match the theater collection to get a list of all theaters in the state of **MN** (Minnesota).

2. Project only the city in which the theater is located.

3. Sort the list by **city** name.

4. Limit the result to the first **three** theaters.

Let's rebuild this command as an aggregation. Don't worry if this looks a little intimidating at first. We'll walk through it step by step:

```
var simpleFindAsAggregate = function() {
    // Aggregation using match, project, sort and limit.
    print ("Aggregation Result:")
    var pipeline = [
        { $match:    { "location.address.state": "MN"} },
        { $project: { "location.address.city": 1    } },
        { $sort:     { "location.address.city": 1    } },
        { $limit: 3 }
    ];
    db.theaters.aggregate(pipeline).forEach(printjson);
};
simpleFindAsAggregate();
```

You should see the following output:

```
MongoDB Enterprise atlas-nb3biv-shard-0:PRIMARY> simpleFindAsAggregate();
Aggregation Result:
{
        "_id" : ObjectId("59a47287cfa9a3a73e51e94f"),
        "location" : {
                "address" : {
                        "city" : "Apple Valley"
                }
        }
}
{
        "_id" : ObjectId("59a47287cfa9a3a73e51eb8f"),
        "location" : {
                "address" : {
                        "city" : "Baxter"
                }
        }
}
{
        "_id" : ObjectId("59a47286cfa9a3a73e51e833"),
        "location" : {
                "address" : {
```

**Figure 7.3: Results of the aggregation (output truncated for brevity)**

If you run these two functions, you will get the same results. Remember, both **find** and **aggregate** commands return a cursor, but we're using **.forEach(printjson);** at the end to print them out to the console for ease of understanding.

If you observe the preceding example, you should be able to match up much of the same functionality from **find**. **project**, **sort**, and **limit** are all there as JSON documents just like in the **find** command. The only noticeable difference with these is that they are now documents in an array instead of functions. The **$match** stage at the very beginning of our pipeline is the equivalent of our filter document. So, let's break it down step by step:

1.  First, search the theater's collection, to locate documents that match the state **MN**:

```
{ $match:   { "location.address.state": "MN"} },
```

2.  Pass this list of theaters to the second stage, which projects only the city the theaters exist in for the selected state:

```
{ $project: { "location.address.city": 1     } },
```

3. This list of cities (and IDs) is then passed to a **sort** stage, which sorts the data alphabetically by city name:

```
{ $sort:     { "location.address.city": 1      } },
```

4. Finally, the list is passed to a **limit** stage, outputting just the first three entries:

```
{ $limit: 3 }
```

Pretty simple, right? You can imagine how large and complex this pipeline could get in production, but one of its strengths is the ability to break down large pipelines into smaller subsections or individual stages. By looking at stages individually and sequentially, seemingly incomprehensible queries can become reasonably straightforward. It's also important to note that the order of the steps is just as important as the stages themselves, not just logically but also to increase performance. The **$match** and **$project** stages execute first because these will reduce the size of the result set at each stage. Although not applicable to every type of query, it is generally good practice to try and reduce the number of documents you are working with early on, disregarding any documents that will add excessive loads to the server.

Although the pipeline structure itself is simple, there are more complex stages and operators required to accomplish advanced aggregations, as well as optimize them. We'll look at many of these over the next few topics.

## EXERCISE 7.01: PERFORMING SIMPLE AGGREGATIONS

Before we begin this exercise, let's revisit the movie company from the scenario outlined in the *Introduction* in which a cinema company runs the classic movie marathon every year. In previous years, they have used a manual process for several subcategories before finally merging all the data by hand. As part of your initial research for this task, you are going to try to recreate one of their smaller manual processes as a MongoDB aggregation. This task will make you more familiar with the dataset and create a foundation for more complex queries.

The process you have decided to recreate is as follows:

*"Return the top three movies in the romance genre sorted by IMDb rating, and return only movies released before 2001."*

This can be done by executing the following steps:

1. Translate your query into sequential stages that you can map to your aggregation stages: limit to three movies, match only romance movies, sort by IMDb rating, and match only movies released before 2001.

2. Simplify your stages wherever possible by merging duplicate stages. In this case, you can merge the two match stages: limit to three movies, sort by IMDb rating, and match romance movies released before 2001.

   It's important to remember that the order of the stages is essential and will produce incorrect results unless we rearrange them. To demonstrate this in action, we'll leave them in the incorrect order for now.

3. Take a quick peek into the structure of the movie documents to help write the stages:

```
db.movies.findOne();
```

The document appears as follows:

```
MongoDB Enterprise atlas-nb3biv-shard-0:PRIMARY> db.movies.findOne()
{
        "_id" : ObjectId("573a1390f29313caabcd4135"),
        "plot" : "Three men hammer on an anvil and pass a bottle of beer around.",
        "genres" : [
                "Short"
        ],
        "runtime" : 1,
        "cast" : [
                "Charles Kayser",
                "John Ott"
        ],
        "num_mflix_comments" : 1,
        "title" : "Blacksmith Scene",
        "fullplot" : "A stationary camera looks at a large anvil with a blacksmith behind
it and one
 on either side. The smith in the middle draws a heated metal rod from the fire, places it
 on the an
vil, and all three begin a rhythmic hammering. After several blows, the metal goes back in
 the fire.
 One smith pulls out a bottle of beer, and they each take a swig. Then, out comes the glow
ing metal
```

Figure 7.4: Looking at the document structure (output truncated for brevity)

For this particular use case, you will need the **imdb.rating**, **released**, and **genres** fields. Now that you know what you're searching for, you can begin writing up your pipeline.

4. Create a file called **Ch7_Activity1.js** and add the following basic stages: **limit** to limit the output to three movies, **sort** to sort them by their rating, and **match** to make sure you only find romantic movies released before 2001:

```
// Ch7_Exercise1.js
var findTopRomanceMovies = function() {
      print("Finding top Classic Romance Movies...");
      var pipeline = [
          { $limit: 3 }, // Limit to 3 results.
            { $sort: {"imdb.rating": -1}}, // Sort by IMDB rating.
      { $match: {. . .}}
        ];
        db.movies.aggregate(pipeline).forEach(printjson);
   }
     findTopRomanceMovies();
```

The **$match** operator functions very similarly to the filter parameter in the **find** command. You can simply pass in two conditions instead of one.

5. For the **older than 2001** condition, use the **$lte** operator:

```
// Ch7_Exercise1.js
   var findTopRomanceMovies = function() {
        print("Finding top Classic Romance Movies...");
        var pipeline = [
            { $limit: 3 },             // Limit to 3 results.
            { $sort: {"imdb.rating": -1}}, // Sort by IMDB rating.
            { $match: {
                genres: {$in: ["Romance"]}, // Romance movies only.
                released: {$lte: new ISODate("2001-01-01T00:00:
                  00Z") }}},
        ];
        db.movies.aggregate(pipeline).forEach(printjson);
   }
   findTopRomanceMovies();
```

Because the **genres** field is an array (movies can belong to multiple genres), you must use the **$in** operator to find arrays containing your desired value.

6. Run this pipeline now; you may notice that it returns no documents:

```
MongoDB Enterprise atlas-nb3biv-shard-0:PRIMARY>
   findTopRomanceMovies();
Finding top Classic Romance Movies...
MongoDB Enterprise atlas-nb3biv-shard-0:PRIMARY>
```

Is it possible that no documents satisfy this query? Of course, there may be no movies that satisfy all these requirements. However, as you may have already guessed, that is not the case here. As stated earlier, it's the order of this pipeline that's producing misleading results. Because your limit stage is the first stage in your pipeline, you are only ever looking at three documents, and the subsequent stages don't have enough data to find a match. Therefore, it is always important to remember:

*When writing aggregation pipelines, the order of operations matters.*

So, rearrange them to make sure that you only limit your documents at the end of your pipeline. Thanks to the array-like structure of the command, this is quite easy: just cut the limit stage and paste it at the end of your pipeline.

7. Arrange the stages so that the limit occurs last and does not produce incorrect results:

```
// Our new pipeline.
var pipeline = [
            { $sort: {"imdb.rating": -1}}, // Sort by IMDB rating.
            { $match: {
                genres: {$in: ["Romance"]}, // Romance movies only.
                released: {$lte: new ISODate("2001-01-01T00:00:
                    00Z") }}},
            { $limit: 3 },  // Limit to 3 results (last stage)
        ];
```

8. Rerun this after the change. This time, the documents are returned:

```
MongoDB Enterprise atlas-nb3biv-shard-0:PRIMARY> findTopRomanceMovies()
Finding top Classic Romance Movies...
{
        "_id" : ObjectId("573a1399f29313caabceeead"),
        "plot" : "Jane Austen's classic novel about the prejudice that occurred between th
e 19th cen
tury classes and the pride which would keep lovers apart.",
        "genres" : [
                "Drama",
                "Romance"
        ],
        "runtime" : 327,
        "cast" : [
                "Jennifer Ehle",
                "Colin Firth",
                "Susannah Harker",
                "Julia Sawalha"
        ],
        "poster" : "https://m.media-amazon.com/images/M/MV5BMDM0MjFlOGYtNTg2ZC00MmRkLTg5OT
QtM2U5ZjUy
YTgxZThiXkEyXkFqcGdeQXVyNTAyODkwOQ@@._V1_SY1000_SX677_AL_.jpg",
        "title" : "Pride and Prejudice",
```

Figure 7.5: Output with valid document return (output truncated for brevity)

This is one of the challenges of writing aggregation pipelines: it is an iterative process and can be cumbersome when dealing with large numbers of complex documents.

One way to relieve this pain point is to add stages during development that simplify the data, and then to remove these stages in your final query. In this case, you will add a stage to project only the data you're querying on. This will make it easier to tell whether you're capturing the right conditions. You must be careful when doing this that you do not affect the results of the query. We will discuss this in more detail later in this chapter. For now, you can simply add the projection stage right at the end to ensure that it will not interfere with your query.

9. Add a projection stage at the end of the pipeline to help debug your query:

```
var pipeline = [
    { $sort:  {"imdb.rating": -1}}, // Sort by IMDB rating.
    { $match: {
    genres: {$in: ["Romance"]}, // Romance movies only.
    released: {$lte: new ISODate("2001-01-01T00:00:00Z") }}},
    { $limit: 3 },       // Limit to 3 results.
    { $project: { genres: 1, released: 1, "imdb.rating": 1}}
];
```

10. Run this query again and you will see a much shorter, more easily understood output, as shown in the following code block:

```
MongoDB Enterprise atlas-nb3biv-shard-0:PRIMARY> findTopRomanceMovies()
Finding top Classic Romance Movies...
{
        "_id" : ObjectId("573a1399f29313caabceeead"),
        "genres" : [
                "Drama",
                "Romance"
        ],
        "released" : ISODate("1996-01-14T00:00:00Z"),
        "imdb" : {
                "rating" : 9.1
        }
}
{
        "_id" : ObjectId("573a1399f29313caabcee607"),
        "imdb" : {
                "rating" : 8.8
        },
        "genres" : [
                "Drama",
                "Romance"
        ],
```

Figure 7.6: Output for the preceding snippet

If you're running the code from a file on your desktop, remember that you can simply copy and paste the entire code snippet (as follows) directly into your shell:

```
// Ch7_Exercise1.js
var findTopRomanceMovies = function() {
    print("Finding top Classic Romance Movies...");
        var pipeline = [
        { $sort: {"imdb.rating": -1}}, // Sort by IMDB rating.
        { $match: {
            genres: {$in: ["Romance"]}, // Romance movies only.
```

```
            released: {$lte: new ISODate("2001-01-01T00:00:
                00Z") }}},
        { $limit: 3 },              // Limit to 3 results.
        { $project: { genres: 1, released: 1, "imdb.rating": 1}}
    ];
        db.movies.aggregate(pipeline).forEach(printjson);
    }
findTopRomanceMovies();
```

The output should be as follows:

```
MongoDB Enterprise atlas-nb3biv-shard-0:PRIMARY> findTopRomanceMovies()
Finding top Classic Romance Movies...
{
        "_id" : ObjectId("573a1399f29313caabceeead"),
        "genres" : [
                "Drama",
                "Romance"
        ],
        "released" : ISODate("1996-01-14T00:00:00Z"),
        "imdb" : {
                "rating" : 9.1
        }
}
{
        "_id" : ObjectId("573a1399f29313caabcee607"),
        "imdb" : {
                "rating" : 8.8
        },
        "genres" : [
                "Drama",
                "Romance"
        ],
```

Figure 7.7: List of the top classic romance movies released before 2001

You can also see that each of the returned movies is in the romance category, was released before 2001, and has a high IMDb rating. So, in this exercise, you have successfully created your first aggregation pipeline. Now, let's take the pipeline we just completed and try to improve it with a little effort. It is often helpful, when you believe you have completed a pipeline, to ask yourself:

*"Can I reduce the number of documents being passed down the pipeline?"*

In the next exercise, we will try to answer this question.

## EXERCISE 7.02: AGGREGATION STRUCTURE

Think of the pipeline as a multi-tiered funnel. It starts broad at the top and becomes thinner as it approaches the bottom. As you pour documents into the top of the funnel, there are many documents, but as you move further down, this number keeps reducing at every stage, until only the documents that you want as output exit at the bottom. Usually, the easiest way to accomplish this is to do your matching (*filtering*) first.

In this pipeline, you will sort all the documents in the collection, and discard the ones that don't match. You are currently sorting documents you don't need. Swap those stages around:

1. Swap the **match** and **sort** stages to improve the efficiency of your pipeline:

```
var pipeline = [
    { $match: {
        genres: {$in: ["Romance"]}, // Romance movies only.
        released: {$lte: new ISODate("2001-01-01T00:00:
            00Z") }}},
    { $sort: {"imdb.rating": -1}}, // Sort by IMDB rating.
    { $limit: 3 },                 // Limit to 3 results.
    { $project: { genres: 1, released: 1,
      "imdb.rating": 1}}
];
```

Another thing to consider is that, although you do have a list of movies matching the criteria, you want your result to be meaningful to your use case. In this case, you want your result to be meaningful and useful to the movie company looking at this data. It is likely that they will care most about the movie title and rating. They may also wish to see that the movie matches their requirements, so let's project those out at the end as well, discarding all other attributes.

2. Add the movie **title** field to your projection stage. Your final aggregation should look like this:

```
// Ch7_Exercise2.js
var findTopRomanceMovies = function() {
    print("Finding top Classic Romance Movies...");
    var pipeline = [
        { $match: {
            genres: {$in: ["Romance"]}, // Romance movies only.
            released: {$lte: new ISODate("2001-01-01T00:00:
                00Z") }}},
        { $sort: {"imdb.rating": -1}}, // Sort by IMDB rating.
```

```
        { $limit: 3 },       // Limit to 3 results.
        { $project: { title: 1, genres: 1, released: 1,
          "imdb.rating": 1}}
    ];
    db.movies.aggregate(pipeline).forEach(printjson);

}
findTopRomanceMovies();
```

3. Rerun your pipeline by copying and pasting the code from *step 2* into your mongo shell. You should see that the top two movies are **Pride and Prejudice** and **Forrest Gump**:

```
MongoDB Enterprise atlas-nb3biv-shard-0:PRIMARY> var findTopRomanceMovies = function() {
...     print("Finding top Classic Romance Movies...");
...     var pipeline = [
...         { $match: {
...             genres: {$in: ["Romance"]}, // Romance movies only.
...             released: {$lte: new ISODate("2001-01-01T00:00:00Z") }}},
...         { $sort: {"imdb.rating": -1}}, // Sort by IMDB rating.
...         { $limit: 3 },     // Limit to 3 results.
...         { $project: { title: 1, genres: 1, released: 1, "imdb.rating": 1}}
...     ];
...     db.movies.aggregate(pipeline).forEach(printjson);
... }
MongoDB Enterprise atlas-nb3biv-shard-0:PRIMARY> findTopRomanceMovies();
Finding top Classic Romance Movies...
{
        "_id" : ObjectId("573a1399f29313caabceeead"),
        "genres" : [
                "Drama",
                "Romance"
        ],
        "title" : "Pride and Prejudice",
        "released" : ISODate("1996-01-14T00:00:00Z"),
```

Figure 7.8: Output for preceding snippet

If you see these results, you have just optimized your first aggregation pipeline.

As you can see, the aggregation pipeline is flexible, robust, and easy to manipulate, but you may be thinking that it seems a little heavy-duty for this use case and that possibly a simple **find** command might do the trick in most cases. Indeed, the aggregation pipeline is not needed for every simple query, but you're just getting started. In the next few sections, you'll see what the **aggregate** command provides that the **find** command does not.

# MANIPULATING DATA

Most of our activities and examples can be reduced to the following: there is a document or documents in a collection that should return some or all the documents in an easy-to-digest format. At their core, the **find** command and aggregation pipeline are just about identifying and fetching the correct document. However, the capability of the aggregation pipeline is much more robust and broader than that of the **find** command.

Using some of the more advanced stages and techniques in the pipeline allows us to transform our data, derive new data, and generate insights across a broader scope. This more extensive implementation of the aggregate command is more common than merely rewriting a find command as a pipeline. If you want to answer complex questions or extract the highest possible value from your data, you'll need to know how to achieve the aggregation part of your aggregation pipelines.

After all, we haven't even begun to aggregate any data yet. In this topic, we'll explore the basics of how you can begin to transform and aggregate your data.

## THE GROUP STAGE

As you may expect from the name, the **$group** stage allows you to group (*or aggregate*) documents based on a specific condition. Although there are many other stages and methods to accomplish various tasks with the **aggregate** command, the **$group** stage serves as the cornerstone of the most powerful queries. Previously, the most significant unit of data we could return was a single document. We can sort these documents to gain insight through a direct comparison of the documents. However, once we master the **$group** stage, we will be able to increase the scope of our queries to an entire collection by aggregating our documents into large logical units. Once we have the larger groups, we can apply our filters, sorts, limits, and projections just as we did on a per-document basis.

The most basic implementation of a **$group** stage accepts only an **_id** key, with the value being an expression. This expression defines the criteria by which the pipeline groups documents together. This value becomes the **_id** of the newly outputted document with one document generated for each unique **_id** that the **$group** stage creates. For example, the following code will group all movies by their rating, outputting a single record for each rating category:

```
var pipeline = [
  {$group: {
     _id: "$rated"
  }}
```

```
        ];
        db.movies.aggregate(pipeline).forEach(printjson);
```

The resultant output will be as follows:

```
{ "_id" : "NC-17" }
{ "_id" : "AO" }
{ "_id" : "X" }
{ "_id" : "M" }
{ "_id" : "Approved" }
{ "_id" : "GP" }
{ "_id" : "PG" }
{ "_id" : "TV-MA" }
{ "_id" : null }
{ "_id" : "PASSED" }
{ "_id" : "Not Rated" }
{ "_id" : "APPROVED" }
{ "_id" : "TV-14" }
{ "_id" : "R" }
{ "_id" : "TV-G" }
{ "_id" : "UNRATED" }
{ "_id" : "TV-PG" }
{ "_id" : "TV-Y7" }
{ "_id" : "NOT RATED" }
{ "_id" : "OPEN" }
{ "_id" : "G" }
{ "_id" : "PG-13" }
```

**Figure 7.9: Resultant output for preceding snippet**

The first thing you may notice in our **$group** stage is the **$** notation before the **rated** field. As stated previously, the value of our **_id** key was an *expression*. In aggregation terms, an expression can be a literal, an expression object, an operator, or a field path. In this case, we are passing in a field path, which tells the pipeline which field to access in the input documents. You may or may not have run into field paths before in MongoDB.

You may be wondering why we can't just pass the field name as we would in a find command. This is because when aggregating, we need to tell the pipeline that we want to access the field of the document that it is currently aggregating. The **$group** stage will interpret **_id: "$rated"** as equivalent to **_id: "$$CURRENT. rated"**. This may seem complicated, but it indicates that for each document, it will fit into the group matching that same (current) document with the **"rated"** key. This will become clearer with practice in the next section.

So far, grouping by a single field has been useful to get a list of unique values. However, this hasn't told us much more about our data. We want to know more about these distinct groups; for example, how many titles fit into each of these groups? This is where our accumulator expressions will come in handy.

## ACCUMULATOR EXPRESSIONS

The **$group** command can accept more than just one argument. It can also accept any number of additional arguments in the following format:

```
field: { accumulator: expression},
```

Let's break this down into its three components:

- **field** will define the key of our newly computed field for each group.

- **accumulator** must be a supported accumulator operator. These are a group of operators, like other operators you may have worked with already – such as **$lte** – except, as the name suggests, they will accumulate their value across multiple documents belonging to the same group.

- **expression** in this context will be passed to the **accumulator** operator as the input of what field in each document it should be accumulating.

Building on the previous example, let's identify the total number of movies in each group:

```
var pipeline = [
  {$group: {
      _id: "$rated",
      "numTitles": { $sum: 1},
  }}
];
db.movies.aggregate(pipeline).forEach(printjson);
```

You can see from this that we can create a new field called **numTitles**, with the value of this field for each group being the sum of the documents. These newly created fields are often referred to as **computed fields**. For each document in a group, we can sum the literal value **1** with the accumulated result so far. Running this in the MongoDB shell will give us the following results:

```
{ "_id" : "NC-17", "numTitles" : 38 }
{ "_id" : "AO", "numTitles" : 3 }
{ "_id" : "X", "numTitles" : 38 }
{ "_id" : "M", "numTitles" : 37 }
{ "_id" : "Approved", "numTitles" : 5 }
{ "_id" : "GP", "numTitles" : 44 }
{ "_id" : "PG", "numTitles" : 1853 }
{ "_id" : "TV-MA", "numTitles" : 60 }
{ "_id" : null, "numTitles" : 9896 }
{ "_id" : "PASSED", "numTitles" : 182 }
{ "_id" : "Not Rated", "numTitles" : 1 }
{ "_id" : "APPROVED", "numTitles" : 711 }
{ "_id" : "TV-14", "numTitles" : 89 }
{ "_id" : "R", "numTitles" : 5538 }
{ "_id" : "TV-G", "numTitles" : 59 }
{ "_id" : "UNRATED", "numTitles" : 751 }
{ "_id" : "TV-PG", "numTitles" : 76 }
{ "_id" : "TV-Y7", "numTitles" : 3 }
{ "_id" : "NOT RATED", "numTitles" : 1354 }
{ "_id" : "OPEN", "numTitles" : 1 }
{ "_id" : "G", "numTitles" : 477 }
{ "_id" : "PG-13", "numTitles" : 2323 }
```

Figure 7.10: Output for preceding snippet

Similarly, instead of accumulating **1** on each document, you can accumulate the value of a given field. For example, let's say we want to find the total runtime of every single film in a rating. We group by the `rating` field and accumulate the runtime of each film:

```
var pipeline = [
 {$group: {
     _id: "$rated",
     "sumRuntime": { $sum: "$runtime"},
 }}
];
db.movies.aggregate(pipeline).forEach(printjson);
```

Remember, we must prefix the runtime field with the **$** symbol to tell MongoDB we are referring to the runtime value of each document we are accumulating. Our new result is as follows:

```
{ "_id" : "Not Rated", "sumRuntime" : 116 }
{ "_id" : "Approved", "sumRuntime" : 472 }
{ "_id" : "OPEN", "sumRuntime" : 85 }
{ "_id" : null, "sumRuntime" : 967127 }
{ "_id" : "TV-PG", "sumRuntime" : 8183 }
{ "_id" : "GP", "sumRuntime" : 4864 }
{ "_id" : "NC-17", "sumRuntime" : 4208 }
{ "_id" : "PASSED", "sumRuntime" : 17886 }
{ "_id" : "UNRATED", "sumRuntime" : 77807 }
{ "_id" : "PG-13", "sumRuntime" : 250843 }
{ "_id" : "PG", "sumRuntime" : 191204 }
{ "_id" : "TV-14", "sumRuntime" : 10527 }
{ "_id" : "G", "sumRuntime" : 43044 }
{ "_id" : "AO", "sumRuntime" : 274 }
{ "_id" : "NOT RATED", "sumRuntime" : 142308 }
{ "_id" : "M", "sumRuntime" : 4107 }
{ "_id" : "TV-MA", "sumRuntime" : 7048 }
{ "_id" : "APPROVED", "sumRuntime" : 74571 }
{ "_id" : "R", "sumRuntime" : 582318 }
{ "_id" : "X", "sumRuntime" : 3960 }
{ "_id" : "TV-Y7", "sumRuntime" : 244 }
{ "_id" : "TV-G", "sumRuntime" : 4653 }
```

Figure 7.11:Output for preceding snippet

Although this is a simple example, you can see that with just a single aggregation stage and two parameters, we can begin to transform our data in exciting ways. Several accumulator operators can be combined and layered to generate much more complex and insightful information about groups. We will see some of these operators in the upcoming examples.

It's important to note that we can use more than just accumulator operators as our expressions. We can also use several other useful operators to transform data after accumulating it. Let's say we want to get the average runtime of the titles for each of our groups. We can change our **$sum** accumulator to **$avg**, which will return the average runtime across each group, so our pipeline becomes as follows:

```
var pipeline = [
  {$group: {
      _id: "$rated",
      "avgRuntime": { $avg: "$runtime"},
  }}
];
db.movies.aggregate(pipeline).forEach(printjson);
```

And our output becomes:

```
MongoDB Enterprise atlas-nb3biv-shard-0:PRIMARY>      var pipeline = [
      ...        {$group: {
      ...           _id: "$rated",
      ...           "avgRuntime": { $avg: "$runtime"},
      ...        }}
      ...      ];
      MongoDB Enterprise atlas-nb3biv-shard-0:PRIMARY>      db.movies.aggregate(pipeline).for
Each(printjson
      );
      { "_id" : "NOT RATED", "avgRuntime" : 105.64810690423162 }
      { "_id" : "TV-14", "avgRuntime" : 128.3780487804878 }
      { "_id" : "G", "avgRuntime" : 90.81012658227849 }
      { "_id" : "AO", "avgRuntime" : 91.33333333333333 }
      { "_id" : "Not Rated", "avgRuntime" : 116 }
      { "_id" : "PG", "avgRuntime" : 103.74606619641888 }
      { "_id" : "TV-G", "avgRuntime" : 80.22413793103448 }
      { "_id" : "X", "avgRuntime" : 104.21052631578948 }
      { "_id" : "APPROVED", "avgRuntime" : 105.17771509167842 }
      { "_id" : "R", "avgRuntime" : 105.53062703878217 }
      { "_id" : "M", "avgRuntime" : 111 }
      { "_id" : "TV-MA", "avgRuntime" : 121.51724137931035 }
      { "_id" : "TV-Y7", "avgRuntime" : 81.33333333333333 }
```

Figure 7.12:Average runtime values based on rating

These average runtime values are not particularly useful in this case. Let's add another stage to project the runtime, using the **$trunc** stage, to give us an integer value:

```
var pipeline = [
  {$group: {
      _id: "$rated",
      "avgRuntime": { $avg: "$runtime"},
  }},
  {$project: {
      "roundedAvgRuntime": { $trunc: "$avgRuntime"}
  }}
];
db.movies.aggregate(pipeline).forEach(printjson);
```

This will give us a much more nicely formatted result, like this:

```
{ "_id" : "PG-13", "avgRuntime" : 108 }
```

This section demonstrated how combining the group stage with operators, accumulators, and other stages can help manipulate our data to answer a much broader number of business questions. Now, let's start aggregating and put this new stage into practice.

## EXERCISE 7.03: MANIPULATING DATA

In the previous scenario, you became accustomed to the shape of the data and recreated one of the client's manual processes as an aggregation pipeline. As part of the lead up to the classic movie marathon, the cinema company has decided to try and run one movie for each genre (one per week until the marathon) and they want to run the most popular genres last to build hype around the event. However, they have a problem. Their schedule for these weeks has already been dictated, meaning the classic movies will have to fit into the gaps in the schedule. So, to accomplish this, they must know the length of the longest movie in each genre, including adding time for trailers on each film.

> **NOTE**
>
> In this scenario, **popularity** is defined by the **IMDb rating**, and trailers run for 12 minutes before any film.

The aim can be summarized as follows:

*"For only movies older than 2001, find the average and maximum popularity for each genre, sort the genres by popularity, and find the adjusted (with trailers) runtime of the longest movie in each genre."*

Translate the query into sequential stages so that you can map to your aggregation stages:

- Match movies that were released before 2001.

- Find the average popularity of each genre.

- Sort the genres by popularity.

- Output the adjusted runtime of each movie.

Since you've learned more about the group stage, elaborate on that step using your new knowledge:

- Match movies that were released before 2001.

- Group all movies by their first genre and accumulate the average and maximum IMDb ratings.

- Sort by the average popularity of each genre.

- Project the adjusted runtime as `total_runtime`.

The following steps will help you complete this exercise.

1. Create the outline for your aggregation first. Create a new file called **Ch7_Exercise3.js**:

```
// Ch7_Exercise3.js
var findGenrePopularity = function() {
  print("Finding popularity of each genre");
  var pipeline = [
          { $match: {}},
          { $group: {}},
          { $sort: {}},
          { $project: {}}
      ];
      db.movies.aggregate(pipeline).forEach(printjson);
  }
    findGenrePopularity();
```

2. Fill in the steps one at a time, starting with **$match**:

```
        { $match: {
            released: {$lte: new ISODate("2001-01-01T00:00:
              00Z") }}},
```

This resembles *Exercise 7.01*, *Performing Simple Aggregations*, where you matched all the documents released before 2001.

3. For the **$group** stage, first identify your new **id** for each output document:

```
{ $group: {
    _id: {"$arrayElemAt": ["$genres", 0]},
}},
```

The **$arrayElemAt** takes an element from an array at the specified index (*in this case, 0*). For this scenario, assume that the first genre in the array is the primary genre of a film.

Next, specify the new computed fields you require in the result. Remember to use the accumulator operators, including **$avg** (*average*) and **$max** (*maximum*). Remember that in **accumulator**, because you are referencing a variable, you must prefix the field with a **$** notation:

```
{ $group: {
    _id: {"$arrayElemAt": ["$genres", 0]},
    "popularity": {  $avg: "$imdb.rating"},
```

```
        "top_movie": { $max: "$imdb.rating"},
        "longest_runtime": { $max: "$runtime"}
}},
```

4. Fill in the **sort** field. Now that you have defined your computed fields, this is simple:

```
{ $sort: { popularity: -1}},
```

5. To get the adjusted runtime, use the **$add** operator and add **12** (minutes). You add 12 minutes because the client (the cinema company) has informed you that this is the length of the trailers running before each movie. Once you have the adjusted runtime, you will no longer need **longest_runtime**:

```
{ $project: {
    _id: 1,
    popularity: 1,
    top_movie: 1,
    adjusted_runtime: { $add: [ "$longest_runtime", 12 ] } } }
```

6. Also add a **$**. Your final aggregation pipeline should look like this:

```
var findGenrePopularity = function() {
    print("Finding popularity of each genre");
    var pipeline = [
        { $match: {
        released: {$lte: new ISODate("2001-01-01T00:00:00Z") }}},
        { $group: {
            _id: {"$arrayElemAt": ["$genres", 0]},
            "popularity": {  $avg: "$imdb.rating"},
            "top_movie": { $max: "$imdb.rating"},
            "longest_runtime": { $max: "$runtime"}
        }},
        { $sort: { popularity: -1}},
        { $project: {
            _id: 1,
            popularity: 1,
            top_movie: 1,
            adjusted_runtime: { $add: [ "$longest_runtime",
                12 ] } } }
    ];
```

```
          db.movies.aggregate(pipeline).forEach(printjson);
  }

  findGenrePopularity();
```

If your results are correct, your top few documents should be as follows:

```
MongoDB Enterprise atlas-nb3biv-shard-0:PRIMARY>       findGenrePopularity();
Finding popularity of each genre
{
        "_id" : "Film-Noir",
        "popularity" : 7.62,
        "top_movie" : 8.3,
        "adjusted_runtime" : 123
}
{
        "_id" : "Documentary",
        "popularity" : 7.555313351498638,
        "top_movie" : 9.4,
        "adjusted_runtime" : 1152
}
{
        "_id" : "Short",
        "popularity" : 7.386,
        "top_movie" : 8.6,
        "adjusted_runtime" : 56
}
```

Figure 7.13:Top few documents returned

The output shows that noir films, documentaries and short films are the most popular, and we can also see the average runtime for each category. In the next exercise, we will select a title from each category based on certain requirements.

## EXERCISE 7.04: SELECTING THE TITLE FROM EACH MOVIE CATEGORY

You have now answered the question posed to you by your client. However, this result won't aid them in picking a specific movie. They must execute a different query to get a list of movies in each genre and pick the best movie to show from the list. Additionally, you have also learned that the maximum time slot available is 230 minutes. You will alter this query to offer the cinema company a recommended title to choose in each category. The following steps will help you complete this exercise:

1. First, increase the first match to filter out films that aren't applicable. Filter out films longer than 218 minutes (230 plus trailers). Also filter out films with a lower rating. To begin, you'll get movies with a rating above 7.0:

```
{ $match: {
  released: {$lte: new ISODate("2001-01-01T00:00:00Z") },
  runtime:  {$lte: 218},
```

```
     "imdb.rating": {$gte: 7.0}
    }
  },
```

2.  To get the recommended title for each category, use the **$first** accumulator in our group stage to get the top document (movie) for each genre. To do this, you will have to first sort by rating in descending order, ensuring that the first document is also the highest rated. Add a new **$sort** stage after the initial **$match** stage:

```
{ $sort: {"imdb.rating": -1}},
```

3.  Now, add the **$first** accumulator to your group stage, adding your new fields. Also add **recommended_rating** and **recommended_raw_runtime** fields for ease of use:

```
{ $group: {
  _id: {"$arrayElemAt": ["$genres", 0]},
   "recommended_title": {$first: "$title"},
   "recommended_rating": {$first: "$imdb.rating"},
   "recommended_raw_runtime": {$first: "$runtime"},
   "popularity": {   $avg: "$imdb.rating"},
   "top_movie": { $max: "$imdb.rating"},
   "longest_runtime": { $max: "$runtime"}
}},
```

4.  Ensure that you add this new field to your final projection:

```
{ $project: {
    _id: 1,
    popularity: 1,
    top_movie: 1,
    recommended_title: 1,
    recommended_rating: 1,
    recommended_raw_runtime: 1,
    adjusted_runtime: { $add: [ "$longest_runtime", 12 ] } } } }
```

Your new final query should look like this:

```
// Ch7_Exercise4js
var findGenrePopularity = function() {
    print("Finding popularity of each genre");
    var pipeline = [
        { $match: {
        released: {$lte: new ISODate("2001-01-01T00:00:00Z") },
            runtime:  {$lte: 218},
            "imdb.rating": {$gte: 7.0}
            }
        },
            { $sort: {"imdb.rating": -1}},
            { $group: {
            _id: {"$arrayElemAt": ["$genres", 0]},
             "recommended_title": {$first: "$title"},
             "recommended_rating": {$first: "$imdb.rating"},
             "recommended_raw_runtime": {$first: "$runtime"},
             "popularity": {   $avg: "$imdb.rating"},
             "top_movie": { $max: "$imdb.rating"},
             "longest_runtime": { $max: "$runtime"}
        }},
            { $sort: { popularity: -1}},
            { $project: {
                _id: 1,
                popularity: 1,
                top_movie: 1,
                recommended_title: 1,
                recommended_rating: 1,
                recommended_raw_runtime: 1,
                adjusted_runtime: { $add: [ "$longest_runtime",
                    12 ] } } }
        ];
        db.movies.aggregate(pipeline).forEach(printjson);
    }
    findGenrePopularity();
```

5. Execute this, and your first two result documents should look something like the following:

```
MongoDB Enterprise atlas-nb3biv-shard-0:PRIMARY> findGenrePopularity()
Finding popularity of each genre
{
        "_id" : "Film-Noir",
        "recommended_title" : "The Third Man",
        "recommended_rating" : 8.3,
        "recommended_raw_runtime" : 93,
        "popularity" : 7.85,
        "top_movie" : 8.3,
        "adjusted_runtime" : 123
}
{

        "_id" : "Documentary",
        "recommended_title" : "Cosmos",
        "recommended_rating" : 9.3,
        "recommended_raw_runtime" : 60,
        "popularity" : 7.69695945945946,
        "top_movie" : 9.3,
        "adjusted_runtime" : 212
}
```

Figure 7.14:First two result documents

You can see that with a few additions to your pipeline, you have extracted the movies with the highest ratings and longest runtimes to create extra value for your client.

In this topic, we saw how we could query data and then sort, limit, and project our results. In this topic, we saw that by using more advanced aggregation stages, we can accomplish much more complicated tasks. Data is manipulated and transformed to create new, meaningful documents. These new stages empower the user to answer a much broader range of more difficult business questions, as well as gain valuable insight into datasets.

# WORKING WITH LARGE DATASETS

So far, we've been working with a relatively small number of documents. The **movies** collection has roughly 23,500 documents in it. This may be a considerable number for a human to work with, but for large production systems, you may be working on a scale of millions instead of thousands. So far, we have also been focusing strictly on a single collection at a time, but what if the scope of our aggregation grows to include multiple collections?

In the first topic, we briefly discussed how you could use the projection stage while developing your pipelines to create more readable output as well as simplify your results for debugging. However, we didn't cover how you can improve performance when working on much, much larger datasets, both while developing and for your final production-ready queries. In this topic, we'll discuss a few of the aggregation stages that you need to master when working with large, multi-collection datasets.

## SAMPLING WITH $SAMPLE

The first step in learning how to deal with large datasets is understanding **$sample**. This stage is simple yet useful. The only parameter to **$sample** is the desired size of your sample. This stage randomly selects documents (up to your specified size) and passes them through to the next stage:

```
{ $sample: {size: 100}}, // This will reduce the scope to
  100 random docs.
```

By doing this, you can significantly reduce the number of documents going through your pipeline. Primarily, this is useful for one of two reasons. The first reason is to speed up the execution time when running against enormous datasets—mainly while you are fine-tuning or building your aggregation. The second is for queries where the use case can tolerate documents missing from the result. For example, if you want to return any five films in a genre, you can use **$sample**:

```
var findWithSample = function() {
    print("Finding all documents WITH sampling")
    var now = Date.now();
    var pipeline = [
        { $sample: {size: 100}},
        { $match: {
            "plot": { $regex: /around/}
        }}
    ];
    db.movies.aggregate(pipeline)
    var duration = Date.now() - now;
    print("Finished WITH sampling in " + duration+"ms");
}
findWithSample();
```

The following result will be achieved after executing your new
**findWithSample()** function:

```
Finding all documents WITH sampling
Finished WITH sampling in 194ms
```

You may be wondering why you wouldn't just use a **$limit** command to achieve
the same result of reducing the number of documents at some stage in your pipeline.
The primary reason is that **$limit** always respects the order of the documents and
thus returns the same documents every time. However, it is important to note that in
some cases, where you do not require the pseudo-random selection of **$sample**, it is
wiser to use **$limit**.

Let's see an example of **$sample** in action. Here is a query to search all movies for a
specific keyword in the **plot** field, implemented both with and without **$sample**:

```
var findWithoutSample = function() {
    print("Finding all documents WITHOUT sampling")
    var now = Date.now();
    var pipeline =[
        { $match: {
            "plot": { $regex: /around/}
        }},
    ]
    db.movies.aggregate(pipeline)
    var duration = Date.now() - now;
    print("Finished WITHOUT sampling in " + duration+ "ms");
}
findWithoutSample();
```

The preceding example is not the best way to measure performance, and there are
much better ways to analyze the performance of your pipelines, such as **Explain**.
However, since we'll cover those in later parts of this book, this will serve as a simple
example. If you run this little script, you will get the following result consistently:

```
Finding all documents WITHOUT sampling
Finished WITHOUT sampling in 862ms
```

A simple comparison of the two outputs of these two commands is as follows:

```
Finding all documents WITH sampling
Finished WITH sampling in 194ms


Finding all documents WITHOUT sampling
Finished WITHOUT sampling in 862ms
```

With sampling, the performance is significantly improved. However, this is because we are only looking at 100 documents. More likely, in this case, we want to sample our result after the **match** statement to make sure we don't exclude all our results in the first stage. In most scenarios, when working on large datasets where the execution time is significant, you may want to sample at the beginning as you construct your pipeline and remove the sample once your query is finalized.

## JOINING COLLECTIONS WITH $LOOKUP

Sampling may assist you when developing queries against extensive collections, but in production queries, you may sometimes need to write queries that are operating across multiple collections. In MongoDB, these collection joins are done using the **$lookup** aggregation step.

These joins can be easily understood by the following aggregation:

```
var lookupExample = function() {
    var pipeline = [
        { $match:  { $or: [{"name": "Catelyn Stark"},
          {"name": "Ned Stark"}]}},
        { $lookup: {
            from: "comments",
            localField: "name",
            foreignField: "name",
            as: "comments"
        }},
   { $limit: 2},
    ];
    db.users.aggregate(pipeline).forEach(printjson);
}
lookupExample();
```

Let's dissect this before we try to run it. First, we are running a **$match** against the **users** collection to get only two users named **Ned Stark** and **Catelyn Stark**. Once we have these two records, we perform our lookup. The four parameters of **$lookup** are as follows:

- **from**: The collection we are joining to our current aggregation. In this case, we are joining **comments** to **users**.

- **localField**: The field name that we are going to use to join our documents in the local collection (*the collection we are running the aggregation on*). In this case, the name of our user.

- **foreignField**: The field that links to **localField** in the **from** collection. These may have different names, but in this scenario, it is the same field: **name**.

- **as**: This is how our new joined data will be labeled.

In this example, the lookup takes the name of our user, searches the **comments** collection, and adds any comments with the same name into a new array field for the original user document. This new array is called **comments**. In this way, we can fetch an array of all related documents in another collection and embed them in our original documents for use in the rest of our aggregation.

If we were to run the pipeline as it is, the beginning of the output would look something like this:

```
MongoDB Enterprise atlas-nb3biv-shard-0:PRIMARY> lookupExample();
{
        "_id" : ObjectId("59b99db4cfa9a34dcd7885b6"),
        "name" : "Ned Stark",
        "email" : "sean_bean@gameofthron.es",
        "password" : "$2b$12$UREFwsRUoyF0CRqGNK0Lz00HM/jLhgUCNNIJ9RJAqMUQ74crlJ1Vu",
        "comments" : [
                {
                        "_id" : ObjectId("5a9427648b0beebeb6957b83"),
                        "name" : "Ned Stark",
                        "email" : "sean_bean@gameofthron.es",
                        "movie_id" : ObjectId("573a1391f29313caabcd8243"),
                        "text" : "Illo nostrum enim sequi doloremque dolore saepe beatae.
Iusto alia
s odit quaerat id dolores. Dolore quaerat accusantium esse voluptatibus. Aspernatur fuga e
xercitatio
nem explicabo.",
                        "date" : ISODate("2000-01-21T03:17:04Z")
                },
                {
                        "_id" : ObjectId("5a9427648b0beebeb6957d08"),
                        "name" : "Ned Stark",
```

Figure 7.15:Output after running the pipeline (truncated for brevity)

Because the output is very large, the preceding screenshot shows only the start of the **comments** array.

In this example, users have made many comments, so the embedded array becomes quite substantial and challenging to view. This issue presents an excellent place to introduce the **$unwind** operator, as these joins can often result in large arrays of related documents. **$unwind** is a relatively simple stage. It deconstructs an array field from an input document to output a new document for each element in the array. For example, if you unwind this document:

```
{a: 1, b: 2, c: [1, 2, 3, 4]}
```

The output will be the following documents:

```
{"a" : 1, "b" : 2, "c" : 1 }
{"a" : 1, "b" : 2, "c" : 2 }
{"a" : 1, "b" : 2, "c" : 3 }
{"a" : 1, "b" : 2, "c" : 4 }
```

We can add this new stage to our join and try running it:

```
var lookupExample = function() {
    var pipeline = [
        { $match:   { $or: [{"name": "Catelyn Stark"},
            {"name": "Ned Stark"}]}},
        { $lookup: {
            from: "comments",
            localField: "name",
            foreignField: "name",
            as: "comments"
        }},
        { $unwind: "$comments"},
        { $limit: 3},
    ];
    db.users.aggregate(pipeline).forEach(printjson);
}
lookupExample();
```

We will see output like this:

```
MongoDB Enterprise atlas-nb3biv-shard-0:PRIMARY> lookupExample();
{
        "_id" : ObjectId("59b99db4cfa9a34dcd7885b6"),
        "name" : "Ned Stark",
        "email" : "sean_bean@gameofthron.es",
        "password" : "$2b$12$UREFwsRUoyFOCRqGNK0LzO0HM/jLhgUCNNIJ9RJAqMUQ74crlJ1Vu",
        "comments" : {
                "_id" : ObjectId("5a9427648b0beebeb6957b83"),
                "name" : "Ned Stark",
                "email" : "sean_bean@gameofthron.es",
                "movie_id" : ObjectId("573a1391f29313caabcd8243"),
                "text" : "Illo nostrum enim sequi doloremque dolore saepe beatae. Iusto al
ias odit quaerat id dolores. Dolore quaerat accusantium esse voluptatibus. Aspernatur fuga
 exercitationem explicabo.",
                "date" : ISODate("2000-01-21T03:17:04Z")
        }
}
{
        "_id" : ObjectId("59b99db4cfa9a34dcd7885b6"),
        "name" : "Ned Stark",
        "email" : "sean_bean@gameofthron.es",
        "password" : "$2b$12$UREFwsRUoyFOCRqGNK0LzO0HM/jLhgUCNNIJ9RJAqMUQ74crlJ1Vu",
```

Figure 7.16:Output for preceding snippet (truncated for brevity)

We can see multiple documents per user with a single document for each comment instead of one embedded array. With this new format, we can add more stages to operate on our new set of documents. For example, we may wish to filter out any comments on a specific movie or sort our comments by their date. This combination of $lookup and $unwind is a powerful combination for answering complex questions across multiple collections in a single aggregation.

## OUTPUTTING YOUR RESULTS WITH $OUT AND $MERGE

Imagine that we've been working on a large, multi-stage aggregation pipeline over the last week. We have been debugging, sampling, filtering, and testing our pipeline to solve a challenging and complex business problem on a tremendously large dataset. We're finally happy with our pipeline, and we want to execute it and then save the results for subsequent analysis and presentation.

We could run the query and export the results into a new format. However, this would mean re-importing the results if we wanted to run subsequent analysis on the result set.

We could save the output in an array and then re-insert it into MongoDB, but that would mean transferring all the data from the server to the client, and then back from the client to the server.

Luckily for us, from MongoDB version 4.2 onward, we are provided with two aggregation stages that solve this problem for us: **$out** and **$merge**. Both stages allow us to take the output from our pipeline and write it into a collection for later use. Importantly, this whole process takes place on the server, meaning that all the data never needs to be transferred to the client across the network. It's not hard to imagine that after creating a complicated aggregation query, you may want to run it once a week and create a snapshot of your result by writing that data into a collection.

Let's look at the syntax of both these stages in their most basic form, and then we can compare how they function:

```
// Available from v2.6
{ $out: "myOutputCollection"}


// Available from version 4.2
{ $merge: {
    // This can also accept {db: <db>, coll: <coll>} to
      merge into a different db
    into: "myOutputCollection",
}}
```

As you can see, the syntax without any optional parameters is almost identical. In every other regard, however, the two commands diverge. **$out** is very simple; the only parameter to specify is the desired output collection. It will either create a new collection or completely replace an existing collection. **$out** also has several constraints not shared with **$merge**. For example, **$out** must output to the same database as the aggregation target.

When running on a MongoDB 4.2 server, **$merge** will probably be the better option. However, for the scope of this book, we will be using the MongoDB free tier, which runs MongoDB 4.0. Therefore, we will focus more on the **$out** stage in these examples.

The syntax for **$out** is very simple. The only parameter is the collection to which we want to output our result. Here is an example of a pipeline with **$out**:

```
var findTopRomanceMovies = function() {
    var pipeline = [
        { $sort:  {"imdb.rating": -1}}, // Sort by IMDB rating.
        { $match: {
            genres: {$in: ["Romance"]}, // Romance movies only.
            released: {$lte: new ISODate("2001-01-01T00:00:
                00Z") }}},
```

```
            { $limit: 5 },                  // Limit to 5 results.
            { $project: { title: 1, genres: 1, released: 1,
              "imdb.rating": 1}},
            { $out: "movies_top_romance"}
        ];

        db.movies.aggregate(pipeline).forEach(printjson);
    }
findTopRomanceMovies();
```

By running this pipeline, you will receive no output. This is because the output has been redirected to our desired collection:

```
MongoDB Enterprise atlas-nb3biv-shard-0:PRIMARY>
  findTopRomanceMovies();
MongoDB Enterprise atlas-nb3biv-shard-0:PRIMARY>
```

We can see that a new collection was created with our result:

```
MongoDB Enterprise atlas-nb3biv-shard-0:PRIMARY> show collections
comments
movies
movies_top_romance
sessions
theaters
users
```

And if we run a find on our new collection, we can see that the results of our aggregation are now stored within it:

```
MongoDB Enterprise atlas-nb3biv-shard-0:PRIMARY> db.movies_top_romance.
findOne({})
{
        "_id" : ObjectId("573a1399f29313caabceeead"),
        "genres" : [
                "Drama",
                "Romance"
        ],
        "title" : "Pride and Prejudice",
        "released" : ISODate("1996-01-14T00:00:00Z"),
        "imdb" : {
                "rating" : 9.1

        }
}
```

By placing our results into a collection, we can store, share, and update new complex aggregation results. We can even run further queries and aggregations against this new collection. **$out** is a simple but powerful aggregation stage.

## EXERCISE 7.05: LISTING THE MOST USER-COMMENTED MOVIES

The cinema company wishes to learn more about which movies generate the most comments from their users. However, given many comments in the database (and your disposition to use your newly learned skills), you have decided that while developing this pipeline, you will use only a sample of the comments. From this sample, you will figure out the most talked-about movies and join these documents with the document in the **movies** collection to get more information about the film. The company has also requested that the final deliverable of your work is a new collection with the output documents. This requirement should be easy to satisfy given that you now know the **$merge** stage.

Some additional information you have gathered is that they wish for the result to be as simple as possible and they wish to know the movie title and rating. Additionally, they would like to see the top five most commented-on movies.

In this exercise, you will help the cinema company to obtain a list of movies that generate the most comments from users. Perform the following steps to complete this exercise:

1.  First, outline the stages in your pipeline; they appear in the following order:

    **$sample** the **comments** collection (while building the pipeline).

    **$group** the comments by the movie for which they are targeted.

    **$sort** the result by the number of total comments.

    **$limit** the result to the top five movies by comments.

    **$lookup** the movie that matches each document.

    **$unwind** the movie array to keep the result documents simple.

    **$project** just the movie title and rating.

    **$merge** the result into a new collection.

    Although this may seem like many stages, each stage is relatively simple, and the process can be followed logically from beginning to end.

2. Create a new file called **Ch7_Exercise5.js** and write up your pipeline skeleton:

```
// Ch7_Exercise5.js
var findMostCommentedMovies = function() {
    print("Finding the most commented on movies.");
    var pipeline = [
                { $sample: {}},
                { $group: {}},
                { $sort: {}},
                { $limit: 5},
                { $lookup: {}},
                { $unwind: },
                { $project: {}},
                { $out: {}}
    ];
    db.comments.aggregate(pipeline).forEach(printjson);
}
findMostCommentedMovies();
```

3. Before deciding on sample size, you should get a sense of how large the **comments** collection is. Run **count** against the **comments** collection:

```
MongoDB Enterprise atlas-nb3biv-shard-0:PRIMARY>
    db.comments.count()
50303
```

4. Sample roughly ten percent of the collection while you're developing. Set the sample size to **5000** for this exercise:

```
{ $sample: {size: 5000}},
```

5. Now that you have the easier steps out of the way, fill in the **$group** statement to group the comments by their associated film, accumulating the total number of comments for each film:

```
{ $group: {
    _id: "$movie_id",
    "sumComments": { $sum: 1}
}},
```

6. Next up, add **sort** so the movies with the highest **sumComments** value are first:

```
{ $sort: { "sumComments": -1}},
```

7. When building pipelines, it's important to periodically run them partially completed to make sure you see the results you're expecting. Since you're about halfway through the stages, quickly comment out the incomplete stages and run the aggregation to list your most-commented movies. Keep in mind that because you are sampling, the results will not be the same each time you run your pipeline. The following output is just an example:

```
MongoDB Enterprise atlas-nb3biv-shard-0:PRIMARY> var findMostCommentedMovies = function ()
{
...    print('Finding the most commented on movies.');
...    var pipeline = [
...      { $sample: { size: 5000 } },
...      {
...        $group: {
...          _id: '$movie_id',
...          sumComments: { $sum: 1 },
...        },
...      },
...      { $sort: { sumComments: -1 } },
...      { $limit: 5 },
...      // { $lookup: {}},
...      // { $unwind: },
...      // { $project: {}},
...      // { $out: {}}
...    ];
...    db.comments.aggregate(pipeline).forEach(printjson);
... };
MongoDB Enterprise atlas-nb3biv-shard-0:PRIMARY> findMostCommentedMovies();
```

Figure 7.17: Example output

Our output will appear as follows:

```
MongoDB Enterprise atlas-nb3biv-shard-0:PRIMARY> findMostCommentedMovies();
Finding the most commented on movies.
{ "_id" : ObjectId("573a1399f29313caabcedb1f"), "sumComments" : 23 }
{ "_id" : ObjectId("573a1399f29313caabcee2fa"), "sumComments" : 21 }
{ "_id" : ObjectId("573a139af29313caabcf0500"), "sumComments" : 21 }
{ "_id" : ObjectId("573a13a5f29313caabd13a18"), "sumComments" : 21 }
{ "_id" : ObjectId("573a13c4f29313caabd6cc80"), "sumComments" : 20 }
```

Figure 7.18: Output after running the aggregation pipeline (truncated for brevity)

You now need to perform a lookup into the **movies** collection to match your comment groups with the movie documents:

```
{ $lookup: {
    from: "movies",
    localField: "_id",
    foreignField: "_id",
    as: "movie"
}},
```

Rerunning this, you can now see a **movie** array with all the movie details embedded within it:

```
MongoDB Enterprise atlas-nb3biv-shard-0:PRIMARY> findMostCommentedMovies();
Finding the most commented on movies.
{
        "_id" : ObjectId("573a13c0f29313caabd60d0d"),
        "sumComments" : 24,
        "movie" : [
                {
                        "_id" : ObjectId("573a13c0f29313caabd60d0d"),
                        "fullplot" : "Peter Klaven's world revolves around his real estate
 work and Zooey, his soon-to-be fiancée. After he pops the question, she calls her best f
riends and they go into wedding planning mode. Peter has no male friends and that poses pr
oblems: will he turn out to be a clingy guy, and who will be his best man? Zooey, her frie
nds, and Peter's brother Robbie offer help that results in awkward moments. Then, at an op
en house Peter's hosting, he meets Sydney, an amiable, low-key guy. They trade business ca
rds, and Peter calls him to meet for drinks. A friendship develops that's great at first b
ut then threatens Peter's engagement and career. Can guys be friends and couples be in lov
e?",
                        "imdb" : {
                                "rating" : 7.1,
                                "votes" : 157277,
                                "id" : 1155056
                        },
```

Figure 7.19: Output after re-running the pipeline

There is only one movie in each **movie** array, so unwind those arrays to simplify the structure. Once it is unwound, you can project out all the fields you don't care to see. Now, fill in these two steps:

```
{ $unwind: "$movie" },
{ $project: {
    "movie.title": 1,
    "movie.imdb.rating": 1,
    "sumComments": 1,
}}
```

8. Your data is now complete, but you still need to output this result into a collection. Add the **$out** step at the end:

```
{ $out: "most_commented_movies" }
```

Your final resulting code should look something like this:

```
// Ch7_Exercise5.js
var findMostCommentedMovies = function() {
    print("Finding the most commented on movies.");
    var pipeline = [
            { $sample: {size: 5000}},
            { $group: {
                _id: "$movie_id",
                "sumComments": { $sum: 1}
            }},
            { $sort: { "sumComments": -1}},
            { $limit: 5},
            { $lookup: {
                from: "movies",
                localField: "_id",
                foreignField: "_id",
                as: "movie"
            }},
            { $unwind: "$movie" },
            { $project: {
                "movie.title": 1,
                "movie.imdb.rating": 1,
                "sumComments": 1,
            }},
            { $out: "most_commented_movies" }
    ];
    db.comments.aggregate(pipeline).forEach(printjson);
}
findMostCommentedMovies();
```

Run this code. If all goes well, you will notice no output from your pipeline in the shell, but you should be able to check your newly created collection using `find()` and see your result. Remember, due to your sampling stage, the results will not be the same every time:

```
MongoDB Enterprise atlas-nb3biv-shard-0:PRIMARY> findMostCommentedMovies();
Finding the most commented on movies.
MongoDB Enterprise atlas-nb3biv-shard-0:PRIMARY> db.most_commented_movies.find({})
{ "_id" : ObjectId("573a139ef29313caabcfd114"), "sumComments" : 25, "movie" : { "imdb" : {
 "rating"
: 8.5 }, "title" : "Gladiator" } }
{ "_id" : ObjectId("573a1398f29313caabceb500"), "sumComments" : 22, "movie" : { "imdb" : {
 "rating"
: 7.8 }, "title" : "Back to the Future Part II" } }
{ "_id" : ObjectId("573a13a7f29313caabd1aa03"), "sumComments" : 22, "movie" : { "imdb" : {
 "rating"
: 7.1 }, "title" : "The Ring" } }
{ "_id" : ObjectId("573a13acf29313caabd289b3"), "sumComments" : 22, "movie" : { "imdb" : {
 "rating"
: 7.3 }, "title" : "Anchorman: The Legend of Ron Burgundy" } }
{ "_id" : ObjectId("573a13bef29313caabd5c293"), "sumComments" : 21, "movie" : { "imdb" : {
 "rating"
: 6.8 }, "title" : "A Christmas Carol" } }
MongoDB Enterprise atlas-nb3biv-shard-0:PRIMARY>
```

**Figure 7.20: Results from preceding snippet (output truncated for brevity)**

With the new phases we have learned about in this topic, we now possess an excellent foundation for performing aggregations on more massive, more complex datasets. Moreover, importantly, we are now able to join data between multiple collections effectively. By doing this, we can increase the scope of our queries and thus satisfy a much broader range of use cases.

With the **out** stage, we can store the result of our aggregations. This allows users to explore the results quickly with normal CRUD operations and allows us to keep updating the results regularly and easily. The unwind stage has also given us the ability to take the joined documents from a lookup and separate them into individual documents that we can feed into further pipeline stages.

With all these stages combined, we are now able to create extensive new aggregations that operate across large, multi-collection datasets.

# GETTING THE MOST FROM YOUR AGGREGATIONS

In the last three topics, we have learned about the structure of aggregation as well as the key stages required to build up complicated queries. We can search large multi-collection datasets with given criteria, manipulate that data to create new insights, and output our results into a new or existing collection.

These fundamentals will allow you to solve most of the problems you will encounter in an aggregation pipeline. However, there are several other stages and patterns for getting the most out of your aggregations. We won't cover them all in this book, but in this topic, we'll discuss a few of the odds and ends that will help you fine-tune your pipelines as well as some other odds and ends that we simply haven't covered so far. We'll be looking at aggregation options using **Explain** to analyze your aggregation.

## TUNING YOUR PIPELINES

In an earlier topic, we timed the execution of our pipeline by outputting the time before and after our aggregation. This is a valid technique, and you may often time your MongoDB queries on the client or application side. However, this only gives us a rough approximation of duration and only tells us the total time the response took to reach the client, not how long the server took to execute the pipeline. MongoDB provides us with a great way of learning exactly how it executed our requested query. This feature is known as **Explain** and is the usual way to examine and optimize our MongoDB commands.

However, there is one catch. **Explain** does not yet support detailed execution plans for aggregations, meaning its use is limited when it comes to the optimization of pipelines. **Explain** and execution plans will be covered in more detail later in this book. Since we can't rely on **Explain** to analyze our pipelines, it becomes even more integral to carefully construct and plan our pipeline to improve the performance of our aggregations. Although there is no single correct method that will work in any situation, there are some heuristics that can generally be helpful. We'll walk through a few of these methods with examples. MongoDB does a lot of performance optimization under the hood, but these are still good patterns to follow.

## FILTER EARLY AND FILTER OFTEN

Each stage of the aggregation pipeline will perform some processing on the input. That means the more significant the input, the larger the processing. If you've designed your pipeline correctly, this processing is unavoidable for the documents you are trying to return. The best you can do is to make sure you're processing *only* the documents you want to return.

The easiest way to accomplish this is by adding or moving pipeline stages that filter out documents. We've already done this in our previous scenarios with **$match** and **$limit**. A common way to ensure this is to have the very first stage in your pipeline be a **$match**, which matches only documents you need later in the pipeline. Let's understand this with the help of the following pipeline example, where the pipeline is not designed to execute as expected:

```
var badlyOrderedQuery = function() {
  print("Running query in bad order.")
  var pipeline = [
    { $sort: {"imdb.rating": -1}}, // Sort by IMDB rating.
    { $match: {
        genres: {$in: ["Romance"]}, // Romance movies only.
        released: {$lte: new ISODate("2001-01-01T00:00:00Z") }}},
    { $project: { title: 1, genres: 1, released: 1,
      "imdb.rating": 1}},
    { $limit: 1 },                  // Limit to 1 result.
  ];
  db.movies.aggregate(pipeline).forEach(printjson);
}
badlyOrderedQuery();
```

The output will be as follows:

```
MongoDB Enterprise atlas-nb3biv-shard-0:PRIMARY>
  badlyOrderedQuery();
Running query in bad order.
{
        "_id" : ObjectId("573a1399f29313caabceeead"),
        "genres" : [
                "Drama",
                "Romance"
        ],
        "title" : "Pride and Prejudice",
        "released" : ISODate("1996-01-14T00:00:00Z"),
        "imdb" : {
                "rating" : 9.1

        }
}
```

Once you have correctly ordered the pipeline, it will look like the following:

```
var wellOrderedQuery = function() {
print("Running query in better order.")
var pipeline = [
    { $match: {
        genres: {$in: ["Romance"]}, // Romance movies only.
        released: {$lte: new ISODate("2001-01-01T00:00:00Z") }}},
    { $sort: {"imdb.rating": -1}}, // Sort by IMDB rating.
    { $limit: 1 },                  // Limit to 1 result.
    { $project: { title: 1, genres: 1, released: 1,
        "imdb.rating": 1}},
];
db.movies.aggregate(pipeline).forEach(printjson);
}
wellOrderedQuery();
```

This will result in the following output:

```
MongoDB Enterprise atlas-nb3biv-shard-0:PRIMARY> wellOrderedQuery();
Running query in better order.
{
        "_id" : ObjectId("573a1399f29313caabceeead"),
        "genres" : [
                "Drama",
                "Romance"
        ],
        "title" : "Pride and Prejudice",
        "released" : ISODate("1996-01-14T00:00:00Z"),
        "imdb" : {
                "rating" : 9.1
        }
}
```

Figure 7.21: Output for preceding snippet (truncated for brevity)

Logically, this change means that the first thing we do is get a list of all our eligible documents before sorting them, and then we take the top five and project only those five documents.

Both pipelines output the same results, but the second is much more robust and easily understood. You may not always see a significant performance increase with this change, particularly on smaller datasets. However, this is an excellent practice to follow because it will assist you in creating logical, efficient, and straightforward pipelines that can be modified or scaled more easily.

## USE YOUR INDEXES

Indexes are another critical element in MongoDB query performance. This book covers indexes and their creation in further depth in *Chapter 9, Performance*. All you need to remember when creating your aggregations is that when utilizing stages such as **$sort** and **$match**, you want to make sure that you are operating on correctly indexed fields. The concepts around using indexes will then become more apparent.

## THINK ABOUT THE DESIRED OUTPUT

One of the most important ways to improve your pipelines is to plan and evaluate them to ensure that you're getting the desired output that solves your business problem. Ask yourself the following questions if you're having trouble creating a finely tuned pipeline:

- Am I outputting all the data to solve my problem?

- Am I outputting only the data required to solve my problem?

- Am I able to merge or remove any intermediate steps?

If you have evaluated your pipeline, tuned it, and still find it to be over-complicated or inefficient, you may need to ask some questions about the data itself. Is the aggregation difficult because the wrong query is being designed, or even the wrong question being asked? Alternatively, perhaps it is a sign that the shape of the data needs to be re-evaluated.

## AGGREGATION OPTIONS

Altering the pipeline is where you may spend most of your time while working with aggregations, and for beginners, you will likely be able to accomplish most of your goals by just writing pipelines. As mentioned earlier in this chapter, several options can be passed into the **aggregate** command to configure its operation. We won't delve too deeply into these options, but it is helpful to recognize them. The following is an example of aggregation with some of our options included:

```
var options = {
    maxTimeMS: 30000,
    allowDiskUse: true
    }
db.movies.aggregate(pipeline, options);
```

To specify these options, a second parameter is passed into the command after the pipeline array. In this case, we've called it **options**. Some of the options to be aware of include the following:

- **maxTimeMS**: The amount of time an operation may be processed before MongoDB kills it. Essentially a timeout for your aggregation. The default for this is **0**, which means operations do not time out.

- **allowDiskUse**: Stages in the aggregation pipeline may only use up a maximum amount of memory, making it challenging to handle massive datasets. By setting this option to **true**, MongoDB can write temporary files to allow the handling of more data.

- **bypassDocumentValidation**: This option is specifically for pipelines that will be writing out to collections using **$out** or **$merge**. If this option is set to **true**, document validation will not occur on documents being written to the collection from this pipeline.

- **comment**: This option is just for debugging and allows a string to be specified that helps identify this aggregation when parsing database logs.

- Let's perform an exercise now, to put the concepts we learnt about till now, into practice.

## EXERCISE 7.06: FINDING AWARD-WINNING DOCUMENTARY MOVIES

After seeing the results of the aggregation pipelines achieved in the previous exercises and the value they are bringing to the cinema company, a few of the company's internal engineers have tried to write up some new aggregations themselves. The cinema company has asked you to review these pipelines to assist in their internal engineers' learning process. You will use some of the preceding techniques and your understanding of aggregations from the last three topics to fix up a pipeline. The goal of this simple pipeline is to get a list of documentary movies with a high rating.

For this scenario, you will also work under the assumption that there is a substantial amount of data in the collection. The pipeline given to you to be reviewed is as follows. The purpose of this exercise is to find a few award-winning documentary movies and then list the movies that have won the most awards:

```
var findAwardWinningDocumentaries = function() {
    print("Finding award winning documentary Movies...");
    var pipeline = [
        { $sort: {"awards.wins": -1}}, // Sort by award wins.
```

```
        { $match: {"awards.wins": { $gte: 1}}},
        { $limit: 20}, // Get the top 20 movies with more than
          one award
        { $match: {
            genres: {$in: ["Documentary"]}, // Documentary
              movies only.
        }},
        { $project: { title: 1, genres: 1, awards: 1}},
        { $limit: 3},
    ];
    var options = { }
    db.movies.aggregate(pipeline, options).forEach(printjson);
}
findAwardWinningDocumentaries();
```

The result can be achieved through the following steps:

1.  First, merge the two **$match** statements and move **match** to the top of the pipeline:

```
var pipeline = [
    { $match: {
        "awards.wins": { $gte: 1},
        genres: {$in: ["Documentary"]},
    }},
    { $sort: {"awards.wins": -1}}, // Sort by award wins.
    { $limit: 20}, // Get the top 20 movies.
    { $project: { title: 1, genres: 1, awards: 1}},
    { $limit: 3},
];
```

2.  **sort** is no longer needed at the beginning, so you can move it to the second-to-last step:

```
var pipeline = [
    { $match: {
        "awards.wins": { $gte: 1},
        genres: {$in: ["Documentary"]},
    }},
    { $limit: 20}, // Get the top 20 movies.
    { $project: { title: 1, genres: 1, awards: 1}},
    { $sort: {"awards.wins": -1}}, // Sort by award wins.
    { $limit: 3},
];
```

3. The two limits are no longer required. Delete the first one:

```
var pipeline = [
    { $match: {
        "awards.wins": { $gte: 1},
        genres: {$in: ["Documentary"]},
    }},
    { $project: { itle: 1, genres: 1, awards: 1}},
    { $sort: {"awards.wins": -1}}, // Sort by award wins.
    { $limit: 3},
];
```

4. Finally, move the projection to the very end, as it only needs to operate on the final three documents:

```
var pipeline = [
    { $match: {
        "awards.wins": { $gte: 1},
        genres: {$in: ["Documentary"]},
    }},
    { $sort: {"awards.wins": -1}}, // Sort by award wins.
    { $limit: 3},
    { $project: { title: 1, genres: 1, awards: 1}},
];
```

5. That's already looking much better. You've been told that the collection is vast, so also add some options to the aggregation:

```
var options ={
        maxTimeMS: 30000,
        allowDiskUse: true,
        comment: "Find Award Winning Documentary Films"
    }
    db.movies.aggregate(pipeline, options).forEach(printjson);
```

6. Run the full query:

```
var findAwardWinningDocumentaries = function() {
    print("Finding award winning documentary Movies...");
    var pipeline = [
        { $match: {
            "awards.wins": { $gte: 1},
            genres: {$in: ["Documentary"]},
```

```
        }},
        { $sort:  {"awards.wins": -1}}, // Sort by award wins.
        { $limit: 3},
        { $project: { title: 1, genres: 1, awards: 1}},
    ];

    var options ={
        maxTimeMS: 30000,
        allowDiskUse: true,
        comment: "Find Award Winning Documentary Films"
    }
    db.movies.aggregate(pipeline, options).forEach(printjson);
}
findAwardWinningDocumentaries();
```

So, your result should be as follows:

```
MongoDB Enterprise atlas-nb3biv-shard-0:PRIMARY> findAwardWinningDocumentaries();
Finding award winning documentary Movies...

{
        "_id" : ObjectId("573a13dcf29313caabdb1463"),
        "genres" : [
                "Documentary",
                "History"
        ],
        "title" : "The Act of Killing",
        "awards" : {
                "wins" : 57,
                "nominations" : 30,
                "text" : "Nominated for 1 Oscar. Another 56 wins & 30 nominations."
        }
}
{
        "_id" : ObjectId("573a13f4f29313caabde1684"),
        "genres" : [
                "Documentary"
        ],
        "title" : "Citizenfour",
```

Figure 7.22: List of award-winning documentaries (truncated for brevity)

With this, you have retrieved the award-winning documentary list as per your cinema company's requirements. We have seen in this topic that to get the most value from your aggregations, you will be required to design, test, and continually re-evaluate your pipeline. The heuristics listed previously are just a small fraction of the patterns for designing useful aggregations, however, and researching other patterns and procedures is always recommended.

We also saw how we could pass in some options to the **aggregate** command to assist us in specific use cases or with massive datasets that may take longer to process.

## ACTIVITY 7.01: PUTTING AGGREGATIONS INTO PRACTICE

The cinema company from previous exercises has been very impressed with the insights you've managed to extract from the data using aggregation pipelines. However, the company is having trouble managing the different queries and combining the data into meaningful results. They have decided that they would like a single, unified aggregation that summarizes the essential information for their upcoming movie marathon campaign.

You aim to design, test, and run an aggregation pipeline that will create this unified view. You should ensure that the final output of the aggregation answers the following business problems:

- For each genre, which movie has the most award nominations, given that they have won at least one of these nominations?

- For each of these movies, what is their appended runtime, given that each movie has 12 minutes of trailers before it?

- An example of the sorts of things users are saying about this film.

- Because this is a classic movie marathon, only movies released before 2001 are eligible.

- Across all genres, list all the genres that have the highest number of award wins.

You may complete this activity in whichever way you choose, but try to focus on creating a simple and efficient aggregation pipeline that can be tweaked or modified in the future. It is sometimes best to try and decide what an output document might look like, and then work backward from there.

Remember, you may also choose to use the **$sample** stage to speed up your query while you're testing, but you must remove these steps in the final solution.

To keep the desired output simple, limit the result to three documents for this scenario.

The following steps will help you to complete this task:

1. Filter out any documents that were not released before 2001.

2. Filter out any documents that do not have at least one award win.

3. Sort the documents by award nominations.

4. Group the documents into a genre.

5. Take the first film in each group.

6. Take the total number of award wins for each group.

7. Join with the **comments** collection to get a list of comments for each film.

8. Reduce the number of comments for each film to one using projection. (Hint: use the **$slice** operator to reduce array length.)

9. Append the trailer time of 12 minutes to each film's runtime.

10. Sort our result by the total number of award wins.

11. Impose a limit of three documents.

The desired output is follows:

```
MongoDB Enterprise atlas-nb3biv-shard-0:PRIMARY> chapter7Activity();
{
        "_id" : "Drama",
        "film_id" : ObjectId("573a139ff29313caabcff499"),
        "film_title" : "Almost Famous",
        "film_awards" : {
                "wins" : 58,
                "nominations" : 95,
                "text" : "Won 1 Oscar. Another 57 wins & 95 nominations."
        },
        "genre_award_wins" : 14020,
        "film_runtime" : 134,
        "comments" : [ ]
}
{

        "_id" : "Comedy",
        "film_id" : ObjectId("573a139bf29313caabcf500b"),
        "film_title" : "Shakespeare in Love",
        "film_awards" : {
                "wins" : 70,
                "nominations" : 77,
                "text" : "Won 7 Oscars. Another 63 wins & 77 nominations."
```

Figure 7.23: Final output after executing activity steps

> **NOTE**
>
> The solution to this activity can be found on page 672.

# SUMMARY

In this chapter, we have covered all the essential components that you need to understand, write, comprehend, and improve MongoDB aggregations. This new functionality will help you to answer more complex and difficult questions about your data. By creating multi-stage pipelines that join multiple collections, you can increase the scope of your queries to the entire database instead of a single collection. We also looked at how to write the results into a new collection to enable further exploration or manipulation of the data.

In the final section, we covered the importance of ensuring that your pipelines are written with scalability, readability, and performance in mind. By focusing on these aspects, your pipelines will continue to deliver value in the future and can act as a basis for further aggregations.

However, what we have covered here is just the beginning of what you can accomplish with the aggregation feature. It is critical that you keep exploring, experimenting, and testing your pipelines to truly master this MongoDB skill.

In the next chapter, we will walk through the creation of an application in Node.js with MongoDB as a backend. Even if you're not a developer, this will give you meaningful insight into how MongoDB applications are built, along with a deeper understanding of building and executing dynamic queries.

# 8

# CODING JAVASCRIPT IN MONGODB

## OVERVIEW

In this chapter, you will learn how to read, understand, and create simple MongoDB applications using the Node.js driver. These applications will help you to programmatically fetch, update, and create data in your MongoDB collections, as well as to handle errors and user inputs. By the end of this chapter, you will be able to create a simple application built on top of MongoDB.

# INTRODUCTION

So far, we have interacted directly with the MongoDB database using the mongo shell. These direct interactions are quick, easy, and a fantastic way to learn or experiment with MongoDB features. However, in many production situations, it will be software that connects with the database in place of the user. MongoDB is a great place to store and query your data, but often, it's most essential use is to serve as a backend for large-scale applications. These applications write, read, and update data programmatically, usually after being triggered by some condition or user interface.

To connect your software with a database, you will typically use a library (often provided by the database creator) known as a driver. This driver will help you connect, analyze, read, and write to your database without having to write multiple lines of code for simple actions. It provides functions and abstractions for common use cases, as well as frameworks for working with data extracted from the database. MongoDB provides several different drivers for different programming languages, one of the most popular (and the one we will explore in this chapter) being the Node.js driver (sometimes known as Node).

To relate this to real life, think about your online shopping experience. The first time you purchase products from a website, you have to enter all your billing and shipping details. If you have signed up for an account, however, the second time you go to the checkout, all your details are already saved on the website. This is a great experience, and, with many websites, this is accomplished by the web application querying a backend database. One such database that can support these applications is MongoDB.

One of the primary reasons why MongoDB has achieved such excellent growth and adoption is its success in persuading software developers to choose it as the database for their applications. Much of this persuasion is derived from how well MongoDB integrates with Node.

Node.js has become one of the primary languages for web-based applications, which we will learn about later in this chapter. However, for now, it is sufficient to know that the ease of integrating Node and MongoDB has proved highly beneficial for both technologies. This symbiotic relationship has also led to the creation of a large numbers of successful Node/MongoDB implementations, from small mobile apps to large-scale web applications. When deciding which programming language to choose when demonstrating MongoDB drivers, Node.js is the preferred choice.

Depending on your job role, you may either be responsible for writing applications that will run against MongoDB or expected to write the occasional line of code. However, regardless of your programming level or professional responsibilities, an understanding of how applications use drivers to integrate with MongoDB will be highly valuable. Most of the MongoDB production queries are run by applications, not by people. Whether you are a data analyst, a frontend developer, or a database administrator, it is highly possible that your production environment will be using one of the MongoDB drivers.

> **NOTE**
>
> For the duration of this chapter, the exercises and activities included are iterations on a single scenario. The data and examples are based on the MongoDB Atlas sample database entitled `sample_mflix`.

For the duration of this chapter, we will follow a set of exercises based on a theoretical scenario. This is an expansion of the scenario we covered in *Chapter 7, Aggregations*.

Building upon the scenario from *Chapter 7, Aggregations*, where a cinema company is running its annual classic movie marathon and wants to decide what their lineup should be, they need a variety of popular movies that meet specific criteria to satisfy their customer base. After exploring the data and assisting them in making business decisions, you have provided them with new insights. The cinema company is pleased with your suggestions and have decided to engage you as part of their next project. This project involves creating a simple Node.js application that will allow their employees to query the film database, without them having to know MongoDB and place votes on which movies should be screened at the cinemas. Over the course of this chapter, you will create this application.

# CONNECTING TO THE DRIVER

At a high level, the process of using the Node.js driver with MongoDB is similar to connecting directly with the shell. You will specify a MongoDB server URI, several connection parameters, and you can execute queries against collections. This should all be quite familiar; the main difference will be that these instructions will be written in JavaScript instead of Bash or PowerShell.

## INTRODUCTION TO NODE.JS

Since the objective of this chapter is not to learn Node.js programming, we will briefly cover the fundamentals to ensure that we can create our MongoDB application. The **js** in Node.js stands for **JavaScript** because JavaScript is the programming language that Node.js understands. JavaScript typically runs in a browser. However, you can think of Node.js as an engine that executes the JavaScript files on your computer.

Over the course of this chapter, you will write JavaScript (`.js`) syntax and execute it with Node.js. Although you can write JavaScript files with any text editor, it is recommended to use an application that will help you with syntax highlighting and formatting, such as **Visual Studio Code** or **Sublime**.

To begin with, let's look at some sample code:

```
// 1_Hello_World.js

var message = "Hello, Node!";
console.log(message);
```

Let's define each term from the preceding syntax, in detail:

- The **var** keyword is used to declare a new variable; in this case, the variable name is **message**.

- The = symbol sets the value of this variable to a string called **Hello, Node!**.

- A semi-colon (`;`) is used at the end of each statement.

- **console.log(message)** is a function used to output the value of **message**.

If you're familiar with programming fundamentals, you may have noticed that we did not have to explicitly declare the **message** variable as **string**. This is because JavaScript is **dynamically typed**, meaning that you don't have to explicitly specify the variable type (number, string, Boolean, and so on).

If you're less familiar with programming fundamentals, some of the terminology in this chapter might confuse you. Because this is not a JavaScript programming book, these concepts will not be covered in depth. The objective of this chapter is to understand how drivers interact with MongoDB; the specifics of Node.js are not important. Although this chapter attempts to keep the programming concepts simple, don't worry if something seems complex.

Let's try running the code sample, saving that code to a file called **1_Hello_World. js** in our current directory, and then running the command in our Terminal or Command Prompt using the following command:

```
> node 1_Hello_World.js
```

You'll see an output that looks like this:

```
Section1> node 1_Hello_World.js
Hello, Node!
Section1>
```

As you can see, it is straightforward to run Node.js scripts since without building or compiling, you can write your code and call it with **node**.

The **var** keyword stores information in a variable and changes it later in the code. However, there is another keyword, **const**, that is used to store information that isn't going to change. So, in our example, we could replace our **var** keyword with the **const** keyword. As a best practice, you can declare anything that won't change as **const**:

```
// 1_Hello_World.js
const message = "Hello, Node!";
console.log(message);
```

Now, let's consider the structure of functions and parameters. It is like the structure from previous chapters' queries in the mongo shell. To begin, let's consider the following example of defining a function:

```
var printHello = function(parameter) {
    console.log("Hello, " + parameter);
}
printHello("World")
```

And here is a preview of some of the types of code we will encounter later in this chapter. You may notice that although it is a much more complex code snippet, there are some common elements from the CRUD operations you have learned in earlier chapters (*Chapter 4, Querying Documents*, in particular), such as the syntax of a **find** command and the MongoDB URI:

```
// 3_Full_Example.js

const Mongo = require('mongodb').MongoClient;
const server = 'mongodb+srv://username:password@server-
  abcdef.gcp.mongodb.net/test?retryWrites=true&w=majority'
const myDB   = 'sample_mflix'
const myColl = 'movies';
const mongo = new Mongo(server);
mongo.connect(function(err) {
    console.log('Our driver has connected to MongoDB!');
    const database = mongo.db(myDB);
    const collection = database.collection(myColl);
    collection.find({title: 'Blacksmith Scene'}).each(function(err, doc) {
        if(doc) {
            console.log('Doc returned: ')
            console.log(doc);
        } else {
            mongo.close();
            return false;
        }
    })
})
```

This may be a little intimidating to begin with, but as we dive deeper into this chapter, this will become more familiar. As we mentioned earlier, there should be some elements that you recognize from the mongo shell, even if they look a little different. Some of the elements in the code that map to mongo shell elements are as follows:

- The **collection** object, like **db.collection** in the shell.

- The **find** command after our **collection**, like the shell.

- The parameter in our **find** command is a document filter, which is precisely what we would use in the shell.

The function declaration in Node.js is done using the **function (parameter) {...}** function and it allows us to create smaller, reusable bits of code that can be run multiple times, such as the **find()** or **insertOne()** functions. Defining a function is easy; you simply use the **function** keyword, followed by the name of the function, its parameters in brackets, and curly braces to define the actual logic for this function.

Here's the code that defines a function. Note that there are two ways to do this: you can declare a function as a variable or pass a function as a parameter to another function. We'll cover this in detail later in this chapter:

```
// 4_Define_Function.js
const newFunction = function(parameter1, parameter2) {
    // Function logic goes here.
    console.log(parameter1);
    console.log(parameter2);
}
```

## GETTING THE MONGODB DRIVER FOR NODE.JS

The easiest way to install the MongoDB driver for Node.js is to use **npm**. **npm**, or the node package manager, is a package management tool used to add, update, and manage different packages used in Node.js programs. In this case, the package you want to add is the MongoDB driver, so, in the directory where the scripts are stored, run the following command in your Terminal or Command Prompt:

```
> npm install mongo --save
```

You may see some output once the package is installed, as follows:

```
Section1> npm install mongo --save
npm WARN  react-redux@6.0.1 requires a peer of react@^16.4.0-0 but none is ins
talled. You must install peer dependencies yourself.
npm WARN  react-redux@6.0.1 requires a peer of redux@^2.0.0 || ^3.0.0 || ^4.0.
0-0 but none is installed. You must install peer dependencies yourself.
npm WARN  Sigma No description
npm WARN  Sigma No repository field.
npm WARN  Sigma No license field.

+ mongo@0.1.0
added 10 packages from 7 contributors and audited 26 packages in 1.606s
found 0 vulnerabilities

Section1> █
```

Figure 8.1: Installing the MongoDB driver with npm

It's as easy as that. Now, let's begin programming against MongoDB.

## THE DATABASE AND COLLECTION OBJECTS

When using the MongoDB driver, there are three main components that you can use for most operations. In the later exercises, we'll see how they all fit together, but before that, let's briefly cover each of them and their purpose.

**MongoClient** is the first object you must create in your code. This represents your connection to the MongoDB server. Think of this as the equivalent of your mongo shell; you pass in the URL and connection parameters for your database, and it will create a connection for you to use. To use **MongoClient**, you must import the module at the top of your script:

```
// First load the Driver module.
const Mongo = require('MongoDB').MongoClient;


// Then define our server.
const server = 'mongodb+srv://username:password@server-
  abcdef.gcp.mongodb.net/test?retryWrites=true&w=majority';
// Create a new client.
const mongo = new Mongo(server);
// Connect to our server.
mongo.connect(function(err) {
    // Inside this block we are connected to MongoDB.
mongo.close(); // Close our connection at the end.
})
```

Next is the **database** object. Like the mongo shell, once the connection is established, run your commands against a specific database in your server. This database object will also determine which collections you may run the queries against:

```
...
mongo.connect(function(err) {
    // Inside this block we are connected to MongoDB.
    // Create our database object.
    const database = mongo.db(«sample_mflix»);
    mongo.close(); // Close our connection at the end.
})
...
```

The third essential object to use in (almost) every MongoDB-based application is the **collection** object. As you may have guessed, a **collection** object is used to send queries. As with the mongo shell, most common operations will run against a single collection:

```
...
mongo.connect(function(err) {
    // Inside this block we are connected to MongoDB.
    // Create our database object.
    const database = mongo.db("sample_mflix");
    // Create our collection object
    const collection = database.collection("movies");
    mongo.close(); // Close our connection at the end.
})
...
```

The **database** and **collection** objects express the same concept as if you were connecting directly with the mongo shell. For the purposes of this chapter, **MongoClient** is only used to create and store connections to the server.

It's important to note that the relationship between these objects is **one-to-many**. This means that, typically, one `MongoClient` object can create multiple `database` objects, and a `database` object can create many `collection` objects for running queries against:

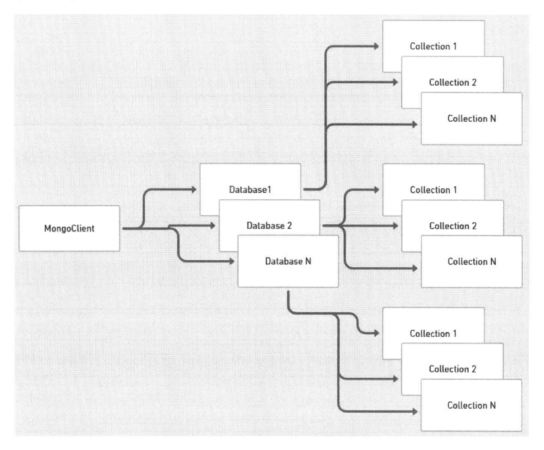

Figure 8.2: Driver entity relationships

The preceding diagram is a visual representation of the entity relationships described in the previous paragraph. Here, there's one `MongoClient` object to multiple `database` objects, each of which may have multiple `collection` objects.

## CONNECTION PARAMETERS

Before we write our code, it's important to know how to establish the connection to **MongoClient**. There are only two parameters when creating a new client: the URL for your server and any additional connection options. The connection options are optional in case you need to create your client, as follows:

```
const serverURL = 'mongodb+srv://username:password@server-
    abcdef.gcp.mongodb.net/test';
const mongo = new Mongo(serverURL);
mongo.connect(function(err) {
    // Inside this block we are connected to MongoDB.
mongo.close(); // Close our connection at the end.
})
```

> **NOTE**
>
> You may be confused by the syntax of this code snippet, particularly the function block in the connect function. This is known as a **callback**. We will cover these in detail later in this chapter. For now, it is enough to use this pattern without having a more in-depth understanding.

Just like the mongo shell, **serverURL** supports all the MongoDB URI options, meaning you can specify a configuration in this connection string itself, rather than in the second optional parameter; for example:

```
const serverURL = 'mongodb+srv://username:password@server-
    abcdef.gcp.mongodb.net/test?retryWrites=true&w=majority';
```

To simplify this string, many of these URI options (and additional options, such as the SSL settings) can be specified in the second parameter when creating the client; for example:

```
const mongo = new Mongo(serverURL, {
    sslValidate: false
});
mongo.connect(function(err) {
    // Inside this block we are connected to MongoDB.
mongo.close(); // Close our connection at the end.
})
```

As with the mongo shell, there are many options for configuration, including SSL, Authentication, and Write Concern options. However, most of them are beyond the scope of this chapter.

> **NOTE**
>
> Remember, you can find a full connection string for Atlas in the user interface at cloud.mongodb.com. You may want to copy this connection string and use it in all your scripts for **serverURL**.

Let's learn how to establish a connection with the Node.js driver through an exercise.

## EXERCISE 8.01: CREATING A CONNECTION WITH THE NODE.JS DRIVER

Before you begin this exercise, revisit the movie company from the scenario outlined in the *Introduction* section. You may recall that the cinema company wants a Node.js application that allows users to query and update records in the movies database. To accomplish this, the first thing your application will need to do is establish a connection to your server. This can be done by executing the following steps:

1. First, in your current working directory, create a new JavaScript file called **Exercise8.01.js** and open it in your chosen text editor (Visual Studio Code, Sublime, and so on):

```
> node Exercise8.01.js
```

2. Import the MongoDB driver library (as described earlier in this chapter) into your script file by adding the following line to the top of the file:

```
const MongoClient = require('mongodb').MongoClient;
```

> **NOTE**
>
> If you did not install the npm MongoDB library earlier in this chapter, you should do so now by running **npm install mongo --save** in your Command Prompt or Terminal. Run this command in the same directory as your script.

3. Create a new variable containing the URL for your MongoDB server:

```
const url = 'mongodb+srv://username:password@server-
   abcdef.gcp.mongodb.net/test';
```

4. Create a new **MongoClient** object called **client** using the **url** variable:

```
const client = new MongoClient(url);
```

5. Open a connection to MongoDB using the **connect** function, as follows:

```
client.connect(function(err) {

    ...

})
```

6. Add a **console.log()** message within the connection block to confirm that the connection is open:

```
console.log('Connected to MongoDB with NodeJS!');
```

7. Finally, at the end of the connection block, close the connection using the following syntax:

```
client.close(); // Close our connection at the end.
```

Your complete script should look like this:

```
// Import MongoDB Driver module.
const MongoClient = require('mongodb').MongoClient;

// Create a new url variable.
const url = 'mongodb+srv://username:password@server-
   abcdef.gcp.mongodb.net/test';

// Create a new MongoClient.
const client = new MongoClient(url);

// Open the connection using the .connect function.
client.connect(function(err) {
    // Within the connection block, add a console.log to confirm the
      connection
    console.log('Connected to MongoDB with NodeJS!');
    client.close(); // Close our connection at the end.
})
```

The following output is generated once you execute the code using **node Exercise8.01.js**:

```
Chapter8> node Excercise8.01.js
Connected to MongoDB with NodeJS!
Chapter8>
```

In this exercise, you established a connection to the server using Node.js driver.

# EXECUTING SIMPLE QUERIES

Now that we have connected to MongoDB, we can run some simple queries against the database. Running queries in the Node.js driver is very similar to running queries in the shell. By now, you should be familiar with the **find** command in the shell:

```
db.movies.findOne({})
```

Here is the syntax for the **find** command in the driver:

```
collection.find({title: 'Blacksmith Scene'}).each(function(err, doc) { … }
```

As you can see, the general structure is the same as the **find** command you would execute in the mongo shell. Here, we get a collection from the database object, and then we run the find command against that collection with a query document. The process itself is straightforward. The main differences concern how we structure our commands and how we handle the results returned from the driver.

When writing Node.js applications, one of the critical concerns is to ensure that your code is written in such a way that it can be modified, extended, or understood easily, either by yourself in the future or by other professionals who may need to work on the application.

## CREATING AND EXECUTING FIND QUERIES

Consider the code from *Exercise 8.01*, *Creating a Connection with the Node.js Driver*, as a reference as it already contains the connection:

```
const MongoClient = require('mongodb').MongoClient;

// Replace this variable with the connection string for your server,
provided by
  MongoDB Atlas.
const url = 'mongodb+srv://username:password@server-abcdef.gcp.mongodb.
net/test';
```

```
const client = new MongoClient(url);

client.connect(function(err) {
    console.log('Connected to MongoDB with NodeJS!');
    // OUR CODE GOES BELOW HERE


    // AND ABOVE HERE
    client.close();
})
```

The logic of our query will be added here:

```
    // OUR CODE GOES BELOW HERE


    // AND ABOVE HERE
```

Now, we have a connection to the MongoDB server. However, there are two other important objects – **db** and **collection**. Let's create our database object (for the **sample_mflix** database), as follows:

```
    // OUR CODE GOES BELOW HERE
    const database = client.db("sample_mflix")
    // AND ABOVE HERE
```

We now have our **database** object. When sending queries in the mongo shell, you must pass a document to the command as a filter for your documents. This is the same in the Node.js driver. You can pass the document directly. However, it is advisable to define the filter as a variable separately and then assign a value. You can see the difference in the following code snippet:

```
// Defining filter first.
var filter = { title: 'Blacksmith Scene'};
database.collection("movies").find(filter).toArray(function(err, docs) {
});

// Doing everything in a single line.
database.collection("movies").find({title: 'Blacksmith
  Scene'}).toArray(function(err, docs) {});
```

As with the mongo shell, you may pass an empty document as a parameter to find all the documents. You may have also noticed **toArray** at the end of our `find` command. This is added because, by default, the `find` command will return a cursor. We'll cover cursors in the next section, but in the meantime, let's look at what this full script would look like:

```
const MongoClient = require('mongodb').MongoClient;


// Replace this variable with the connection string for your server,
provided by
  MongoDB Atlas.
const url = 'mongodb+srv://mike:password@myAtlas-
  fawxo.gcp.mongodb.net/test?retryWrites=true&w=majority'
const client = new MongoClient(url);


client.connect(function(err) {
    console.log('Connected to MongoDB with NodeJS!');
    const database = client.db("sample_mflix");
    var filter = { title: 'Blacksmith Scene'};
    database.collection("movies").find(filter).
toArray(function(err, docs) {
        console.log('Docs results:');
        console.log(docs);
    });
    client.close();
})
```

If you were to save this modified script as **2_Simple_Find.js** and run it with the command **node 2_Simple_Find.js**, the following output would result:

```
Chapter8> node 2_Simple_Find.js
Connected to MongoDB with NodeJS!
Docs results:
[
  {
    _id: 573a1390f29313caabcd4135,
    plot: 'Three men hammer on an anvil and pass a bottle of beer around.',
    genres: [ 'Short' ],
    runtime: 1,
    cast: [ 'Charles Kayser', 'John Ott' ],
    num_mflix_comments: 1,
    title: 'Blacksmith Scene',
    fullplot: 'A stationary camera looks at a large anvil with a blacksmith behind it and
one on either side. The smith in the middle draws a heated metal rod from the fire, places
 it on the anvil, and all three begin a rhythmic hammering. After several blows, the metal
 goes back in the fire. One smith pulls out a bottle of beer, and they each take a swig. T
hen, out comes the glowing metal and the hammering resumes.',
    countries: [ 'USA' ],
    released: 1893-05-09T00:00:00.000Z,
    directors: [ 'William K.L. Dickson' ],
    rated: 'UNRATED',
    awards: { wins: 1, nominations: 0, text: '1 win.' },
```

*Figure 8.3: Output for the preceding snippet (truncated for brevity)*

The preceding output is very similar to the output from a MongoDB query executed through the mongo shell rather than the driver. When executing queries through the driver, we have learned that although the syntax may differ from the mongo shell, the fundamental elements in a query and its output are the same.

## USING CURSORS AND QUERY RESULTS

In the previous examples, we used the **toArray** function to transform our query output into an array we could output with **console.log**. When working with small amounts of data, this is a simple way to work with the results; however, with larger result sets, you should use cursors. You should be somewhat familiar with cursors from your mongo shell queries in *Chapter 5, Inserting, Updating, and Deleting Documents*. In the mongo shell, you could use the **it** command to iterate through your cursor. In Node.js, there are many ways to access your cursor, of which three are more common patterns, as follows:

- **toArray**: This will take all the results of the query and place them in a single array. This is easy to use but not very efficient when you are expecting a large result from your query. In the following code, we're running a **find** command against the movies collection and then using **toArray** to log the first element in the array to the console:

```
database.collection("movies").find(filter).
toArray(function(err, docsArray) {
    console.log('Docs results as an array:');
    console.log(docsArray[0]); // Print the first entry in the array.
 });
```

- **each**: This will iterate through each document in the result set, one at a time. This is a good pattern if you want to inspect or use each document in the result. In the following code snippet, we're running a **find** command against the movies collection, using **each** to log every document that's returned until there are no documents left:

```
database.collection("movies").find(filter).each(function(err, doc) {
    if(doc) {
        console.log('Current doc');
        console.log(doc);
    } else {
        client.close(); // Close our connection.
        return false;   // End the each loop.
    }
 });
```

When there are no more documents to return, the document will be equal to **null**. Hence, it is important to check whether the document exists (using **if(doc)**) every time we inspect a new document.

- **next**: This will allow you to access the next document in the result set. This is the best pattern to use if you are only looking for a single document or a subset of your results without having to iterate through the entire result. In the following code snippet, we're running a **find** command against the movies collection, using **next** to get the first document returned, and then outputting that document to the console:

```
database.collection("movies").find(filter).next(function(err, doc) {
    console.log("First doc in the cursor");
    console.log(doc);
});
```

Because **next** only returns one document at a time, in this example, we run it three times to inspect the first three documents.

In the examples, exercises, and activities in this chapter, we will learn how all three methods are being used. However, it is essential to note that there are other, more advanced, patterns.

You can also accomplish the same **sort** and **limit** functionality from the mongo shell by placing these commands after **find(…)**; this should be familiar to you from your previous queries in the shell:

```
database.collection("movies").find(filter).limit(5).sort([['title', 1]]).
next
    (function(err, doc) {…}
```

## EXERCISE 8.02: BUILDING A NODE.JS DRIVER QUERY

In this exercise, you will build upon the scenario in *Exercise 8.01*, *Creating a Connection with the Node.js Driver*, which allows you to connect to the mongo server. If you are going to deliver a Node.js application that allows cinema employees to query and vote on movies, your script will need to query the database with given criteria and return the results in an easily readable format. For this scenario, the query you must get results for is as follows:

*Find two movies in the romance category, projecting only the title for each.*

You can accomplish this in Node.js by executing the following steps:

1. Create a new JavaScript file called **Exercise8.02.js**.

2. So that you don't have to rewrite everything from scratch, copy the content of **Exercise8.01.js** into your new script. Otherwise, rewrite the connection code in your new file.

3. To keep the code clean, create new variables to store **databaseName** and **collectionName**. Remember, since these won't change throughout our script, you must declare them as constants using the **const** keyword:

```
const databaseName = "sample_mflix";
const collectionName = "movies";
```

4. Now, create a new **const** to store our query document; you should be familiar with creating these from the previous chapters:

```
const query = { genres: { $all: ["Romance"]} };
```

5. With all your variables defined, create our database object:

```
const database = client.db(databaseName);
```

Now, you can send your query with the following syntax. Use the **each** pattern, passing in a callback function to handle each document. Don't worry if this appears strange; you will learn about this in detail in the upcoming section. Remember to use **limit** to only return two documents and **project** to output only **title**, as they are requirements for our scenario:

```
database.collection(collectionName).find(query).limit(2).
project({title:
  1}).each(function(err, doc) {

    if(doc) {

    } else {
        client.close(); // Close our connection.
        return false;   // End the each loop.

    }
});
```

6. Inside your callback function, use **console.log** to output each of the documents that was returned by our query:

```
if(doc){
        console.log('Current doc');
        console.log(doc);

}
```

Your final code should look like this:

```
const MongoClient = require('mongodb').MongoClient;
const url = 'mongodb+srv://username:password@server-
  abcdef.gcp.mongodb.net/test';
const client = new MongoClient(url);
const databaseName = "sample_mflix";
const collectionName = "movies";


const query = { genres: { $all: ["Romance"]} };


// Open the connection using the .connect function.
client.connect(function(err) {
    // Within the connection block, add a console.log to confirm the
      connection
    console.log('Connected to MongoDB with NodeJS!');


    const database = client.db(databaseName);
    database.collection(collectionName).find(query).limit(2).
project({title:
        1}).each(function(err, doc) {
        if(doc) {
            console.log('Current doc');
            console.log(doc);
        } else {
            client.close(); // Close our connection.
            return false;   // End the each loop.
        }
    });
})
```

7. Now, run the script using **node Exercise8.02.js**. You should get the
   following output:

```
Connected to MongoDB with NodeJS!
Our database connected alright!
Current doc
{ _id: 573a1390f29313caabcd548c, title: 'The Birth of a Nation' }
Current doc
{ _id: 573a1390f29313caabcd5b9a, title: "Hell's Hinges" }
```

In this exercise, you built a Node.js program that executes a query against MongoDB and returns the results to us in the console. Although this is a small step that we could easily accomplish in the mongo shell, this script will serve as a foundation for more advanced and interactive Node.js applications for MongoDB.

## CALLBACKS AND ERROR HANDLING IN NODE.JS

So, we have managed to open a connection to MongoDB and run some simple queries, but there were probably a couple of elements of the code that seemed unfamiliar; for example, the syntax here:

```
.each(function(err, doc) {
    if(doc) {
        console.log('Current doc');
        console.log(doc);
    } else {
        client.close(); // Close our connection.
        return false;   // End the each loop.
    }
});
```

This is what is known as a **callback**. It's a method for creating code that executes in a specific order. For example, in the preceding code snippet, we instruct **MongoClient** that once it completes its own internal logic, it should execute the code in the function we passed in as a second parameter. That second parameter is known as a callback. Callbacks are extra functions (blocks of code) that are passed as parameters to another function that executes first.

Callbacks allow you to specify the logic to execute only after a function has completed. The reason we have to use callbacks in Node.js instead of simply having the statements be in order is that Node.js is asynchronous, meaning that when we call functions such as **connect**, it doesn't block execution. Whatever is next in the script will be executed. That's why we use callbacks: to ensure that our next steps wait for the connection to complete. There are other modern patterns that can be used instead of callbacks, such as **promises** and **await/async**. However, considering the scope of this book, we will only cover callbacks in this chapter and learn how to handle errors returned from the driver.

# CALLBACKS IN NODE.JS

Callbacks can often be visually confusing and hard to conceptualize; however, fundamentally, they are quite simple. A callback is a function provided as a parameter to a second function, which allows both functions to be run in order.

Without using callbacks (or any other synchronization pattern), both functions would start executing right after the other. When using a driver, this would create errors, because the second function may be dependent on the first function finishing before it begins. For example, you cannot query your data until the connection is established. Let's look at a breakdown of a callback:

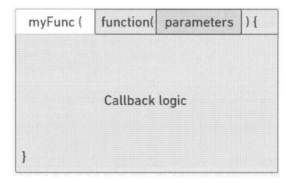

Figure 8.4: Breakdown of a callback

And now, compare this to our **find** query code:

```
.each(   function(   err, doc   ) {

    if(doc) {
        console.log('Current doc');
        console.log(doc);
    } else {
        client.close(); // Close our connection.
        return false;   // End the each loop.
    }
});
```

Figure 8.5: Breakdown of a MongoDB callback

As you can see, the same structure exists, just with different parameters to the callback function. You may be wondering how we know which parameters to use in a specific callback. The answer is that the parameters passed into our callback function are determined by the first function that we provide our callback function to. That's perhaps a confusing sentence, but what it means is this: when passing a function, fA, as a parameter to a second function, fB, the parameters of fA are provided by fB. Let's examine our practical example again to make sure we understand this:

```
database.collection(collectionName).find(query).limit(2).
project({title: 1}).each
    (function(err, doc) {

        if(doc) {

            console.log('Current doc');
            console.log(doc);

        } else {

            client.close(); // Close our connection.
            return false;   // End the each loop.

        }

    });
```

So, our callback function, **function(err, doc) { … }**, is provided as a parameter to the driver function, **each**. This means that **each** will run our callback function for each document in the result set, passing the **err** (error) and **doc** (document) parameters in for each execution. Here's the same code, but with some logging to demonstrate the order of execution:

```
console.log('This will execute first.')

database.collection(collectionName).find(query).limit(2).
project({title: 1}).each
    (function(err, doc) {

console.log('This will execute last, once for each document in the
result.')
        if(doc) {

        } else {

            client.close(); // Close our connection.
            return false;   // End the each loop.

        }

    });
console.log('This will execute second.');
```

And if we run this code using **node 3_Callbacks.js**, we can see the order of execution in the output:

```
Connected to MongoDB with NodeJS!
This will execute first.
This will execute second.
This will execute last, once for each doc.
This will execute last, once for each doc.
This will execute last, once for each doc.
```

Callbacks are sometimes complicated patterns to become familiar with and are increasingly being replaced by more advanced Node.js patterns, such as **promises** and **async/await**. The best way to become more familiar with these patterns is by using them, so if you don't feel 100% comfortable with them yet, don't worry.

## BASIC ERROR HANDLING IN NODE.JS

As we've been examining our callbacks, you may have noticed that there was a parameter we have not described yet: **err**. In the MongoDB driver, most commands that can return an error in the mongo shell can also return an error in the driver. In the case of callbacks, the **err** parameter will always exist; however, if there is no error, the value of **err** is **null**. This "error-first" pattern to catch errors in asynchronous code is standard practice in NodeJS.

For example, imagine you have created an application that enters users' phone numbers into a customer database, and two different users enter the same phone number. MongoDB will return a duplicate key error when you attempt to run the insert. At this point, it is your responsibility, as the creator of the Node.js application, to properly handle that error. To check any errors in our query, we can check whether **err** is not **null**. You can easily check this by using the following syntax:

```
database.collection(collectionName).find(query).limit(2).
project({title: 1}).each
    (function(err, doc) {
        if(err) {
            console.log('Error in query.');
            console.log(err);
            client.close();
            return false;
        }
        else if(doc) {
            console.log('Current doc');
            console.log(doc);
```

```
        } else {
            client.close(); // Close our connection.
            return false;   // End the each loop.
        }
    });
```

You may recognize that this was the same syntax we used to check whether we have more documents when using **each**. Similar to how we're checking the error for a query, the **connect** function in our client also provides an error to our **callback** function, which should be checked before we run any further logic:

```
// Open the connection using the .connect function.
client.connect(function(err) {
    if(err) {
        console.log('Error connecting!');
        console.log(err);
        client.close();
    } else {
        // Within the connection block, add a console.log to confirm the
            connection
        console.log('Connected to MongoDB with NodeJS!');
        client.close(); // Close our connection at the end.
    }
})
```

> **NOTE**
>
> It is advisable to use callbacks to check the parameters that are passed in before we try to use them. In the case of a **find** command, this would mean checking whether there is an error and checking that a document was returned. When writing code against MongoDB, it is good practice to validate everything that was returned from the database and log errors for debugging purposes.

But it's not just in callbacks that we can validate the accuracy of our code. We can also check non-callback functions to make sure everything worked out, for example, when we create our **database** object:

```
const database = client.db(databaseName);
if(database) {
    console.log('Our database connected alright!');
}
```

Depending on what you are trying to accomplish with MongoDB, your error handling might be as simple as the preceding examples, or you may need much more advanced logic. However, for the scope of this chapter, we'll only be looking at basic error handling.

## EXERCISE 8.03: ERROR HANDLING AND CALLBACKS WITH THE NODE.JS DRIVER

In *Exercise 8.02*, *Building a Node.js Driver Query*, you created a script that successfully connected to a MongoDB server and resulted a query. In this exercise, you will add error handling to your code—meaning that if anything goes wrong, it allows you to identify or fix the issue. You will test this handling by modifying your query so that it fails. You can accomplish this in Node.js by going through the following steps:

1. Create a new JavaScript file called **Exercise8.03.js**.

2. So that you don't have to rewrite everything from scratch, copy the content of **Exercise8.02.js** into your new script. Otherwise, rewrite the connection and query code in your new file.

3. Within the connect callback, check the **err** parameter. If you do have an error, make sure to output it using **console.log**:

```
client.connect(function(err) {
    if(err) {
        console.log('Failed to connect.');
        console.log(err);
        return false;
    }

    // Within the connection block, add a console.log to confirm the
       connection
    console.log('Connected to MongoDB with NodeJS!');
```

4. Add some error checks before running the query to ensure that the database object was created successfully. If you do have an error, output it using `console.log`. Use the **!** syntax to check whether something does not exist:

```
const database = client.db(databaseName);
if(!database) {
    console.log('Database object doesn't exist!');
    return false;
}
```

5. In the **each** callback, check the **err** parameter to make sure each document was returned without error:

```
database.collection(collectionName).find(query).limit(2).
project({title: 1}).each(function(err, doc) {
    if(err) {
        console.log('Query error.');
        console.log(err);
        client.close();
        return false;
    }
    if(doc) {
        console.log('Current doc');
        console.log(doc);
    } else {
        client.close();   // Close our connection.
        return false;     // End the each loop.
    }
});
```

At this point, your entire code should look like this:

```
const MongoClient = require('mongodb').MongoClient;
const url = 'mongodb+srv://username:password@server-
    fawxo.gcp.mongodb.net/test?retryWrites=true&w=majority';
const client = new MongoClient(url);
const databaseName = "sample_mflix";
const collectionName = "movies";
const query = { genres: { $all: ["Romance"]} };

// Open the connection using the .connect function.
client.connect(function(err) {
    if(err) {
```

```
        console.log('Failed to connect.');
        console.log(err);
        return false;
    }


    // Within the connection block, add a console.log to confirm the
      connection
    console.log('Connected to MongoDB with NodeJS!');


    const database = client.db(databaseName);
    if(!database) {
        console.log('Database object doesn't exist!');
        return false;
    }
    database.collection(collectionName).find(query).limit(2).
project({title:
        1}).each(function(err, doc) {
        if(err) {
            console.log('Query error.');
            console.log(err);
            client.close();
            return false;
        }
        if(doc) {
            console.log('Current doc');
            console.log(doc);
        } else {
            client.close(); // Close our connection.
            return false;    // End the each loop.
        }
    });
})
```

6. Before adding an error, run the script using node **Exercise8.03.js**. You should get the following output:

```
Connected to MongoDB with NodeJS!
Current doc
{ _id: 573a1390f29313caabcd548c, title: 'The Birth of a Nation' }
Current doc
{ _id: 573a1390f29313caabcd5b9a, title: "Hell's Hinges" }
```

7. Modify the query to ensure that you produce an error:

```
const query = { genres: { $thisIsNotAnOperator: ["Romance"]} };
```

8. Run the script using node **Exercise8.03.js**. You should get the following output:

```
Connected to MongoDB with NodeJS!
Query error.
MongoError: unknown operator: $thisIsNotAnOperator
    at Connection.<anonymous> (/Users/mike/Personal/projects/The-MongoDB-Workshop/Chapter_
8_Coding_JavaScript/node_modules/mongodb/lib/core/connection/pool.js:451:61)
    at Connection.emit (events.js:315:20)
    at processMessage (/Users/mike/Personal/projects/The-MongoDB-Workshop/Chapter_8_Coding
_JavaScript/node_modules/mongodb/lib/core/connection/connection.js:452:10)
    at TLSSocket.<anonymous> (/Users/mike/Personal/projects/The-MongoDB-Workshop/Chapter_8
_Coding_JavaScript/node_modules/mongodb/lib/core/connection/connection.js:621:15)
    at TLSSocket.emit (events.js:315:20)
    at addChunk (_stream_readable.js:295:12)
    at readableAddChunk (_stream_readable.js:271:9)
    at TLSSocket.Readable.push (_stream_readable.js:212:10)
    at TLSWrap.onStreamRead (internal/stream_base_commons.js:186:23) {
  operationTime: Timestamp { _bsontype: 'Timestamp', low_: 2, high_: 1597978152 },
  ok: 0,
  code: 2,
  codeName: 'BadValue',
  '$clusterTime': {
    clusterTime: Timestamp { _bsontype: 'Timestamp', low_: 2, high_: 1597978152 },
    signature: { hash: [Binary], keyId: [Long] }
```

Figure 8.6: Output after the script is run (truncated for brevity)

In this exercise, you extended your Node.js application so that it catches and handles errors that you may run into when running MongoDB queries in a Node.js environment. This will allow you to create more robust, error-tolerant, and scalable applications.

## ADVANCED QUERIES

In the previous section, we connected to a MongoDB server, queried some data, outputted it, and handled any errors we encountered. However, an application or script would have limited utility if it could only perform read operations. In this section, we will apply **write** and **update** operations in the MongoDB driver. Furthermore, we will examine how we can use the function syntax to create reusable code blocks for our final application.

# INSERTING DATA WITH THE NODE.JS DRIVER

Similar to the mongo shell, we can use either the **insertOne** or **insertMany** function to write data into our collection. These functions are called on the collection object. The only parameter we need to pass into these functions is a single document in the case of **insertOne**, or an array of documents in the case of **insertMany**. The following is a code snippet that includes how to use **insertOne** and **insertMany** with callbacks. By now, you should be able to recognize that this is an incomplete snippet. To execute the following code, you will need to add the basic connection logic we learned about earlier in this chapter. This should look very familiar by now:

```
database.collection(collectionName).insertOne({Hello:
  "World"}, function(err, result) {
    // Handle result.
})


database.collection(collectionName).insertMany([{Hello: "World"},
  {Hello: "Mongo"}], function(err, result) {
    // Handle result.
})
```

As with **find**, we pass a callback to these functions to handle the result of the operation. Insert operations will return an error (which may be **null**) and a result, which details how the insert operation executed. For example, if we were to build on top of the result of the previous exercise and log the result of an **insertMany** operation, this would produce the following output:

```
database.collection(collectionName).insertOne({Hello: "World"},
  function(err, result) {
    console.log(result.result);
client.close();
})
```

We may see a **result** object like *Figure 8.7* in the output.

> **NOTE**
>
> We are only outputting a subset of the overall **result** object, which contains much more information about our operation. For example, we are logging **result.result**, which is a sub-document within the entire **result** object. This is just for the scope of this example. In other use cases, you may want more information about the result of your operation:

```
Connected to MongoDB with NodeJS!
{
  n: 1,
  opTime: {
    ts: Timestamp { _bsontype: 'Timestamp', low_: 6, high_: 1597978219 },
    t: 5
  },
  electionId: 7fffffff0000000000000005,
  ok: 1,
  '$clusterTime': {
    clusterTime: Timestamp { _bsontype: 'Timestamp', low_: 6, high_: 1597978219 },
    signature: { hash: [Binary], keyId: [Long] }
  },
  operationTime: Timestamp { _bsontype: 'Timestamp', low_: 6, high_: 1597978219 }
}
```

Figure 8.7: Output showing a subset of the overall result object

## UPDATING AND DELETING DATA WITH THE NODE.JS DRIVER

Updating and deleting documents with the driver follows the same pattern as the **insert** function, where the **collection** object passes through a callback, checks for errors, and analyzes the results of the operation. All these functions will return a results document. However, between the three operations, the format and information contained within a result document may differ. Let's look at some examples.

Here is an example of some sample code (also built on top of our earlier connection code) that updates a document. We can use either **updateOne** or **updateMany**:

```
    database.collection(collectionName).
updateOne({Hello: "World"}, {$set: {Hello
    : "Earth"}}, function(err, result) {
        console.log(result.modifiedCount);
        client.close();
    })
```

And if we were to run this code, our resulting output may look something like this:

```
Connected to MongoDB with NodeJS!
1
```

Now, let's look at an example of deleting a document. As with our other functions, we can use either **deleteOne** or **deleteMany**. Remember that this snippet exists as part of the larger code we created for *Exercise 8.03, Error Handling and Callbacks with the Node.js Driver*:

```
    database.collection(collectionName).
deleteOne({Hello: "Earth"}, function(err, result) {
        console.log(result.deletedCount);
        client.close();
    })
```

And if we were to run this code, our output would be as follows:

```
Connected to MongoDB with NodeJS!
1
```

As you can see, all these operations follow similar patterns and are very close in structure to the same commands you would send to the mongo shell. The main difference comes in the callback, where we can run our custom logic on the results of our operations.

## WRITING REUSABLE FUNCTIONS

In our examples and exercises so far, we have always executed a single operation and outputted the result. However, in larger, more complex applications, you will want to run many different operations in the same program, depending on the context. For example, in your application, you may want to run the same query multiple times and compare the respective results, or you may want the second query to be modified depending on the output of the first.

This is where we will create our own functions. You have already written a few functions to use as callbacks, but in this case, we are going to write functions we can call at any time, either for utility or to keep our code clean and separated. Let's look at an example.

Let's understand this better through the following code snippet, which runs three very similar queries. The only difference between these queries is a single parameter (rating) in each of the queries:

```
database.collection(collectionName).find({name: "Matthew"}).
each(function(err,
  doc) {});

database.collection(collectionName).find({name: "Mark"}).
each(function(err, doc)
  {});

database.collection(collectionName).find({name: "Luke"}).
each(function(err, doc)
  {})
```

Let's try to simplify and clean up this code with a function. We declare a new function using the same syntax we would use for a variable. Because this function does not change, we can declare it as **const**. For the value of the function, we can use the syntax we have become familiar with from callbacks in previous examples (examples from the *Callbacks* section, earlier in this chapter):

```
const findByName = function(name) {


}
```

Now, let's add our logic to this function, between the curly braces:

```
const findByName = function(name) {
    database.collection(collectionName).find({name:
      name}).each(function(err, doc) {})
}
```

But something isn't quite right. We're referencing the database object before we have created one. We will have to pass that object into this function as a parameter, so let's adjust our function to do that:

```
const findByName = function(name, database) {
    database.collection(collectionName).find({name: name}).
each(function(err,
        doc) {})
}
```

We can now replace our three queries with three function calls:

```
const findByName = function(name, database) {
    database.collection(collectionName).find({name: name}).
each(function(err, doc
        ) {})
}

findByName("Matthew", database);
findByName("Mark", database);
findByName("Luke", database);
```

In this chapter, we won't be going too far into creating modular, functional code for the sake of simplicity. However, if you wanted to improve this code even further, you could use an array and a **for** loop to run the function for each value, without having to call it three times.

## EXERCISE 8.04: UPDATING DATA WITH THE NODE.JS DRIVER

Considering the scenario from the *Introduction* section, you have made considerable progress from where you started. Your final application for the cinema company will need to be able to add votes to movies by running update operations. You're not quite ready to add this logic yet. However, to prove that you can accomplish this, write a script that updates several different documents in the database, and create a reusable function to do this. In this exercise, you will need to update the following names in the **chapter8_Exercise4** collection. You will use this unique collection to ensure that data is not corrupted for other activities during the updates:

*Ned Stark to Greg Stark, Robb Stark to Bob Stark, and Bran Stark to Brad Stark.*

You can accomplish this in Node.js by executing the following steps:

1. First, make sure the correct documents exist to update. Connect to the server directly with the mongo shell and execute the following code snippet to check for these documents:

```
db.chapter8_Exercise4.find({ $or: [{name: "Ned Stark"}, {name: "Robb
Stark"}, {name: "Bran Stark"}]});
```

2. If the result of the preceding query is empty, use this snippet to add the documents for updating:

```
db.chapter8_Exercise4.insert([{name: "Ned Stark"}, {name: "Bran
Stark"}, {name: "Robb Stark"}]);
```

3. Now, to create the script, exit the mongo shell connection and create a new JavaScript file called **Exercise8.04.js**. So that you don't have to rewrite everything from scratch, copy the content of **Exercise8.03.js** into your new script. Otherwise, rewrite the connection code in your new file. If you copied your code from *Exercise 8.03, Error Handling and Callbacks with the Node.js Driver*, then remove the code for the find query.

4. Change the collection from movies to **chapter8_Exercise4**:

```
const collectionName = "chapter8_Exercise4";
```

5. At the start of your script, before you connect, create a new function called **updateName**. This function will take the database object, the client object, and **oldName** and **newName** as parameters:

```
const updateName = function(client, database, oldName, newName) {

}
```

6. Within the **updateName** function, add the code for running an update command that will update a document containing a name field of **oldName** and update the value to **newName**:

```
const updateName = function(client, database, oldName, newName) {
    database.collection(collectionName).
updateOne({name: oldName}, {$set: {name: newName}},
function(err, result) {
        if(err) {
            console.log('Error updating');
            console.log(err);
            client.close();
            return false;
        }
```

```
        console.log('Updated documents #:');
        console.log(result.modifiedCount);
        client.close();
    })
};
```

7. Now, within the connect callback, run your new function three times, one for each of the three names you are updating:

```
    updateName(client, database, "Ned Stark", "Greg Stark");
    updateName(client, database, "Robb Stark", "Bob Stark");
    updateName(client, database, "Bran Stark", "Brad Stark");
```

8. At this point, your entire code should look like this:

```
const MongoClient = require('mongodb').MongoClient;
const url = 'mongodb+srv://mike:password@myAtlas-fawxo.gcp.mongodb.
net/test?retryWrites=true&w=majority';
const client = new MongoClient(url);
const databaseName = "sample_mflix";
const collectionName = "chapter8_Exercise4";

const updateName = function(client, database, oldName, newName) {
    database.collection(collectionName).
updateOne({name: oldName}, {$set: {name: newName}},
function(err, result) {
        if(err) {
            console.log('Error updating');
            console.log(err);
            client.close();
            return false;
        }
        console.log('Updated documents #:');
        console.log(result.modifiedCount);
        client.close();
    })
};


// Open the connection using the .connect function.
client.connect(function(err) {
    if(err) {
        console.log('Failed to connect.');
        console.log(err);
```

```
        return false;
    }


    // Within the connection block, add a console.log to confirm the
connection
    console.log('Connected to MongoDB with NodeJS!');

    const database = client.db(databaseName);
    if(!database) {
        console.log('Database object doesn't exist!');
        return false;
    }

    updateName(client, database, "Ned Stark", "Greg Stark");
    updateName(client, database, "Robb Stark", "Bob Stark");
    updateName(client, database, "Bran Stark", "Brad Stark");


})
```

9. Run the script using **node Exercise8.04.js**. You should get the
following output:

```
Connected to MongoDB with NodeJS!
Updated documents #:
1
Updated documents #:
1
Updated documents #:
1
```

Over the last four sections, you have learned how to create a Node.js script that
connects to MongoDB, run queries in easy-to-use functions, and handle any errors we
might encounter. This serves as a foundation upon which you can build many scripts
to perform complex logic using your MongoDB database. However, in our examples
so far, our query parameters have always been hardcoded into our scripts, meaning
each of our scripts can only satisfy a specific use case.

This is not ideal. One of the great strengths of using something like the Node.js driver is the ability to have a single application that solves a vast number of problems. To expand the scope of our scripts, we will take user input to create dynamic queries, capable of solving users' questions, without us having to rewrite and distribute a new version of our program. In this section, we will learn how to accept user input, handle it, and build dynamic queries from it.

> **NOTE**
>
> In most large, production-ready applications, user input will come in the form of a **Graphical User Interface** (**GUI**). These GUIs transform simple user selections into complex, relevant queries. However, building GUIs is quite tricky, and beyond the scope of this book.

## READING INPUT FROM THE COMMAND LINE

In this section, we will be obtaining inputs from the command line for our application. Fortunately, Node.js provides some simple ways for us to read input from the command line and use it in our code. Node.js provides a module called **readline** that will allow us to ask the user for input, accept that input, and then use it. You can load **readline** into your script by adding the following lines at the top of your file. You must always create an interface when using **readline**:

```
const readline = require('readline');

const interface = readline.createInterface({
    input: process.stdin,
    output: process.stdout,
});
```

Now, we can ask the user for some input. **readline** provides us with multiple ways to handle input. However, the simplest way, for now, is to use the **question** function, as in the example here:

```
interface.question('Hello, what is your name? ', (input) => {
    console.log(`Hello, ${input}`);

    interface.close();
});
```

> **NOTE**
>
> The `${input}` syntax allows us to embed a variable within a string. When using this, make sure to use backticks, ` (if you're not sure where to find this, on a standard QWERTY keyboard, it shares a key with the ~ symbol, to the left of the **1** key.)

If we run this example, we will get an output resembling this:

```
Chapter_8> node example.js
Hello, what is your name? Michael
Hello, Michael
```

If you want to create a longer prompt, it is better to use **console.log** to output the bulk of your output, and then provide just a smaller question for the **readline**. For example, say we have a long message that we send before we ask for user input. We can define it as a variable and log it before we ask our question:

```
const question = "Lorem ipsum dolor sit amet, consectetur adipiscing
elit, sed do eiusmod tempor incididunt ut labore et dolore magna
aliqua. Ut enim ad minim veniam, quis nostrud exercitation ullamco
laboris nisi ut aliquip ex ea commodo consequat. Duis aute irure dolor
in reprehenderit in voluptate velit esse cillum dolore eu fugiat nulla
pariatur. Excepteur sint occaecat cupidatat non proident, sunt in culpa
qui officia deserunt mollit anim id est laborum?"
interface.question(question, (input) => {
    console.log(`Hello, ${input}`);


    interface.close();
});
```

In this way, it is easy to modify and reuse our messages across multiple inputs.

> **NOTE**
>
> There are many different libraries and modules for handling inputs in Node.js. However, to keep things simple, we'll use **readline** in this chapter.

## CREATING AN INTERACTIVE LOOP

So, we have an easy way of asking a user a question and accepting some input from them. However, our application won't be very useful if we have to run it from the command line every time we want to use it. It would be much more useful if we could run the program once, and execute many runs of it based on different inputs.

To accomplish this, we can create an interactive loop, meaning the application will keep asking for input until an exit condition is met. To make sure we keep looping, we can place our prompt in a function that calls itself, which will keep running the code inside its block until the exit condition stated becomes **true**. This will provide a much better experience for users of our code. Here is an example of an interactive loop using our aforementioned **readline**:

```
const askName = function() {
    interface.question("Hello, what is your name?", (input) => {
        if(input === "exit") {
            return interface.close(); // Will kill the loop.
        }

        console.log(`Hello, ${input}`);
        askName();

    });
}
askName(); // First Run.
```

Note the exit condition here:

```
        if(input === "exit") {
            return interface.close(); // Will kill the loop.
        }
```

It is vitally important to ensure that, in any loop, you have an exit condition, as this allows users to quit the application. Otherwise, they will be stuck in a loop forever, and it may consume the resources of your computer.

> **NOTE**
>
> When writing loops in your code, it is possible that you could accidentally create an infinite loop without an exit condition. If this does happen, you may have to kill your shell or Terminal. You can try *Ctrl+C*, or *Cmd+C* on a macOS, to exit.

If you were to run the preceding example, you would be able to answer the question multiple times before exiting; for example:

```
Chapter_8> node examples.js
Hello, what is your name?Mike
Hello, Mike
Hello, what is your name?John
Hello, John
Hello, what is your name?Ed
Hello, Ed
Hello, what is your name?exit
```

## EXERCISE 8.05: HANDLING INPUTS IN NODE.JS

For this exercise, you're going to create a small Node.js application that allows you to ask users their name. You can think of this as a rudimentary login system. This application should run in an interactive loop; the options for the user are as follows:

- **login** (*Ask and store the user's name*)

- **who** (*Output the user's name*)

- **exit** (*End the application*)

Create this application by performing the following steps:

1. Create a new JavaScript file called **Exercise8.05.js**.

2. Import the **readline** module:

```
const readline = require('readline');
const interface = readline.createInterface({
    input: process.stdin,
    output: process.stdout,
});
```

3. Define the choice and user variables.

4. Now, define a new function called **login** that takes user as parameters. The function first asks for a user and stores it in a variable:

```
const login = function() {
    interface.question("Hello, what is your name?", (name) => {
        user = name;
    prompt();
        });
}
```

5. Create a new function called **who** that outputs **user**:

```
const who = function () {
    console.log(`User is ${user}`);
    prompt();
}
```

6. Create an input loop with the condition that choice is not equal to exit:

```
const prompt = function() {
    interface.question("login, who OR exit?", (input) => {
        if(input === "exit") {
            return interface.close(); // Will kill the loop.
        }

        prompt();
        });
}
```

7. After that, use the if keyword to check whether their choice matches "**login**". If we find a match, then run the **login** function:

```
        if(input === "login") {
            login();
        }
```

8. Then, use the if keyword to check whether their choice matches "**who**". If we find a match, then print out the **user** variable:

```
        if(input === "who") {
            who();
        }
```

Your final code should look something like this:

```javascript
const readline = require('readline');
const interface = readline.createInterface({
    input: process.stdin,
    output: process.stdout,
});

var choice;
var user;
var cinema;

const login = function() {
    interface.question("Hello, what is your name?", (name) => {
        user = name;
        prompt();
    });
}
const who = function () {
    console.log(`User is ${user}`)
    prompt();
}
const prompt = function() {
    interface.question("login, who OR exit?", (input) => {
        if(input === "exit") {
            return interface.close(); // Will kill the loop.
        }
        if(input === "login") {
            login();
        }
        if(input === "who") {
            who();
        }
    });
}
prompt();
```

9. Run the code using **node Exercise8.05.js** and enter some input. Now, you should be able to interact with the application. The following is an example:

```
Chapter_8> node .\Exercise8.06.js
login, who OR exit?login
Hello, what is your name?Michael
login, who OR exit?who
User is Michael
login, who OR exit?exit
```

In this exercise, you created a basic interactive application using Node.js that lets the user choose from three inputs and outputs the result accordingly.

## ACTIVITY 8.01: CREATING A SIMPLE NODE.JS APPLICATION

You have been engaged by a cinema company to create an application that allows customers to list the highest rated movies in a selected category. Customers should be able to provide a category and the responses within a named command-line list. They also need to provide details of their favorite movie to be captured within the favorite field. Finally, once all this is done, the customer should be able to **exit** the application, as follows:

- **"list"**: Ask the user for a genre, and then query the database for the top five movies in that genre, outputting the **ID**, **title**, and **favourite** fields.

- **"favourite"**: Ask the user for a film ID, and then update that film with a favorite field.

- **"exit"**: Quit the interactive loop and the application.

This activity aims to create a small Node.js application that exposes an interactive input loop to the user. Within this loop, users can query information in the database by genre, as well as update records by ID. You will need to ensure that you also handle any errors that may occur from users' input.

You may complete this objective in several ways, but remember what we have learned throughout this chapter and attempt to create simple, easy-to-use code.

The following high-level steps will help you to complete this task:

1.  Import the **readline** and MongoDB libraries.

2.  Create your **readline** interface.

3.  Declare any variables you will need.

4.  Create a function called list that will fetch the top five highest rated films for a given genre, returning the **title**, **favorite**, and **ID** fields.

> **NOTE**
>
> You will need to ask for the category in this function. Look at the login method in *Exercise 8.05*, *Handling Inputs in Node.js*, for more information.

5.  Create a function called **favourite** that will update a document by title and add a key called **favourite** with a value of **true** to the document. (*Hint: You will need to ask for the title in this function using the same method you used for your list function.*)

6.  Create the MongoDB connection, database, and collection.

7.  Create an interactive while loop based on the user's input. If you're unsure how to do this, refer to our prompt function from *Exercise 8.05*, *Handling Inputs in Node.js*.

8.  Inside the interactive loop, use if conditions to check for the input. If a valid input is found, run the relevant function.

9.  Remember, you will need to pass the database and client objects through to each of your functions, including any time you call **prompt()**. To test your output, run the following commands:

```
list

Horror

favourite

list

exit
```

The expected output is as follows:

> **NOTE**
>
> You may notice that the title **Nosferatu** appears twice in the output.
> If you look at the **_id** values, you will see that these are actually two
> separate films with the same title. In MongoDB, you may have many
> different documents that share the same values in their fields.

```
Activity8.01> node .\Activity8.01.js
(node:6748) DeprecationWarning: current Server Discovery and Monitoring engine is deprecat
ed, and will be removed in a future version. To use the new Server Discover and Monitoring
 engine, pass option { useUnifiedTopology: true } to the MongoClient constructor.      Con
nected to MongoDB with NodeJS!list, favourite OR exit: listPlease enter a category: Horror
Docs Array
[
  { _id: 573a1391f29313caabcd75b5, title: 'Nosferatu' },
  { _id: 573a1391f29313caabcd806b, title: 'The Phantom of the Opera' },
  { _id: 573a1391f29313caabcd8978, title: 'The Unknown' },
  {
    _id: 573a1391f29313caabcd8acf,
    title: 'The Fall of the House of Usher'
  },
  { _id: 573a1391f29313caabcd956e, title: 'Nosferatu' }
]
list, favourite OR exit: favourite
Please enter a movie title: Nosferatu
Updated documents #:
1list, favourite OR exit: listPlease enter a category: HorrorDocs Array[  {
    _id: 573a1391f29313caabcd75b5,
    title: 'Nosferatu',
```

Figure 8.8: Final output (truncated for brevity)

> **NOTE**
>
> The solution to this activity can be found on page 676.

# SUMMARY

In this chapter, we have covered the basic concepts that are essential to the creation of a MongoDB-powered application using the Node.js driver. Using these fundamentals, a vast number of scripts can be created to perform queries and operations on your database. We even learned to handle errors and create interactive applications.

Although you may not be required to write or read applications like these as part of your day-to-day responsibilities, having a thorough understanding of how these applications are built gives you a unique insight into MongoDB development and how your peers may interact with your MongoDB data.

However, if you are looking to increase your expertise with regards to the Node.js driver for MongoDB, this is just the beginning. There are many different patterns, libraries, and best practices you can use to develop Node.js applications against MongoDB. This is just the beginning of your Node.js journey.

In the next chapter, we will dive deeper into improving the performance of your MongoDB interactions and create efficient indexes that will speed up your queries. Another useful feature we will cover is the use of **explain** and how to best interpret its output.

# 9

# PERFORMANCE

## OVERVIEW

This chapter introduces you to the concepts of query optimization and performance improvement in MongoDB. You will first explore the internal workings of query execution and identify the factors that can affect query performance, before moving on to database indexes and how indexes can reduce query execution time. You will also learn how to create, list, and delete indexes, and study the various types of indexes and their benefits. In the final sections, you will be introduced to various query optimization techniques that can help you use indexes effectively. By the end of this chapter, you will be able to analyze queries and use indexes and optimization techniques to improve query performance.

# INTRODUCTION

In the previous chapters, we learned about the MongoDB query language and various query operators. We learned how to write queries to retrieve data. We also learned about various commands used to add and delete data and also to update or modify a piece of data. We ensured that the queries bring us the desired output; however, we did not pay much attention to their execution time and their efficiency. In this chapter, we will focus on how to analyze a query's performance and optimize its performance further, if needed.

Real-world applications are made up of multiple components, such as a user interface, processing components, databases, and more. The responsiveness of an application is dependent on the efficiency of each of these components. The database component performs different operations, such as saving, reading, and updating data. The amount of data a database table or collection stores, or the amount of data being pushed into or retrieved from a database, can affect the performance of the entire system. Therefore, it is important to know how efficiently database operations are executed and whether further optimization is possible to improve the speed of those operations.

In the next section, you will learn how to analyze queries based on the detailed statistics provided by the database and use them to identify problems.

# QUERY ANALYSIS

In order to write efficient queries, it is important to analyze them, find any possible performance issues, and fix them. This technique is called performance optimization. There are many factors that can negatively affect the performance of a query, such as incorrect scaling, incorrectly structured collections, and inadequate resources such as RAM and CPU. However, the biggest and most common factor is the difference between the number of records scanned and the number of records returned during the query execution. The greater the difference is, the slower the query will be. Thankfully, in MongoDB, this factor is the easiest to address and is done using indexes.

Creating and using indexes on a collection narrows down the number of records being scanned and improves the query performance noticeably. Before we delve further into indexes, though, we first need to cover the details of query execution.

Say you want to find a list of the movies released in the year 2015. The following snippet shows the command for this:

```
db.movies.find(
    {
        "year" : 2015
    },
    {
        "title" : 1,
        "awards.wins" : 1
    }
).sort(
    {"awards.wins" : -1}
)
```

The query filters the **movies** collection based on the **year** field, projects the movie title and awards won in the output, and sorts the results so that the movies with the greatest number of wins appear at the top. If we execute this query by connecting to the MongoDB Atlas **sample_mflix** database, it returns **484** records.

To execute any such query, the MongoDB query execution engine prepares one or more query execution plans. The database has an inbuilt query optimizer that chooses the most efficient plan for the execution. A plan is usually composed of multiple processing stages that are executed in sequence to produce the final output. The previous query we created has a query condition, a projection expression, and a sort specification. For the queries with similar shapes, a typical execution plan will look as shown in *Figure 9.1*:

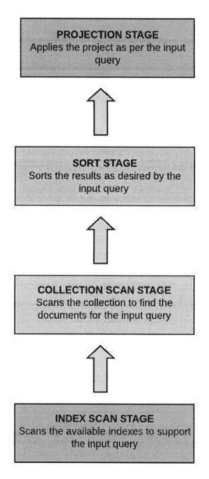

**Figure 9.1: Query execution stages**

At first, if there is a supporting index for the given query condition, the index is scanned to identify the matching records. In our case, the **year** field does not have an index, and so the index scan stage will be ignored. In the next stage, the full collection is scanned to find the matching records. The matched records are then passed to the sort stage, where the records are sorted in memory. Finally, projection is applied to the sorted records and the final output is delivered to the client.

MongoDB provides a query analysis mechanism with which we can fetch some useful stats about query execution. In the next section, we will learn how to use query analysis and stats to identify performance issues in the previous query.

## EXPLAINING THE QUERY

The **explain()** function is extremely useful for exploring the internal workings of a query. The function can be used along with a query or a command to print detailed statistics pertinent to their execution. The most important metrics it can give us are as follows:

- Query execution time

- Number of documents scanned

- Number of documents returned

- The index that was used

The following code snippet shows an example of using the **explain** function on a query using the same query that you created previously:

```
db.movies.explain().find(
    {
        "year" : 2015
    },
    {
        "title" : 1,
        "awards.wins" : 1
    }
).sort(
    {"awards.wins" : -1}
)
```

Note that the **explain** function can also be used with the following commands:

- **remove()**

- **update()**

- **count()**

- **aggregate()**

- **distinct()**

- **findAndModify()**

By default, the **explain** function prints the query planner details—that is, details of various execution stages. This can be seen in the following snippet:

```
"queryPlanner" : {
    "plannerVersion" : 1,
    "namespace" : "mflix.movies",
    "indexFilterSet" : false,
    "parsedQuery" : {
        "year" : {
            "$eq" : 2015
        }
    },
    "queryHash" : "9A7F8C29",
    "planCacheKey" : "9A7F8C29",
    "winningPlan" : {
        "stage" : "PROJECTION_DEFAULT",
        "transformBy" : {
            "title" : 1,
            "awards.wins" : 1
        },
        "inputStage" : {
            "stage" : "SORT",
            "sortPattern" : {
                "awards.wins" : -1
            },
            "inputStage" : {
                "stage" : "SORT_KEY_GENERATOR",
                "inputStage" : {
                    "stage" : "COLLSCAN",
                    "filter" : {
                        "year" : {
                            "$eq" : 2015
                        }
                    },
                    "direction" : "forward"
                }
            }
        }
    },
```

```
        "rejectedPlans" : [ ]
    },
```

The output shows the winning plan and a list of rejected plans. In the case of the preceding query, the execution began with **COLLSCAN** as there was no suitable index. Thus, the query does not have any rejected plans, and the only plan available was the winning plan. In the winning plan, there are multiple nested `inputStage` objects, which clearly shows the execution sequence of different stages.

The first stage is **COLLSCAN**, where a filter is applied to the `year` field. The next stage, **SORT**, performs the sorting based on the `awards.wins` field—that is, the number of awards won. Finally. in the **PROJECTION_DEFAULT** stage, the `title` and `awards.wins` fields are selected and returned in the output.

The `explain` function can take an optional argument called verbosity mode, which controls what information is returned by the function. The following list details the three different verbosity levels:

1. `queryPlanner`: This is the default option and prints query planner details such as rejected plans, the winning plan, and the execution stages of the winning plan.

2. `executionStats`: This option prints all the information provided by `queryPlanner` along with detailed execution statistics for the query execution. This option is useful for finding any performance-related problems in queries.

3. `allPlansExecution`: This option outputs the details provided by `executionStats` along with the details of the rejected execution plans.

## VIEWING EXECUTION STATS

In order to view the execution stats, you need to pass `executionStats` as an argument to the `explain()` function. The following snippet shows `executionStats` for your query:

```
    "executionStats" : {
        "executionSuccess" : true,
        "nReturned" : 484,
        "executionTimeMillis" : 85,
        "totalKeysExamined" : 0,
        "totalDocsExamined" : 23539,
        "executionStages" : {
            "stage" : "PROJECTION_DEFAULT",
            "nReturned" : 484,
            "executionTimeMillisEstimate" : 3,
```

```
            "works" : 24027,
            "advanced" : 484,
            "needTime" : 23542,
            "needYield" : 0,
            "saveState" : 187,
            "restoreState" : 187,
            "isEOF" : 1,
            "transformBy" : {
                "title" : 1,
                "awards.wins" : 1
            },
            "inputStage" : {
                "stage" : "SORT",
                "nReturned" : 484,
                "executionTimeMillisEstimate" : 3,
                "works" : 24027,
                "advanced" : 484,
                "needTime" : 23542,
                "needYield" : 0,
                "saveState" : 187,
                "restoreState" : 187,
                "isEOF" : 1,
                "sortPattern" : {
                    "awards.wins" : -1
                },
                "memUsage" : 613758,
                "memLimit" : 33554432,
                "inputStage" : {
                    "stage" : "SORT_KEY_GENERATOR",
                    "nReturned" : 484,
                    "executionTimeMillisEstimate" : 3,
                    "works" : 23542,
```

```
                    "advanced" : 484,
                    "needTime" : 23057,
                    "needYield" : 0,
                    "saveState" : 187,
                    "restoreState" : 187,
                    "isEOF" : 1,
                    "inputStage" : {
                            "stage" : "COLLSCAN",
                            "filter" : {
                                    "year" : {
                                            "$eq" : 2015
                                    }
                            },
                            "nReturned" : 484,
                            "executionTimeMillisEstimate" : 3,
                            "works" : 23541,
                            "advanced" : 484,
                            "needTime" : 23056,
                            "needYield" : 0,
                            "saveState" : 187,
                            "restoreState" : 187,
                            "isEOF" : 1,
                            "direction" : "forward",
                            "docsExamined" : 23539
                    }
            }
        }
    }
},
```

The execution stats provide useful metrics pertinent to each execution phase, along with some top-level fields where some metrics are aggregated over the total execution of the query. The following are some of the most important metrics from the execution stats:

- **executionTimeMillis**: This is the total time (in milliseconds) taken for query execution.

- **totalKeysExamined**: This indicates the number of indexed keys that were scanned.

- **totalDocsExamined**: This indicates the number of documents examined against the given query condition.

- **nReturned**: This is the total number of records returned in the query output.

Now, let's analyze the execution stats in the next section.

## IDENTIFYING PROBLEMS

The execution stats (as seen from the preceding snippet) tell us that there are a few problems with the querying process. To return **484** matching records, the query examined **23539** documents, which is also the total number of documents in the collection. Having to scan a large number of documents slows down the query execution. Looking at the query execution time of **85** milliseconds, it seems like it is fast enough. However, the query execution time can vary based on the network traffic, the RAM and CPU loads on the server, and the number of records getting scanned. The reason the number of scanned documents slows down the performance is explained in the following section.

## LINEAR SEARCH

When we execute a **find** query with a search criterion on a collection, the database search engine picks the first record in the collection and checks whether it matches the given criteria. If no match is found, the search engine moves on to the next record to find a match, and the process is repeated till a search is found.

This search technique is called a sequential or linear search. Linear searches perform better when they are applied to a small amount of data, or in the best-case scenarios, where the required term is found within the first search. Thus, the search performance will be good when searching for a document in a small collection. However, it will be noticeably poorer if there is a large amount of data, or in the worst-case scenario, when the required term exists at the end of the collection.

Most of the time, when a newly built system goes live, the collections are either empty or they hold a very small amount of data. Thus, all the database operations are instant. But, over time, as the collections grow in size, the same operations start taking longer. The primary reason for the slowness is linear search, which is the default search algorithm used by most databases, including MongoDB. Linear searches can be avoided or at least limited by creating indexes on specific fields of a collection. In the next section, we will explore this concept in detail.

# INTRODUCTION TO INDEXES

Databases can maintain and use indexes to make searches more efficient. In MongoDB, indexes are created on a field or a combination of fields. The database maintains a special registry of indexed fields and some of their data. The registry is easily searchable, as it maintains a logical link between the value of an indexed field and the respective documents in the collection. During a search operation, the database first locates the value in the registry and identifies the matching documents in the collection accordingly. The values in a registry are always sorted in ascending or descending order of the values, which helps during a range search and also while sorting the results.

To better understand how the index registry helps during searches, imagine you are searching for a theater by its ID, as follows:

```
db.theaters.find(
    {"theaterId" : 1009}
)
```

When the query is executed on the **sample_mflix** database, it returns a single record. Note that the total number of theaters in the collection is 1,564. The following diagram depicts the difference between document searches with and without an index:

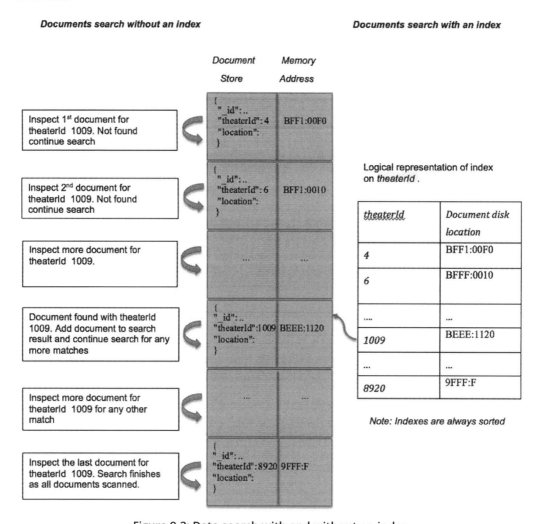

Figure 9.2: Data search with and without an index

The following table represents the number of documents scanned against the number of documents returned in these two different scenarios.

| Scenario | Scanned | Returned | Additional Info |
|---|---|---|---|
| No index available on the `theaterId` field | 1,564 | 1 | The `theaterId` field is neither indexed nor unique, so all 1,564 documents in the collections were scanned. |
| Index available on the `theaterId` field | 1 | 1 | Since the `theaterId` field is indexed, MongoDB quickly locates the document without performing any scans. The number of documents scanned is only 1 because only 1 document has a `theaterId` value equal to 1,009. |

Figure 9.3: Details about the documents scanned and the documents returned

Looking at the preceding table, it is clear that searching with an index is preferable to searching without one. In this section, we learned that databases support indexes for the faster retrieval of data and how the index registry helps avoid complete collection scans. We will now learn how to create an index and find indexes in a collection.

# CREATING AND LISTING INDEXES

Indexes can be created by executing a **createIndex()** command on a collection, as follows:

```
db.collection.createIndex(
keys,
options
)
```

The first argument to the command is a list of key-value pairs, where each pair consists of a field name and sort order, and the optional second argument is a set of options to control the indexes.

In a previous section, you wrote the following query to find all the movies released in 2015, sort them in descending order of the number of awards won, and print the title and number of wins:

```
db.movies.find(
    {
        "year" : 2015
    },
    {
        "title" : 1,
        "awards.wins" : 1
    }
```

```
).sort(
    {"awards.wins" : -1}
)
```

As the query uses a filter on the **year** field, you need to create an index on that field. The next command creates an index on the **year** field by passing a sort order of **1**, which indicates ascending order:

```
db.movies.createIndex(
    {year: 1}
)
```

The next snippet shows the output after executing the command on the mongo shell:

```
{
    "createdCollectionAutomatically" : true,
    "numIndexesBefore" : 2,
    "numIndexesAfter" : 3,
    "ok" : 1,
    "$clusterTime" : {
        "clusterTime" : Timestamp(1596352285, 3),
        "signature" : {
            "hash" : BinData(0,"Ce9YztoqHYaBhubyzM3SsujEYFY="),
            "keyId" : NumberLong("6853300587753111555")
        }
    },
    "operationTime" : Timestamp(1596352285, 3)
}
```

The output indicates that the index was successfully created. It also mentions the number of indexes present before and after the execution of this command (see the highlighted part in the code) and the time the index was created.

## LISTING INDEXES ON A COLLECTION

You can list the indexes of a collection by using the **getIndexes()** command. This command does not take any parameters. It simply returns an array of indexes with some basic details.

Executing the following command will list all the indexes present in the **movies** collection:

```
db.movies.getIndexes()
```

The output for this will be as follows:

```
[
    {
        "v" : 2,
        "key" : {
            "_id" : 1
        },
        "name" : "_id_",
        "ns" : "sample_mflix.movies"
    },
    {
        "v" : 2,
        "key" : {
            "_fts" : "text",
            "_ftsx" : 1
        },
        "name" : "cast_text_fullplot_text_genres_text_title_text",
        "default_language" : "english",
        "language_override" : "language",
        "weights" : {
            "cast" : 1,
            "fullplot" : 1,
            "genres" : 1,
            "title" : 1
        },
        "ns" : "sample_mflix.movies",
        "textIndexVersion" : 3
    },
    {
        "v" : 2,
        "key" : {
            "year" : 1
        },
        "name" : "year_1",
        "ns" : "sample_mflix.movies"
    }
]
```

The output indicates that there are three indexes on the collection, including the one you just created. For each index, it displays the version, indexed fields and their sort order, the index name, and a namespace made up of the index name and database name. Note that, while creating the index on the **year** field, you did not specify its name. You will see how index names are derived in the next section.

## INDEX NAMES

MongoDB assigns a default name to an index if a name is not provided explicitly. The default name of an index consists of the field name and the sort order, separated by underscores. If there is more than one key in the index (known as a compound index), all the keys are concatenated in the same manner.

The following command creates an index for the **theaterId** field without providing a name:

```
db.theaters.createIndex(
    {theaterId : 1}
)
```

This command will result in the creation of an index with the default name **theaterId_1**.

However, you can also create an index with a specific name. To do so, you can use the **name** attribute to provide a custom name to the index, as follows:

```
db.theaters.createIndex(
    {theaterId : -1},
    {name : "myTheaterIdIndex"}
);
```

The preceding command will create an index with the name **myTheaterIdIndex**. In the next exercise, you will use MongoDB Atlas to create an index.

## EXERCISE 9.01: CREATING AN INDEX USING MONGODB ATLAS

In the previous section, you learned how to create an index using the mongo shell. In this exercise, you will use the MongoDB Atlas portal to create an index on the **accounts** collection, which is present in the **sample_analytics** database. Perform the following steps to complete this exercise:

1. Sign in to your account at https://www.mongodb.com/cloud/atlas.

2. Go to the **sample_analytics** database and select the **accounts** collection. On the collection screen, select the **Indexes** tab, and you should see one index.

Figure 9.4: The Indexes tab in the accounts collection in the sample_analytics database

3. Click on the **CREATE INDEX** button in the top-right corner. You should be presented with a modal, as shown in the following figure:

Figure 9.5: The Create Index page

4.  To create an index on **account_id**, remove the default field and type entries from the **FIELDS** section. Introduce **account_id** as the field and type with value **1** for ascending index order. The following is a screenshot showing the updated **FIELDS** section:

FIELDS

```
1▾ {
2      "account_id": "1"
3  }
```

Figure 9.6: Updated FIELDS section

5.  Pass the **name** parameter to provide a custom name for this index in the **OPTIONS** section, as shown here:

OPTIONS

```
{ "name" : "accountIdIndex"}
```

Figure 9.7: Passing the name parameter in the OPTIONS section

6.  Once you update the fields section, the **Review** button should turn green. Click on it to go to the next step:

Figure 9.8 The Review button

7. A confirmation screen will be presented to you. Click the **Confirm** button on the following screen to finish creating the index:

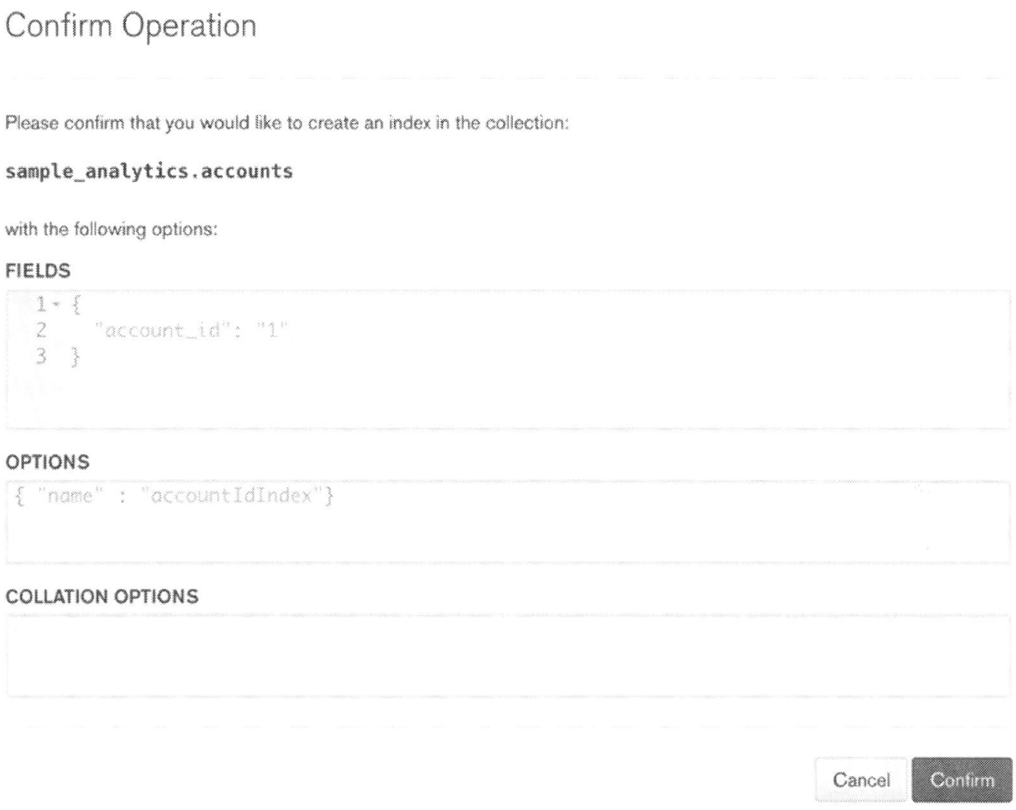

## Confirm Operation

Please confirm that you would like to create an index in the collection:

**sample_analytics.accounts**

with the following options:

**FIELDS**

```
1 ▾ {
2     "account_id": "1"
3 }
```

**OPTIONS**

```
{ "name" : "accountIdIndex"}
```

**COLLATION OPTIONS**

Cancel    Confirm

Figure 9.9: Confirmation screen

Once the index creation is finished, the index list will be updated, as follows:

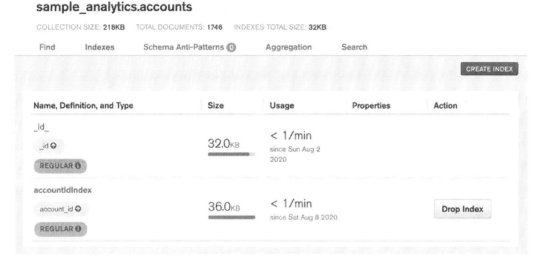

Figure 9.10: Updated index list

In this exercise, you have successfully created indexes using the MongoDB Atlas portal.

You have now learned how to create an index on a collection. Next, you will see how an indexed field improves query performance.

## QUERY ANALYSIS AFTER INDEXES

In the *Query Analysis* section, you analyzed the performance of a query that did not have suitable indexes to support its query condition. Because of this, the query scanned all **23539** documents in the collection to return **484** matching documents. Now that you have added an index on the **year** field, let's see how the query execution stats have changed.

The following query prints the execution statistics for the same query:

```
db.movies.explain("executionStats").find(
    {
        "year" : 2015
    },
    {
        "title" : 1,
        "awards.wins" : 1
    }
```

```
).sort(
    {"awards.wins" : -1}
)
```

The output for this is slightly different than the previous one, as shown in the following snippet:

```
"executionStats" : {
    "executionSuccess" : true,
    "nReturned" : 484,
    "executionTimeMillis" : 7,
    "totalKeysExamined" : 484,
    "totalDocsExamined" : 484,
    "executionStages" : {
        "stage" : "PROJECTION_DEFAULT",
        "nReturned" : 484,
        "executionTimeMillisEstimate" : 0,
        "works" : 971,
        "advanced" : 484,
        "needTime" : 486,
        "needYield" : 0,
        "saveState" : 7,
        "restoreState" : 7,
        "isEOF" : 1,
        "transformBy" : {
            "title" : 1,
            "awards.wins" : 1
        },
        "inputStage" : {
            "stage" : "SORT",
            "nReturned" : 484,
            "executionTimeMillisEstimate" : 0,
            "works" : 971,
            "advanced" : 484,
            "needTime" : 486,
            "needYield" : 0,
            "saveState" : 7,
            "restoreState" : 7,
            "isEOF" : 1,
            "sortPattern" : {
                "awards.wins" : -1
```

```
            },
            "memUsage" : 613758,
            "memLimit" : 33554432,
            "inputStage" : {
                "stage" : "SORT_KEY_GENERATOR",
                "nReturned" : 484,
                "executionTimeMillisEstimate" : 0,
                "works" : 486,
                "advanced" : 484,
                "needTime" : 1,
                "needYield" : 0,
                "saveState" : 7,
                "restoreState" : 7,
                "isEOF" : 1,
                "inputStage" : {
                    "stage" : "FETCH",
                    "nReturned" : 484,
                    "executionTimeMillisEstimate" : 0,
                    "works" : 485,
                    "advanced" : 484,
                    "needTime" : 0,
                    "needYield" : 0,
                    "saveState" : 7,
                    "restoreState" : 7,
                    "isEOF" : 1,
                    "docsExamined" : 484,
                    "alreadyHasObj" : 0,
                    "inputStage" : {
                        "stage" : "IXSCAN",
                        "nReturned" : 484,
                        "executionTimeMillisEstimate" : 0,
                        "works" : 485,
                        "advanced" : 484,
                        "needTime" : 0,
                        "needYield" : 0,
                        "saveState" : 7,
                        "restoreState" : 7,
                        "isEOF" : 1,
                        "keyPattern" : {
                            "year" : 1
```

```
                            },
                            "indexName" : "year_1",
                            "isMultiKey" : false,
                            "multiKeyPaths" : {
                                "year" : [ ]
                            },
                            "isUnique" : false,
                            "isSparse" : false,
                            "isPartial" : false,
                            "indexVersion" : 2,
                            "direction" : "forward",
                            "indexBounds" : {
                                "year" : [
                                    "[2015.0, 2015.0]"
                                ]
                            },
                            "keysExamined" : 484,
                            "seeks" : 1,
                            "dupsTested" : 0,
                            "dupsDropped" : 0
                        }
                    }
                }
            }
        }
    },
```

The first difference is that the first stage (that is, **COLLSCAN**) is now replaced by **IXSCAN** and **FETCH** stages. This means that first, an index scan stage was performed, and then, based on the retrieved index references, the data was fetched from the collection. Also, the top-level fields indicate that only **484** documents were examined, and the same number of documents were returned.

Thus, we see that query performance is greatly improved by reducing the number of documents being scanned. This is evident here as the query execution time is now reduced to **7** milliseconds from **85** milliseconds. Even as more and more documents are pushed into the collection every year, the performance of the query will remain consistent.

We have seen how to create indexes and also how to list the indexes from a collection. MongoDB also provides a way to remove or drop an index. The following section will explore this in detail.

## HIDING AND DROPPING INDEXES

Dropping an index means removing the values of the fields from the index registry. Thus, any searches on the related fields will be performed in a linear fashion, provided there are no other indexes present on the field.

It is important to note that MongoDB does not allow updating an existing index. Thus, to fix an incorrectly created index, we need to drop it and recreate it correctly.

An index is deleted using the **dropIndex** function. It takes a single parameter, which can either be the index name or the index specification document, as follows:

```
db.collection.dropIndex(indexNameOrSpecification)
```

The index specification document is the definition of the index that is used to create it (like the following snippet, for example):

```
db.movies.createIndex(
    {title: 1}
)
```

Consider the following snippet:

```
db.movies.dropIndex(
    {title: 1}
)
```

This command drops the index on the **title** field of the **movies** collection:

```
{
    «nIndexesWas» : 4,
    "ok" : 1,
    "$clusterTime" : {
        "clusterTime" : Timestamp(1596885249, 1),
        "signature" : {
            "hash" : BinData(0,"WNi8vLv+MUP5F7bUg6ZGAbhbT1o="),
            "keyId" : NumberLong("6853300587753111555")
        }
    },
    "operationTime" : Timestamp(1596885249, 1)
}
```

The output contains **nIndexesWas** (highlighted), which refers to the index count before the command was executed. The **ok** field shows the status as **1**, which indicates the command was successful.

## DROPPING MULTIPLE INDEXES

You can also drop multiple indexes using the **dropIndexes** command. The command syntax is as follows:

```
db.collection.dropIndexes()
```

This command can be used to drop all the indexes on a collection except the default **_id** index. You can use the command to drop a single index by passing either the index name or the index specification document. You can also use the command to delete a group of indexes by passing an array of index names. The following is an example of the **dropIndexes** command:

```
db.theaters.dropIndexes()
```

The preceding command generates the following output:

```
{
    "nIndexesWas" : 3,
    «msg» : «non-_id indexes dropped for collection»,
    "ok" : 1,
    "$clusterTime" : {
        "clusterTime" : Timestamp(1596887253, 1),
        "signature" : {
            "hash" : BinData(0,"+OYwY3X1upiuad63SOAYOe0uPXI="),
            "keyId" : NumberLong("6853300587753111555")
        }
    },
    "operationTime" : Timestamp(1596887253, 1)
}
```

All the indexes except the default **_id** index were dropped, as confirmed in the **msg** attribute (highlighted).

## HIDING AN INDEX

MongoDB provides a way to hide indexes from the query planner. Creating and deleting indexes are expensive operations in terms of time. For large collections, these operations take longer to finish. So, before you decide to remove an index, you can first hide it to analyze the performance impact and then decide accordingly.

To hide an index, the **hideIndex()** command can be used on the collection, as follows:

```
db.collection.hideIndex(indexNameOrSpecification)
```

The argument to the command is similar to that for the **dropIndex()** function. It takes either the name of the index or an index specification document.

An important thing to note is that hidden indexes appear only on the **getIndexes()** function call. They are updated after every write operation on the collection. However, the query planner won't see these indexes, and so they cannot be used for executing queries.

Once an index is hidden, you can analyze the impact on the queries and drop the indexes if they are truly unneeded. However, if hiding an index has an adverse effect on performance, you can restore or unhide them by using the **unhideIndex()** function, as follows:

```
db.collection.unhideIndex(indexNameOrSpecification)
```

The **unhideIndex()** function takes a single argument, which can either be the index name or an index specification document. Since hidden indexes are always updated after write operations, they are always in a ready state. Unhiding them can immediately put them back in operation.

## EXERCISE 9.02: DROPPING AN INDEX USING MONGO ATLAS

In this exercise, you will remove an index from the **accounts** collection of the **sample_analytics** database using the Atlas portal. The following steps will help you complete this exercise:

1. Sign in to your account at https://www.mongodb.com/cloud/atlas.

2. Go to the **sample_ analytics** database and select the **accounts** collection. On the collection screen, select the **Indexes** tab and you should see the existing indexes. Click on the **Drop Index** button next to the index that you want to remove:

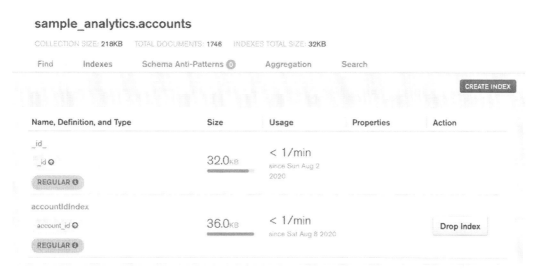

Figure 9.11: The Indexes tab for the accounts collection of the sample_analytics database

3. A confirmation dialog box should be presented as shown in the following figure. Enter the index name, which is also displayed in bold in the dialog message:

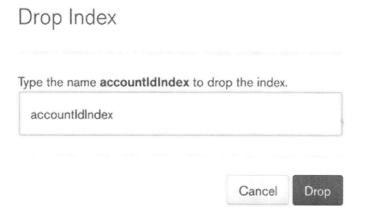

Figure 9.12: Entering the name of the index to be dropped

4. The index should be removed from the list of indexes, as indicated by the following screen. Note the absence of the **accountIdIndex** index:

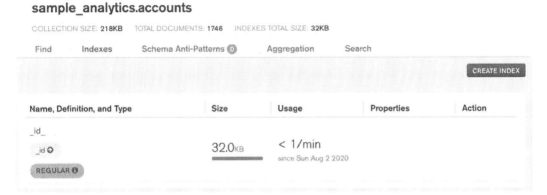

Figure 9.13: The Indexes tab indicating that accountIdIndex was successfully removed

In this exercise, you practiced dropping an index on the collection by using the MongoDB Atlas portal. In the next section, we will look at the types of indexes available in MongoDB.

# TYPE OF INDEXES

We have seen how indexes help with query performance and how we can create, drop, and list indexes in the collection. MongoDB supports different types of indexes, such as single key, multikey, and compound indexes. Each of these indexes has different advantages that you will need to know before deciding which type is suitable for your collection. Let's start with a brief overview of default indexes.

## DEFAULT INDEXES

As seen in the previous chapters, each document in a collection has a primary key (namely, the **_id** field) and is indexed by default. MongoDB uses this index to maintain the uniqueness of the **_id** field, and it is available on all the collections.

## SINGLE-KEY INDEXES

An index created using a single field from a collection is called a single-key index. You used a single-key index earlier in this chapter. The syntax is as follows:

```
db.collection.createIndex({ field1: type}, {options})
```

## COMPOUND INDEXES

Single-key indexes are preferable when using the key in a search significantly reduces the number of documents to be scanned. However, in some scenarios, single-key indexes are not sufficient to reduce the collection scans. This typically happens when the query is based on more than one field.

Consider the query you wrote to find movies released in 2015. You saw that adding a single-key index on the **year** field improved the query performance. You will now modify the query and add a filter based on the **rated** field, as follows:

```
db.movies.find(
    {
        "year" : 2015,
        "rated" : "UNRATED"
    },
    {
        "title" : 1,
        "awards.wins" : 1
    }
).sort(
    {"awards.wins" : -1}
)
```

Use **explain("executionStats")** on this query and analyze the execution stats:

```
"executionStats" : {
        "executionSuccess" : true,
        "nReturned" : 3,
        "executionTimeMillis" : 1,
        "totalKeysExamined" : 484,
        "totalDocsExamined" : 484,
        "executionStages" : {
```

The preceding snippet is from the execution stats of the query. The following are important observations from these stats:

- Because of the indexes, only **484** documents were scanned.

- Indexes helped locate the **484** documents and the second filter, based on the **rated** field, was applied by doing the collection scan.

From these points, it is clear that we have again widened the difference between the number of documents to be scanned and the number of documents returned. This could be a potential performance issue when the same query is used with some other year that has thousands of records. For such cases, the database allows you to create an index based on more than one field (called compound indexes). The **createIndex** command can be used to create a compound index using the following syntax:

```
db.collection.createIndex({ field1: type, field2: type, ...}, {options})
```

This syntax is similar to that of a single-field index, except that it accepts multiple pairs of fields and their respective sort orders. Note that a compound index can consist of a maximum of **32** fields.

Now, create a compound index on both the **year** and **rated** fields:

```
db.movies.createIndex(
    {year : 1, rated : 1}
)
```

This command generates the following output:

```
{
    "createdCollectionAutomatically" : false,
    "numIndexesBefore" : 3,
    "numIndexesAfter" : 4,
    "ok" : 1,
    "$clusterTime" : {
        "clusterTime" : Timestamp(1596932004, 4),
        "signature" : {
            "hash" : BinData(0,"y8fxEd0oLD6+OkLmhCjirg2Cm14="),
            "keyId" : NumberLong("6853300587753111555")
        }
    },
    "operationTime" : Timestamp(1596932004, 4)
}
```

The default name of a compound index contains the field names and their sort order, separated by an underscore. The index name for the index created by the last index will be **year_1_rated_1**. You can give a custom name to the compound indexes as well.

Now that you have created an additional index on the two fields, observe what execution stats the query gives:

```
"executionStats" : {
        "executionSuccess" : true,
        "nReturned" : 3,
        "executionTimeMillis" : 2,
        "totalKeysExamined" : 3,
        "totalDocsExamined" : 3,
        "executionStages" : {
```

The preceding snippet indicates that the compound index is used to execute this query and not the single-key index you created earlier. The number of documents scanned, and the number of documents returned are the same. Since only **3** documents are scanned, the query execution time is reduced as well.

## MULTIKEY INDEXES

An index created on the fields of an array type is called a multikey index. When an array field is passed as an argument to the **createIndex** function, MongoDB creates an index entry for each element of the array. The syntax of the **createIndex** element is the same as that for creating an index of a regular (non-array) field:

```
db.collectionName.createIndex( { arrayFieldName: sortOrder } )
```

MongoDB inspects the input field, and if it is an array, a multikey index will be created. For example, consider the following command:

```
db.movies.createIndex(
    {"languages" : 1}
)
```

This query adds an index on the **languages** field, which is an array. In MongoDB, you can find documents based on an element of their array fields. Multikey indexes help accelerate such queries:

```
db.movies.explain("executionStats").count(
    {"languages": "Cantonese"}
)
```

Let's see how the preceding query performs:

```
"executionStats" : {
    "executionSuccess" : true,
    "nReturned" : 361,
    "executionTimeMillis" : 1,
    "totalKeysExamined" : 361,
    "totalDocsExamined" : 361,
    "executionStages" : {
```

The snippet of the execution stats shows **361** documents are returned and the same number of documents were scanned. It proves that the multikey index is correctly created and used.

## TEXT INDEXES

An index defined on a string field or an array of string elements is called a text index. Text indexes are not sorted, meaning that they are faster than normal indexes. The syntax to create a text index is as follows:

```
db.collectionName.createIndex({ fieldName : "text"})
```

The following is an example of a text index to be created on the **users** collection on the **name** field:

```
db.users.createIndex(
    { name : "text"}
)
```

The command should generate output as follows:

```
{
    "createdCollectionAutomatically" : false,
    "numIndexesBefore" : 2,
    "numIndexesAfter" : 3,
    "ok" : 1,
    "$clusterTime" : {
        "clusterTime" : Timestamp(1596889407, 2),
        "signature" : {
            "hash" : BinData(0,"B4Ro1V1WTwkGUMGEImtxvctR9C4="),
            "keyId" : NumberLong("6853300587753111555")
        }
```

```
    },
    "operationTime" : Timestamp(1596889407, 2)
}
```

> **NOTE**
>
> You cannot drop a text index by passing the index specification document, and such indexes can only be deleted by passing the name of the index in the **dropIndex** function.

## INDEXES ON NESTED DOCUMENTS

A document can contain nested objects to group a few attributes. For example, the **theaters** collection in the **sample_mflix** database contains the **location** field, which has a nested object:

```
{
    "_id" : ObjectId("59a47286cfa9a3a73e51e72c"),
    "theaterId" : 1000,
    "location" : {
        "address" : {
            "street1" : "340 W Market",
            "city" : "Bloomington",
            "state" : "MN",
            "zipcode" : "55425"
        },
        "geo" : {
            "type" : "Point",
            "coordinates" : [
                -93.24565,
                44.85466
            ]
        }
    }
}
```

Using a dot (.) notation, you can create an index on any of the nested document fields, just like any other field in the collection, as in the following example:

```
db.theaters.createIndex(
    { "location.address.zipcode" : 1}
)
```

You can also create an index on the embedded document. For example, you can create an index on the **location** field instead of its attributes, as follows:

```
db.theaters.createIndex(
    { "location" : 1}
)
```

Such indexes can be used when searching for a location by passing the entire nested document.

## WILDCARD INDEXES

MongoDB supports flexible schema, and different documents can have fields of varying types and quantities. It can be difficult to create and maintain indexes on non-uniform fields that are not present in all documents. Also, when a new field is introduced into a document, it remains unindexed.

To put this in perspective, consider the following documents from a hypothetical **products** collection. The following table displays two different product documents:

| A product document representing a shoe | A product document representing a shampoo |
| --- | --- |
| ```{   "_id": 2323,   "name": "shoes",   "brand": "Asics",   "specifications": {       "color": "White",       "size": "9"   } }``` | ```{   "_id": 3232,   "name": "shampoo",   "brand": "Pantene",   "specifications": {       "quantity": "300ml",       "fragrance": "Mint"       "expiry": "15 Feb 2025"   } }``` |

Figure 9.14: Two different product specification documents

As you can see, the fields under **specifications** are dynamic in nature. Different products can have different specifications. Defining an index on each of these fields will result in too many index definitions. As new products with new fields get added all the time, the idea of creating an index on all fields is not practical. MongoDB provides wildcard indexes to resolve this problem. For instance, consider the following query:

```
db.products.createIndex(
    { "specifications.$**"  : 1}
)
```

This query uses special wildcard characters (**$\*\***) to create indexes on the **specifications** field. It will create indexes on all the fields under **specifications**. If new nested fields are added in the future, they will be automatically indexed.

Similarly, wildcard indexes can be created on the top-level fields of a collection as well:

```
db.products.createIndex(
    { "$**" : 1 }
)
```

The preceding command creates indexes on all fields of all documents. Thus, all the new fields added to the documents will be indexed by default.

You can also select or omit specific fields from the wildcard indexes by passing a **wildcardProjection** option and one or more field names, as shown in the following snippet:

```
db.products.createIndex(
    { "$**" : 1 },
    {
        "wildcardProjection" : { "name" : 0 }
    }
)
```

The preceding query creates a wildcard index on all the fields of a collection, excluding the **name** field. To explicitly include the **name** field, excluding all the others, you can pass it with a value of **1**.

> **NOTE**
>
> MongoDB provides a couple of indexes to support the geometric fields: **2dsphere** and **2d**. It is beyond the scope of this book to cover these indexes but interested readers can find out more about them at https://docs. mongodb.com/manual/geospatial-queries/#geospatial-indexes.

Now that we have covered the types of indexes, we will explore index properties in the next section.

# PROPERTIES OF INDEXES

In this section, we will cover different properties of indexes in MongoDB. An index property can influence the usage of an index and can also enforce some behavior on the collection. Index properties are passed as an option to the **createdIndex** function. We will be looking at unique indexes, TTL (time to live) indexes, sparse indexes, and finally, partial indexes.

## UNIQUE INDEXES

A unique index property restricts the duplication of the index key. This is useful if you want to maintain the uniqueness of a field in a collection. The unique fields are useful for avoiding any ambiguity in identifying documents precisely. For example, in a **license** collection, a unique field such as **license_number** can help identify each document individually. This property enforces the behavior on the collection to reject duplicate entries. Unique indexes can be created on a single field or on a combination of fields. The following is the syntax to create a unique index on a single file:

```
db.collection.createIndex(
    { field: type},
    { unique: true }
)
```

The **{ unique: true }** option is used to create a unique index.

In some cases, you may want a combination of fields to be unique. For such cases, you can define a unique compound index by passing the **unique: true** flag while creating a compound index, as follows:

```
db.collection.createIndex(
    { field1 : type, field2: type2, ...},
    { unique: true }
)
```

## EXERCISE 9.03: CREATING A UNIQUE INDEX

In this exercise, you will enforce the uniqueness of the **theaterId** field in the **theaters** collection in the **sample_mflix** database:

1.  Connect your shell to the Atlas cluster and choose the **sample_mflix** database.

2.  Confirm whether the **theaters** collection enforces any uniqueness of the **theaterId** field. To do so, find a record and try to insert another record using the same **theaterId** present in the fetched record. The following is the command to retrieve a document from the **theaters** collection:

```
db.theaters.findOne();
```

This results in the following output, though you may get a different record:

```
{
        "_id" : ObjectId("59a47286cfa9a3a73e51e733"),
        "theaterId" : 1012,
        "location" : {
            "address" : {
                    "street1" : "1207 W Century Ave",
                    "city" : "Bismarck",
                    "state" : "ND",
                    "zipcode" : "58503"
            },
            "geo" : {
                    "type" : "Point",
                    "coordinates" : [
                            -100.81213,
                            46.829876
                    ]
            }
        }
}
```

Figure 9.15: The result of retrieving a document from the theaters collection

3. Now, insert a record with the same **theaterId** (that is, **1012**):

```
db.theaters.insertOne(
    {theaterId : 1012}
);
```

The document is inserted successfully, which proves that **theaterId** is not a unique field.

4. Now, create a unique index on the **theaterId** field using the following command:

```
db.theaters.createIndex(
    {theaterId : 1},
    {unique : true}
)
```

The preceding command will return an error response as it is a prerequisite that there should be no duplicate records existing in the collection. The following is the output, confirming this:

```
{
        "operationTime" : Timestamp(1596939398, 1),
        "ok" : 0,
        "errmsg" : "E11000 duplicate key error collection:
5f261717eae2b55842a6aff0_sample_mflix.theaters index: theaterId_1 dup
key: { theaterId: 1012.0 }",
        "code" : 11000,
        "codeName" : "DuplicateKey",
        "keyPattern" : {
            "theaterId" : 1
        },
        "keyValue" : {
            "theaterId" : 1012
        },
        "$clusterTime" : {
            "clusterTime" : Timestamp(1596939398, 1),
            "signature" : {
                "hash" : BinData(0,"hzOmtVWMNJkF3fkISbf3kJLLZIA="),
                "keyId" : NumberLong("6853300587753111555")
            }
        }
}
```

5. Now, remove the duplicate record that was inserted in *step 3* using its **_id** value:

```
db.theaters.remove(
    {_id : ObjectId("5dd9c2d9de850e38c5cfc6dd")}
)
```

6. Try creating the unique index once again, as follows:

```
db.theaters.createIndex(
    {theaterId : 1},
    {unique : true}
)
```

This time, you should receive a successful response, as shown here:

```
{
    "createdCollectionAutomatically" : false,
    "numIndexesBefore" : 1,
    "numIndexesAfter" : 2,
    "ok" : 1,
    "$clusterTime" : {
        "clusterTime" : Timestamp(1596939728, 2),
        "signature" : {
            "hash" : BinData(0,"hdejOvB7dqQojg46DRWRLJVwblM="),
            "keyId" : NumberLong("6853300587753111555")
        }
    },
    "operationTime" : Timestamp(1596939728, 2)
}
```

7. Now that the field has a unique index, try inserting a duplicate record, as follows:

```
db.theaters.insertOne(
    {theaterId : 1012}
);
```

This command will fail due to the duplicate key error:

```
2020-08-09T12:24:11.584+1000 E   QUERY    [js] WriteError({
    "index" : 0,
    "code" : 11000,
    "errmsg" : "E11000 duplicate key error collection: sample_mflix.
theaters index: theaterId_1 dup key: { theaterId: 1012.0 }",
    "op" : {
        "_id" : ObjectId("5f2f5e4b78436de2a47da0e4"),
```

```
                "theaterId" : 1012
        }
}) :
WriteError({
        "index" : 0,
        "code" : 11000,
        "errmsg" : "E11000 duplicate key error collection: sample_mflix.
theaters index: theaterId_1 dup key: { theaterId: 1012.0 }",
        "op" : {
            "_id" : ObjectId("5f2f5e4b78436de2a47da0e4"),
            "theaterId" : 1012
        }
})
```

In this exercise, you enforced the property of uniqueness on an index.

## TTL INDEXES

**TTL** (or **Time to Live**) indexes put an expiry on documents. Once the documents have expired, they are deleted. This index can only be created on a field of the date type. To create the index, you pass the field details and the **expireAfterSeconds** attribute. The following snippet shows the syntax for creating a TTL index:

```
db.collection.createIndex({ field: type}, { expireAfterSeconds: seconds })
```

Here, the **{ expireAfterSeconds: seconds }** option is used to create a TTL index. MongoDB removes the documents that have passed the threshold of the **expireAfterSeconds** value.

### EXERCISE 9.04: CREATING A TTL INDEX USING MONGO SHELL

In this exercise, you will create a TTL index on a collection called **reviews**. A field called **reviewDate** will be used to capture the current date and time of the review. You will introduce a TTL index to check whether the records that have passed the thresholds are removed:

1. Connect the mongo shell to the Atlas cluster and switch to the **sample_mflix** database.

2. Create the **reviews** collection by inserting two documents, as follows:

```
db.reviews.insert(
    {"reviewer" : "Eliyana A" , "movie" : "Cast Away","review" :
"Interesting plot", "reviewDate" : new Date() }
```

```
);

db.reviews.insert(
    {"reviewer" : "Zaid A" , "movie" : "Sully","review" :
"Captivating", "reviewDate" : new Date() }
);
```

3. Fetch these documents from the **reviews** collection to confirm they exist in the collection:

```
db.reviews.find().pretty();
```

This command results in the following output:

```
{
    "_id" : ObjectId("5f2f65d978436de2a47da0e5"),
    "reviewer" : "Eliyana",
    "movie" : "Cast Away",
    "review" : "Interesting plot",
    "reviewDate" : ISODate("2020-08-09T02:56:25.415Z")
}
{
    "_id" : ObjectId("5f2f65dd78436de2a47da0e6"),
    "reviewer" : "Zaid",
    "movie" : "Sully",
    "review" : "Captivating",
    "reviewDate" : ISODate("2020-08-09T02:56:29.144Z")
}
```

4. Introduce a TTL index to expire documents older than 60 seconds, using the following command:

```
db.reviews.createIndex(
    { reviewDate: 1},
    { expireAfterSeconds: 60 }
)
```

This results in the following output:

```
{
    "createdCollectionAutomatically" : false,
    "numIndexesBefore" : 1,
    "numIndexesAfter" : 2,
    "ok" : 1,
    "$clusterTime" : {
```

```
            "clusterTime" : Timestamp(1596941915, 2),
            "signature" : {
                    "hash" : BinData(0,"s5DU9ZElN+N2cCZ8d27pV5802Uk="),
                    "keyId" : NumberLong("6853300587753111555")
            }
        },
        "operationTime" : Timestamp(1596941915, 2)
    }
```

5.  After 60 seconds, execute the **find** query again:

```
db.reviews.find().pretty();
```

The query will not return any records, and it proves both documents are deleted after 60 seconds.

In this exercise, you created a TTL index on a collection and saw that the documents expired after the specified time—that is, 60 seconds.

## SPARSE INDEXES

When an index is created on a field, all the values of that field from all documents are maintained in the index registry. If the field does not exist in a document, a **null** value is registered for that document. Conversely, if an index is marked as **sparse**, then only those documents are registered in which the given field exists with some value including **null**. A sparse index will not have entries from the collection where the indexed field does not exist, and that is why this type of index is called sparse.

Compound indexes can also be marked as sparse. For a compound sparse index, only those documents are registered where the combination of fields exists. Sparse indexes are created by passing a flag of **{ sparse: true }** to the **createIndex** command, as shown in the following snippet:

```
db.collection.createIndex({ field1 : type, field2: type2, ...}, { sparse:
true })
```

MongoDB does not provide any command to list the documents that are maintained by an index. This makes it difficult to analyze the behavior of a sparse index. This is where the **db.collection.stats()** function can be really useful, as you will observe in the next exercise.

## EXERCISE 9.05: CREATING A SPARSE INDEX USING MONGO SHELL

In this exercise, you will create a sparse index on the **review** field in the **reviews** collection. You will verify that the index maintains entries only for those documents that have the **review** field present. To do so, you will use the **db.collection. stats()** command to check the size of the index by first inserting the documents with the indexed field, and then again without the field. The size of the index should remain the same when a document is inserted without the **review** field:

1. Connect the mongo shell to the Atlas cluster and switch to the **sample_mflix** database.

2. Create a sparse index on the **review** field:

```
db.reviews.createIndex(
    {review: 1},
    {sparse : true}
)
```

3. Check the size of the index on the current collection:

```
db.reviews.stats();
```

This command results in the following output:

```
{
    "ns" : "sample_mflix.reviews",
    "size" : 0,
    "count" : 0,
    "storageSize" : 36864,
    "capped" : false,
    "nindexes" : 3,
    "indexBuilds" : [ ],
    "totalIndexSize" : 57344,
    "indexSizes" : {
        "_id_" : 36864,
        "reviewDate_1" : 12288,
        «review_1» : 8192
    },
    "scaleFactor" : 1,
    "ok" : 1,
    "$clusterTime" : {
        "clusterTime" : Timestamp(1596943433, 1),
        "signature" : {
```

```
                    "hash" : BinData(0,"9zOSj95cZplzIj5JQv+IgYfMIPI="),
                    "keyId" : NumberLong("6853300587753111555")
            }
        },
        "operationTime" : Timestamp(1596943433, 1)
    }
```

Note the size (8,192 bytes, as highlighted in the snippet) of the newly created index **review_1** under the **indexSizes** section of the preceding output.

4. Insert a document that does not have the **review** field, as follows:

```
db.reviews.insert(
    {"reviewer" : "Jamshed A" , "movie" : "Gladiator"}
);
```

5. Check the size of the index using the **stats()** function:

```
db.reviews.stats()
```

The output for this is as follows:

```
        "indexSizes" : {
            "_id_" : 36864,
            "reviewDate_1" : 12288,
            "review_1" : 8192
        }
```

You can see that the size of the **review_1** index (highlighted) has not changed. This is because the last document was not registered in the index.

6. Now, insert a document that contains the **review** field:

```
db.reviews.insert(
    {"reviewer" : "Javed A" , "movie" : "The Pursuit of Happyness",
"review": "Inspirational"}
);
```

7. Check the size of the index after a couple of minutes using the **stats()** function once again:

```
db.reviews.stats()
```

The **indexSizes** portion from the output is as follows:

```
        "indexSizes" : {
            "_id_" : 36864,
            "reviewDate_1" : 36864,
```

```
        "review_1" : 24576
    },
```

As you can see, the sparse index size has changed. This is because the last insert contained the **reviews** field, which is part of the sparse index.

> **NOTE**
>
> Index updates can take some time, depending on the size of the index. So, give it a few moments before you view the updated size of the index.

In this exercise, you created a sparse index and proved that documents without the indexed fields are not indexed.

## PARTIAL INDEXES

An index can be created to maintain documents that match a given filter expression. Such an index is called a partial index. As the documents are filtered depending on the input expression, the size of the index is smaller than a normal index. The syntax to create a partial index is as follows:

```
db.collection.createIndex(
    { field1 : type, field2: type2, ...},
    { partialFilterExpression: filterExpression }
)
```

In the preceding snippet, the **{ partialFilterExpression: filterExpression }** option is used to create a partial index. **partialFilterExpression** can only accept an expression document that contains operations from the following list:

- Equality expressions (that is, **field: value** or using the **$eq** operator)
- The **$exists: true** expression
- **$gt**, **$gte**, **$lt**, and **$lte** expressions
- **$type** expressions
- The **$and** operator at the top level only

To get a better idea of how partial indexes work, let's perform a simple exercise.

## EXERCISE 9.06: CREATING A PARTIAL INDEX USING THE MONGO SHELL

In this exercise, you will introduce a compound index on **title** and **type** fields for all the movies released after 1950. You will then verify whether the index contains the desired entries, using **partialFilterExpression**:

1. Connect the mongo shell to the Atlas cluster and switch to the **sample_mflix** database.

2. Introduce a partial index on the **title** and **type** fields in the **movies** collection, using **partialFilterExpression**, as follows:

```
db.movies.createIndex(
    {title: 1, type:1},
    {
        partialFilterExpression: {
            year : { $gt: 1950}
        }
    }
)
```

The preceding command creates a partial compound index on the given fields for all the movies released after 1950. The following snippet shows the output of this command:

```
{
    "createdCollectionAutomatically" : false,
    "numIndexesBefore" : 2,
    "numIndexesAfter" : 3,
    "ok" : 1,
    "$clusterTime" : {
        "clusterTime" : Timestamp(1596945704, 2),
        "signature" : {
            "hash" : BinData(0,"jaL6CDJrPPntbo5LibWl+Yv74Zo="),
            "keyId" : NumberLong("6853300587753111555")
        }
    },
    "operationTime" : Timestamp(1596945704, 2)
}
```

3. Check and note down the index size on the collection using the **stats()** function:

```
db.movies.stats();
```

The following is the **indexSizes** section of the resulting output:

```
"indexSizes" : {
        "_id_" : 368640,
        "cast_text_fullplot_text_genres_text_title_text" :
13549568,
        «title_1_type_1» : 618496
    },
```

Note the size of your newly created **index**, **title_1_type_1**, is 618,496 bytes (highlighted).

4. Insert a movie that was released before 1950:

```
db.movies.insert(
    {title: "In Old California", type: "movie", year: "1910"}
)
```

5. Check the index size and ensure it is unchanged using the **stats()** function:

```
db.movies.stats()
```

The next snippet shows the **indexSizes** portion of the output:

```
"indexSizes" : {
        "_id_" : 368640,
        "cast_text_fullplot_text_genres_text_title_text" :
13615104,
        «title_1_type_1» : 618496
    },
```

The output snippet proves that the index size remained unchanged, as can be seen from the highlighted part.

6. Now, insert a movie that was released after 1950:

```
db.movies.insert(
    {title: "The Lost Ground", type: "movie", year: "2019"}
)
```

7. Check the index size again, with the help of the **stats()** function:

```
db.movies.stats()
```

The following is the **indexSizes** portion from the output of the preceding command:

```
    "indexSizes" : {
        "_id_" : 258048,
        "cast_text_fullplot_text_genres_text_title_text" :
13606912,
        "title_1_type_1" : 643072
    },
```

As shown, the size of the index increases when a record is inserted that passes **partialFilterExpression**.

In this exercise, you introduced a partial index and verified that it worked as desired.

## CASE-INSENSITIVE INDEXES

Case-insensitive indexes allow you to find data using indexes in a case-insensitive manner. This means that the index will match the documents even if the values of a field are written in a different case from the values in the search expression. This is possible due to the collation feature in MongoDB, which allows the input of language-specific rules, such as case and accent marks, to match documents. To create the case-insensitive index, you need to pass the field details and the **collation** parameter.

The syntax to create a case-insensitive index is as follows:

```
db.collection.createIndex(
    { "field" : 1 },
    {
        collation: { locale : <locale>, strength : <strength> }
    }
)
```

Note that **collation** is made up of **locale** and **strength** parameters:

- **locale**: This refers to the language to be used, such as **en** (English), **fr** (French), and more. The full list of locales can be found at https://docs.mongodb. com/manual/reference/collation-locales-defaults/#collation-languages-locales.

- **strength**: A value of 1 or 2 indicates a case-level collation. You can find the details about collation **International Components for Unicode (ICU)** levels at http://userguide.icu-project.org/collation/concepts#TOC-Comparison-Levels.

To use an index that specifies a collation, the query and the sort specification must have the same collation as the index.

## EXERCISE 9.07: CREATING A CASE-INSENSITIVE INDEX USING THE MONGO SHELL

In this exercise, you will create a case-insensitive index by connecting the mongo shell to the Atlas cluster. This feature is immensely useful for web-based applications because database querying is executed in a case-sensitive manner in the backend. On the frontend though, the user will not necessarily use the same case for searches as the one used in the backend. Therefore, it is important to make sure that searches are case-insensitive. Perform the following steps to complete this exercise:

1. Connect the mongo shell to the Atlas cluster and switch to the **sample_mflix** database.

2. Perform a case-insensitive search and verify that the expected document is not returned:

```
db.movies.find(
    {"title" : "goodFEllas"},
    {"title" : 1}
)
```

The preceding query returns no result.

3. To solve this problem, create a case-insensitive index on the **title** attribute of the **movies** collection, as follows:

```
db.movies.createIndex(
    {title: 1},
    {
        collation: {
            locale: 'en', strength: 2
        }
    }
)
```

This command results in the following output:

```
{
        "createdCollectionAutomatically" : false,
        "numIndexesBefore" : 3,
        "numIndexesAfter" : 4,
        "ok" : 1,
        "$clusterTime" : {
                "clusterTime" : Timestamp(1596961452, 2),
                "signature" : {
                        "hash" : BinData(0,"9cdM8c3neW3oRd9A/IFGn5gZiic="),
                        "keyId" : NumberLong("6856698413690388483")
                }
        },
        "operationTime" : Timestamp(1596961452, 2)
}
```

4.  Rerun the command in *step 2* to confirm that the correct movie is returned:

```
db.movies.find(
    {"title" : "goodFEllas"}
).collation({ locale: 'en', strength: 2});
```

The command returns the correct movie, as shown in the next snippet:

```
{ "_id" : ObjectId("573a1398f29313caabcebf8e"), "title" :
"Goodfellas" }
```

In this exercise, you created a case-insensitive index and verified that it worked as desired.

> **NOTE**
>
> The `collation` option allows us to perform case-insensitive searches on unindexed fields as well. The only difference is that such queries will do a full collection scan.

In this section, you reviewed different index properties and learned how to create indexes with each of these properties. In the next section, you will explore some query optimization techniques that can be used along with indexes.

# OTHER QUERY OPTIMIZATION TECHNIQUES

So far, we have seen the internal workings of queries and how indexes help limit the number of documents to be scanned. We have also explored various types of indexes and their properties and learned how we can use the correct index and correct index properties in specific use cases. Creating the right index can improve query performance, but there are a few more techniques that are required to fine-tune the query performance. We will cover those techniques in this section.

## FETCH ONLY WHAT YOU NEED

The performance of a query is also affected by the amount of data it returns. The database server and client communicate over a network. If a query produces a large amount of data, it will take longer to transfer it over a network. Moreover, to transfer the data over the network, it needs to be transformed and serialized by the server and deserialized by the receiving client. This means that the database client will have to wait longer to get the final output of the query.

To improve the overall performance, consider the following factors.

### Correct Query Condition and Projection

An application can have a variety of use cases, and each of them may need a different subset of data. Therefore, it is important to analyze all such use cases and to make sure we have optimal queries or commands to satisfy each of them. This can be done by using optimal query conditions and correctly using projections to return only the essential fields pertinent to the use case.

### Pagination

Pagination is about serving only a small subset of data to the client in each subsequent request. It is also the best method of performance optimization, especially when serving a large amount of data to the client. It improves user experience by limiting the amount of data being returned and serving faster results.

## SORTING USING INDEXES

Queries often need to return the data in some order. For example, if the user chooses an option to view the latest movies, the resulting movies can be sorted on the basis of the release date. Similarly, if the user wants to view popular movies, we may sort the movies based on their ratings.

By default, sort operations for a query are carried out in memory. First, all the matching results are loaded in memory, and then the sort specification is applied to them. For a large dataset, such a process requires a lot of memory. MongoDB reserves only **100 MB** of memory to perform sort operations and throws an error if the memory limit is exceeded. To avoid the error, you can use the `allowDiskUse` flag, so that when the memory limit is reached the records are written on the disk and then sorted. However, writing records on disk and reading them back slows down the query.

To avoid this, you can use indexes for sorting, since indexes are created and maintained with a specific sort order. This means that for an indexed field, the index registry is always sorted based on the values of that field. When a sort specification is based on such an index field, MongoDB refers to the indexes to retrieve an already sorted dataset and returns it.

## FITTING INDEXES IN THE RAM

Indexes are much more efficient when they are fit in memory. If they exceed the available memory, they are written to the disk. As you already know, disk operations are slower than in-memory ones. MongoDB intelligently makes use of both disk and memory by keeping the most recently added records in the memory and older ones on the disk. This logic assumes that the most recent records will be queried more than the old ones. To fit indexes in memory, you can use the `totalIndexSize` function on a collection, as follows:

```
db.collection.totalIndexSize()
```

If the size exceeds the available memory on the server, you can choose to increase the memory or optimize the indexes. This way, you ensure that all the indexes always remain in memory.

## INDEX SELECTIVITY

Indexes are more effective when they can considerably narrow down the actual collection scans. This depends on the **selectivity** of an index field. For example, consider the following records from a collection. The `isRunning` field holds a Boolean value, which means it will have either **true** or **false** as its value:

```
{_id: ObjectId(..), name: "motor", type: "electrical", isRunning:
"true"};
{_id: ObjectId(..), name: "gear", type: "mechanical",  isRunning:
"false"};
{_id: ObjectId(..), name: "plug", type: "electrical",  isRunning:
"false"};
```

```
{_id: ObjectId(..), name: "starter", type: "electrical", isRunning:
"false"};
{_id: ObjectId(..), name: "battery", type: "electrical", isRunning:
"true"};
```

Now, add an index on the **isRunning** field and execute the following query to find a running device by its name:

```
db.devices.find({
    "name" : "motor",
    "isRunning" : false
})
```

MongoDB will first use the **isRunning** index to locate all the running devices before the collection scan to find documents with a matching **name** value. Since **isRunning** can have only **true** or **false** values, a significant part of the collection will have to be scanned.

Hence, to make the preceding query more efficient, we should put an index on the **name** field as there will not be too many documents with the same name. Indexes are more efficient on fields that have a broader range of values or unique values.

## PROVIDING HINTS

MongoDB query planner picks an index for a query depending on its own internal logic. When there are multiple indexes available to perform a query execution, the query planner uses its default query optimization technique to select and use the most appropriate index. However, we can use a **hint()** function to specify which index should be used for the execution:

```
db.users.find().hint(
    { index }
)
```

This command shows a syntax for providing an index hint. The argument to the **hint** function can simply be an index name or an index specification document.

## OPTIMAL INDEXES

After learning about the benefits of indexes, you might be wondering if we can create indexes on all fields and their various combinations. However, indexes have some overheads as well. Each index requires a dedicated index registry, which stores a subset of data in memory or on the disk. Too many indexes consume a lot of space. Hence, before adding indexes to the collection, we should first analyze the requirements, listing the use cases and the possible queries our application will be executing. Then, based on this information, a minimal number of indexes should be created.

Although indexes make queries faster, they slow down every write operation on the collection. Because of indexes, every write operation on the collection involves the overhead of updating the respective index registries. Whenever documents are added, removed, or updated in a collection, all the respective index registries need to be updated, rescanned, and resorted, which takes longer than the actual collection write operations. Hence, before deciding to use indexes, it is recommended to check whether the database operations are read-heavy or write-heavy. For write-heavy collections, indexes are an overhead, hence they should be created only after a careful evaluation.

In short, indexes have their benefits as well as overheads. A higher number of indexes generally means faster read operations and slower write operations. Hence, we should always use indexes in an optimal fashion.

## ACTIVITY 9.01: OPTIMIZING A QUERY

Imagine your organization has retail stores throughout the world. Details about all the items sold are stored in a MongoDB database. The data analytics team uses the sales data to identify the purchase trends of different customers based on their age and location. Recently, one of the team members has complained about the performance of a query they wrote. The query, which is shown in the following snippet, queries the **sales** collection to find the email address and age of the customers who have purchased one or more backpacks in the Denver store. Then, it sorts the results in descending order of the customers' ages:

```
db.sales.find(
    {
        "items.name" : "backpack",
        "storeLocation" : "Denver"
    },
    {
```

```
        "_id" : 0,
        "customer.email": 1,
        "customer.age": 1
    }
).sort({
    "customer.age" : -1
})
```

Your task for this activity is to analyze the given query, identify the problems, and create correct indexes to make it faster. The following steps will help you complete this activity:

1. Connect to the **sample_supplies** dataset using mongo shell.

2. Find the query execution stats and identify the problems.

3. Create correct indexes on the collection.

4. Analyze the query performance again to see if the problems are fixed.

> **NOTE**
>
> The solution to this activity can be found on page 680.

## SUMMARY

In this chapter, you practiced improving query performance. You first explored the internal workings of query execution and the query execution stages. You then learned how to analyze a query's performance and identify any existing problems based on the execution statistics. Next, you reviewed the concept of indexes; how they solve performance issues for a query; various ways to create, list, and delete indexes; different types of indexes; and their properties. In the final sections of this chapter, you studied query optimization techniques and got a brief look at the overheads associated with indexes. In the next chapter, you will learn about the concept of replication and how it is implemented in Mongo.

# 10

# REPLICATION

## OVERVIEW

This chapter will introduce MongoDB cluster concepts and administration. It starts with a discussion on the concepts of high availability and the load sharing of a MongoDB database. You will configure and install MongoDB replica sets in different environments, manage and monitor MongoDB replica set clusters, and practice cluster switchover and failover steps. You will explore high-availability clusters in MongoDB and connect to a MongoDB cluster to perform typical administration tasks on MongoDB cluster deployments.

# INTRODUCTION

From a MongoDB developer perspective, it is probably true that the MongoDB database server is some sort of black box, living somewhere in the cloud or in a data center room. Details are not important if the database is up and running when needed. From a business perspective though, things look slightly different. For example, when a production application needs to be available online for customers 24/7, those details are very important. Any outage can have a negative impact on service availability for customers, and ultimately, if the failure is not recovered quickly, the business' financial results.

Outages happen from time to time, and they can be attributed to a wide variety of reasons. These are often the result of common hardware failures, such as disk or memory failures, but they may also be caused by network failures, software failures, or even application failures. For example, a software failure such as an OS bug can render the server unresponsive to users and applications. Outages can also be caused by disasters such as flooding and earthquakes. Even though the probability of a disaster is much smaller, they could still have a devastating impact on businesses.

Predicting failures and disasters is an impossible task, as it is not possible to guess the exact time when they will strike. Therefore, the business strategy should focus on solutions for these, by allocating redundant hardware and software resources. In the case of MongoDB, the solution to high availability and disaster recovery is to deploy MongoDB clusters instead of a single-server database. As opposed to other third-party database solutions, MongoDB doesn't require expensive hardware to build high-availability clusters, and they are relatively easy to deploy. This is where replication comes in handy. This chapter explores the idea of replication in detail.

First, it is important to learn about the basics of high-availability clusters.

## HIGH-AVAILABILITY CLUSTERS

Before we delve into the technical details of MongoDB clusters, let's first clarify the basic concepts. There are many different technical implementations of high-availability clusters, and it is important to find out how a MongoDB cluster solution is different from other third-party cluster implementations.

Computer clusters are a group of computers, connected to provide a common service. Compared to single servers, clusters are designed to provide better availability and performance. Clusters have redundant hardware and software that permits the continuation of services in the event of failures, so that, from the user perspective, the cluster appears as a single unified system rather than a group of different computers.

## CLUSTER NODES

A cluster node is a server computer system (or virtual server) that is part of the cluster. It takes at least two different servers to make a cluster, with each cluster node having its own hostname and IP address. MongoDB 4.2 clusters can have a maximum of 50 nodes. In practice, most MongoDB clusters have at least 3 members and they rarely reach more than 10 nodes, even for very large clusters.

## SHARE-NOTHING

In other third-party clusters, cluster nodes share common cluster resources, such as disk storage. MongoDB has a "share-nothing" cluster model instead, where nodes are independent computers. Cluster nodes are connected only by the MongoDB software, and data replication is performed over the internet. The advantage of this model is that MongoDB clusters are easier to build with just commodity server hardware, which is not expensive.

## CLUSTER NAMES

A cluster name is defined in the Atlas Console, and it is used to manage the cluster from the Atlas web interface. As mentioned in some of the previous chapters, in Atlas Free Tier, you can create only one cluster (M0), which has three cluster nodes. The default name for a new cluster is `Cluster0`. The name of the cluster cannot be changed after the cluster is created.

## REPLICA SETS

A MongoDB cluster is based on data replication between cluster nodes. Data is replicated among nodes or replica set members with the purpose of keeping data in sync across all MongoDB database instances.

## PRIMARY-SECONDARY

Data replication in MongoDB replica set clusters is a master-slave replication architecture. The primary node sends data to secondary nodes. The replication is always unidirectional, from primary to secondary. There is no option for multi-master replication in MongoDB, so there can be only one primary node at a time. All other members of the MongoDB replica set cluster must be secondary nodes.

> **NOTE**
>
> It is possible to have multiple **mongod** processes on the same server. Each **mongod** process can be a standalone database instance, or it can be a member of a replica set cluster. For production servers, it is recommended to deploy just one **mongod** process per server.

## THE OPLOG

One database component that is essential for MongoDB replication is the **Oplog** (**Operation Log**). The Oplog is a special circular buffer in which all data changes are saved for cluster replication. Data changes are generated by CRUD operations (insert/update/delete) on the primary database. Nevertheless, database queries don't generate any Oplog records because queries don't modify any data:

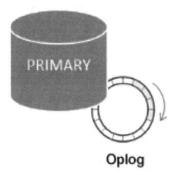

Figure 10.1: Mongo DB Oplog

Therefore, all CRUD database writes are applied to datafiles by changing JSON data in database collections (just like on non-clustered databases) and are saved in the Oplog buffer for replication. Data change operations are converted into a special idempotent format that can be applied multiple times with the same result.

At the database logical level, the Oplog appears as a capped (circular) collection in the local system database. The size of the Oplog collection is particularly important for cluster operations and maintenance.

By default, the maximum allocated size for the Oplog is 5% of the server's free disk space. To check the size of the currently allocated Oplog (in bytes), use the **local** database to query replication stats, as shown in the following example:

```
db.oplog.rs.stats().maxSize
```

The following JS script will print the size of the Oplog in megabytes:

```
use local
var opl = db.oplog.rs.stats().maxSize/1024/1024
print("Oplog size: " + ~~opl + " MB")
```

This results in the following output:

```
MongoDB Enterprise atlas-rzhbg7-shard-0:PRIMARY>
MongoDB Enterprise atlas-rzhbg7-shard-0:PRIMARY> use local
switched to db local
MongoDB Enterprise atlas-rzhbg7-shard-0:PRIMARY> var opl = db.oplog.rs.stats().maxSize/1024/1024
MongoDB Enterprise atlas-rzhbg7-shard-0:PRIMARY> print("Oplog size: " + ~~opl + " MB")
Oplog size: 3258 MB
MongoDB Enterprise atlas-rzhbg7-shard-0:PRIMARY>
```

Figure 10.2: Output after running the JS script

As shown in *Figure 10.2*, the Oplog size for this Atlas cluster is **3258 MB**.

> **NOTE**
>
> Sometimes, the Oplog is mistaken for WiredTiger journaling. Journaling is also a log for database changes, but with a different scope. While the Oplog is designed for cluster data replication, database journaling is a low-level log needed for database recovery. For example, if MongoDB crashes unexpectedly, datafiles can become corrupted because the last changes were not saved. Journal records are needed to perform database recovery after the instance restarts.

# REPLICATION ARCHITECTURE

The following diagram depicts the architecture diagram of a simple replica set cluster with only three server nodes – one primary node and two secondary nodes:

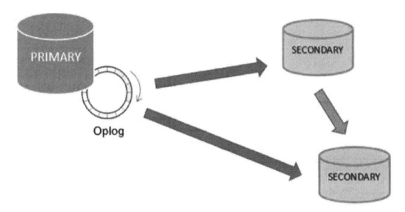

Figure 10.3: MongoDB replication

- In the preceding model, the PRIMARY database is the only active replica set member that receives write operations from database clients. The PRIMARY database saves data changes in the Oplog. Changes saved in the Oplog are sequential—that is, saved in the order that they are received and executed.

- The SECONDARY database is querying the PRIMARY database for new changes in the Oplog. If there are any changes, then Oplog entries are copied from PRIMARY to SECONDARY as soon as they are created on the PRIMARY node.

- Then, the SECONDARY database applies changes from the Oplog to its own datafiles. Oplog entries are applied in the same order they were inserted in the log. As a result, datafiles on SECONDARY are kept in sync with changes on PRIMARY.

- Usually, SECONDARY databases copy data changes directly from PRIMARY. Sometimes a SECONDARY database can replicate data from another SECONDARY. This type of replication is called *Chained Replication* because it is a two-step replication process. Chained replication is useful in certain replication topologies, and it is enabled by default in MongoDB.

It is important to understand that, once a MongoDB instance is part of a replica set cluster, all changes are copied to the Oplog for data replication. It is not possible to use a replica set to replicate only some parts, such as just a few database collections. For this reason, all user data is replicated and kept in sync across all cluster members.

Cluster members can have different states, such as PRIMARY and SECONDARY in the preceding diagram. Node states can change in time, depending on cluster activity. For example, a node can be in the PRIMARY state at one point in time, and in the SECONDARY state, another time. PRIMARY and SECONDARY are the most common states of a node in the cluster configuration, although other states are possible. To understand their possible roles and how they can change, let's explore the technical details of cluster election.

## CLUSTER MEMBERS

In Atlas, you can see the cluster member list from the **Clusters** page, as shown in the following screenshot:

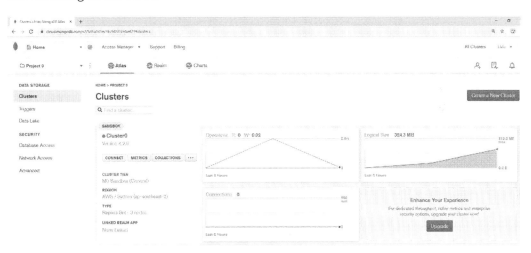

Figure 10.4: Atlas web interface

Click on the cluster name **Cluster0** from **SANDBOX**. Then the list of servers and their roles will be displayed in the Atlas application:

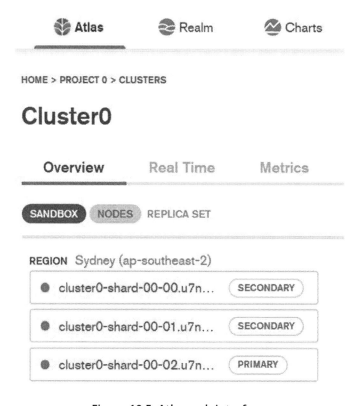

Figure 10.5: Atlas web interface

As shown in *Figure 10.5*, this cluster has three cluster members, which are named with the same prefix as the Atlas cluster name (in this case, **Cluster0**). For MongoDB clusters that are installed without using the Atlas PaaS web interface (or that are installed locally, on premises), you can check the cluster members using the following mongo shell command:

```
rs.status().members
```

An example of using the cluster status command will be provided in *Exercise 10.01, Checking Atlas Cluster Members*.

## THE ELECTION PROCESS

One feature specific to all cluster implementations is the ability to survive (or fail over) in the event of failures. The MongoDB replica set is protected against any type of failure, be it a hardware failure, software failure, or network outage. The MongoDB software responsible for this process is called **cluster election**—a name derived from the action of electing using votes. The purpose of a cluster election is to "elect" a new primary.

The election process is initiated by an event. For example, consider that the primary member is lost. Analogous to political elections, the MongoDB cluster members participate in a vote to elect a new primary member. The election is validated only if it obtains the majority of all votes in the cluster. The formula is remarkably simple: the surviving cluster has a majority of ($N/2 + 1$), where $N$ is the total number of nodes. Therefore, half plus one of the votes is enough to elect a new primary. This majority is necessary to avoid split-brain syndrome:

> **NOTE**
>
> Split-brain syndrome is the terminology used to define a situation where two parts of the same cluster are isolated and they both "believe" that they are the only surviving part of the cluster. Enforcing the "half plus one" rule ensures that only the largest part of the cluster can elect a new primary.

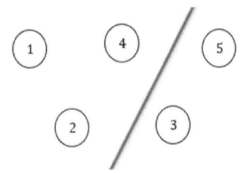

Figure 10.6: MongoDB election

Consider the preceding diagram. After a network partition incident, nodes 3 and 5 are isolated from the rest of the cluster. In this situation, the left side (nodes 1, 2, and 4) form a majority, whereas nodes 3 and 5 form a minority. So, nodes 1, 2, and 4 can elect a primary, since they form the majority cluster. Nevertheless, there are situations where a network partition could split the cluster into halves, with identical numbers of nodes. In this case, none of the halves have a majority necessary to elect a new primary. Therefore, one of the key factors in MongoDB cluster design is that clusters should always be configured with an odd number of nodes to avoid a perfect half split.

Not all cluster members can participate in an election. There can be a maximum of seven votes, regardless of the total number of members in a MongoDB cluster. This is designed to limit the network traffic between cluster nodes during the election process. Non-voting members cannot participate in elections, but they can replicate data from the primary as secondary nodes. By default, each node can have one vote.

## EXERCISE 10.01: CHECKING ATLAS CLUSTER MEMBERS

In this exercise, you will connect to the Atlas cluster using mongo shell and identify the cluster name and all cluster members, together with their current state. Use JavaScript to list the cluster members:

1.  Connect to your Atlas database using mongo shell:

```
mongo "mongodb+srv://cluster0.u7n6b.mongodb.net/test" --username
admindb
```

2.  The replica set status function **rs.status()** gives detailed information about the cluster that is not visible from the Atlas web interface. A simple JS script to list all nodes and their member roles for **rs.status** is as follows:

```
var rs_srv = rs.status().members
for (i=0; i<rs_srv.length; i++) {
    print (rs_srv[i].name, '  -  ', rs_srv[i].stateStr)
}
```

> **NOTE**
>
> The script can run from any node of the cluster if you are connected to one secondary instead of the primary.

```
MongoDB Enterprise atlas-rzhbg7-shard-0:PRIMARY>
MongoDB Enterprise atlas-rzhbg7-shard-0:PRIMARY> for (i=0; i<rs_srv.length; i++) {
...    print (rs_srv[i].name, ' - ', rs_srv[i].stateStr)
... }
cluster0-shard-00-00.u7n6b.mongodb.net:27017    -    SECONDARY
cluster0-shard-00-01.u7n6b.mongodb.net:27017    -    SECONDARY
cluster0-shard-00-02.u7n6b.mongodb.net:27017    -    PRIMARY
MongoDB Enterprise atlas-rzhbg7-shard-0:PRIMARY>
```

Figure 10.7: Output after running the JS script

We have learned about the basic concepts of MongoDB replica set clusters. The MongoDB primary-secondary replication technology protects the database from any hardware and software failures. In addition to providing high availability and disaster recovery for applications and users, MongoDB clusters are also easy to deploy and manage. Thanks to the Atlas managed database service, users can easily connect to Atlas and test applications, without the need to install and configure the cluster locally.

# CLIENT CONNECTIONS

The MongoDB connection string was covered in *Chapter 3*, *Servers and Clients*. Database services deployed in Atlas are always replica set clusters, and the connection string can be copied from the Atlas interface. In this section, we will explore the connections between clients and MongoDB clusters.

## CONNECTING TO A REPLICA SET

In general, the same rules apply for the MongoDB connection string. Consider the following screenshot, which shows such a connection:

```
Command Prompt - mongo "mongodb+srv://cluster0.u7n6b.mongodb.net/test" --username admindb        —    □    ✕
C:\>
C:\>mongo "mongodb+srv://cluster0.u7n6b.mongodb.net/test" --username admindb
MongoDB shell version v4.4.0
Enter password:
connecting to: mongodb://cluster0-shard-00-00.u7n6b.mongodb.net:27017,cluster0-shard-00-01.u7n6b.mongodb.net:27017,cluster0-s
hard-00-02.u7n6b.mongodb.net:27017/test?authSource=admin&compressors=disabled&gssapiServiceName=mongodb&replicaSet=atlas-rzhb
g7-shard-0&ssl=true
Implicit session: session { "id" : UUID("3cb7d1c4-24f4-4082-88a0-4a6034ac4256") }
MongoDB server version: 4.2.8
WARNING: shell and server versions do not match
MongoDB Enterprise atlas-rzhbg7-shard-0:PRIMARY>
```

Figure 10.8: An example of a connection string in mongo shell

As shown in *Figure10.6*, the connection string looks like this:

```
"mongodb+srv://cluster0.<id#>.mongodb.net/<db_name>"
```

As explained in *Chapter 3, Servers and Clients*, this type of string needs DNS to resolve the actual server names or IP addresses. In this example, the connection string contains the Atlas cluster name **cluster0** and the ID number **u7n6b**.

> **NOTE**
>
> In your case, the connection string could be different. That is because your Atlas cluster deployment is likely to have a different ID number and/or a different cluster name. Your actual connection string can be copied from your Atlas web console.

Following a careful inspection of the text in the shell, we see the following details:

```
connecting to: mongodb://cluster0-shard-00-00.u7n6b.mongodb.
net:27017,cluster0-shard-00-01.u7n6b.mongodb.net:27017,cluster0-
shard-00-02.u7n6b.mongodb.net:27017/test?authSource=admin&compressors=dis
abled&gssapiServiceName=mongodb&replicaSet=atlas-rzhbg7-shard-0&ssl=true
```

The first thing to notice is that the second string is significantly longer than the first. That is because the original connection string is substituted (after a successful DNS SRV lookup) into the equivalent string with the **mongodb://** URI prefix. The following table explains the structure of the cluster connection string:

| URI prefix | mongodb:// |
| --- | --- |
| **Server list (hostname:port)** | cluster0-shard-00-00.u7n6b.mongodb.net:27017, cluster0-shard-00-01.u7n6b.mongodb.net:27017, cluster0-shard-00-02.u7n6b.mongodb.net:27017 |
| **Database** | test |
| **Connection parameters (after the "?" character)** | authSource=admin& compressors=disabled& gssapiServiceName=mongodb& replicaSet= atlas-rzhbg7-shard-0& ssl=true |

Figure 10.9: Structure of the collection string

Following a successful connection and user authentication, the shell prompt will have the following format:

```
MongoDB Enterprise atlas-rzhbg7-shard-0:PRIMARY>
```

- **MongoDB Enterprise** here specifies the version of the MongoDB server running in the cloud.

- **atlas-rzhbg7-shard-0** indicates the MongoDB replica set name. Note that in the current version of Atlas, the MongoDB replica set name is different from the cluster name, which is **Cluster0** in this case.

- **PRIMARY** refers to the database instance role.

There is a clear distinction in MongoDB between a cluster connection and a single server connection. The connection shows the MongoDB cluster, in the following form:

```
replicaset/server1:port1, server2:port2, server3:port3...
```

To verify the current connection from mongo shell, use the following function:

```
db.getMongo()
```

This results in the following output:

```
Command Prompt - mongo "mongodb+srv://cluster0.u7n6b.mongodb.net/test" --username admindb          —    □    ×
MongoDB Enterprise atlas-rzhbg7-shard-0:PRIMARY>
MongoDB Enterprise atlas-rzhbg7-shard-0:PRIMARY> db.getMongo()
connection to atlas-rzhbg7-shard-0/cluster0-shard-00-00.u7n6b.mongodb.net:27017,cluster0-shard-00-01.u7n6b.mongodb.net:27017,
cluster0-shard-00-02.u7n6b.mongodb.net:27017
MongoDB Enterprise atlas-rzhbg7-shard-0:PRIMARY>
```

Figure 10.10: Verifying the connection string in mongo shell

> **NOTE**
>
> The replica set name connection parameter **replicaSet** indicates that the connection string is for a cluster instead of a simple MongoDB server instance. In this case, the shell will attempt to connect to all server members of the cluster. From the application perspective, the replica set is behaving as a single system, rather than a collection of separate servers. When connected to a cluster, the shell will always indicate the **PRIMARY** read-write instance.

The next section looks at single-server connections.

## SINGLE-SERVER CONNECTIONS

In the same way we connect to a non-clustered MongoDB database, we have the option to connect to individual cluster members separately. In this case, the target server name (cluster member) needs to be contained in the connection string. Also, the **replicaSet** parameter needs to be removed. Here is an example for the Atlas cluster:

```
mongo "mongodb://cluster0-shard-00-00.u7n6b.mongodb.net:27017/
test?authSource=admin&ssl=true" --username admindb
```

> **NOTE**
>
> The other two parameters, **authSource** and **ssl**, need to be retained for Atlas server connections. As described in *Chapter 3*, *Servers and Clients*, Atlas has authorization and SSL network encryption activated for cloud security protection.

The following screenshot shows an example of this:

```
C:\>mongo "mongodb://cluster0-shard-00-00.u7n6b.mongodb.net:27017/test?authSource=admin&ssl=true" --username admindb
MongoDB shell version v4.4.0
Enter password:
connecting to: mongodb://cluster0-shard-00-00.u7n6b.mongodb.net:27017/test?authSource=admin&compressors=disabled&gssapiServic
eName=mongodb&ssl=true
Implicit session: session { "id" : UUID("972385b0-ff46-4251-abe6-e768e448a606") }
MongoDB server version: 4.2.8
WARNING: shell and server versions do not match
MongoDB Enterprise atlas-rzhbg7-shard-0:SECONDARY>
MongoDB Enterprise atlas-rzhbg7-shard-0:SECONDARY> db.getMongo()
connection to cluster0-shard-00-00.u7n6b.mongodb.net:27017
MongoDB Enterprise atlas-rzhbg7-shard-0:SECONDARY>
```

Figure 10.11: Connecting to individual cluster members

This time, the shell prompt indicates **SECONDARY**, which indicates that we are connected to the secondary node. Also, the **db.getMongo()** function returns a simple server and port number connection.

As described earlier, data changes are not allowed on secondary members. This is because a MongoDB cluster needs to maintain a consistent copy of data across all cluster nodes. Therefore, changing data is allowed only on the primary node of the cluster. For example, if we try to modify, insert, or update a collection while connected on a secondary member, we will get the **not master** error message, as shown in the following screenshot:

```
Command Prompt - mongo "mongodb://cluster0-shard-00-00.u7n6b.mongodb.net:27017/test?authSource=admin&ssl=true" --username admindb    —   □   ×
MongoDB Enterprise atlas-rzhbg7-shard-0:SECONDARY> use sample_mflix
switched to db sample_mflix
MongoDB Enterprise atlas-rzhbg7-shard-0:SECONDARY> db.new_collection.insert({info:"I can't write anything on secondary!"})
WriteCommandError({
        "operationTime" : Timestamp(1598665375, 1),
        "ok" : 0,
        "errmsg" : "not master",
        "code" : 10107,
        "codeName" : "NotMaster",
        "$clusterTime" : {
                "clusterTime" : Timestamp(1598665375, 1),
                "signature" : {
                        "hash" : BinData(0,"fAzSpq2IdpRH+eu4ZGFAUf8/7/U="),
                        "keyId" : NumberLong("6817874997416034306")
                }
        }
})
MongoDB Enterprise atlas-rzhbg7-shard-0:SECONDARY>
```

Figure 10.12: Getting the "not master" error message in mongo shell

However, read-only operations are allowed on secondary members, and this is precisely the scope of the next exercise. In this exercise, you will learn how to read collections while connected on secondary cluster members.

> **NOTE**
>
> To enable read operations while connected to a secondary node, it is necessary to run the shell command **rs.slaveOk()**.

## EXERCISE 10.02: CHECKING THE CLUSTER REPLICATION

In this exercise, you will connect to the Atlas cluster database using mongo shell and observe the data replication between the primary and secondary cluster nodes:

1. Connect to your Atlas cluster with mongo shell and user **admindb**:

```
mongo "mongodb+srv://cluster0.u7n6b.mongodb.net/test" --username
admindb
```

> **NOTE**
>
> The connection string could be different in your case. You can copy the connection string from the Atlas web interface.

2. Execute the following script to create a new collection on the primary node and insert a few new documents with random numbers:

```
use sample_mflix


db.createCollection("new_collection")


for (i=0; i<=100; i++) {
    db.new_collection.insert({_id:i, "value":Math.random()})
}
```

The output for this is as follows:

```
Command Prompt - mongo "mongodb+srv://cluster0.u7n6b.mongodb.net/test" --username admindb                        —  □  ×
MongoDB Enterprise atlas-rzhbg7-shard-0:PRIMARY> use sample_mflix
switched to db sample_mflix
MongoDB Enterprise atlas-rzhbg7-shard-0:PRIMARY>
MongoDB Enterprise atlas-rzhbg7-shard-0:PRIMARY> db.createCollection("new_collection")
{
        "ok" : 1,
        "$clusterTime" : {
                "clusterTime" : Timestamp(1598667036, 1),
                "signature" : {
                        "hash" : BinData(0,"fzRkuSNbqA0GfC2V7nQe20fFODw="),
                        "keyId" : NumberLong("6817874997416034306")
                }
        },
        "operationTime" : Timestamp(1598667036, 1)
}
MongoDB Enterprise atlas-rzhbg7-shard-0:PRIMARY>
MongoDB Enterprise atlas-rzhbg7-shard-0:PRIMARY> for (i=0; i<=100; i++) {
...     db.new_collection.insert({_id:i, "value":Math.random()})
... }
WriteResult({ "nInserted" : 1 })
MongoDB Enterprise atlas-rzhbg7-shard-0:PRIMARY>
```

Figure 10.13: Inserting new documents with random numbers

3. Connect to a secondary node by entering the following code:

```
mongo "mongodb://cluster0-shard-00-00.u7n6b.mongodb.net:27017/
test?authSource=admin&ssl=true" --username admindb
```

> **NOTE**
>
> The connection string could be different in your case. Make sure you edit the correct server node in the connection string. The connection should indicate a **SECONDARY** member.

4. Query the collection to see whether data is replicated on the secondary nodes. To enable the reading of data on the secondary nodes, run the following command:

```
rs.slaveOk()
```

The output for this is as follows:

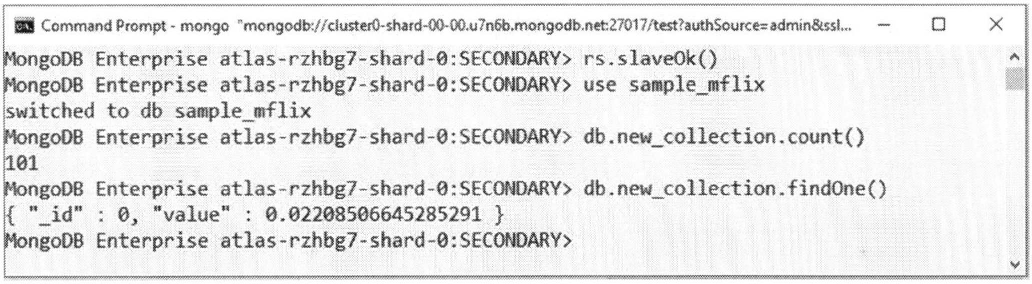

```
Command Prompt - mongo "mongodb://cluster0-shard-00-00.u7n6b.mongodb.net:27017/test?authSource=admin&ssl...  —  ☐  ✕
MongoDB Enterprise atlas-rzhbg7-shard-0:SECONDARY> rs.slaveOk()
MongoDB Enterprise atlas-rzhbg7-shard-0:SECONDARY> use sample_mflix
switched to db sample_mflix
MongoDB Enterprise atlas-rzhbg7-shard-0:SECONDARY> db.new_collection.count()
101
MongoDB Enterprise atlas-rzhbg7-shard-0:SECONDARY> db.new_collection.findOne()
{ "_id" : 0, "value" : 0.02208506645285291 }
MongoDB Enterprise atlas-rzhbg7-shard-0:SECONDARY>
```

Figure 10.14: Reading data on the secondary nodes

In this exercise, you verified the cluster MongoDB replication by inserting documents on the primary node and querying them on secondary nodes. You may notice that the replication is almost instantaneous, even though MongoDB replication is asynchronous.

## READ PREFERENCE

While it is possible to read data from a secondary node (as shown in the previous exercise), it is not ideal for applications because it requires a separate connection. **Read preference** is a term in MongoDB that defines how clients can redirect read operations to secondary nodes automatically, without connecting to individual nodes. There are a few reasons why the client may choose to redirect read operations to secondary nodes. For example, running large queries on the primary node will slow down overall performance for all operations. Offloading the primary node by running queries on secondary nodes is a good idea to optimize performance for inserts and updates.

By default, all operations are performed on the primary node. While write operations must be executed only on the primary node, read operations can be performed on any secondary node (except an arbiter node). The client can set a read preference at the session or statement level while connected to a MongoDB cluster. The following command helps check the current read preference:

```
db.getMongo().getReadPrefMode()
```

The following table shows the various **read preferences** in MongoDB:

| | |
|---|---|
| `null` | This is the default for database sessions if the read preference is not set. All operations are performed on a local connection. |
| `primary` | All operations are performed on `primary`. This option is similar to the default `null` option if you are connected to a cluster or primary node.<br><br>Please note that the `primary` read preference option can only be used if the cluster has a majority and has already elected a primary node. Otherwise, all nodes will remain in the secondary role. |
| `primaryPreferred` | Using this option will redirect reads to secondary nodes, but only if the primary node is not available. |
| `secondary` | All read operations are redirected to secondary nodes in this case. |
| `secondaryPreferred` | All read operations are redirected to secondary nodes. However, if no secondary node is available, then the queries are run on the primary node. |
| `nearest` | Reads are directed to a member with the least network latency (reply time in milliseconds), irrespective of their state as primary or secondary nodes. |

Figure 10.15: Read preferences in MongoDB

The following code shows an example of setting the read preference (in this case, **secondary**):

```
db.getMongo().setReadPref('secondary')
```

> **NOTE**
>
> Make sure you have a current cluster connection, with DNS SRV or a cluster/server list. The read preference setting doesn't work correctly with a single node connection.

The following is an example of using a read preference from mongo shell:

```
Command Prompt - mongo "mongodb+srv://cluster0.u7n6b.mongodb.net/test" --username admindb              —   □   ×
MongoDB Enterprise atlas-rzhbg7-shard-0:PRIMARY>
MongoDB Enterprise atlas-rzhbg7-shard-0:PRIMARY> db.getMongo().getReadPrefMode()
MongoDB Enterprise atlas-rzhbg7-shard-0:PRIMARY> db.getMongo().setReadPref('secondary')
MongoDB Enterprise atlas-rzhbg7-shard-0:PRIMARY> db.getMongo().getReadPrefMode()
secondary
MongoDB Enterprise atlas-rzhbg7-shard-0:PRIMARY> use sample_mflix
switched to db sample_mflix
MongoDB Enterprise atlas-rzhbg7-shard-0:PRIMARY> db.theaters.findOne()
{
        "_id" : ObjectId("59a47286cfa9a3a73e51e734"),
        "theaterId" : 1009,
        "location" : {
                "address" : {
                        "street1" : "6310 E Pacific Coast Hwy",
                        "city" : "Long Beach",
                        "state" : "CA",
                        "zipcode" : "90803"
                },
                "geo" : {
                        "type" : "Point",
                        "coordinates" : [
                                -118.11414,
                                33.760353
                        ]
                }
        }
}
MongoDB Enterprise atlas-rzhbg7-shard-0:PRIMARY>
```

Figure 10.16: Read preference from mongo shell

Note that once the read preference is set to **secondary**, the shell client automatically redirects the read operations to secondary nodes. After the query is performed, the shell returns to **primary** (shell prompt: **PRIMARY**). All further queries will be redirected to **secondary**.

> **NOTE**
>
> The read preference is lost if the client disconnects from the replica set. This is because the read preference is a client-side setting (not server). In this case, you will need to set the read preference again, after reconnecting to the MongoDB cluster.

The read preference can also be set as an option in the connection string URI, with the **?readPreference** parameter. For example, consider the following connection string:

```
"mongodb+srv://atlas1-u7n6b.mongodb.net/?readPreference=secondary"
```

> **NOTE**
>
> MongoDB offers even more sophisticated features for setting the read preference in a cluster. In more advanced configurations, the administrator can set tag names for each cluster member. For example, a tag name can indicate that the cluster member is located in a specific geographical region or data center. The tag name can then be used as a parameter to the **db.setReadPref()** function to redirect reads to a specific geographical region in the proximity of the client's location.

# WRITE CONCERN

By default, a Mongo client receives a confirmation for each write operation (insert/update/delete) on the primary node. The confirmation return code can be used in applications to make sure that data is securely written into the database. In the case of replica set clusters, though, the situation is more complex. For example, it is possible to insert rows in a primary instance, but if the primary node crashes before replication Oplog records are applied to secondary nodes, then there is a risk of data loss. Write concern addresses this issue by ensuring that the write is confirmed on multiple cluster nodes. Therefore, in the event of an unexpected crash of the primary node, the inserted data will not be lost.

By default, the write concern is `{w: 1}`, which indicates acknowledgment from the primary instance only. `{w: 2}` will require confirmation from two nodes for each write operation. Multiple node confirmation comes at a cost, however. A large number for the write concern can lead to slower write operations on the cluster. `(w: "majority")` indicates the majority of cluster nodes. This setting helps ensure data safety in unexpected failure scenarios.

Write concern can be set at the cluster level or at the write statement level. In Atlas, we cannot see or configure the write concern, as it is preset by MongoDB to `{w: "majority"}`. The following is an example of write concern at the statement level:

```
db.new_collection.insert({"_id":1, "info": "test writes"},
                              {w:2})
```

All CRUD operations (except queries) have an option for write concern. Optionally, a second parameter can be set, **wtimeout: 1000**, to configure the maximum timeout in milliseconds.

The following screenshot shows an example of this:

```
Command Prompt - mongo  "mongodb+srv://cluster0.u7n6b.mongodb.net/test" --username admindb      —    □    ×
MongoDB Enterprise atlas-rzhbg7-shard-0:PRIMARY>
MongoDB Enterprise atlas-rzhbg7-shard-0:PRIMARY> db.new_collection.insert({"_id":102, "info": "test writes"}
,{w:2,wtimeout:1000})
WriteResult({ "nInserted" : 1 })
MongoDB Enterprise atlas-rzhbg7-shard-0:PRIMARY>
```

Figure 10.17: Write concern in mongo shell

The MongoDB client has many options for replication-set clusters. Understanding the basics of a client session in the cluster environment is essential for application development. It can lead to mistakes if developers overlook the cluster configuration. For example, one common mistake is to run all queries on the primary node or to assume that secondary reads are executed by default without any configuration. Setting up the read preference can significantly improve the performance of applications while reducing the load on the primary cluster node.

# DEPLOYING CLUSTERS

Setting up a new MongoDB replica set cluster is an operational task that is usually required at the start of a new development project. Depending on the complexity of the new environment, the deployment of a new replica set cluster can vary from a relatively easy, straightforward, simple configuration to more complex and enterprise-grade cluster deployments. In general, deploying MongoDB clusters requires more technical and operational knowledge than installing a single server database. Planning and preparation are essential and should never be overlooked before cluster deployments. That is because users need to carefully plan the cluster architecture, the underlying infrastructure, and database security to provide the best performance and availability for their database.

Regarding the method used for MongoDB replica set cluster deployments, there are a few tools that can help with the automatization and management of the deployments. The most common method is manual deployment. Nevertheless, the manual method is probably the most laborious option—especially for complex clusters. Automatization tools are available from MongoDB and other third-party software providers. The next section looks at the most common methods used for MongoDB cluster deployments and the advantages of each method.

## ATLAS DEPLOYMENT

Deploying MongoDB clusters on the Atlas cloud is the easiest option available for developers as it saves on effort and money. The MongoDB company manages the infrastructure, including the server hardware, OS, network, and **mongod** instances. As a result, users can focus on application development and DevOps, rather than spending time on the infrastructure. In many cases, this is the perfect solution for fast-delivery projects.

Deploying a cluster on Atlas requires nothing more than a few clicks in the Atlas web application. You are already familiar with database deployments in Atlas from *Chapter 1, Introduction to MongoDB*. The free-tier Atlas M0 cluster is a great free-of-charge environment for learning and testing. As a matter of fact, all deployments in Atlas are replica set clusters. In the current Atlas version, it is not possible to deploy single-server clusters in Atlas.

Atlas offers more cluster options for larger deployments, which are charged services. If required, Atlas clusters can scale up easily—both vertically (adding server resources) and horizontally (adding more members). It is possible to build multi-region, replica set clusters on dedicated Atlas servers M10 and higher. Therefore, high availability can extend across geographical regions, between Europe and North America. This option is ideal for allocating read-only secondary nodes in a remote data center.

The following screenshot shows an example of a multi-region cluster configuration:

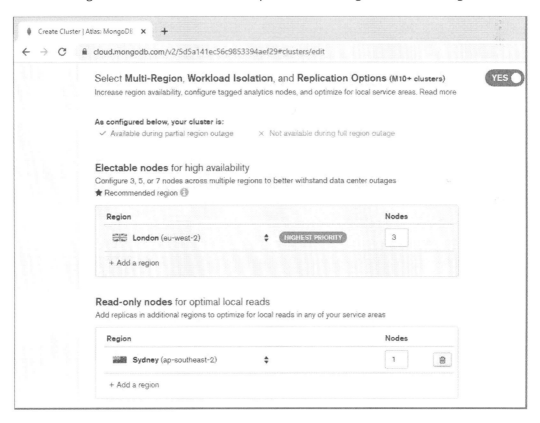

Figure 10.18: Multi-region cluster configuration

In the preceding example, the primary database is in London, together with two other secondary nodes, while in Sydney, Australia, one additional secondary node is configured for read-only access.

## MANUAL DEPLOYMENT

Manual deployment is the most common form of MongoDB cluster deployment. For many developers, building a MongoDB cluster manually is also the preferred option for database installation because this method gives them full control over the infrastructure and cluster configuration. Manual deployment is more laborious compared with other methods, however, which makes this method less scalable for large environments.

You would perform the following steps to manually deploy MongoDB clusters:

1.  Choose the server members of the new cluster. Whether they are physical servers or virtual, they must meet the minimum requirements for the MongoDB database. Also, all cluster members should have identical hardware and software specifications (CPU, memory, disk, and OS).

2.  MongoDB binaries must be installed on each server. Use the same installation path on all servers.

3.  Run one **mongod** instance per server. Servers should be on separate hardware with a separate power supply and network connections. For testing, however, it is possible to deploy all cluster members on a single physical server.

4.  Start the Mongo server with the **--bind_ip** parameter. By default, **mongod** binds only to the localhost IP address (**127.0.0.1**). In order to communicate with other cluster members, **mongod** must bind to external private or public IP addresses.

5.  Set the network properly. Each server must be able to communicate freely with other members without firewalls. Also, servers' IPs and DNS names must match in the DNS domain configuration.

6.  Create the directory structure for database files and database instance logs. Use the same path on all servers. For example, use **/data/db** for database files (WiredTiger storage) and **/var/log/mongodb** for log files on Unix/macOS systems, and in the case of Windows OSes, use **C:\data\db** directories for datafiles and **C:\log\mongo** for log files. Directories must be empty (create a new database cluster).

7. Start up the **mongod** instance on each server with the replica set parameter **replSet**. To start a **mongod** instance, start an OS Command Prompt or terminal and execute the following command for Linux and macOS:

```
mongod --replSet cluster0 --port 27017 --bind_ip <server_ip_address>
--dbpath /data/db --logpath /var/log/mongodb/cluster0.log --oplogSize
100
```

For Windows OSes, the command is as follows:

```
mongod --replSet cluster0 --port 27017 --bind_ip <server_ip_
address> --dbpath C:\mongo\data --logpath C:\mongo\log\cluster0.log
--oplogSize 100
```

The following table lists the parameters and the description for each:

| Parameter | Description |
|---|---|
| `--replSet cluster0` | Start mongod as part of a replica set cluster (not a single server). cluster0 is the name of the replica set. |
| `--port 27017` | TCP port number where the mongod member is listening for new connections. |
| `--dbpath /data/db`<br>For Windows OSes:<br>`--dbpath c:\mongo\data` | Database path on disk for WiredTiger datafiles. |
| `--logpath /var/log/mongodb/cluster0.log`<br>For Windows OSes:<br>`--logpath C:\mongo\log\cluster0.log` | Database log file, for mongod instance log messages. |
| `--oplogSize 100` | Size of the Oplog buffer. In this example, Oplog is created with an initial size of 100 MB. The Oplog size can be changed later, and it is recommended to have the same size on all cluster members. |

*Figure 10.19: Description of the parameters in the commands*

8. Connect to the new cluster with mongo shell:

```
mongo mongodb://hostname1.domain/cluster0
```

9. Create the cluster config JSON document and save it in a JS variable (**cfg**):

```
var cfg = {
    _id : "cluster0",
    members : [
        { _id : 0, host : "hostname1.domain":27017"},
```

```
            { _id : 1, host : "hostname2.domain":27017"},
            { _id : 2, host : "hostname3.domain":27017"},
            ]
  }
```

> **NOTE**
>
> The preceding configuration steps are not real commands. `hostname1.domain` should be replaced with the real hostname and domain that matches DNS records.

10. Activate the cluster as follows:

```
rs.initiate( cfg )
```

Cluster activation saves the configuration and starts the cluster configuration. During the cluster configuration, there is an election process where member nodes decide on the new primary instance.

Once the configuration is activated, the shell prompt will display the cluster name (for example, `cluster0 : PRIMARY>`). Moreover, you can check the cluster status with the `rs.status()` command, which gives detailed information about the cluster and member servers. In the next exercise, you will set up a MongoDB cluster.

## EXERCISE 10.03: BUILDING YOUR OWN MONGODB CLUSTER

In this exercise, you will set up a new MongoDB cluster that will have three members. All **mongod** instances will be started on the local computer, and you need to set different directories for each server so that instances will not clash on the same datafiles. You will also need to use a different TCP port for each instance:

1. Create the file directories. For Windows OSes, this should be as follows:

   `C:\data\inst1`: For instance 1 datafiles

   `C:\data\inst2`: For instance 2 datafiles

   `C:\data\inst3`: For instance 3 datafiles

   `C:\data\log`: Log file destination

For Linux, the file directories are the following. Note that for MacOS, you can use any directory name of your choice instead of **/data**.

**/data/db/inst1**: For instance 1 datafiles

**/data/db/inst2**: For instance 2 datafiles

**/data/db/inst3**: For instance 3 datafiles

**/var/log/mongodb**: Log file destination

The following screenshot shows an example of this in Windows Explorer:

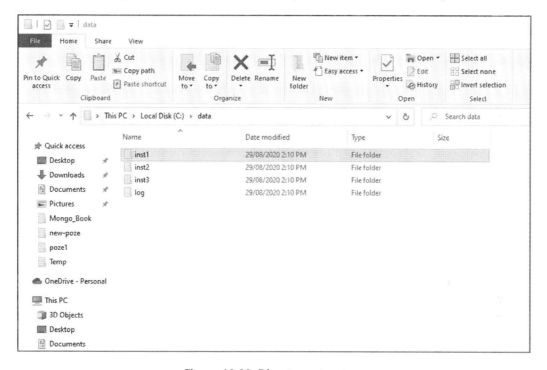

Figure 10.20: Directory structure

For the various instances, use the following TCP ports:

Instance 1: 27001

Instance 2: 27002

Instance 3: 27003

Use the replica set name **my_cluster**. The Oplog size should be 50 MB.

2. Start the **mongod** instances from Windows Command Prompt. Use **start** to run the **mongod** startup command. This will create a new window for the process. Otherwise, the **start mongod** command might hang, and you will need to use another Command Prompt window. Note that you will need to use **sudo** instead of **start** for MacOS.

```
start mongod --replSet my_cluster --port 27001 --dbpath C:\data\inst1
-- logpath C:\data\log\inst1.log --logappend --oplogSize 50

start mongod --replSet my_cluster --port 27002 --dbpath C:\data\inst2
-- logpath C:\data\log\inst2.log --logappend --oplogSize 50

start mongod --replSet my_cluster --port 27003 --dbpath C:\data\inst3
-- logpath C:\data\log\inst3.log --logappend --oplogSize 50
```

> **NOTE**
>
> The **--logappend** parameter adds log messages at the end of the log file. Otherwise, the log file will be truncated each time you start the **mongod** instance.

3. Check the startup messages in the log destination folder (**C:\data\log**). Each instance has a separate log file, and at the end of the log, there should be a message as shown in the following code snippet:

```
16.613+1000 I  NETWORK  [initandlisten] waiting for connections on
port 27001
```

4. In a separate terminal (or Windows Command Prompt), connect to the cluster using mongo shell using the following command:

```
mongo mongodb://localhost:27001/replicaSet=my_cluster
```

The following screenshot shows an example using mongo shell:

```
Command Prompt - mongo mongodb://localhost:27001/replicaSet=my_cluster        —   □   ×

C:\>mongo mongodb://localhost:27001/replicaSet=my_cluster
MongoDB shell version v4.4.0
connecting to: mongodb://localhost:27001/replicaSet%3Dmy_cluster?compressors=disabled&gssapiServiceName=mongodb
Implicit session: session { "id" : UUID("de805cf9-883e-48ee-a110-499f09a84e64") }
MongoDB server version: 4.4.0
---
The server generated these startup warnings when booting:
        2020-08-29T14:16:34.398+10:00: Access control is not enabled for the database. Read and write access to
data and configuration is unrestricted
        2020-08-29T14:16:34.398+10:00: This server is bound to localhost. Remote systems will be unable to conne
ct to this server. Start the server with --bind_ip <address> to specify which IP addresses it should serve respo
nses from, or with --bind_ip_all to bind to all interfaces. If this behavior is desired, start the server with -
-bind_ip 127.0.0.1 to disable this warning
---
---
        Enable MongoDB's free cloud-based monitoring service, which will then receive and display
        metrics about your deployment (disk utilization, CPU, operation statistics, etc).

        The monitoring data will be available on a MongoDB website with a unique URL accessible to you
        and anyone you share the URL with. MongoDB may use this information to make product
        improvements and to suggest MongoDB products and deployment options to you.

        To enable free monitoring, run the following command: db.enableFreeMonitoring()
        To permanently disable this reminder, run the following command: db.disableFreeMonitoring()
---
>
```

Figure 10.21: Output in mongo shell

Notice that the shell command prompt is just **>**, even though you connected with the **replicaSet** parameter in the connection string. That is because the cluster is not configured yet.

5. Edit the cluster configuration JSON document (in the JS variable **cfg**):

```
var cfg = {
    _id : "my_cluster",        //replica set name
    members : [
        { _id : 0, host : "localhost:27001"},
        { _id : 1, host : "localhost:27002"},
        { _id : 2, host : "localhost:27003"},
    ]
}
```

**NOTE**

This code can be typed directly into mongo shell.

6. Activate the cluster configuration as follows:

```
rs.initiate( cfg )
```

Note that it usually takes some time for the cluster to activate the configuration and elect a new primary:

```
Command Prompt - mongo  mongodb://localhost:27001/replicaSet=my_cluster          —    □    ×
>
> var cfg = {
...     _id : "my_cluster",      //replica set name
...     members : [
...         { _id : 0, host : "localhost:27001"},
...         { _id : 1, host : "localhost:27002"},
...         { _id : 2, host : "localhost:27003"},
...         ]
... }
> rs.initiate(cfg)
{
        "ok" : 1,
        "$clusterTime" : {
                "clusterTime" : Timestamp(1598674782, 1),
                "signature" : {
                        "hash" : BinData(0,"AAAAAAAAAAAAAAAAAAAAAAAAAAA="),
                        "keyId" : NumberLong(0)
                }
        },
        "operationTime" : Timestamp(1598674782, 1)
}
my_cluster:SECONDARY>
my_cluster:PRIMARY>
```

Figure 10.22: Output in mongo shell

The shell prompt should indicate the cluster connection (initially **mycluster: SECONDARY** and then **PRIMARY**) after the election process is completed and successful. If your prompt still shows **SECONDARY**, then try to reconnect or check the server logs for errors.

7. Verify the cluster configuration. For this, connect with mongo shell and verify that the prompt is **PRIMARY>**, and then run the following command to check the cluster status:

```
rs.status()
```

Run the following command to verify the current cluster configuration:

```
rs.conf()
```

Both commands return a long output with many details. The expected results are in the following screenshot (which shows a partial output):

```
Command Prompt - mongo  mongodb://localhost:27001/replicaSet=my_cluster        —    □    ×
my_cluster:PRIMARY>
my_cluster:PRIMARY> rs.status()
{
        "set" : "my_cluster",
        "date" : ISODate("2020-08-29T04:21:24.021Z"),
        "myState" : 1,
        "term" : NumberLong(1),
        "syncSourceHost" : "",
        "syncSourceId" : -1,
        "heartbeatIntervalMillis" : NumberLong(2000),
        "majorityVoteCount" : 2,
        "writeMajorityCount" : 2,
        "votingMembersCount" : 3,
        "writableVotingMembersCount" : 3,
        "optimes" : {
                "lastCommittedOpTime" : {
                        "ts" : Timestamp(1598674883, 1),
                        "t" : NumberLong(1)
                },
                "lastCommittedWallTime" : ISODate("2020-08-29T04:21:23.475Z"),
                "readConcernMajorityOpTime" : {
                        "ts" : Timestamp(1598674883, 1),
                        "t" : NumberLong(1)
```

Figure 10.23: Output in mongo shell

In this exercise, you manually deployed all members of a replica set cluster on your local system. This exercise is for testing purposes only and should not be used for real applications. In real life, MongoDB cluster nodes should be deployed on separate servers, but the exercise gave a good inside look at a replica set's initial configuration and is especially useful for quick tests.

## ENTERPRISE DEPLOYMENT

For large-scale enterprise applications, MongoDB provides integrated tools for managing deployments. It is easy to imagine why deploying and managing hundreds of MongoDB cluster servers could be an incredibly challenging task. Therefore, the ability to manage all deployments in an integrated interface is essential for large, enterprise-scale MongoDB environments.

MongoDB provides two different interfaces:

- **MongoDB OPS Manager** is a package available for MongoDB Enterprise Advanced. It typically requires installation on-premises.

- **MongoDB Cloud Manager** is a cloud-hosted service to manage MongoDB Enterprise deployments.

> **NOTE**
>
> Both Cloud Manager and Atlas are cloud applications, but they provide
> different services. While Atlas is a fully managed database service, Cloud
> Manager is a service to manage database deployments, including local
> server infrastructure.

Both applications provide similar functionality for enterprise users, with integrated automation for deployments, advanced graphical monitoring, and backup management. Using Cloud Manager, administrators are able to deploy all types of MongoDB servers (both single and clusters), while maintaining full control over the underlying infrastructure.

The following diagram shows the Cloud Manager architecture:

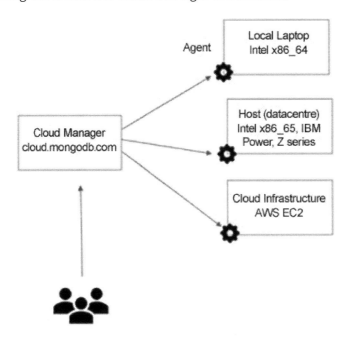

Figure 10.24: Cloud Manager architecture

The architecture is based on a central management server and MongoDB Agent. Before a server can be managed in Cloud Manager, the MongoDB Agent needs to be deployed on the server.

> **NOTE**
>
> MongoDB Agent software should not be confused with MongoDB database software. MongoDB Agent software is used for Cloud Manager and OPS Manager centralized management.

With regard to Cloud Manager, users are not actually required to download and install MongoDB databases. All MongoDB versions are managed automatically by the deployment server once the agent is installed and the server is added to Cloud Manager configuration. MongoDB Agent will automatically download, stage, and install MongoDB server binaries on the server.

The following screenshot shows an example from MongoDB Cloud Manager:

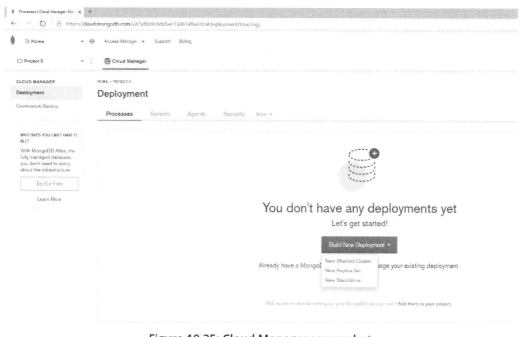

Figure 10.25: Cloud Manager screenshot

The Cloud Manager web interface is similar to the Atlas application. One major difference between them is that Cloud Manager has more features. While Cloud Manager can manage your Atlas deployments, it has more complex options available for MongoDB Enterprise deployments.

The first step is to add a deployment (the **New Replica Set** button), and then to add servers to the deployment and install MongoDB agents. Once the MongoDB agent is installed on cluster members, the deployment is performed automatically by the agent.

> **NOTE**
>
> You can test Cloud Manager for free for 30 days on MongoDB Cloud. The registration process is similar to the steps were shown in *Chapter 1*, *Introduction to MongoDB*.

The MongoDB Atlas managed DBaaS cloud service is a great platform for quick and easy deployments. Most users will find Atlas their preferred choice for database deployments because the cloud environment is fully managed, secure, and always available. On the downside, the Atlas cloud service has some limitations for users when compared with Mongo DB on-premises. For example, Atlas does not allow users to access or tune the hardware and software infrastructure. If users want to have full control over the infrastructure, they can choose to manually deploy MongoDB databases. In the case of large enterprise database deployments, MongoDB provides software solutions such as Cloud Manager, which is useful for managing many cluster deployments while still having full control of the underlying infrastructure.

# CLUSTER OPERATIONS

Consider a scenario where one of your servers that is running a MongoDB database has reported memory errors. You are a bit worried because the computer is running the primary active member of your cluster. The server needs maintenance to replace the faulty **DIMM (Dual In-Line Memory Module)**. You decide to switch over the primary instance to another server. The maintenance should take less than an hour, but you want to make sure that users can use their applications during the maintenance.

MongoDB cluster operations refer to such day-to-day administration tasks that are necessary for cluster maintenance and monitoring. This is especially important for clusters deployed manually, where users must fully manage and operate replica set clusters. In the case of the Atlas DBaaS managed service, the only interaction is through the Atlas web application and most of the work is done behind the scenes by MongoDB. Therefore, our discussion will be limited to MongoDB clusters deployed manually, either in the local infrastructure or in cloud IaaS (Infrastructure as a Service).

## ADDING AND REMOVING MEMBERS

New members can be added to replica sets with the command **rs.add()**. Before we can add a new member, the **mongod** instance needs to be prepared and started with the same **—replSet** cluster name option. The same rules apply to new cluster members. For example, starting the new **mongod** instance would look as follows:

```
mongod --dbpath C:\data\inst4 --replSet <cluster_name>  --bind_ip
<hostname> --
   logpath <disk path>
```

Before we add a new member to an existing replica set, though, we need to decide on the type of cluster member. The following options are available for this:

| Member Type | Description |
| --- | --- |
| SECONDARY | Add a new member to a replica set as a secondary member. This is the most common scenario. |
| READ ONLY | READ ONLY is a SECONDARY database that is never elected as the primary database. The main purpose of a READ ONLY instance is to report client query routing, using the read preference secondary. |
| HIDDEN | Similar to READ ONLY, but with one difference. Hidden instances do not participate in the normal client read preference. They are designed for isolated applications (such as data warehousing) that do not need to interfere with normal client activity. |
| DELAY | Sometimes, reporting applications need an older snapshot of the database (a delayed copy; 12 hours for example), which is continuously updated from the primary. A DELAY instance must also be hidden. |
| ARBITER | ARBITER is a special type of member that has no user data. Therefore, arbiter nodes do not replicate Oplog operations from the primary and they never become the primary. The purpose of an arbiter is to help during the election to create a majority of cluster nodes. |
| PRIMARY | While it is possible to add a new primary member (added with higher priority that will initiate election), this is NOT recommended because the new instance needs time to synchronize datafiles from the former primary. Always add new members as secondary first and switch over later when they are in sync. |

Figure 10.26: Descriptions for the member types

## ADDING A MEMBER

There are a few arguments that can be passed when we add a new cluster member, depending on the member type. In its simplest form, the **add** command has only one parameter—a string containing the hostname and port of the new instance:

```
rs.add ( "node4.domain.com:27004" )
```

Keep in mind the following while adding a member:

- A **SECONDARY** member should be added to the cluster.

- Priority can be any number between **0** and **1000**. If this instance were to be elected as the primary, the priority must be set greater than **0**. Otherwise, the instance is considered **READ ONLY**. Moreover, the priority must be **0** for the **HIDDEN**, **DELAY**, and **ARBITER** instance types. The default value is **1**.

- All nodes have one vote by default. In version 4.4, a node can have either 0 votes or 1 vote. There can be a maximum of 7 voting members—with one vote each. The rest of the nodes are not participating in the election process, having 0 votes. The default value is 1.

The following screenshot shows an example of adding a member:

```
Command Prompt - mongo  mongodb://localhost:27001/replicaSet=my_cluster          —    □    ×
my_cluster:PRIMARY>
my_cluster:PRIMARY> rs.add("localhost:27004")
{
        "ok" : 1,
        "$clusterTime" : {
                "clusterTime" : Timestamp(1598675156, 1),
                "signature" : {
                        "hash" : BinData(0,"AAAAAAAAAAAAAAAAAAAAAAAAAAA="),
                        "keyId" : NumberLong(0)
                }
        },
        "operationTime" : Timestamp(1598675156, 1)
}
my_cluster:PRIMARY>
my_cluster:PRIMARY>
```

Figure 10.27: Example of adding a member

In the preceding screenshot, **"ok" : 1** indicates that the add member operation was successful. In the new instance logs, the initial sync (database copy) is started for the new replica set member:

```
INITSYNC [replication-0] Starting initial sync (attempt 1 of 10)
```

0 adds a different member type, but the **add** command can be different. For example, to add a hidden member with a vote, add the following:

```
rs.add ( {host: "node4.domain.com:27017", hidden : true,
  votes : 1})
```

If successful, the **add** command will do the following:

- Change the cluster configuration by adding the new member node
- Perform the initial sync—the database is copied to the new member instance (except in the case of **ARBITER**)

In some situations, adding a new member can change the current primary.

> **NOTE**
>
> The new member cluster must have an empty database (empty data directory) before joining the replica set cluster. Oplog operations that are generated on the primary node during the sync process are also copied and applied to the new cluster member. The synchronization process may take a long time, especially if synchronization is running over the internet.

## REMOVING A MEMBER

Cluster members can be removed by connecting to the cluster and running the following command:

```
rs.remove({ <hostname.com> })
```

> **NOTE**
>
> Removing a cluster member does not remove the instance and datafiles. The instance can be started in single-server mode (without the **—replSet** option), and datafiles will contain the latest updates from before it was removed.

## RECONFIGURING A CLUSTER

Cluster reconfiguration may be necessary if you want to make more complex changes to a replica set, such as adding multiple nodes in one step or editing the default values for votes and priority. Clusters can be reconfigured by running the following command:

```
rs.reconfig()
```

The following is a step-by-step breakdown of a cluster reconfiguration with a different priority for each node:

- Save the configuration in a JS variable as follows:

```
var new_cfg = rs.config()
```

- Edit **new_conf** to change the default priority by adding the following snippet:

```
new_conf.members[0].priority=1
new_conf.members[1].priority=0.5
new_conf.members[2].priority=0
```

- Enable the new configuration as follows:

```
rs.reconfig(new_cfg)
```

The following screenshot shows an example of cluster reconfiguration:

```
Select Command Prompt - mongo  mongodb://localhost:27001/replicaSet=my_cluster        —    □    ×
my_cluster:PRIMARY>
my_cluster:PRIMARY> var new_conf=rs.conf()
my_cluster:PRIMARY> new_conf.members[0].priority=1
1
my_cluster:PRIMARY> new_conf.members[1].priority=0.5
0.5
my_cluster:PRIMARY> new_conf.members[2].priority=0
0
my_cluster:PRIMARY> rs.reconfig(new_conf)
{
        "ok" : 1,
        "$clusterTime" : {
                "clusterTime" : Timestamp(1598675337, 1),
                "signature" : {
                        "hash" : BinData(0,"AAAAAAAAAAAAAAAAAAAAAAAAAAA="),
                        "keyId" : NumberLong(0)
                }
        },
        "operationTime" : Timestamp(1598675337, 1)
}
```

**Figure 10.28: Example of cluster reconfiguration**

# FAILOVER

In certain situations, the MongoDB cluster could initiate an election process. In data center operations terminology, these types of events are usually called **Failover** and **Switchover**:

- **Failover** is always a result of an incident. When one or more cluster members become unavailable (usually because of a failure or network outage) the cluster fails over. The replica set detects that some of the nodes become unavailable, and the replica set election is automatically started.

  > **NOTE**
  >
  > How does a replica set cluster detect an incident? Member servers regularly communicate between themselves—sending/receiving a heartbeat network request every couple of seconds. If one member does not reply for a longer time (the default is 10 seconds), then the member is declared unavailable and a new cluster election is initiated.

- **Switchover** is a user-initiated process (that is, initiated by a server command). The purpose of switchover is to perform planned maintenance on the cluster. For example, the server running the primary member needs to restart for OS patching, and the administrator switches the primary over to another cluster member.

Regardless of whether it is a failover or a switchover, the election mechanism is started, and the cluster aims to achieve a new majority and, if successful, a new primary node. During the election process, there is a transition period when writes are not possible on the database and client sessions will reconnect to the new primary member. Application coding should be able to handle MongoDB failover events transparently for users.

In Atlas, failovers are managed automatically by MongoDB, so no user involvement is required. In larger Atlas deployments (such as M10+), the `Test Failover` button is available in the Atlas application. The `Test Failover` button will force a cluster failover for application testing. If the new cluster majority cannot be achieved, then all nodes will stay in the secondary state and no primary will be elected. In this situation, the clients will not be able to modify any data in the database. However, the read-only operations are still possible on all secondary nodes regardless of the cluster status.

## FAILOVER (OUTAGE)

In the event of outages, usually, messages such as the one in the following code snippet can be seen in the instance logs:

```
2019-11-25T15:08:05.893+1000  REPL      [replexec-0] Member
localhost:27003 is now in state RS_DOWN - Error connecting to
localhost:27003 (127.0.0.1:27003) :: caused by :: No connection could be
made because the target machine actively refused it.
```

The client session (in other words, the connection pool) will automatically reconnect to the remaining nodes, and the activity can continue as normal. Once the missing node is restarted, it will rejoin the cluster automatically. If the cluster cannot successfully complete election with the available nodes, then the failover is not considered successful. In the logs, we can see a message like this:

```
2019-11-25T15:08:05.893+1000 I  ELECTION [replexec-4] not becoming
primary, we received insufficient votes
...Election failed.
```

In this case, the client connection is dropped, and users are not able to reconnect unless the read preference is set to **secondary**:

```
2019-11-25T15:09:45.928+1000 W  NETWORK  [ReplicaSetMonitor-TaskExecutor]
Unable to reach primary for set my_cluster
2019-11-25T15:09:45.929+1000 E  QUERY    [js] Error: Could not find host
matching read preference { mode: "primary", tags: [ {} ] } for set my_
cluster :
```

Even if election is not successful, the users are able to connect with a read preference **secondary** setting, as in the following connection string:

```
mongo mongodb://localhost:27001/?readPreference=secondary&replicaSet=my_
cluster
```

> **NOTE**
>
> It is not possible to open the database instance in read-write mode (the primary state) unless there are sufficient nodes to form a cluster majority. One typical mistake is to reboot many secondary members at the same time. If the cluster detects that the majority is lost, then the primary state member will step down to secondary.

## ROLLBACK

In some situations, failover events could generate rollbacks of writes on the former primary node. This may happen if writes on the primary were performed with the default write concern (**w:1**), and the former primary crashed before it had the chance to replicate changes to any secondary node. The cluster forms a new majority, and the activity will continue with a new primary. When the former primary is back up, it needs to roll back those (previously un-replicated) transactions before it can get in sync with the new primary.

The chances of rollback could be reduced by setting write concern to **majority** (**w: 'majority'**)—that is, by obtaining acknowledgment from most cluster nodes (the majority) for every database write. On the downside, this could slow down the writes for the application.

Normally, failures and outages are remedied quickly, and the affected nodes rejoin the cluster when they are back up. However, if the outage is taking a long time (for example, a week), then the secondary instances could become **stale**. A stale instance will not be able to resynchronize data with the primary member after a restart. In that case, the instance should be added as a new member (empty data directory) or from a recent database backup.

## SWITCHOVER (STEPDOWN)

For maintenance activities, we often need to transfer the primary state from one instance to another. For this, the user admin command to be executed on the primary is as follows:

```
rs.stepDown()
```

The **stepDown** command will force the primary node to step down and cause the secondary node with the highest priority to step up as the new primary node. The primary node will step down only if the secondary node is up to date. Therefore, switchover is a safer operation compared to failover. There is no risk of losing writes on a former primary member.

The following screenshot shows an example of this:

```
Command Prompt - mongo mongodb://localhost:27001/replicaSet=my_cluster            —  ☐  ✕
my_cluster:PRIMARY> rs.isMaster().ismaster
true
my_cluster:PRIMARY> rs.stepDown()
{
        "ok" : 1,
        "$clusterTime" : {
                "clusterTime" : Timestamp(1598675553, 1),
                "signature" : {
                        "hash" : BinData(0,"AAAAAAAAAAAAAAAAAAAAAAAAAAA="),
                        "keyId" : NumberLong(0)
                }
        },
        "operationTime" : Timestamp(1598675553, 1)
}
my_cluster:SECONDARY> rs.isMaster().ismaster
false
my_cluster:SECONDARY>
```

Figure 10.29: Using the stepDown command

You can verify the current master node by running the following command:

```
rs.isMaster()
```

Note that in order for a switchover to be successful, the target cluster member must be configured with a higher priority. A member with a default priority (**priority =** **0**) will never become a primary.

## EXERCISE 10.04: PERFORMING DATABASE MAINTENANCE

In this exercise, you will perform cluster maintenance on a primary node. First, you will switch over to the secondary server, **inst2**, so that the current primary server will become secondary. Then, you will shut down the former primary server for maintenance and restart the former primary and switch over:

> **NOTE**
>
> Before you start this exercise, prepare the cluster script and directories as per the steps given in *Exercise 10.02, Checking the Cluster Replication*.

1. Start up all cluster members (if not already started), connect with mongo shell, and verify the configuration and the current master node with **rs.isMaster().primary**.

2. Reconfigure the cluster. For this, copy the existing cluster configuration into a variable, **sw_over**, and set the read-only member priority. For **inst3**, the priority should be set to **0** (read-only).

```
var sw_over = rs.conf()
sw_over.member[2].priority = 0
rs.reconfig(sw_over)
```

3. Switch over to **inst2**. On the primary node, run the **stepDown** command as follows:

```
rs.stepDown()
```

4. Verify that the new primary is **inst2** by using the following command:

```
rs.isMaster().primary
```

Now, **inst1** can be stopped for hardware maintenance.

5. Shut down the instance locally using the following command:

```
db.shutdownServer()
```

The output for this should be as follows:

```
Command Prompt - mongo  mongodb://localhost:27001,localhost:27002,localhost:27003/replicaSet=my_cluster          —    □    ×
my_cluster:PRIMARY>
my_cluster:PRIMARY> rs.isMaster().primary
localhost:27001
my_cluster:PRIMARY> rs.stepDown()
{
        "ok" : 1,
        "$clusterTime" : {
                "clusterTime" : Timestamp(1598744038, 1),
                "signature" : {
                        "hash" : BinData(0,"AAAAAAAAAAAAAAAAAAAAAAAAAAA="),
                        "keyId" : NumberLong(0)
                }
        },
        "operationTime" : Timestamp(1598744038, 1)
}
my_cluster:SECONDARY> rs.isMaster().primary
localhost:27002
my_cluster:SECONDARY>
```

Figure 10.30: Output in mongo shell

In this exercise, you practiced the switchover steps in a cluster. The commands are quite simple. Switchover is a good practice to test how applications handle MongoDB cluster events.

## ACTIVITY 10.01: TESTING A DISASTER RECOVERY PROCEDURE FOR A MONGODB DATABASE

Your company is about to become public, and as a result, some certifications are necessary to prove that a business continuity plan is in place in case of disaster. One of the requirements is to implement and test a disaster recovery procedure for a MongoDB database. The cluster architecture is distributed between the main office (primary instance) and a remote office (secondary instance), which is the disaster recovery location. To help with MongoDB replica set elections in case of a network split, an arbiter node is installed in a third separate location. Once a year, the DR plan is tested by simulating a crash of all cluster members in the main office, and this year, that task falls to you. The following steps will help you to complete this activity:

> **NOTE**
>
> If you have multiple computers, it is a good idea to try the activity with two or three computers, with each computer emulating a physical location. In the solution, however, this activity will be completed by starting all instances on the same local computer. All secondary databases (including DR) should be in sync with the primary database when the activity is started.

1. Configure a **sale-cluster** cluster with three members:

   **sale-prod**: Primary

   **sale-dr**: Secondary

   **sale-ab**: Arbiter (third location)

2. Insert test data records into the primary collection.

3. Simulate a disaster. Reboot the primary node (that is, kill the current **mongod** primary instance).

4. Perform testing on DR by inserting a few documents.

5. Shut down the DR instance.

6. Restart all nodes for the main office.

7. After 10 minutes, start up the DR instance.

8. Observe the rollback of inserted test records and re-sync with the primary.

After restarting **sales_dr**, you should see a rollback message in the logs. The following code snippet shows an example of this:

```
ROLLBACK [rsBackgroundSync] transition to SECONDARY
2019-11-26T15:48:29.538+1000 I  REPL      [rsBackgroundSync] transition to
SECONDARY from ROLLBACK
2019-11-26T15:48:29.538+1000 I  REPL      [rsBackgroundSync] Rollback
successful.
```

> **NOTE**
>
> The solution to this activity can be found on Page 687.

## SUMMARY

In this chapter, you learned that MongoDB replica sets are essential for providing high availability and load sharing in a MongoDB database environment. While Atlas transparently provides support for infrastructure and software (including for replica set cluster management), not all MongoDB clusters are deployed in Atlas. In this chapter, we discussed the concepts and operations of replica set clusters. Learning about simple concepts for clusters, such as read preference, can help developers build more reliable, high-performance applications in the cloud. In the next chapter, you will learn about backup and restore operations in MongoDB.

# 11

# BACKUP AND RESTORE IN MONGODB

## OVERVIEW

In this chapter, we will examine exactly how to load backups, samples, and test databases into a target MongoDB instance, and just as importantly, you will learn how to export an existing dataset for backup and restoration at a later date. By the end of this chapter, you will be able to backup, export, import, and restore MongoDB data into an existing server. This allows you to recover data from disasters as well as quickly load known information into a system for testing.

# INTRODUCTION

In the previous chapters, we have relied primarily on the sample data preloaded into a MongoDB Atlas instance. Unless you are working on a new project, this is generally the way a database will first appear to you. However, when you are hired or moved to a different project with a MongoDB database, it will contain all the data that was created before you started there.

Now, what if you require a local copy of this data to test your applications or queries? It is often not safe or feasible to run queries directly against production databases, so the process of duplicating datasets onto a testing environment is quite common. Similarly, when creating a new project, you may wish to load some sample data or test data into the database. In this chapter, we will examine the procedures for migrating, importing or exporting for an existing MongoDB server and setting up a new database with existing data.

> **NOTE**
>
> Throughout this chapter, the exercises and activities included are iterations on a single scenario. The data and examples are based on the MongoDB Atlas sample database titled `sample_mflix`.

For the duration of this chapter, we will follow a set of exercises based on a theoretical scenario. This is an expansion of the scenario covered in *Chapter 7, Data Aggregation* and *Chapter 8, Coding JavaScript in MongoDB*. As you may recall, a cinema chain asked you to create queries and programs that would analyze their database to produce a list of movies to screen during their promotional season.

Over the course of these chapters, you built up some aggregations whose output was a new collection containing summary data. You also created an application that enabled users to update movies programmatically. The company has been so delighted with your work that they have decided to migrate the entire system to more significant, better hardware. Although the system administrators feel they are confident in migrating the existing MongoDB instance to the new hardware, you have decided it would be best if you manually test the procedure to ensure you can assist if required.

# THE MONGODB UTILITIES

The mongo shell does not include functions for exporting, importing, backup or restore. However, MongoDB has created methods for accomplishing this, so that no scripting work or complex GUIs are needed. For this, several utility scripts are provided that can be used to get data in or out of the database in bulk. These utility scripts are:

- `mongoimport`
- `mongoexport`
- `mongodump`
- `mongorestore`

We will cover each of these utilities in detail in the upcoming sections. As their names suggest, these four utilities correspond to importing documents, exporting documents, backing up a database and restoring a database. We will start with the topic of exporting data.

## EXPORTING MONGODB DATA

When it comes to moving data in and out of MongoDB in bulk, the most common and generally useful utility is **mongoexport**. This command is useful because it is one of the primary ways to extract large amounts of data from MongoDB in a usable format. Getting your MongoDB data out into a JSON file allows you to ingest it with other applications or databases and share data with stakeholders outside of MongoDB.

It is important to note that **mongoexport** must run on a single specified database and collection. You cannot run **mongoexport** on an entire database or multiple collections. We will see how to accomplish larger scope backups like these later in the chapter. The following snippet is an example of **mongoexport** in action:

```
mongoexport --uri=mongodb+srv://USERNAME:PASSWORD@provendocs-fawxo.
gcp.mongodb.net/sample_mflix -quiet --limit=10 --sort="{theaterId:1}"
--collection=theaters --out=output.json
```

This example is a more complex command, which includes some optional parameters and explicitly sets others. In practice though, your export commands may be much more straightforward. The structure and parameters used here are explained in detail in the following section.

## USING MONGOEXPORT

The best way to learn the **mongoexport** syntax is to build up a command parameter by parameter. So let's do that, beginning with the simplest possible version of an export:

```
mongoexport --collection=theaters
```

As you can see, in its simplest form, the command only requires a single parameter: **--collection**. This parameter is the collection for which we wish to export our documents.

If you execute this command, you may encounter some puzzling results, as follows:

```
2020-03-07-T13:16:09.152+1100 error connecting to db server: no reachable
servers
```

We get this result because we have not specified a database or URI. In such cases, where these details are not specified, **mongoexport** defaults to using a local MongoDB on port 27017 and the default database. Since we have been running our MongoDB server on Atlas in previous chapter examples and exercises, let's update our command to specify these parameters.

> **NOTE**
>
> You cannot specify both database and URI; this is because the database is a part of the URI. In this chapter, we will use URI for our exports.

The updated command would look as follows:

```
mongoexport --uri=mongodb+srv://USERNAME:PASSWORD@myAtlasServer.gcp.
mongodb.net/sample_mflix --collection=theaters
```

Now that you have a valid command, run it against the MongoDB Atlas database. You will see the following output:

```
2020-08-17T11:07:23.302+1000    connected to: mongodb+srv://
[**REDACTED**]@performancetuning.98afc.gcp.mongodb.net/sample_mflix
{"_id":{"$oid":"59a47286cfa9a3a73e51e72c"},"theaterId":1000,"location":
  {"address":{"street1":"340 W
Market","city":"Bloomington","state":"MN","zipcode":"55425"},"geo":
  {"type":"Point","coordinates":[-93.24565,44.85466]}}}
{"_id":{"$oid":"59a47286cfa9a3a73e51e72d"},"theaterId":1003,"location":
  {"address":{"street1":"45235 Worth
Ave.","city":"California","state":"MD","zipcode":"20619"},"geo":
  {"type":"Point","coordinates":[-76.512016,38.29697]}}}
```

```
{"_id":{"$oid":"59a47286cfa9a3a73e51e72e"},"theaterId":1008,"location":
   {"address":{"street1":"1621 E Monte Vista
Ave","city":"Vacaville","state":"CA","zipcode":"95688"},"geo":
   {"type":"Point","coordinates":[-121.96328,38.367649]}}}
{"_id":{"$oid":"59a47286cfa9a3a73e51e72f"},"theaterId":1004,"location":
   {"address":{"street1":"5072 Pinnacle
Sq","city":"Birmingham","state":"AL","zipcode":"35235"},"geo":
   {"type":"Point","coordinates":[-86.642662,33.605438]}}}
```

At the end of the output, you should see the number of exported records:

```
{"_id":{"$oid":"59a47287cfa9a3a73e51ed46"},"theaterId":952,"location":
   {"address":{"street1":"4620 Garth
Rd","city":"Baytown","state":"TX","zipcode":"77521"},"geo":
   {"type":"Point","coordinates":[-94.97554,29.774206]}}}
{"_id":{"$oid":"59a47287cfa9a3a73e51ed47"},"theaterId":953,"location":
   {"address":{"street1":"10 McKenna
Rd","city":"Arden","state":"NC","zipcode":"28704"},"geo":
   {"type":"Point","coordinates":[-82.536293,35.442486]}}}
2020-08-17T11:07:24.992+1000    [#######################]   sample_mflix.
theaters  1564/1564  (100.0%)
2020-08-17T11:07:24.992+1000    exported 1564 records
```

With your URI specified, the export operation worked, and you can see all the documents from the **theatres** collection. However, it's not very useful having all these documents flooding your output. You could use some shell commands to pipe or append this output into a file, but the **mongoexport** command provides another parameter in its syntax for outputting to a file automatically. You can see this parameter (**--out**) in the following command:

```
mongoexport --uri=mongodb+srv://USERNAME:PASSWORD@myAtlasServer.gcp.
mongodb.net/sample_mflix --collection=theaters --out=output.json
```

After running this command, you will see the following output:

```
2020-08-17T11:11:44.499+1000    connected to: mongodb+srv://
[**REDACTED**]@performancetuning.98afc.gcp.mongodb.net/sample_mflix
2020-08-17T11:11:45.634+1000    [.......................]   sample_mflix.
theaters  0/1564  (0.0%)
2020-08-17T11:11:45.694+1000    [#######################]   sample_mflix.
theaters  1564/1564  (100.0%)
2020-08-17T11:11:45.694+1000    exported 1564 records
```

Now, there is a new file created in that directory called **output.json**. If you look inside this file, you can see our documents exported from the theatres collection.

The parameters **uri**, **collection**, and **out** enable the majority of use cases for exporting. Once you have your data in a file on the disk, it is easy to integrate it with other applications or scripts.

## MONGOEXPORT OPTIONS

We now know about the three most important options for a **mongoexport**. However, there are several other useful options that are helpful for exporting data from MongoDB. Here are some of these options and their effects:

- **--quiet**: This option reduces the amount of output sent to the command line during export.

- **--type**: This will affect how the documents are printed in the console and defaults to JSON. For example, you can export the data in **Comma-Separated Value** (**CSV**) format by specifying CSV.

- **--pretty**: This outputs the documents in a nicely formatted manner.

- **--fields**: This specifies a comma-separated list of keys in your documents to be exported, similar to an export level projection.

- **--skip**: This works similar to a query level skip, skipping documents in the export.

- **--sort**: This works similar to a query level sort, sorting documents by some keys.

- **--limit**: This works similar to a query level limit, limiting the number of documents outputted.

Here is an example with some of these options used, in this case outputting ten **theatre** documents, sorted by id, into a file called **output.json**. Additionally, the **--quiet** parameter has also been used:

```
mongoexport --uri=mongodb+srv://USERNAME:PASSWORD@provendocs-fawxo.gcp.
mongodb.net/sample_mflix --quiet --limit=10 --sort="{theaterId:1}"
--collection=theaters --out=output.json
```

Since we have used the **--quiet** option, we will not see any output at all.

```
> mongoexport --uri=mongodb+srv://testUser:testPassword@performancet
uning.98afc.gcp.mongodb.net/sample_mflix --quiet --limit=10 --sort="
{theaterId:1}" --collection=theaters --out=output.json

>
```

However, if we look inside the **output.json** file, we can see the ten documents sorted by ID:

```
{"_id":{"$oid":"59a47287cfa9a3a73e51eb78"},"theaterId":4,"location":{"address":{"street1":"13513 Rid
gedale Dr","city":"Hopkins","state":"MN","zipcode":"55305"},"geo":{"type":"Point","coordinates":[-93
.449539,44.969658]}}}
{"_id":{"$oid":"59a47287cfa9a3a73e51ebff"},"theaterId":6,"location":{"address":{"street1":"1350 50th
 Street E","city":"Inver Grove Heights","state":"MN","zipcode":"55077"},"geo":{"type":"Point","coord
inates":[-93.077156,44.879314]}}}
{"_id":{"$oid":"59a47287cfa9a3a73e51ec20"},"theaterId":7,"location":{"address":{"street1":"1643 Coun
ty Road B2","city":"Roseville","state":"MN","zipcode":"55113"},"geo":{"type":"Point","coordinates":[
-93.168518,45.01651]}}}
{"_id":{"$oid":"59a47287cfa9a3a73e51ed33"},"theaterId":8,"location":{"address":{"street1":"14141 Ald
rich Ave S","city":"Burnsville","state":"MN","zipcode":"55337"},"geo":{"type":"Point","coordinates":
[-93.288039,44.747404]}}}
{"_id":{"$oid":"59a47286cfa9a3a73e51e786"},"theaterId":10,"location":{"address":{"street1":"1795 Cou
nty Rd D E","city":"Maplewood","state":"MN","zipcode":"55109"},"geo":{"type":"Point","coordinates":[
-93.025986,45.036556]}}}
{"_id":{"$oid":"59a47286cfa9a3a73e51e7e2"},"theaterId":11,"location":{"address":{"street1":"300 Nort
htown Dr Ne","city":"Blaine","state":"MN","zipcode":"55434"},"geo":{"type":"Point","coordinates":[-9
3.261429,45.126179]}}}
{"_id":{"$oid":"59a47286cfa9a3a73e51e7f9"},"theaterId":12,"location":{"address":{"street1":"4130 W D
ivision St","city":"Saint Cloud","state":"MN","zipcode":"56301"},"geo":{"type":"Point","coordinates"
:[-94.209656,45.55275]}}}
{"_id":{"$oid":"59a47286cfa9a3a73e51e801"},"theaterId":13,"location":{"address":{"street1":"1615 38t
h St S","city":"Fargo","state":"ND","zipcode":"58103"},"geo":{"type":"Point","coordinates":[-96.8427
43,46.857113]}}}
{"_id":{"$oid":"59a47287cfa9a3a73e51e866"},"theaterId":14,"location":{"address":{"street1":"4050 Hwy
 52 N","city":"Rochester","state":"MN","zipcode":"55901"},"geo":{"type":"Point","coordinates":[-92.4
96895,44.064365]}}}
{"_id":{"$oid":"59a47287cfa9a3a73e51e890"},"theaterId":15,"location":{"address":{"street1":"8301 3rd
```

Figure 11.1: Contents of output.json file (truncated)

There is another option that can be used for more advanced exports, and that is the query option. The query option allows you to specify a query, using the same format as your standard MongoDB queries. Only documents matching this query will be exported. Using this option in combination with other options like --fields, **--skip**, and **--limit** allows you to define a complete query with formatted output and then export that into a file.

The following is an export that uses the query option to return a specific subset of documents. In this case, we are getting all cinemas with a **theaterId** of **4**.

```
mongoexport --uri=mongodb+srv://USERNAME:PASSWORD@provendocs-fawxo.gcp.
mongodb.net/sample_mflix --query="{theaterId: 4}" --collection=theaters
```

> **NOTE**
>
> On MacOS you may need to wrap the **theaterId** in quotation marks, for example: **--query="{\"theaterId\": 4}"**

We will now see the document we're looking for as follows:

```
2020-08-17T11:22:48.559+1000    connected to: mongodb+srv://
[**REDACTED**]@performancetuning.98afc.gcp.mongodb.net/sample_mflix
{"_id":{"$oid":"59a47287cfa9a3a73e51eb78"},"theaterId":4,"location":
  {"address":{"street1":"13513 Ridgedale
Dr","city":"Hopkins","state":"MN","zipcode":"55305"},"geo":
  {"type":"Point","coordinates":[-93.449539,44.969658]}}}
2020-08-17T11:22:48.893+1000    exported 1 record
```

Let us use these options in the next Exercise.

## EXERCISE 11.01: EXPORTING MONGODB DATA

Before you begin this exercise, let's revisit the movie company from the scenario outlined in the *Introduction* section. Say your client (the cinema company) is going to migrate their existing data, and you're worried about any loss of valuable information. One of the first things you decide to do is export the documents from the database as JSON files, which can be stored in inexpensive cloud storage in case of a disaster. Additionally, you are going to create a different export for each film category.

> **NOTE**
>
> To demonstrate knowledge of **mongoexport**, we will not create an export for each category, but just for a single category. You will also only export the top three documents.

In this exercise, you will use **mongoexport** to create a file called **action_movies. json**, which contains three action movies, sorted by release year. The following steps will help you accomplish the task:

1. Fine-tune your export and save it for later. Create a new file called **Exercise11.01.txt** to store your export command.

2. Next, type the standard **mongoexport** syntax with just the URI and **movies** collection:

```
mongoexport --uri=mongodb+srv://USERNAME:PASSWORD@myAtlas-fawxo.gcp.
mongodb.net/sample_mflix --collection=movies
```

3. Add extra parameters to satisfy your conditions. First, output your export into a file called **action_movies.json**. Use the **--out** parameter as follows:

```
mongoexport --uri=mongodb+srv://USERNAME:PASSWORD@myAtlas-fawxo.gcp.
mongodb.net/sample_mflix --collection=movies --out=action_movies.json
```

4. Next, add your sort condition to sort the movies by release year as per the specifications of this exercise. You can accomplish this using `--sort`:

```
mongoexport --uri=mongodb+srv://USERNAME:PASSWORD@myAtlas-fawxo.gcp.
mongodb.net/sample_mflix --collection=movies --out=action_movies.json
--sort='{released: 1}'
```

5. If you were to run this command at its current intermediary stage, you would encounter the following error:

```
2020-08-17T11:25:51.911+1000      connected to: mongodb+srv://
[**REDACTED**]@performancetuning.98afc.gcp.mongodb.net/sample_mflix
2020-08-17T11:25:52.581+1000      Failed: (OperationFailed) Executor
error during find command :: caused by :: Sort operation used more
than the maximum 33554432 bytes of RAM. Add an index, or specify a
smaller limit.
```

This is because there are a large number of documents that the MongoDB server is trying to sort for us. To improve the performance of your exports and imports, you can limit the number of documents you retrieve, so MongoDB doesn't have to sort so many for you.

6. Add a `--limit` parameter to reduce the number of documents being sorted and satisfy the three-document condition:

```
mongoexport --uri=mongodb+srv://USERNAME:PASSWORD@myAtlas-fawxo.gcp.
mongodb.net/sample_mflix --collection=movies --out=action_movies.
json --sort='{released: 1}' --limit=3
```

Finally, you need to add your query parameter to filter out any documents not in the movie genre.

> **NOTE**
>
> Depending on your operating system and shell, you may have to modify the single and double quotes to ensure the quoted values do not interfere with your shell. For example when using a query against a string, you may have to use double quotes around the filter document and single quotes around the values. For command prompt users, try escaping the double quotes with the backslash character, for example, `query="{\"genres\": \"Action\"}"`

The query is as follows:

```
mongoexport --uri=mongodb+srv://USERNAME:PASSWORD@myAtlas-fawxo.gcp.
mongodb.net/sample_mflix --collection=movies --out=action_movies.
json --sort='{released : 1}' --limit=3 --query="{'genres': 'Action'}"
```

> **NOTE**
>
> On MacOS and Linux, you may need to change the quotation marks around strings within parameters, for example in the preceding query you will need to use: `--query='{"genres": "Action"}'`

7. With your command complete, copy it from your **Exercise11.01.txt** file into your terminal or command prompt to run it:

```
2020-08-18T12:35:42.514+1000    connected to: mongodb+srv://
[**REDACTED**]@performancetuning.98afc.gcp.mongodb.net/sample_mflix
2020-08-18T12:35:42.906+1000    exported 3 records
```

The output looks good so far, but you need to check your output file to ensure the correct documents have been exported. In the directory in which you just executed your command, you should see the new file **action_movies.json**. Open this file and view the contents inside.

> **NOTE**
>
> The plot field is removed to improve the clarity of the output.

You should see the following documents:

```
{"_id":{"$oid":"573a1394f29313caabce0e40"},"num_mflix_comments":1,"genres":["Action","Adventure"],"runtime":105
,"title":"Le Bossu","poster":"https://m.media-amazon.com/images/M/MV5BMzJjNTIwMDAtNmI2NS00N2UxLThmNzYtNmFlYzBhM
jJhMTFjXkEyXkFqcGdeQXVyMjc1NDA2OA@@._V1_SY1000_SX677_AL_.jpg","countries":["France","Italy"],"lastupdated":"201
5-08-10 00:49:05.363000000","languages":["French"],"cast":["Jean Marais","Bourvil","Sabine Sesselmann","Jean Le
 Poulain"],"directors":["Andr┤¿ Hunebelle"],"writers":["Pierre Foucaud","Paul F┤¿val (novel)","Jean Halain","An
dr┤¿ Hunebelle"],"awards":{"wins":1,"nominations":0,"text":"1 win."},"year":1959,"imdb":{"rating":7.0,"votes":6
90,"id":52644},"type":"movie","tomatoes":{"viewer":{"rating":4.0,"numReviews":1},"lastUpdated":{"$date":"2015-0
8-26T18:14:36.000Z"}}}
{"_id":{"$oid":"573a1395f29313caabce2a08"},"plot":"After the Civil War, desperadoes led by a renegade named Rol
lins, following the settlers moving westward, try to drive a wedge in the friendship between the whites and the
 Indians. Apache ...","genres":["Action","Adventure","Western"],"runtime":93,"rated":"APPROVED","title":"Winnet
ou: The Last Shot","num_mflix_comments":1,"poster":"https://m.media-amazon.com/images/M/MV5BMjAxNjczNDcxNV5BMl5
BanBnXkFtZTcwODE0NDkxMQ@@._V1_SY1000_SX677_AL_.jpg","countries":["West Germany","Italy","Yugoslavia"],"fullplot
":"After the Civil War, desperadoes led by a renegade named Rollins, following the settlers moving westward, tr
y to drive a wedge in the friendship between the whites and the Indians. Apache chief Winnetou and his frontier
 friend, Old Shatterhand, do what they can to keep the peace. Rollins' henchmen try to keep Winnetou away from
the warring Jicarillos' chief, White Buffalo, but he fights his way through, only to be confronted by Rollins c
arrying the chief's son, stabbed in the back with Winnetou's knife. Winnetou is accused of the killing. It is u
p to Old Shatterhand to save his friend.","languages":["German"],"cast":["Lex Barker","Pierre Brice","Rik Batta
glia","Ralf Wolter"],"directors":["Harald Reinl"],"writers":["Karl May (novel)","J. Joachim Bartsch (screenplay
)","Harald G. Petersson (screenplay)"],"awards":{"wins":3,"nominations":0,"text":"3 wins."},"lastupdated":"2015
-08-13 01:06:42.600000000","year":1965,"imdb":{"rating":6.7,"votes":1525,"id":59915},"type":"movie","tomatoes":
{"viewer":{"rating":3.9,"numReviews":8},"lastUpdated":{"$date":"2015-08-11T18:42:14.000Z"}}}
{"_id":{"$oid":"573a1396f29313caabce4122"},"plot":"At the end of the 16th century Wallachian ruler Prince Micha
el the Brave overcame the adversity of the Ottoman and Austrian Empires to unite Wallachia, Moldavia and Transy
lvania into one country.","genres":["Action","Biography","Drama"],"runtime":203,"title":"Michael the Brave","co
untries":["Romania","France","Italy"],"fullplot":"An epic fresco depicting the reign (1593-1601) of Mihai P┤¿tr
ascu (better known as \"Mihai Viteazul\" / \"Michael the Brave\"), the famous prince who united the three provi
```

Figure 11.2: Contents of the action_movies.json file (truncated for brevity)

This exercise illustrated the fundamentals required to export your documents from MongoDB in a robust and flexible way. Combining the parameters learned here, most basic exports will now be easy. To master data exports in MongoDB, it is helpful to keep experimenting and learning.

# IMPORTING DATA INTO MONGODB

You now know how to get your collection data out of MongoDB and into an easy-to-use format on disk. But say that you have this file on disk, and you want to share it with someone with their own MongoDB database? This situation is where **mongoimport** comes in handy. As you may have guessed from the name, this command is essentially the reverse of **mongoexport**, and it is designed to take the output of **mongoexport** as an input into **mongoimport**.

However, it is not only data exported from MongoDB that you can use with **mongoimport**. The command supports JSON, CSV and TSV formats, meaning data extracted from other applications or manually created can still be easily added to the database using **mongoimport**. By supporting these widespread file formats, the command becomes an all-purpose way to load bulk data into MongoDB.

As with **mongoexport**, **mongoimport** operates on a single target collection within the specified database. This means that if you wish to import data into multiple collections, you must separate the data into individual files.

Following is an example a complex **mongoimport**. We'll go through the syntax in detail during the next section.

```
mongoimport --uri=mongodb+srv://USERNAME:PASSWORD@myAtlas-fawxo.gcp.
mongodb.net/imports  --collection=oldData --file=old.csv --type=CSV
--headerline --ignoreBlanks --drop
```

## USING MONGOIMPORT

The following is a **mongoimport** command with the fewest possible parameters. This is significantly simpler than preceding command.

```
mongoimport --db=imports --collection=contacts --file=contacts.json
```

This example should also look very similar to some of the snippets we saw in the previous section. It is almost identical to our **mongoexport** syntax, except, instead of providing a location to create a new file using **--out**, we're entering a **--file** parameter which specifies the data we wish to load in. Our database and collection parameters are provided with the same syntax as in the **mongoexport** examples.

As you may have guessed, another similarity that **mongoimport** shares with **mongoexport** is that, by default, it would run against a MongoDB database running on your local machine. We use the same **--uri** parameter to specify that we are loading data into a remote MongoDB server—in this case, on MongoDB Atlas.

> **NOTE**
>
> As with **mongoexport**, the **db** and **uri** parameters are mutually exclusive as the database is defined in the **uri** itself.

The **mongoimport** command, when using the **--uri** parameter, will look as follows:

```
mongoimport --uri=mongodb+srv://USERNAME:PASSWORD@myAtlasServer-fawxo.
gcp.mongodb.net/imports --collection=contacts --file=contacts.json
```

Before you can execute this command against your MongoDB database and import, you require a file containing valid data. Let's create one now. One of the simplest ways to create importable data is to run a **mongoexport**. However, to improve your knowledge of importing files, we'll create one from scratch.

You would begin by creating a file called **contacts.json**. Open the file in a text editor and create some very simple documents. When importing JSON files, each line within the file must contain exactly one document.

The **contacts.json** file should look as follows:

```
//contacts.json
{"name": "Aragorn","location": "New Zealand","job": "Park Ranger"}
{"name": "Frodo","location": "New Zealand","job": "Unemployed"}
{"name": "Ned Kelly","location": "Australia","job": "Outlaw"}
```

Execute the following import:

```
mongoimport --uri=mongodb+srv://USERNAME:PASSWORD@myAtlasServer-fawxo.
gcp.mongodb.net/imports --collection=contacts --file=contacts.json
```

This will result in the following output:

```
2020-08-17T20:10:38.892+1000    connected to: mongodb+srv://
[**REDACTED**]@performancetuning.98afc.g
cp.mongodb.net/imports
2020-08-17T20:10:39.150+1000    3 document(s) imported successfully. 0
document(s) failed to import.
```

You can also use a JSON array format for your file, meaning your import file contains an array of many different JSON documents. In that case, you must specify the **--jsonArray** option in your command. This JSON array structure should be very familiar to you by now, as it matches both the **mongoexport** output as well as the results you receive from MongoDB queries. For example, if your file contains an array as follows:

```
[
    {
        "name": "Aragorn",
        "location": "New Zealand",
        "job": "Park Ranger"
    },
    {
        "name": "Frodo",
        "location": "New Zealand",
```

```
        "job": "Unemployed"
    },
    {
        "name": "Ned Kelly",
        "location": "Australia",
        "job": "Outlaw"
    }
]
```

You could still import the file using the **mongoimport** command with the **--jsonArray** option as follows:

```
mongoimport --uri=mongodb+srv://USERNAME:PASSWORD@myAtlasServer-fawxo.
gcp.mongodb.net/imports --collection=contacts --file=contacts.json
--jsonArray
```

This will result in the following output:

```
2020-08-17T20:10:38.892+1000     connected to: mongodb+srv://
[**REDACTED**]@performancetuning.98afc.g
cp.mongodb.net/imports
2020-08-17T20:10:39.150+1000     3 document(s) imported successfully. 0
document(s) failed to import.
```

> **NOTE**
>
> In the preceding example, you will notice that you can provide **_id** values for documents in the import. If no **_id** is provided, one will be generated for the document. You must ensure that the **_id** you provide is not already used; otherwise, the **mongoimport** command will throw an error.

These two imports have shown us simple ways to get data into our MongoDB database, but let's have a look at what happens when things go wrong. Let's modify our file to specify the **_id** for a few of our documents.

```
[
    {
        "_id": 1,
        "name": "Aragorn",
        "location": "New Zealand",
        "job": "Park Ranger"
    },
    {
```

```
        "name": "Frodo",
        "location": "New Zealand",
        "job": "Unemployed"
    },
    {
        "_id": 2,
        "name": "Ned Kelly",
        "location": "Australia",
        "job": "Outlaw"
    }
]
```

Execute this once, and you should get an output without error.

```
mongoimport --uri=mongodb+srv://USERNAME:PASSWORD@myAtlasServer-fawxo.
gcp.mongodb.net/imports --collection=contacts --file=contacts.json
--jsonArray
```

You will see the following output:

```
2020-08-17T20:12:12.164+1000      connected to: mongodb+srv://
[**REDACTED**]@performancetuning.98afc.g
cp.mongodb.net/imports
2020-08-17T20:12:12.404+1000      3 document(s) imported successfully. 0
document(s) failed to import.
```

Now, if you rerun the same command, you see an error because that **_id** value already exists in your collection.

```
2020-08-17T20:12:29.742+1000      connected to: mongodb+srv://
[**REDACTED**]@performancetuning.98afc.g
cp.mongodb.net/imports
2020-08-17T20:12:29.979+1000      continuing through error: E11000
duplicate key error collection: imp
orts.contacts index: _id_ dup key: { _id: 1 }
2020-08-17T20:12:29.979+1000      continuing through error: E11000
duplicate key error collection: imp
orts.contacts index: _id_ dup key: { _id: 2 }
2020-08-17T20:12:29.979+1000      1 document(s) imported successfully. 2
document(s) failed to import.
```

You can see the error in your output. Another thing you may notice is that the documents without problems are still imported successfully. **mongoimport** will not fail on a single document if you're importing a ten-thousand document file.

Say you did want to update this document without changing its **_id**. You couldn't use this **mongoimport** command because you would receive a duplicate key error every time.

You can log into MongoDB using the mongo shell and manually remove this document before importing, but this would be a slow way to do it. With **mongoimport**, we can use the --drop option to drop the collection before the import takes place. This is a great way to ensure that what exists in your file exists in the collection.

For example, consider that you have the following documents in our collection before our import:

```
MongoDB Enterprise PerformanceTuning-shard-0:PRIMARY> db.contacts.find({})
{ "_id" : ObjectId("5e0c1db3fa8335898940129ca8"), "name": "John Smith"}
{ "_id" : ObjectId("5e0c1db3fa8335898940129ca8"), "name": "Jane Doe"}
{ "_id" : ObjectId("5e0c1db3fa8335898940129ca8"), "name": "May Sue"}
```

Now, run the following **mongoimport** command with **--drop**:

```
mongoimport --uri=mongodb+srv://USERNAME:PASSWORD@myAtlasServer-fawxo.
gcp.mongodb.net/imports --collection=contacts --file=contacts.json
--jsonArray --drop


2020-08-17T20:16:08.280+1000     connected to: mongodb+srv://
[**REDACTED**]@performancetuning.98afc.g
cp.mongodb.net/imports
2020-08-17T20:16:08.394+1000     dropping: imports.contacts
2020-08-17T20:16:08.670+1000     3 document(s) imported successfully. 0
document(s) failed to import.
```

You will see that the collection has the following documents once the command is executed, view these documents using the find command.

```
db.contacts.find({})
```

You should see the following output:

```
{ "_id" : ObjectId("5f3a58e8fd0803fc3dec8cbf"), "name" : "Frodo",
"location" : "New Zealand", "job" : "Unemployed" }
{ "_id" : 1, "name" : "Aragorn", "location" : "New Zealand", "job" :
"Park Ranger" }
{ "_id" : 2, "name" : "Ned Kelly", "location" : "Australia", "job" :
"Outlaw" }
```

In the next section, we will look at the options we can use with **mongoimport**.

## MONGOIMPORT OPTIONS

We now know about the fundamental options you need to use **mongoimport** with the **--uri**, **--collection**, and **--file** parameters. But, just as with **mongoexport** in our last section, there are several additional options you may wish to use when running the command. Many of these options are the same as from **mongoexport**. The following list describes some of the options and their effects.

- **--quiet**: This reduces the amount of output messaging from the import.

- **--drop**: This drops the collection before beginning import.

- **--jsonArray**: A JSON type only, this specifies if the file is in a JSON array format.

- **--type**: This can be either JSON, CSV, or TSV to specify what type of file will be imported, but the default type is JSON.

- **--ignoreBlanks** TSV and CSV only, this will ignore empty fields in your import file.

- **--headerline** : TSV and CSV only, this will assume the first line of your import file is a list of field names.

- **--fields**: TSV and CSV only, this will specify a comma-separated list of keys in your documents for CSV and TSV formats. This is only needed if you do not have a header line.

- **--stopOnError**: If specified, the import will stop on the first error it encounters.

Here is an example with some more of these options used—specifically, a CSV import with a header line. We will also have to ignore blanks so that a document is not given a blank **_id** value.

Here is our **.csv** file, called **contacts.csv**:

```
_id,name,location,job
1,Aragorn,New Zealand,Park Ranger
,Frodo,New Zealand,Unemployed
2,Ned Kelly,Australia,Outlaw
```

We will use the following command to import the CSV:

```
mongoimport --uri=mongodb+srv://USERNAME:PASSWORD@myAtlasServer-fawxo.
gcp.mongodb.net/imports --collection=contacts --file=contacts.csv --drop
--type=CSV --headerline --ignoreBlanks

2020-08-17T20:22:39.750+1000    connected to: mongodb+srv://
[**REDACTED**]@performancetuning.98afc.gcp.mongodb.net/imports
2020-08-17T20:22:39.863+1000    dropping: imports.contacts
2020-08-17T20:22:40.132+1000    3 document(s) imported successfully. 0
document(s) failed to import.
```

The preceding command results in the following documents in our collection:

```
MongoDB Enterprise atlas-nb3biv-shard-0:PRIMARY> db.contacts.find({})
{ "_id" : 2, "name" : "Ned Kelly", "location" : "Australia", "job" :
"Outlaw" }
{ "_id" : 1, "name" : "Aragorn", "location" : "New Zealand", "job" :
"Park Ranger" }
{ "_id" : ObjectId("5f3a5a6fc67ba81a6d4bcf69"), "name" : "Frodo",
"location" : "New Zealand", "job" : "Unemployed" }
```

Of course, these are only some of the more common options you may encounter. There is a full list available in the documentation. It is useful to familiarize yourself with these in case you need to run a more advanced import to a differently configured MongoDB server.

## EXERCISE 11.02: LOADING DATA INTO MONGODB

In this scenario, you have successfully created an export of the clients' data on your local machine. You have set up a new server on a different version and would like to make sure the data imports correctly into the new configuration. Additionally, you have been given some data files from another, older database in CSV format that will be migrated to the new MongoDB server. You want to ensure this different format also imports correctly. With that in mind, your goal is to import two files (shown as follows) into your Atlas database and test that the documents exist in the correct collections.

In this exercise, you will use **mongoimport** to import two files (**old.csv** and **new.json**) into two separate collections (**oldData** and **newData**) and use drop to ensure no leftover documents exist.

This aim can be accomplished by executing the following steps:

1. Fine-tune your import and save it for later. Create a new file called **Exercise11.02.txt** to store your export command.

2. Create your **old.csv** and **new.json** files that contain the data to be imported. Either download the files from GitHub at https://packt.live/2LsgKS3 or copy the following into identical files in your current directory.

   The **old.csv** file should look as follows:

   ```
   _id,title,year,genre
   54234,The King of The Bracelets,1999,Fantasy
   6521,Knife Runner,1977,Science Fiction
   124124,Kingzilla,1543,Horror
   64532,Casabianca,1942,Drama
   23214,Skyhog Day,1882,Comedy
   ```

   The **new.json** file should look as follows:

   ```
   [
        {"_id": 54234,"title": "The King of The Bracelets","year":
   1999,"genre": "Fantasy"},
        {"_id": 6521, "title": "Knife Runner","year": 1977,"genre":
   "Science Fiction"},
        {"
   id": 124124,"title": "Kingzilla","year": 1543,"genre": "Horror"},
        {"
   id": 64532,"title": "Casabianca","year": 1942,"genre": "Drama"},
        {"
   id": 23214,"title": "Skyhog Day","year": 1882,"genre": "Comedy"}
   ]
   ```

3. Enter the standard **mongoimport** syntax into your **Exercise11.02.txt** file, with just the URI, collection, and file location. Import your data into the **"imports"** database, importing the old data first:

   ```
   mongoimport --uri=mongodb+srv://USERNAME:PASSWORD@myAtlas-fawxo.gcp.
   mongodb.net/imports --collection=oldData --file=old.csv
   ```

4. Now, start adding your extra parameters to satisfy the conditions for your CSV file. Specify **type=CSV**:

   ```
   mongoimport --uri=mongodb+srv://USERNAME:PASSWORD@myAtlas-fawxo.gcp.
   mongodb.net/ imports  --collection=oldData --file=old.csv --type=CSV
   ```

5. Next, because you have a header row in your old data, use the **headerline** parameter.

```
mongoimport --uri=mongodb+srv://USERNAME:PASSWORD@myAtlas-fawxo.gcp.
mongodb.net/imports  --collection=oldData --file=old.csv --type=CSV
--headerline
```

6. When you saw a CSV import in some of the examples earlier in the chapter, the **--ignoreBlanks** parameter was used to ensure empty fields were not imported. This is a good practice, so add it here too.

```
mongoimport --uri=mongodb+srv://USERNAME:PASSWORD@myAtlas-fawxo.gcp.
mongodb.net/imports  --collection=oldData --file=old.csv --type=CSV
--headerline --ignoreBlanks
```

7. Finally, for this exercise, you need to make sure you don't import on top of the existing data, as this may cause conflicts. To ensure your data is imported cleanly, use the **--drop** parameter as follows:

```
mongoimport --uri=mongodb+srv://USERNAME:PASSWORD@myAtlas-fawxo.gcp.
mongodb.net/imports  --collection=oldData --file=old.csv --type=CSV
--headerline --ignoreBlanks --drop
```

8. That should be everything you need for your CSV import. Start writing your JSON import  by copying your existing command on to a new line and then removing the CSV specific parameters.

```
mongoimport --uri=mongodb+srv://USERNAME:PASSWORD@myAtlas-fawxo.gcp.
mongodb.net/imports  --collection=oldData --file=old.csv --drop
```

9. Now, change the **file** and **collection** parameters by importing your **new. json** file into a **newData** collection as follows:

```
mongoimport --uri=mongodb+srv://USERNAME:PASSWORD@myAtlas-fawxo.gcp.
mongodb.net/imports  --drop --collection=newData --file=new.json
```

10. You can see that the data in your **new.json** file is in a JSON array format, so add the matching parameter, as follows:

```
mongoimport --uri=mongodb+srv://USERNAME:PASSWORD@myAtlas-fawxo.gcp.
mongodb.net/imports --collection=newData --file=new.json --drop
--jsonArray
```

11. You should now have the following two commands in your **Exercise11.02. txt** file.

```
mongoimport --uri=mongodb+srv://USERNAME:PASSWORD@myAtlas-fawxo.gcp.
mongodb.net/imports  --collection=newData --file=new.json --drop
--jsonArray
```

```
mongoimport --uri=mongodb+srv://USERNAME:PASSWORD@myAtlas-fawxo.gcp.
mongodb.net/imports  --collection=oldData --file=old.csv --type=CSV
--headerline --ignoreBlanks --drop
```

12. Run your **newData** import using the following command:

```
mongoimport --uri=mongodb+srv://USERNAME:PASSWORD@myAtlas-fawxo.
gcp.mongodb.net/imports  --collection=newData --file=new.json --drop
--jsonArray
```

The output is as follows:

```
2020-08-17T20:25:21.622+1000    connected to: mongodb+srv://
[**REDACTED**]@performancetuning.98afc.gcp.mongodb.net/imports
2020-08-17T20:25:21.734+1000    dropping: imports.newData
2020-08-17T20:25:22.019+1000    5 document(s) imported successfully.
0 document(s) failed to import.
```

13. Now, execute the **oldData** import as follows:

```
mongoimport --uri=mongodb+srv://USERNAME:PASSWORD@myAtlas-fawxo.gcp.
mongodb.net/imports  --collection=oldData --file=old.csv --type=CSV
--headerline --ignoreBlanks --drop
```

The output is as follows:

```
2020-08-17T20:26:09.588+1000    connected to: mongodb+srv://
[**REDACTED**]@performancetuning.98afc.gcp.mongodb.net/imports
2020-08-17T20:26:09.699+1000    dropping: imports.oldData
2020-08-17T20:26:09.958+1000    5 document(s) imported successfully.
0 document(s) failed to import.
```

14. Check the two new collections in MongoDB by running the following command:

```
show collections
```

The output is as follows:

```
MongoDB Enterprise atlas-nb3biv-shard-0:PRIMARY> show collections
contacts
newData
oldData
MongoDB Enterprise atlas-nb3biv-shard-0:PRIMARY> db.newData.find({})
{ "_id" : 54234, "title" : "The King of The Bracelets", "year" : 1999, "genre" : "Fantasy" }
{ "_id" : 6521, "title" : "Knife Runner", "year" : 1977, "genre" : "Science Fiction" }
{ "_id" : 124124, "title" : "Kingzilla", "year" : 1543, "genre" : "Horror" }
{ "_id" : 64532, "title" : "Casabianca", "year" : 1942, "genre" : "Drama" }
{ "_id" : 23214, "title" : "Skyhog Day", "year" : 1882, "genre" : "Comedy" }
MongoDB Enterprise atlas-nb3biv-shard-0:PRIMARY> db.oldData.find({})
{ "_id" : 54234, "title" : "The King of The Bracelets", "year" : 1999, "genre" : "Fantasy" }
{ "_id" : 23214, "title" : "Skyhog Day", "year" : 1882, "genre" : "Comedy" }
{ "_id" : 6521, "title" : "Knife Runner", "year" : 1977, "genre" : "Science Fiction" }
{ "_id" : 124124, "title" : "Kingzilla", "year" : 1543, "genre" : "Horror" }
{ "_id" : 64532, "title" : "Casabianca", "year" : 1942, "genre" : "Drama" }
```

Figure 11.3: Displaying the new collections

First, we learned how to export our data from our MongoDB server. Now we are able to take that external data and enter it back into MongoDB using the import command. By combining these two simple commands, we can also shift data between instances of MongoDB or create data using external tools before importing them into MongoDB.

# BACKING UP AN ENTIRE DATABASE

Using **mongoexport**, we could theoretically take an entire MongoDB server and extract all the data in each database and collection. However, we would have to do this with one collection at a time, ensuring that the files correctly mapped to the original database and collection. Doing this manually is possible but difficult. A script could accomplish this reliably for an entire MongoDB server even with hundreds of collections

Fortunately, along with **mongoimport** and **mongoexport**, the MongoDB tools package also provides a tool for exporting the entire contents of a database. This utility is called **mongodump**. This command creates a backup of the entire MongoDB instance. All you need to provide is the URI (or host and port numbers), and the **mongodump** command does the rest. This export creates a binary file that can be restored using **mongorestore** (a command covered in the next section). By combining **mongodump** and **mongorestore**, you have a reliable way of backing up, restoring, and migrating your MongoDB databases across different hardware and software configurations.

## USING MONGODUMP

The following is a **mongodump** command in its simplest possible form:

```
mongodump
```

Interestingly enough, you can run **mongodump** without a single parameter. This is because the only piece of information the command needs to use is the location of your MongoDB server. If no URI or host is specified, it will attempt to create a backup of a MongoDB server running on your local system.

We can specify a URI using the `--uri` parameter to specify the location of our MongoDB server.

> **NOTE**
>
> As with **mongoexport**, the `--db`/`--host` and `--uri` parameters are mutually exclusive.

If we did have a local MongoDB server running, however, this is the sort of output we may receive:

```
2020-08-18T12:38:43.091+1000        writing imports.newData to
2020-08-18T12:38:43.091+1000        writing imports.contacts to
2020-08-18T12:38:43.091+1000        writing imports.oldData to
2020-08-18T12:38:43.310+1000        done dumping imports.newData (5
documents)
2020-08-18T12:38:44.120+1000        done dumping imports.contacts (3
documents)
2020-08-18T12:38:44.120+1000        done dumping imports.oldData (5
documents)
```

At the end of this command, we can see there is a new folder in our directory containing the dump of our database. By default, **mongodump** exports everything in our MongoDB server. However, we can be more selective with our exports, and we see an example of this in the next section.

## MONGODUMP OPTIONS

The **mongodump** command requires very minimal options to function; in most cases, you may only be using the `--uri` parameter. However, there are several options we can use to get the most out of this utility command. Following is a list of some of the most useful options.

- `--quiet`: This reduces the amount of output messaging from the dump.

- `--out`: This allows you to specify a different location for the export to be written to disk, by default it will create a directory called "dump" in the same directory the command is run.

- `--db`: This allows you to specify a single database for the command to backup, by default it will back up all databases.

- **--collection**: This allows you to specify a single collection to backup, by default it will back up all collections.

- **--excludeCollection**: This allows you to specify a collection to exclude from the backup.

- **--query**: This allows you to specify a query document which will limit the documents being backed up to only those matching the query.

- **--gzip**: If enabled, the output of the export will be a compressed file in **.gz** format instead of a directory.

We'll look at creating a dump of a single database, with users and roles, to a specific location on disk. Because we are doing a single database dump, we can use **--uri** with the database we want to use.

```
mongodump --uri=mongodb+srv://USERNAME:PASSWORD@myAtlas-fawxo.gcp.
mongodb.net/imports --out="./backups"
        2020-08-18T12:39:51.457+1000     writing imports.newData to
2020-08-18T12:39:51.457+1000     writing imports.contacts to
2020-08-18T12:39:51.457+1000     writing imports.oldData to
2020-08-18T12:39:51.697+1000     done dumping imports.newData (5
documents)
2020-08-18T12:39:52.472+1000     done dumping imports.contacts (3
documents)
2020-08-18T12:39:52.493+1000     done dumping imports.oldData (5
documents)
```

As you can see in the preceding screenshot, only the collections existing in our specified database were exported. You can even see this if you have a look at the folder containing our exports:

```
⌐ ~/backups
└ ls

    imports/


⌐ ~/backups
└ ls imports

    contacts.bson          contacts.metadata.json newData.bson
    newData.metadata.json  oldData.bson           oldData.metadata.json
```

You can see in the imports directory that two files are created for each collection in the dump, a **.bson** file containing our data and a **.metadata.json** file for the collection metadata. All **mongodump** results will match this format.

Next, use your **--query** parameter to dump only specific documents in a collection. You can specify your collection using a standard query document. For example, consider the following command on Windows:

```
mongodump --uri=mongodb+srv://USERNAME:PASSWORD@myAtlasServer-
fawxo.gcp.mongodb.net/sample_mflix --collection="movies" --out="./
backups" --query="{genres: 'Action'}"
```

On MacOS/Linux, you will have to modify the quotation marks to the following:

```
mongodump --uri=mongodb+srv://USERNAME:PASSWORD@myAtlasServer-
fawxo.gcp.mongodb.net/sample_mflix --collection="movies" --out="./
backups" --query='{"genres": "Action"}'
```

The output is as follows:

```
2020-08-18T12:57:06.533+1000        writing sample_mflix.movies to
2020-08-18T12:57:07.258+1000        sample_mflix.movies   101
2020-08-18T12:57:09.109+1000        sample_mflix.movies   2539
2020-08-18T12:57:09.110+1000        done dumping sample_mflix.movies (2539
documents)
```

The movies collection has over 20,000 documents in it, but we have exported only the **2539** matching documents.

Now, execute this same export without the **--query** parameter:

```
mongodump --uri=mongodb+srv://USERNAME:PASSWORD@myAtlasServer-fawxo.gcp.
mongodb.net/sample_mflix --collection="movies" --out="./backups"
```

The output is as follows:

```
2020-08-18T12:57:45.263+1000        writing sample_mflix.movies to
2020-08-18T12:57:45.900+1000        [........................]  sample_mflix.
movies   101/23531   (0.4%)
2020-08-18T12:57:48.891+1000        [........................]  sample_mflix.
movies   101/23531   (0.4%)
2020-08-18T12:57:51.894+1000        [##########..............]  sample_mflix.
movies   10564/23531   (44.9%
)
2020-08-18T12:57:54.895+1000        [##########..............]  sample_mflix.
movies   10564/23531   (44.9%)
2020-08-18T12:57:57.550+1000        [########################]  sample_mflix.
movies   23531/23531   (100.0%)
2020-08-18T12:57:57.550+1000        done dumping sample_mflix.movies (23531
documents)
```

We can see in the preceding output that the number of documents dumped is significantly higher without the **--query** parameter, meaning we have reduced the number of documents exported from our collection to only those matching the query.

As with the commands we learned earlier, these options only represent a small subset of the parameters you can provide to **mongodump**. By combining and experimenting with these options, you will be able to create a robust backup and snapshot solution for your MongoDB server.

By using **mongoimport** and **mongoexport**, you have been able to get specific collections in and out of a database easily. However, as part of the backup strategy for your MongoDB server, you may want to back up the entire state of your MongoDB database. In the next exercise, we will create a dump of only the **sample_mflix** database, rather than creating a larger dump of the many different databases we may have within our MongoDB server.

## EXERCISE 11.03: BACKING UP MONGODB

In this exercise, you will use **mongodump** to create a backup of the **sample_mflix** database. Export the data to a **.gz** file in a folder called **movies_backup**.

Perform the following steps to complete this exercise:

1. To fine-tune your import and save it for later, create a new file called **Exercise11.03.txt** to store your **mongodump** command.

2. Next, type the standard **mongodump** syntax with just the **--uri** parameter set. Remember, the **--uri** includes the target database within it.

```
mongodump --uri=mongodb+srv://USERNAME:PASSWORD@myAtlas-fawxo.gcp.
mongodb.net/sample_mflix
```

3. Next, add the parameter which specifies the location your dump should be saved to. In this case, that is a folder called **movies_backup**:

```
mongodump --uri=mongodb+srv://USERNAME:PASSWORD@myAtlas-fawxo.gcp.
mongodb.net/sample_mflix --out=movies_backup
```

4. Finally, to automatically place your dump file in a **.gz** file, use the **--gzip** parameter and run the command.

```
mongodump --uri=mongodb+srv://USERNAME:PASSWORD@myAtlas-fawxo.gcp.
mongodb.net/sample_mflix --out=movies_backup --gzip
```

> **NOTE**
>
> Because this command will dump the entire **sample_mflix** database, it may take a little bit of time depending on your internet connection.

Once the command executes, you should see output similar to the following screenshot:

```
2020-08-18T12:59:03.331+1000    writing sample_mflix.comments to
2020-08-18T12:59:03.331+1000    writing sample_mflix.theaters to
2020-08-18T12:59:03.331+1000    writing sample_mflix.movies to
2020-08-18T12:59:03.331+1000    writing sample_mflix.users to
2020-08-18T12:59:04.750+1000    done dumping sample_mflix.users (185 documents)
2020-08-18T12:59:04.750+1000    writing sample_mflix.movies_top_romance to
2020-08-18T12:59:04.983+1000    done dumping sample_mflix.movies_top_romance (5 documents)
2020-08-18T12:59:04.983+1000    writing sample_mflix.most_commented_movies to
2020-08-18T12:59:05.157+1000    done dumping sample_mflix.theaters (1564 documents)
2020-08-18T12:59:05.157+1000    writing sample_mflix.sessions to
2020-08-18T12:59:05.212+1000    done dumping sample_mflix.most_commented_movies (5 documents)
2020-08-18T12:59:05.422+1000    done dumping sample_mflix.sessions (1 document)
2020-08-18T12:59:05.723+1000    [........................]  sample_mflix.comments  101/50303   (0.2%)
2020-08-18T12:59:05.723+1000    [........................]   sample_mflix.movies   101/23531   (0.4%)
2020-08-18T12:59:05.723+1000
2020-08-18T12:59:08.677+1000    [########################]  sample_mflix.comments  50303/50303  (100.0%)
2020-08-18T12:59:08.677+1000    done dumping sample_mflix.comments (50303 documents)
2020-08-18T12:59:08.723+1000    [........................]  sample_mflix.movies   101/23531   (0.4%)
2020-08-18T12:59:11.724+1000    [........................]  sample_mflix.movies   101/23531   (0.4%)
2020-08-18T12:59:14.724+1000    [##########..............]  sample_mflix.movies  10564/23531  (44.9%)
2020-08-18T12:59:17.723+1000    [##########..............]  sample_mflix.movies  10564/23531  (44.9%)
2020-08-18T12:59:20.725+1000    [####################....]  sample_mflix.movies  20708/23531  (88.0%)
2020-08-18T12:59:21.683+1000    [########################]  sample_mflix.movies  23531/23531  (100.0%)
2020-08-18T12:59:21.683+1000    done dumping sample_mflix.movies (23531 documents)
```

Figure 11.4: Output after the mongodump command is executed

5. Check your dump directory. You can see all the **mongodump** data has been written into the correct directory.

```
└ ls movies_backup
    sample_mflix/


└ ls movies_backup/sample_mflix
    comments.bson.gz                      comments.metadata.json.gz
    most_commented_movies.bson.gz         most_commented_movies.
metadata.json.gz
    movies.bson.gz                        movies.metadata.json.gz
    movies_top_romance.bson.gz            movies_top_romance.
metadata.json.gz
    sessions.bson.gz                      sessions.metadata.json.gz
    theaters.bson.gz                      theaters.metadata.json.gz
    users.bson.gz                         users.metadata.json.gz
```

Over the course of this exercise, you have learned how to write a **mongodump** command that will correctly create a compressed backup of your database. You will now be able to integrate this technique as part of a database migration or backup strategy.

# RESTORING A MONGODB DATABASE

In the previous section, we learned how to create a backup of an entire MongoDB database using **mongodump**. However, these exports would not be beneficial in our backup strategy unless we possess a method for loading them back into a MongoDB server. The command that complements **mongodump** by putting our export back into the Database is **mongorestore**.

Unlike **mongoimport** which allows us to import commonly used formats into MongoDB, **mongorestore** is only used to importing **mongodump** results. This means it is most commonly used for restoring most or all of a database to a specific state. The **mongorestore** command is ideal for restoring a dump after a disaster or for migrating an entire MongoDB instance to a new configuration.

When put in combination with our other commands, it should be clear that **mongorestore** completes the import and export lifecycle. With the three commands (**mongoimport**, **mongoexport**, and **mongodump**), we have learned we can export collection-level data, import collection-level data, export at the server level, and now finally, with **mongorestore**, we can import server-level information.

## USING MONGORESTORE

As with the other commands, let's have a look at a simple implementation of the **mongorestore** command.

```
mongorestore .\dump\
```

Or on MacOS/Linux, you can enter the following:

```
mongorestore ./dump/
```

The only required parameter we need to pass in is the location of the dump we are restoring. However, as you may have guessed from our other commands, by default **mongorestore** attempts to restore the backup to the local system.

> **NOTE**
>
> The dump location does not require a **--parameter** format and, instead, can be passed in as the last value of the command.

Here again, we can specify a URI using the **--uri** parameter to specify the location of our MongoDB server.

As an example, let's say that we did have a local MongoDB server running. To complete a restore we would need a previously created dump . Here is the dump command based off *Exercise 11.03, Backing up MongoDB*:

```
mongodump --uri=mongodb+srv://USERNAME:PASSWORD@myAtlas-fawxo.gcp.
mongodb.net/imports --out=./dump
```

If we now run **mongorestore** against this dump using the **--drop** option, you might see an output similar to the following:

```
> mongorestore --uri=mongodb+srv://testUser:DBEnvy2016@performancetuning.98afc.gcp.mongodb.net/imports  --drop
./dump
2020-08-18T13:09:43.221+1000    preparing collections to restore from
2020-08-18T13:09:43.451+1000    reading metadata for imports.newData from dump/imports/newData.metadata.json
2020-08-18T13:09:43.599+1000    restoring imports.newData from dump/imports/newData.bson
2020-08-18T13:09:43.720+1000    no indexes to restore
2020-08-18T13:09:43.720+1000    finished restoring imports.newData (5 documents, 0 failures)
2020-08-18T13:09:44.259+1000    reading metadata for imports.oldData from dump/imports/oldData.metadata.json
2020-08-18T13:09:44.266+1000    reading metadata for imports.contacts from dump/imports/contacts.metadata.json
2020-08-18T13:09:44.391+1000    restoring imports.oldData from dump/imports/oldData.bson
2020-08-18T13:09:44.400+1000    restoring imports.contacts from dump/imports/contacts.bson
2020-08-18T13:09:44.508+1000    no indexes to restore
2020-08-18T13:09:44.508+1000    finished restoring imports.oldData (5 documents, 0 failures)
2020-08-18T13:09:44.528+1000    no indexes to restore
2020-08-18T13:09:44.529+1000    finished restoring imports.contacts (3 documents, 0 failures)
2020-08-18T13:09:44.529+1000    13 document(s) restored successfully. 0 document(s) failed to restore.
```

Figure 11.5: Output after mongorestore is run using the –drop option

As you would expect, this output should be most similar to the output from **mongoimport**, telling us exactly how many documents and indexes were restored from the dump file. If your use case is to restore as part of a backup strategy, this simple command with minimal parameters is all you need.

By default, **mongorestore** restores every database, collection and document in the targeted dump. If you wish to be more specific with your restore, there are several handy options which allow you to restore only specific collections or even rename collections during the restore. Examples of these options are provided in the next section.

## THE MONGORESTORE OPTIONS

Like **mongodump**, the **mongorestore** command can satisfy most use cases with just its fundamental parameters such as **--uri** and the location of the dump file. If you wish to accomplish a more specific type of restore, you can use some of the following options:

- **--quiet**: This reduces the amount of output messaging from the dump.

- **--drop**: Similar to **mongoimport**, the **--drop** option will drop the collections to be restored before restoring them, allowing you to ensure no old data remains after the command has run.

- **--dryRun**: This allows you to see the output of running a **mongorestore** without actually changing the information in the database, this is an excellent way to test your command before executing potentially dangerous operations.

- **--stopOnError**: If enabled, the process stops as soon as a single error occurs.

- **--nsInclude**: Instead of providing a database and collection specifically, this option allows you to define which namespaces (databases and collections) should be imported from the dump file. We will see an example of this later in the chapter.

- **--nsExclude**: This is the complimentary option for **nsInclude**, allowing you to provide a namespace pattern that is not imported when running the restore. There is an example of this in the next section.

- **--nsFrom**: Using the same namespace pattern as in **nsInclude** and **nsExclude**, this parameter can be used with **--nsTo** to provide a mapping of namespaces in the export to new namespaces in the restored backup. This allows you to change the names of collections during your restore.

Now, let us look at some examples of these options being used. Note that for these examples, we are using the dump file created in the previous section. As a reminder, this is the command required to create this dump file:

```
mongodump --uri=mongodb+srv://USERNAME:PASSWORD@myAtlas-fawxo.gcp.
mongodb.net/sample_mflix --out=dump
```

Firstly, assume you have a full **mongodump** created from the **sample_mflix** database. The following is an example of the command required to restore just a subset of our collections. You may notice the parameter is in the format of **{database}.{collection}**, but you can use the wild-star (**\***) operator to match all values. In the following example, we are including any collections that match the namespace **"sample_mflix.movies"** (only the movies collection of the **sample_mflix** database).

```
mongorestore --uri=mongodb+srv://USERNAME:PASSWORD@myAtlasServer-fawxo.
gcp.mongodb.net --drop --nsInclude="sample_mflix.movies" dump
```

Once this command finishes running, you should see an output similar to the following:

```
2020-08-18T13:12:28.204+1000     [###################.....]    sample_mflix.
movies   7.53MB/9.06MB   (83.2%)
2020-08-18T13:12:31.203+1000     [######################.]    sample_mflix.
movies   9.04MB/9.06MB   (99.7%)
2020-08-18T13:12:33.896+1000     [#######################]    sample_mflix.
movies   9.06MB/9.06MB   (100.0%)
2020-08-18T13:12:33.896+1000     no indexes to restore

2020-08-18T13:12:33.902+1000     finished restoring sample_mflix.movies
(6017 documents, 0 failures)
2020-08-18T13:12:33.902+1000     6017 document(s) restored successfully. 0
document(s) failed to restore.
```

In the output, you can see that only the matching namespaces are restored. Now let's examine how the **nsFrom** and **nsTo** parameters can be used to rename collections, using the same format as in the preceding example. We will rename collections in the **sample_mflix** database to the same collection name but in a new database called backup:

```
mongorestore --uri=mongodb+srv://USERNAME:PASSWORD@myAtlasServer-fawxo.
gcp.mongodb.net --drop --nsFrom="sample_mflix.*" --nsTo="backup.*" dump
```

Once execution of this command is complete, the final few lines should look similar to the following:

```
2020-08-18T13:13:54.152+1000     [#################........]     backup.
movies   6.16MB/9.06MB   (68.0%)
2020-08-18T13:13:54.152+1000
2020-08-18T13:13:56.916+1000     [#######################]    backup.
comments   4.35MB/4.35MB   (100.0%)
2020-08-18T13:13:56.916+1000     no indexes to restore
2020-08-18T13:13:56.916+1000     finished restoring backup.comments (16017
documents, 0 failures)
2020-08-18T13:13:57.153+1000     [###################.....]    backup.movies
```

```
7.53MB/9.06MB    (83.1%)
2020-08-18T13:14:00.152+1000    [#####################.]   backup.movies
9.04MB/9.06MB    (99.7%)
2020-08-18T13:14:02.929+1000    [######################]   backup.movies
9.06MB/9.06MB    (100.0%)
2020-08-18T13:14:02.929+1000    no indexes to restore
2020-08-18T13:14:02.929+1000    finished restoring backup.movies (6017
documents, 0 failures)
2020-08-18T13:14:02.929+1000    23807 document(s) restored successfully.
0 document(s) failed to restore.
```

Now, if we observe the collections in our MongoDB database, we will see that the **sample_mflix** collections exist in a database called **backup** as well, for example:

```
MongoDB Enterprise atlas-nb3biv-shard-0:PRIMARY> use backup
switched to db backup
MongoDB Enterprise atlas-nb3biv-shard-0:PRIMARY> show collections
comments
most_commented_movies
movies
movies_top_romance
sessions
theaters
users
```

Finally, let's have a quick look at how the **dryRun** parameter works. Take a look at the following command:

```
mongorestore --uri=mongodb+srv://USERNAME:PASSWORD@myAtlasServer-fawxo.
gcp.mongodb.net --drop --nsFrom="imports.*" --nsTo="backup.*" --dryRun .\
dump\
```

You will notice an output about the command preparing the restore. However, it will not load any data. None of the underlying data in MongoDB has changed. This serves as an excellent way to make sure your command will run without error before executing it.

The **mongorestore** command completes our four commands, that is, **mongoimport**, **mongoexport**, **mongodump**, and **mongorestore**. Although it is straightforward to use **mongorestore**, if your backup strategy has a more complicated setup, you may need to use multiple options and to refer the documentation.

## EXERCISE 11.04: RESTORING MONGODB DATA

In the previous exercise, you used **mongodump** to create a backup of the **sample_mflix** database. As part of the backup strategy for your MongoDB server, you now need to place this data back into the database. In this exercise, pretend that the database you exported from and imported to are different databases. So, to prove to the client that the backup strategy works, you will use **mongorestore** to import that dump back into a different namespace.

> **NOTE**
>
> You need to create a dump from *Exercise 11.03*, *Backing up MongoDB*, before completing this exercise.

In this exercise, you will use **mongorestore** to restore the **sample_mflix** database from the **movies_backup** dump created in the previous exercise, changing the namespace of each collection to **backup_mflix**.

1.  Fine-tune your import and save it for later. Create a new file called **Exercise11.04.txt** to store your restore command.

2.  Make sure the **movies_backup** dump from *Exercise 11.03*, *Backing up MongoDB*, is in your current directory as well. Otherwise, you can create a new backup using the following command:

```
mongodump --uri=mongodb+srv://USERNAME:PASSWORD@myAtlas-fawxo.gcp.
mongodb.net/sample_mflix --out=./movies_backup --gzip
```

3.  Next, type the standard **mongorestore** syntax with just the URI and location of the dump file being provided. Remember, the URI includes the target database within it:

```
mongorestore --uri=mongodb+srv://USERNAME:PASSWORD@myAtlas-fawxo.gcp.
mongodb.net ./movies_backup
```

4.  Since the dump file is in **gzip** format, you also need to add the **--gzip** parameter to your restore command so that it can decompress the data.

```
mongorestore --uri=mongodb+srv://USERNAME:PASSWORD@myAtlas-fawxo.gcp.
mongodb.net --gzip ./movies_backup
```

5. To ensure the restore ends up with a clean result, use your **--drop** parameter to drop the relevant collections before you try and restore them:

```
mongorestore --uri=mongodb+srv://USERNAME:PASSWORD@myAtlas-fawxo.gcp.
mongodb.net --gzip --drop ./movies_backup
```

6. Now, add the parameters that modify your namespace. Because you are restoring a dump of the **sample_mflix** database, **"sample_mflix"** will be the value of your **nsFrom** parameter:

```
mongorestore --uri=mongodb+srv://USERNAME:PASSWORD@myAtlas-fawxo.gcp.
mongodb.net --nsFrom="sample_mflix.*" --gzip --drop ./movies_backup
```

7. This use case dictates that these collections will be restored in a database named **backup_mflix**. Provide this new namespace with the **nsTo** parameter as follows.

```
mongorestore --uri=mongodb+srv://USERNAME:PASSWORD@myAtlas-fawxo.
gcp.mongodb.net --nsFrom="sample_mflix.*" --nsTo="backup_mflix.*"
--gzip --drop ./movies_backup
```

8. Your command is now complete. Copy and paste this code into your Terminal or Command Prompt and run it. There will be a lot of output to show you the progress of the restore, but at the end, you should see an output like the following:

```
2020-08-18T13:18:08.862+1000    [####################....]   backup_
mflix.movies  10.2MB/11.7MB  (86.7%)
2020-08-18T13:18:11.862+1000    [####################...]   backup_
mflix.movies  10.7MB/11.7MB  (90.8%)
2020-08-18T13:18:14.865+1000    [####################..]   backup_
mflix.movies  11.1MB/11.7MB  (94.9%)
2020-08-18T13:18:17.866+1000    [####################.]   backup_
mflix.movies  11.6MB/11.7MB  (98.5%)
2020-08-18T13:18:20.217+1000    [####################]   backup_
mflix.movies  11.7MB/11.7MB  (100.0%)
2020-08-18T13:18:20.217+1000    restoring indexes for collection
backup_mflix.movies from metadata
2020-08-18T13:18:26.389+1000    finished restoring backup_mflix.movies
(23531 documents, 0 failures)
2020-08-18T13:18:26.389+1000    75594 document(s) restored
successfully. 0 document(s) failed to restore.
```

From reading the output, you can see that the restoration completed, restoring each existing collection into a new database titled **backup_mflix**. The output will even tell you exactly how many documents were written as part of the restore. For example, **23541** documents were restored into the **movies** collection.

Now if you log into your server with the mongo shell, you should be able to see your newly restored **backup_mflix** database and relevant collections as follows:

```
MongoDB Enterprise atlas-nb3biv-shard-0:PRIMARY> use backup_mflix
switched to db backup_mflix
MongoDB Enterprise atlas-nb3biv-shard-0:PRIMARY> show collections
comments
most_commented_movies
movies
movies_top_romance
sessions
theaters
users
```

And that's it. You have successfully restored your backup into the MongoDB server. With your working knowledge of **mongorestore**, you will now be able to backup, and migrate entire MongoDB databases or servers efficiently. As noted earlier in this chapter, you might have been able to manage this same task with **mongoimport**, but being able to use **mongodump** and **mongorestore** will make your task significantly simpler.

With the four key commands you've learned about in this chapter (**mongoexport**, **mongoimport**, **mongodump** and **monogrestore**), you should now be able to accomplish the majority of backup, migration and restoration tasks that you will encounter when working with MongoDB.

## ACTIVITY 11.01: BACKUP AND RESTORE IN MONGODB

Your client (the cinema company) already has several scripts that run nightly to export, import, backup, and restore data. They run both backups and exports to ensure there are redundant copies of the data. However, due to their lack of experience with MongoDB, these commands are not functioning correctly. To resolve this, they have asked you to assist them with fine-tuning their backup strategy. Follow these steps to complete this activity:

> **NOTE**
>
> The four commands in this activity must be run in the correct order, as the **import** and **restore** commands depend on the output from the **export** and **dump** commands.

9. **Export**: Export all theater data, with location and **theaterId** fields, sorted by **theaterId**, into a CSV file called **theaters.csv**:

```
mongoexport --uri=mongodb+srv://USERNAME:PASSWORD@myAtlas-fawxo.
gcp.mongodb.net/sample_mflix --db=sample_mflix --collection=theaters
--out="theaters.csv" --type=csv --sort='{theaterId: 1}'
```

10. **Import**: Import the **theaters.csv** file into a new collection called **theaters_import**:

```
mongoimport --uri=mongodb+srv://USERNAME:PASSWORD@myAtlas-fawxo.gcp.
mongodb.net/imports --collection=theaters_import --file=theaters.csv
```

11. **Dump**: Dump every collection except the **theaters** collection into a folder called **backups** in **gzip** format:

```
mongodump --uri=mongodb+srv://USERNAME:PASSWORD@myAtlas-fawxo.gcp.
mongodb.net/sample_mflix --out=./backups -gz --nsExclude=theaters
```

12. **Restore**: Restore the dump in the backups folder. Each collection should be restored into a database called **sample_mflix_backup**:

```
mongorestore --uri=mongodb+srv://USERNAME:PASSWORD@myAtlas-fawxo.gcp.
mongodb.net --from="sample_mflix" --to="backup_mflix_backup" --drop ./
backups
```

Your goal is to take the provided scripts from the client, determine what is wrong with these scripts, and fix these problems. You can test that these scripts are running correctly on your own MongoDB server.

You can complete this objective in several ways, but remember what we have learned throughout the chapter and attempt to create simple, easy to use code. The following steps will help you to complete this task:

1. The target database is specified twice, try removing the redundant parameter.

2. Rerun the **export** command. We are missing an option specific to the CSV format. Add this parameter to ensure we export the **theaterId** and location fields.

   Now looking at the **import** command, you should immediately notice there are some missing parameters required for CSV imports.

3. Firstly for the **dump** command, one of the options is not correct; run the command for the hint.

4. Secondly, the **nsInclude** option is not available for the dump command, as this is a **mongorestore** option. Replace it with the appropriate option for **mongodump**.

5. In the **restore** command, there are some options with incorrect names. Fix these names.

6. Also in the **restore** command, restore a **gzip** format dump from the preceding command. Add an option to your restore command to support this format.

7. Finally, in the **restore** command, look at values of the **nsFrom** and **nsTo** options and check whether they are in the correct namespace format.

To test your results, run the four resulting commands in order (export, import, dump, restore.)

The output from the **mongoexport** command would look as follows:

```
2020-08-18T13:21:29.778+1000      connected to: mongodb+srv://
[**REDACTED**]@performancetuning.98afc.gcp.mongodb.net/sample_mflix
2020-08-18T13:21:30.891+1000      exported 1564 records
```

The output from the **mongoimport** command will look as follows:

```
2020-08-18T13:22:20.720+1000      connected to: mongodb+srv://
[**REDACTED**]@performancetuning.98afc.g
cp.mongodb.net/imports
2020-08-18T13:22:22.817+1000      1564 document(s) imported successfully. 0
document(s) failed to import.
```

The output from the **mongodump** command will look as follows:

```
2020-08-18T13:33:14.575+1000    writing sample_mflix.comments to
2020-08-18T13:33:14.576+1000    writing sample_mflix.users to
2020-08-18T13:33:14.576+1000    writing sample_mflix.movies to
2020-08-18T13:33:14.834+1000    done dumping sample_mflix.users (183 documents)
2020-08-18T13:33:17.211+1000    [........................]  sample_mflix.comments  101/50304  (0.2%)
2020-08-18T13:33:17.211+1000    [........................]   sample_mflix.movies  101/23539  (0.4%)
2020-08-18T13:33:17.211+1000
2020-08-18T13:33:19.010+1000    [########################]  sample_mflix.comments  50304/50304  (100.0%)
2020-08-18T13:33:19.011+1000    done dumping sample_mflix.comments (50304 documents)
2020-08-18T13:33:20.213+1000    [#######.................]  sample_mflix.movies  7623/23539  (32.4%)
2020-08-18T13:33:23.212+1000    [#########.............]  sample_mflix.movies  10574/23539  (44.9%)
2020-08-18T13:33:25.123+1000    [########################]  sample_mflix.movies  23539/23539  (100.0%)
2020-08-18T13:33:25.123+1000    done dumping sample_mflix.movies (23539 documents)
```

Figure 11.6 Output from the mongodump command

The start of the output from the **mongorestore** command will look as follows:

```
2020-08-18T13:40:38.860+1000    preparing collections to restore from
2020-08-18T13:40:38.881+1000    reading metadata for backup_mflix_backup.movies from backups/sample_mflix/movie
s.metadata.json.gz
2020-08-18T13:40:38.900+1000    reading metadata for backup_mflix_backup.comments from backups/sample_mflix/com
ments.metadata.json.gz
2020-08-18T13:40:38.918+1000    reading metadata for backup_mflix_backup.users from backups/sample_mflix/users.
metadata.json.gz
2020-08-18T13:40:38.937+1000    reading metadata for backup_mflix_backup.sessions from backups/sample_mflix/ses
sions.metadata.json.gz
2020-08-18T13:40:38.981+1000    restoring backup_mflix_backup.sessions from backups/sample_mflix/sessions.bson.
gz
2020-08-18T13:40:39.008+1000    restoring indexes for collection backup_mflix_backup.sessions from metadata
2020-08-18T13:40:39.034+1000    restoring backup_mflix_backup.movies from backups/sample_mflix/movies.bson.gz
```

Figure 11.7: Start of the output from the mongorestore command

The end of the output from the **mongorestore** command will look as follows:

```
2020-08-18T13:40:50.110+1000    no indexes to restore
2020-08-18T13:40:50.110+1000    finished restoring backup_mflix_backup.comments (50304 documents, 0 failures)
2020-08-18T13:40:50.821+1000    [######.................]  backup_mflix_backup.movies  3.43MB/11.8MB  (29.2%)
2020-08-18T13:40:53.822+1000    [##########.............]  backup_mflix_backup.movies  4.95MB/11.8MB  (42.2%)
2020-08-18T13:40:56.825+1000    [#############..........]  backup_mflix_backup.movies  6.55MB/11.8MB  (55.8%)
2020-08-18T13:40:59.824+1000    [################.......]  backup_mflix_backup.movies  8.20MB/11.8MB  (69.8%)
2020-08-18T13:41:02.823+1000    [###################....]  backup_mflix_backup.movies  9.70MB/11.8MB  (82.6%)
2020-08-18T13:41:05.822+1000    [#####################..]  backup_mflix_backup.movies  11.1MB/11.8MB  (94.9%)
2020-08-18T13:41:07.868+1000    [#######################]  backup_mflix_backup.movies  11.8MB/11.8MB  (100.0%)
2020-08-18T13:41:07.868+1000    no indexes to restore
2020-08-18T13:41:07.868+1000    finished restoring backup_mflix_backup.movies (23539 documents, 0 failures)
2020-08-18T13:41:07.869+1000    74037 document(s) restored successfully. 0 document(s) failed to restore.
```

Figure 11.8: End of the output from the mongorestore command

> **NOTE**
>
> The solution to this activity can be found on page 690.

# SUMMARY

In this chapter, we have covered four separate commands. However, these four commands all serve as elements in a complete backup and restore lifecycle for MongoDB. By using these fundamental commands in combination with their advanced options, you should now be able to ensure that any MongoDB server you are responsible for can be appropriately snapshotted, backed up, exported, and restored in case of data corruption, loss, or disaster.

You may not be responsible for backing up your MongoDB data, but these commands can also be used for a vast array of utilities. For example, being able to export the data into a CSV format will be very handy when trying to explore the information as a spreadsheet visually or even to present it to colleagues who are unfamiliar with the document model. By using `mongoimport`, you can also reduce the amount of manual work required to import data that is not provided in MongoDB format as well as import MongoDB data from other servers in bulk.

The next chapter covers data visualization, an incredibly important concept for transforming MongoDB information into easily understood results that can provide insight and clarity for business problems as well as integrating them into presentations to persuade or convince stakeholders of hard to explain trends in the data.

# 12

# DATA VISUALIZATION

## OVERVIEW

This chapter will introduce you to MongoDB Charts, which offers the best way to create visualizations using data from a MongoDB database. You will start by learning the basics of the MongoDB Charts data visualization engine, then go on to create new dashboards and charts to understand the difference between the various types of graphs. You will also integrate and customize graphs with other external applications. By the end of this chapter, you will be well versed in the basic concepts of the Charts PaaS cloud interface and be able to perform the steps necessary to build useful graphs.

# INTRODUCTION

The visual representation of data is extremely useful for reporting as well as for business presentations. The advantages of using charts for data visualization in science, statistics, and mathematics cannot be overstated. Graphs and charts can effectively communicate essential information for business decisions to be made, in much the same way that movies can tell stories by using images in motion.

MongoDB has developed a new, integrated tool for data visualization, called MongoDB Charts. This is a relatively new feature, with its first release in the second quarter of 2018. MongoDB Charts allows users to perform quick data representation from a MongoDB database without writing code in a programming language such as Java or Python. Currently, there are two different implementations of MongoDB Charts:

- **MongoDB Charts PaaS** (**Platform as a Service**): This refers to the cloud service for Charts. This version of Charts is fully integrated with Atlas cloud projects and databases. It does not require any installation on the client side, and is free to use with an Atlas cloud account.

- **MongoDB Charts Server**: This refers to the on-premises MongoDB Charts tools, installed locally. The Charts server needs to be downloaded from MongoDB and installed on a dedicated server installation with Docker. On-premises Charts is included as part of MongoDB Enterprise Advanced, and it will not be covered in this course.

The features available for users are similar in both versions of MongoDB Charts. Using just a simple browser client, users can create dashboards and a variety of charts. Mongo DB continuously expands upon the Charts tools by adding new features in the application and bug-fixes with each new release.

Throughout this chapter, we will consider a scenario wherein John, an employee at XYZ organization, has been assigned to create a dashboard with information from a database containing a collection of movies. John is a beginner with limited experience in MongoDB. He wonders whether there is an easy way to build graphics without writing code in a programming language. And that is where MongoDB Charts comes into play. First, we will learn about **Menus and Tabs** in MongoDB Charts.

## EXPLORING MENUS AND TABS

To start the MongoDB Charts GUI application, users need to first log into the Atlas cloud web application. MongoDB Charts (the PaaS version) is bound to one Atlas project (the "per project" option), so if there are multiple Atlas projects, the user needs to select the currently active Atlas project. As described in previous chapters, the name of the Atlas project is chosen when the project is created. For this chapter, the name of the project is the default project name in Atlas: **Project 0**. The **Charts** tab is visible in the Atlas web application as shown in the following figure:

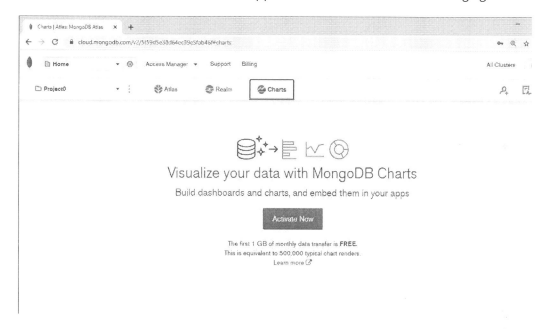

Figure 12.1: Charts tab

The MongoDB Charts option needs to be activated before the first use. To do so, you need to click on the **Activate Now** button to activate the Charts application, as shown in *Figure 12.1*. The activation process will only take a minute. During the activation, the Atlas application will set up Charts and will generate the database metadata necessary to create and run Charts.

As you can see from *Figure 12.1*, in MongoDB Charts, there is a maximum limit of 1 GB data transfer per month that can be used for sandpit testing and for learning about Charts. Once the limit is reached, MongoDB Charts cannot be used until the end of the month. However, the limit can be increased by upgrading the free-tier service to a paid Atlas service. You can find more details regarding this at https://www.mongodb.com/pricing.

Note that, once activated, the MongoDB Charts option will remain activated for the entire lifetime of your Atlas project. You will be asked if you wish to populate with sample data or connect an existing cluster in ATALS cloud. If you wish to remove the Charts option, you can do so by going to the Atlas project settings. This could be useful if you want to re-activate a fresh new version of Charts for an existing project. Nevertheless, removing Charts should be done with caution because it will automatically delete all charts and dashboards saved in the cloud. Once Atlas Charts is activated, the application starts and it can be used to create charts, as shown in the following screenshot:

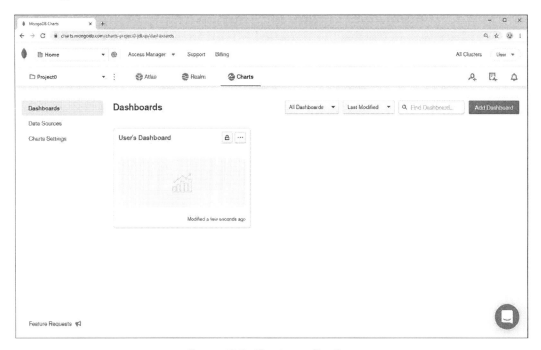

**Figure 12.2: Charts application**

The option buttons are displayed on the left side of the application:

- **Dashboards**: As the name suggests, this option helps manage dashboards. A dashboard is a set of different charts combined into a single page for business reporting purposes.

- **Data Sources**: Using this option, you can manage the data source, which is simply a reference to the MongoDB database collection from which data is processed to display charts.

- **`Charts Settings`**: This option allows users to manage chart authentication providers and to monitor the network bandwidth usage of the Charts application.

> **NOTE**
>
> To return to the main Atlas web application, you can click the **`Atlas`** tab link on the top bar in the Charts application.

## DASHBOARDS

In business presentations, information is usually displayed that's pertinent to subject areas. A subject area is a category, such as human resources or real estate. A subject display contains all the relevant data indicators for the respective business area, but data from one subject area is often not correlated with database structures. That is how data is stored in the MongoDB database. Therefore, dashboards are a chart grouping feature for when we need to present data in a centralized and meaningful way for businesses.

In the current version of Charts, the cloud application automatically creates an empty dashboard for us. The default dashboard has a name, **`User's Dashboard`**, as shown in *Figure 12.2*, where **`User`** is the Atlas login username.

You can delete the default dashboard and create additional dashboards for your business presentations. To create a new dashboard, you can click on the **Add Dashboard** button as shown in *Figure 12.2*. A dialog box will open in which you need to add details about the new dashboard:

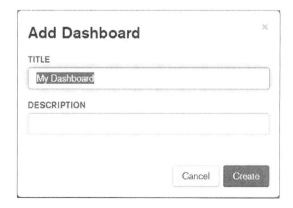

Figure 12.3: Add Dashboard dialog box

To access dashboard properties, click on the ... button from the dashboard box, as shown in the following figure:

## Dashboards

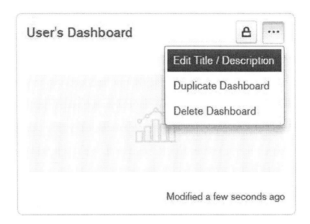

**Figure 12.4: Dashboard properties drop-down menu**

There are a few buttons and options available in the dashboard context:

- **Edit Title / Description**: This option is used to change the current title or description of the dashboard.

- **Duplicate Dashboard**: This option copies the dashboard to a new one, with a different name.

- **Delete Dashboard**: This option removes the dashboard from MongoDB Charts.

- **Lock**: This option assigns dashboard permissions for Atlas project users. This option is not useful for free-tier Atlas Charts, as MongoDB does not allow you to manage project users and teams with the free tier.

To view a dashboard, click on the dashboard name link (for example, **User's Dashboard**). The dashboard will open and show all charts contained in it. If no charts are created, then an empty dashboard is displayed as in the following screenshot:

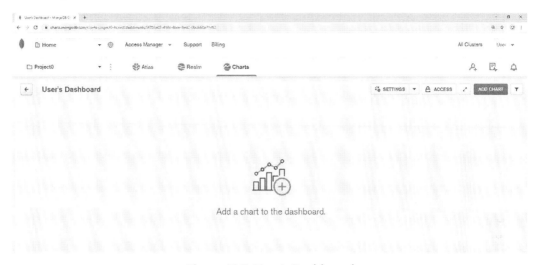

Figure 12.5: User's Dashboard

Later in this chapter, we will go through the steps to add charts to our dashboards. But before we can add new charts, we must ensure that database documents are available for our charts. This is the topic of the next section.

## DATA SOURCES

Data sources represent the interface between MongoDB database structures and the MongoDB Charts presentation engine. A data source is a pointer to a specific database collection (or collections) from which the data is processed to create a graph. As MongoDB Charts is integrated with the Atlas web application, all data sources are configured to connect to Atlas database deployments. Therefore, a data source contains a description of the Atlas cluster deployment, the database, and the collection that will be used for Charts.

A data source also enables a level of isolation between the MongoDB database and MongoDB Charts application users. It is guaranteed that data sources do not modify MongoDB databases because they access databases in read-only mode. Without a data source, Charts cannot access JSON documents from a MongoDB database.

> **NOTE**
>
> MongoDB Charts (the PaaS version) permits data sources to reference data only from Atlas cloud cluster deployments. Therefore, it is not possible to create a data source from your local MongoDB database installation. Before you can generate a new data source, database collections and documents must be uploaded to your Atlas database cluster.

To access the data sources, click on the **Data Sources** tab on the left, as shown in the following figure:

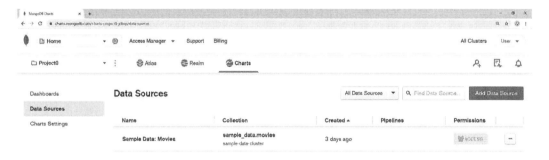

Figure 12.6: Data Sources tab

In the middle, you can observe a list with existing data sources and the **Add Data Source** button in the upper-right corner of the page.

As you can see, in the current version of Charts, one sample data source is automatically populated by your application. The name of this sample data source is **Sample Data: Movies**. MongoDB tries to facilitate a quick introduction to Charts by providing a sample data source and sample dashboards/charts, so that users can see some charts without learning how to use the Charts interface.

> **NOTE**
>
> The sample data source **Sample Data: Movies** cannot be changed or deleted by users. That is because the sample data source is pointing to a special Atlas database, which is external to your project and not accessible to users. As it is not guaranteed that this data source will exist in future versions, you should ignore this data source and continue as if there are none.

To create a new data source, you must provide the connection details to your cloud MongoDB database. A data source usually points to a single database collection. As you are already familiar with the MongoDB database structure, it should be relatively easy to create a new data source in Charts.

However, data sources can be more complicated to deal with than a single database collection. More complex options (which are called **data source preprocessing**) are available for Charts users. Complex data sources include features such as filtering, joining, and aggregation. More details about preprocessing features will be covered later in this chapter. For the moment, let's focus on creating a new data source in Charts.

To create a data source, click on the **Add Data Source** button as shown in *Figure: 12.6*. A new window with the **Add Data Sources** wizard will appear on the screen:

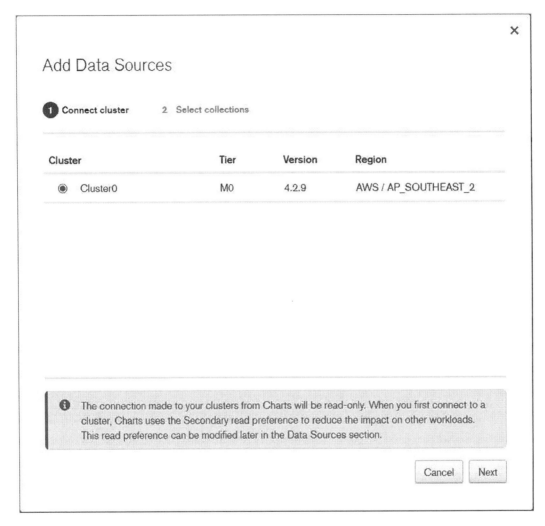

Figure 12.7: Add Data Sources window

You will be presented with a list of cloud databases available for Charts (*Figure 12.7*). In the case of free-tier Atlas, there will be one **M0** cluster available. As you can see, the footer says **The connection made to your clusters from Charts will be read-only**. This is to reassure you that the data source will not alter the database information. You can choose **Cluster0** from the cluster list and then click on the **Next** button.

Next, a list of available databases is displayed. You can expand each database, display all collections within, and select a specific collection from the respective database, as shown in the following screenshot:

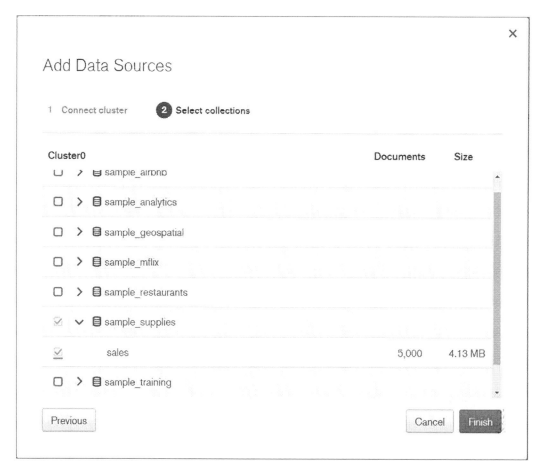

Figure 12.8: Select collections window

You can select the entire database or expand the database section and select one or more collections from within the database. If you select multiple collections (or multiple databases), Atlas will generate multiple data sources—one data source for each database collection. It is therefore possible to create multiple data sources without going through this setup assistant multiple times. The limitation in this case is that all data sources will point to a single database cluster that was selected previously.

Once the data source is configured and saved, it will appear in the list, as shown in *Figure 12.9*:

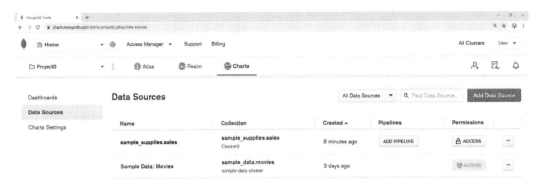

Figure 12.9: Data Sources tab shows that sample_supplies database is configured

## EXERCISE 12.01: WORKING WITH DATA SOURCES

In this exercise, you will create new data sources for Charts. These will reappear in examples later in this chapter, so it is important to follow the steps here carefully:

> **NOTE**
>
> Please ensure that you have uploaded the Atlas sample data in your **M0** cluster as it was shown in the first three chapters of this book. As explained before, a new data source cannot be defined without a valid MongoDB database collection.

1. In the **Data Source** tab, click on **Add Data Source**, as shown in *Figure 12.6*.

2. Select your own cluster, as shown in *Figure 12.7*. Then, click Next:

3.  From the database list, click on the **`sample_mflix`** database. If you wish, you can expand the database section to see the list of all collections from the **`sample_mflix`** database:

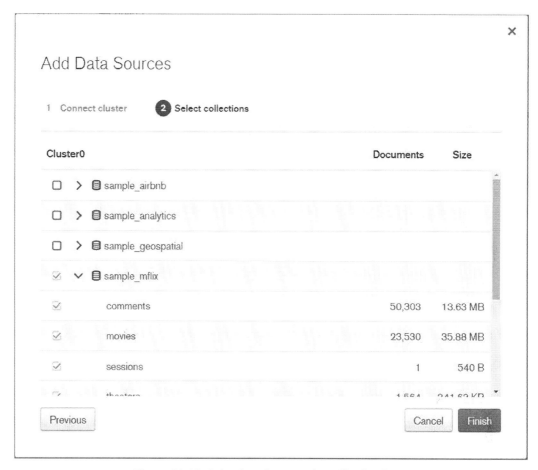

Figure 12.10: Selecting the sample_mflix database

4. Click on the **Finish** button. You should be able to see five additional data sources (one for each collection) created in your interface, as shown in the following figure:

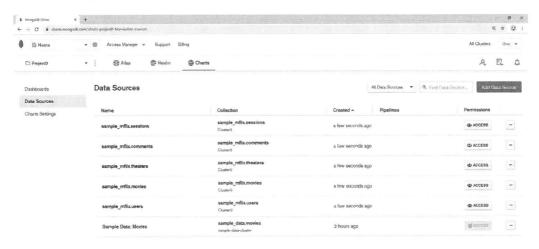

Figure 12.11: Data Sources list updated

In this example, you added a new data source in MongoDB Charts.

## DATA SOURCE PERMISSIONS

Complex MongoDB projects can have many developers and business users working together with Charts. In such cases, the Atlas user who creates a new data source may need to share it with other Atlas project users. As explained in previous chapters, Atlas applications can manage multiple users for large Atlas deployments. However, this concept is not applicable for the free-tier Atlas sandpit projects in which most of the examples in this book are presented.

Once a user creates a new data source, they become the owner of that data source and can share it with other project members by clicking on the **ACCESS** button in the **Charts** tab in the **Data Sources** window (see *Figure 12.9*). Here is a screenshot example from the **M0** free-tier cluster:

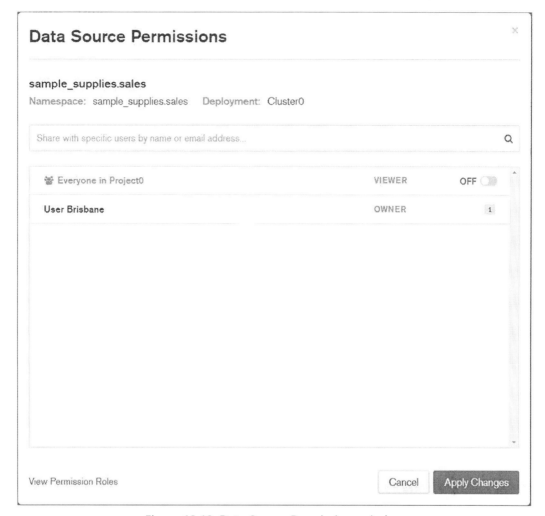

Figure 12.12: Data Source Permissions window

As can be seen from the preceding screenshot, the owner can enable or disable the **VIEWER** permission for **Everyone in Project0**. The **VIEWER** permission allows users to "use" the data source to build their own charts. Other users are not allowed to modify or delete the data source.

For large projects, the data source owner can grant permission to a specific Atlas group or users that are invited to the project. These advanced permissions, which are specific to large Atlas projects, are not covered in this introductory course.

## BUILDING CHARTS

New charts can be created in MongoDB Charts using the Chart Builder. To start the Chart Builder, open a dashboard. You can open your own user dashboard by clicking on the **User's Dashboard** link in the dashboard tab, as shown in *Figure 12.5*. Then, click on the **ADD CHART** button.

The following is a screenshot of the Chart Builder:

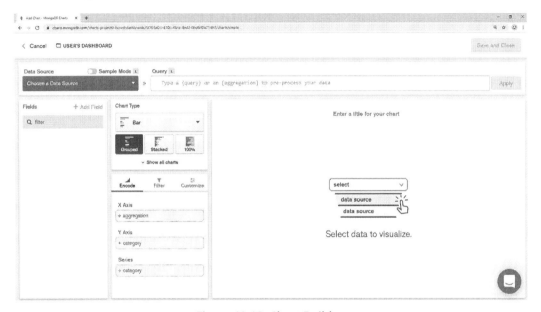

Figure 12.13: Chart Builder

The first step is to choose the data source. The **Choose a Data Source** button appears highlighted in green in the top-left corner. Note that a valid data source needs to be created and published before you can assign it to a chart. Also, it is not possible to assign more than one data source to a chart. By default, all documents from a collection are retrieved for the Chart Builder.

There is an option to click the **Sample Mode** radio button. This mode enables Charts to retrieve only a subset of documents from the database. There is no rule about the maximum number of JSON documents that should be loaded in the Chart Builder. For example, if the goal is to display precise aggregation values, then we may need to retrieve all the documents. On the other hand, if the goal is to display a trend or a correlation graph, then just a sample of documents should suffice. Nevertheless, loading an extremely high amount of data in Charts (more than 1 GB) will have a negative impact on Charts' performance and is discouraged.

## FIELDS

On the left side of the Chart Builder page, you can see the list of collection fields:

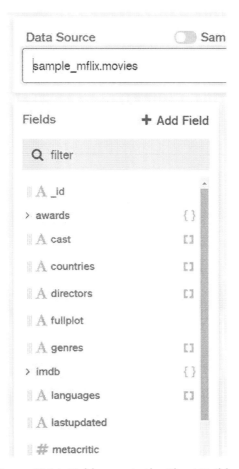

Figure 12.14: Fields area in the Chart Builder

Each field has a name and a data type, as you have already seen in *Chapter 2, Documents and Data Types*.

The following is the list of data types in the Chart Builder:

- **A** – String
- **#** – Numeric (integer or float)
- Date

- **[]** – Array

- **{}** – Sub-document

> **NOTE**
>
> In the example screenshot (*Figure 12.14*), the movies data source has been selected for **sample_mflix.movies**.

## TYPES OF CHARTS

There are various types of charts available that you can choose from. They all could represent similar views. However, some chart types are better suited to a particular scenario or database data type. The following table enlists all the chart types and their respective functions:

| Type / Name | Description | Data Usage |
|---|---|---|
| Bar and Column | These display a sequence of rectangular bars (vertical) or columns (horizontal).<br><br>The bar chart can display single or multiple values, either grouped with different colors or stacked one on top of the other. | These are preferable for discrete values or categories—for example, high, medium, and low.<br><br>A bar or column chart is effective for low-cardinality (*) variables with only a few categories or distinct values. |
| Line and Area | These display lines between discrete points on the graph. This chart type can also display multiple values, either as separate lines or stacked one on top of the other. | These are preferable for continuous variables or variables with many different values. For example, a line chart is especially useful to display how values change over time. |
| Grid | These are graphs represented in the form of regular tiles that display data on a grid with two axes. | These are preferable for datasets without a set trend or a category. A grid graph is also called a "heatmap" because each tile can be represented with a different color intensity. |
| Circular | A circular chart (also called a donut or pie chart) is a round, colored circle, which is often sub-divided into slices.<br><br>There are no axes—horizontal or vertical. Slices can have values or percentages from the whole pie value. | Pie charts provide a full perspective for one domain and illustrate how the total value is distributed. For example, you can use a pie chart to display the number of sales per category: wholesales, direct sales, retail, and more. |
| Text | Here, the data is listed in an alphanumeric format, either free text or in tables, with lines and columns. | Sometimes, a table is more useful than a graph. When you need to know precise values or to compare pairs of values, a table is the perfect solution. |
| Geospatial | This type of chart uses a map to display data. The geospatial graph is therefore applicable for data that can be correlated with geographical locations. | Geospatial charts are useful to display how data is geographically distributed. It is more visually impactful to present data on a geographical map for users who need to see the geographical distribution for specific data metrics; for example, total sales per location is a great graph for sales managers. |

Figure 12.15: Types of charts in MongoDB

Each chart type could have one or more sub-types that are visual variations of the main chart and are useful in different presentations. Since a chart sub-type is dependent on the main chart type, we will discuss them for each type of chart.

A chart sub-type can be selected from the same menu, just under **Chart Type**, as shown in the following screenshot for the **Bar** chart type:

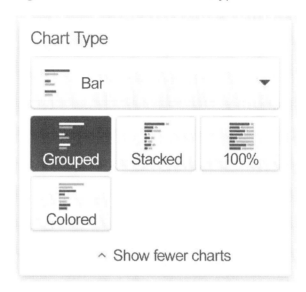

Figure 12.16: Bar chart sub-types

Note that there are four different sub-types for bar and column charts as shown in *Figure 12.16*. While most sub-types are only variations of the same chart type, some sub-types can be useful to focus on different aspects of data. For example, the **Grouped** sub-type is useful to compare values in different categories while **Stacked** is useful to see the cumulated values for all categories. The simplest way to identify the right sub-type for you is to quickly navigate through them. The Charts engine will automatically re-display the chart in your chosen sub-type form.

Just under the **Chart Type** selection menu, there is a submenu with other tabs that is used to define chart channels or dimensions. The following screenshot shows these:

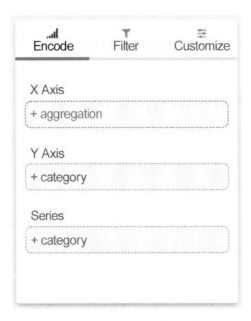

Figure 12.17: Chart channels

The following list gives a brief description of each tab:

- **Encode**: This is for defining the chart channels. A channel describes how the data is translated into a chart visualization item. Different chart types have different encode channels. For example, bar and line graphs have channels represented by Cartesian coordinates (an X axis and a Y axis).

- **Filter**: This is for defining data filters. This option helps filter input documents, so only the required documents are considered for the chart plotting. This is useful if we want to exclude non-relevant data from our graph.

- **Customize**: This is used to define functional and aesthetical customizations of charts, such as chart colors and labels. While this option is non-essential, it often makes a big difference in terms of graph readability.

More detailed information about channel utilization is presented later in this chapter. For now, let's go through some of the chart types and practical examples.

## BAR AND COLUMN CHARTS

Bar and column charts are probably the most common type of charts used in presentations. The basic format of the chart is comprised of a set of bars with different values for height and thickness, arranged in a bi-dimensional graph.

Bar charts are especially useful to represent aggregated values for categorical data. The main designation for bar charts is therefore data categorization or classification. While this material is not a comprehensive theory on data science, a short introduction will help you to understand the basics. Here is a description of how categorical data can be defined:

- **Data classification**: This pertains to data that can be identified based on a category or label, for example, quality (high, average, low) or color (white, red, blue). This could also include a few distinct numerical values or numbers used as categories (not values).

- **Data binning**: This means grouping data in a category based on an interval. For example, numerical values between 0 and 9.99 could be grouped in the first bin, and numbers between 10 and 19.99 in the second bin, and so on. In this way, we can group many values into relatively few categories. Binning is the method used to represent graphs for statistical analysis, called histograms.

Once we have defined data categories, our bi-dimensional bar chart can be built from there. The data category will populate one dimension of the chart, while the calculated (aggregated) values will populate the other dimension of the chart.

## EXERCISE 12.02: CREATING A BAR CHART TO DISPLAY MOVIES

The goal of this exercise is to create a bar chart and to get familiar with the MongoDB Charts interface menu and options:

1.  First, choose the chart type and then drag and drop fields into the **Encode** area. For example, if you choose the chart type **Bar** and **Grouped**, you can see the X and Y axes in the **Encode** area.

   > **NOTE**
   >
   > Select `sample_mflix.movies datasource` for this chart (top-left drop down menu)

2. Click on the field named **title** (movie title) and drag it to **Y Axis**:

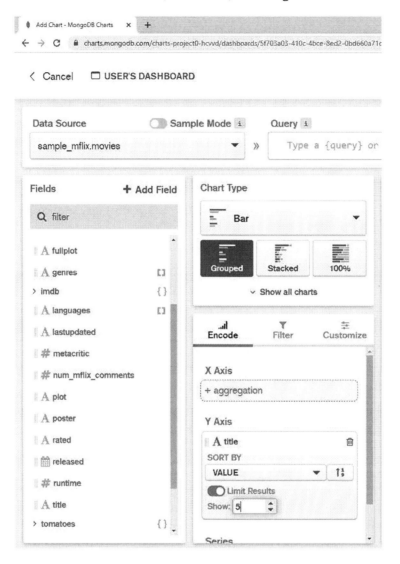

Figure 12.18: Dragging the title field to the Y Axis

3.  To limit the number of values, click **Limit Results** and enter **5** in the **Show** box.

> **NOTE**
>
> Accept the default option for **SORT BY**, which is **VALUE** (see *Figure 12.17*). We will explain the various options in the encoding channels in the upcoming sections.

4.  The next step is to define values for the X axis. Expand the **awards** field sub-document, then click and drag and drop **wins** to **X Axis**. Keep the default setting for **AGGREGATE**, which is **SUM**:

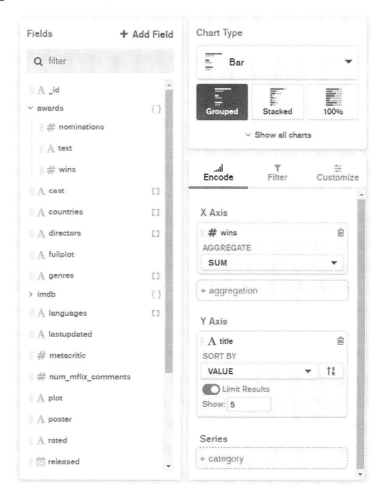

Figure 12.19: Adding the wins field to the X Axis

The graph should now automatically appear on the right side of the Chart Builder screen:

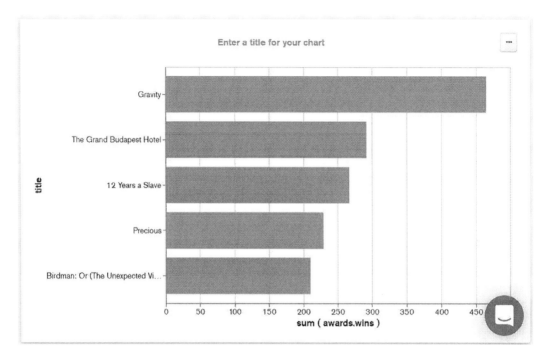

Figure 12.20: Top five movies sorted by the number of awards

5.  Now, group the bars based on database fields. For this feature, add multiple fields to the **X Axis** channel while keeping **title** as the only **Y Axis** value. To add a second set of values on the X axis (**Grouped** bar), drag and drop **nominations** to **X Axis**:

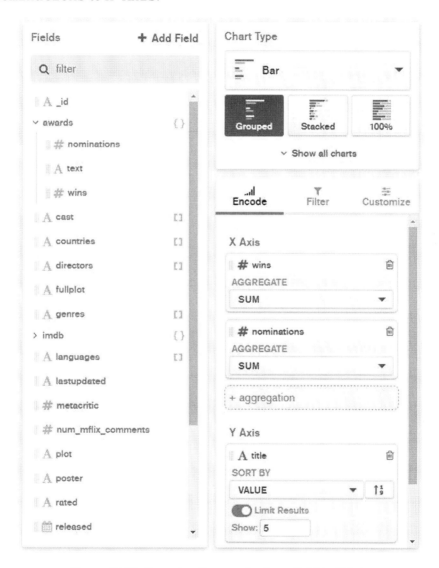

Figure 12.21: Dragging the nominations field to X Axis

The chart is then automatically updated to show both **nominations** and **wins** for each movie:

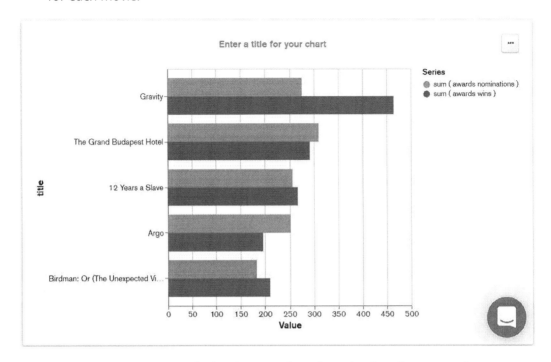

**Figure 12.22: Bar graph showing awards and nominations for top movies**

This graph sub-type is particularly useful if you want to compare values. In this case, you compared the number of nominations and wins for each movie. As you can see, the values are "grouped." This is exactly the meaning of the **Grouped** tab in the **Chart Type** selection menu.

If you prefer to see them "stacked" instead of grouped, then just click on the **Stacked** button (*Figure 12.21*) and the chart will be automatically updated. This option is useful if we want to see the total cumulated values of movie award nominations and wins:

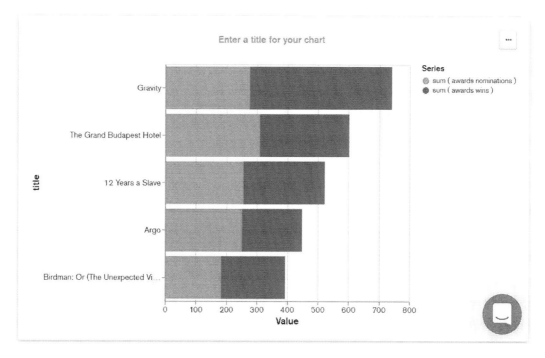

Figure 12.23: Result with stacked bars (instead of grouped)

As you can see, switching from one sub-type to another in MongoDB Charts comes down to one click. As a result, the chart is automatically redrawn in the new format without any other user input. This feature is extremely useful once we decide whether our initial sub-type choice was the right one for our presentation.

Now, let's look at other types of charts that are available in Atlas.

## CIRCULAR CHARTS

Circular charts are colored round circles or semi-circles, often sub-divided into slices to represent values or percentages. The circular chart is also "unidimensional," which means that the graph can only represent a single set of scalar values and not values that can be represented in a Cartesian coordinate system. Considering this limitation, we need to be aware that there is little information that we can represent using this type of chart. Nevertheless, a circular chart provides a powerful visual representation of data proportions, by putting an emphasis on the ratio between one slice and the whole. Because of its simplicity and visual impact, this type of chart is also highly effective for presentations.

There are two sub-types of circular charts: **Donut** and **Gauge**:

- **Donut**: This represents a full, colored circle (pie), which is divided into slices that represent values or percentages. There could be many values or slices. However, it is recommended to limit the number of values, so that the donut is divided into a relatively small number of slices.

- **Gauge**: This represents a semi-circle, with a ratio from the total. This type of graph is a simplified version of the donut type because it can represent a single value proportion.

In the next exercise, you will learn how to build a donut chart.

## EXERCISE 12.03: CREATING A PIE CHART GRAPH FROM THE MOVIES COLLECTION

Say you need to represent the movies based on their country of origin. As a pie representation is generally more intuitive than a table, you decide to use a donut chart to represent this data. This will also allow you to put an emphasis on the top movie-producing countries in the world:

1. Select the **Donut** sub-type from the **Chart Type** drop-down menu:

Figure 12.24: Selecting donut chart sub-type

2. Click and drag the **countries** field to the **Label** channel, as in the following screenshot:

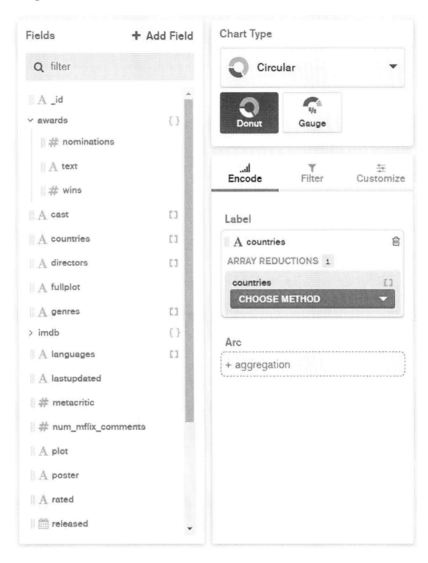

Figure 12.25: Dragging the countries field to the Label channel

3. Click on the **CHOOSE METHOD** dropdown and select `Array element by index (index = 0)` to choose the first element of the array in all documents. Accept the default option for **SORT BY**—that is, **VALUE**.

> **NOTE**
>
> Because the `countries` field is a JSON array data type, your best option will be an **ARRAY REDUCTION** method, so that Charts will know how to interpret the data. In this example, you are focusing on the primary country producer (`index = 0`) and ignoring co-producers.

4. Reduce the number of results (using the `Limit Results` option) to **10**. In this way, your pie will have only **10** slices, which will correspond to the top 10 movie producers:

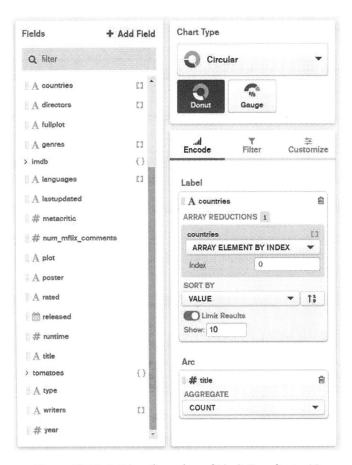

Figure 12.26: Setting the value of Limit Results to 10

5.  Drag and drop the **title** field into the **Arc** channel and select the option of **COUNT** for the **AGGREGATE** dropdown. The circular chart should appear on the right side of the screen as follows:

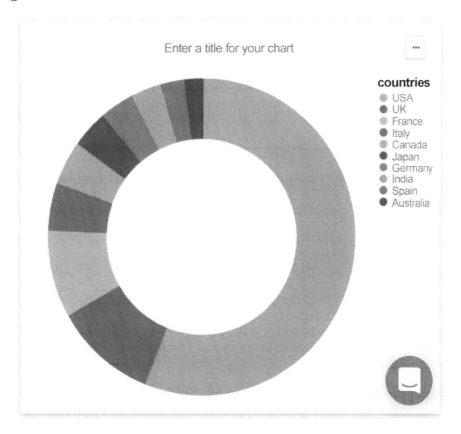

Figure 12.27: Donut chart for the top movie-producing countries

This exercise walked you through the few simple steps needed to build a donut or pie chart. Almost any presentation or dashboard contains at least one pie chart because of how attractive they look. But attractiveness is not the only reason donut charts are so popular. The donut chart is also a powerful tool to represent ratios and proportions in visual graphs. The following section will take a look at another type of chart, that is, geospatial charts.

## GEOSPATIAL CHARTS

Geospatial charts are a special category of charts wherein geographical data is the main ingredient for building the graph. The simplest definition of geographical (or geospatial) data is that it contains information about a specific location on the planet. The location details are pinpointed on a map to build a geospatial chart.

Geospatial information can be specific or more general. The following are a few examples of geospatial data that can be mapped easily using a map engine, such as Google Maps:

- Precise longitude and latitude coordinates

- An address that can be mapped using a map engine

- Broader locations such as cities, regions, or countries

For example, say that we have a database that contains information about cars. The main database collection contains millions of documents about cars, such as the model, odometer details, and other attributes. A few other attributes will also describe the physical address where the vehicle is registered. That information can then be used to build a geospatial chart using a city map.

There are a few chart sub-types for geospatial charts as follows:

- **Choropleth** charts: This chart shows colored geographical areas, such as regions and countries. This type of chart is less specific and, in general, is useful for high-level aggregations—for example, a chart that displays the total number of COVID-19 cases per country.

- **Scatter** charts: This chart requires a precise address or location. The chart marks the location with a dot or a small circle on the map. This chart is useful if we want to display a chart with a relatively small number of precise locations.

- **Heatmap** charts: A heatmap displays colors with different intensities on a map. A higher intensity corresponds to a higher density of database entities in that location. Heatmap charts are useful to display large numbers of objects on a map, where users are more interested in density rather than a precise location.

In the next section, you will complete an exercise using the `sample_mflix` database, which contains sample geospatial information to further practice using geo-point information in a new geospatial chart.

# EXERCISE 12.04: CREATING A GEOSPATIAL CHART

The purpose of this exercise is to create a geospatial chart that represents a map of all movie theaters located in the United States of America. You will use the **theaters** collection to map geographical data:

1. For **Data Source**, choose **sample_mflix.theaters**:

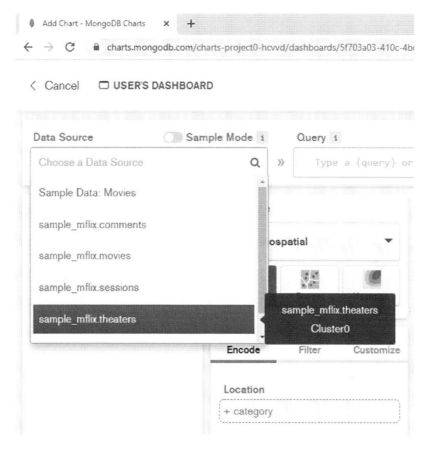

Figure 12.28: Selecting sample_mflix.theaters as the data source

2. Select the **Geospatial** chart and, from the sub-type categories, select **Heatmap**:

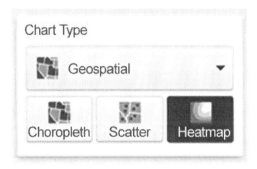

Figure 12.29: Selecting Heatmap from the list of geospatial chart sub-types

3. Click on the **geo** field and drag it into the **Coordinates** encoding channel:

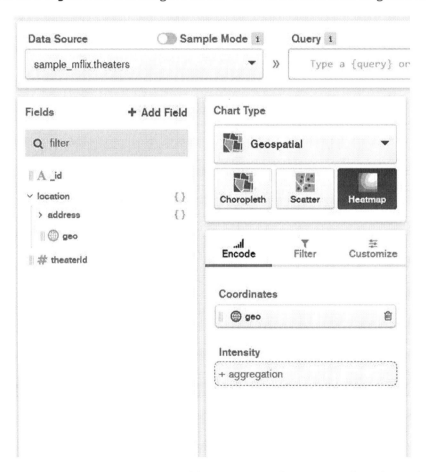

Figure 12.30: Dragging the geo field into the Coordinates encoding channel

4.  Next, click on the **theatreId** field and drag it into the **Intensity** channel:

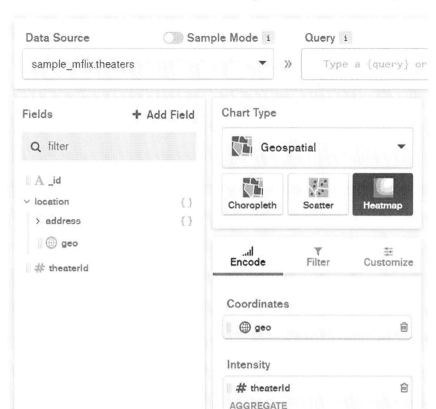

Figure 12.31: Dragging theatreId field into the Intensity channel

When switching to the **Heatmap** chart type, you should notice an immediate chart update with color areas, instead of dots—with red intensity around large US cities.

The USA map should appear on the right side of the window and will show the theaters' density using different color gradients. The color coding is displayed on the right side of the chart. The highest density of movie theaters (around New York City) will appear in red on the map (see *Figure 12.32*):

Figure 12.32: Heatmap chart

In this exercise, you practiced building a geospatial chart of all movie theaters in the USA. You started with data analysis to see whether the database information was suitable for presenting via a geospatial chart. Once data is available in the MongoDB database, building a chart is relatively easy.

# COMPLEX CHARTS

In previous sections, you saw how easy it is to use MongoDB Charts in Atlas. While the user interface is very intuitive and easy to use, it is also very powerful. There are many options available in MongoDB Charts so that data from the database can be preprocessed, grouped, and displayed in various ways. We'll take a look at more advanced configuration topics in this section.

## PREPROCESSING AND FILTERING DATA

As discussed previously, charts access the database through data sources that are defined in Charts. By default, all documents from a database collection are selected to build a new chart. Moreover, the data fields in Charts will inherit the original database JSON document data format.

Also note that a data source cannot alter or modify the database. In a real-life scenario, it happens quite often that the data format is not ideal for presenting via a chart. The data must be prepared, or the data format needs to be altered in some way before it is ready to be used for our chart. This category of data preparation for plotting is called preprocessing.

Data preprocessing includes the following:

- **Data filtering**: Filtering the data such that only certain documents are selected

- **Data type change**: Modifying the data type so that it fits the Chart Builder better

- **Adding new fields**: Adding custom fields that do not exist in the MongoDB database

## FILTERING DATA

Data filtering allows users to select only a subset of documents from a MongoDB collection. Sometimes, the database collection is just too large, which makes the operation in the Chart Builder slower and less effective. One of the ways this can be overcome is to sample the data. Another method is to simply filter the data based on some categories so that only a subset of documents is considered for the chart.

There are a few ways in which a user can control the number of documents processed in a chart. These are listed in the following table:

| Filtering Method | Level/Type | Description |
|---|---|---|
| `Filter` Tab | Chart Builder | The easiest method to filter data is to use the filter tab in the chart builder. With just a few clicks, we can add the database attribute to the chart filter box and choose the filter. |
| `Query` Bar | Chart Builder | The query bar is situated at the top of the Chart Builder window. The query bar allows developers to write powerful JSON queries to filter and process data. |
| Pipeline | Data Source | A pipeline is another option for data preprocessing. A pipeline can be configured at the data source level, so data is processed before it comes to the Chart Builder. |
| | | Developers can write JavaScript code for filtering and aggregation, and also for joining multiple database collections. Another advantage of this method is that a data source is external to the Chart Builder, and therefore can be used by multiple charts. |
| View or M-View | Database (external charts) | Views created in the database can be accessed by MongoDB Charts just like normal collections. |
| | | This method is easy to use and does not require any configuration in Charts. |

Figure 12.33: Ways in which a user can control the number
of documents processed in a chart

> **NOTE**
>
> It is recommended that you choose one filter method that is the most appropriate for the chart's requirements and use just that filter. Mixing two or three filtering methods into the same chart could lead to confusion and should be avoided.

Except for the **Filter Tab** method, which is a part of the UI, all other methods require JavaScript code to define the filter. The query syntax was presented in detail in *Chapter 4, Querying Documents*. The same format of querying can be used in Charts too. For example, to define a filter for all Italian or French movies released after 1999, the following JSON query can be written:

```
{ countries: { $in: ["Italy", "France"]},
  year: { $gt : 1999}}
```

Once this query is entered into the **Query** bar, the **Apply** button should be clicked, as shown in the following screenshot:

Figure 12.34: Query bar example screenshot

> **NOTE**
>
> Filtering documents may lead to a delayed chart response, especially when working with large databases. To help with performance, you can create indexes on collection fields that are involved in filter expressions, as seen in *Chapter 9, Performance*.

## ADDING CUSTOM FIELDS

Charts allows users to add custom fields that can be used to build charts. Sometimes raw data from MongoDB does not offer the right attributes for creating a new chart and it becomes important to add custom fields. Most of these custom fields are either derived or calculated using the source database values.

Custom fields can be added by clicking the **+ Add Field** button in the **Fields** area of the Chart Builder, as shown in the following screenshot:

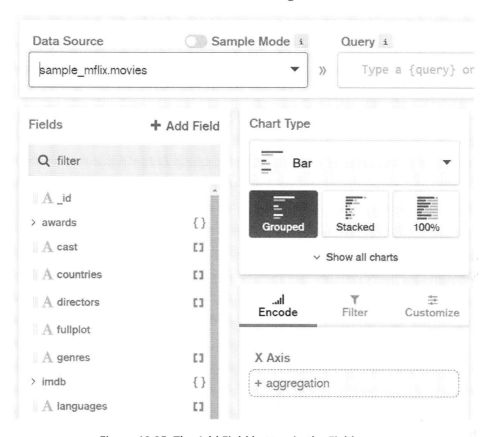

Figure 12.35: The Add Field button in the Fields area

There are two types of fields that can be added:

- **MISSED**: This option is used to add a field that is missing from the list of fields. For example, imagine a new field has been added to the application and only a few documents in the database have the new field. In such a case, MongoDB Charts can add the missing field to the initial load.

- **CALCULATED**: This is used to add a new field that does not exist in the collection. For example, the source database for a ride-sharing app can have fields for the number of hours and the tariff per hour. However, the total value (hours multiplied by the tariff) might not be in the database. Therefore, we can add a new custom field that is calculated from other values in the database.

> **NOTE**
>
> It is not possible to add a **MISSED** field if the field does not exist in any collection document. In this case, you need to add/update the collection document first.

To better understand this concept, consider this practical example. In this example, you will add a new calculated field in Charts. Perform the following steps:

1. Click on the **Add Field** button, and then click on the **CALCULATED** button, as in the following screenshot:

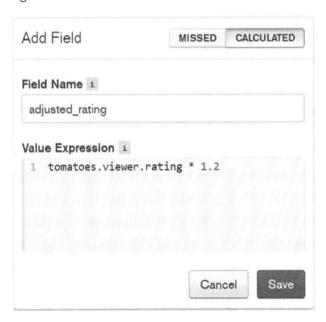

Figure 12.36: Adding a new field

2. Type the new field name in as **adjusted_rating**.

3. Type in the formula for calculating the total value, that is, **tomatoes.viewer. rating * 1.2**.

4.  Click on the **Save** button. You should now be able to see the new calculated field and use it in charts, just like any other data-type attribute.

> **NOTE**
>
> Calculated fields are not saved in the database. Their scope is only within the MongoDB Chart Builder. Moreover, a calculated field can be deleted from the **Fields** list.

## CHANGING FIELDS

Sometimes, the data from the database is not the right data type. In such cases, MongoDB Charts allows users to change fields to a data type appropriate for chart plotting. For example, a chart channel may require data to be in numeric format to aggregate **SUM** or **AVERAGE**. To change a field, drag the mouse pointer over the field name in the **Fields** list (on the left side of the **Chart Builder** window):

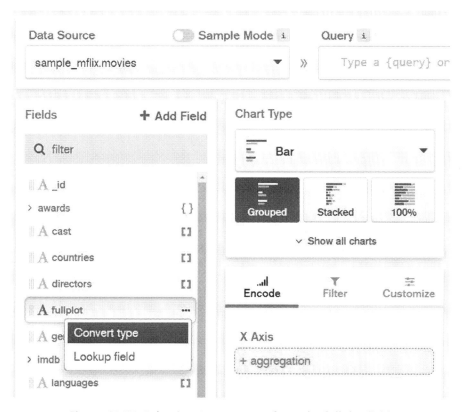

Figure 12.37: Selecting Convert type from the fullplot field

Upon clicking on the `. . .` menu and selecting the **Convert type** option (the only one available), a list of JSON data types will be displayed. Then, you can choose the desired data type and click on the **SAVE** button.

For example, if you want to change the **metacritic** numerical field (**#**) into a string field (**A**), you can click on **metacritic** and a new **Convert type** window will appear as shown here:

Figure 12.38: Convert type window

Note that changing a field's data type will have an effect only on the current chart and will not change the data type in the database.

> **NOTE**
>
> In the most recent version of Charts, there is another option in the context field menu [...], which is called `lookup`. The `lookup` field allows us to build a chart by joining a second collection from the same database. More details on how to join collections were given in *Chapter 4, Querying Documents*.

## CHANNELS

The encoding channels are one of the most important aspects of data visualization. The channel decides how the data is visualized in the chart. Users can get confusing charts or totally unexpected results if they select the wrong channel type. Therefore, a proper understanding of encoding channels is essential for efficient chart building and data visualization.

As shown in previous examples, the encoding channels lie under the **Encode** tab in the Chart Builder, just under the chart sub-type selection buttons:

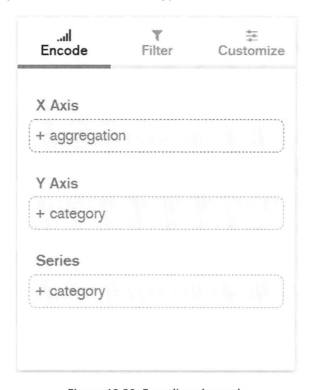

Figure 12.39: Encoding channels

Each encoding channel has a name and a type. The channel name defines the target in the graph—that is, the end to which the channel will be used. For example, the **X Axis** channel name indicates that the channel is providing the values for the horizontal axis of the graph. It is clear in this case that we are going to have a Cartesian bi-dimensional chart. The channel type defines what type of data is expected as the channel input. Finding the right data type for the channel input is important. Also, as you have probably noticed by now, not all data types can be accepted as channel input.

There are four channel types available in MongoDB Charts, as listed in the following table:

| Channel | Accepted Data Type | Description |
| --- | --- | --- |
| + category | Numeric, Date, or String | This is a channel that accepts a categorical type of data, as described before in the *Bar Charts* section. A chart element will be plotted for each unique occurrence of a value. The dataset must have unique values (no duplicates). Values in this category channel can be sorted if required. |
| + value | Numeric or Date | This channel accepts data values (not categories). The dataset can have duplicate values. One example where this channel type is used is in continuous line charts. |
| + aggregation | Numeric, Date, or String | An aggregation expression is applied to group elements based on a specific category. We will learn more details about these in the next section, *Aggregation and Binning*. |
| + geopoint | Geodata (X, Y) | This is used for longitude and latitude coordinates that can be mapped on a geographical map. This type of channel is valid only for geospatial scatter and heatmap charts. |

Figure 12.40: List of channel types in MongoDB Charts

**NOTE**

It is possible to assign channel values from sub-documents or array fields in a JSON document. In this case, MongoDB charts will ask you to identify the element that is considered for the channel encoding—for example, array index `[0]` (which points to the first element in the array, for each document).

## AGGREGATION AND BINNING

Data in one channel is often combined with a category data type channel so that it can calculate aggregate values for each category. For example, we can **SUM** aggregate all awards for French films. In the Chart Builder, when a field is dragged and dropped into an aggregation channel, it is assumed that the values will be aggregated in the chart. The Chart Builder does this transparently without requiring you to write the code for an aggregation pipeline.

The aggregation type will depend on the data type that we provide on the channel input. For example, it is not possible to **SUM** if the data type provided to the channel is text.

There are a few types of aggregations, as listed in the following table:

| Data Type | Aggregation Function |
|---|---|
| Numerical fields | SUM: This function calculates the sum of all elements. |
| | MIN: This function finds the minimum value. |
| | MAX: This function finds the maximum value. |
| | Other statistical functions (example: Standard Deviation). |
| String and Date fields | COUNT: This function counts the total number of occurrences. |
| | DISTINCT: This function counts the distinct occurrences. |

Figure 12.41: Types of aggregations

> **NOTE**
>
> Some channels can have the **Series** type. This option allows users to add a second dimension to a chart, either unique or binning, by grouping data in a range of values.

## EXERCISE 12.05: BINNING VALUES FOR A BAR GRAPH

In this exercise, you will build another bar chart that shows movies produced in Italy. In this graph, you need to aggregate data per movie release year. Also, the chart should only consider movies released after 1970. To build this chart, you need to filter the documents and choose the encoding fields for representing movies aggregated per year. The following steps will help you complete this exercise:

1. From the dashboard window, click on **Add Chart**, and then choose the **Bar** chart type.

2. Drag and drop the **year** field to the categorical channel **Y Axis**. The chart builder will detect that there are too many categorical distinct values (years) and will propose binning them (grouping them in 10-year periods). Now, toggle **Binning** on and for **Bin Size**, enter the value **10** (see the following figure):

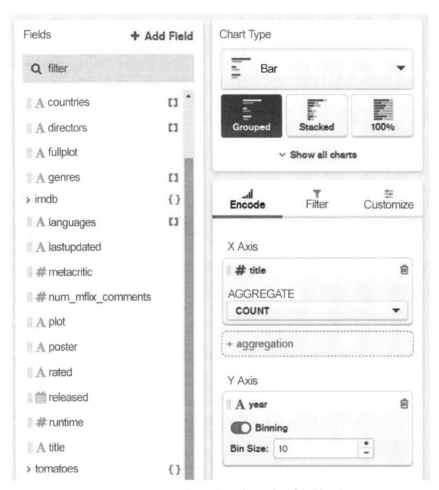

Figure 12.42: Entering 10 as the value for Bin Size

3. Drag and drop the **title** field to the categorical channel **X Axis**. Then, choose the **AGGREGATE** function option **COUNT** and click the **Filter** tab.

4. Drag and drop the **countries** field to the chart filter.

5. Select **Italy** from the chart filter as follows:

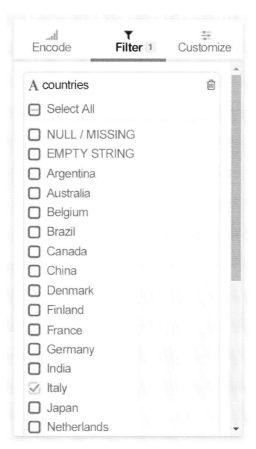

Figure 12.43: Selecting Italy from the list of countries

6. Drag and drop the second field, **year**, to the chart filter, and set **Min** to **1970** as follows:

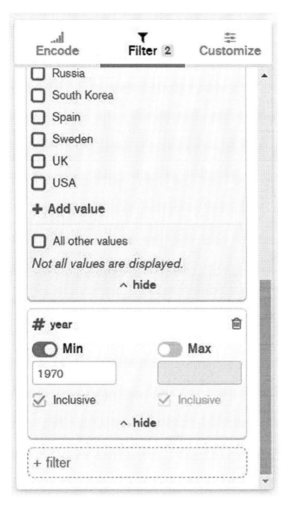

Figure 12.44: Selecting 1970 as the Min value for the year field

7.  Edit the chart title to **Movies from Italy**, as follows:

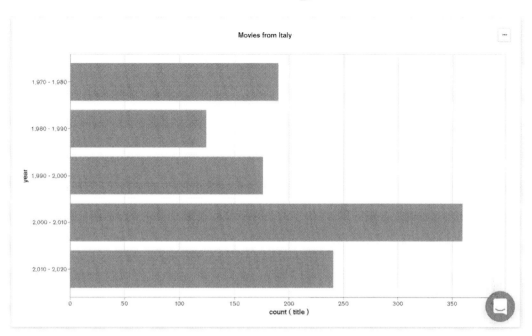

Figure 12.45: The final Movies from Italy bar chart

8.  Save the chart.

In this exercise, you created a chart using both filtering and aggregation techniques in a simple manner and without writing any JavaScript code. The new chart is saved on the dashboard, so it can be loaded and edited later. The MongoDB Chart Builder has an efficient web GUI, which helps users to create complex charts. Besides being simple to use, the interface also has numerous options and configuration items you can choose from.

# INTEGRATION

So far, the topics in this chapter have focused on describing the functionality of MongoDB Charts PaaS. We have learned that users can easily build dashboards and charts using data sources from the Atlas cloud database. The last topic of this chapter addresses the end result of a MongoDB chart—that is, how the dashboards and charts can be used for presentations and applications.

One option is to save the charts as images and integrate them into MS PowerPoint presentations or to publish them as web page content. While this option is very simple, it has one main disadvantage in that the chart image is static. Therefore, the chart is not updated when the database is updated.

Another option is to use MongoDB Charts as a presentation tool. This option guarantees that charts are refreshed and rendered each time the database is updated. Nevertheless, this option is probably not ideal, as the content is limited to the MongoDB Charts user interface and cannot be easily integrated.

Fortunately, MongoDB Charts has an option to publish charts as dynamic content for web pages and web applications. It can also be easily integrated into an MS PowerPoint presentation. This integration feature is called **Embedded Charts** and allows charts to be automatically refreshed after a pre-established time interval.

## EMBEDDED CHARTS

Embedding charts is an option you can use to share charts outside of the MongoDB Charts tool by providing web links that can be used in data presentations and applications.

There are three methods to share charts:

- **Unauthenticated**: With this method, users are not required to authenticate themselves to access the chart. They only need to have the access link. This option is appropriate for public data or information that is not sensitive.

- **Authenticated**: With this method, users are required to authenticate themselves to access the chart. This option is appropriate for charts with non-public data.

- **Verified Signature**: With this method, users are required to provide a signature key to access the chart. This option is appropriate for sensitive data and requires additional configuration and code to verify the signature.

Choosing the method depends on data security requirements and policies. The **Unauthenticated** method is acceptable for learning or testing with non-sensitive data. In applications with real or sensitive data, the **Verified Signature** method should always be used for integration with other applications.

There are a few options for embedded charts, as shown in the screenshot here:

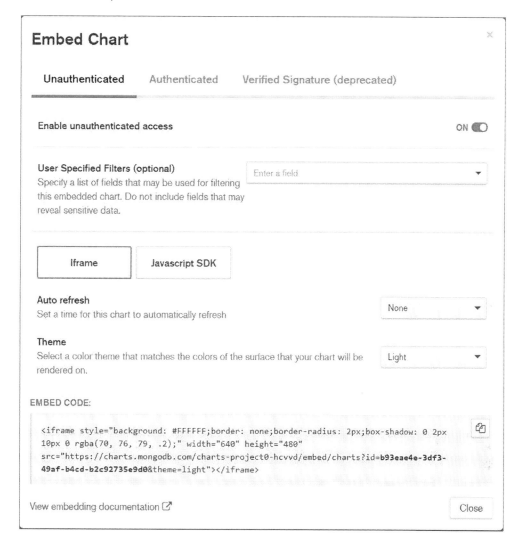

Figure 12.46: Embed Chart window

For example, say you want to configure **Unauthenticated** access for users. After selecting the **Unauthenticated** option, you can specify the following details:

- **User Specified Filters (optional)**: You can specify the fields that are not visible for sharing.

- **Auto refresh**: You can specify the time interval at which the chart is automatically refreshed.

- **Theme**: You can specify a **Light** or **Dark** chart theme.

The embedded code is automatically generated and can be copied to the application code as you can see from *Figure 12.46*.

## EXERCISE 12.06: ADDING CHARTS TO HTML PAGES

In this exercise, you will create a simple HTML report containing embedded charts created with MongoDB Atlas Charts. Use the saved chart **Movies from Italy**, created in *Exercise 12.05*, *Binning Values for a Bar Graph*:

1.  As you have done in the preceding sections, enable access to the data source by navigating to the **Data Source** tab and select the data source **sample_ mflix.movies**.

2.  Click on the right side of the menu (...) and choose **External Sharing Options**.

3.  Click **Unauthenticated or Authenticated Access**, and then click on **Save**, as shown in the following figure:

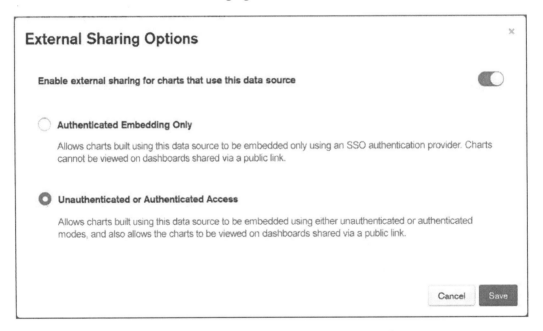

Figure 12.47: External Sharing Options screenshot

4. Go to the **Dashboards** tab and open the **Movies** dashboard. You should be able to see charts created and saved, including the **Movies from Italy** bar chart.

5. Click on the right side of the chart (...) and then click **Embed Chart** as shown in the following figure:

Figure 12.48: Selecting the Embed Chart option

The **Embed Chart** window will appear as can be seen in the following figure:

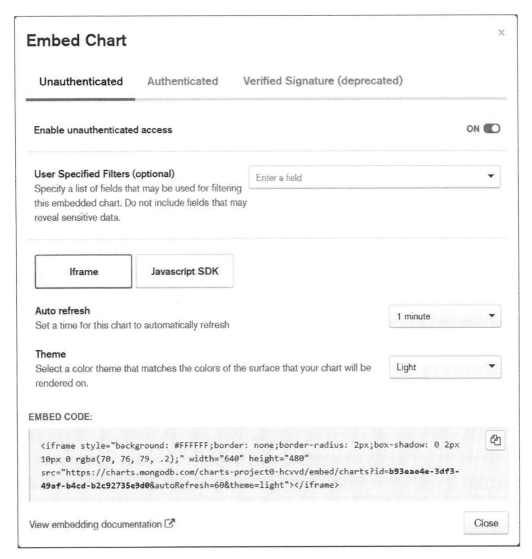

**Figure 12.49: Embed Chart page**

6. Click the **Unauthenticated** tab and change the settings as follows:

**Auto refresh**: 1 minute

**Theme**: Light

7. Copy the **EMBED CODE** content that appears at the bottom of the page.

> **NOTES**
>
> Users can interact with the embedded chart by selecting filters. To activate this optional feature, click on **User Specified Filters (optional)** and select the field that can be used to determine the chart filters. The JavaScript SDK allows integrating MongoDB charts using a coding library. This option is developer-driven, and it is not presented in this chapter.

8. Create a simple HTML page, using a text editor such as Notepad, and save it with the **.html** extension:

```
<hr />

<h3 style="text-align: left;">Introduction to MongoDB - Test
HTML </h3>
<p align="center">


<! - Paste here the embedded code copied from MongoDB Chart -- >


</p>
<h3 style="text-align: center;"> </h3>
<hr />
<p> </p>
```

9. Now, consider the following line of code:

```
<!-- Paste here the embedded code copied from MongoDB chart -->
```

10. In its place, add the code copied in *step 7*. The end code result should look as follows:

```
<hr />

<h3 style="text-align: left;">Introduction to MongoDB - Test
HTML </h3>
<p align="center">
<iframe style="background: #FFFFFF;border: none;border-radius:
2px;box-
   shadow: 0 2px 10px 0 rgba(70, 76, 79, .2);" width="640"
height="480"
      src="https://charts.mongodb.com/charts-project-0-
        paxgp/embed/charts?id=772fcf16-f0ec-467d-b2bf-
          d6a49e665511&tenant=e6ffce97-1ff7-4430-9bb2-
            8b8fb32917c5&theme=light"></iframe>
```

```
</p>
<h3 style="text-align: center;"> </h3>
<hr />
<p> </p>
```

11. Save the Notepad file. Then, open the file using an internet browser, such as Google Chrome or Microsoft Edge. The browser should display the page with dynamic chart content, as the following screenshot shows:

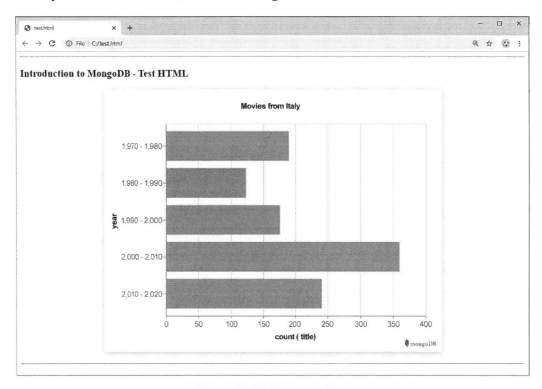

Figure 12.50: Browser view

This exercise is a good example of how MongoDB charts can be integrated into HTML web pages so that the content is dynamically updated every time the data changes. In this case, if the database records are updated and the chart is changed, the web page will also be updated after an interval of 1 minute, to reflect the changes.

In this section, we have discussed the options available for chart presentation and integration with external applications. In most business use cases, static images are not appropriate for dynamic web content and applications. The **Embed Chart** option from MongoDB allows users to integrate charts in presentations and web applications. Both secure and non-secure chart publishing options are available. However, the secure option should always be used for data-sensitive presentations.

## ACTIVITY 12.01: CREATING A SALES PRESENTATION DASHBOARD

In this activity, you will create a new chart with sales statistics from a sample database. Specifically, the analysis must help identify sales in Denver, Colorado, based on the sales item type. The following steps will help you complete this activity:

1. Create a donut circular chart to plot the top sales aggregated per sales item.

2. Create a new data source from the **sample_supplies** database.

3. Filter data so that only documents from Denver stores are considered in the report. The chart should display a donut with the top 10 items (by value) and should be named **Denver Sales (million $)**.

4. Use chart label formatting to display the values in millions and interpret the data based on the resulting charts.

The final output should appear as follows:

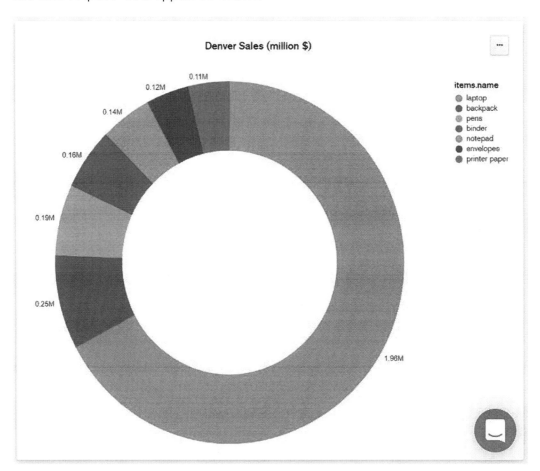

Figure 12.51: Sales chart

**NOTE**

The solution to this activity can be found on Page 692.

# SUMMARY

This chapter differed from previous chapters in that it focused on the Charts user interface rather than MongoDB programming. The results that can be achieved using the Atlas cloud Charts module are impressive, allowing users to focus on data rather than programming and presentation.

There are various chart types and sub-types to choose from, which makes Charts both more effective and easier to work with. MongoDB Charts can also be easily integrated with other web applications using the **EMBED CODE** option, which is an advantage for developers because they do not need to deal with another programming module to plot graphs in their applications. In the next chapter, we will look at a business use case in which MongoDB will be used for managing the backend.

# 13

# MONGODB CASE STUDY

## OVERVIEW

In this chapter, you will learn how MongoDB can be used in a business use case. It begins with a scenario wherein an imaginary city council and a local start-up jointly develop a mobile-application-based bike-sharing platform. It will then cover a detailed project proposal and a few challenges, and how the challenges are solved by using a MongoDB Atlas-based Database-as-a-Service solution. Finally, you will explore how MongoDB can be used for some use cases, go through each of them, and verify that the database design covers all the requirements.

# INTRODUCTION

So far in this book, we have successfully mastered various aspects of MongoDB, from a basic introduction to disaster recovery. For any tool or technology that you choose to learn, it is important to learn how it is used, and that is what we have achieved in the previous chapters. This final chapter, then, will focus on using this technology to solve real-life problems and to make life easier.

In this chapter, we will study a use case of an imaginary city council and their upcoming bike-sharing project. First, we will look at the details of the project and see why it is needed; then, we will cover the requirements and find out how MongoDB can solve their problem.

# FAIR BAY CITY COUNCIL

Fair Bay is a city located on the east coast of North Roseland and is traditionally known for its pleasant climate and historical significance. It is also one of the major business hubs of the country. Over the last two decades, this city has generated tremendous job opportunities and attracted talent from all over the country and across the globe. Consequently, it has seen a huge population rise over the last decade, which in turn has boosted the city's real estate market.

The city is expanding at a fast pace, and the local city council is working hard to assess and redevelop the city's basic infrastructure and facilities to maintain its ease of living index. They frequently conduct surveys and assessments of their public infrastructures to identify some of the most common issues raised by the public.

In past assessments and surveys, the following concerns were repeatedly raised by the residents of the local communities:

- Local transport is always crowded.

- There is frequent traffic congestion.

- Fuel and parking prices are rising.

- There is bad air quality in the central parts of the city.

- Commute times are increasing.

To resolve these complaints, the council invites corporates, start-ups, and even the public to come forward with smart and innovative ideas and related project proposals. Upon close review and approval, the best proposals are sent to the Development and Planning Commission of the state for funding. The council's initiative has been a big success so far, as they have several popular ideas. This year, one of the submitted project proposals caught everyone's attention. One of the local start-ups has proposed a rollout of Fair Bay City Bikes, which is an online bike-sharing platform. Besides being a unique, innovative solution, it is also one of the most environmentally friendly project proposals. The details of their proposal are outlined in the following sections.

# FAIR BAY CITY BIKES

Densely populated metropolitan cities often suffer from traffic congestion and overcrowded public transport. A bike-sharing program is a sustainable way of traveling for several reasons. It provides a healthier and cheaper mode of transportation than using cars, public transport, or private bikes. It involves procuring and parking bikes in various locations across the city. These bikes can be used by the public, on a first come first serve basis, to travel into the city. Typically, the booking and tracking of the bikes are controlled via an online platform. Studies and surveys have concluded that a well-implemented bike-sharing program can:

- Reduce traffic congestion

- Improve air quality

- Reduce car and public transport usage

- Help people save money spent on other vehicles

- Encourage healthier lifestyles

- Improve the sense of community

For these reasons, many cities are actively encouraging bike riding by providing bike-sharing platforms and dedicated cycle lanes in the city. The Fair Bay City Bikes project is a next-generation bike-sharing platform with some unique qualities, such as automated self-locking and a user-friendly mobile app. Next, we will look at some of the major highlights of their proposal.

## PROPOSAL HIGHLIGHTS

Some of the highlights of the Fair Bay City Bikes project are as follows.

## DOCKLESS BIKES

The Fair Bay City Bike project is a dockless bike-sharing project. Generally, bikes need dedicated docking stations where they remain locked. Users need to access these docking stations to start and end their rides. The major drawback of such systems is setting up docking station infrastructure evenly across the city. Establishing such a network involves finding a safe and suitable place in every area, which is often unaffordable. Secondly, people tend to find it difficult to locate and access the docking stations. Not finding an empty docking station close to the destination is a common problem for users, which discourages them from using the system.

On the other hand, dockless bikes have a built-in automated self-locking and unlocking mechanism. They can be picked up, parked, and left in any safe place or any dedicated parking area. Users can pick up any of the bikes that are parked in their surrounding area and leave them in any safe parking space close to their destination.

## EASE OF USE

The users can download and access the City Bikes app on their mobile phones. Upon providing a few personal details, such as name, phone number, and a government-issued photo ID such as a driver's license, they are free to use the bikes anytime they want.

To start a bike ride, users can use the find function in the app and, based on their location, a list of the closest available bikes will be displayed in a map view. The user can then select any of the available bikes and use the in-app navigation assistance to reach it. Next, the user needs to scan a unique Quick Response (QR) code located on the bike and then simply click to unlock it.

Figure 13.1: QR code that the user can scan to unlock a bike

Once the bike is unlocked, it becomes temporarily associated with the user's account. Upon finishing the journey, the user needs to park the bike at a safe location, open the app, and click to lock the bike, which will in turn release it from the user's account.

## REAL-TIME TRACKING

All bikes have an inbuilt GPS tracking device, which enables real-time tracking of their locations. With this tracking ability, a user can easily search for available bikes in their surrounding area and use navigation assistance to access the bike.

Also, once the ride has started, each bike's location is tracked and logged into the system every 30 seconds. The logs will be used for reporting, analytics, and tracking the bikes in case of emergency or theft. Users can take the bikes 24/7 to any part of the city and the real-time tracking helps them feel safe, no matter the time of the day.

## MAINTENANCE AND CARE

All bikes need periodic maintenance and careful inspections to ensure they work efficiently. This maintenance is done every 15 days, during which the bike is cleaned, the moving parts are lubricated, tire pressure is checked and regulated, and the brakes are inspected and adjusted. Every day, the system identifies the bikes that are due for maintenance, takes them out of the list of available bikes on the system, and notifies a team of technicians.

# TECHNICAL DISCUSSIONS AND DECISIONS

The proposal is highly appreciated by the council members, and they are impressed with its cutting-edge features and low-cost implementations, as the dockless system is a lot cheaper than using docking bikes. The council is ready to procure the bikes, construct cycle lanes, and implement the signaling system throughout the city. They will also prepare the usage and safety guidelines as well as handling advertising. The team at the start-up is responsible for building the IT infrastructure and mobile application.

The council has insisted that the team keep the IT infrastructure cost to a minimum, reduce the overall rollout time, and build a scalable and flexible system for future requirement changes. The technical team at the start-up did some research to address these conditions, as detailed in the following sections.

## QUICK ROLLOUT

The team is on a tight schedule and needs to find a way to *build fast and ship fast*. The key to achieve this is to reduce research time and go with well-known and proven technologies. The technical team already has the mobile application and the backend application ready. The only thing they need to do now is to decide on a suitable database platform. A database is required to persist customer details, bike details, real-time locations of the bikes, and ride details. This database platform should be quick to set up without worrying much about the infrastructure, integrations, security, or backups. The team has decided to go for a **Database-as-a-Service** (**DBaaS**) solution to provide a reliable, scalable solution, and reduce the time to market.

## COST EFFECTIVE

As the council is simultaneously funding numerous projects, there is a bit of a budget crunch. For this reason, they have decided to start with 200 bikes first, observe the effectiveness, and seek public feedback. Based on this feedback, they are willing to increase the fleet size to 1,000, or even 2,000 if required. This increase in fleet size will in turn lead to an increase in the data to be managed. For this, **DBaaS** platforms are a great choice as it allows you to start with minimal setup and scale as and when you need.

The initial 200 bikes mean at any time there will be 200 rides at most. Therefore, there will not be any need for large dataset processing, and so the team has decided to go for low RAM and low CPU clusters. As the fleet size grows, they can scale up or scale out and the costs will always be optimized to the usage requirements.

## FLEXIBLE

During a council meeting, a few members made the following suggestions:

- Charge fees: Only residents can use it free of charge, while tourists and visitors will be charged for each ride.

- Use passport as valid proof of ID: Add passport to the list of valid IDs. Customers who do not have a photo ID provided by the government use their passports to enroll in the system.

- Add scooters into the fleet: The system should support bike-sharing and scooter sharing.

These suggestions will certainly improve the system by making it more user friendly. However, before they are incorporated into the system, some analysis needs to be carried out. Charging fees and supporting different types of ID verification requires integration with federal and external systems. This integration needs to comply with different rules, regulations, and safety and privacy policies issued by the concerned departments.

Considering these challenges, the council has decided to stick to the current plan for phase 1 of the rollout. The requirements for the suggested changes will be finalized and incorporated in phase 2 of the project.

The technical team understands that the system needs to be flexible enough to incorporate any future changes that are still unknown or uncertain. With the current technical design, the user has a driving license number as ID, but it needs to be more flexible to store other types of ID. Also, to charge the fees, the schema needs to be flexible enough to incorporate users' bank accounts or credit card details. Similarly, to introduce scooters in the fleet (which may have different maintenance requirements or a different fee structure), the system needs to be able to differentiate between a cycle and a scooter.

In this scenario, traditional database entities, which are bound to strict schema definitions, are not a good choice. To incorporate some of the future changes, their schema definitions need to be updated first. With traditional databases, the schema changes are difficult to roll out and roll back. Upon careful consideration and comparison, the team has decided to go for a MongoDB Atlas cluster. MongoDB provides a flexible schema and horizontal as well as vertical scaling capabilities. The Atlas cluster helps to roll out a production-level system with just a few clicks and saves significantly on cost and time. In the next section, we will look at the detailed database design.

# DATABASE DESIGN

As per the requirements described in the previous sections, the three basic entities to be persisted are **user**, **vehicle**, and **ride**. The **user** and **vehicle** entities will store the attributes of users and vehicles respectively, while the **ride** entity will be created whenever a new ride is commenced.

Apart from the basic entities, an additional entity is needed to track the bike ride logs. For each active ride, the system captures and logs the bike's location. The logs will be used for reporting and analytics purposes.

Because of the document-based dataset offered by MongoDB, all the entities can easily be designed as collections. These collections and some of their sample records will be explored in the next sections.

## USERS

The **users** collection holds data for all who have registered in the system. The following code snippet shows a sample document that represents one of the registered users:

```
{
    "_id" : "a6e36e30-41fa-45bf-93c5-83da4efeed37",
    "email_address" : "ethel.112@example.com",
    "first_name" : "Ethel",
    "last_name" : "Carter",
    "date_of_birth" : ISODate("1993-06-01T00:00:00Z"),
    "address" : {
        "street" : "51 Thornridge Cir",
        "city" : "Fair Bay",
        "state" : "North Roseland",
        "post_code" : 9924,
        "country" : "Roseland"
    },
    "registration_date" : ISODate("2020-11-24T00:00:00Z"),
    "id_documents" : [
    {
        "drivers_license" : {
            "license_number" : 2771556252,
            "issue_date" : ISODate("2011-04-18T00:00:00Z")
        }
    }],
    "payments" : [
    {
        "credit_card" : {
            "name_on_card" : "Ethel Carter",
            "card_number" : 342610644867494,
            "valid_till" : "3/22"
        }
    }]
}
```

The primary key in the document is a randomly generated unique UUID string. There are other fields to hold the user's basic information, such as their first name, last name, date of birth, address, email address, and system registration date. The **id_documents** field is an array and currently stores driving license details. In the future, when other ID types such as passports are enabled, the user will be able to provide multiple ID details. The payment details are currently collected as a precaution. Customers will not be charged unless the bike is damaged or stolen during a ride. The **payments** field is an array and currently stores credit card details. Once the system is integrated with other payment gateways, the user will be given an option for other means of payment.

## VEHICLES

The **vehicles** collection represents the bikes in the fleet. City Bikes will have 200 bikes initially. The structure of a vehicle document with all the fields and example values is shown in the following snippet:

```
{
    "_id" : "227fe7e0-76c7-410b-afe8-6ae5785ac937",
    "vehicle_type" : "bike|scooter",
    "status" : "available",
    "rollout_date" : ISODate("2020-10-20T00:00:00Z"),
    "make" : {
        "Manufacturer" : "Compass Cycles",
        "model_name" : "Unisex - Flatbar Carbon Frame Road Bike",
        "model_code" : "CBUFLATR101",
        "year" : 2020,
        "frame_number" : "FWJ166K23683958E"
    },
    "gears" : 3,
    "has_basket" : true,
    "has_helmet" : true,
    "bike_type" : "unisex|men|women",
    "location" : {
        "type" : "Point",
        "coordinates" : [
            111.189631,
            -72.454577
```

```
        ]
    },
    "last_maintenance_date" : ISODate("2020-11-05T00:00:00Z")
}
```

The primary key in this document is a unique UUID string. This ID is used to uniquely refer to the vehicle—for example, in the QR code or vehicle ride details. There are other static fields to represent the vehicle's rollout date, manufacturer name, model, frame number, number of gears, and more. Considering the council's plan to roll out scooters in the future, a field named **vehicle_type** is introduced. This field differentiates between a bike and a scooter. The **status** field denotes whether the bike is currently available, on a ride, or under maintenance (in this case, it is available). This field can hold any of these three values: **available**, **on_ride**, and **under_maintenance**. The last maintenance date helps identify whether the vehicle is due for maintenance. The **location** field represents the current geographical location of the vehicle, and it is represented in MongoDB's geospatial index of **Point** type. The other optional fields, such as **has_basket**, **has_helmet**, and **bike_type**, are useful for serving customers with specific requirements. Note that the bike models can be categorized as **men**, **women**, or unisex bikes, while scooters are always **unisex**. Hence, the **bike_type** field will be present only if the **vehicle_type** is **bike**.

## RIDES

The **rides** collection represents the trips, and the total number of documents in this collection denotes the number of rides taken through the system:

```
{
    "_id" : "ebe89a65-ee02-4fa8-aba7-88c33751d487",
    "user_id" : "a6e36e30-41fa-45bf-93c5-83da4efeed37",
    "vehicle_id" : "227fe7e0-76c7-410b-afe8-6ae5785ac937",
    "start_time" : ISODate("2020-11-25T02:10:00Z"),
    "start_location" : {
        "type" : "Point",
        "coordinates" : [
            111.189631,
            -72.454577
        ]
    },
    "end_time" : ISODate("2020-11-25T03:17:00Z"),
    "end_location" : {
        "type" : "Point",
```

```
        "coordinates" : [
            111.045789,
            -72.456144
        ]
    },
    "feedback" : {
        "stars" : 5,
        "comment" : "Navigation helped me locate the bike quickly,
 enjoyed my
            ride. Thank you City Bikes"
    }
}
```

Each ride has a primary key of a randomly generated UUID string. The **user_id** and **vehicle_id** fields denote the user currently availing themself of the ride and the vehicle, respectively. The **ride** document is created when the user unlocks the bike and the **start_time** and **start_location** fields are inserted upon creation. The **end_time** and **end_location** fields are created when the user locks the bike at the end of the trip. There is an optional field to represent the feedback, where the star rating and user comments are recorded.

## RIDE LOGS

The **ride_logs** collection records the progress of each active ride at 30-second intervals. This collection is mainly used for analytics and reporting purposes. By using the data in this collection, any ride's complete path can be traced in real time. While on a ride, if the bike is involved in an accident or if the bike goes missing, the last logged entry of the bike can help to locate it. The following code snippet shows three consecutive log entries for the same bike ride:

```
{
    "_id" : "6b868a75-5c47-4b36-a706-e84b486d4c40",
    "ride_id" : " -ee02-4fa8-aba7-88c33751d487",
    "time" : ISODate("2020-11-25T02:10:00Z"),
    "location":{
        "type":"Point",
        "coordinates":[111.189631, -72.454577]
    }
}
{
    "_id" : "e33f9d94-8787-4b0d-aa52-08795fab2b38",
    "ride_id" : "ebe89a65-ee02-4fa8-aba7-88c33751d487",
```

```
        "time" : ISODate("2020-11-25T02:10:30Z"),
        "location":{
            "type":"Point",
            "coordinates":[111.189425 -72.454582]
        }
    }
    {
        "_id" : "8d39567b-efc5-43d4-9034-f636c97c97b3",
        "ride_id" : "ebe89a65-ee02-4fa8-aba7-88c33751d487",
        "time" : ISODate("2020-11-25T02:11:00Z"),
        "location":{
            "type":"Point",
            "coordinates":[111.189291, -72.454585]
        }
    }
}
```

Each of these log entries has a primary key of a unique UUID string. The document contains **ride_id**, which helps trace the ride, user, and vehicle details. The **time** and **location** fields help track the geographic coordinates of the vehicle at a given time. For analytics purposes, this collection can be used in numerous ways to generate useful statistics to identify and address existing issues or carry out future improvements. For example, this collection helps find the average bike speed for all rides, the average speed in certain areas, or the average speed of riders within certain age groups. By comparing these statistics, the council can identify the areas of the city in which riders tend to ride more slowly and provide adequate cycle lanes. Also, they can examine bike usage and speed patterns by the age of riders and designate safe speed limits. The collection also helps to find the most and least popular areas of the city for bike riders. Based on this information, the council can take appropriate measures to make more bikes available in popular areas and fewer bikes available in unpopular ones.

This section covered the details of the MongoDB database structure and the anatomy of the collections. In the next section, we will run through the various use cases using some example scenarios.

# USE CASES

The preceding sections provided an overview of the City Bikes system, the requirements and considerations, and the database structure. Now, we will list the system use cases using some example scenarios and the database queries to run through them. This will help verify the correctness of the design and help ensure that no requirement is missed.

## USER FINDS AVAILABLE BIKES

Consider a situation in which a user opens the app on their mobile phone and clicks to find a bike in a radius of 300 meters from their location. The user's current coordinates are *Longitude 111.189528 and Latitude -72.454567*. The next snippet shows the corresponding database query:

```
db.vehicles.find({
    "vehicle_type" : "bike",
    "status" : "available",
    "location" : {
        $near : {
            $geometry : {
                "type" : "Point",
                "coordinates" : [111.189528, -72.454567]
            },
            $maxDistance : 300
        }
    }
})
```

The query finds all the bikes that are currently available and located within the requested 300-meter radius.

## USER UNLOCKS A BIKE

The user scans the QR code on the bike (**227fe7e0-76c7-410b-afe8-6ae5785ac937**) and clicks to unlock it. Unlocking a bike starts the ride and makes the bike unavailable to the other users.

Using our database, this scenario can be implemented in two steps. First, the status of the bike should be changed, and then, a new ride entry should be created. The following snippet shows how to do this:

```
db.vehicles.findOneAndUpdate(
    {"_id" : "227fe7e0-76c7-410b-afe8-6ae5785ac937"},
    {
        $set : {"status" : "on_ride"}
    }
)
```

The preceding command sets the status of the bike to **on_ride**. As the status of the bike is no longer set to **available**, it will not appear in bike searches performed by other users. The next snippet shows the **insert** command on the **rides** collection:

```
db.rides.insert({
    "_id" : "ebe89a65-ee02-4fa8-aba7-88c33751d487",
    "user_id" : "a6e36e30-41fa-45bf-93c5-83da4efeed37",
    "vehicle_id" : "227fe7e0-76c7-410b-afe8-6ae5785ac937",
    "start_time" : new Date("2020-11-25T02:10:00Z"),
    "start_location" : {
        "type" : "Point",
        "coordinates" : [
            111.189631,
            -72.454577
        ]
    }
})
```

This **insert** command creates a new ride entry and associates the user, the bike, and the ride together. It also captures the start time and the start location of the ride.

## USER LOCKS THE BIKE

At the end of the trip, the user parks the bike at a safe location, opens the application, and clicks on the screen to finish the ride. This also requires two steps. First, the ride entry needs to be updated with the end-of-trip details. Second, the status and new location of the vehicle need to be updated:

```
db.rides.findOneAndUpdate(
    {"_id" : "ebe89a65-ee02-4fa8-aba7-88c33751d487"},
    {
        $set : {
            "end_time" : new Date("2020-11-25T03:17:00Z"),
            "end_location" : {
                "type" : "Point",
                "coordinates" : [
                    111.045789,
                    -72.456144
                ]
            }
        }
    }
)
```

The preceding command sets the end time and the coordinates in the ride. Note that the absence of an end location and end time indicates that the ride is still in progress:

```
db.vehicles.findOneAndUpdate(
    {"_id" : "227fe7e0-76c7-410b-afe8-6ae5785ac937"},
    {
        $set : {
            "status" : "available",
            "location" : {
                "type" : "Point",
                "coordinates" : [
                    111.045789,
                    -72.456144
                ]
            }
        }
    }
)
```

The preceding command marks the vehicle as available and updates its location with the new coordinates.

## SYSTEM LOGS THE GEOGRAPHICAL COORDINATES OF RIDES

Every 30 seconds, a scheduled job queries for all the bikes from active rides, gathers their latest geographical coordinates through GPS, and creates ride log entries for each of them. The next snippet shows an **insert** command for the **logs** collection:

```
db.ride_logs.insert({
    "_id" : "8d39567b-efc5-43d4-9034-f636c97c97b3",
    "ride_id" : "ebe89a65-ee02-4fa8-aba7-88c33751d487",
    "time" : new Date(),
    "location":{
        "type":"Point",
        "coordinates":[
            111.189291,
            -72.454585
        ]
    }
})
```

The preceding command demonstrates how a new ride log is created. It uses **new Date()** to log the current timestamp in *GMT* and inserts the latest location coordinates for the given bike ride.

## SYSTEM SENDS BIKES FOR MAINTENANCE

All the bikes need regular maintenance every two weeks. The technicians perform regular checks on the bikes and fix any identified problems. A scheduled job is carried out every night at midnight, and the last maintenance dates of all bikes are checked. The job helps find all the bikes whose maintenance has not been done in the last 15 days and marks them as due for maintenance. The bikes then become unavailable. The following command finds all the bikes where the last maintenance date is more than 15 days prior to the current date:

```
db.vehicles.updateMany(
    {
        "last_maintenance_date" : {
            $lte : new Date(new Date() - 1000 * 60 * 60 * 24 * 15)
        }
```

```
    },
    {
        $set : {"status" : "under_maintenance"}
    }
)
```

The **1000 * 60 * 60 * 24 * 15** expression represents 15 days in milliseconds. The calculated number of milliseconds is then subtracted from the current date to find that date 15 days ago. If the bike's **last_maintenance_date** field is older than 15 days, its status is marked as **under_maintenance**.

## TECHNICIAN PERFORMS FORTNIGHTLY MAINTENANCE

The technician team finds all the bikes with the **under_maintenance** status, performs the maintenance, and makes the bikes available:

```
db.vehicles.findOneAndUpdate(
    {"_id" : "227fe7e0-76c7-410b-afe8-6ae5785ac937"},
    {
        $set : {
            "status" : "available",
            "last_maintenance_date" : new Date()
        }
    }
)
```

This command sets the bike status as available and sets **last_maintenance_date** to the current timestamp.

## GENERATING STATS

The analysts are tasked with using the various stats generated by the app to identify areas of improvement and optimization as well as to assess the system benefits in terms of the money being spent. They can use the database in more than one way; however, we will use a sample use case for demonstration.

The city's Central Park (located at *108.146337, -78.617716*) is a very popular and crowded place. To make riding easy for cyclists, the council has built special cycle lanes in the area surrounding the park. The council wants to know how many City Bike riders have traveled on these lanes.

The analysts execute a quick query to find bike rides traveled through the area within a 200-meter radius of Central Park:

```
db.ride_logs.distinct(
    "ride_id",
    {
        "location" : {
            $near : {
                $geometry : {
                    "type" : "Point",
                    "coordinates" : [108.146337, -78.617716]
                },
                $maxDistance : 200
            }
        }
    }
)
```

This distinct query on the **ride_logs** filters all the log entries to find how many bike rides were geographically close to the given location and prints their ride IDs.

In this section, we discussed various scenarios where the app could be used and satisfied them with MongoDB queries and commands.

## SUMMARY

This chapter explored the City Bikes project implemented by an imaginary city council. This began with a consideration of the predicted problems faced by the council and how the project proposal might address those problems. Among these considerations were the council's time and budget, uncertain requirements, and the technical team's decision to use a MongoDB Atlas-based **Database-as-a-Service (DBaaS)** solution to address all these issues. You studied the database design in detail and reviewed MongoDB queries to log, implement, and resolve several example scenarios in this example system.

Throughout this course, you have been introduced to various features and benefits of MongoDB through practical examples and applications. You started with the basics of MongoDB, looking at its nature and function, and how it differs from traditional RDBMS databases. You then uncovered the benefits offered by its JSON-based data structure and flexible schema. Next, you learned the core database operations and operators to find, aggregate, insert, update, and delete data from collections, as well as more advanced concepts such as performance improvement, replication, backup and restore, and data visualization. You also created your own MongoDB database cluster in the cloud using MongoDB Atlas, then loaded a real-life example dataset into the cluster, which you used throughout the book. Finally, this chapter concluded this course by demonstrating how MongoDB solutions can solve real-life problems.

With the knowledge and skills that you have gained over the course of this book, you will be able to implement a highly scalable, robust database design that meets business requirements at your workplace, or for your own personal projects.

# APPENDIX

# CHAPTER 1: INTRODUCTION TO MONGODB

## ACTIVITY 1.01: SETTING UP A MOVIES DATABASE

**Solution:**

The following steps will help you complete this activity:

1. First, connect to your MongoDB cluster that was set up as part of *Exercise 1.04, Setting Up Your First Free MongoDB Cluster on Atlas*. It should look something like this:

```
mongo "mongodb+srv://cluster0-zlury.mongodb.net/test" –username
   <yourUsername>
```

2. Enter the preceding command on your command prompt and provide the password when prompted. Upon successful login, you should see a shell prompt with your cluster name, something like this:

```
MongoDB Enterprise Cluster0-shard-0:PRIMARY>
```

3. Now, create the movies database and call it **moviesDB**. Utilize the **use** command:

```
use moviesDB
```

4. Create the **movies** collection with a few relevant attributes. Create the collection by inserting the documents into a non-existent collection. You are encouraged to think and implement collections with attributes that you find most suitable:

```
db.movies.insertMany(
    [
        {
            "title": "Rocky",
            "releaseDate": new Date("Dec 3, 1976"),
            "genre": "Action",
            "about": "A small-time boxer gets a supremely rare
               chance to fight a heavy-weight champion in a bout
                  in which he strives to go the distance for his
                     self-respect.",
            "countries": ["USA"],
            "cast" : ["Sylvester Stallone","Talia Shire",
               "Burt Young"],
            "writers" : ["Sylvester Stallone"],
            "directors" : ["John G. Avildsen"]
        },
        {
```

```
                "title": "Rambo 4",
                "releaseDate ": new Date("Jan 25, 2008"),
                "genre": "Action",
                "about": "In Thailand, John Rambo joins a group of
                    mercenaries to venture into war-torn Burma, and rescue
                        a group of Christian aid workers who were kidnapped
                            by the ruthless local infantry unit.",
                "countries": ["USA"],
                "cast" : [" Sylvester Stallone", "Julie Benz", "Matthew
                    Marsden"],
                "writers" : ["Art Monterastelli","Sylvester Stallone"],
                "directors" : ["Sylvester Stallone"]
            }

        ]

    )
```

This should result in the following output:

```
{
    "acknowledged" : true,
    "insertedIds" : [
        ObjectId("5f33d027592962df72246aed"),
        ObjectId("5f33d027592962df72246aee")
    ]
}
```

5. Use the **find** command to fetch the documents you inserted in the previous step, that is, **db.movies.find().pretty()**. It should return the following output:

```
{
        "_id" : ObjectId("5f33d027592962df72246aed"),
        "title" : "Rocky",
        "releaseDate" : ISODate("1976-12-02T13:00:00Z"),
        "genre" : "Action",
        "about" : "A small-time boxer gets a supremely rare chance to
            fight a heavy-weight champion in a bout in which he strives to
                go the distance for his self-respect.",
        "countries" : [
                "USA"
        ],
        "cast" : [
                "Sylvester Stallone",
                "Talia Shire",
```

```
                "Burt Young"
        ],
        "writers" : [
                "Sylvester Stallone"
        ],
        "directors" : [
                "John G. Avildsen"
        ]
}
{
        "_id" : ObjectId("5f33d027592962df72246aee"),
        "title" : "Rambo 4",
        "releaseDate " : ISODate("2008-01-24T13:00:00Z"),
        "genre" : "Action",
        "about" : "In Thailand, John Rambo joins a group of mercenaries
           to venture into war-torn Burma, and rescue a group of
              Christian aid workers who were kidnapped by the ruthless
                 local infantry unit.",
        "countries" : [
                "USA"
        ],
        "cast" : [
                " Sylvester Stallone",
                "Julie Benz",
                "Matthew Marsden"
        ],
        "writers" : [
                "Art Monterastelli",
                "Sylvester Stallone"
        ],
        "directors" : [
                "Sylvester Stallone"
        ]
}
{
```

```
        "_id" : ObjectId("5f33d050592962df72246aef"),
        "title" : "Rocky",
        "releaseDate" : ISODate("1976-12-02T13:00:00Z"),
        "genre" : "Action",
        "about" : "A small-time boxer gets a supremely rare chance to
          fight a heavy-weight champion in a bout in which he strives to
            go the
            distance for his self-respect.",
        "countries" : [
                "USA"
        ],
        "cast" : [
                "Sylvester Stallone",
                "Talia Shire",
                "Burt Young"
        ],
        "writers" : [
                "Sylvester Stallone"
        ],
        "directors" : [
                "John G. Avildsen"
        ]
}
{

        "_id" : ObjectId("5f33d050592962df72246af0"),
        "title" : "Rambo 4",
        "releaseDate " : ISODate("2008-01-24T13:00:00Z"),
        "genre" : "Action",
        "about" : "In Thailand, John Rambo joins a group of mercenaries
          to venture into war-torn Burma, and rescue a group of
            Christian aid
            workers who were kidnapped by the ruthless local
              infantry unit.",
        "countries" : [
                "USA"
        ],
        "cast" : [
                " Sylvester Stallone",
                "Julie Benz",
```

```
                "Matthew Marsden"
        ],
        "writers" : [
                "Art Monterastelli",
                "Sylvester Stallone"
        ],
        "directors" : [
                "Sylvester Stallone"
        ]
}
```

6. You may also like to store awards information in your movies database. Create an **awards** collection with a few records. You are encouraged to think and come up with your own collection name and attributes. Here are the commands to insert a few sample documents in your **awards** collection:

```
db.awards.insertOne(
    {
        "title": "Oscars",
        "year": "1976",
        "category": "Best Film",
        "nominees": ["Rocky","All The President's Men","Bound For
          Glory","Network","Taxi Driver"],
        "winners" :
        [
            {
                "movie" : "Rocky"
            }
        ]
    }
)

db.awards.insertOne(
    {
        "title": "Oscars",
        "year": "1976",
        "category": "Actor In A Leading Role",
```

```
        "nominees": ["PETER FINCH","ROBERT DE NIRO","GIANCARLO
          GIANNINI"," WILLIAM HOLDEN","SYLVESTER STALLONE"],
        "winners" :
        [

            {
                "actor" : "PETER FINCH",
                "movie" : "Network"
            }
        ]
    }
)
```

Each of these commands should generate an output like the following:

```
{
    "acknowledged" : true,
    "insertedId" : ObjectId("5f33d08e592962df72246af1")
}
```

Each of these commands should generate an output like the following:

```
{
  "acknowledged" : true,
  "insertedId" : ObjectId("5f33d08e592962df72246af1")
}
```

> **NOTE**
>
> The inserted ID is the unique ID for the document that is inserted, so it will
> not be the same for you as mentioned in the preceding output.

7.  Run the **find** command to get the documents from the **awards** collection. The lines starting with **//** (a double slash) are comments, which are only for the purpose of description; the database does not execute them as commands:

```
// find all the documents from the awards collection
db.awards.find().pretty()
```

Here is the output of the preceding command:

```
{
        "_id" : ObjectId("5fbcde49afd316e9e7c93dfe"),
        "title" : "Oscars",
        "year" : "1976",
        "category" : "Best Film",
        "nominees" : [
                "Rocky",
                "All The President's Men",
                "Bound For Glory",
                "Network",
                "Taxi Driver"
        ],
        "winners" : [
                {
                        "movie" : "Rocky"
                }
        ]
}
{
        "_id" : ObjectId("5fbcde4bafd316e9e7c93dff"),
        "title" : "Oscars",
        "year" : "1976",
        "category" : "Actor In A Leading Role",
        "nominees" : [
                "PETER FINCH",
                "ROBERT DE NIRO",
                "GIANCARLO GIANNINI",
                " WILLIAM HOLDEN",
                "SYLVESTER STALLONE"
        ],
        "winners" : [
                {
                        "actor" : "PETER FINCH",
                        "movie" : "Network"
                }
        ]
}
```

Figure 1.39: Documents from the awards collection

> **NOTE**
>
> This exercise was for you to add as many collections/documents as you think are required to store the movie data effectively and efficiently. Feel free to add any more relevant collections and documents.

In this activity, you have found a relevant database solution for the movies database. You have also created a database on MongoDB Atlas for storing collections and documents.

In the next chapter, you will be provided with steps to import another sample dataset about movies. It is advisable that you think realistically about what other collections or attributes in the collections are required for a movies database. You will also see in the next chapter how your dataset is different from the sample provided.

# CHAPTER 2: DOCUMENTS AND DATA TYPES

## ACTIVITY 2.01: MODELING A TWEET INTO A JSON DOCUMENT

**Solution:**

Perform the following steps to complete the activity:

1. Identify and list the following fields from the tweet that can be included in the JSON document:

```
creation date and time
user id
user name
user profile pic
user verification status
hash tags
mentions
tweet text
likes
comments
retweets
```

2. Group the related fields such that they can be placed as embedded objects or arrays. Since a tweet can have multiple hashtags and mentions, it can be represented as an array. The modified list appears as follows:

```
creation date and time
user
  id
  name
  profile pic
  verification status
hash tags
  [tags]
mentions
  [mentions]
tweet text
likes
comments
retweets
```

3. Prepare the user object and add the values from the tweet:

```
{
    "id": "Lord_Of_Winterfell",
    "name": "Office of Ned Stark",
    "profile_pic": "https://user.profile.pic",
    "isVerified": true
}
```

4. List all the hashtags as an array:

```
[
    "north",
    "WinterfellCares",
    "flueshots"
]
```

5. Include all the mentions as an array:

```
[
    "MaesterLuwin",
    "TheNedStark",
    "CatelynTheCat"
]
```

Once you combine all the documents with the rest of the fields, the final output will appear as follows:

```
{
    "id": 1,
    "created_at": "Sun Apr 17 16:29:24 +0000 2011",
    "user": {
        "id": "Lord_Of_Winterfell",
        "name": "Office of Ned Stark",
        "profile_pic": "https://user.profile.pic",
        "isVerified": true
    },
    "text": "Tweeps in the #north. The long nights are upon us. Do
            stock enough warm clothes, meat and mead...",
    "hashtags": [
        "north",
        "WinterfellCares",
        "flueshots"
    ],
```

```
    "mentions": [
      "MaesterLuwin",
      "TheNedStark",
      "CatelynTheCat"
    ],
    "likes_count": 14925,
    "retweet_count": 12165,
    "comments_count": 0
  }
```

6. Click on **Validate JSON** to validate the code from any text editor as follows:

```
1 ▼ {
2      "id": 1,
3      "created_at": "Sun Apr 17 16:29:24 +0000 2011",
4 ▼    "user": {
5          "id": "Lord_Of_Winterfell",
6          "name": "Office of Ned Stark",
7          "profile_pic": "https://user.profile.pic",
8          "isVerified": true
9      },
10     "text": "Tweeps in the #north. The long nights are upon us. Do stock er
11 ▼   "hashtags": [
12         "north",
13         "WinterfellCares",
14         "flueshots"
15     ],
```

Figure 2.21: Validated JSON document

In this activity, you modeled data from a tweet into a valid JSON document.

# CHAPTER 3: SERVERS AND CLIENTS

## ACTIVITY 3.01: MANAGING YOUR DATABASE USERS

**Solution:**

The following are the detailed steps for the activity:

1. Go to http://cloud.mongodb.com to connect to the Atlas console.

2. Log on to your new MongoDB Atlas web interface using your username and password, which was created when you registered for the Atlas Cloud:

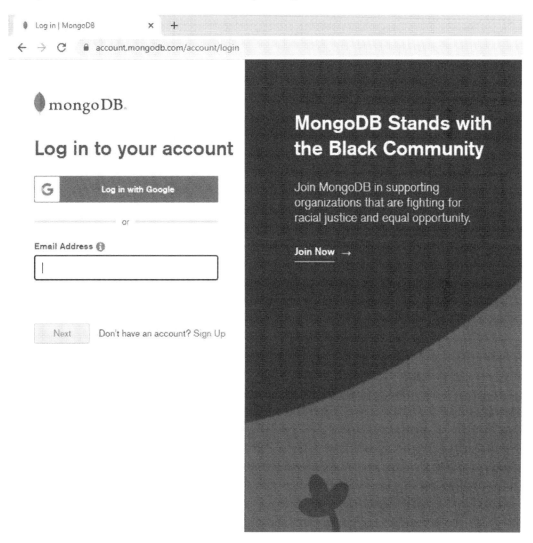

Figure 3.40: MongoDB Atlas login page

3. Create a new database called **dev_mflix** and, on the Atlas clusters page, click the **COLLECTIONS** button:

Figure 3.41: MongoDB Atlas Clusters Page

A window with all the collections will appear, as shown in *Figure 3.42*:

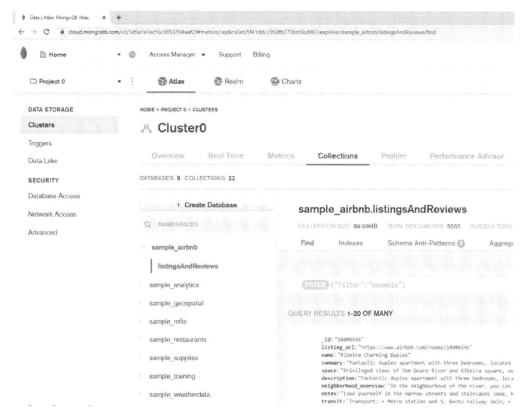

Figure 3.42: MongoDB Atlas data explorer

4.  Next, click the **+Create Database** button, at the top of the database list. The following window will appear:

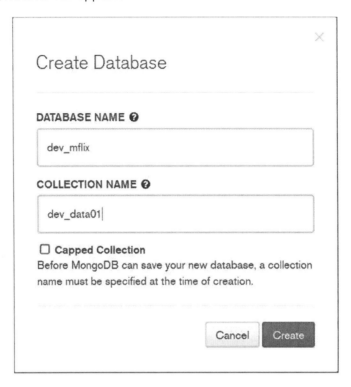

Figure 3.43: MongoDB Create Database window

5.  Set **DATABASE NAME** to `dev_mflix` and **COLLECTION NAME** to `dev_data01`, and then click the **CREATE** button.

6.  Create a custom role called **Developers**. Click on **Database Access** (on the left side). On the **Database Access** page, click on the **Custom Role** tab.

7.  Click on the **Add Custom Role** button. The **Add Custom Role** window will appear, as in the following screenshot:

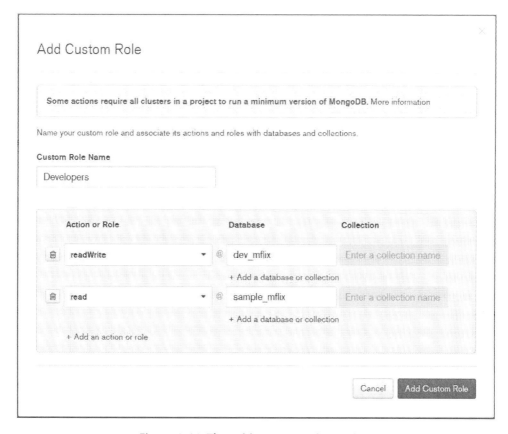

Figure 3.44: The Add Custom Role window

8. Within new **Developers** role, add the **readWrite** role on **dev_mflix**
database. Then, add the **read** role on **sample_mflix** database and click on
the **Add Custom Role** button. The new **Developers** role will appear in
the list:

Figure 3.45: Database Access – Custom Roles

9. Create the new Atlas user, **Mark**. In the **Database Access** menu, click the **+Add New Database User** button. The **Add New Database User** window will appear as follows:

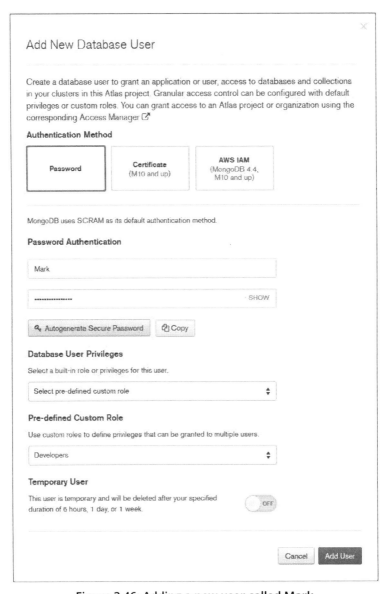

Figure 3.46: Adding a new user called Mark

10. Fill in the details as follows:

Username: **Mark**

Authentication Method: **SCRAM**

Pre-defined Custom Role: **Developers**

Now, a new user named **Mark** should appear in the Atlas user list:

Figure 3.47: Atlas database users

11. Connect to the MongoDB cloud database as user **Mark** and run the **db.getUser()** shell function. The expected shell output is shown in the following screenshot:

```
Command Prompt - mongo "mongodb+srv://cluster0.u7n6b.mongodb.net/admin" --username Mark
C:\>mongo "mongodb+srv://cluster0.u7n6b.mongodb.net/admin" --username Mark
MongoDB shell version v4.4.0
Enter password:
connecting to: mongodb://cluster0-shard-00-00.u7n6b.mongodb.net:27017,cluster0-shard-00-01.u7n6b.mongodb.
erviceName=mongodb&replicaSet=atlas-rzhbg7-shard-0&ssl=true
Implicit session: session { "id" : UUID("238da0ec-fbc0-4e4f-88d2-68589a70d861") }
MongoDB server version: 4.2.8
WARNING: shell and server versions do not match
Error while trying to show server startup warnings: user is not allowed to do action [getLog] on [admin.]
MongoDB Enterprise atlas-rzhbg7-shard-0:PRIMARY> db.getUser("Mark")
{
        "_id" : "admin.Mark",
        "user" : "Mark",
        "db" : "admin",
        "roles" : [
                {
                        "role" : "Developers",
                        "db" : "admin"
                }
        ]
}
MongoDB Enterprise atlas-rzhbg7-shard-0:PRIMARY>
MongoDB Enterprise atlas-rzhbg7-shard-0:PRIMARY>
```

Figure 3.48: Shell output (example)

This concludes the activity. A new developer called Mark has been added to the Atlas system and the appropriate access permissions have been granted.

# CHAPTER 4: QUERYING DOCUMENTS

## ACTIVITY 4.01: FINDING MOVIES BY GENRE AND PAGINATING RESULTS

**Solution:**

The most important part of the **findMoviesByGenre** function is the underlying MongoDB query. You will take a step-by-step approach to solving the problem, starting with creating the query on a mongo shell. Once the query has been prepared, you will wrap it into a function:

1.  Create a query to filter results by **genre**. For this activity, we are using the **Action** genre:

```
db.movies.find(
    {"genres" : "Action"}
)
```

2.  The requirement is to return only the titles of the movies. For this, add a projection to project only the **title** field and exclude the rest, including **_id**:

```
db.movies.find(
    {"genres" : "Action"},
    {"_id" : 0, "title" :1}
)
```

3.  Now, sort the results in descending order of IMDb ratings. Add a **sort()** function to the query:

```
db.movies.find(
    {"genres" : "Action"},
    {"_id" : 0, "title" :1})
.sort({"imdb.rating" : -1})
```

4.  Add the **skip** function and, for now, provide any value you want (**3**, in this case):

```
db.movies.find(
    {"genres" : "Action"},
    {"_id" : 0, "title" :1})
.sort({"imdb.rating" : -1})
.skip(3)
```

5.  Next, add a **limit** to the query, as follows. The limit value indicates the page size:

```
db.movies.find(
    {"genres" : "Action"},
    {"_id" : 0, "title" :1})
.sort({"imdb.rating" : -1})
.skip(3)
.limit(5)
```

6.  Finally, convert our resulting cursor into an array by using the **toArray()** function:

```
db.movies.find(
    {"genres" : "Action"},
    {"_id" : 0, "title" :1})
.sort({"imdb.rating" : -1})
.skip(3)
.limit(5)
.toArray()
```

7.  Now that the query has been written, open a text editor and write an empty function that accepts a genre, a page number, and a page size, as follows:

```
var findMoviesByGenre = function(genre, pageNumber, pageSize){

}
```

8.  Copy and paste the query inside the function, assigning it to a variable, as follows:

```
var findMoviesByGenre = function(genre, pageNumber, pageSize){
    var movies = db.movies.find(
        {"genres" : "Action"},
        {"_id" : 0, "title" :1})
    .sort({"imdb.rating" : -1})
    .skip(3)
    .limit(5)
    .toArray()
}
```

9. The result you will get is an array. Write the logic needed to iterate through the elements and print the **title** fields, as follows:

```
var findMoviesByGenre = function(genre, pageNumber, pageSize){

    var movies = db.movies.find(
        {"genres" : "Action"},
        {"_id" : 0, "title" :1})
    .sort({"imdb.rating" : -1})
    .skip(3)
    .limit(5)
    .toArray()


    print("************* Page : " + pageNumber)
    for(var i =0; i < movies.length; i++){
        print(movies[i].title)
    }
}
```

10. The query still has hardcoded values that need to be replaced with the variables that are received as function arguments, so put the **genre** and **pageSize** variables in the correct places:

```
var findMoviesByGenre = function(genre, pageNumber, pageSize){

    var movies = db.movies.find(
        {"genres" : genre},
        {"_id" : 0, "title" :1})
    .sort({"imdb.rating" : -1})
    .skip(3)
    .limit(pageSize)
    .toArray()


    print("************* Page : " + pageNumber)
    for(var i =0; i < movies.length; i++){
        print(movies[i].title)
    }
}
```

11. Now, you need to derive the skip value based on the page number and page size. When the user is on the first page, the skip value should be zero. On the second page, the skip value should be the page size. Similarly, if the user is on the third page, the skip value should be page size multiplied by 2. Write this logic as follows:

```
var findMoviesByGenre = function(genre, pageNumber, pageSize){
    var toSkip = 0;
    if(pageNumber < 2){
        toSkip = 0;
    } else{
        toSkip = (pageNumber -1) * pageSize;
    }

    var movies = db.movies.find(
        {"genres" : genre},
        {"_id" : 0, "title" :1})
    .sort({"imdb.rating" : -1})
    .skip(toSkip)
    .limit(pageSize)
    .toArray()


    print("************* Page : " + pageNumber)
    for(var i =0; i < movies.length; i++){
        print(movies[i].title)
    }
}
```

Now, use the newly calculated skip value in the limit function. This makes the function complete.

12. Copy and paste the function into the mongo shell and execute it. You should see the following result:

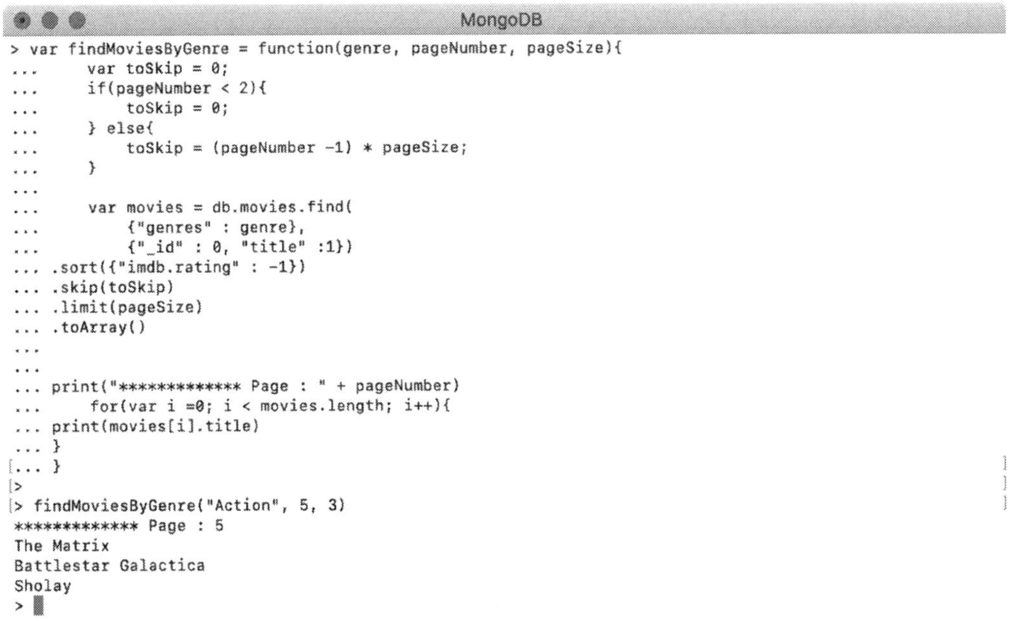

```
● ● ●                          MongoDB
> var findMoviesByGenre = function(genre, pageNumber, pageSize){
...      var toSkip = 0;
...      if(pageNumber < 2){
...          toSkip = 0;
...      } else{
...          toSkip = (pageNumber -1) * pageSize;
...      }
...
...      var movies = db.movies.find(
...          {"genres" : genre},
...          {"_id" : 0, "title" :1})
... .sort({"imdb.rating" : -1})
... .skip(toSkip)
... .limit(pageSize)
... .toArray()
...
...
... print("************* Page : " + pageNumber)
...      for(var i =0; i < movies.length; i++){
... print(movies[i].title)
... }
[... }
|>
|> findMoviesByGenre("Action", 5, 3)
************* Page : 5
The Matrix
Battlestar Galactica
Sholay
> ▊
```

Figure 4.46: Final output

In this activity, by using the **sort()**, **skip()**, and **limit()** functions, you implemented pagination for your movie service, vastly improving the user experience.

# CHAPTER 5: INSERTING, UPDATING, AND DELETING DOCUMENTS

## ACTIVITY 5.01: UPDATING COMMENTS FOR MOVIES

**Solution:**

Perform the following steps to complete the activity:

1.  First, update the **movie_id** field in all three comments. As we need to apply the same update to all three comments, we will use the **findOneAndUpdate()** function along with the **$set** operator to change the value of the field:

```
db.comments.updateMany(
  {
    "_id" : {$in : [
      ObjectId("5a9427658b0beebeb6975eb3"),
      ObjectId("5a9427658b0beebeb6975eb4"),
      ObjectId("5a9427658b0beebeb6975eaa")
    ]}
  },
  {
    $set : {"movie_id" : ObjectId("573a13abf29313caabd25582")}
  }
)
```

Using the update command, we find three movies by their **_id**, providing their primary keys using the **$in** operator. Then, we use **$set** to update the value of the field **movie_id**.

2.  Connect to the MongoDB Atlas cluster, use the database **sample_mflix**, and then execute the command in the previous step. The output should be as follows:

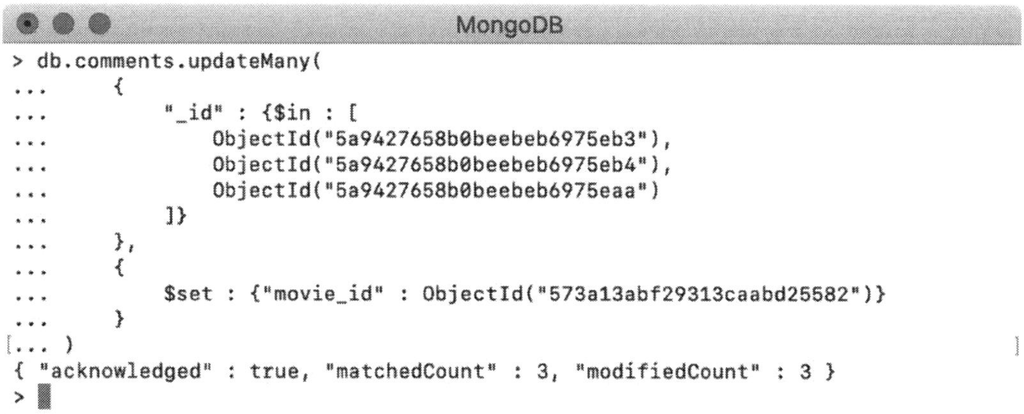

```
> db.comments.updateMany(
...    {
...         "_id" : {$in : [
...             ObjectId("5a9427658b0beebeb6975eb3"),
...             ObjectId("5a9427658b0beebeb6975eb4"),
...             ObjectId("5a9427658b0beebeb6975eaa")
...         ]}
...    },
...    {
...         $set : {"movie_id" : ObjectId("573a13abf29313caabd25582")}
...    }
... )
{ "acknowledged" : true, "matchedCount" : 3, "modifiedCount" : 3 }
>
```

Figure 5.30: Assigning the correct movie to the comments

The output confirms that all three comments are updated correctly.

3.  Find the movie **Sherlock Holmes** by **_id** and reduce the count of comments by **3**:

```
db.movies.findOneAndUpdate(
  {"_id" : ObjectId("573a13bcf29313caabd57db6")},
  {$inc : {"num_mflix_comments" : -3}},
  {
    "returnNewDocument" : true,
    "projection" : {"title" : 1, "num_mflix_comments" : 1}
  }
)
```

The update command here finds the movie by **_id** and uses **$inc** with a negative number to reduce the **num_mflix_comments** count by 3. It returns the modified document containing the fields **title** and **num_mflix_comments**.

4.  Execute the command on the same mongo shell, as follows:

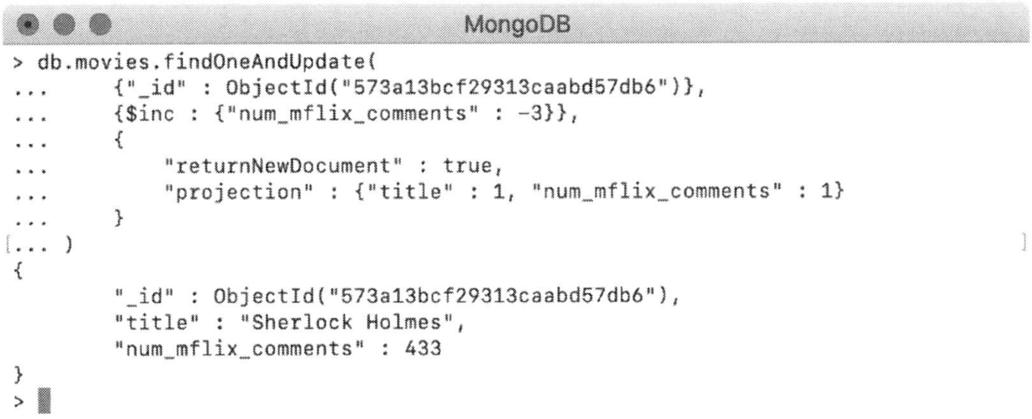

```
●  ●  ●                          MongoDB
> db.movies.findOneAndUpdate(
...      {"_id" : ObjectId("573a13bcf29313caabd57db6")},
...      {$inc : {"num_mflix_comments" : -3}},
...      {
...          "returnNewDocument" : true,
...          "projection" : {"title" : 1, "num_mflix_comments" : 1}
...      }
[... )                                                                 ]
{
         "_id" : ObjectId("573a13bcf29313caabd57db6"),
         "title" : "Sherlock Holmes",
         "num_mflix_comments" : 433
}
>  ▮
```

**Figure 5.31: Incrementing the count of comments on Sherlock Holmes**

The output shows that the number of comments is correctly reduced by **3**.

5.  Finally, prepare a similar command on **50 First Dates** and increase the number of comments by **3**. The following command should be used for this:

```
db.movies.findOneAndUpdate(
  {"_id" : ObjectId("573a13abf29313caabd25582")},
  {$inc : {"num_mflix_comments" : 3}},
  {
    "returnNewDocument" : true,
    "projection" : {"title" : 1, "num_mflix_comments" : 1}
  }
)
```

In this update operation, we are finding the movie by its **_id** and using **$inc** with a positive value of 3 to increase the number of comments. It also returns the updated document and returns only the fields **title** and **num_mflix_comments**.

6. Now, execute the command on the mongo shell:

```
●  ●  ●                          MongoDB
> db.movies.findOneAndUpdate(
...        {"_id" : ObjectId("573a13abf29313caabd25582")},
...        {$inc : {"num_mflix_comments" : 3}},
...        {
...            "returnNewDocument" : true,
...            "projection" : {"title" : 1, "num_mflix_comments" : 1}
...        }
[... )
{
        "_id" : ObjectId("573a13abf29313caabd25582"),
        "title" : "50 First Dates",
        "num_mflix_comments" : 406
}
> ▌
```

**Figure 5.32: Decrementing the count of comments on 50 First Dates**

The output shows that the number of comments has been increased correctly. In this activity, we have practiced modifying the fields of different collections and incrementing and decrementing values of numeric fields during the update operations.

# CHAPTER 6: UPDATING WITH AGGREGATION PIPELINES AND ARRAYS

## ACTIVITY 6.01: ADDING AN ACTOR'S NAME TO THE CAST

**Solution:**

Perform the following steps to complete the activity:

1. Since only one movie document must be updated, use the **findOneAndUpdate()** command. Open a text editor and type the following command:

```
db.movies.findOneAndUpdate({"title" : "Jurassic World"})
```

This query uses a query expression based on the movie title.

2. Prepare an update expression to insert an element into the array. As the cast array must be unique, use **$addToSet**, as follows:

```
db.movies.findOneAndUpdate(
    {"title" : "Jurassic World"},
    {$addToSet : {"cast" : "Nick Robinson"}}
)
```

This query inserts **Nick Robinson** into **cast** and also ensures that no duplicates are inserted.

3. Next, you need to sort the array. Since sets are unordered collections, you cannot use **$sort** in an **$addToSet** expression. Instead, first add the element to the set and then sort it. Open the mongo shell and connect to the **sample_ mflix** database:

```
db.movies.findOneAndUpdate(
    {"title" : "Jurassic World"},
    {$addToSet : {"cast" : "Nick Robinson"}},
    {
        "returnNewDocument" : true,
        "projection" : {"_id" : 0, "title" : 1, "cast" : 1}
    }
)
```

In this command, the **returnNewDocument** flag has been set to **true** and only the **title** and **cast** fields have been projected. Execute the query in the **sample_mflix** database:

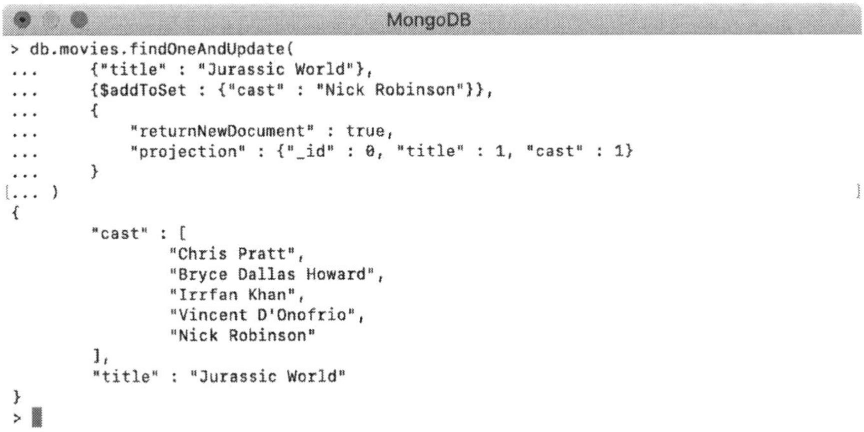

```
> db.movies.findOneAndUpdate(
...     {"title" : "Jurassic World"},
...     {$addToSet : {"cast" : "Nick Robinson"}},
...     {
...         "returnNewDocument" : true,
...         "projection" : {"_id" : 0, "title" : 1, "cast" : 1}
...     }
... )
{
    "cast" : [
        "Chris Pratt",
        "Bryce Dallas Howard",
        "Irrfan Khan",
        "Vincent D'Onofrio",
        "Nick Robinson"
    ],
    "title" : "Jurassic World"
}
>
```

Figure 6.23: Adding the missing cast member's name

The screenshot confirms that the element **Nick Robinson** has been correctly added to the end of the array.

4. Open a text editor and write a basic update command, along with the same query expression:

```
db.movies.findOneAndUpdate(
    {"title" : "Jurassic World"}
)
```

5. Modify the command, add a **$push** expression to the array, and provide the **$sort** option:

```
db.movies.findOneAndUpdate(
    {"title" : "Jurassic World"},
    {$push : {
        "cast" : {
            $each : [],
            $sort : 1
        }}
    }
)
```

As no new element needs to be pushed, an empty array has been passed to the **$each** operator.

6. Add the **returnNewDocument** flag, add the projection to the **title** and **cast** fields, and execute the command, as follows:

```
db.movies.findOneAndUpdate(
    {"title" : "Jurassic World"},
    {$push : {
        "cast" : {
            $each : [],
            $sort : 1
        }}
    },
    {
        "returnNewDocument" : true,
        "projection" : {"_id" : 0, "title" : 1, "cast" : 1}
    }
)
```

7. Open the mongo shell, connect to the **sample_mflix** database, and execute the command:

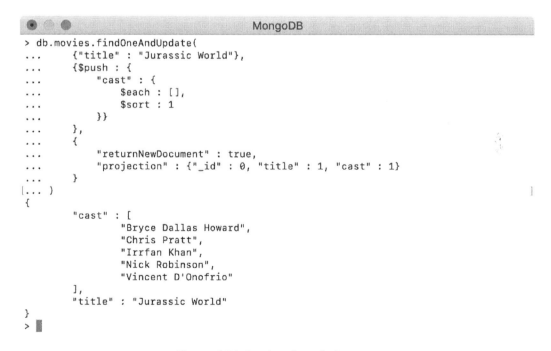

```
MongoDB
> db.movies.findOneAndUpdate(
...     {"title" : "Jurassic World"},
...     {$push : {
...         "cast" : {
...             $each : [],
...             $sort : 1
...         }}
...     },
...     {
...         "returnNewDocument" : true,
...         "projection" : {"_id" : 0, "title" : 1, "cast" : 1}
...     }
... )
{
        "cast" : [
                "Bryce Dallas Howard",
                "Chris Pratt",
                "Irrfan Khan",
                "Nick Robinson",
                "Vincent D'Onofrio"
        ],
        "title" : "Jurassic World"
}
>
```

Figure 6.24: Sorting the missing cast

The output confirms that the **cast** array is now alphabetically sorted in the ascending order of the elements.

# CHAPTER 7: DATA AGGREGATION

## ACTIVITY 7.01: PUTTING AGGREGATIONS INTO PRACTICE

**Solution:**

Perform the following steps to complete the activity:

1. First, create the scaffold code:

```
// Chapter_7_Activity.js
var chapter7Activity = function() {
    var pipeline = [];
    db.movies.aggregate(pipeline).forEach(printjson);
}
Chapter7Activity()
```

2. Add the first match for documents older than 2001:

```
var pipeline = [
   {$match: {
       released: {$lte: new ISODate("2001-01-01T00:00:00Z")}
   }}
 ];
```

3. Add a second match condition for movies with at least one award win:

```
   {$match: {
       released: {$lte: new ISODate("2001-01-01T00:00:00Z")},
       "awards.wins": {$gte: 1},
   }}
```

4. Add a **sort** condition for award nominations. This is to ensure that the **$first** operator in our **$group** statement fetches the highest nominated film for each genre:

```
   {$sort: {
       "awards.nominations": -1
   }},
```

5.  Add the **$group** stage. Create groups based on the first genre and output the **$first** film in each group, along with the sum of award wins for that genre:

```
{ $group: {
    _id: {"$arrayElemAt": ["$genres", 0]},
    "film_id": {$first: "$_id"},
    "film_title": {$first: "$title"},
    "film_awards": {$first: "$awards"},
    "film_runtime": {$first: "$runtime"},
    "genre_award_wins": {$sum: "$awards.wins"},
}},
```

Perform a join on the **comments** collection to retrieve comments for the film in each group. This joins our computed **film_id** field with the **movie_id** comments field. Call this new array **comments**:

```
{ $lookup: {
    from: "comments",
    localField: "film_id",
    foreignField: "movie_id",
    as: "comments"
}},
```

6.  Project just the first comment from your new array, as well as any fields you want to output at the end. Use the **$slice** operator to return only the first entry in the **comments** array. Remember also to add the trailers to the film runtime:

```
{ $project: {
    film_id: 1,
    film_title: 1,
    film_awards: 1,
    film_runtime: { $add: [ "$film_runtime", 12]},
    genre_award_wins: 1,
        "comments": { $slice: ["$comments", 1]}
}},
```

7.  Finally, sort by **genre_award_wins** and limit to three documents:

```
{ $sort: {
    "genre_award_wins": -1}},
{ $limit: 3}
```

Your final pipeline should now look like this:

```
var chapter7Activity = function() {
    var pipeline = [
        {$match: {
            released: {$lte: new ISODate("2001-01-01T00:00:00Z")},
            "awards.wins": {$gte: 1},
        }},
        {$sort: {
            "awards.nominations": -1}},
        { $group: {
            _id: {"$arrayElemAt": ["$genres", 0]},
            "film_id": {$first: "$_id"},
            "film_title": {$first: "$title"},
            "film_awards": {$first: "$awards"},
            "film_runtime": {$first: "$runtime"},
            "genre_award_wins": {$sum: "$awards.wins"},
        }},
        { $lookup: {
            from: "comments",
            localField: "film_id",
            foreignField: "movie_id",
            as: "comments"}},
        { $project: {
            film_id: 1,
            film_title: 1,
            film_awards: 1,
            film_runtime: { $add: [ "$film_runtime", 12]},
            genre_award_wins: 1,
            "comments": { $slice: ["$comments", 1]}
        }},
        { $sort: {
            "genre_award_wins": -1
        }},
        { $limit: 3}
    ];
    db.movies.aggregate(pipeline).forEach(printjson);
}
Chapter7Activity();
```

Your output will be as follows:

```
MongoDB Enterprise atlas-nb3biv-shard-0:PRIMARY> chapter7Activity();
{
        "_id" : "Drama",
        "film_id" : ObjectId("573a139ff29313caabcff499"),
        "film_title" : "Almost Famous",
        "film_awards" : {
                "wins" : 58,
                "nominations" : 95,
                "text" : "Won 1 Oscar. Another 57 wins & 95 nominations."
        },
        "genre_award_wins" : 14020,
        "film_runtime" : 134,
        "comments" : [ ]
}
{

        "_id" : "Comedy",
        "film_id" : ObjectId("573a139bf29313caabcf500b"),
        "film_title" : "Shakespeare in Love",
        "film_awards" : {
                "wins" : 70,
                "nominations" : 77,
                "text" : "Won 7 Oscars. Another 63 wins & 77 nominations."
```

**Figure 7.24: Final output after running the pipeline (truncated for brevity)**

In this activity, we have put together all the different aspects of aggregation pipelines to query, transform, and join data across collections. By combining the methods learned in this chapter, you will now be able to confidently design and write efficient aggregation pipelines to solve complex business problems.

# CHAPTER 8: CODING JAVASCRIPT IN MONGODB

## ACTIVITY 8.01: CREATING A SIMPLE NODE.JS APPLICATION

**Solution:**

Perform the following steps to complete the activity:

1. Import the **readline** and MongoDB libraries:

```
const readline = require('readline');
const MongoClient = require('mongodb').MongoClient;
```

2. Create your **readline** interface:

```
const interface = readline.createInterface({
    input: process.stdin,
    output: process.stdout,
});
```

3. Declare any variables you will need:

```
const url = 'mongodb+srv://mike:password@myAtlas-
  fawxo.gcp.mongodb.net/test?retryWrites=true&w=majority';
const client = new MongoClient(url);
const databaseName = "sample_mflix";
const collectionName = "movies";
```

4. Create a function called **list** that will fetch the top five films for a given genre, returning their **title**, **favourite**, and **ID** fields. *You will need to ask for the category in this function. Look at the* **login** *method in Exercise 7.05, Handling Inputs in Node.js, for more information. Combine this with the* **find** *code from our earlier exercises*:

```
const list = function(database, client) {
    interface.question("Please enter a category: ", (category) => {
        database.collection(collectionName).find({genres: { $all:
[category]
        }}).limit(5).project({title: 1, favourite:
        1}).toArray(function(err, docs) {
        if(err) {
            console.log('Error in query.');
            console.log(err);
        }
        else if(docs) {
            console.log('Docs Array');
```

```
            console.log(docs);
        } else {
        }
        prompt(database, client);
        return;
    });
    });
}
```

5.  Create a function called **favourite** that will update a document by title, and add a key called **favourite** with a value of **true** to the document. You will need to ask for the title in this function using the same method you used for your **list** function. Combine this with the updated code from our earlier exercises:

```
const favourite = function(database, client) {
    interface.question("Please enter a movie title: ", (newTitle) =>
    {
        database.collection(collectionName).updateOne({title:
    newTitle},
            {$set: {favourite: true}}, function(err, result) {
                if(err) {
                    console.log('Error updating');
                    console.log(err);
                    return false;
                }
                console.log('Updated documents #:');
                console.log(result.modifiedCount);
                prompt(database, client);
            })
        })
}
```

6.  Create an interactive **while** loop based on the user's input. If you're unsure how to do this, refer to the **prompt** function from *Exercise 8.05, Handling Inputs in Node.js*:

```
const prompt = function(database, client) {
    interface.question("list, favourite OR exit: ", (input) => {
        if(input === "exit") {
            client.close();
            return interface.close(); // Will kill the loop.
        }
```

```
        else if(input === "list") {
            list(database, client);
        }
        else if(input === "favourite") {
            favourite(database, client);
        }
        else { // If input matches none of our options.
            prompt(database, client)
        }
    });
}
```

7.  Create the MongoDB connection and database, calling your **prompt** function if the database creates successfully:

```
client.connect(function(err) {
    if(err) {
        console.log('Failed to connect.');
        console.log(err);
        return false;
    }

    // Within the connection block, add a console.log to confirm the
      connection
    console.log('Connected to MongoDB with NodeJS!');

    const database = client.db(databaseName);
    if(!database) {
        console.log('Database object doesn\'t exist!');
        return false;
    } else {
        prompt(database, client);
    }
})
```

Remember, you will need to pass the **database** and **client** objects through to each of your functions, including any time you call the **prompt** function.

8.  Run your code using **node Activity8.01.js**.

```
Activity8.01> node .\Activity8.01.js
(node:6748) DeprecationWarning: current Server Discovery and Monitoring engine is deprecat
ed, and will be removed in a future version. To use the new Server Discover and Monitoring
 engine, pass option { useUnifiedTopology: true } to the MongoClient constructor.      Con
nected to MongoDB with NodeJS!list, favourite OR exit: listPlease enter a category: Horror
Docs Array
[
  { _id: 573a1391f29313caabcd75b5, title: 'Nosferatu' },
  { _id: 573a1391f29313caabcd806b, title: 'The Phantom of the Opera' },
  { _id: 573a1391f29313caabcd8978, title: 'The Unknown' },
  {
    _id: 573a1391f29313caabcd8acf,
    title: 'The Fall of the House of Usher'
  },
  { _id: 573a1391f29313caabcd956e, title: 'Nosferatu' }
]
list, favourite OR exit: favourite
Please enter a movie title: Nosferatu
Updated documents #:
1list, favourite OR exit: listPlease enter a category: HorrorDocs Array[  {
    _id: 573a1391f29313caabcd75b5,
    title: 'Nosferatu',
```

Figure 8.9: Final output (truncated for brevity)

In this activity, you created an application with an interactive input loop and implemented error handling to handle invalid input types entered by the user.

# CHAPTER 9: PERFORMANCE

## ACTIVITY 9.01: OPTIMIZING A QUERY

**Solution:**

Perform the following steps to complete the activity:

1.  Open your mongo shell and connect to the **sample_supplies** database on the Atlas cluster. First, you need to find how many records the query returns. The following snippet shows a **count** query, which gives the number of backpacks sold at the Denver store:

```
db.sales.count(
    {
        "items.name" : "backpack",
        "storeLocation" : "Denver"
    }
)
```

2.  The query returns a count of **711** records.

3.  Next, analyze the query given by the analytics team using the **explain()** function, and print the execution stats, as follows:

```
db.sales.find(
        {
            "items.name" : "backpack",
            "storeLocation" : "Denver"
        },
        {
            "_id" : 0,
            "customer.email": 1,
            "customer.age": 1
        }
    ).sort({
        "customer.age" : -1
    }).explain("executionStats")
```

The query invokes the **explain()** function by passing **executionStats** as an argument. The following snippet shows the **executionStats** section of the output:

```
"executionStats" : {
    "executionSuccess" : true,
    "nReturned" : 711,
    "executionTimeMillis" : 10,
    "totalKeysExamined" : 0,
    "totalDocsExamined" : 5000,
    executionStages" : {
        "stage" : "PROJECTION_DEFAULT",
        "nReturned" : 711,
        "executionTimeMillisEstimate" : 1,
        "works" : 5715,
        "advanced" : 711,
        "needTime" : 5003,
        "needYield" : 0,
        "saveState" : 44,
        "restoreState" : 44,
        "isEOF" : 1,
        "transformBy" : {
            "_id" : 0,
            "customer.email" : 1,
            "customer.age" : 1
        },
        "inputStage" : {
            "stage" : "SORT",
            "nReturned" : 711,
            "executionTimeMillisEstimate" : 1,
            "works" : 5715,
            "advanced" : 711,
            "needTime" : 5003,
            "needYield" : 0,
            "saveState" : 44,
            "restoreState" : 44,
            "isEOF" : 1,
            "sortPattern" : {
                "customer.age" : -1
            },
```

```
                "memUsage" : 745392,
                "memLimit" : 33554432,
                "inputStage" : {
                    "stage" : "SORT_KEY_GENERATOR",
                    "nReturned" : 711,
                        "executionTimeMillisEstimate" : 1,
                        "works" : 5003,
                        "advanced" : 711,
                        "needTime" : 4291,
                        "needYield" : 0,
                        "saveState" : 44,
                        "restoreState" : 44,
                        "isEOF" : 1,
                        "inputStage" : {
                            "stage" : "COLLSCAN",
                            "filter" : {
                                "$and" : [
                                    {
                                        "items.name" : {
                                                "$eq" : "backpack"
                                            }
                                    },
                                    {
                                            "storeLocation" : {
                                                "$eq" : "Denver"
                                            }
                                    }
                                ]
                            },
                            "nReturned" : 711,
                            "executionTimeMillisEstimate" : 1,
                            "works" : 5002,
                            "advanced" : 711,
                            "needTime" : 4290,
                            "needYield" : 0,
                            "saveState" : 44,
                            "restoreState" : 44,
                            "isEOF" : 1,
                            "direction" : "forward",
                            "docsExamined" : 5000
```

```
                    }
                }
            }
        }
    }
},
```

The output indicates that to return **711** records, all **5000** records were scanned. It also indicates the execution started with the **COLLSCAN** stage, which means no index was initially present to support the fields in the query.

To improve the query performance, you can create an index on the collection. As the query uses two fields in the filter criteria, use both fields in the index. However, the query also has a sort specification and as denoted by the execution stat, the sort is performed in memory. To avoid the in-memory scan, include the sort field in the index.

4.  Create a compound index on the collection and include **items.name**, **storeLocation**, and **customer.age** fields. The following query creates a compound index on the **sales** collection:

```
db.sales.createIndex(
    {
        "items.name" : 1,
        "storeLocation" : 1,
        "customer.age" : -1
    }
)
```

The output indicates that the index is created correctly, as follows:

```
{
    "createdCollectionAutomatically" : false,
    "numIndexesBefore" : 1,
    "numIndexesAfter" : 2,
    "ok" : 1,
    "$clusterTime" : {
        "clusterTime" : Timestamp(1603246555, 1),
    "signature" : {
        "hash" : BinData(0,"yLQFK4QAJOciOMOPzZTex+K73LU="),
        "keyId" : NumberLong("6827475821280624642")
    }
},
```

```
            "operationTime" : Timestamp(1603246555, 1)
}
```

Execute the **explain()** query executed in *step 2* again. The following snippet shows the **executionStats** section of the output:

```
    "executionStats" : {
        "executionSuccess" : true,
        "nReturned" : 711,
        "executionTimeMillis" : 2,
        "totalKeysExamined" : 711,
        "totalDocsExamined" : 711,
        "executionStages" : {
            "stage" : "PROJECTION_DEFAULT",
            "nReturned" : 711,
            "executionTimeMillisEstimate" : 0,
            "works" : 712,
            "advanced" : 711,
            "needTime" : 0,
            "needYield" : 0,
            "saveState" : 5,
            "restoreState" : 5,
            "isEOF" : 1,
            "transformBy" : {
                "_id" : 0,
                "customer.email" : 1,
                "customer.age" : 1
            },
            "inputStage" : {
                "stage" : "FETCH",
                "nReturned" : 711,
                "executionTimeMillisEstimate" : 0,
                "works" : 712,
                "advanced" : 711,
                "needTime" : 0,
                "needYield" : 0,
                "saveState" : 5,
                "restoreState" : 5,
                "isEOF" : 1,
                "docsExamined" : 711,
                "alreadyHasObj" : 0,
```

```
"inputStage" : {
    "stage" : "IXSCAN",
    "nReturned" : 711,
    "executionTimeMillisEstimate" : 0,
    "works" : 712,
    "advanced" : 711,
    "needTime" : 0,
    "needYield" : 0,
    "saveState" : 5,
    "restoreState" : 5,
    "isEOF" : 1,
    "keyPattern" : {
        "items.name" : 1,
        "storeLocation" : 1,
        "customer.age" : -1
    },
    "indexName" : "items.name_1_storeLocation_1_
customer.age_-1",
    "isMultiKey" : true,
    "multiKeyPaths" : {
        "items.name" : [
            "items"
        ],
        "storeLocation" : [ ],
        "customer.age" : [ ]
    },
    "isUnique" : false,
    "isSparse" : false,
    "isPartial" : false,
    "indexVersion" : 2,
    "direction" : "forward",
    "indexBounds" : {
        "items.name" : [
            "[\"backpack\", \"backpack\"]"
        ],
        "storeLocation" : [
            "[\"Denver\", \"Denver\"]"
        ],
        "customer.age" : [
            "[MaxKey, MinKey]"
        ]
```

```
                },
                "keysExamined" : 711,
                "seeks" : 1,
                "dupsTested" : 711,
                "dupsDropped" : 0
            }
        }
      }
    }
```

From the output, it is evident that the first stage of the execution is **IXSCAN**, which means that the correct indexes were used. Also notice that there is no sorting phase. This means that no further sorting is required because of the correct index on the **customer.age** field. The top-level execution stats show that only **711** records were scanned, and the same number of records were returned. This proves that the query is correctly optimized.

In this activity, you analyzed the performance stats of a query, identified problems, and created the correct index to solve the performance problems.

# CHAPTER 10: REPLICATION

## ACTIVITY 10.01: TESTING A DISASTER RECOVERY PROCEDURE FOR A MONGODB DATABASE

**Solution:**

Perform the following steps to complete the activity:

1. Create the directories as follows: **C:\sale\sale-prod**, **C:\sale\sale-dr**, **C:\sale\sale-ab**, and **C:\sale\log**.

> **NOTE**
>
> For Linux and macOS, the directory names would be like **/data/sales/sale-prod**, **/data/sales/sale-dr**...

2. Start the cluster nodes as follows:

```
start mongod --port 27001 --bind_ip_all --replSet sale-cluster
--dbpath C:\sale\sale-prod --logpath C:\sale\log\sale-prod.log
--logappend --oplogSize 50

start mongod --port 27002 --bind_ip_all --replSet sale-cluster
--dbpath C:\sale\sale-dr --logpath C:\sale\log\sale-dr.log
--logappend --oplogSize 50

start mongod --port 27003 --bind_ip_all --replSet sale-cluster
--dbpath C:\sale\sale-ab --logpath C:\sale\log\sale-ab.log
--logappend --oplogSize 50
```

3. Connect with mongo shell:

```
mongo mongodb://localhost:27001/?replicaSet=sale-cluster
```

4. Create and activate the cluster configuration:

```
var cfg = {
    _id : "sale-cluster",
    members : [
        { _id : 0, host : "localhost:27001"},
        { _id : 1, host : "localhost:27002"},
        { _id : 2, host : "localhost:27003", arbiterOnly:true},
    ]
}

rs.initiate(cfg)
```

> **NOTE**
>
> You should be able to see **PRIMARY** on the shell prompt following a successful cluster election.

5. Insert **100** documents into the **sample_mflix** database. Use the following script on the primary to create a **sales_data** collection and insert **100** documents:

```
use sample_mflix


db.createCollection("sales_data")


for (i=0; i<=100; i++) {
    db.new_sales_data.insert({_id:i, "value":Math.random()})
}
```

6. Shut down the primary by adding the following command:

```
use admin
db.shutdownServer()
```

7. Check that the primary is the DR instance by adding the following command (first disconnect and then connect again)

```
rs.isMaster().primary
```

The result should show **sales_dr**.

8. Use the following script to insert an additional 10 documents on the new primary instance (**sales_dr**):

```
use sample_mflix


for (i=101; i<=110; i++) {
    db.new_sales_data.insert({_id:i, "value":Math.random()})
}
```

9.  Shut down the DR database and arbiter with the following command:

```
use admin
db.shutdownServer()
```

10. After you have made sure that both are shut down, restart the former primary as follows:

```
start mongod --port 27001 --bind_ip_all --replSet sale-cluster
--dbpath C:\sale\sale-prod --logpath C:\sale\log\sale-prod.log
--logappend --oplogSize 50
```

11. Restart the arbiter as follows:

```
start mongod --port 27003 --bind_ip_all --replSet sale-cluster
--dbpath C:\sale\sale-ab --logpath C:\sale\log\sale-ab.log
--logappend --oplogSize 50
```

Connect to the cluster. You should not be able to see the 10 documents that were inserted on **sales_dr**, and **db.new_sales_data.count()** should rerun only 100.

12. After 5 minutes, restart the DR database as follows:

```
start mongod --port 27002 --bind_ip_all --replSet sale-cluster
--dbpath C:\sale\sale-dr --logpath C:\sale\log\sale-dr.log
--logappend --oplogSize 50
```

13. Verify the steps in the **sales_dr log** file after a restart. In the DR logs, you should be able to see a message like this:

```
ROLLBACK [rsBackgroundSync] transition to SECONDARY
2019-11-26T15:48:29.538+1000 I  REPL      [rsBackgroundSync]
transition to SECONDARY from ROLLBACK
2019-11-26T15:48:29.538+1000 I  REPL      [rsBackgroundSync] Rollback
successful.
```

# CHAPTER 11: BACKUP AND RESTORE IN MONGODB

## ACTIVITY 11.01: BACKUP AND RESTORE IN MONGODB

**Solution:**

Perform the following steps to complete the activity:

1. Start with **mongoexport**. Remove the **--db** option, since you are providing it in the URI.

```
mongoexport --uri=mongodb+srv://USERNAME:PASSWORD@myAtlas-fawxo.
gcp.mongodb.net/sample_mflix --collection=theaters --out="theaters.
csv" --type=csv --sort='{theaterId: 1}'
```

2. Add the fields option to the **mongoexport** command

```
mongoexport --uri=mongodb+srv://USERNAME:PASSWORD@
myAtlas-fawxo.gcp.mongodb.net/sample_
mflix --fields=theaterId,location --collection=theaters
--out="theaters.csv" --type=csv --sort='{theaterId: 1}'
```

3. Add the necessary CSV options to the import command, that is, **type**, **ignoreBlanks**, and **headerline**.

```
mongoimport --uri=mongodb+srv://USERNAME:PASSWORD@
myAtlas-fawxo.gcp.mongodb.net/imports
--type=CSV --headerline --ignoreBlanks --collection=theaters_
import --file=theaters.csv
```

4. Fix the **gzip** option for the **dump** command.

```
mongodump --uri=mongodb+srv://USERNAME:PASSWORD@myAtlas-fawxo.gcp.
mongodb.net/sample_mflix --out=./backups –gzip --nsExclude=theaters
```

5. Change **nsExclude** to **excludeCollection**:

```
mongodump --uri=mongodb+srv://USERNAME:PASSWORD@myAtlas-
fawxo.gcp.mongodb.net/sample_mflix --out=./backups –gzip
--excludeCollection=theaters
```

6. In the **mongorestore** command, fix the names of the options:

```
mongorestore --uri=mongodb+srv://USERNAME:PASSWORD@myAtlas-fawxo.
gcp.mongodb.net --nsFrom="sample_mflix" --nsTo="backup_mflix_
backup" --drop ./backups
```

7. Also in **mongorestore**, add the **gzip** option as your dump was a **gzip**:

```
mongorestore --uri=mongodb+srv://USERNAME:PASSWORD@myAtlas-fawxo.
gcp.mongodb.net --nsFrom="sample_mflix" --nsTo="backup_mflix_
backup" --gzip --drop ./backups
```

8.  Finally, make sure your namespace uses the wildcard for proper name migration:

```
mongorestore --uri=mongodb+srv://USERNAME:PASSWORD@myAtlas-fawxo.
gcp.mongodb.net --nsFrom="sample_mflix.*" --nsTo="backup_mflix_
backup.*" --gzip --drop ./backups
```

9.  The final **mongoexport** command should look as follows:

```
mongoexport --uri=mongodb+srv://USERNAME:PASSWORD@
myAtlas-fawxo.gcp.mongodb.net/sample_
mflix --fields=theaterId,location --collection=theaters
--out="theaters.csv" --type=csv --sort='{theaterId: 1}'
```

10. The final **mongoimport** command should look as follows:

```
mongoimport --uri=mongodb+srv://USERNAME:PASSWORD@myAtlas-fawxo.
gcp.mongodb.net/imports --type=CSV -headerline -ignoreBlanks
--collection=theaters_import --file=theaters.csv
```

11. The final **mongodump** command should look as follows:

```
mongodump --uri=mongodb+srv://USERNAME:PASSWORD@myAtlas-
fawxo.gcp.mongodb.net/sample_mflix --out=./backups -gzip
--excludeCollection=theaters
```

12. The final **mongorestore** command should look as follows:

```
mongorestore --uri=mongodb+srv://USERNAME:PASSWORD@myAtlas-fawxo.
gcp.mongodb.net --nsFrom="sample_mflix.*" --nsTo="backup_mflix_
backup.*" --gzip --drop ./backups
```

> **NOTE**
>
> It is important to note that because **mongoimport** and **mongorestore**
> will both create new documents in the database, you will have to execute
> these commands using credentials with write access.

# CHAPTER 12: DATA VISUALIZATION

## ACTIVITY 12.01: CREATING A SALES PRESENTATION DASHBOARD

**Solution:**

Perform the following steps to complete the activity:

1.  Before you can start building the charts for this new presentation, you must define the appropriate data source in the application. Follow the steps from *Exercise 12.01, Working with Data Sources*, to create a new sales data source on the sales collection from the **sample_supplies** database, as shown in the following figure:

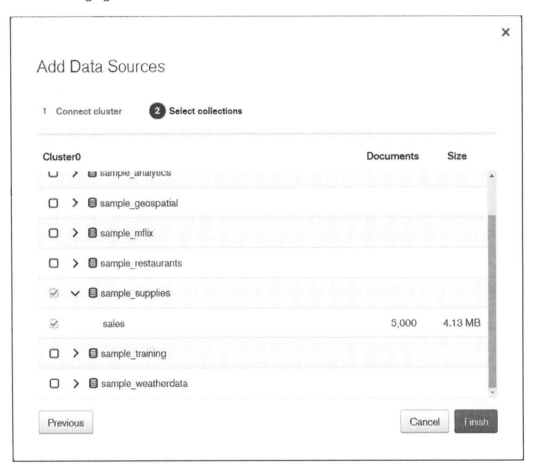

Figure 12.52: Creating a new sales data source

2. Click **Finish** to save. The new data source will appear in the list as can be seen in the following figure:

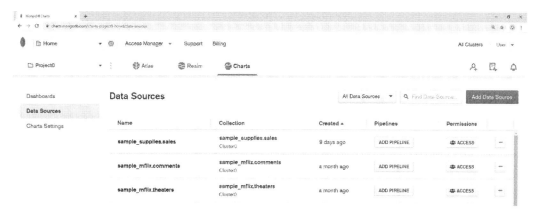

Figure 12.53: Sales Data Sources

3. From the dashboard, click on the **ADD CHART** button as shown in the following screenshot:

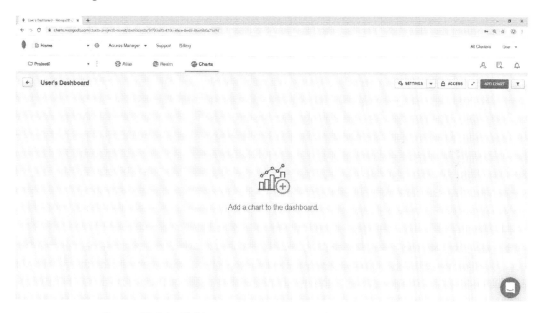

Figure 12.54: Clicking on ADD CHART in the User's Dashboard

In the **Chart Builder**, choose the sales data source, that was created in *step 2* (that is, `sample_supplies.sales`) and then select the **Circular** chart type and the **Donut** chart sub-type, as can be seen in the following screenshot:

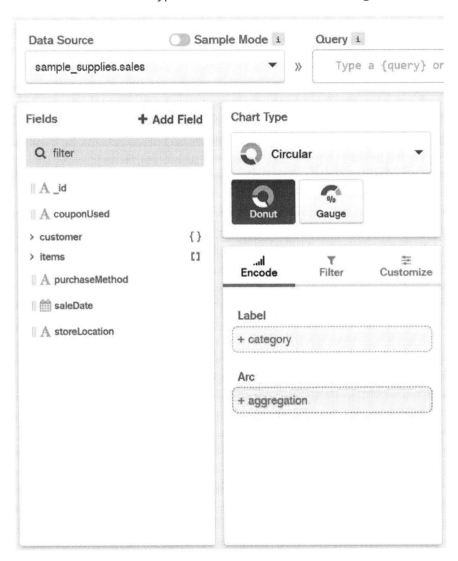

Figure 12.55: Selecting the Circular chart type and the Donut chart sub-type

4. Unwind the **items** array. This step is important because the sales data is in an array format inside the JSON database. So, the **unwind** function will create a virtual document for each item in the array. To do so, add the following JSON code to the **Query** bar:

```
[{$unwind:"$items"}]
```

Then click the **Apply** button, as shown in the following screenshot:

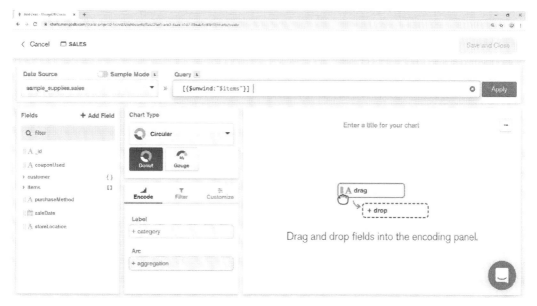

Figure 12.56: Writing the unwind function in the Query bar

5. The next step is to add a new calculated field—that is, **items.value**. To do this, click on the **+ Add Field** button and add the new field as **items. value = items.price * items.quantity**, as can be seen in the following screenshot:

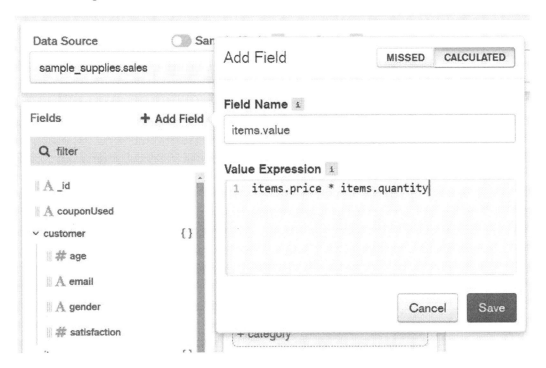

Figure 12.57: Ading the items.value field

6. Add a filter so that only items from stores in **Denver** are considered for the chart. From the **Filter** tab, define the new filter for the store location by checking only the **Denver** location checkbox:

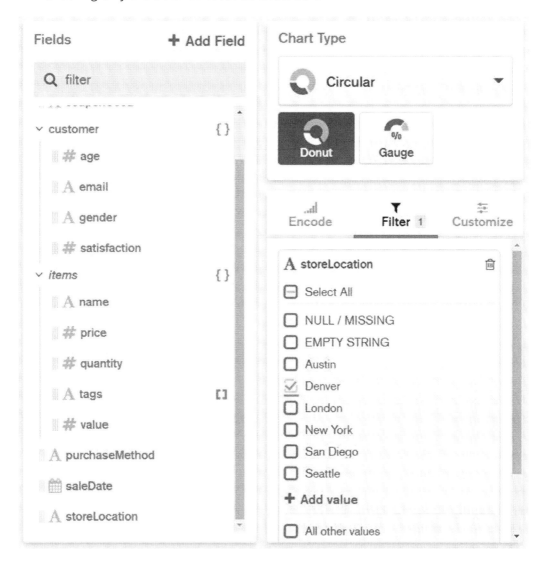

Figure 12.58: Selecting only Denver from the list of locations

7. Add channels in the **Encode** tab. As can be seen from the following figure, drag the field `items.name` into the `Label` channel. Select **VALUE** from the **SORT BY** dropdown and limit it to **10** results. That will split our donut into 10 slices. Similarly, drag `items.value` (the new calculated field) into the `Arc` channel, and choose the **SUM** function from the **AGGREGATE** dropdown:

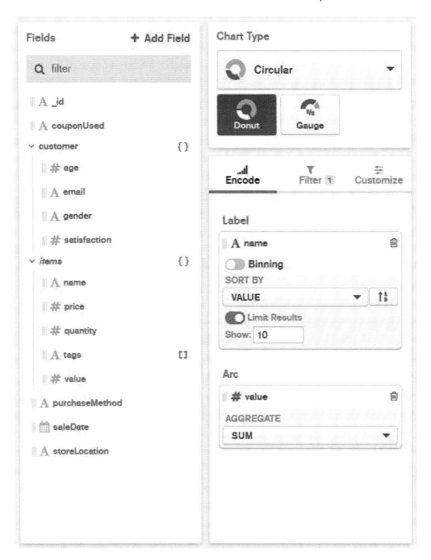

Figure 12.59: Dragging items.value into the Arc channel and choosing the SUM function

8. The chart should appear on the right side of the screen as follows:

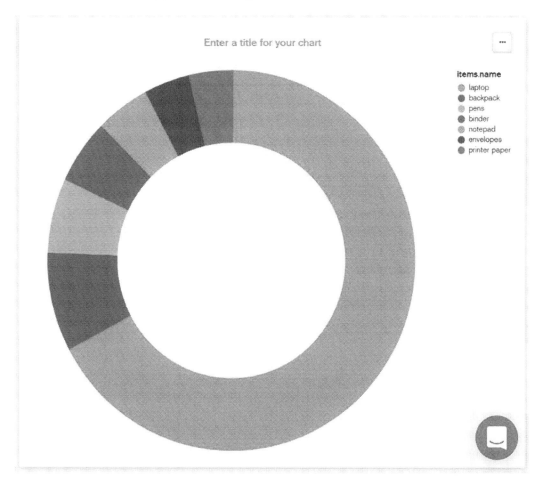

Figure 12.60: Final chart

9. Edit the chart name to **Denver Sales (million $)** as follows:

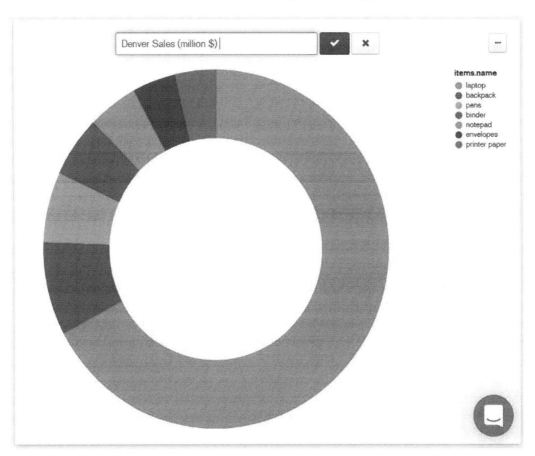

Figure 12.61: Editing the chart title

10. Edit the chart labels. From the **Customize** tab, click to enable **Data Value Labels**, as follows:

Figure 12.62: Customizing the data labels

11. Next, from the **Number Formatting** dropdown, choose **CUSTOM** with a maximum of **2** decimals, as follows:

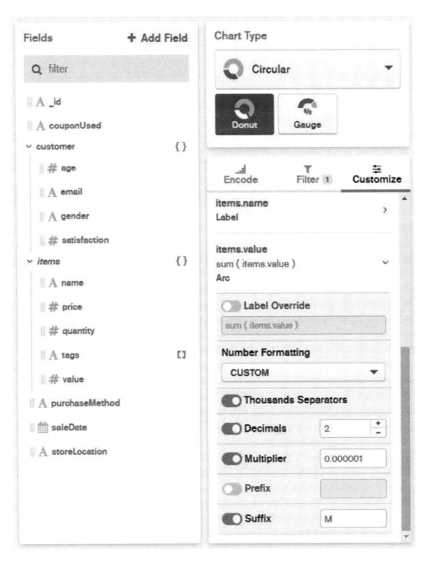

Figure 12.63: Customizing the chart formatting

12. The chart will appear with the right title and label formatting, as can be seen in the following figure:

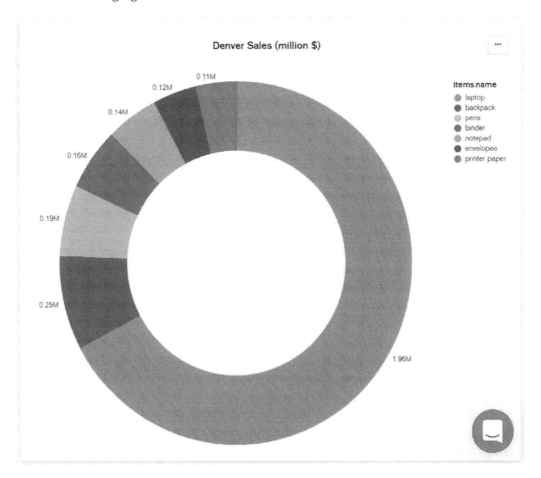

**Figure 12.64: Final Denver Sales chart**

The results are quite self-explanatory. As expected, the laptop sales value of almost 2 million dollars tops the sales and is by far the most valuable item in the sales report. The next item by sales is backpacks, with only a $250,000 value.

The activity is now complete. In only 10 simple steps, you were able to create a top sales report for items from stores in Denver, Colorado. Your chart build is now finished and the chart can be saved on your dashboard. Lessons learned here could be applied by students and professionals alike, to make presentations using real data.

# INDEX

Made in the USA
Monee, IL
11 September 2021